Where Food
And People Meet

Where Food And People Meet

Enjoy Your Journey

Phyllis Watts

Phyllis Watts

To order additional copies of this book, contact:
Xlibris Corporation
1-888-795-4274
www.Xlibris.com
Orders@Xlibris.com
54999

A THOUSAND THANK YOUS ARE NEVER ENOUGH

There's always a supportive group behind any project or person making it possible for them to accomplish what seems to be an impossible task.

First and foremost to my husband Joe—besides the obvious help, he has always encouraged my creativity, my love for cooking, the ups and downs and is a driving force in getting each project completed. He has put projects together, spent hours troubleshooting with computers, printers and getting supplies. Truly without him, I could not have done this and so much more.

To all the people contributing ideas, recipes, proof-reading, proof-tasting and encouragement. Your words, trust and belief in my ability and strengths sustained and fortified me to make every part of this possible. God Bless you all ten-fold and more.

I'm so grateful to the vast help available over the Internet, without it, my activity restrictions would've prevented me from completing the necessary research and communications required for this project. I appreciate the cooking shows, bakers, chefs, cooks and writers who helped me with the phraseology and recipe instructions. The technology of computers, software and web has helped bring back some of our past and keep them a part of our future.

Without any doubt, my extreme humbleness to God for the opportunity to travel; meeting the incredible people who shared their lives and knowledge; the time and circumstances that made it possible for me to get this done; for His directing us to Alaska; for my family in Alaska, Montana, Missouri, Texas, Maryland and Florida; and His everyday leading and blessings.

*"This one is dedicated to
My Joey and my puppy Marlowe—
Forever and ever, Amen."*

FOOD & PEOPLE --->MEETING<---

This cookbook is a long time in coming: a lifetime . . . actually many lifetimes. Included are my recipes, ones given to me and those adapted as family favorites. Some are very old with additions or suggestions to rework them. The others were given to me and meant to be shared.

The thing they all have in common and why they are included: they have a story. Either the food or the people or situation created a time in history and all three made a memory. They represent periods in time when the food and the people were highlighted.

I'm not a professional chef or baker, I've never attended any culinary schooling. I admire those who have; their techniques, details and specialties. I know I could never do what they do. I have, however, traveled in 49 states (Hawaii to go yet) and most of Canada, which greatly expanded my knowledge about both people and food with everyday folk.

Being a Professional nurse, I learned to not only listen to what's said and what people think is important, but to also hear what wasn't said; to watch individuals interacting and cherish the stories shared. I heard what people like, what they fix their families, how they fix to celebrate and what they think is good.

My love of history and cookbooks is reflected in this gathering. This cookbook is my travel diary and personal life scrapbook. I *finally* assembled all the recipe cards, notes, scraps, instructions, emails, letters, footnotes, margin scribbles, journals, torn newspapers, magazine pieces, and memories. I've added my understanding and experience about the people and food to put it all here in one book. It really is just a sample of the good times and fantastic people.

I've included answers to some frequently asked questions to help those who are new at this wonderful art of preparing food. Yes I consider it an art. A cook or baker is creating something; using their resourcefulness to be enjoyed. Just like quilts, collages, scrapbooks and photo albums; we're putting a part of ourselves into following a format with the intent for the result to be "used" and shared with others.

I've met people from all walks of life, in every occupation, education level and economic status. The one subject I can always count on opening a discussion with absolutely anyone is food. It's the common denominator everywhere.

Even if someone doesn't cook or bake, they eat. Everyone who eats has an opinion about what they like and dislike. Food has opened more doors of fellowship than absolutely any other, as you will see by the following stories and anecdotes.

The point is, no matter who we are, what we believe, where we're from or where we're headed, we all have experiences with food.

This is about passing along the pieces of once in a lifetime events, reminiscences of those now gone or those I will never see again; bits of my life entwined with other lives. What I discovered—Life Happens Where Food and People Meet.

Phyllis
Wasilla, Alaska—2009

BEVERAGES

Cooking and baking are some of the most satisfying activities and outlets in my life. It'll be a great surprise to those who know me to find out there was a time when I hated to cook. Really, it's true.

LEARN

At first, I merely made meals with sustenance the only goal and a chore to accomplish. Dinner had to be ready or close to it by the time Mom got home. She gave the directions and I followed them.

TO COOK

That all changed the day I walked into my first cooking class. Eighth Grade home economics teacher Mrs. Kees explored and explained the kitchen and its tools like they were treasures in a chest. Her voice filled with drama and suspense while she read the recipes and explained the ingredients. She spoke the culinary terms like they were a fantastic foreign language. Cooking was exciting and an adventure she loved and her joy was catching. An easy thing like a beverage had animation in her hands. Punch should create a punch to your meal. A beverage could stimulate the drinker to look forward to a wonderful eating experience or be the signal of a satisfying end to a delectable feast. Preparing meals could be creative, joyful, fulfilling. She generously shared her enthusiasm for making delicious crowd-pleasing creations. Thank you, Mrs. Kees.

Since that class, I've attempted, conquered, succeeded and failed, but never stopped trying and learning because her love of the adventure passed to me. I'm grateful to say there have been more delights than disasters. Some failures were tolerable and still got politely eaten; others never made it past the wastebasket. Even with the miserable failures, I never stopped loving the endeavor; exploring what works and doesn't work.

One of the funniest mistakes was a rather simple thing. Coffee. As a new bride

LOVE TO COOK

I wanted to show my husband how much I loved him, by giving him something he enjoyed. I'm not a coffee drinker, but my husband loves it. The stronger the better and no cream, no sugar, so the actual coffee taste is important, no camouflages.

The very first pot of coffee I made him was so strong, when I served him a cup of it, his eyes tear-ed up and he politely gasped, "I think we need to dilute it with some water"

My pathetic answer back was, "I already did". We ended up with eight pots of coffee from that one pot and Joe drank every drop; bless his heart.

I knew then that I had the perfect soul mate: someone who would tolerate a lot of experimenting. Of course with the multiple attempts and failures, comes great winners. He's enjoyed a few incredibly fabulous dishes that *will never* be repeated—one of the drawbacks of creating as you go. Now, I keep a piece of paper and pen close by—most of the time. From trials and tribulations we have many family traditions and frequently requested favorites.

BANANA STRAWBERRY SMOOTHIE

These were always refreshing while Paula and I chatted after our mall walks.

2 cups strawberry nectar	**1 ripe banana**
1 cup frozen strawberries chopped	**6-10 ice cubes**
2 scoops fat-free vanilla yogurt	

Combine ½ of ingredients in blender and blend on high speed until ice is crushed and drink is smooth. Repeat with remaining ingredients. Share with friend.

BLOOD MARY

Leave out the vodka and enjoy a spicy tomato juice before a meal.

1 ¼ ounces vodka	**Celery salt**
Tomato juice	**Crushed ice**
¼ ounce Worcestershire sauce	**Dash hot sauce**
Salt and black pepper	

Pour vodka, Worcestershire sauce, seasonings and hot sauce into glass (usually a Collins glass or specialty glass) over crushed ice. Add tomato juice and stir well. Garnish with celery stalk, lemon or lime wedge. May also garnish with stalk of spiced asparagus and lemon or lime wedge.

CITRUS PUNCH

This is an easy way to remember the punches I enjoyed made fresh from backyard citrus trees.

6 ounces frozen lemonade
    concentrate
6 ounces frozen limeade concentrate
6 ounces frozen orange juice
    concentrate

1 quart club soda 1 quart ginger ale
3 quarts lemon-lime soda
Lime slices

Let all concentrates thaw before using. Combine all ingredients except lemon-lime soda and lime slices. Refrigerate until ready to serve. Add lemon-lime soda and float thinly sliced lime to punch bowl or pitcher.

COLD HARVEST PUNCH

This is the best drink for those warm Autumn days when the leaves are being raked.

1 cup lemon juice
½ cup sugar
2 cups cranberry juice
2 cups orange juice

2 cups strong—spiced tea
Orange and lemon slices
Whole cloves

Mix all ingredients except tea, citrus slices and cloves. Pour mixture into mold and freeze overnight. Brew tea long enough ahead to allow it to cool; pour over ice mold in punch bowl. Add slices and cloves. Increase as needed for size of group.

CRANBERRY ORANGE SLUSH COCKTAIL

2 cups brandy

32 ounces cranberry juice

12 ounces frozen orange juice
concentrate

1 can frozen cranberry juice
concentrate

2 liters lemon-lime soda

Mix all ingredients except soda in nonmetal container. Divide among pint containers. Cover and freeze at least 8 hours or until slushy. For each serving, mix equal amounts of slush mixture and soda in glass.

DAIQUIRI

Depending on where you live, add the fresh fruit of choice to make a popular drink.

1 ¼ ounces rum

1 ounce fresh lime juice

1 teaspoon powdered sugar

Crushed ice

Shake or blend all ingredients with ice, strain into cocktail glass (most people prefer this drink blended). Garnish with lime slice

EGGNOG PUNCH

For those who've never tried eggnog, this will introduce you to its unique taste.

1 quart eggnog

2 liters bottle lemon-lime soda

1 pint vanilla ice cream

Mix all ingredients together in chilled punch bowl. Sprinkle with nutmeg to taste and serve cold.

FRUIT FLAVORED TEA

This is becoming popular now in restaurants across the country.

2 cups fresh or frozen strawberries,   6 tea bags
    raspberries, blueberries or   6 cups boiling water
    mixed berries

Place fruit of choice and tea bags in large glass bowl. Pour boiling water over fruit and tea bags. Cover and let stand 5-10 minutes. Remove tea bags. Strain fruit from mixture into pitcher. Serve warm, cooled or over ice. Add sugar or artificial sweetener after pouring into pitcher or when served if a sweeter drink is desired.

FRUIT PUNCH

6 ounces frozen lemonade   3 quarts chilled ginger ale
    concentrate   Ice
8 ounce can crushed pineapple
1 16-ounce bag frozen strawberries

Combine lemonade concentrate, pineapple and strawberries in blender. Blend on medium-high speed until mixture is smooth. Pour mixture into punch bowl over ice. Add ginger ale. Punch mixture (minus ginger ale) can be made in advance and stored in refrigerator in covered container and finished later by adding ginger ale just before serving.

FRUIT SMOOTHIE

4 ounces each orange and apple juice	¼ cup frozen or fresh peaches
or 8 ounces orange or apple juice	1 banana
8 fresh or frozen strawberries	4 ounces low-fat milk
4 frozen or fresh raspberries	3-4 ice cubes

Pour juice into blender. Add frozen fruits first and blend well. Add other fruits and blend again. Add milk and ice cubes to correct thickness. Pour into tall glasses. Only juice enough fruit to equal about 1 quart at a time. How much you juice depends on how much you believe you will use in 2-3 days.

HOLIDAY EGGNOG

If you have never had homemade, try it once—you will be surprised.

Custard:	Eggnog:
⅓ cup sugar	1 cup heavy cream
3 eggs slightly beaten	2 tablespoons powdered sugar
Dash salt	½ teaspoon vanilla extract
2 ½ cups milk	½ cup rum or 2 teaspoons rum
1 teaspoon vanilla extract	extract in cup of water
	Ground nutmeg

Custard: Mix eggs, sugar and salt in heavy saucepan. Gradually stir in milk. Cook over low heat 15-20 minutes, stirring constantly, just until mixture coats metal spoon; remove from heat. Stir in vanilla. Place saucepan in cold water until custard is cool. (if custard curdles, beat vigorous with beater until smooth) Cover and refrigerate at least 2 hours but no longer than 24 hours. Eggnog: Beat cream, sugar and vanilla in chilled small bowl until stiff. Stir rum into chilled custard and gently stir 1 cup of whipped cream into custard and rum. Pour eggnog into small punch bowl. Drop remaining whipped cream in 4-5 rounds onto eggnog. Sprinkle with nutmeg. Serve immediately. Refrigerate any remaining eggnog.

HOT AUTUMN PUNCH

Warms the body after a hayride, in front of a campfire, wood stove or fireplace munching on popcorn.

6 cups apple juice

½ cup orange juice concentrate

2 sticks cinnamon

8 wholes cloves

½ teaspoon ground nutmeg

¼ cup lemon juice

¼ cup honey

2 ¼ cups pineapple juice

Combine apple juice, cinnamon stick and whole cloves in slow cooker. Cover and cook on high 1 hour. Add remaining ingredients. Cover and cook on low 2-3 hours. Serve from cooker on warm.

HOT BUTTERED RUM (FOR LOIS)

Think "warming your frozen insides" after caroling in the snow. The essential ingredients are: a hot beverage such as tea, coffee, cocoa, water, lemonade or apple cider; an alcohol such as brandy, rum, or whisky; and usually a sweetener, such as honey, sugar or syrup.

1 cup butter

1 cup brown sugar

1 cup heavy cream

2 cups powdered sugar

⅛ teaspoon ground cloves

⅛ teaspoon ground cinnamon

¼ teaspoon ground nutmeg

1 ounce (2 tablespoons) rum

½ cup boiling water

Beat butter and brown sugar in medium bowl on medium speed about 5 minutes or until fluffy. Beat in heavy cream and powdered sugar alternately on low speed until smooth. Stir in cloves, cinnamon and nutmeg. Spoon into 1 quart freezer container. Cover and freeze for up to 3 months. For each serving: Place rum and 2 tablespoons frozen batter in mug. Stir in boiling water.

HOT COCOA MIX

Nothing creates memories like "liquid chocolate" or warms the toes on freezing days. Keeping this in the pantry is just as easy as the store kind and so much better.

3 ½ cups nonfat dry milk powder

2 cups sifted powdered sugar

1 cup powdered non-dairy coffee creamer

½ cup sifted unsweetened cocoa

Mocha Cocoa:

½ cup instant coffee

In bowl combine milk powder, sugar, creamer and cocoa powder. Store in airtight container. For Mocha: add instant coffee. Store in airtight container. For each serving: Place ⅓ cup of mix in mug and add ¾ cup boiling water. For a large party: Pour 8 cups water into slow cooker. Gradually add milk powder until blended. Cover and cook on high 2-3 hours. Stir in coffee creamer and cocoa. Turn on low 1 hour. Serve in mugs from cooker on warm.

HOT MULLED CIDER

Mulled cider gets its name from the definition of mull, which means to flavor a beverage by heating it and adding spices and includes either slices or the zest of citrus fruits like oranges.

2 quarts apple cider

⅓ cup brown sugar

¼ teaspoon salt

6 whole cloves

6 wholes allspice

4 cinnamon sticks

Combine above ingredients in large saucepan. Place over low heat and bring to boiling point. Simmer for 5 minutes and strain. Serve hot in cups or mugs.

HOT SPICED CIDER

This is a very popular cold weather party beverage. For a party double or triple the recipe and place in slow cooker on warm for duration of party.

8 cups apple juice	1 teaspoon cloves
1 cup orange juice or orange liqueur	8 thin oranges wedges
⅓ cup brown sugar	8 whole cloves
6 cinnamon sticks	6 inch 100% cotton cheesecloth
1 teaspoon allspice	double thick

Combine cider, orange juice and brown sugar in saucepan. To make spice bag, cut double-thick square from cheesecloth. Place spices in center of cheesecloth. Gather corners of cloth together and tie with clean string. Add bag to cider mixture. Bring to boiling; reduce heat. Cover and simmer for 10 minutes. Meanwhile, if desired, stud orange wedges with cloves. Remove spice bag; discard. Serve cider in mugs with studded orange wedges. This can also be fixed in slow cooker. Combine cider, orange juice, brown sugar and spice bag in slow cooker. Cover and cook on high 2 hours or low for 5 hours. Remove spice bag and place studded orange wedges, place slow cooker on warm and place cooker on table.

JOEY'S IRISH DRINK

My husband will splurge on one of these for the Irish holidays or the long Alaskan deep freeze winter nights.

LATTE:	**Irish Coffee:**
¼ cup Irish cream liqueur	⅔ cup hot, strong coffee
½ cup espresso	1 tablespoon Irish whiskey
8 ounces steamed (heated) milk	1 teaspoon brown sugar
	Whipped cream (optional)
	Nutmeg (optional)

Latte: Put espresso in 16 ounce cup. Add liqueur followed by steamed milk—or heat in microwave. Stir, top off drink with dollop of whipped cream and sprinkle of nutmeg. Dessert Coffee: Stir together coffee and whiskey and brown sugar. If desired, top with whipped cream and sprinkle of nutmeg

LIME COKE SLUSHIE

Just add the cola and lime for the kids and for an adult drink add the whiskey

2 12-ounce cans cola soda pop   6 ounces bourbon whiskey chilled
6 ounces frozen limeade concentrate

Combine cola and limeade with a whisk; freeze in an ice cream machine according to manufacturers directions. Divide frozen mixture into four chilled glasses. Serve to any kids. Then make another batch and drizzle each serving with 1 shot of bourbon. Serve with a spoon or a straw.

MARGARITA

This has become a very popular drink that is easy to make at home and saves your pocket book.

½ cup fresh lime juice   1 cup tequila
Lime wedges and slices   1 cup triple sec
2 tablespoons fresh lemon juice   1-2 cups ice

Pour all ingredients including ice into large pitcher and stir. Salt rims of glasses (if desired). For blended margarita: Pour all ingredients including ice into blender and blend until ice is crushed, pour into rim-salted glasses garnish with lime as above and serve.

MEXICAN HOT COCOA

This drink is almost a dessert in of itself. It makes the perfect late night drink with a simple cookie as well as a great finish to a nice southwestern meal. Have it on your pantry shelf to mix up quickly.

1 ¾ cups dry milk powder
¼ cup baking cocoa powder
3 tablespoons brown sugar

½ cup instant chocolate milk mixes
½ teaspoon cinnamon

Mix all together and store in pint jar. To make drink, mix 3 heaping teaspoons with 6 ounces boiling water.

MOCHA BANANA SMOOTHIE

Here's your liquid chocolate banana, strong flavors and cool going down.

1 cup ice cubes
¾ cup milk
½ cup cooled double strength coffee

1 ripe banana
1 tablespoon chocolate syrup
1 tablespoon sugar or Splenda

Process all ingredients in blender until smooth.

MULLED WINE

This is wine, usually red, combined with spices and typically served warm. Historically, wine often went bad. By adding spices and honey made it drinkable again. Nowadays, it's a traditional drink during winter, especially around Christmas. Different states and different types of winter create different recipes.

2 cups pineapple juice	2 cinnamon sticks
1 cup water	6 whole cloves
½ cup orange juice	3 whole allspice
1 cup brown sugar	Orange slices
½ teaspoon salt	1 750-milliliter bottle dry red wine

Place pineapple juice, water, orange juice, sugar, salt, cinnamon, cloves, and allspice in slow cooker. Place on high for 1 hour. Remove spices and stir in wine. Add orange slices and heat just until warm, serve hot.

OLD FASHIONED LEMONADE

Ah, the beverage that means Summer, who can resist a tall cold glass on those 80-plus humidity days.

1 ½ cups (8 large) lemons	3 cups cold water
½ cup sugar	1 lemon cut in small wedges
2 cups warm water	Freshly made ice cubes

In small saucepan, combine freshly squeezed lemon juice, sugar and 2 cups of cold water; heat and stir briskly to dissolve sugar. In large pitcher, add lemon syrup and cold water; stir briskly until all mixed. Add ice and wedge to each glass served. Honey Lemonade: Substitute "honey" sugar. Adjust more or less to taste.

PEACH PLEASURE

I still remember sipping this drink in the humid heat of Georgia on an old front porch swing, the peaches were fresh off the tree then, no such luck in Alaska, but this is close enough.

12 ounces peach nectar   2 scoops orange sherbet
1 cup frozen sliced peaches   1 cup ice
½ cup bananas

Combine all ingredients in blender and blend on high until drink is smooth.

PINA COLADA

Omit the rum and it's nonalcoholic and close your eyes and feel the cool breeze of the tropics.

1 ½ ounces rum   Pineapple wedges
3 ounces pineapple juice   Maraschino cherry
3 ounces cream of coconut   Crushed ice

Pour all ingredients into blender with ice and blend well. Pour into Hurricane glass or specialty glass and garnish with pineapple wedge and maraschino cherry

PINEAPPLE SHERBET PUNCH

My friend swears this is the easiest and most popular punch she serves at parties.

½ gallon pineapple sherbet   24 ounces pineapple juice
2 2-liter bottles lemon-lime soda   24 ounces club soda

Two to three hours before serving time, place sherbet in punch bowl; pour club soda and pineapple juice over sherbet (it will foam). Mix well, then scoop out ⅓ of the mix into ice trays and freeze. Refrigerate mixture in punch bowl until serving time. Add lemon-lime soda just before serving and stir. Add frozen mixture cubes every now and then to keep the punch chilled.

POMEGRANATE SPRITZ

This fruit is the newest craze for health benefits, but was introduced into Latin America and California by Spanish settlers in 1769, pomegranate is now cultivated in parts of California and Arizona for juice production. Here are several ways to enjoy the delicious juice.

1 cup pomegranate juice with the your choice of the following

3 cups ginger ale or lemon-lime soda	OR 2 cups orange juice
OR 3 cups sparkling white grape juice	1 cup club soda
OR 3 cups grapefruit flavored soda	OR 2 cups lemonade
	1 cup club soda

Mix and serve in a clear glasses.

SANGRIA

Sangria is a popular wine punch at bars, pubs and restaurants in Portugal, Mexico, southern Spain and Mexican restaurants in the US. It's easy to make, a refreshing drink and a hit with even for those who are not "into wine."

1 lemon	1 can citrus-flavored carbonated
1 orange	drinks
½ cup sugar	2 tablespoons brandy
½ cup water	Ice
1 bottle white wine or red wine, chilled	

Cut lemon and orange into ¼ inch thick slices. Place the end slices from fruit in saucepan. Set aside remaining slices. Add sugar and water to saucepan. Bring to boil. Stir until sugar dissolves. Remove from heat; cool for 30 minutes. Squeeze juice from cooked fruit into syrup. Discard cooked fruit. In pitcher, combine remaining fruit slices, syrup, wine, carbonated drink and brandy. Serve over ice.

SLOE-GIN FIZZ

Sloe gin is a red colored liqueur flavored with sloe berries, a relative of the plum- and what a plum.

2 ounces Sloe Gin

2 ounces Gin

2 ounces fresh grapefruit juice

1 tablespoon fresh lemon juice

1 ½ teaspoons Blackberry liqueur

1 ½ teaspoons simple syrup sugar
   and water, equal parts

Shake all ingredients with ice and strain into chilled glasses.

SOUTHERN SWEET TEA

3 family size tea bags

¼ teaspoon baking soda

1 ⅓ cups sugar

Bring 4 cups water to boil. Add pinch of baking soda to water and add tea bags. Remove from heat and cover. Allow to sit for at least 10-15 minutes; pour into gallon pitcher and add sugar, mixing well. Fill pitcher with cold water. Refrigerate.

SPARKLING PINEAPPLE PUNCH

Pineapple has become associated with the notion of welcome and that's what this wonderful punch says too.

½ cup sugar

½ cup water

2 cinnamon sticks

¼ cup lime juice

46 ounces chilled pineapple juice

1 liter sparkling water

1 bottle chilled sparkling white wine

Heat sugar, water and cinnamon to boiling; reduce heat. Cover and simmer 15 minutes. Cover and refrigerate at least 2 hours or until chilled. Remove cinnamon from syrup. Just before serving, mix syrup and remaining ingredients in large punch bowl.

STRAWBERRY PINK DRINK

This such a simple mix of tart and sweet and so refreshing.

1 10-ounce bag frozen strawberries   3 cups chilled grapefruit juice

Break up strawberries. Place strawberries and 1 cup of juice in blender. Cover and blend on high about 30 seconds or until smooth. Add remaining grapefruit juice. Cover and blend until mixed. Serve over ice

SUN TEA

Making sun tea became popular in the 1980's and can be safe if done right. The tea will taste more mellow than what you are used to from using boiling water. The slow seeping has a way of bringing out a slightly different flavor from the tea whichever way you do it.

3 Family size tea bags   Translucent or Glass Jar with Lid
1 quart cold water

Put water and tea bags in jar and put lid on. Set jar in sun for about an hour. If it's a cloudy day, leave it out for 2 hours (Do not leave tea to brew for more than 3 hours). Add ice and water to jar. Refrigerate right away and keep no longer than 2 days. Or you can fill the jar with the water and tea bags and place it in your refrigerator at least 6 hours or overnight, then squeeze out the tea bags and add ice. Either way, be sure to use a container scrubbed in warm soapy water and dipped in a bleach solution made with 1 tablespoon bleach per gallon of water before each batch made. Discard tea if it appears thick or syrupy.

SWEET FLAVORED ICE TEAS

Tea is an inexpensive and versatile way to enjoy your water intake. There are so many types to try and experiment with, enjoy the discovery.

Basic Tea:
2 quarts (8 cups) water
6 tea bags
⅓ cup sugar or
16 packets artificial sweetener
Cranberry:
⅓ cup plus 2 Tablespoons lemon
    juice
2 tablespoons cranberry juice
Lemon:
⅓ cup bottled lemon juice
Orange:
⅓ cup bottled lemon juice
⅛ teaspoon orange extract
Peach:
¼ cup plus 1 tablespoon lemon juice
3 tablespoons peaches flavored
    syrup
Raspberry:
¼ cup plus 1 tablespoon lemon juice
2 tablespoons raspberries flavored
    syrup
Strawberry:
⅓ cup bottled lemon juice
1 tablespoon strawberries extract

Bring water to rapid boil in saucepan. Turn off heat, add tea bags, cover saucepan and let tea steep for an hour. Pour sugar or sweetener into 2 quart pitcher. Remove tea bags and pour tea into pitcher. Stir to dissolve sugar or sweetener. Add lemon juice and your desired fruit flavoring ingredients. Stir, cover and chill.

WARMING TOMATO DRINK

5 cups beef broth
1 cup tomato juice
1 cup water
1 ½ teaspoons horseradish
½ teaspoon dried dill weed

Heat all ingredients to simmering. Serve hot or cold. More spicy: Use spicy tomato juice or add drops of hot sauce to taste.

WASSAIL

Wassail is a hot, spiced punch often associated with Christmas. Particularly popular in Germanic countries, this drink would be the equivalent to beer or wine in many cultures of today. People drank it at parties and it was the main ale of the day.

1 quart apple juice	¼ cup brown sugar
1 quart orange juice	4 cinnamon sticks
2 cups cranberry juice	8 whole cloves
¼ cup lemon juice	8 whole allspice
½ cup honey	Orange slices

Combine all ingredients in listed order to crockpot (4 qt. or larger) and cook on low setting for about 4 hours or until heated to desired temperature. You may also cook on high initially for an hour and reduce heat to save time. This reheats well for 3 days.

WASSAIL WITH BRANDY

1 gallon apple cider	2 teaspoons ground nutmeg
2 cups cranberry juice	1 tablespoon whole cloves
1 6-ounce can orange juice concentrate	1 tablespoon allspice
1 6-ounce can lemonade concentrate	1 cup brandy
½ cup honey	Orange
½ cup sugar	8 cinnamon sticks

Set crockpot to lower setting; pour in apple cider, cranberry juice, orange juice, lemonade, honey and sugar; mix carefully. As it heats up, stir so honey and sugar dissolve. Stud orange with cloves; place in pot (they'll float). Add allspice, nutmeg; snap cinnamon sticks in half and add. Cover pot and allow to simmer 2-4 hours on low heat. About half hour prior to serving, add brandy

COOKIES

I wanted to take my new skills and use them for my family, but we were a meat and potatoes kind of family and not really open to much change in meal preparation. Besides, I needed to start off easy and work my way up, so I chose a simple thing everyone liked: cookies. No one turned down the offer of a cookie.

Surprisingly, as the aroma of baking cookies arose, so did the memories. Pleasant, recollections of grandma's nut cake and oatmeal cookies and mom's sugar free apple pies for dad, fried apricot pies, potato candy, blackberry cobbler and cinnamon scraps. I wanted to create those kinds of recollections; things that produced a smell in the house that people associated with familiar, fuzzy, caring feelings.

Good FRIENDS

Good FOOD

Good FUN

Fancy cookies are usually associated with holidays, special occasions, parties and exclusive festivities. I found if I made these small treats for no reason, people's moods and attitudes changed to party mode. It automatically made them smile and lifted spirits. It turned a mundane hour into something unique and made people feel special and relaxed. Laughter seemed to always quickly follow the first bite or two. It still remains a simple enough way to generate and establish memories lasting much longer than the cookies.

So I now believe there is a cookie for every situation. From the most formal setting

COLLECTED AND

to the most casual, "a cookie can be found". Cookies are associated with countries, regions, cultures, religions, families, rituals, schools, holidays, companies, social functions, festivals,

PERFECTED

organizations, events, climates and life's milestones. The simplest change can make it a new favorite.

Cookie-like hard wafers have existed for as long as baking is documented, in part because they travel very well. Cookies have always made a natural travel companion, which may be why we associate them with so many places and things. They are the piece of an event that we can take with us or the portion of us, we can send to others. They can remind us of home, a goal, a purpose, a celebration or communicate love, pride or concern. All from that little wafer like cake.

Whether you choose drop, molded, rolled, pressed, bar, sandwich or fried cookies—concoct your own recipe. Invent or name one after every friend, they will be thrillede. Always have some on hand for any unexpected situation or when you need to smile or laugh. Use them as a way to hug someone long distance or to form a tradition. Fill your own personall "**Life's Cookie Jar**".

ALABAMA COOKIES

The only place I ever had these cookies was in a small town in Alabama. They were so good, I just had to take the recipe with me. Since then, I've fixed them for people in several states and never had leftovers to take home. They make fun gifts too.

1 cup shortening	1 tablespoon salt
1 cup sugar	2 cups oats
1 cup brown sugar	2 cups chopped pecans
2 eggs	1 cup crispy rice cereal
1 teaspoon vanilla extract	1 cup flaked coconut
½ cup flour	

Cream shortening, gradually add sugars, beating well at medium speed of mixer. Add eggs and vanilla, beating well. Combine flour and salt, add to creamed mixture, mixing well. Stir in oats and remaining ingredients. Drop dough by heaping teaspoons onto sprayed cookie sheets. Bake in 325° oven for 10 to 12 minutes. Let cool slightly on cookie sheets, remove to wire rack to cool completely.

BUTTER PECAN SHORTBREAD

The sound just "melts in your mouth" as should the cookie. Butter pecan is a flavor, prominent especially in the United States, used to make cakes, cookies, and ice cream.

2 ½ cups flour	¼ cup finely chopped pecans, roasted
6 tablespoons brown sugar	1 teaspoon vanilla extract
1 cup butter	

Combine flour and sugar in bowl. Cut in butter until mixture resembles fine crumbs and starts to cling. Stir in pecans and vanilla. Form mixture into ball and knead until smooth. Divide dough into 2 halves. On lightly floured surface roll each half of dough to 6 x 8 rectangle, ½ inch thick. Use sharp knife or pizza cutter to cut dough into strips. Each rectangle makes 24-2x1 inch strips. Place 1 inch apart on ungreased baking sheet. Bake in 325° oven for 20-25 minutes. Cool on cookie sheet for 5 minutes. Transfer to wire rack; cool.

CHEWY BUTTER COOKIES

2 ½ cups flour	1 egg
¾ cups brown sugar	2 teaspoons vanilla extract
¼ teaspoon salt	2 tablespoons cream cheese
2 sticks butter cut into 16 pieces	

Soften cream cheese and butter to room temperature. With mixer, combine flour, sugar and salt on low speed. Keep mixer on low and add butter 1 piece at a time until crumbly and slightly wet. Add egg, vanilla and cream cheese; mix on low until dough just begins to form a ball. Knead dough by hand in bowl to form cohesive ball. Divide dough in half, pat into 2 4-inch disks, wrap each with plastic wrap; refrigerate until begins to firm up, 20-30 minutes. Roll out dough disks between parchment paper and chill in refrigerator 10 minutes before cutting cookies out. Keep dough firm, refrigerate as needed. Pat together scraps, re-roll and refrigerate before cutting cookies. Place cut outs on parchment-lined cookie sheet, bake in 375° oven about 10 minutes, until golden brown. Cool cookies on wire rack before decorating.

CHEWY MACAROON DROPS

Too simple not to make and serving them just makes the gathering special.

1 14-ounce can sweetened condensed milk	2 teaspoons vanilla extract
1 14-ounce bag coconut	

Mix all ingredients into large bowl. Drop by teaspoonfuls onto very well greased cookie sheet. Bake in 400° oven until golden brown. Remove and cool.

CHEWY OATMEAL COOKIES

Some people just prefer a nice chewy cookie and this one's been a favorite for many years.

2 cups old-fashioned oatmeal	1 teaspoon baking soda
2 cups flour	1 tablespoon cinnamon
½ cup sugar	¼ teaspoon salt
½ cup brown sugar	1 ½ teaspoons vanilla extract
1 ¼ cups shortening	1 cup evaporated milk
2 eggs	2 cups raisins

Blend all dry ingredients into large bowl, add shortening, eggs; add milk and vanilla. Mix very well and add raisins. Form into balls size of golf balls. Place on ungreased pan about 1-inch apart. Press center down slightly of each ball. Bake 350° oven for 15-20 minutes; don't over bake them. Check them often. They will be a little brown but look shiny and wet when taken out of oven. Remove from oven and cool on cookie sheet before removing to store.

CHOCOLATE BISCOTTI

Homemade biscotti is well received gift; it looks perfect and stays fresh for days and because it does take some time to prepare, most people don't make their own. Packaged in little cellophane bags tied with a colorful ribbon; people will think you spent a fortune on them at a fancy bakery and be delighted when told they were made by hand.

⅔ cup semisweet chocolate chips	2-2 ¼ cups flour
½ cup butter	½ cup unsweetened cocoa
2 eggs	1 ½ teaspoons baking powder
1 cup sugar	1 teaspoon salt
1 teaspoon vanilla extract	1 beaten egg white for glazing

Melt butter and chocolate together in microwave and set aside. Beat eggs and sugar until light yellow color, about 2 minutes with electric mixer. Add vanilla and cooled chocolate mixture. Mix flour, cocoa, baking powder and salt together; add to wet ingredients just until combined. Dough needs to be soft, but not sticky. Add extra ¼ cup of flour if dough is too sticky. Divide dough in half. On lightly floured surface, form each half into a log that is 3-½ inches by 9 inches. Place logs on a large baking sheet and brush with egg white. Bake in 350° oven for 25 minutes or until tops are set, remove from oven. Reduce oven to 275° while you let logs cool. (the cooler they are, the easier to cut and slice into ½-inch thick slices) Arrange slices on baking sheet and bake for 20 minutes. Remove from oven, carefully turn slices over and bake for another 20 minutes. Cool on wire rack. Store in an airtight container or freeze.

CHOCOLATE CANDY COOKIES

Whatever chocolate candy you use, changes the recipe to a new cookie. This one is easy to make for lots of different people without ever "repeating" the same cookie.

1 ½ cups brown sugar	3 ½ cups flour
1 cup shortening	2 teaspoons baking soda
1 cup butter	1 teaspoon salt
1 ½ tablespoons vanilla extract	3 cups candy-coated chocolate
2 eggs	candies

In large bowl, combine sugar, shortening, butter, vanilla and eggs; beat well. In separate bowl combine flour, baking soda and salt. Add to butter mixture; stir in 2 cups of candy. Cover bowl and refrigerate 1 hour. Shape dough into 2 inch balls; place on ungreased cookie sheet. Press remaining candies into balls to decorate tops. Bake in 350° oven for 15-20 minutes or until light golden brown. Cool 2 minutes; remove from cookie sheet to wire rack to cool.

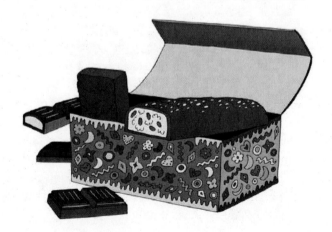

CRISP BUTTER COOKIES

Each crunchy bite just oozes with the rich taste.

2 ½ cups flour	2 sticks butter cut into 16 pieces
¾ cup granulated sugar	2 teaspoons vanilla extract
¼ teaspoon salt	2 tablespoons cream cheese

Soften cream cheese and butter to room temperature. With mixer, combine flour, sugar and salt on low speed. Keep mixer on low speed and add butter 1 piece at a time until mixture is crumbly and slightly wet. Add vanilla and cream cheese and mix on low until dough just begins to form large clumps. Knead dough by hand in bowl to form cohesive ball. Divide dough in half, pat into 2 4-inch disks, wrap each with plastic wrap and refrigerate until they begin to firm up; 20-30 minutes. Roll out dough disks between parchment paper; chill in refrigerator 10 minutes before cutting cookies out. Keep dough firm, refrigerate as needed. Pat together scraps, re-roll and refrigerate before cutting cookies. Place cut out shapes on sprayed baking sheet in 375° oven about 10 minutes, until golden brown. Cool cookies on wire rack before decorating.

CZECH FRIENDSHIP COOKIES

These cookies are just as special as my Czech "family" and friends.

2 sticks butter (not margarine)	2 cups flour
1 cup sugar	½ cup grape or strawberry jam
2 egg yolk	1 cup chopped walnuts

In electric mixing bowl cream butter until soft. Gradually add sugar and beat until light and fluffy. Add egg yolks and blend well. Gradually add flour and mix thoroughly; fold in nuts. Spoon half of batter into well-sprayed 8-inch baking pan. Top with jam keeping it away from pan edges. Cover jam with remaining dough. Drop by tablespoons and pat down lightly to flatten surface to edge of pan. Bake in 325° oven for 1 hour or until lightly brown. Remove from oven, cool and cut into bars.

DATE BARS

Probably one of the oldest fruits and still a winner in this cookie I first tasted in Minnesota.

1 cup butter	½ teaspoon allspice
2 cups sugar	1 cup chopped walnuts
3 eggs	2 tablespoons sugar
1 teaspoon baking soda	Icing:
2 teaspoons water	6 ounces almond bark
8 ounces chopped dates	1 teaspoon almond extract
3 ¼ cups flour	1 teaspoon instant coffee
1 teaspoon vanilla extract	3 tablespoons water
1 teaspoon cinnamon	¾ cup butter softened
1 teaspoon nutmeg	¼ cup powdered sugar
¼ teaspoon cloves	

Cream together butter and sugar; add eggs, baking soda, water and vanilla. Blend well and stir in dates. In separate bowl whisk together flour and spices; add to butter mixture and stir. Stir in chopped nuts. On lightly floured board, shape dough into 10 inch long and ¾ inch diameter rolls. Place rolls on sprayed cookie sheet; flatten with fingers to ½ inch thickness; sprinkle with sugar. Bake in 350° oven for about 25 minutes; remove from oven and allow to cool before icing. Icing: In small saucepan, melt almond bark over low heat, stirring constantly. Remove saucepan from heat. In small bowl stir together extract, instant coffee and water until mixed thoroughly. Stir into melted bark. Cool for 30 minutes. In separate bowl with electric mixer, beat sugar and butter until light and fluffy, beat in cooled candy until smooth. Ice bars and serve.

FIG AND GINGER COOKIES

These Jewish cookies are recognizable by the three-cornered shape and eaten during the holiday of Purim. They are made with many different flavors, including prune, nut, poppy, date, apricot, fruit preserves, chocolate, caramel or cheese. All are great and should be tried.

1 stick butter room temperature	2 cups flour
1 8-ounce package cream cheese	1 teaspoon baking powder
½ cup sugar	¾ cup figs preserves or filling
1 egg room temperature	3 tablespoons minced candied ginger

Mix fig preserves or jarred fig filling with minced candied ginger; set aside. In large bowl, cream together butter and cream cheese; add sugar and mix thoroughly. Add egg and mix thoroughly. In small bowl, combine flour and baking powder; gradually add to butter mixture; mix thoroughly. Refrigerate dough for 1 hour or until firm. On lightly floured surface, roll out small amount of dough about ¼ inch thick. If dough gets warm and hard to work with, refrigerate for a few minutes and re-roll. Use round cookie cutter or drinking glass to cut out circles. Arrange cut circles on cookie sheets. Spoon teaspoon of preserves into center of each cookie. Pinch edges of cookies to make 3 corners, but don't seal dough up completely. Bake in 350° oven for 15 to 18 minutes or until lightly golden brown. Cool on wire rack

FUDGE CRACKER COOKIES

This is like having crunchy fudge, a very different sensation with an old familiar flavor.

1 ½ cups semisweet chocolate chips	2-14-ounce can sweetened condensed milk
2-ounce unsweetened baking chocolate	3 ¾ cups graham cracker crumbs
	1 cup finely chopped walnuts

Grate chocolate squares and place chocolate in slow cooker. Cover and cook on high 1 hour, stirring every 15 minutes. Continue to cook on low, stirring until chocolate is melted. Stir milk into melted chocolate. Add 3 cups of graham cracker crumbs, 1 cup at a time, stir after each addition. Stir in nuts. Mixture will be thick but not stiff. Stir in remaining crumbs until cookie dough consistency. Drop by teaspoonfuls onto lightly sprayed cookie sheet. Keep remaining mixture warm by covering and turning slow cooker to warm. Bake in 325° oven for 7-9 minutes or until tops of cookies begin to crack. Remove from oven, let cool on baking sheet for 1 minute before transferring to waxed paper.

GENERATIONAL JUMBLE

This is the oldest cookie recipe in writing that has been found. When something is good, it will last the generations. The texture is delicate, so handle gently. Feel free to adjust the spices to suit your own taste.

2 cups softened butter	**2 teaspoons ginger**
2 cups sugar	**3 eggs**
2 teaspoons nutmeg	**6 cups flour**
2 teaspoons cinnamon	

In large bowl, cream together butter and sugar until very light and fluffy; stir in spices. In separate bowl whisk eggs until creamy and pale yellow in color. Whisk eggs into butter mixture. Sift in flour, one cup at a time until a tender but not sticky ball of dough is formed; add more flour if necessary. Roll out with rolling pin on floured surface. Slice pieces off with knife, roll them with your fingertips into ropes and twist them into a knot. Bake in 350° oven on ungreased baking sheets for 12 to 15 minutes. Cool on wire rack. They can be glazed if a sweeter treat is your desire.

Nothing made all of the people, surroundings, sounds and feelings of home rush over me like opening a "care package" filled with the homemade cookies I grew up eating.

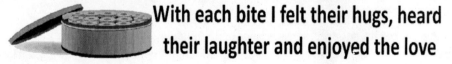

With each bite I felt their hugs, heard their laughter and enjoyed the love

GINGERSNAP

If there is a list of America's favorite cookies, gingersnaps must be on it. This highly addictive, sugar coated cookie gets its chewy texture and spicy flavor from adding brown sugar, molasses, cinnamon, ginger and cloves to the batter. There are differences of opinion as to how 'spicy' a gingersnap should be. Being one of my husband's favorite snacks, he gets to choose the level of spiciness at our house.

¾ cup butter room temperature	½ teaspoon baking soda
½ cup brown sugar	¼ teaspoon salt
½ cup sugar	1 ½ teaspoons cinnamon
¼ cup molasses	2 teaspoons ground ginger
1 egg	½ teaspoon ground cloves
½ teaspoon vanilla extract	Garnish:
2 cups flour	1 cup raw sugar or coarse sugar

In bowl with electric mixer cream butter and sugars until light and fluffy 2-3 minutes. Add molasses, egg, and vanilla extract and beat until combined. In separate bowl whisk together flour, baking soda, salt, and spices. Add to butter mixture and mix until well combined. Cover and chill batter for 30 minutes. Line two baking sheets with parchment paper. Place raw or coarse sugar in medium sized bowl. When dough has chilled, roll into 1 inch balls. Roll balls of dough into sugar, coating them thoroughly. Place on baking sheet, spacing about 2 inches apart; with bottom of glass, flatten cookies slightly. Bake in 350° oven for 12-15 minutes or until cookies feel dry and firm on top. The longer the cookies bake, the more crisp they will be. Cool on wire rack.

GRANNY'S OATMEAL COOKIES

Grandma would mix the batter with her hand and never measured anything. It took a long time to finally work out the exact measurements so our family could enjoy them after she was gone. Making them still reminds me of her kitchen and sticky hands.

2 cups flour	2 teaspoons cinnamon
2 cups 1-minute oatmeal (not instant)	¼ teaspoon salt
	1 ½ teaspoons vanilla extract
1 cup white sugar (not brown)	6 tablespoons evaporated milk
1 cup shortening	1 ½ cups raisins
2 eggs	
1 teaspoon baking soda	

Blend all dry ingredients into large bowl, add shortening, eggs, mix well and then add milk and vanilla. Add raisins and form into balls walnut size. Place on ungreased pan about 1 inch apart. Bake 350° oven for 15-20 minutes. Don't over bake them; check them often. They will be turning a little brown but should look shiny and still wet when you take them out of oven. Remove from cookie sheet and cool on wire rack.

HARVEST COOKIES

Harvest time is full of frenzied activities before the long winter in many parts of the country and a simple but substantial cookie is always a welcome snack or quick break from the work. These went well with the fresh apple cider we were pressing the old fashioned way one cold September in Wenatchee Washington.

2 ¼ cups flour	¾ cup brown sugar
1 teaspoon salt	1 teaspoon vanilla extract
1 teaspoon baking soda	2 eggs
¼ teaspoon apple pie spice	2 cups white chocolate chips
1 cup butter softened	1 cup dried cranberries
¾ cup sugar	1 cup chopped pecans

Combine flour, salt, baking soda and spice in small bowl. Beat butter, sugars and vanilla in large bowl until creamy. Add eggs, one at a time, beating well after each addition. Gradually beat in flour mixture; stir in chips, cranberries and pecans. Drop by rounded tablespoonfuls onto ungreased baking sheet. Bake in 375° oven for 9-10 minutes or until slightly brown.

HEAVENLY PEANUT BUTTER BARS

I was playing with recipes one day; took batches into work and these got the most votes that day. Complicated isn't always best. Simple, quick and good, who could ask for more.

1 box cake mix yellow or white	1 cup peanut butter
1 beaten egg	1 cup chopped peanuts
4 tablespoons melted butter	

Mix all ingredients together and press into lightly sprayed 13x9 baking pan. Bake in 350° oven for 15 minutes, just until golden brown. Do NOT overcook. Let stand 5 minutes, cut into squares. One cup semi-sweet chocolate chips can be melted in microwave for 1 minute and spread on top before they are cut to make a Chocolate Peanut Butter Bar.

HOLIDAY SHORTBREAD COOKIES

A true shortbread cookie recipe is the most basic of all cookie recipes. Butter, flour and sugar with maybe some salt. This one has a crisp and yet crumbly texture and will absolutely melt in your mouth. I first ate this cookie in Kansas around a huge fireplace while toasting chestnuts.

1 ⅓ cups cornstarch	2 ½ teaspoons lemon peels divided
2 cups flour	½ teaspoon vanilla extract
4 ⅔ cups powdered sugar divided	¼ teaspoon almond extract
2 ⅓ cups butter divided (no margarine)	⅓ cup lemon juice

Shortbread: In large bowl, combine cornstarch, flour and ⅔ cup of powdered sugar; set aside. With electric mixer on medium, beat 2 cups butter until fluffy and smooth. Add flour mixture, 1 ½ teaspoon lemon peel, vanilla and almond. Beat until well blended. Shape dough in to 1-inch balls and place on ungreased cookie sheet. Bake 10-12 minutes or until edges are lightly browned. Remove from oven; cool completely on wire racks.

Icing: With electric mixer, beat together ⅓ cup butter and 1 teaspoon lemon peel until smooth. Add remaining 4 cups sugar and beat until well combined. Stir in lemon juice and beat well. Ice cookies.

HOLIDAY SWIRLS

Swirls have been a festive favorite for generations and recipes are found in most of my 1950's cookbooks. For colored layers: Christmas use red and green; for Valentine's use pink and red; for Fall time try shades of brown, golden yellow and orange.

1 cup butter	1 teaspoon baking soda
1 ½ cups powdered sugar	1 teaspoon cream of tartar
1 egg	¼ teaspoon salt
1 teaspoon vanilla extract	Food coloring
2 ½ cups flour	1 beaten egg

In large bowl with electric mixer on medium speed, cream butter, sugar and egg. In separate bowl combine flour, baking soda, cream of tartar and salt. At low speed add flour mixture to butter mixture. Remove ⅓ of dough; tint one color with a few drops at a time until you have desired color. Remove another ⅓ of the dough and repeat with second color. Keep remaining dough uncolored. Chill dough for 30 minutes. On lightly floured board, roll each color of dough out in rectangle of equal size, ¼-inch thick. Lightly brush one rectangle of dough with beaten egg; be careful not to leave puddles. Stack second rectangle directly on top of first one, pressing lightly to adhere. Brush second layer with beaten egg and stack white layer on top. Press lightly to adhere. Roll lengthwise into tight log. Wrap in plastic wrap and chill for 4 hours or overnight. When ready to bake, spray two cookie sheets. Cut log into ¼-inch slices and arrange 1-inch apart. Bake 8-10 minutes or until lightly colored. Let cool in pans for 5 minutes; transfer to wire rack and cool completely.

ITALIAN ALMOND BISCOTTI

Biscotti has been around since Roman times. Traditional Italian biscotti does not contain butter, it's flavored with anise and break-your-teeth hard because it's meant to be dunked in coffee before eating. This version is a hit for holiday treats.

3 cups whole almonds	2 ½ cups flour
1 cup sugar	4 eggs
1 cup brown sugar	1 teaspoon vanilla extract
½ teaspoon brown sugar	2 teaspoons grated orange peel
½ teaspoon cinnamon	1 beaten egg for egg wash
2 teaspoons baking powder	

Line two large baking sheets with parchment paper. Place almonds in single layer on baking sheet and toast in 350° oven for 10 minutes, or until light golden. Remove and set aside to cool. In large bowl, hand mix toasted almonds, sugars, cinnamon, baking powder and flour. In small bowl, whisk eggs. Add vanilla and orange peel; whisk until well blended. Add to flour mixture. Work batter together with lightly floured hands. Mixture will be sticky; keep squeezing batter until dough starts to form. Once dough is firm, form into ball. Divide ball into four equal pieces. Place one piece of dough on lightly floured surface. Using hands, roll into log approximately 8 inches long, 2 inches wide and ¾ of an inch high. Repeat with remaining three pieces of dough. Place two logs on each baking sheet. Brush loaves with egg wash. Bake for 40 minutes, rotating pans midway through. Tops of loaves will be shiny and deep golden. Cool on rack for about 20 minutes. Place loaf on cutting board and using large serrated knife, slice cookies ¾ of an inch thick on diagonal. If cookie crumbles, let it cool for a few more minutes. Don't let it rest too long, it could become too hard to slice. Place slices on sides on baking sheets. Place in still-warm oven with temperature off and door closed for 30 to 60 minutes. The longer they stay in the oven, the harder they will become. Remove from oven and cool completely before storing in air-tight container, preferably metal tin, which helps keep them crisp. Stored properly, biscotti will last up to a month.

MACADAMIA COOKIES

Friends brought back some of these heavenly Hawaiian gifts to us. I searched and experimented until I found the right combination so we could enjoy a little of the islands here in Alaska all year round.

1 stick butter	**½ teaspoon cinnamon**
½ cup corn syrup	**1 cup flour**
½ cup brown sugar	**½ cup chopped macadamia nuts**
4 teaspoons unsweetened cocoa	

Bring butter, corn syrup and brown sugar to boil in medium saucepan, stirring constantly.

Combine cocoa powder, cinnamon, flour and chopped macadamia nuts in small bowl; gradually stir into hot butter mixture. Drop dough by level tablespoons, about 3 inches apart, on sprayed cookie sheets. Bake in 375° oven for 5 to 6 minutes, until golden brown and bubbling. Cool on sheets for 1 to 2 minutes then remove to wire rack to cool completely.

MACAROON BARS

I can't resist trying coconut in all sorts of things and just seems to make anything "richer" and "moister"—these are fabulous for a party and so easy to make.

1 cup graham cracker crumbs	¼ cup flour
1 cup sugar divided	3 egg whites
¼ cup butter melted	1 egg
3 ¾ cups coconut	1 teaspoon almond extract
¼ teaspoon salt	

In bowl, stir together crumbs, ¼ cup of sugar and melted butter. Press mixture into bottom of 13 x 9 inch baking pan. Bake in 350° oven for 5 minutes, remove from oven and set aside to cool. In same bowl, mix together rest of sugar, coconut, salt, flour, egg whites, egg and almond extract. Spread batter over crumb bottom. Bake in 350° oven for 30-35 minutes or until lightly brown. Cool before cutting into bars.

MADEL "BREAD"

*Mandelbrot, which literally means **almond bread**, is a twice-baked hard treat similar to Italian biscotti, but requires no additional sauces or dips in order to be enjoyed. The second baking at the lower temperature depends on how toasty you like the final cookie. I've made them baked only once and baked twice and enjoyed both. Plain or adding either cherries, raisins or chips or a combination gives you several varieties to serve. These also pack and travel well for gift giving and people absolutely love getting them.*

3 eggs	2 teaspoons baking powder
½ cup canola oil	1 cup almond slices
1 cup sugar	1 cup dried cherries or raisins
1 teaspoon vanilla extract	(optional)
2 tablespoons lemon juice	1 cup semisweet chocolate chips
3 cups flour	(optional)
	Sugar and cinnamon

By hand or mixer, beat eggs, oil and sugar into a yellow, creamy mixture. Whisk in vanilla and juice. Combine dry ingredients and mix in by hand. Dough should be firm and a little stiff, consistency of play dough. If dough is too moist to handle, add up to ½ cup more flour. Knead in almonds, raisins and/or chocolate chips. Knead into a ball then slice ball into four wedges. Roll each wedge into a loaf about 12 inches long. Prepare baking sheet with foil; Spray foil with oil or non-stick spray. Place loaves on sheet, about four inches apart. Sprinkle with cinnamon-sugar mixture. Bake in 350° oven for 30 minutes and remove from oven, slice while warm. You'll get about a dozen slices per loaf. Turn pieces on sides and sprinkle with remaining cinnamon sugar. Toast in oven 2-4 minutes. Cool. The cookies are fine to eat like this, but if you want the more traditional and crispy cookies then reduce oven heat to 250° when you remove them from the oven after the first baking. Wait and when loaves are cool, slice on a diagonal. Lay the slices flat on the foil of the baking pan. Sprinkle again with cinnamon-sugar. Return to oven for the second baking of 20 minutes. Flip slices after 10 minutes. Try them both ways to see which you like better.

MENNONITE PEANUT BUTTER COOKIES

This unusual recipe was one I had while in Ohio with a very giving family. They are eggless, which was important to their son who had allergies.

1 ½ cups brown sugar
1 ½ cups sugar
1 ¼ cups butter
1 ½ teaspoons vanilla extract

1 tablespoon baking soda
3 ¾ cups flour
1 ¼ cups peanut butter

Combine all ingredients and mix together well. Drop by teaspoonfuls onto a cookie sheet. Press cookies flat with fork. Bake in 350° oven for 8-10 minutes.

MOUND BALLS

Most people love the combination of coconut and chocolate. I've tried lots of different recipes and each one has little variations, this is the one I get the most compliments on.

½ pound butter

1 pound powdered sugar

1 pound flaked coconut

½ cup sweetened condensed milk

1 cup chopped walnuts

1 teaspoon vanilla extract

12 ounces semisweet chocolate chips

4 ounces unsweetened baking chocolate

In mixing bowl, cream together butter and sugar; add coconut, milk, walnuts and vanilla; stir until well blended. Chill until slightly firm; roll into walnut size balls. Insert toothpick in each ball. Place balls on cookie sheet and freeze. In double boiler over simmering water, melt chocolate and chips. Using toothpicks as handles, dip frozen balls into chocolate mixture. Stick upright onto wax paper covered Styrofoam sheet. Chill until firm.

NEIMAN MARCUS COOKIES

There are several variations of this recipe, but I researched and believe this to be the original type of cookie that was served at Neiman Marcus.

1 cup butter softened

2 cups brown sugar

6 tablespoons sugar

2 eggs

1 ½ tablespoons vanilla extract

3 ½ cups flour

1 teaspoon baking powder

1 teaspoon baking soda

1 teaspoon salt

1 tablespoon instant espresso powder

3 cups semisweet chocolate chips

Cream butter with sugars using electric mixer on medium speed until fluffy about 30 seconds. Beat in egg and vanilla extract for 30 seconds. In mixing bowl, sift together dry ingredients; beat into butter mixture at low speed for about 15 seconds. Stir in espresso coffee powder and chocolate chips. Using tablespoon, drop cookie dough onto greased cookie sheet about 3 inches apart. Gently press down on dough with back of spoon to spread out into 2-inch circle. Bake in 300° oven for 20 minutes or until nicely browned around edges. Bake little longer for crispier cookie.

ORIGINAL CHOCOLATE CHIP COOKIES PLUS

Everyone has a favorite chocolate chip cookie recipe, most variations come from the Toll House recipe developed in 1937 by Ruth Wakefield—now declared the most popular cookie of all time. Here's the original and just one different way to fix them. Using different oatmeals, breakfast cereals, peanut butter, raisins different nuts and dried fruits create wonderful variations to these cookies. Bake them in a pan and cut into bars for a different texture and to save time with preparation.

2 ¼ cups flour
1 teaspoon baking soda
1 teaspoon salt
1 cup soft butter
¾ cup sugar
¾ cup brown sugar
1 teaspoon vanilla extract
2 eggs
12 ounces semisweet chocolate chips

1 cup chopped nuts (optional)
One Popular Variation:
Use only ½ teaspoon baking soda and
Use only 1 egg and only ½ teaspoon salt
Add 1 teaspoon baking powder
Use ½ cup milk chocolate chips
½ cup semisweet chocolate chips
½ cup white chocolate chips

Toll House: Sift together flour, baking soda and salt in small bowl. Beat butter, sugar, brown sugar and vanilla in large mixer bowl until creamy. Add eggs one at a time, beating well after each addition. Gradually beat in flour mixture on low speed, don't over do it. Fold in chips and nuts. Drop by rounded tablespoon onto ungreased baking sheets. Bake in 375° oven for 9-11 minutes or until golden brown. Cool on baking sheets for 2 minutes; remove to wire racks to cool completely.

Variation: Sift together flour, baking powder, baking soda and salt in small bowl. Beat butter, sugar and brown sugar in large mixer bowl until creamy. Add vanilla and eggs and mix on medium speed. Gradually beat in flour mixture on low speed, don't over do it. Fold in chips and nuts. Drop by rounded tablespoon onto ungreased baking sheets. Bake in 350° oven for 18-20 minutes or until golden brown. Cool on baking sheets for 2 minutes; remove to wire racks to cool completely.

PARTY COOKIES

I first tasted these at a football party in Missoula Montana. It's been a favorite at game nights and potlucks for over 25 years.

1 cup shortening	1 teaspoon baking soda
1 cup sugar	1 teaspoon cinnamon
1 cup molasses	4 cups flour
1 cup strong hot coffee	1 teaspoon salt
2 eggs	1 teaspoon ground ginger

In large bowl, combine shortening and sugar; blend in molasses, coffee and eggs. Sift baking soda, cinnamon, flour, salt and ginger together. Mix dry ingredients into wet ingredients. Drop by teaspoonfuls on sprayed cookie sheet. Bake in 375° oven for 10 minutes. Frost with a vanilla, maple or orange glaze while still warm.

PEANUT BUTTER COOKIES

These came from experimenting with a lot of reliable recipes and taste testing parties. So far these measurements and ingredients seem to please the most and bring back the memories of childhood for those who enjoyed this wonderful cookie before all the nut allergies developed over the years.

1 cup butter	2 eggs
1 ½ cups peanut butter	3 cups flour
1 cup sugar	1 teaspoon baking powder
1 cup brown sugar	½ teaspoon salt
1 teaspoon vanilla extract	1 ½ teaspoons baking soda

Cream together butter, peanut butter and sugars. Beat in eggs and vanilla. In separate bowl, sift together flour, baking powder, baking soda, and salt. Stir into batter. Put batter in refrigerator for 1 hour. Roll into 1-inch balls and put on baking sheets. Flatten each ball with fork, making a crisscross pattern. Bake in 375° oven for about 10 minutes or until cookies begin to brown. Do not over-bake.

RAISIN COOKIES

An incredible family in Ohio introduced me to this cookie, it was a many generation favorite. Raisins are sweet due to their high concentration of sugars. If they are stored for a long period, the sugar inside the fruit crystallizes. This makes the dry raisins gritty, but won't affect their usability. The sugar grains dissolve when the raisins are swelled in hot water. So if you have some old raisins around, try this one.

2 cups raisins
1 cup boiling water
1 cup shortening
1 cup sugar
1 cup brown sugar
3 eggs
1 ½ teaspoons vanilla extract

4 cups flour
1 teaspoon baking powder
1 teaspoon baking soda
1 teaspoon salt
1 ½ teaspoons cinnamon
½ teaspoon allspice

Cook raisins in boiling water for 5 minutes. Set aside to cool. In mixing bowl, cream shortening; add sugar and beat well. Add eggs and beat until well blended. Add vanilla and cooled raisins. In another bowl, combine flour, baking powder, soda, salt, and spices. Add flour mixture to creamed mixture; mix well. Drop raisin cookie dough by spoonfuls on greased cookie sheet. Bake in 325° oven for 10 to 14 minutes, depending on size of cookies.

RHUBARB COCONUT COOKIE

I mixed rhubarb with my wonderful coconut and it was irresistible even to me.

½ cup shortening
1 ⅓ cups brown sugar
1 egg
2 cups flour
½ teaspoon baking soda
1 teaspoon cinnamon
½ teaspoon cloves

½ teaspoon nutmeg
½ teaspoon salt
¼ cup milk
1 cup finely chopped rhubarb
1 cup chopped walnuts
1 cup raisins
½ cup coconut

Cream shortening and brown sugar; beat in egg. Mix together flour, baking soda, spices and salt. Add dry mixture to creamed mixture alternating with milk. Stir in rhubarb, nuts, raisins and coconut. Drop by tablespoons onto sprayed cookie sheet. Bake in 375° oven for 12-15 minutes or until golden. Cool on racks.

RHUBARB SHORTBREAD SQUARES

Rhubarb being inexpensive and easy to grow, I started developing recipes to put it in.

1 cup flour
2 tablespoons sugar
¼ teaspoon salt
½ cup cold butter
Filling:
4 cups diced rhubarb
1 ¼ cups sugar

¼ cup water
⅛ teaspoon salt
2 envelopes unflavored gelatin
⅓ cup cold water
4 drops red food coloring
1 cup whipping cream whipped

In bowl, combine flour, sugar and salt; cut in butter until crumbly. Press into sprayed 8-inch square baking dish. Bake in 350° oven for 15-20 minutes or until edges are lightly browned. Cool on wire rack. In saucepan, bring rhubarb, sugar, water and salt to boil. Reduce heat; simmer, uncovered, for 8-10 minutes or until rhubarb is tender, stirring occasionally. In small bowl, sprinkle gelatin over cold water; let stand for 1 minute. Stir into rhubarb mixture. Cook and stir until gelatin is dissolved; stir in food coloring. Cover and refrigerate until cooled, 2 hours. Fold in whipped cream; spread over crust. Cover and refrigerate for 3 hours or until set. Cut into squares.

RICE KRISPY BARS

Here are 3 different ways I've prepared this snack and all get rave reviews. In different parts of the country, each is considered The One and only Rice Krispy Treat recipe.

¼ cup butter
6 cups crispy rice cereal
4 cups miniature marshmallows
Peanut Butter:

Add ¼ cup peanut butter
Scotch Bars:
¼ cup peanut butter
1 cup butterscotch chips

Melt butter in 3-quart saucepan. Add marshmallows and cook over low heat, stirring constantly, until marshmallows are melted and mixture is syrupy. Remove from heat. Add cereal and stir until well coated. Press warm mixture evenly and firmly into buttered 13 X 9-inch pan. Cut into squares when cool. Peanut Butter: When melted marshmallow mixture is removed from heat, stir in peanut butter before adding cereal. Scotch: Melt chips in microwave; when melted marshmallow mixture is removed from heat, stir in peanut butter and chips before adding cereal.

SCOTTISH SHORTBREAD

The story has it that medieval Scots baked shortbread in the winter months and put cuts in it to represent the suns rays. In Alaska I call them my "Winter Solstice" Cookie—to celebrate the shortest day of the year.

½ cup superfine sugar
2 teaspoons cinnamon
½ teaspoon cardamom
½ teaspoon ginger

¾ teaspoon allspice
½ teaspoon salt
3 cups flour
1 cup softened butter

In medium bowl, stir together sugar, cinnamon, cardamom, ginger, allspice and salt. Divide into two equal parts; set one aside. Add flour and butter to other half; stir until blended. It should be slightly grainy. Press dough evenly into 8-inch square pan. Cut into 1x2 inch pieces using knife; prick with tines of a fork. This will keep shortbread from warping while baking. Sprinkle reserved sugar and spice liberally over top, brush into all of cuts and holes. Bake for 25 to 30 minutes in 350° oven, or until firm and golden at edges. Do not brown. Cool completely in pan, and break into pieces along the lines to serve

SIMPLE PUMPKIN FRIED COOKIES

Fried was the only way to make homemade cookies since there were no ovens in family homes until late in the twentieth century. They're still an authentic type treat to fix for "Western Days" celebrations and "Wild West" parties.

1 cup raisins	1 tablespoon baking powder
2 ⅔ cup pumpkin puree	1 teaspoon grated lemon peels
⅔ cup flour	2 cups vegetable oil for frying
¼ cup sugar	⅓ cup powdered sugar
⅛ teaspoon salt	

Soak raisins in hot water for 10 minutes, drain water off and pat dry with paper towels. In large bowl, mix together pumpkin puree, flour, sugar, salt, baking powder and lemon peel. Fold in raisins. Roll dough into balls size of walnuts. Heat vegetable oil in large deep skillet or deep fryer to 365°. Fry cookies in small batches until golden brown all over. Test with toothpick for doneness. Drain off excess oil with paper towels and dust with powdered sugar. Pumpkin Puree: ¾ pound baked pumpkin makes about 1 cup puree. Cut top from pumpkin and scrape out stringy membranes and seeds. Cut pumpkin into large pieces and place skin side down on a baking sheet. Bake in 350° oven for about 45 minutes or until pumpkin is soft. Let baked pumpkin pieces cool until they can be handled. Scoop and scrape out pumpkin flesh. Mash well with fork in bowl, or pulse in food processor or blender to puree. Pureed pumpkin can be added to pancakes, mousse, soups, frostings and breads.

SMART TREASURE COOKIES

Originally conceived of as a health food, modern commercial grahams have remained popular as a snack food and breakfast cereal. With greater amounts of sugar and other sweeteners than in the original recipe, and far less graham flour, these crackers are no longer considered a health food but are still special.

1 ½ cups graham cracker crumbs
½ cup flour
2 teaspoons baking powder
1 14-ounce can sweetened
    condensed milk

½ cup margarine softened
2 cups raisins
1 ⅓ cups coconut
1 cup chopped walnuts

Mix crumbs, flour and baking powder in small bowl, set aside. In another bowl, beat margarine and milk until smooth. Add crumb mixture, mix well. Stir in raisins, coconut and walnuts. Drop by spoonfuls onto lightly sprayed cookie sheet. Bake in 375° oven for 9-10 minutes or until lightly browned. Cool 2-3 minutes; remove from cookie sheets.

I never imagined it would be so hard to order a simple beverage.

I love ice tea in any type of weather and got very hooked on drinking fresh Sun Tea. Then I started traveling through the southern states. If you've ever traveled in the south you know how sweet they drink their tea. First taste and I learned to ask specifically for mine to be "unsweetened" but some restaurants didn't have any and offered to give me a glass of ice, hot water and a tea bag to make my own.  Times have changed and now most places offer several flavored teas, all kinds of sweeteners and numerous kinds of tea bags.

In a restaurant on the East Coast, I asked for my favorite drink a 'diet soda'. The waitress was polite but obviously confused and finally explained they didn't have diet ice cream, but they could put the diet pop in with regular ice cream.

At another eatery I again ordered a "diet soda" and they asked if I wanted the ice cream to be diet or the pop to be diet or both.

In another part of the country I requested a 'pop or soda' trying to keep from confusing anyone. This server looked perplexed and asked me if I meant 'a coke'. I said yes and she asked me 'what kind of 'coke' I wanted. Now I was confused. She said they had, 'orange, lemon-lime, root beer, diet and regular'. I just smiled.

VEGETABLES

Once I graduated from nursing school I moved into an apartment and looked forward to cooking in my own kitchen. But I had no idea how to cook for one person. I snacked, ate fast foods and gained weight. Unfortunately the emphasis for weight control groups in the 1970's was on "diet" foods and substitutes for the high calorie goodies.

The cookbooks had strange ingredients with complicated, strict and difficult instructions to follow. I worked at it with gusto, attempting to cook vegetables and items I'd never heard of or wanted to taste. I filled my refrigerator with the "good stuff".

The dishes required lots of spices to imitate familiar foods. I knew about salt, pepper, garlic salt and cinnamon, that was it. Suddenly I had a whole cabinet full of strange spices to use. There were other unfamiliar ingredients available only at health food places. At the time in St. Louis, "health food" stores were not easy to find or plentiful. There were no substitutions usually and I didn't have the knowledge to make recipe changes.

The finished dishes lacked texture or had unfamiliar after taste from the only artificial sweeteners available leaving a lingering bitterness in your mouth. The dishes weren't something you would serve to guest or take to a potluck. I grew very tired of eating alone and the social restrictions.

Nutrition was an up and coming field, so I plowed through the difficult science of it and studied calories, fats, sugars, fruit, protein, and veggies. The best discovery was raw, fresh, crunchy vegetables. Bags and bowls of them could be found in my car, my fridge, at work and in my tote. Some days, vegetables were all I ate with my diet

soda. I was free of the complicated kitchen recipes, but not for long. Soon it became clear I wasn't getting all the nutrients I needed. I had a lot more to learn about healthy eating; it has been a process.

In the 1990's, Joe and I joined a weight reduction class together. In twenty years, a lot of things about "diet food and theories" had changed. Gone were the long lists of totally forbidden foods or special ingredients to make the "pretend" entrees and desserts. The new emphasis was on eating everything, but all in moderation. We planned out our meals and watched the quantities. The whole approach was more natural and conducive to entertaining company and eating with others in their homes or at restaurants. I was totally relieved and encouraged when my husband announced after our first meeting, "Any diet that includes peanut butter and jelly sandwiches sounds doable."

We loved snacking on vegetables and eating salads for meals. I made "chips" out of all kinds of those versatile vegetables. We learned to grill, bake, broil, steam, stir-fry, roast and dip those veggies. Different dip, sauces and seasonings made it easy to vary the taste. To this day we still love to throw some protein in a large bowl of salad and let that be our supper or dinner. Living in Alaska we miss our long growing seasons, until we moved to the area of Alaska where the majority of produce is grown for the whole state. With sunshine 24 hours a day for 2-3 months, we squeeze in the summer and accelerate our growing season while loving every crunchy minute.

AMISH CHOW CHOW

Chow-chow is regionally associated with Pennsylvania and southern United States, though the recipes vary greatly. Pennsylvania chow-chow is generally much sweeter than the southern types. It can be eaten by itself or can be used as a condiment on biscuits and gravy, pinto beans, hot dogs, hamburgers and other foods.

2 cups cucumbers	1 cup green bell peppers
2 cups corn	1 cup red bell peppers
1 cup green beans	½ cup small onions
1 cup yellow wax beans	1 tablespoon dry mustard
2 cups lima beans	1 cup sugar
2 cups cauliflower	2 cups cider vinegar
1 cup celery	

Chop vegetables in varying sizes and cook until just tender (DO NOT OVERCOOK). Do this by cooking all vegetables separately, then mix them together. Combine sugar, vinegar and dry mustard in large pot; bring to boil. Add vegetables; bring to boil again. Remove from heat, place into jars or tight lid containers and refrigerate

BAKED CHEESE GRITS

I prefer my grits plain with butter and stirred into my eggs, but this dish has made believers of my dinner guest from many northern states that grits aren't exclusively a southern food.

2 cups chicken broth	1 cup shredded Cheddar cheese
½ cup quick cooking grits	1 tablespoon margarine
1 beaten egg	

In saucepan bring chicken broth to boiling. Slowly add grits, stir constantly. Gradually stir ½ cup grits into egg. Return egg mixture to saucepan and stir to combine. Remove from heat, stir in cheese and margarine until all is melted. Spoon grits into casserole dish. Bake in 325° oven for 25-30 minutes. A knife inserted near center should come out clean. Let stand 5 minutes before serving.

BAKED ZUCCHINI FRIES

What a great substitute to French fries or even the new favorite dish sweet potato fries. Zucchini is so plentiful in gardens everywhere, you can never have too many ways to fix it.

3 cups unseasoned bread crumbs	1 cup flour
½ teaspoon kosher salt	2 eggs beaten
¼ teaspoon black pepper	3 medium zucchini

Cut peeled zucchini lengthwise into 2 inch long and ¼ inch thick pieces. Combine bread crumbs, salt and pepper in bowl. Place flour in another bowl and beaten eggs in another bowl. Dip zucchini sticks first in flour until lightly coated, then in beaten eggs. Roll in bread crumbs until well covered. Transfer zucchini pieces onto nonstick baking sheet. Bake in 350° oven until tender but coating is crisp, about 20 minutes. Let fries cool slightly before eating. (Try adding different seasonings to our bread crumbs and find your favorite way to enjoy this simple dish)

BROCCOLI SALAD

Most store deli's have this salad, but making it at home is easy and keeps too much sugar being added.

2 bunches fresh broccoli chopped	1 cup frozen green peas
¾ cup red onions chopped	Salt and black pepper to taste
1 cup chopped celery	½ cup grated Cheddar cheese
⅔ cup raisins	(optional)
1 cup hulled sunflower seeds	1 cup mayonnaise
12-16 ounces bacon cooked,	¼ cup honey
crumbled	2 tablespoons cider vinegar

Toss together broccoli, onion, celery, raisins, sunflower seeds, peas and bacon in large bowl. Set aside. In separate bowl, beat together vinegar, honey and mayonnaise. Pour dressing over salad and toss to coat. Refrigerate at least 2 hours before serving

COLLARD GREENS

Collard greens are a very nutritious and inexpensive treat. Traditional pork-seasoned turnip greens, kale, collards, or mustard greens are served up with freshly baked corn bread to dip. If you like spinach, just try these once, you'll be surprised by the flavor.

½ pound smoked meat: ham hocks, turkeys wings or neck bones	1 tablespoon seasoned salt
2 teaspoons salt	1-3 teaspoons hot sauce
½ teaspoon black pepper	1 bunch collard greens
½ teaspoon garlic powder	1 tablespoon butter
	Barbecue sauce (optional)

In large pot, bring 3 quarts of water to boil and add smoked meat, salt, pepper, garlic powder, seasoned salt and hot sauce. Reduce heat to medium and cook for 1 hour. Wash collard greens thoroughly. Easiest way to clean them is in the sink or a very large pot filled with cold water. After cutting stems and heavy ribs out, place leaves in cold water. Soak for few minutes; swish around to loosen grit and sand; drain. Repeat process two or three times, depending on how gritty leaves are. Remove stems that run down center by holding leaf in left hand and strip leaf down with right hand. Tender young leaves in heart of collards don't need to be stripped. Stack 6 to 8 leaves on top of one another and roll up, cut into ½ to 1-inch thick slices. Place greens in pot with meat and add butter. Cook for 45 to 60 minutes, stirring occasionally. When done taste and adjust seasoning.

CORN ON THE COB GRILLED—2 WAYS

This a popular menu item for barbecues and clambakes and it's easy to do. It never fails to impress guests and especially delicious when you add other herbs and spices to the ear of corn before grilling it.

6 ears fresh corn in their husk	Salt and black pepper
6 tablespoons softened butter	Herbs and Spices

Prepare grill, gas or charcoal, with direct, high heat, about 550° and lightly oil grate. First Way: Place corn in their husks on hot grill. Cover. Turn corn occasionally, until husks are charred on all sides, about 15 to 20 minutes.

Remove corn from grill. Let sit 5 minutes. Use a hand towel to protect hands while removing silks and charred husks from corn. Serve hot, with butter. Second Way: Peel back husks and remove silk. Place 1 tablespoon butter, salt and pepper on each piece of corn. Close husks. Wrap each ear of corn tightly in aluminum foil. Place on prepared grill. Cook approximately 30 minutes, turning until corn is tender.

CREAMY SUMMER SQUASH FOR PASTA

2 pounds summer squash or
   zucchini
1 tablespoon kosher salt
4 quarts water
1 tablespoon table salt
1 pound bow tie pasta
5 tablespoons olive oil
1 tablespoon minced garlic

½ teaspoon red pepper flakes
1 pint grape or cherry tomatoes cut
   in half
½ cup chopped fresh basil
2 tablespoons balsamic vinegar
¼ cup chopped pine nuts toasted
Parmesan cheese

Toss zucchini/squash with kosher salt in medium bowl. Place in large colander, set colander over bowl and let stand 30 minutes. Spread squash over paper towels and pat dry. Wipe off residual salt. Boil water and table salt until rolling boil, add pasta and cook until al dente. Drain and return to pot. Heat 1 tablespoon of oil in skillet over high heat until just beginning to smoke. Coat pan with oil, add half of squash and cook, stir until golden brown, transfer to plate. Add another tablespoon oil to skillet and cook last half of squash. Place on plate. Using same skillet, add tablespoon of oil. Heat on medium high heat and add garlic and pepper flakes; cook about 30 seconds. Place squash in skillet and stir well to combine and heat, about 30 more seconds. Place squash mixture, remaining oil, tomatoes, basil, vinegar and pine nuts to pot with pasta. Toss and combine. Serve with Parmesan cheese to sprinkle as desired.

CRUNCHY FRIED OKRA

My niece Heather first ordered these at a fast food place and I nearly lost my head when it snapped to look at her in disbelief. To this day, I'm not sure she really believes okra is a vegetable. Who'd a thought a non-veggie kid would love this one so much.

⅓ cup flour	½ teaspoon black pepper
⅓ cup cornmeal	1 slightly beaten egg
½ teaspoon salt	½ pound whole okra cut ½ inch thick

In plastic zip lock bag combine flour, cornmeal, salt and pepper. In small mixing bowl combine egg and milk. Toss okra pieces in egg mixture. Add ¼ of okra to plastic bag; shake to coat okra well. Remove coated okra, repeat with remaining okra. In large skillet heat ¼ inch oil. Fry okra, ¼ batch at a time, over medium heat 3-4 minutes or until golden, turn once. Remove from oil, drain on paper towels and keep warm in 300° oven while frying remaining batches. Serve warm.

DILL BUTTERED CARROTS

1 16-ounce bag tiny whole baby carrots	1 tablespoon lemon juice
	¼ teaspoon salt
2 tablespoons margarine softened	¼ teaspoon black pepper
½ teaspoon dried dill weed	

In medium saucepan cook carrots, covered in small amount of boiling water about 10 minutes or until crisp tender; drain. Stir margarine, dill, lemon juice, salt and pepper into carrots; toss lightly to coat.

FRIED GREEN TOMATOES

These are a side dish made from unripe (green) tomatoes. Fried green tomatoes are usually considered a southern dish, but can be found in northern homes as well. The northern version is more likely to be made with white flour rather than corn meal. Also, green tomatoes tend to appear at the end of the season in the north when the remaining fruit is harvested before the first frosts.

3 medium firm green tomatoes	2 beaten eggs
⅓ cup milk	¾ cup fine dry bread crumbs
½ cup flour	¼ cup vegetable oil

Cut unpeeled tomatoes into ½ inch thick slices. Sprinkle both sides with salt and pepper. Dip slices in milk, then flour. Dip in eggs, then bread crumbs. In skillet fry slices half at a time in hot oil over medium heat 8 minutes on each side or until brown

FRIED GRITS

5 cups water	½ cup flour
Salt	Vegetable oil
1 cup stone ground quick cooking grits	

Bring water and salt to boil in large saucepan. Add grits and continue to simmer, stirring constantly, over medium heat until grits are cooked and thick like mush, about 15-20 minutes. If needed, add more boiling water. Pour hot grits on to large plate to make layer about ¾ inch deep. Cover and let stand to cool. Refrigerate to chill thoroughly. When grits are cold and firm, cut into pieces. Dredge grit pieces in flour and shake off excess flour. Heat oil at depth ½ inch in heavy skillet. Fry grit pieces until golden brown on both sides, about 4-5 minutes total. Drain on paper towels and sprinkle with salt. Serve hot.

FRIED VEGETABLES

Any type of dipping sauce can be enjoyed with these veggies.

2 cups flour	Vegetable oil for frying
1 ½ cups beer	1 carrot cut in thick strips
2 eggs	1 onion sliced into rings
1 cup milk	6 fresh mushrooms stems removed
Salt and black pepper to taste	1 green bell pepper sliced in rings

In medium bowl, mix together 1 ½ cup flour and beer with a wooden spoon; let stand for at least 3 hours at room temperature. Mix eggs and milk in small bowl. In separate bowl mix together ½ cup flour, salt and pepper. Heat oil to 375°. Dip each vegetable in egg and milk mixture. Next dip vegetables into flour and seasoning mixture, finally dip vegetables in beer and flour mixture. Place vegetables into oil and fry until golden brown.

GARLIC BEAN DISH

2 tablespoons olive oil	1 can black beans drained, rinsed
1 sweet onion chopped	1 can pinto beans drained, rinsed
1 stalk celery chopped	½ cup diced tomatoes
1 carrot chopped	½ teaspoon dried thyme
1 tablespoon minced garlic	2 teaspoons white wine
1 can kidney beans drained, rinsed	Salt and black pepper

Heat oil in medium skillet. Add onions, celery and carrots. Cook over medium heat until tender. Add garlic. Add beans, tomato, thyme and wine. Salt and pepper to taste and serve with any meat or poultry.

GREEN BEAN AMANDINE

I finally found a vegetable the kids would eat! They called it Green beans Almond-dine.

1 bag frozen French-style green
　　beans
2 tablespoons slivered almonds

1 tablespoon margarine
1 teaspoon lemon juice

Cook frozen beans according to package directions drain and keep warm. In small skillet, cook and stir almonds in melted margarine over medium heat until golden. Remove from heat; stir in lemon juice. Stir almond mixture into beans and serve.

GREEN BEANS AND BACON DRESSING

2 pounds fresh or frozen green
　　beans
4 slices bacon
½ cup diced onions

2 tablespoons cider vinegar
¼ teaspoon salt
¼ teaspoon black pepper

In large pot, bring green beans and small amount water to boil. Cook until crisp-tender and drain. Cook bacon in large skillet until crisp, drain on paper towel. Remove all but 2 tablespoons bacon fat from skillet. Add onions and sauté 1-2 minutes until slightly golden. Remove from heat; stir in vinegar. Add green beans, salt and pepper; toss to coat. Crumble bacon on top.

GRILLED ITALIAN VEGETABLES

Grilling vegetables keeps the fresh taste in them and keeps your kitchen cool.

½ pound whole button mushrooms	½ cup olive oil
2 carrots cut in wide strips	3 teaspoons minced garlic
1 red bell pepper quartered	Salt and black pepper
1 yellow bell pepper quartered	¼ cup chopped basil
3 green onions	¼ cup balsamic vinegar
2 zucchinis cut in wide strips	3 tablespoons brown sugar

In bowl combine mushrooms, carrots, green onions red and yellow peppers. Whisk together olive oil, garlic, balsamic vinegar and brown sugar. Season vegetables with salt and pepper to taste. Pour in oil mixture and toss to coat. Place vegetables on medium-hot grill; cook on both sides until vegetables are marked with grill marks, but still firm to the bite. Transfer to a platter and serve.

GRILLED PORTOBELLO MUSHROOM

Portobellos gained incredible popularity in the 1980s. Distinguished by their large size, thick cap and stem and distinctive musky smell, the caps can be cooked in many ways, including as a substitute for the "meat" in sandwiches.

8 Portobello mushroom caps	1 tablespoon minced garlic
¼ cup balsamic vinegar	⅛ teaspoon salt
2 tablespoons olive oil	⅛ teaspoon black pepper
1 teaspoon dried basil	4 slices provolone cheese
1 teaspoon dried oregano	

Place mushroom caps smooth side up, in shallow dish. In small bowl, whisk together vinegar, oil, basil, oregano, garlic, salt, and pepper; pour over mushrooms. Let stand at room temperature for 15 minutes or so, turning twice. Preheat grill for medium-high heat. Brush grate with oil. Place mushrooms on grill, reserving marinade for basting. Grill for 5 to 8 minutes on each side, or until tender. Brush with marinade frequently. Top with cheese during last 2 minutes of grilling.

MUSTARD COLESLAW

1 cup mustard
1 cup mayonnaise
1 cup vinegar
1 ½ cups sugar
1 tablespoon salt
1 teaspoon white pepper

5 pounds finely chopped cabbage
½ cup diced sweet red bell pepper
2 tablespoons celery seed
1 cup finely chopped sweet onion
1 cup finely chopped carrot

In large mixing bowl, mix mustard, mayonnaise, vinegar, sugar, white pepper and salt together until smooth. Place cabbage in large mixing bowl then pour the liquid dressing over the cabbage. Add red bell pepper, onion, carrot and celery seed. Mix until all ingredients are evenly blended. Chill well before serving.

ISLAND SNAP PEAS

3 cups frozen snap peas
2 tablespoons orange marmalade
½ teaspoon cider vinegar

¼ teaspoon ground ginger
1 tablespoon butter
⅛ teaspoon black pepper

Cook frozen peas according to package directions; drain. In small saucepan heat and stir marmalade until melted, stir in vinegar, ginger and pepper. Pour sauce over hot cooked peas, add butter and toss lightly to coat.

MASHED CAULIFLOWER

This recipe has developed from several low carbohydrate diets and the idea was to use it as a substitute for mashed potatoes. Now days I don't hide the cauliflower taste but enhance it with the different extras and enjoy it smooth or chunky.

1 head cauliflower or	Ranch salad dressing mix
16-ounce bag frozen cauliflower	Sharp cheddar cheese
¼ cup milk	Parmesan cheese
2 tablespoons butter	Chili powder
Salt and black pepper	Horseradish
Extras:	Chopped onion
Paprika	Onion powder
Garlic salt	Cayenne pepper

Break cauliflower up into florets or chop. Microwave or steam; cook it until it's tender—a fork should easily pierce it. Add milk, butter, salt and pepper to cauliflower blend or mash up, if you prefer a chunkier dish, until smooth or desired consistency. Add seasoning to taste. A few shakes of Ranch dressing powder can spice it up. Or add garlic, cheddar cheese, or a dash of chili powder. Pour cauliflower into small baking dish. Bake in 350° oven until bubbly.

COOKED MUSTARD DRESSING COLESLAW

Perfect on a Memphis barbeque pulled pork sandwich and grilled chicken.

1 bag shredded cabbage	¼ cup ketchup or chili sauce
or coleslaw mix	¼ cup mayonnaise
2 shredded carrots	¼ cup cider vinegar
1 finely chopped onion	¼ cup sour cream
2 teaspoons salt	1 teaspoon celery seeds
¼ cup mustard	⅔ cup brown sugar
2 tablespoons Dijon style mustard	

Combine cabbage, carrot, onion and salt together in strainer over sink. Let sit at least 1-2 hours to drain. This keeps finished slaw from being watery. Rinse vegetables under cold water and let dry. In bowl or plastic bag, place in refrigerator until ready to use, up to one day. Dressing: combine mustards, vinegar, chili sauce, mayonnaise, sour cream and sugar in medium, non-reactive saucepan. Bring to boil. Add celery seed. Reduce heat and simmer about 3-5 minutes, until sugar has dissolved. Cool to room temperature. Pour over veggies in a large serving bowl. Mix well. Refrigerate at least an hour before serving.

NIFTY SUCCOTASH

The secret to great succotash is not overcooking the corn and not undercooking the lima beans, but don't let the beans turn mushy and soupy.

1 10-ounce package frozen whole
    kernel corn
2 16-ounce bags baby lima beans
1 teaspoon dried minced onion

1 tablespoon margarine
½ teaspoon salt
½ teaspoon black pepper

In large saucepan cook corn and lima beans in small amount of boiling, lightly salted water for 10 minutes. Add onions, cook 5-10 minutes more; drain well. Stir in margarine, salt and pepper.

OVEN ROASTED CARROTS

2 pounds baby carrots
¼ teaspoon onion salt
¼ teaspoon garlic salt
⅛ teaspoon black pepper

2 tablespoons olive oil
2 teaspoons cider vinegar
1 teaspoon dried thyme

Place carrots in sprayed baking dish. Mix together salts, olive oil and vinegar. Drizzle over carrots. Sprinkle with pepper and thyme. Toss to coat carrots. Cover and bake in 450° oven for 10 minutes. Stir carrots, bake uncovered for 10 minutes. Stir again and bake uncovered for 10 more minutes. Stir before serving.

OVEN ROASTED VEGGIES

This is just as easy as grilling but a nice winter way to warm up the kitchen.

1 pound vegetables	¼ teaspoon salt
2 teaspoons olive oil	¼ teaspoon black pepper

Heat oven to 450°. Line rimmed baking pan with foil. Toss vegetables of choice with olive oil, salt and pepper in pan. Roast 10 minutes: Asparagus or ½-inch thick red onion wedges or ½-inch thick zucchini slices Roast 15 minutes: ¾-inch cubes peeled butternut squash or 1-inch strips red pepper or 1-inch cauliflower florets. Roast 20 minutes: ½-inch thick fennel slices or peeled, halved baby carrots or halved brussels sprouts. Experiment with other types of vegetables, thickness and sizes: cauliflower, eggplant, mushrooms, tomatoes, garlic

PENNSYLVANIA RED CABBAGE

2 tablespoons brown sugar	2 cups shredded red cabbage
2 tablespoons vinegar	¾ cup coarsely chopped apples
2 tablespoons water	¼ teaspoon salt
1 tablespoon oils	Dash black pepper
¼ teaspoon caraway seeds	

In large skillet combine sugar, vinegar, water, oil, caraway, salt and pepper. Cook for 2-3 minutes or until hot, stirring occasionally. Stir in cabbage and apple. Cook, covered, over medium heat until cabbage is crisp-tender, about 5 minutes, stirring occasionally.

PICKLED RED BEETS

This is an old farmhouse side dish that adds a lot of color and flavor to a meal.

5 beets
¼ cup cider vinegar
1 tablespoon sugar

1 tablespoon olive oil
½ teaspoon dry mustard
Salt and Black pepper

Remove greens from beets. Cut beets to uniform sizes so they will cook evenly. Steam or boil around 30 minutes or until done or roast them by wrapping them whole in foil and cook in 350° oven for about an hour. A fork easily inserted into the beet will tell you if the beets are done or not. Drain the beets, rinsing them in cold water. Use your fingers to slip the peels off of the beets. Peels should come off easily. Discard peels. Slice beets. Combine cider vinegar, sugar, olive oil and dry mustard. Whisk ingredients together with fork. Add salt and pepper to taste. Combine beets and vinaigrette in bowl and allow to marinate for half-hour at room temperature.

SAUTE VEGETABLES

1 tablespoon olive oil
2 red bell peppers julienned
2 green bell peppers julienned
1 zucchini julienned
1 summer squash julienned
4 carrots julienned
1 large sweet onion julienned
1 cup snow peas

4 cups thinly sliced red cabbage
¼ teaspoon salt
¼ teaspoon black pepper
1 tablespoon minced garlic
¼ cup water
4 teaspoons cider vinegar
2 tablespoons sesame seeds

In large skillet, sauté in oil peppers, zucchini, squash, carrots, onions and snow peas for 5 minutes. Add cabbage, salt, pepper and garlic; cook for 1 minute. Combine water and vinegar; pour over vegetables. Sauté for 3 more minutes. Sprinkle with sesame seeds, cook for 1 minute and serve.

SAUTEED WINTER SQUASH

Cutting the raw squash into small cubes reduces the cooking time while maintaining the rich taste of baked squash. Cut squash in half, lengthwise, and remove seeds and stringy pulp. Then cut crosswise into large chunks. Roasted squash seeds make a tasty snack.

2 pounds winter squash smooth skinned	1 tablespoon brown sugar omit if squash is sweet
2 tablespoons butter	Salt and black pepper

Peel and cut squash meat into ½-inch cubes. Over medium heat, melt butter in large skillet. When hot, add squash cubes in single layer and cook without stirring for about 5 minutes, to brown the bottom sides. Stir to turn cubes and cook another 5 minutes. Sprinkle on brown sugar, if using, stir to mix well, and cook 5 minutes or until squash is tender. Add salt and pepper to taste. Serve warm.

SCALLOPED RHUBARB

5 cups rhubarb cut in chunks	3 cups corn bread crumbs
½ cup sugar	½ cup chopped walnuts
½ cup butter	¼ cup blackberry liqueur
1 chopped onion	

In large mixing bowl, toss together rhubarb and sugar. Melt 2 tablespoons of butter in medium skillet over medium-high heat. Add onion and sauté until quite soft, 10-15 minutes. Remove onion from skillet and combine with rhubarb. Melt remaining 6 tablespoons butter in skillet and add it to rhubarb mixture along with cornbread crumbs and walnuts. Stir to combine well. Spread mixture in sprayed 10-inch shallow casserole dish. Drizzle liqueur evenly over top. Bake in 325° oven until rhubarb juices are bubbling and crumbs are lightly browned, 40-45 minutes. Serve immediately.

SIMPLE GLAZED CARROTS

Making sure you don't overcook carrots keeps them from being mushy and unappealing.

6 medium peeled carrots ¼ inch slices	**½ cup chicken broth**
½ teaspoon salt	**1 tablespoon butter cut into 4 pieces**
3 tablespoons sugar	**2 teaspoons lemon juice**
	Black pepper

In skillet on medium high heat, place carrots, salt, 1 tablespoon sugar and broth. Cover with lid and bring to boil. Reduce heat to medium and simmer, stirring occasionally until carrots are almost tender. Uncover, increase heat to high, simmer rapidly for 1-2 minutes, until liquid is reduced, stirring occasionally. Add butter and remaining sugar to skillet, toss carrots to coat and cook, stirring frequently until carrots are completely tender and glaze is light gold, about 3 minutes. Remove from heat and add lemon juice. Stir to coat.

Scrape glaze from pan when placing in serving dish. Season to taste with salt and pepper.

SPINACH CREAMY STYLE

1 tablespoon olive oil	**¼ teaspoon nutmeg**
1 pound fresh spinach leaves	**4 ounces cream cheese softened**
2 teaspoons dried minced onion	

Rinse spinach and nearly dry by patting with paper towels. Heat oil in large skillet and place spinach leaves, large stems trimmed or removed, on top. Sprinkle with onion and nutmeg. Cover tightly and steam with just moisture clinging to leaves. Spinach will wilt in about 3 minutes. Stir in cream cheese until melted.

SQUASH CASSEROLE

This creamy crowd-pleasing side dish is crispy on top and creamy in the center.

3 cups cornbread stuffing	**2 shredded yellow squash**
1 ½ cups cream of chicken soup	**2 shredded zucchini**
¼ cup melted butter	**¼ cup shredded carrots**
½ cup sour cream	**½ cup shredded Cheddar cheese**

Mix stuffing and butter. Reserve ½ cup stuffing mixture and spoon remaining into 2-quart shallow baking dish. Mix soup, sour cream, yellow squash, zucchini, carrot and cheese. Spread over stuffing mixture and sprinkle with reserved stuffing mixture. Bake in 350° oven for 40 minutes or until hot.

STIR FRY MEDLEY

1 large bag frozen stir-fry vegetables	**2 ¼ teaspoons Worcestershire sauce**
¼ cup butter	**¼ cup soft bread crumbs**
½ teaspoon minced garlic	

Place vegetables in large saucepan with small amount salted water and cook for directed amount of time; drain. In small saucepan melt butter, add garlic and Worcestershire sauce and simmer for 2 minutes. Take 3 tablespoons of butter mixture and toss with cooked vegetables. Place vegetables in serving dish. Add breadcrumbs to remaining butter mixture and mix well. Sprinkle over vegetables and serve.

FRESH STIR FRY VEGETABLES

4 cups frozen broccoli thawed
1 cup chopped green bell peppers
1 cup chopped red bell peppers
2 cans sliced water chestnuts
    drained
1 cup sliced fresh mushrooms
1 cup julienned carrots

2 cups chopped onions
1 cup diced celery
1 cup snow peas
2 cups rinsed bean sprouts
4 tablespoons olive oil
4 teaspoons minced garlic
4 teaspoons minced ginger

In large skillet, heat oil, add broccoli, peppers, chestnuts, mushrooms, carrots, onions, celery and peas. Add garlic and ginger; stir well. Cook over medium high heat for 9 minutes or until barely crispy, add bean sprouts and cook for 1 more minute. Serve immediately.

SUMMER SQUASH SKILLET

This is a scrumptious way to enjoy summer squash and zucchini from the garden.

2 yellow summer squash
2 zucchini
3 tablespoons olive oil
3 teaspoons minced garlic
1 teaspoon dried basil

1 teaspoon cried oregano
Dash dried marjoram
2 tablespoons chopped fresh parsley
10 grape or cherry tomatoes cut in
    quarters or any kind of tomatoes
    cut up

Cut zucchini and summer squash into quarters, lengthwise, cut in thin slices. Heat olive oil over medium heat; add zucchini, summer squash, and garlic and sauté, stirring frequently, until tender. Meanwhile, combine remaining ingredients. When squash is tender add tomato and herb mixture to pan. Continue cooking, stirring, for just couple of minutes, until hot and well combined.

TREASURING THE MEASURING

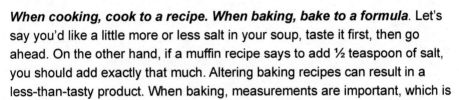

Microwave a lemon for 15 seconds, then before cutting the lemon, roll it back and forth between the hand ~ this will double the juice you get before squeezing.

When cooking, cook to a recipe. When baking, bake to a formula. Let's say you'd like a little more or less salt in your soup, taste it first, then go ahead. On the other hand, if a muffin recipe says to add ½ teaspoon of salt, you should add exactly that much. Altering baking recipes can result in a less-than-tasty product. When baking, measurements are important, which is why some "chefs" prefer not to bake. If you're trying a new recipe, try it exactly as written the first time. Make adjustments once you have tasted it and you know how it works.

There is a difference between liquid and dry measures; use the appropriate one for each task. While they hold the same volume, they are used differently. Measuring spoons are interchangeable, but use liquid measuring cups for water, milk or oil. Fill the cup to the appropriate line, place it on a level surface, and read it with your eye at the level of the liquids.

Molasses substitutions in an emergency:
For 1 cup of molasses use 1 cup of honey or ¾ cup brown sugar or 1 cup dark corn syrup or 1 cup granulated sugar with ¼ cup water or 1 cup of pure maple syrup.

Many pie recipes involve blind baking: it refers to the process of baking a piecrust or other pastry without the filling. Generally, the piecrust is lined with tin foil or parchment paper, and then filled with dried peas, lentils, beans or ceramic "baking beans", so that it will keep its shape when baking. Metal or ceramic pie weights are also used. After the piecrust is done, the beans are replaced with the regular filling, Blind-baking is used also when the pie filling can't be cooked as long as the crust requires or if the filling in the pies would make the piecrust too soggy if added immediately as it does with quiches.

Pastry is different from bread because it has a higher fat content that contributes to a flaky or crumbly texture. A good pastry is light and airy, but firm enough to support the weight of it's filling. Over mixing and too much handling of the dough will cause your crust to be tough.

In Danish pastry or croissant pastry, the flaky texture is achieved by repeatedly rolling out dough into many thin layers and folding it. This can be a laborious

process, which is why the croissant dough available in the store's refrigerator section is an easier and acceptable substitute.

Ice With Your Meal?

My husband and I had a meal served to us when we camped out overnight on Mendenhall Glacier in Juneau Alaska. We had our own sleeping tent, which was warm and comfortable and the best sleep I'd been able to enjoy in a long time. We trekked all over the glacier for a couple of hours first and developed quite a hunger by the time the sun was setting that day in mid August. In the main tent, a feast had been prepared for us. Appetizers, soup, salad, entrée and desert and it was not the usual camp out fare. This was something you would expect in a restaurant. We shared it with another couple and our two guides who prepared the meal.

Now, lots of people have done what we did. It was fun and trekking down the glacier the next day was gorgeous and the trip of a lifetime. The really unusual part for me was that not a bit of the meal or garbage

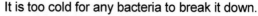

was left on the glacier. Even the water they cooked the meal in was not left. Anything left on the glacier; even a piece of chewed gum will stay there, forever. It is too cold for any bacteria to break it down.

So everything, absolutely everything, has to be brought back with you. Now we didn't have to do that task, they did. But it made me so aware of some of the garbage and excess we deal with when we fix a dish or meal. We waste a lot and take so much of the conveniences for granted. I also learned that if we could have a fabulous meal where nothing exists, anything is possible when it comes to fixing meals.

SWEET FRUIT

We bought our home in Montana at the beginning of October. That winter ended up being one of the coldest Montana had in the 1990's with record snowfall. Right next to the driveway, the very first plant looked strong poking through the snowy mud reaching for the warmth of the first spring sun. We had no idea what kind of plant it was, we were just glad to see anything green signaling the end of that long, extremely hard winter.

Our blissful ignorance didn't last long. Too busy that summer to identify or prune it, suddenly we had huge thick stalks where some big spiders took up residence under even bigger leaves. It took 3 major frosts and 3 inches of snow for that plant to die in November. The whole next year we had a car parked on top of the plant. I assumed the dirt in that area meant the grass and plant were gone.

Cleaning up for spring, I lifted pieces of wood lying on that spot since the car had been removed. No grass was growing, but poking through the dirt was the beginnings of not just that plant, but

Hidden Treasure

two others like it. Not only was it not dead, it had multiplied. That year I identified my indestructible plant; it was rhubarb. The only thing I knew about rhubarb was from my first weight loss program 25 years earlier where they used it as a low calorie dessert substitute. I never found a recipe I liked and didn't have any use for it now.

It's actually a very beautiful plant, but if you don't trim it, it'll turn into a massive monster that houses all kinds of little creatures until early winter. I finally cut all three plants down to the ground and gave the cut stalks to eager co-workers. Some of them brought me samples of the sweet things they were making from my contribution. I actually enjoyed the samples, but I cut it down twice more and gave away the stalks before the winter snow. Back then, I never made peace with that plant the whole 8 years we were there.

Several years later, we were moving into our new home in Alaska and I was enjoying our landscaped yard when I noticed something familiar growing in a shaded corner. There it was, already 3 feet high, my old nemesis: the indestructible rhubarb.

When I trimmed it and took in to work, everyone was grateful and more than willing to share recipes with me. Since then rhubarb and I have formed a friendship. So far I haven't figured out anything that the rhubarb can't be used to make.

Grow and Glow

I was actually sad when we moved to Wasilla Alaska and there wasn't a rhubarb plant in my new yard this time. I can't believe I'm saying this, but I'm actually going to plant rhubarb on purpose, because I know it will grow, no matter how short or cold the summer. I also have quite a collection of recipes for that durable plant and I intend to use every one of them.

ALASKA RHUBARB TART

A tart is a pastry dish that has a sweet or savory filling baked in a straight edged crust with no top layer.

1 ½ cups flour divided	2 ¼ cups sugar
½ cup powdered sugar	1 ⅛ teaspoons baking powder
Pinch salt	4 ½ cups sliced rhubarb
¾ cup butter	Frozen whipped topping
3 eggs	

In mixing bowl, combine 1 cup of flour, powdered sugar and salt. Cut in butter as for pastry. Pat into a 9x13 baking pan and bake crust in 375° for 10 minutes. Meanwhile, beat eggs, sugar, remaining flour and baking powder. Fold in rhubarb and spread over baked crust. Return to oven and bake for 35-40 minutes. Cool. Serve with dollop of whipped cream.

AMISH STYLE APPLE BUTTER

Apple butter is a highly concentrated form of applesauce, produced by long, slow cooking of apples with cider or water to a point where the sugar in the apples caramelizes, turning the apple butter a deep brown. The concentration of sugar gives apple butter a much longer shelf life as a preserve than applesauce.

5 pounds peeled, cored, apples cut in chunks	1 ½ cups honey
	2 teaspoons cinnamon
3 cups apple cider	¾ teaspoon ground cloves
¾ cup vinegar	¾ teaspoon ground allspice

Place all ingredients in slow cooker and cook on low for 14 hours. Place in tight lid containers and refrigerate or freeze.

APPLE BROWN BETTY

A Betty consist of a fruit, most commonly apples, baked between layers of buttered crumbs, this one uses a skillet. It makes a great summer dessert without heating the house baking in an oven. I found it also stays crunchier for a lighter summer treat.

CRUMBS:
5 ⅓ ounces sandwich bread
2 ½ tablespoons brown sugar
5 ½ tablespoons butter
5 ⅓ cups Granny Smith apples
    peeled, cut into ½ inch cubes
5 ⅓ cups Golden Delicious apples
    peeled, cut into ½ inch cubes

¼ cup brown sugar
⅓ teaspoon ground ginger
1 ⅓ teaspoons lemon juice
⅓ teaspoon cinnamon
Pinch salt
2 ½ tablespoons butter
1 cup apple cider

Pulse bread, sugar and butter in a processor until coarsely ground. Transfer crumbs into 12-inch skillet, cook over medium heat, stirring constantly until crumbs are deeply brown, about 5 minutes. Transfer to paper towel, wipe skillet clean. Combine sugar, spices and salt in small bowl. Heat 1 tablespoon butter in skillet over medium high heat. Stir in 4 cups of apples and ½ of sugar mixture. Distribute apples in even layer and cook, stirring 2 or 3 times, until mediums down, about 5 minutes. Transfer to medium bowl. Repeat with remaining butter, apples and sugar mixture, returning first batch of apples to skillet when second batch is done. Add apple cider and scrape bottom and sides of skillet with wooden spoon to lessen browned bits; cook until about ⅔ cups liquid remains and apples are tender but not mushy, 2-4 minutes. Remove skillet from heat; stir in lemon juice and ½ cup toasted breadcrumbs. Using wooden spoons, lightly flatten apples into even layer in skillet and evenly sprinkle with remaining toasted breadcrumbs. Let cool 5 minutes. Spoon warm Betty into individual bowls and serve.

APPLE FRITTERS

A fritter is any kind of food coated in batter and deep-fried. There is some debate as to how to properly classify a fritter: some say it's a doughnut, others say it belongs in the pastry family.

2 cups flour	2 quarts vegetable oil for frying
½ cup sugar	Powdered sugar
½ teaspoon vanilla extract	Maple Sauce:
1 tablespoon baking powder	2 cups applesauce
2 teaspoons apple pie spice	⅓ cup maple syrup
1 teaspoon salt	1 teaspoon cinnamon
2 eggs	Glaze:
1 cup milk	2 cups powdered sugar
3 cups chopped apples	1 ½ tablespoons milk

Place in dish, microwave 4 minutes to soften them; set aside to cool. Combine flour, sugar, salt, baking powder and apple pie spice. Whisk together milk and egg; stir into flour mixture until just combined. Fold in apples. Pour oil into skillet approximately 1 ½ deep. Heat oil on high. Oil is ready when dough floats to top. Carefully add dough to oil in heaping tablespoons. Cook until brown, about 3 minutes, then flip. Cook another 2-3 minutes, until both sides are browned. Transfer briefly to paper towels to absorb excess oil; transfer to cooling rack. Dust with sugar or make glaze by stirring milk and powdered sugar together in small bowl. Drizzle over fritters. Wait 3 minutes for glaze to harden; flip fritters and drizzle glaze over other side; served warm. If desired, mix applesauce, syrup and cinnamon together and serve with fritters.

APPLE KUCHEN

This is a quick and versatile recipe for the classic kuchen cake. To make Pear Kuchen: use 32 ounce can of pears and devil's food cake mix. For a Peach Kuchen use canned peaches and white cake mix.

1 box yellow cake mix	½ cup sugar
¼ cup margarine softened	1 teaspoon cinnamon
½ cup flaked coconut	1 cup sour cream
4 Granny Smith apples	1 egg

Peel, core and cut each apple into 8 wedges. Set aside. In medium bowl, combine cake mix, coconut and margarine until crumbly. Pat mixture lightly into sprayed 9x13 baking pan, building up edges slightly to form crust. Arrange apple wedges on top. Mix together cinnamon and sugar; sprinkle over apples and cake mixture. In small bowl, whisk together egg and sour cream. Drizzle over top of the cake. Bake in 350° oven for 35 minutes, or until edges of cake are golden and apples are tender.

APPLE STRUDEL

A strudel is a pastry made with fruit or cheese rolled up in layers of thin sheets of dough and then baked.

6 cups tart apples sliced	¾ cup ground almonds
¾ cup seedless raisins	8 ounces frozen phyllo pastry leaves
1 tablespoon grated lemon peels	thawed
¾ cup sugar	1 ¾ cups melted butter (not
2 teaspoons cinnamon	margarine)
	1 cup finely crushed breadcrumbs

Mix apples with raisins, lemon rind, sugar, cinnamon, and almonds. Set aside. Place 1 phyllo sheet on kitchen towel and brush with melted butter. Place second sheet on top and brush with butter again. Repeat until 5 sheets have been used, using about ½ cup of butter. In a large skillet, heat and stir breadcrumbs with ¼ cup of butter until crumbs are lightly browned. Sprinkle ¾ cup crumbs on the layered phyllo sheets. Mound ½ of the filling in a 3-inch strip along the narrow end of the phyllo, leaving a 2-inch border. Lift towel, using it to roll sheets over apples, jelly roll fashion. Brush top of strudel with butter and sprinkle with 2 tablespoons of crumbs. Repeat entire procedure for second strudel. Bake strudels in 400° oven for 20 to 25 minutes, until browned.

APPLESAUCE LAYERED TORTE

This torte is a multi-layered pastry with sweet fruit in between layers, creating the affect of a cake torte

2 cups flour
4 tablespoons sugar divided
1 teaspoon salt
⅔ cup shortening

6 tablespoons water
3 cups chunky unsweetened apple juice
1 12-ounce container frozen whipped topping

Combine flour, half sugar and salt in medium bowl; cut in shortening until mixture resembles cornmeal. With fork, blend in water, 1 tablespoon at a time, until dough holds together. Form dough into ball, flatten and divide into fifths. Roll each part into 8-inch circle and gently place them on ungreased baking sheets. Prick all over with fork, brush lightly with water and sprinkle with remaining sugar. Bake in 400° oven for 10 to 12 minutes or until evenly browned. Remove to wire racks to cool. Mix applesauce and cinnamon together in a mixing bowl. About 30 minutes before serving, place one baked pastry circle on serving plate, top with ¼ of applesauce mixture. Continue layering torte with pastry and apple mixture ending with baked pastry on top. Sprinkle with powdered sugar; serve with whipped topping.

BANANA NUT BREAD

Banana bread is a sweet cake-like quick bread that uses baking soda as the leavening agent instead of yeast. The history of banana bread is quite short; this memory-provoking edible became popular in 1960's and 70's. Some say banana bread is not bread, but a cake. True, the texture and taste of this bread is more like a cake or muffin, but most of us don't care about the distinctions, we just enjoy the sweet taste.

3 cups flour	1 cup chopped nuts
1 teaspoon baking soda	3 eggs
1 teaspoon cinnamon	1 ½ cups canola oil
1 teaspoon ginger	1 8-ounce can crushed pineapple
1 teaspoon nutmeg	un-drained
2 cups sugar	1 ½ teaspoons vanilla extract
1 teaspoon salt	2 cups mashed bananas

Whisk dry ingredients together in bowl. Mix in another bowl, eggs, oil, pineapple, vanilla, bananas and add remaining ingredients. Stir with a wooden spoon only until well blended. Pour into two sprayed loaf pans and bake in 350° oven for 60-80 minutes.

BERRY BLUEBERRY GRUNT

Brambles and grunts are all old-fashioned New England desserts, usually made with berries and topped with a type of sweet dumpling mixture. A grunt is a steamed pudding with berries. The theory is a tightly covered skillet will 'grunt' while this traditional dessert cooks

2 16-ounce packages frozen	2 teaspoons grated lemon peels
blueberries	¼ teaspoon nutmeg
1 cup water	½ teaspoon cinnamon
½ cup sugar	¼ teaspoon salt
1 ½ cups flour	¾ cup milk
2 teaspoons baking powder	

Pour blueberries and water into skillet or kettle. Stir in sugar. Cook until juice begins to boil, reduce heat. In medium mixing bowl, mix flour, baking powder, lemon peel, spices, and salt. Stir in milk until dry particles are just moistened. Drop dough by spoonfuls (8 dumplings) on top of simmering berry mixture and cover skillet. Cook over medium-low heat until dough is puffed and cooked through.

BERRY DESSERT SAUCE

Use over cheesecake, pound cake, ice cream, cakes, pancakes, waffles or French toast.

3 cups fresh or frozen raspberries, strawberries blueberries, raspberries, huckleberries or blackberries	¼ cup water 6 tablespoons sugar ⅛ teaspoon salt 2 teaspoons juice from 1 lemon

Bring berries, water, sugar and salt to simmer over medium heat, stirring occasionally. Cook until sugar is dissolved and berries are heated through, about 1 minute longer. Transfer mixture to blender, puree until smooth. Strain through fine mesh strainer into small bowl. Press and stir puree with rubber spatula to extract as much seedless puree as possible. Stir in lemon juice. Cover with plastic wrap and refrigerate until cold. Stir before serving.

CINNAMON RHUBARB BARS

A number of varieties of rhubarb have been domesticated both as medicinal plants and for human consumption. While the leaves are toxic, the stalks are used in pies and other foods for their tart flavor.

½ cup shortening	1 teaspoon baking soda
1 cup brown sugar	½ teaspoon salt
1 cup sugar divided	1 cup buttermilk
1 egg	2 cups diced rhubarb
1 teaspoon vanilla extract	1 teaspoon cinnamon
2 cups flour	

In large mixing bowl, cream together shortening, brown sugar and ½ cup of sugar until light and fluffy. Add egg and vanilla, beat for 2 minutes. Combine flour, baking soda and salt in a bowl. Add flour mixture to butter mixture alternating with buttermilk. Beat well after each addition. Stir in rhubarb. Pour batter into sprayed 9x13 baking pan. Combine ½ cup of sugar and cinnamon, sprinkle over batter. Bake in 350° oven for 40-45 minutes or until wooden pick inserted near center comes out clean. Serve warm.

COMPANY RASPBERRY TARTLETS

Tartlets are small pastry shells with shallow sides, no top crust and various fillings.

Pastry:
1 cup flour
4 ounces cream cheese softened
½ cup butter softened
¼ teaspoon salt
Filling:

8 ounces cream cheese softened
½ cup powdered sugar
1 tablespoon lemon juice
2 ½ cups raspberries, blackberries
    or blueberries

Using electric mixer, mix together flour, cream cheese, butter and salt until dough forms. Wrap dough in plastic and refrigerate at least 30 minutes and up to 24 hours. If chilled longer than 1 hour, let the dough warm up at room temperature for about 20 minutes. Divide dough into 10 balls and place them in a standard size muffin pan. Press each dough ball into bottom and up sides of muffin cup to form a shell. Bake in 350° oven until browned, about 20-25 minutes. Carefully invert pan to remove baked shells and cool on wire rack. Filling: With electric mixer, beat cream cheese with powdered sugar until smooth. Beat in lemon juice. Spread heaping tablespoon of cream cheese mixture on bottom of each cooled pastry shell. Arrange berries on top. Refrigerate until ready to serve.

CRANBERRY BREAD

Most cranberries are processed into products such as juice, sauce and sweetened dried cranberries, with the remainder sold fresh to consumers. Cranberry sauce is regarded as an indispensable part of traditional American and Canadian Thanksgiving menus and European winter festivals.

2 cups flour	¼ cup orange juice
1 cup sugar	3 tablespoons grated orange peel
1 ½ teaspoons baking powder	3 tablespoons canola oil
½ teaspoon baking soda	½ cup chopped walnuts
1 teaspoon salt	2 cups coarsely chopped cranberries
1 egg well beaten	

Mix flour, sugar, baking powder, baking soda and salt in large bowl. In smaller bowl, combine egg, orange juice, orange peel and oil. Add egg mixture to dry ingredients and mix only to dampen. Carefully fold in nuts and cranberries. Place batter in 2 sprayed loaf pans and bake in 350° oven for 1 hour.

FRUIT COFFEE CAKE

Like most foods, coffee cake is an item that evolved over hundreds of years and across continents. People prepared honey cakes since biblical times. Gradually the French came up with galettes, the forerunner of Christmas fruitcake. Galettes also lead to the invention of sweet yeast rolls that eventually resulted in Danish coffee cakes, which really did contain coffee. Over the years, people experimented with those recipes and began adding creamy fillings, cheese, yogurt and sugared fruit.

1 ½ cups sugar	2 tablespoons flour
½ cup soft shortening	1 tablespoon cinnamon
2 eggs	Topping:
1 cup evaporated milk	¼ cup brown sugar
3 cups flour	¼ cup butter
1 ½ tablespoons baking powder	1 tablespoon cream
1 teaspoon salt	1 cup peach preserves or peach jam
Filling:	or Apricot preserves or orange
½ cup brown sugar	marmalade

Mix sugar, shortening and egg thoroughly; stir in milk. Sift together flour, baking powder and salt, and stir in to sugar batter. Beat until smooth. FILLING: Mix brown sugar, flour and cinnamon. Spread half of cake batter in sprayed 13x9 inch pan and sprinkle filling mixture evenly over batter. Add remaining batter. TOPPING: Mix brown sugar, butter, cream and fruit until smooth. Spread on top of batter. Bake in 375° oven for 25 to 35 minutes. Serve while still warm.

FRUIT FOOL

Fool, which dates to the 16th century, is a simple combination of fruit and cream or whipped cream. Sometimes the fruit is stewed, then folded into the whipped cream. Originally "fool" was a term of endearment, which might be how this dessert got its name. With its origins in England, it was probably made with gooseberries.

1 cup fruit puree	Strawberry, blackberries,
1 cup heavy whipping cream	huckleberries blueberries
1 tablespoon sugar	or 4 sliced kiwi fruits
Fruit Puree:	⅓ to ½ cup sugar
1 pound bag frozen unsweetened	
fruit	

Puree: Thaw frozen fruit or with kiwi, peel and quarter. Place fruit in a food processor or blender and blend until the berries are pureed. Transfer to a bowl and stir in sugar. Taste and add more sugar if necessary. Refrigerate for several hours or overnight.

Fool: Place mixing bowl and whisk attachment in refrigerator or freezer for about 15 minutes or until very cold. Whip cream until soft peaks form. Add sugar and continue to whip until stiff peaks form. With a rubber spatula gently fold in fruit puree, leaving some streaks of white whipping cream. Pour fool into four—individual long stemmed parfait or wine glasses. Cover and refrigerate until serving time. Can be made about 4 hours before serving. Garnish with a fresh fruit

FRUIT PIZZA

If you prefer, melt 1 cup semisweet chocolate chips in microwavable bowl—on high for 1 minute, then stir, if needed microwave 15 seconds at a time, stir after each time until all are melted. Drizzle over fruit and let set 5-10 minutes to set chocolate.

1 18-ounce tube sugar cookie dough	3 cups Fruit: bananas, apple,
1 8-ounce package cream cheese	pineapple, Strawberries,
softened	peaches, orange or berries
½ teaspoon almond extract	½ cup orange marmalade

Roll out cookie dough to cover round pizza pan. Bake in 350° oven for 8-15 minutes or until firm. Cool completely. Mix together cream cheese and extract; spread mixture over cooled cookie crust. Arrange fruit in circles on crust. Slightly warm marmalade and brush over fruit.

FRUITY TUTTI BARS

Whether tutti-fruiti reminds you of a 1955 song or a colorful ice cream—all over the world the term informs people the dessert or treat will have lots of candied, dried and maybe brandy soaked fruit in it.

1 cup fruit cocktail	½ teaspoon salt
1 cup mixed candied fruit	1 ½ cups flaked coconut
2 eggs beaten to fluffy	½ cup chopped pecans
½ teaspoon baking soda	1 stick butter softened
2 ¼ cups flour	¼ cup evaporated milk
1 teaspoon vanilla extract	¾ cup sugar
1 cup sugar	1 cup chopped candied cherries

Blenderize fruit cocktail, including juice. Pour fruit in large bowl; add candied fruit, beaten eggs, baking soda, flour, vanilla, sugar and salt. Mix until well blended. Place mixture in sprayed jellyroll pan. Mix together coconut and pecan; sprinkle on top of batter. Bake in 350° oven for 25-30 minutes or until toothpick comes out clean. In small saucepan, stir butter, milk and sugar; bring to boil and cook for 2 minutes, stirring constantly. Remove from heat and cool. When cooled, beat until smooth; spread over bars. Sprinkle cherries over top of glaze.

GRILLED FRUIT

If you haven't tried grilling fruit, you are missing out on a very delectable indulgence.

2 bananas   1 stick butter
2 peaches   1 tablespoon sugar
1 pound fresh strawberries

Peel bananas. Rinse peaches and strawberries; pat dry. Slice peaches into quarters (make sure they are big enough to put straight on the grill). Cut off tops of strawberries. Place strawberries on aluminum foil. Sprinkle with sugar and wrap. Put some butter on each banana and on each peach slice. Place all of fruit on grill. Monitor fire. If flames get too high, place cover on grill. Cook until there are visible grill marks or black crisps. Depending on heat, do not cook longer than 15 minutes. Bananas take least amount of time and are usually done in about 10 minutes. Strawberries take longest. Remove fruit as soon as it's done. Cover until ready to serve.

HALO TROPICAL BAR

Heavenly and luscious, it will remind you of a Caribbean sun beach indulgence.

⅓ cup sugar   2 cups biscuit baking mix
¼ cup softened butter   ½ cup coconut
2 eggs   ½ cup chopped nuts
½ cup mashed bananas
1 8-ounce can crushed pineapple
    drained

Mix sugar, butter and eggs until blended. Stir in bananas and pineapple. Stir in remaining ingredients until moistened. Spread in sprayed loaf pan. Bake in 350° oven for 55 minutes until toothpick comes out clean. Cool 5 minutes. Loosen sides of loaf from pan and cool completely before cutting.

HEFTY PEACH COBBLER

Cobbler is a deep-dish fruit dessert topped with a biscuit crust. Depending on the region, it might also be called a bramble, grunt or slump. It can be made with almost any type of fruit—for cherry substitute almond extract for lemon juice, add cinnamon for apple flavored and mixed berries can just be substituted for the peaches.

2 ½ pounds fresh or frozen peaches	3 tablespoons plus 1 teaspoon sugar
¼ cup sugar	¾ teaspoon baking powder
1 teaspoon cornstarch	¼ teaspoon baking soda
1 tablespoon lemon juice	¼ teaspoon salt
Pinch salt	5 tablespoons cold butter cut in
Topping:	cubes
1 cup flour	⅓ cup plain yogurt

Filling: Gently toss peaches and sugar in large bowl, let stand 30 minutes tossing several times. Drain off accumulated juice, save ¼ cup of juice, discard rest. Whisk drained juice, cornstarch, lemon juice and salt together in small bowl. Toss peach juice mixture with peach slices and transfer to 8-inch square baking dish. Bake in 425° oven for about 10 minutes or until peaches begin to bubble. Remove from oven. Topping: Whisk flour, 3 tablespoons sugar, baking powder, baking soda and salt together. Cut butter cubes into flour mixture just until resembles coarse meal; add yogurt and toss with rubber spatula until dough is formed. Don't over mix. Divided dough into 6 evenly sized but roughly shaped mounds. Place dough mounds on top, space at least ½ inch apart, don't let them touch. Sprinkle 1 teaspoon of sugar evenly over the 6 mounds. Bake until topping is golden brown and fruit is bubbling, about 16-18 minutes. Cool on wire rack about 20 minutes. Serve warm.

HOLY NORTH CAROLINA SONKER

A sonker is a deep-dish pie or cobbler served in many flavors including strawberry, peach, sweet potato, and cherry. This same dish is called zonker and seems to be a dish unique to North Carolina, although I've shared my recipe with those all over the US.

6 tablespoons butter	1 ¼ cups sugar
½ teaspoon salt	¾ cup milk
2 cups sliced peaches or berries or	¾ cup flour
cherries	1 teaspoon baking powder

Melt butter in deep-dish pie pan in oven while it's heating. Toss ¼ cup of sugar with peaches or fruit. Whisk together remaining sugar, flour and milk. Pour batter into pie pan once butter is melted. Add fruit to batter, distributing evenly, but do not stir. Bake in 350° oven for 50-60 minutes until deep golden brown. Serve warm with ice cream.

HUCKLEBERRY BUCKLE

Buckle or crumple is a type of cake made in a single layer with berries added to the batter. It is usually made with blueberries. The batter is quite thick and as it bakes, it forms a thin bottom layer. The topping is similar to a streusel, which gives it a buckled or crumpled appearance.

¼ cup butter	**Fruit Filling:**
½ cup sugar	2 ½ cups huckleberries or
1 cup flour	blackberries, raspberries
1 teaspoon baking powder	¾ cup sugar
¼ teaspoon salt	½ cup boiling water
½ cup milk	1 tablespoon butter

In a large bowl, cream butter and sugar. In a separate small bowl, combine flour, baking powder and salt. Stir into butter mixture. Stir in milk; mixture will be thick and lumpy. Spread batter into a sprayed 9-inch square pan. In large bowl, combine berries, sugar and boiling water. Pour over the batter in the pan. Dot top with remaining butter. Bake in 375° oven for 45 to 50 minutes.

LAYMAN PEACH PANDOWDY

Pandowdy is a deep-dish dessert that can be made with a variety of fruit, sweetened with molasses or brown sugar. The topping is a crumbly type of biscuit.

6 cups thick sliced fresh or frozen peaches	DOUGH: 1 cup flour
1 tablespoon lemon juice	2 tablespoons sugar
6 tablespoons white sugar	1 teaspoon baking powder
2 tablespoons brown sugar	¼ teaspoon salt
1 tablespoon cornstarch	1 tablespoon butter
	½ cup heavy cream

Place peaches in medium bowl. Sprinkle lemon juice over them. Mix together sugars and cornstarch. Sprinkle over peaches and stir to coat, spoon into 2-quart casserole dish. In medium bowl, stir together flour, sugar, baking powder and salt. Cut in butter with a fork or pastry cutter until fine crumbs. Make a well in center and pour in cream. Stir with fork until dough pulls away from sides of bowl. Roll out dough on floured surface until just big enough to cover baking dish. Cut 2-inch cross in the center. Place over peaches and tuck in dough around sides. Turn back corners of cross to reveal filling. Bake in 375° oven 40 to 45 minutes, until filling is bubbly and top is golden brown.

RASPBERRY PEACH CRUMBLE

Crumble has a crispy topping that doesn't have flour.

2 cups fresh or frozen raspberries	¼ cup brown sugar
3 cups fresh or frozen peaches chopped	¼ cup sugar
2 tablespoons lemon juice	1 teaspoon vanilla extract
⅔ cup sugar divided	1 teaspoon salt
½ teaspoon cinnamon divided	Shortbread Crust:
1 cup rolled oats	1 cup butter
½ cup butter	½ cup brown sugar
	2 ¼ cups flour

Crust: Cream butter and brown sugar, add 2 cups flour and mix well. Knead for 5 minutes, adding enough flour to make a soft dough. Pat crust evenly into bottom sprayed 13x9 inch baking dish. In a bowl, mix the raspberries, peaches, lemon juice, ⅓ cup white sugar, and ¼ teaspoon cinnamon. In a separate bowl, mix oats, butter, brown sugar, rest of white sugar, vanilla, salt, and rest of cinnamon. Spoon raspberry and peach mixture evenly over crust and top with oats mixture. Bake in 350° oven for 35 minutes, until crisp and golden brown. Cool 10 minutes before serving.

LOW CARB LEMON CHEESECAKE

Cheesecake is a decadent, delicious dessert; smooth and creamy, the tastiest and most elegant way to end a meal. No wonder people have been perfecting the cheesecake recipe since early Roman times. This one is refreshingly lemony.

3 cups almonds finely ground

1 stick butter melted

⅓ cup splenda or sugar

Filling:

1 package unflavored jello

1 cup boiling water

3 8-ounce packages cream cheese
   cut into chunks

¼ cup sour cream

Dash salt

1 ½ teaspoons vanilla extract

1 teaspoon lemon extract

1 teaspoon lemon juice

½ cup splenda or sugar

Place crust ingredients together in sprayed 13 x 9 baking dish, mix well and press on to bottom of dish. Place in refrigerator to set. Mix gelatin in boiling water, stir well until dissolved; set aside to cool. Place cream cheese in mixing bowl and beat on low. Slowly add cooled dissolved gelatin. When mixed well, add sour cream, salt, extracts, juice and sugar/splenda. Beat well until creamy and smooth. Pour onto crust, chill until firm at least 4 hours.

MIXED FRUIT COBBLER

Cobblers are an American deep-dish fruit dessert or pie with a thick crust, usually a biscuit and a filling of peaches, apples or berries.

1 cup sliced fresh or frozen sliced
   peaches
¾ cup peeled sliced apples
¾ cup peeled sliced pears
½ cup blueberries
½ cup pitted, sliced sweet cherries
½ cup pitted, sliced plums
½ cup sugar
1 tablespoon cornstarch
2 tablespoons lemon juice

⅛ teaspoon salt
Topping:
2 cups flour
7 tablespoons sugar
1 ½ teaspoons baking powder
¾ teaspoon baking soda
½ teaspoon salt
10 tablespoons cold butter cut into
   cubes
⅔ cup plain yogurt

Filling: Gently toss peaches, apple, pear, blueberries, cherries, plums and sugar in large bowl, let stand 30 minutes tossing several times. Drain off juice, save ¾ cup of juice, discard rest. Whisk drained juice, cornstarch, lemon juice and salt together in small bowl. Toss fruit juice mixture with fruit slices and transfer to sprayed 13x9 inch baking dish. Bake in 425° oven for about 10 minutes or until fruit begins to bubble; remove from oven. Topping: Whisk flour, 6 tablespoons sugar, baking powder, baking soda and salt together. Cut butter cubes into flour mixture just until resembles coarse meal. Add yogurt and toss with rubber spatula until dough is formed; don't over mix. Divide dough into 12 evenly sized but roughly shaped mounds. Place dough mounds on top, space them out at least ½ inch apart, don't let them touch. Sprinkle 1 tablespoon of sugar evenly over 12 mounds. Bake until topping is golden brown and fruit is bubbling, about 16-18 minutes. Cool on wire rack about 20 minutes. Serve warm.

MOIST BANANA BREAD

The banana is possibly the most popular fruit in the world. A staple in most kitchens in America, it does have a very short shelf life. If you ever buy too many bananas and some don't get eaten; the over-ripened bananas make the best bread, muffin or cake.

2 cups sugar	1 teaspoon salt
1 cup butter	1 teaspoon baking powder
4 eggs beaten	2 teaspoons baking soda
4 cups flour	6 mashed bananas

Cream butter and sugar. Beat eggs until light and add to butter mixture. In separate bowl, sift together flour, salt, baking powder, and soda. Add to creamed mixture a little at a time. Add banana alternately with flour; beat well. Spray 2 loaf pans. Bake in 350° oven for 40-45 minutes until a toothpick comes out clean. Cool in pans. Wrap in foil and refrigerate or freeze.

ORANGE CRANBERRY CRISP

There's a rapidly growing popularity of cranberries for their nutrient content and antioxidant qualities and usually add a nice tartness to most dishes.

4 cups fresh or frozen cranberries	½ cup softened butter
1 cup orange marmalade	Maple Apple Crisp:
Crisp:	Omit both cranberries and
½ cup flour	marmalade
½ cup rolled oats	5 cups peeled and sliced apples
½ cup brown sugar	¾ cup maple syrup
Pinch salt	

Place cranberries (apples) in an sprayed 8-inch baking dish. Toss fruit with marmalade (syrup). In separate bowl, mix together flour, oats, sugar, and salt. Cut in butter until mixture is crumbly. Sprinkle mixture evenly over fruit. Bake in 375° oven for 35 minutes, until topping is golden brown. Serve warm or at room temperature.

PANTRY DELIGHT

Last minute company had me scrambling to put together a simple treat. Delight is what everyone expressed when I served this dessert from what I had on hand in the pantry.

2 cans refrigerated biscuits	**½ cup regular or sugar free maple**
2 tart apple peeled and diced	**syrup**
1 teaspoon apple pie spice	**6 tablespoons butter melted**
2 teaspoons cinnamon	**¼ cup unsweetened applesauce**

Separate biscuits and cut each biscuit into 4 equal pieces. Stir butter, apple pie spice, cinnamon and maple syrup until smooth. Add applesauce and mix. Place biscuits and apples in well sprayed Bundt pan, evenly mixing them. Bake in 350° oven for 30 minutes. Let stand for 10 minutes, invert on to plate and use spoon to serve.

PEACH OR APPLE CRISP

Fresh fruit crisps can match fruit pies in terms of flavor—and they are so much easier to make. Using the slow cooker makes this an unexpected summer treat without turning on the oven.

⅔ cup sugar	**½ teaspoon ground allspice**
1 ¼ cups water	**¾ cup quick oatmeal**
3 tablespoons cornstarch	**½ cup brown sugar**
4 cups sliced and peeled apples or	**½ cup flour**
4 cups peaches fresh or frozen	**¼ cup margarine at room**
½ teaspoon cinnamon	**temperature**

Combine sugar, water, cornstarch, apples or peaches, cinnamon and allspice and place in slow cooker. Combine oatmeal, brown sugar, flour and margarine until crumbly. Sprinkle over fruit filling. Cover with lid and cook on low 2-3 hours.

PEAR CRUNCH

The crunch is helped along by using oats, nuts and less liquid in the topping making a crunchy yummy combination.

3 peeled, sliced pears	⅛ teaspoon cinnamon
2 teaspoons lemon juice	⅛ teaspoon ginger
3 tablespoons sugar	Dash nutmeg
3 tablespoons old fashioned oats	1 tablespoon cold butter
2 tablespoons flour	2 tablespoons chopped nuts

Place pear slices in a sprayed 1-quart baking dish. Sprinkle with lemon juice. In a bowl, combine the sugar, oats, flour, cinnamon, ginger and nutmeg. Cut in butter until crumbly, add nuts. Sprinkle over pears. Bake in 350° oven for 25-30 minutes or until bubbly.

QUICK RHUBARB BROWN BETTY

Betty was a popular baked pudding made during Colonial times. It's made by layering spiced fruit with buttered breadcrumbs. It can be made with all sorts of fruit. The microwave makes this much easier and quicker to make last minute.

5 cups chopped rhubarb	4 cups cubed cinnamon bread
¾ cup sugar	¼ cup melted butter
½ teaspoon cinnamon	

In a medium bowl, toss together the rhubarb, sugar and cinnamon. Add half of the bread cubes, and toss lightly to distribute. Transfer to an ungreased 2 quart microwave-safe baking dish. Top with remaining bread cubes. Drizzle melted butter over the top. Cook in the microwave for 12 minutes, or until the rhubarb is tender. Serve warm.

RHUBARB CRUNCH

Easy, fast crisps, crunches and cobblers are a perfect way to showcase seasonal and regional fruits, as well as utilizing the abundant crops in our garden, lowering the cost.

3 cups diced rhubarb	1 cup quick cooking oats
1 cup sugar	1 ½ cups flour
3 tablespoons flour	1 cup butter
1 cup brown sugar	

In large mixing bowl combine rhubarb, white sugar and flour. Stir well and spread evenly into lightly sprayed 9x13 inch baking dish. Set aside. In large mixing bowl combine brown sugar, oats, and 1 ½ cups flour. Stir well; cut in butter until mixture is crumbly. Sprinkle mixture over rhubarb layer. Bake in 375° oven for 40 minutes. Serve hot or cold.

RHUBARB JAM

5 cups rhubarb cut in to pieces	1 3-ounce box strawberry gelatin
4 cups sugar	

Combine rhubarb and sugar, stir well. Let set overnight. Place in saucepan, bring to boil and add dry gelatin. Stir very well until dissolved and well mixed. Place in tight lid containers and refrigerate or freeze.

RHUBARB STRAWBERRY GELATIN

1 cup chopped rhubarb	1 tablespoon strawberry jam
¾ cup water	1 cup pineapple juice
1 3 ounce package strawberry gelatin	1 tart apple peeled and diced
	½ cup chopped walnuts
⅓ cup sugar	

In saucepan over medium heat bring rhubarb and water to boil. Reduce heat, cover and simmer for 10 minutes, or until rhubarb is tender. Remove from heat, add gelatin powder, sugar and jam. Stir until gelatin is dissolved completely.

Stir in pineapple juice. Chill in refrigerator until partially set. Stir in apple and nuts. Pour into 1-quart bowl coated with cooking spray. Chill until set. Unmold onto lettuce leaves and topped with mayonnaise.

SIMPLE BIRD'S NEST PUDDING

A VERY old recipe for pudding containing apples whose cores have been replaced by sugar. The apples are nestled in a bowl created by the crust and the first recipe appears in pages from an 1894 cook book. Enjoy the updated version.

6 large tart apples	**½ teaspoon salt**
½ cup brown sugar	**Sauce:**
1 ½ cups evaporated milk	**½ teaspoon nutmeg**
3 eggs	**¾ cup powdered sugar**
1 cup flour	**3 tablespoons melted butter**

Peel apples; remove core by cutting from end into middle, leave apple whole; place them in a deep pie dish with opening upward. Press even amounts of brown sugar in each apple hole. Make thin batter, using milk, eggs, salt and flour; pour this into dish around apples. Bake in 350° oven until crust has browned, about 60 minutes. Mix butter, sugar and nutmeg together for sauce, set aside. Take cooked pudding directly to table before it falls. Turn each serving onto a plate so apple is nested in fluffy crust. Pour sauce over each dessert.

SLUMP

A slump is a dessert that is basically the same as a grunt, it consists of fruit or berries. The difference is the slump is baked uncovered instead of steamed. Some recipes call for it to be cooked on the stovetop and others use the oven. The slump was given its name because when served on a plate it has a tendency to slump.

8 cups thinly sliced apples, peaches or pears	¼ cup cold butter
¼ cup brown sugar	½ cup sour cream
½ cup sugar	Melted butter
½ teaspoon cinnamon	Sugar and cinnamon
½ teaspoon almond extract	Sauce:
Dough:	1 cup sugar
1 ⅔ cups flour	1 cup boiling water
2 tablespoons sugar	½ teaspoon nutmeg
2 teaspoons baking powder	1 tablespoon flour
¼ teaspoon baking soda	1 tablespoon butter
¼ teaspoon salt	

Lightly spray bottom and sides of 9x13 inch baking dish. In large bowl, combine fruit slices, sugars, cinnamon, and almond extract. Toss together until evenly mixed. Pour fruit into baking dish. Place dish in 375° oven and bake for 20 minute. Fruit should be hot when topping is added. Prepare topping while fruit is baking. Combine flour, sugar, baking powder, baking soda, and salt together in bowl and whisk until evenly mixed. Cut cold butter into 4 slabs and add to dry ingredient mixture. Cut butter into mixture using a pastry blender or knives until small pea size pieces. Add sour cream and work into dough until it forms one or two lumps of fairly dry dough. Place dough on un-floured work surface. If there are two lumps of dough, work dough with hands until they are combined into one piece. Dough will be slightly sticky. Work dough into rectangle approximately 8 x 8 inches. Turn several times adding flour if needed to make dough less sticky. Cut into 8 equal squares. Place squares on top of hot fruit dish, do not overlap. Brush surface of dough with melted butter. Sprinkle cinnamon and sugar evenly over dough, Place baking dish back in oven and bake for 40 to 45 minutes. The slump is done when fruit is bubbling and topping is well browned. Also, check topping for doneness by lifting one of biscuits in middle of dish to make sure biscuit is not still doughy. If serving warm, allow slump to cool slightly before serving. The slump can also be cooled completely and serve at room temperature if desired. It can also be served with nutmeg sauce. Nutmeg sauce: In a saucepan, mix sugar and flour. Stir in boiling water and cook, stirring constantly until sauce bubbles. Add butter and simmer gently 5 minutes. Remove from heat and stir in nutmeg. Serve over each serving of slump.

STRAWBERRY SHORTCAKE

Shortcake is a classic American dessert made with a rich biscuit, split in two, topped with fruit and whipped cream. Strawberries are traditional, but peaches, other berries and apricots are also quite tasty.

3 cups flour	½ cup milk
4 teaspoons baking powder	¾ cup shortening
¾ teaspoon salt	Strawberry Filling:
¼ teaspoon cream of tartar	1 quart strawberries
2 tablespoons sugar	⅓ cup sugar
2 eggs	1 ½ cups frozen whipped topping

Sift together dry ingredients. Beat eggs with milk and set aside. Mix shortening with dry ingredients until pea-size crumbs. Add milk and eggs; knead for few minutes on board. Roll ¾ inch thick. Cut and bake in 425° oven for 10 to 15 minutes on sprayed cookie sheet. Rinse berries under cold water; drain well. Hull and slice berries; place in a bowl. Sprinkle with sugar; cover and let stand at room temperature for about 1 hour. Split each biscuit horizontally with serrated knife. Place bottom biscuits on plate; top with about ⅓ cup of berry mixture. Replace tops and top with a tablespoon or so of berries. Serve with thawed whipped topping.

SAUCES & RUBS

In September 1989, Joe and I had just finished our summer camp nurse jobs in Maine. We were headed home and stopped in a small town at the border of New York and Pennsylvania for the night. It was late, the hotel restaurant was closed, but the bar was open and served food. We ordered Buffalo wings, something we both enjoyed all over the country.

I can't handle spicy hot food so I always get the mild. My husband on the other hand hasn't found anything too hot for his palate and always orders the hottest available. As we ate, he started sniffing and blowing his nose. I was afraid he was coming down with a cold, but it wasn't a virus, it was the spices. Those hot wings were the hottest he'd ever eaten. He enjoyed every bite despite the tears and extra fluids needed. Eating hot wings all over the US, he has yet to find them any spicier than those at that little motel bar. Until just recently—it has taken me 20 years to beat out those New York wings.

On our travels Joe buys hot sauces and I read labels to pick up ingredient combination ideas. After multiple attempts with blends and concoctions, I fixed a wing sauce that was too hot even for my husband to eat in one sitting. He took some to a co-worker who couldn't believe something was too spicy to eat. She wanted to call him "hot sauce weakling", until she tasted the wings I made. She too, tear-ed up and needed a lot of liquids to eat just one wing. Now that I have found the top of the ladder of spiciness, I can work my way down the ladder and rate the different levels. It will take a year or so; I don't want to burn out Joe's taste buds.

When we joined a weight loss program in the 1990's, a lot of things about dieting had changed. "Diet" foods weren't popular anymore and the long list of forbidden foods was gone with portion control the emphasis. That was good because if my husband couldn't have his bacon and peanut butter, no diet change would work.

ENTICE WITH SPICE

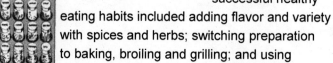 

The ways to successful healthy eating habits included adding flavor and variety with spices and herbs; switching preparation to baking, broiling and grilling; and using healthier oils and sugars. With those changes, I could still cook delicious, flavorful meals for my husband and not hurt him. It was fun to find new sweets and desserts to eat and then share them with our friends and co-workers without telling them the calorie, fat and sugar levels had been reduced. No one suspected the food was healthier and loved the recipes even more when they found out.

Once we moved to Alaska, my task was making our dishes taste fresher. We use mostly canned goods and frozen foods since fresh is expensive, not very "fresh" or always available. I discover that herbs can easily be grown in our heated garage in very small space. The difference using them and the homemade dried spices is the big difference between bland or garden fresh taste—increasing the satisfaction of the meal and keeping a healthier diet innovative and creative. Being inventive with ingredients makes things more satisfying and less likely for us to crave unhealthy fats, carbohydrates and sugars. Use fresh herbs and spices whenever possible, I've included equivalents so you can adjust any recipe.

Experiment With All the Flavored Oils, Vinegars, Juices, Wines, Beers, Sodas and Liquids to Create Your Own Favorite Flavored Marinades

ALABAMA WHITE BBQ SAUCE

This sauce is great for basting pork or chicken while cooking or used as a dipping sauce for meats (at a fondue party) or on a submarine sandwich or as the base for a chicken white sauce pizza.

Spicy:
1 cup mayonnaise
½ cup apple cider vinegar
1 teaspoon horseradish
1 teaspoon salt
1 teaspoon white pepper
¼ cup apple juice

Peppery:
2 cups mayonnaise
2 tablespoons black pepper
2 teaspoons salt
⅓ cup lemon juice
⅓ cup white vinegar
4 tablespoons sugar

For either sauce, whisk together ingredients in bowl. Refrigerate to allow flavors to combine. Baste on chicken, ribs, or pork, and set some aside (not touching the raw meat) for dipping.

CALIFORNIA RUB

1 tablespoon salt
1 ½ teaspoons garlic salt
½ teaspoon celery salt
¼ teaspoon lemon pepper
¼ teaspoon onion powder

¼ teaspoon paprika
¼ teaspoon dried dill
¼ teaspoon dried sage
¼ teaspoon dried rosemary

Mix together salt, garlic salt, celery salt, pepper, onion powder, paprika, dill, sage and rosemary in a bowl. Store in airtight container at room temperature until ready to use. When you do use the rub, use a squeeze of fresh lemon juice with the rub.

CAROLINA RUB

A classic-style Carolina barbecue rub for traditional Carolina Pulled Pork.

2 tablespoons salt

2 tablespoons sugar

2 tablespoons brown sugar

2 tablespoons ground cumin

2 tablespoons chili powder

2 tablespoons black pepper

1 tablespoon cayenne pepper

¼ cup paprika

Combine all ingredients in small bowl and mix well; use as dry rub on beef, chicken, lamb or pork.

CAROLINA STYLE BBQ SAUCE

This style sauce has vinegar and mustard bases, as opposed to ketchup and molasses. The combination of sweet and tangy brings out the best in grilled pork or chicken.

1 cup mustard

½ cup sugar

¼ cup brown sugar

¾ cup cider vinegar

¼ cup water

2 tablespoons chili powder

1 teaspoon black pepper

1 teaspoon white pepper

¼ teaspoon cayenne pepper

½ teaspoon soy sauce

2 tablespoons butter

1 tablespoon liquid smoke

Mix together mustard, sugar, brown sugar, vinegar, water, chili powder, black pepper, white pepper and cayenne pepper in saucepan; simmer for 30 minutes. Stir in soy, butter and smoke; and simmer for 10 more minutes.

GEORGIA BBQ SAUCE

Careful this one can be hot!

1 cup white vinegar	1 tablespoon sugar
½ tablespoon dry mustard	2 tablespoons butter
1 tablespoon black pepper	6 ounces tomato paste
1 tablespoon crushed red pepper	1-2 teaspoons hot sauce
1 tablespoon salt	

Combine vinegar, mustard, black pepper, red pepper, salt, sugar, and butter in medium saucepan. Bring to a boil over medium heat, stirring frequently. Stir in tomato paste and hot sauce until well blended. Allow to cool.

HONEY BBQ SAUCE

¾ cup honey	1 tablespoon soy sauce
½ cup ketchup	2 teaspoons minced garlic
1 stick butter	¼ cup minced onions
1 tablespoon vinegar	2 teaspoons chili powder
1 tablespoon mustard	¼ teaspoon salt
2 tablespoons brown sugar	

Saute onion and garlic over medium low heat for about 2 minutes, until slightly translucent. Add remaining ingredients; bring to simmer for 5-10 minutes, until hot and slightly thickened. Leftover sauce will keep in fridge for several weeks.

HOT DOG CHILI SAUCE

½ finely chopped onion	1 teaspoon minced garlic
1 tablespoon olive oil	½ teaspoon garlic powder
2 pounds ground beef chuck	¼ teaspoon cayenne pepper
2 teaspoons chili powder	½ teaspoon black pepper
1 teaspoon paprika	½ teaspoon salt

Melt butter in skillet over medium heat. Add onions and cook, stirring occasionally, for 5 minutes or until translucent. Remove onions from skillet; add ground chuck to skillet. Cook 6 to 8 minutes until beef is browned. Return onions to skillet, cook with beef over medium-low heat for 5 minutes. Using slow cooker, place contents of skillet into cooker set on high, add spices and mix thoroughly, cook for 4 to 6 hours depending on desired consistency.

KANSAS CITY BBQ SAUCE

A thick sweet sauce with a touch of heat and a good example of a KC sauce used on ribs and pork

1 ¼ cups ketchup
1 cup water
⅓ cup cider vinegar
¼ cup brown sugar
2 tablespoons molasses
1 tablespoon onion powder

1 tablespoon garlic powder
1 tablespoon black pepper
1 teaspoon celery salt
1 teaspoon allspice
1 tablespoon chili powder
1 teaspoon cayenne pepper

Combine all ingredients in saucepan over medium heat. Stir constantly for 5 minutes. Reduce heat to low and simmer 20 minutes, stirring occasionally. Sauce should be thick. Allow to cool. Store in airtight container. Refrigerate.

KANSAS CITY RUB

This sweet, smoky blend on steaks, pork tenderloin, pork chops, or chicken is superb.

¼ cup paprika
2 tablespoons black pepper
1 tablespoon brown sugar
1 teaspoon kosher salt

2 teaspoons garlic salt
1 ½ teaspoons chili powder
½ teaspoon celery salt

Combine all ingredients. Store in airtight container for up to one month

KANSAS POULTRY BBQ SAUCE

A poultry farm on the East Coast gave me this recipe as the one they use for the yearly barbecue chicken festival. You can adjust the "heat" by increasing or decreasing the amount of hot sauce.

¼ teaspoon allspice	½ teaspoon paprika
¼ teaspoon cinnamon	1 teaspoon hot sauce
¼ teaspoon mace	¼ cup white vinegar
½t black pepper	⅓ cup molasses
½ teaspoon chili powder	1 cup ketchup

Sift together all dry ingredients. Combine hot sauce, vinegar, molasses and ketchup in large saucepan. Add dry ingredients and mix well. Bring to boil on top of stove. Serve with chicken or turkey legs. Store up to 3 weeks in refrigerator.

KENTUCKY BBQ RUB

This rub is exceptional and creates a succulent meal when used on barbecued lamb. My friend who helped me with the recipe gets rave reviews when he lightly glazes his grilled white fish.

½ cup black pepper	2 cloves crushed garlic
2 ½ tablespoons brown sugar	½ teaspoon ground allspice
2 tablespoons kosher salt	¼ cup Worcestershire sauce

Combine all ingredients except Worcestershire sauce and store in airtight container. This is enough rub for a 12 pound roast and best applied the night before cooking. Before putting rub on meat or poultry, coat it with Worcestershire sauce to hold rub on good. Wrap in plastic and refrigerate until it's time to go in smoker.

KENTUCKY BBQ SAUCE

It took quite a lot of sauce making to find something that matched the wonderful State Fair meal I had many years ago—our tongues were sore licking all the goodness from our fingers.

2 ½ cups beef broth or beer
¼-½ cup Kentucky bourbon
2 tablespoons brown sugar
2 tablespoons canola oil
¼ cup white vinegar
2 ½ teaspoons salt
2 tablespoons onion powder

2 ½ teaspoons black pepper
2 teaspoons Worcestershire sauce
1 teaspoon dry mustard
2 teaspoons chili powder
½ teaspoon hot pepper sauce
½ teaspoon red pepper flakes
1 tablespoon garlic powder

Combine all ingredients in saucepan and bring to rolling boil. Remove from heat and cool. Refrigerate sauce overnight to blend flavors.

KEYNOTE STEAK RUB

The cocoa in this seems an odd ingredient and is one of those mistakes that ends up being a huge success. It made our grilled game meat flavors explode and so did all the high praise.

1 tablespoon unsweetened cocoa
4 tablespoons ground cumin
2 teaspoons ground allspice

1 tablespoon ground black pepper
2 teaspoons salt

Mix ingredients and use on beef, buffalo, venison, elk or moose steak.

MEMPHIS BARBEQUE RUB

In Memphis, ribs are traditionally served up dry. This doesn't mean that the meat is tough and dried out, there just isn't a barbecue sauce on it. This traditional Memphis barbecue rub recipe is the base of a great rack of pork ribs but also awesome on chicken.

¼ cup paprika	½ teaspoon crushed red pepper
2 tablespoons brown sugar	flakes
2 teaspoons kosher salt	1 teaspoon dry mustard
1 teaspoon black pepper	1 teaspoon garlic powder
1 teaspoon chili powder	1 teaspoon onion powder

Combine all ingredients in small bowl. Mix with fork. Store until needed. Keeps in cool, dry place for six months.

MEMPHIS STYLE BBQ SAUCE

If you don't like chunks of onion and garlic in your sauce, place in blender after it's cooled to smooth it out.

2 cups ketchup	1 teaspoon chili powder
¼ cup mustard	½ teaspoon hot sauce
½ cup brown sugar	1 teaspoon black pepper
¼ cup apple cider vinegar	1 tablespoon minced garlic
¾ cup red wine vinegar	1 teaspoon celery salt
2 cups chopped onions	1 teaspoon liquid smoke

Combine all ingredients in medium saucepan. Bring to simmer and cook over low heat about 25 minutes, stirring occasionally, until smooth and thickened. Let cool slightly and serve. It gets better as it sits.

NORTH CAROLINA BBQ SAUCE

This tangy vinegar-based sauce, popular in Eastern North Carolina, is great for all meats, but best on pork

1 quart apple cider vinegar	2 tablespoons red pepper flakes
2 tablespoons garlic salt	1 cup brown sugar
1 tablespoon cayenne pepper	1 tablespoon hot pepper sauce

In large bowl, mix together cider vinegar, salt, cayenne pepper, red pepper flakes, brown sugar and hot pepper sauce. Stir until salt and brown sugar have dissolved. Cover and let stand at least 3 hours before using as basting sauce or serving on meat.

OZARK BBQ SAUCE

The Ozarks in southern Missouri and northern Arkansas, is full of recreation, entertainment and incredible food.

½ cup finely chopped onions	2 tablespoons molasses
2 teaspoons minced garlic	1 tablespoon paprika
1 teaspoon oils	1 tablespoon horseradish
¾ cup apple juice	1 tablespoon Worcestershire sauce
⅓ cup tomato paste	1 teaspoon salt
¼ cup cider vinegar	½ teaspoon black pepper
2 tablespoons brown sugar	

In saucepan, cook onion and garlic in oil over medium heat until onion is tender. Stir in juice, tomato paste, vinegar, sugar, molasses, paprika, horseradish, Worcestershire sauce, salt and pepper. Bring to a boil, reduce heat to simmer and cook uncovered, stirring occasionally, for 30 minutes or until sauce is desired consistency.

PEACH BBQ SAUCE

This may not count as a fruit serving for your daily diet, but this peach could convince a non-fruit eater to change their mind, at least about peaches.

1 tablespoon olive oil	3 tablespoons brown sugar
2 cups spicy v8 vegetable juice	2 teaspoons hot sauce
1 ½ cups peach nectar	Black pepper
1 teaspoon Worcestershire sauce	3 cups chopped frozen peaches
¼ cup cider vinegar	

In skillet whisk together olive oil, vegetable juice, peach nectar, Worcestershire sauce, cider vinegar, brown sugar, garlic, hot sauce, black pepper, and chopped peaches; simmer over medium heat for 8 to 10 minutes. Remove sauce from heat, pour sauce over seared meat or poultry in baking dish. Place in oven and cook until dish is cooked.

SIMPLE BBQ SAUCE

Barbecue sauces can be any combination of sour, sweet, spicy, smoky flavor and tangy ingredients. Some common items are tomato paste, vinegar, spices and sweeteners. Variations are often due to regional traditions, types of meat or poultry, available ingredients, health issues and family recipes or traditions.

1 cup ketchup	2 teaspoons Worcestershire sauce
1 cup diced onions	½ teaspoon garlic powder
¼ cup brown sugar	½ teaspoon red pepper flakes
2 tablespoons mustard	

In saucepan stir all ingredients together and cook 2 minutes over medium heat.

SOUTHWEST BBQ RUB

This wet rub packs a lot of flavor; adjust heat by using the cayenne pepper.

1 tablespoon chili powder

1 teaspoon ground cumin

1 teaspoon minced garlic

2 tablespoons Worcestershire sauce

1 teaspoon coarse salt

1 teaspoon sugar

¾ teaspoon black pepper

¼ teaspoon allspice

Pinch cayenne pepper (optional)

1 tablespoon vegetable oil

Mash garlic and salt together to form paste. Mix together chili powder, cumin, garlic paste, Worcestershire sauce, sugar, pepper, allspice, cayenne pepper and oil. Let rub sit on meat for 30 minutes to 2 hours.

SPICY HOT BBQ SAUCE

2 cups ketchup

2 cups vinegar

1 cup corn syrup

¼ cup molasses

1 tablespoon finely diced red bell
    peppers

4 teaspoons sugar

2 tablespoons liquid smoke

1 teaspoon salt

1 teaspoon crushed red pepper

1 teaspoon hot pepper sauce

½ teaspoon cayenne pepper

½ teaspoon black pepper

½ teaspoon garlic powder

½ teaspoon onion powder

Combine all ingredients in saucepan over high heat; whisk and stir until smooth. Bring mixture to boil, reduce heat and simmer, uncovered. Simmer for 30-45 minutes, until desired thickness. Remove from heat and store in tightly covered container in refrigerator.

SPICY MAPLE BBQ SAUCE

This is especially good on chicken, turkey, salmon fillets and white fishes.

1 ¼ cups ketchup

¾ cup apple cider vinegar

2 minced onions

2 ½ cups chicken broth

½ cup real maple syrup

2 tablespoons margarine

2 tablespoons Worcestershire sauce

1 tablespoon Dijon style mustard

1 teaspoon red pepper flakes

Combine all ingredients in medium saucepan. Bring to boil then reduce heat. Simmer about 50 minutes, stirring occasionally, until thickened and reduced.

ST LOUIS BBQ

St. Louis barbecue preparation involves slow open grilling until done, then simmering in a pan of barbecue sauce placed on the grill.

2 cups ketchup

½ cup water

½ cup apple cider vinegar

¼ cup brown sugar

3 tablespoons mustard

1 tablespoon onion powder

1 tablespoon garlic powder

1 teaspoon cayenne pepper

Combine all ingredients in saucepan over low heat. Stirring occasionally and simmer for 20 minutes. Sauce should be thin, but not watery. Store in an airtight container and refrigerate. Sauce is better 24 hours later.

ST. LOUIS FAMILY BBQ SAUCE

St. Louis sauce is thinner and more tangy than Kansas City sauce. There are lots of variations, but this is a good example of the basic BBQ in the "Gateway City".

2 cups ketchup
1 can beer
½ cup minced onion
2 tablespoons minced garlic
½ cup cider vinegar

¼ cup spicy mustard
2 tablespoons Worcestershire sauce
2 tablespoons soy sauce
½ teaspoon hot sauce

Whisk all ingredients in saucepan over a low heat. Stirring, simmer for 20 minutes. Let it cool to room temperature. Use to baste or brush on during cooking and serve additional sauce on the side.

SWEET SMOKEY BBQ SAUCE

2 cups ketchup
2 cups vinegar
1 cup molasses
1 cup honey
2 teaspoons liquid smoke

1 teaspoon salt
½ teaspoon garlic powder
½ teaspoon onion powder
½ teaspoon hot pepper sauce

Combine all ingredients in saucepan over high heat. Whisk and stir until smooth. When mixture comes a boil, reduce heat and simmer, uncovered. Simmer for 30-45 minutes, until desired thickness. Remove from heat and store in tightly covered container in refrigerator until needed.

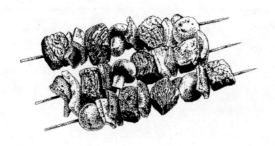

TEXAS BBQ SAUCE

Texas BBQ recipes usually use some type of hot pepper—the secret ingredient.

1 cup tomato sauce

½ cup cider vinegar

¼ cup Worcestershire sauce

1 cup brown sugar

2 tablespoons dry mustard

3 tablespoons margarine

1 tablespoon hot sauce

2 cloves crushed garlic

¼ cup chopped onions

Salt and black pepper

2 jalapeño peppers seeded and
    chopped

1 teaspoon liquid smoke

First, sauté onions in medium saucepan until onions are translucent; add remaining ingredients. Cook on medium heat until mixture is smooth. Use sauce to baste meat prior to cooking and during cooking.

TEXAS STYLE BBQ SAUCE

2 cups ketchup

2 cups vinegar

1 cup corn syrup

4 teaspoons sugar

1 teaspoon salt

½ teaspoon garlic powder

½ teaspoon onion powder

½ teaspoon hot pepper sauce

Combine all ingredients in saucepan over high heat. Whisk and stir until smooth. When mixture comes to boil, reduce heat and simmer, uncovered. Simmer for 30-45 minutes, until desired thickness. Remove from heat and sore in tightly covered container in refrigerator until needed.

VIRGINIA BBQ SAUCE

You'll notice this one doesn't contain any tomato base, it gives a very different flavor to your meat or poultry.

1 cup white vinegar	1 tablespoon hot sauce
1 cup cider vinegar	1 teaspoon salt
1 tablespoon brown sugar	1 teaspoon black pepper
1 tablespoon cayenne pepper	

Combine vinegars, brown sugar, cayenne pepper, hot pepper sauce, salt and pepper in jar or bottle with tight fitting lid. Refrigerate for 1-2 days before using so flavors will blend. Shake occasionally and store for up to 2 months in refrigerator.

WHISKY GLAZE

Apply this glaze toward the end of cooking so the meat surface won't burn.

1 cup whiskey	2 teaspoons Worcestershire sauce
1 cup ketchup	3 teaspoons mince garlic
½ cup brown sugar	½ teaspoon dry mustard
¼ cup vinegar	Salt and black pepper
1 tablespoon lemon juice	

Combine ingredients and mix well. Store in an airtight container in refrigerator. Make it a few days in advance so flavors will have more time to blend together.

WHITE BBQ SAUCE

Great as a white pizza sauce or on pork, chicken and even fish.

2 cups mayonnaise	⅓ cup lemon juice
2 tablespoons black pepper	⅓ cup white vinegar
1 teaspoon salt	4 tablespoons sugar

Whisk together ingredients in bowl. Refrigerate to allow flavors to combine.

^BURGER SAUCE

¼ cup mayonnaise

1 tablespoon ketchup

1 small diced onion

Dill pickle slices

Lettuce leaves

Mix mayonnaise and ketchup together and add onions. Use on top of hamburgers with dill pickles and leaf or 2 of lettuce.

^CONEY ISLAND HOT DOG SAUCE

Many say that Coney Island is the birthplace of the hotdog, and there is no shortage of places to eat them. Coney Island is a New York City neighborhood that features an amusement area that has over 35 separately owned rides and attractions.

½ pound ground beef

⅓ cup chopped onions

1 8-ounce can tomato sauce

⅛ teaspoon black pepper

¾ teaspoon salt

2 teaspoons minced garlic

1 tablespoon water

1 teaspoon chili powder

Mix ground beef and onion in frying pan, breaking up beef finely and brown. Drain off grease. Add tomato sauce, pepper, salt, garlic, water and chili powder. Simmer until thoroughly heated.

^CRANBERRY SAUCE

There are many who believe you can't call it a Thanksgiving meal without this sauce on the table. Fix this ahead of time and skip the store bought stuff. The difference in flavor will catch everyone by surprise.

2 12-ounce bags fresh cranberries

2 cups water

1 ¾ cups sugar

1 teaspoon grated orange peel

Place all ingredients in large saucepan and bring to boil. Reduce heat and simmer 15 minutes or until most of cranberries have burst. Remove from heat. Cool slightly, then refrigerate covered up to 2 weeks.

^CUCUMBER SAUCE

Once I tasted real Greek Tzatziki sauce, I had to find my own recipe to use this wonderful cucumber infused sauce to try on everything: meats, poultry, potatoes and all raw or cooked vegetables

1 cup sour cream
2 diced cucumbers
½ cup finely chopped onions
½ teaspoon celery flakes

1 teaspoon salt
½ teaspoon black pepper
1 teaspoon minced garlic

Mix all ingredients together, place in covered container and refrigerate for at least 2 hours.

^HONEY SAUCE

I use this for pork, chicken, nuggets or strips and even to dip potatoes or other vegetables—baked, grilled or fried. No preservatives and less sugar makes it healthier and more flavorsome than the fast food dips.

1 tablespoon canola oil
1 ¼ teaspoons chili powder
1 teaspoon garlic powder
½ teaspoon liquid smoke
1 teaspoon black pepper

½ cup ketchup
½ cup water
¾ cup white vinegar
⅓ cup honey

Combine all ingredients in to saucepan. Bring to boil while stirring. Then reduce heat and simmer sauce uncovered for 20 minutes. Serve this warm, room temperature or chilled.

^MILD TACO SAUCE

Nothing beats making your own tacos at home and it makes sense that homemade sauce elevates the fiesta to superior levels—the added work is minimal compared to the taste.

3 cups water	4 teaspoons chili powder
2 teaspoons cornstarch	2 teaspoons salt
1 6-ounce can tomato paste	1 teaspoon cayenne pepper
1 tablespoon white vinegar	

Dissolve cornstarch in water in saucepan. Add remaining ingredients, bring mixture to boil, stirring well, over medium heat. Reduce heat and simmer for 5 minutes. Cover and cool. Store in Refrigerator.

^MUSHROOM SAUCE

¼ cup minced onions	1 ½ cups chicken broth
3 tablespoons oils	1 6-ounce can mushrooms drained
3 tablespoons flour	

Sauté onion in oil until golden. Add flour and blend to smooth paste. Gradually add broth and cook, stirring, until sauce thickens. Add mushrooms and simmer gently until heated through.

^MUSTARD SAUCE

Anything you put mustard on can be a candidate for this sauce. I use it as a dip with fondue cooked meats and poultry.

1 cup whipping cream	2 tablespoons mustard
2 tablespoons Dijon style mustard	3 tablespoons horseradish

Beat whipping cream until forms soft peaks. Fold in horseradish and mustards. Cover and refrigerate before serving. Store up to 24 hours.

^PIZZA SAUCE

Great as a dipping sauce for meats, cheeses, potatoes and I use it at the "Italian Fondue" parties.

1 15-ounce can tomato purée
½ teaspoon salt
¼ teaspoon black pepper
½ teaspoon garlic powder
¼ teaspoon onion powder

¼ teaspoon dried basil
¼ teaspoon dried marjoram
¼ teaspoon dried oregano
¼ teaspoon dried thyme

Combine all ingredients in saucepan. Cook over medium heat uncovered until begins to bubble. Reduce heat and simmer for 30 minutes. Remove from heat, cool. Store in tightly sealed container in refrigerator up to 4 weeks. Heat to serve.

^PIZZA SAUCE 2

1 8-ounce can tomato sauce
1 14 ½-ounce can tomatoes don't
   drain off the juice
½ cup onions chopped
1 tablespoon dried basil

1 teaspoon dried oregano
1 teaspoon sugar
2 cloves garlic minced
¼ teaspoon black pepper

Combine all ingredients into saucepan and bring to boil. Reduce heat and simmer uncovered for about 10 minutes or until desired thickness

^RESORT TARTAR SAUCE

The resort that inspired me to make this was the first time I had mustard in my tartar sauce—it was a subtle surprise that I wanted to reproduce. Since I've made my own tartar sauce for years, adding a touch of mustard wasn't that big a deal. Leave the mustard out if you prefer the regular tartar sauce we all love.

1 cup mayonnaise
½ teaspoon mustard
1 tablespoon sweet pickle relish

½ tablespoon dill pickle relish
½ teaspoon lemon juice
Salt and black pepper

Blend all ingredients in bowl, cover and refrigerate at least an hour before serving. Keep refrigerated up to 3 days. If you like it spicy, add 1-2 teaspoons horseradish. For hot and spicy also add a dash or two of hot sauce.

^RHUBARB STEAK SAUCE

Who would a thought using the leftover rhubarb from my baking would make such a difference on our steak dinner that night.

8 cups chopped rhubarb	1 teaspoon allspice
4 cups chopped onions	½ teaspoon cloves
2 cups white vinegar	1 teaspoon salt
2 ⅓ cups brown sugar	½ teaspoon black pepper
1 teaspoon cinnamon	

Combine all ingredients in large saucepan and bring to boil. Reduce heat; simmer 1 hour or until thickened. Cool. Store in refrigerator.

^SWEET CHERRY SAUCE

The flavor of this recipe changes depending on what state my cherries are from and sometimes I use black cherries since my husband prefers their taste.

½ cup sugar	1 tablespoon orange or cherry
2 tablespoons cornstarch	liqueur or cherry brandy or
½ cup water	orange juice
2 cups fresh pitted or frozen cherries	

In saucepan stir sugar and cornstarch; stir in water. Add cherries; cook and stir over medium heat until thick and bubbly. Cook and stir for 2 minutes. Remove from heat. Stir in juice, brandy or liqueur.

^SWEET ONION SAUCE

½ cup corn syrup

1 tablespoon minced onions

1 tablespoon red wine vinegar

2 teaspoons white vinegar

1 teaspoon balsamic vinegar

1 teaspoon brown sugar

1 teaspoon buttermilk powder

¼ teaspoon lemon juice

¼ teaspoon poppy seeds

⅛ teaspoon salt

⅛ teaspoon black pepper

⅛ teaspoon garlic powder

Combine all ingredients in microwave bowl and heat uncovered in microwave for 1-2 minutes until mixture boils. Whisk well, cover and cook before using over sandwiches, beef, chicken, fish or vegetables.

^SWEET AND SOUR SAUCE

There are more variations of this sauce then there are countries in the world. After many different ingredients and attempts, this one has lasted the test of time in our house.

1 tablespoon canola oil

¼ cup pineapple juice (drained from chunks)

2 tablespoons cornstarch

¼ cup ketchup

½ teaspoon ginger

1 teaspoon soy sauce

¼ cup white vinegar

½ cup water

⅓ cup brown sugar

1 can pineapple chunks

1 small onion cut into 1-inch chunks

1 green bell pepper cut into 1-inch chunks

Mix oil with pineapple juice and cook over low heat for 5 minutes. Mix cornstarch with ketchup, ginger, soy sauce, vinegar, water and sugar. Add to hot pineapple juice and stir until thickened. Add onions and green pepper, cook for 2-3 minutes. Stir in pineapple pieces and simmer until hot.

^TERIYAKI SAUCE

The interest in Teriyaki anything has boomed, so experiment with this on everything.

½ cup sherry
⅓ cup soy sauce
¼ cup brown sugar
¾ cup chicken broth
3 tablespoons minced garlic

3 tablespoons minced ginger
4 teaspoons balsamic vinegar
6 tablespoons lemon juice
½ teaspoon red pepper flakes

In saucepan combine all ingredients. Heat over medium heat to boiling, stirring constantly. Reduce heat to simmer and cook about 3 minutes or until reduced to syrup.

^TOMATO SAUCE

Whether you think of the tomato as a vegetable or a fruit, its close cousins are potatoes, chili peppers, tobacco and eggplants. Tomatoes are used especially in Italian and Middle Eastern cuisines and their acidic nature maks them easy to preserve in home canning or to vacuum seal and freeze. Being so healthy for us to eat just increases the pleasure of enjoying our garden bounty all year round.

1 sweet onion cut in chunks
5 ripe tomatoes quartered
½ cup chopped basil
¼ cup chopped parsley
2 teaspoons minced garlic

Dash red pepper flakes
2 teaspoons brown sugar
⅛ teaspoon salt
⅛ teaspoon white pepper
¼ teaspoon celery flakes

In large pot, add onions, tomatoes, basil, parsley, garlic, pepper flakes, sugar, salt, pepper and celery flakes. Bring to simmer over medium high heat, stirring often. Reduce heat to low and cook covered for 10 minutes. Using hand held blender carefully beat mixture in pot until everything is smooth. Place back over heat and cook on low uncovered for 10 more minutes or until thickened.

PORK

A Nurse's family accepts the fact that holidays are never going to be the same if you work in a hospital. Hospitals are open 24/7 and staff has to take their turns working on the holidays. We didn't celebrate Thanksgiving on the Thursday Holiday until both Joe and I stopped working in hospitals. Having no children afforded us the luxury of being flexible when we ate our holiday meals.

Whether you have family at home or not, around major holidays everyone ends up with some sleep deprivation. Joe and I volunteered to work most holidays attempting to give the families with children and less flexibility the time off. Working so many holidays I discovered that if I fixed a holiday style dish for everyone, it produced a mood of celebration at work and helped energize those who were tired or just disheartened because they had to work.

Lemon to Lemonade

In Juneau Alaska, we worked at the only hospital in town. It was very small with 60 patient beds. On the night shift, we had no cafeteria, housekeeping, surgical, respiratory or maintenance staff on duty, so there were only about 30-35 employees working nights in the whole hospital. My best friend Paula loves cooking and baking like I do. She and her husband, both nurse, are like many Alaskans—transplants from other states and countries. We all have family too far away to travel for every holiday. Celebrating at work caught on in a big way because of her help, the small staff size and our love for holidays and to observe special occasions.

The holiday potlucks we had on our unit became hospital wide in a very short time. We shared a meal, socialized and made a depressing situation into a party. One year, there were people who *requested* to work the holiday shifts Paula and I did, knowing it would be festive instead of an inconvenience.

Quickly it became monthly potlucks. People who weren't working would come in with a dish or just to have a family type meal and hang out. It created a camaraderie that carried over into our work compatibility and strengths. Our productivity and outlook was showing in our workload and in the patient care. We became a community, developed friendships, socialized outside our jobs and crossed cultural barriers. It didn't take too long for a good thing to be noticed by the day shift staff, physicians and administration.

Paula and I were experienced cooks already, but the night get-togethers gave us the opportunity to taste unfamiliar food from Juneau's large Filipino community. We worked with some superb nurses who prepared their native Philippine dishes. Southeast Alaska is the home of the Alaskan Native community of Haida and Tlingit tribes and we expanded our recipe repertoire from their contributions to the parties. There were workers from all over the lower 48, many well traveled and all of them generously shared their specialties and favorites. I hadn't learned so much about different recipes and histories since my own traveling days.

A RAINBOW OF TASTE, PEOPLE & MEMORIES

It all started with bringing one dish to work. Food lifts spirits and encourages a good-humored atmosphere. It reminds us all of pleasant times and being nurtured. We got our share and were able to share with others. We all benefited, in more ways than we could ever imagine.

BBQ BABY BACK RIBS

There are two schools of thought about how ribs should end up: one group that says they should fall off the bone and the other insist they should be more like steak texture and require a good chewing to get off the bone. Making them fall off the bone means boiling your ribs and finishing them on the grill or oven. Those who prefer steak texture wouldn't think of boiling them first, they insist on roasting ribs slow at low temps with smoke and humidity. Steaming or microwaving the ribs and finishing on the grill is a good compromise when you don't have the time to slow cook.

2 wholes slabs pork baby back ribs	½ teaspoon dried thyme
Dry Rub:	½ teaspoon onion powder
8 tablespoons brown sugar	Braising:
3 tablespoons kosher salt	1 cup white wine
1 tablespoon chili powder	2 tablespoons white wine vinegar
½ teaspoon black pepper	2 tablespoons Worcestershire sauce
½ teaspoon cayenne pepper	1 tablespoon honey
½ teaspoon jalapeno seasoning	2 teaspoons minced garlic
½ teaspoon Old Bay seasoning	1 teaspoon liquid smoke

In bowl, combine all dry ingredients and mix well. Place each slab of baby back ribs on piece of heavy-duty aluminum foil, shiny side down. Sprinkle each side generously with dry rub. Pat dry rub into meat. Refrigerate ribs for minimum of 1 hour. In microwavable container, combine all ingredients for braising liquid. Microwave on high for 1 minute. Place ribs on baking sheet. Open one end of foil on each slab and pour half of braising liquid into each foil packet. Tilt baking sheet in order to equally distribute braising liquid. Braise ribs in 250° oven for 2 ½ hours. Transfer braising liquid into medium saucepot. Bring liquid to simmer and reduce by half or until thick syrup consistency. Brush glaze onto ribs. Place under broiler just until glaze caramelizes lightly. Slice each slab into 2 rib bone portions. Place remaining hot glaze into bowl and toss rib portions in the glaze.

CAROLINA STYLE PULLED PORK SHOULDER

Pulled pork is the perfect slow-cooked winter dish, warm and spicy. But try to pick one up with your hands and it should completely fall apart, hardly adhering to the "sandwich" rule. The sauce soaks into the buns and most likely will need to be eaten with a fork. You could try a sturdier bun or wrapping it in foil to eat, but a real pulled pork is going to be soaked with sauce and worth the effort to eat, no matter how you choose to do that task.

5 pounds boneless pork shoulder
   roast
Rub:
2 tablespoons salt
2 tablespoons paprika
1 tablespoon black pepper
2 teaspoons cayenne pepper
Baste:
½ cup bourbon whiskey

2 tablespoons molasses
1 ½ cups cider vinegar
1 cup water
1 teaspoon hot pepper sauce
2 tablespoons salt
1 tablespoon crushed red pepper
   flakes
1 tablespoon black pepper

Soak wood chips in water for 1 hour. In small bowl, mix together rub ingredients, set aside. In saucepan, mix together baste ingredients, simmer for 5 minutes. Divide into two portions; set aside. Rub pork shoulder on all surfaces with rub mixture; cover and refrigerate up to 24 hours. In charcoal grill with cover, place preheated coals around drip pan for medium indirect heat. Sprinkle half of wood chips over coals. Place meat on grill rack over drip pan. Cover and grill about 5-6 hours or until meat is very tender. Add more preheated coals (use a hibachi or a metal chimney starter to preheat coals), wood chips every 1 to 1 ½ hours, to maintain medium-low heat. Smoke until internal temperature is about 170°. Baste shoulder with one portion of sauce every 20 to 30 minutes during last 2 hours of cooking. Remove meat from grill; cover with foil and let stand for 20 to 30 minutes. Using fork, shred meat into long, thin strands. Pour remaining sauce over shredded meat; toss to coat. Serve on sandwich buns or rolls.

CITRUS BRAISED PORK ROAST

The Caribbean is where this recipe comes from, a specialty served on cruise ships. This also has the basis for being a Cubano if you have any leftovers, which is highly unlikely.

2 pounds bone in pork shoulder roast	1 lime zest and juice
1 teaspoon fennel seeds	¼ cup rum
1 teaspoon coriander seeds	2 teaspoons minced garlic
2 oranges zest and juice	½ teaspoon salt
2 lemons zest and juice	½ teaspoon black pepper
	1-2 cups chicken broth

Heat fennel and coriander seed in small, dry skillet over low heat until fragrant; set aside. In gallon size zip loc bag, combine zest and juice from oranges, lemons and lime. Add to bag the heated seeds, rum, garlic, salt and pepper; mix well. Add pork, flip bag to cover meat well and marinate 12-24 hours in refrigerator. Place pork and marinade in slow cooker; add enough chicken broth to bring liquid half way up sides of meat. Cover and set on low; cook for 6-7 hours or until meat is falling off the bones. Let pork cool; pull it apart in long strands. Serve pulled pork on top of white rice and drizzle with cooking liquid.

CORNMEAL SCRAPPLE

Scrapple is a mush of pork scraps, typically made with the head, heart, liver, and trimmings combined with cornmeal and flour. Scraps of meat left over from butchering were made into scrapple to avoid waste. The mush is formed into a loaf and slices of the scrapple are then fried before serving. A breakfast favorite on the East Coast, I'd never heard of it until I met my husband Joe from Maryland. He and his Pennsylvania buddy craved their childhood meat when we all moved to Alaska and none of the "delicacy" could be found. I decided to find and refine a recipe. This a healthier version, making it easier for me to serve; I know what meat is in it and has less fat than the store version.

1 cup cornmeal	2 ¾ cups boiling water
1 cup milk	½ pound pork sausages cook, drained
1 teaspoon sugar	Flour
1 teaspoon salt	2 tablespoons butter

Combine cornmeal, milk, sugar and salt in a saucepan. Gradually stir in boiling water; cook over medium heat, uncovered and stir until thickened and bubbly. Reduce heat to low, cover saucepan and cook about 10 minutes. Crumble sausage finely and add to cornmeal mixture. Pour into loaf pan. Cover with plastic wrap and chill. Cut scrapple into ⅓ inch thick slices; dip slices in flour. Fry slowly in skillet with butter for 15-20 minutes or until lightly browned, turning once. Serve with butter and maple syrup.

COUNTRY PORK AND SAUERKRAUT

Our German family favorite that never gets old. We serve this with a big pile of mash potatoes or baked potato. I make my mashed potatoes for this dinner with less milk so they can soak up the sauerkraut juices.

1-17-ounce jar sauerkraut
1 diced onion
3-4 pounds pork spare ribs or pork
    shoulder steaks

1 can beer
1 teaspoon black pepper

Place pork, onion, beer and black pepper in slow cooker. Cook on low 8 hours. About an hour before serving, drain and discard liquid from sauerkraut. Stir sauerkraut into meat mixture and continue to cook on low for 1 hour.

CREAMY PORK CHOPS

This a quick and crowd pleasing recipe any night of the week.

4 boneless pork loin chops
2 tablespoons olive oil
1 chopped onion
8 fresh mushrooms sliced
¼ cup water
2 teaspoons mustard

½ teaspoon salt
¼ teaspoon black pepper
1 tablespoon flour
1 cup sour cream
4 cups cooked egg noodles
4 cups frozen French-style green
    beans—steamed or cooked

In skillet over medium heat, brown pork chops in oil, about 4-5 minutes on each side. Drain on paper towels. In same skillet and without removing any oil, sauté onion and mushrooms until tender. Add water and scrape bottom with wooden spoon, add mustard, salt and pepper. Bring liquids to boil. Return chops to skillet, reduce heat; cover skillet and simmer for 15-20 minutes or until pork is tender. Remove only chops and keep warm. Combine flour and sour cream until smooth. Add to skillet and stir into vegetables. Bring to boil, cook and stir for 1-2 minutes or until slightly thickened. Serve by placing pork chops on bed of noodles, green beans and top with sauce.

GOLDEN GLAZED HAM

Ham, considered by many to be only a holiday entree, shouldn't be strictly for special occasions. Domestication of pigs for food dates back to 4900 B.C. in China. Although Christopher Columbus had eight pigs on board when he left Spain for the new world, it's explorer Hernando de Soto whose 13 pigs became the breeding stock for America's pork industry. By the 17th century, most American farmers raised pigs. The shelf-life of salt pork and bacon made them staples in most kitchens, as well as meat to travel with when settling the West. George A. Hormel & Company pioneered canned hams in America in 1926 allowing for more "city" folks to enjoy an old farm favorite.

1 ham	¼ teaspoon nutmeg
1 tablespoon molasses	¼ teaspoon ginger
1 tablespoon mustard	20 whole cloves
4 tablespoons brown sugar	1 20-ounce can pineapple slices
3 tablespoons corn syrup	4 tablespoons brown sugar
¼ teaspoon cinnamon	

Line large roasting or baking pan with aluminum foil. Place ham in pan, score and place whole cloves in slits. In saucepan, mix molasses, mustard, brown sugar, corn syrup, cinnamon, nutmeg and ginger. Heat over medium until all melted together. Pour mixture over ham. Cover ham with foil and place in 250° oven for 1 hour. Baste ham every 15 minutes. Add small amounts of water to drippings if needed. In meantime, drain can of pineapple and reserve juice. Mix brown sugar in juice. Remove ham from oven and place brown sugared pineapple juice over top of ham. Bake additional 20-30 minutes. Remove from oven and let ham sit for 15 minutes before slicing. Slice into ham steaks, serve with pineapple ring and pan drippings over to of each slice.

ITALIAN PINEAPPLE PORK ROAST

1-3 pound pork roast
Pineapple juice from pineapple can
1 tablespoon minced garlic
2 ½ tablespoons honey
3 cups pineapple chunks
½ cup chopped red bell peppers

3 tablespoons chopped red onions
3 tablespoons chopped fresh basil
4 teaspoons white wine vinegar
1 tablespoon balsamic vinegar
¼ teaspoon red pepper flakes
⅛ teaspoon salt

Combine pineapple juice, garlic and honey, set aside as glaze. Combine pineapple, pepper, onion, basil, vinegars, pepper flakes and salt; cover and chill at least an hour to let flavors blend. Place roast on rack in shallow roasting pan; insert meat thermometer. Roast in 325° oven for 1 hour. Brush glaze over meat and roast for another 30 minutes or until thermometer registers 155°. Cover meat with foil; let stand 15 minutes before carving. Slice and top with refrigerated pineapple mix.

KAHLUA PORK

Traditional kahlua pork involves a whole pig, an underground oven and two days of cooking. This will come close enough for an island themed party or those Hawaiian backyard or inside Luaus.

7 pounds pork shoulder roast
3 tablespoons kosher salt

5 tablespoons liquid smoke
1 package onion soup mix

Lay large sheet of heavy aluminum foil on a work surface. Place pork on top; season meat with salt, dry onion mix and liquid smoke. Cover with additional foil and seal tightly. Place meat in deep roasting pan, fill with 2 inches of water, and cover pan with several sheets of aluminum foil to seal in steam. Cook in 300° oven for 5 hours, until pork falls apart easily. An instant-read thermometer tucked into thickest part of roast should read 170°; when cool, shred using two forks.

PERFECT BBQ RIBS

4 pounds pork baby back ribs   **4 pieces aluminum foil**

Take full racks of ribs and cut in half to get perfect serving size, about 4-6 rib bones per rack. Coat front and back of ribs with any flavor BBQ sauce and place each rack of ribs onto a piece of foil and wrap tightly. Place in foil packs in refrigerator overnight or up to 24 hours. Next day, preheat oven to 300°, remove foil packs from refrigerator and place in oven with seam of foil wrap facing up. Cook for 2-2 ½ hours or until you see meat of ribs shrinking from cut ends of bones. Remove ribs from foil and smother them with more BBQ sauce. Grill ribs on hot grill for 2-4 minutes per side, don't burn them. Use sharp knife to slice meat between each bone about halfway down and serve hot with additional BBQ sauce on the side.

PHILIPPINES MENUDO

Thanks to my Filipino friends, I discovered this wonderfully hearty and satisfying dish.

2 ½ cups pork diced	**½ cup diced tomatoes**
2 cups water	**1 teaspoon garlic salt**
2 tablespoons corn or vegetable oil	**½ cup pimiento**
2 tablespoons minced garlic	**2 cups diced potatoes**
¼ cup chopped onions	**⅓ cup boiled and peeled chickpeas**

In medium pot, place water and pork; cook until pork is tender. Reserve ½ cup of broth. In large skillet, heat oil and sauté garlic, onions and tomatoes until onion is transparent. Add cooked pork, sauté for 5 minutes. Add reserved broth, salt, pimento, potatoes and chickpeas. Bring to boil and reduce heat to simmer for 10 minutes.

PORK ADOBO

This recipe popular in Southeast Asia has many variations and gaining great popularity in the US.

1 pound pork roast cut into chunks	1 teaspoon black pepper
4 teaspoons minced garlic	2 tablespoons canola oil
¼ cup soy sauce	½ cup white vinegar

Place pork, in large pot with 2 teaspoons of garlic, soy sauce, pepper, 1 tablespoon of oil and vinegar. Let stand for 2 hours. Place pot on stove and slowly cook until pork is tender, about 30 minutes. In large skillet, heat on high remaining minced garlic in oil. Transfer all of pork from pot to skillet and brown pork. Add broth to skillet of fried pork and garlic. Simmer for 10 minutes and serve.

PORK CHOPS AND GRAVY

If you prefer non-creamy gravy, substitute the 1 cup of milk with 1 cup of chicken or beef broth stirred into skillet.

1 ½ cups milk	¼ teaspoon salt
1 egg	¼ teaspoon pepper
1 ½ cups breadcrumbs	¼ cup olive oil
2 teaspoons dried parsley	4 center-cut pork chops—1-inch
2 teaspoons ground sage	thickness

In pie plate or wide bowl, whisk ½ cup of milk with egg. In shallow dish, combine breadcrumbs, with 1 teaspoon of parsley and 1 teaspoon of sage. Season chops with salt and pepper; coat each chop with egg mixture, breadcrumbs and shake off excess. In large skillet, heat oil over medium high heat. Add chops and cook 3-4 minutes per side. Transfer to rack set over baking sheet. Bake chops in 400° until golden and just cooked through, 8-10 minutes. Meanwhile in skillet, with wooden spoon stir in remaining milk, sage and parsley. Scrape bottom of skillet and continue to stir on medium heat until begins to thicken. Remove from heat and serve with chops

PORK AND RHUBARB CHUTNEY

Chutney:
4 cups cubed rhubarb
½ cup brown sugar
⅓ cup cider vinegar
1 tablespoon ground ginger
3 teaspoons grated orange peel
½ teaspoon cinnamon
1 red onion chopped
½ cup raisins
2 pounds pork tenderloin

Rub:
1 teaspoon ground ginger
1 teaspoon red pepper flakes
1 teaspoon minced garlic
1 teaspoon garlic salt
¼ teaspoon black pepper
½ cup red wine
⅛ cup cider vinegar

Put rhubarb, sugar, vinegar, ginger, orange peel, cinnamon, onion and raisins in medium, heavy saucepan. Bring to boil; lower heat and simmer until rhubarb is tender, 20-30 minutes. Serve warm or at room temperature. Place pork in shallow pan. Mix together ginger, pepper flakes, garlic, salt, pepper, wine and vinegar in small bowl and pour over pork. Marinate at room temperature, basting frequently, for an hour. Cook under preheated broiler, 7-8 minutes per side. Remove from oven and let sit for 10 minutes before slicing. Put a little chutney on pork slices and pass the rest separately.

PORK AND RHUBARB STIR FRY

The cooked rhubarb makes a nice glaze over the finished dish. No one ever guesses they are eating rhubarb.

2 cups chopped rhubarb ½-inch
    pieces
½ cup sugar
1 tablespoon canola oil
1 pork tenderloin ½ inch slices
1 red onion sliced
1 cup coarsely chopped broccoli
½ cup sliced carrots

½ cup coarsely chopped cabbage
Teaspoon ground ginger
2 teaspoons minced garlic
2 tablespoons cider vinegar
2 tablespoons soy sauce
Salt and black pepper

Put rhubarb and sugar in heavy saucepan over medium high heat and stir occasionally until rhubarb is just-tender, sugar melts and resulting syrup bubbles vigorously, 5 minutes or so. Remove from heat and set aside. Heat tablespoon of oil in heavy skillet over medium-high heat. When hot, add tenderloin pieces in single layer and brown without disturbing for several minutes. Flip pork and add onion, vegetables, garlic, ginger, salt and pepper. When pork is golden-brown, add vinegar and soy sauce. Cover and cook until vegetables are barely tender, about 5 minutes. Reduce heat and add reserved rhubarb and sugar syrup. Stir to combine. Serve hot, over rice.

SANGRIA PORK CHOPS

I mixed two of my favorite ingredients: sangria and ranch dressing—sheer delight.

4 boneless pork loin chops	1 tablespoon onion powder
1 tablespoon canola oil	2 cups sangria or red wine
Salt and black pepper	¼ cup ranch salad dressing
1 tablespoon garlic powder	

Heat oil in ovenproof skillet over medium high. Place chops in skillet, sprinkle salt, pepper, garlic powder and onion powder over top of the chops. Sear on one side, turn with tongs and sear on other side. In small bowl, whisk together sangria and ranch dressing until blended. Pour over chops in skillet. Cover skillet and place in preheated 300° oven. Cook for 1 hour. Remove from oven, place chops on warm plate. Cook liquid over stove top on high heat to reduce the sauce; stir often. Pour sauce over chops and serve.

SANTE FE PORK ROAST

4 pounds boneless pork loin roast	2 tablespoons salt
8 cups water	1 tablespoon dried thyme
1 cup sugar	1 tablespoon ground cumin
4 tablespoons paprika	2 teaspoons lemon pepper
1 tablespoon cayenne pepper	2 teaspoons dried oregano
1 teaspoon garlic powder	

In large saucepan, heat all ingredients EXCEPT pork loin to boiling, stirring to dissolve ground spices and mix ingredients thoroughly. Remove from heat and cool to room temperature. Place pork loin in glass container large enough to immerse roast in cooked solution, cover and refrigerate 2 to 4 days. Remove pork roast and discard solution. Pat pork gently dry with paper towels. Prepare covered grill with coals heated to medium-hot. Place roast over drip pan and cook over indirect heat for 45 minutes to an hour, until thermometer inserted reads 155° to 160°. Remove from grill, let set for 15 minutes before slicing and serving.

SAUERKRAUT SAUSAGE BAKE

This one came about to take to potlucks and lunches for Joe. Old favorites made easy to carry.

1 pound kielbasa or polish sausages	**2 cups mashed potatoes**
2 cups sauerkraut drained	**1 cup shredded Cheddar cheese**
1 large onion chopped	**(optional)**

Cut sausage into 1 inch thick rounds. Mix ½ of chopped onions into mashed potatoes. In 9-inch baking dish, layer ingredients: sauerkraut, rest of onions, sausage, potatoes and top with cheese if using. Bake in 400° oven for 20-25 minutes or until heated.

SAUSAGE STUFFING

This stuffing goes with any poultry or pork entrée. It's very moist and even people who weren't fond of bread stuffing, found this tasty.

1 pound pork sausages	**1 teaspoon dried sage**
1 tablespoon butter	**1 teaspoon poultry seasoning**
2 stalks celery chopped	**12 cups cubed stale bread**
1 large onion chopped	**1 14 ½-ounce can chicken broth**
¼ cup chopped fresh parsley	

Crumble sausage over medium heat in skillet. Cook until no longer pink and lightly browned. Remove sausage from skillet with slotted spoon. Add butter to skillet and when melted, cook celery and onion about 5 minutes; stir in parsley, sage and poultry seasoning. Remove from heat; add sausage, cubed bread and chicken broth. Stir well. Pour mixture into sprayed 13 x 9 inch baking pan and cover with foil. Bake in 350° oven for 50 minutes. Remove foil and bake another 10 minutes or until top is lightly browned.

SLOW COOKED PORK ROAST

3-4 pounds pork roast
1 packet onion soup mix
¼ cup Worcestershire sauce
⅛ cup brown sugar

⅛ teaspoon black pepper
1 teaspoon poultry seasoning
1 can stewed or diced tomatoes

Place roast in sprayed slow cooker. Mix together dry soup mix, Worcestershire sauce, sugar, pepper, poultry seasoning and tomatoes; pour over roast. Cover and cook on high for 1 hour, reduce heat to low and cook for 8-10 hours. Serve sliced topped with broth from cooker.

SOUTH CAROLINA BBQ PORK

4 pounds boneless pork loin roast
⅔ cup mustard
½ cup brown sugar
½ cup white vinegar
¼ cup water

1 tablespoon soy sauce
1 teaspoon garlic powder
½ teaspoon hot pepper sauce
3 cups hickory or oak wood chips

At least 1 hour before grilling, soak wood chips in enough water to cover; drain before using. In charcoal grill with cover, place preheated coals around drip pan for medium-low indirect heat. Sprinkle half of wood chips over coals. In small saucepan, combine mustard, brown sugar, vinegar, water, soy sauce, garlic powder and hot pepper sauce. Bring to boil; reduce heat and simmer, uncovered, for 5-10 minutes or until desired consistency, stirring occasionally. Divide into two portions; set aside. Place meat on grill rack over drip pan. Cover and grill for 1 ½ to 2 hours, until internal temperature; measured with meat thermometer is 155°, basting meat with one portion of reserved sauce last 15 minutes. Add more preheated coals (use hibachi or metal chimney starter to preheat coals) and wood chips halfway through grilling. Remove meat from grill. Cover and let rest for 15 minutes before slicing. Serve second portion of reserved sauce with meat. For gas grills, preheat and turn off any burners directly below where food will go. Heat circulates inside grill, so turning food is not necessary.

SOUTHWESTERN GRILLED PORK TENDERLOIN

2 whole pork tenderloin
5 teaspoons chili powder
1 ½ teaspoons dried oregano
¾ teaspoon ground cumin
2 teaspoons minced garlic
1 tablespoon vegetable oil

Vegetable Bed:
1 can of corn, drained of liquid
1 medium, sweet, chopped onion
2 green peppers, seeded and diced
2 stalks of celery diced
1 teaspoon minced garlic
1 teaspoon chili powder
1/2 teaspoon cumin
1 large carrot chopped
1 small yellow squash sliced

In small bowl, mix together seasonings and vegetable oil together. Rub mixture over all surfaces of tenderloins. Cover and refrigerate 2 to 24 hours. Preheat grill; lightly oil grill rack. Place pork over medium-hot coals, turning occasionally, for 15 to 20 minutes, until thermometer inserted reads 155 to 160°. Let rest for 10 minutes before slicing. For Vegetable Bed: Sauté all vegetables and spices lightly to marry flavors together, about 6 minutes over medium low heat, stirring often and not to let the veggies get soggy, you'll still want a crisp bed of vegetables to serve the sliced pork on.

SPAM BAKE

If you enjoy spam like my husband does, this will only add to the love fest.

1 can spam
⅓ cup brown sugar
1 teaspoon mustard
½ teaspoon vinegar

1 teaspoon water
½ teaspoon ground cloves
½ teaspoon onion powder
½ teaspoon garlic powder

Place Spam in shallow pan; score top. Bake in 350° oven for 10 minutes. Combine sugar, mustard, vinegar, water and seasonings. Pour sauce over Spam and bake another 15 minutes, base every 5 minutes.

SUMMER GRILLED PORK

1 cup apple juice	2 teaspoons minced garlic
1 medium onion chopped	½ teaspoon black pepper
3 tablespoons honey	3 pounds boneless pork roast
2 teaspoons dried rosemary	Sweet and sour sauce

In saucepan combine all ingredients except pork and bring to boil. Reduce heat and simmer uncovered for 5 minutes; cool completely. Place mixture in large zip loc bag, add pork roast. Refrigerate overnight, turning occasionally. Remove roast and place on grill. Cover grill well and shut any air vents. Use grill thermometer to monitor internal temperature of grill. It should hover around 275° to 300°. Use instant-read cooking thermometer to monitor internal temperature of roast. Cooking times will vary, so begin checking temperature after about 45 minutes of cooking. Take roast off grill when it's done—internal temperature is 155°. Let it rest away from heat for 15 minutes before carving. Serve with Sweet and Sour Sauce.

SWEET MAPLE PORK ROAST

⅓ cup maple syrup	¾ teaspoon salt
⅛ teaspoon cinnamon	½ teaspoon black pepper
Pinch ground cloves	2 teaspoons vegetable oil
Pinch cayenne pepper	
2 ½ pounds boneless pork loin roast, tied at even intervals	

Combine maple syrup, cinnamon, cloves and cayenne pepper in bowl and set aside. Pat roast dry, sprinkle evenly with salt and pepper. Heat oil in ovenproof nonstick skillet over medium high heat until just begins to smoke. Place roast fat side down in skillet. Use tongs to rotate roast until well browned on all sides. Transfer roast to plate. Reduce heat to medium and pour off fat from skillet. Add maple mixture and cook about 30 second. Remove skillet from heat and roll roast in skillet using tongs to coat with glaze on all sides. Place skillet in oven and roast in 325° oven until roast registers about 135° on thermometer; about 35-45 minutes and spin roast to coat with glaze twice during roasting time. Transfer roast to carving board. Set skillet aside to cook slightly and allow glaze to thicken, about 5 minutes. Pour glaze over roast and let rest 15 minutes longer. Snip twine off roast and cut into ¼ inch slices and serve.

TENNESSEE BBQ PORK RIBS

Tennessee typical side dishes include french fries, baked potatoes, potato salad, corn on the cob, barbecue beans, coleslaw, green beans, white beans, dinner rolls, and collard greens.

1 tablespoon chili powder	4 pounds pork spare ribs cut in 4
1 tablespoon dried parsley	pieces
2 teaspoons onion powder	Sauce:
2 teaspoons garlic powder	3 cups any barbecue sauce
2 teaspoons dried oregano	¼ cup cider vinegar
2 teaspoons paprika	¼ cup honey
2 teaspoons black pepper	2 teaspoons onion powder
1 ½ teaspoons salt	2 teaspoons garlic powder
	Dash hot pepper sauce

Combine chili powder, parsley, onion powder, garlic powder, oregano, paprika, pepper and salt in small bowl; mix well. Rub spice mixture onto ribs. Cover; refrigerate at least 2 hours or overnight. Sauce: Combine all ingredients in medium bowl; mix well. Reserve 1 cup sauce for dipping. Preheat oven to 350°. Place ribs in foil-lined shallow roasting pan. Bake 45 minutes. Meanwhile, prepare grill for direct cooking. Place ribs on grill. Cook, covered, over medium heat 10 minutes. Brush with sauce. Continue grilling 10 minutes or until ribs are tender, brushing with sauce occasionally. Serve reserved sauce on the side for dipping.

SOUPS & CHILIS

WARM AND COMFORTING

In 1984, we'd just traveled the only road between Marquette and Sault Sainte-Marie in Upper Peninsula Michigan. It was 10 degrees below zero and it took us 8 hours to travel 160 miles. The blowing snowstorm and occasional white out made us loose sight of the actual road several times.

As we pulled in the parking lot, the pastor exclaimed, "How did you get here? They just closed the highway. This is the worst blizzard we've had in 5 years. We cancelled the performance for tonight."

A generous family offered to house all five of us weary traveling missionaries. Not ready for this kind of winter deluge, we were cold, wet, hungry and exhausted by the time we pulled up to a blue farmhouse and finally unpacked the van. It was dark and much colder by the time we got beds made, dry clothes on and settled around the warm and welcoming fireplace.

"I hope everyone likes soup", announced our gracious hostess. "That and homemade bread is what we live on in weather like this. Besides, no matter who gets caught in the storm and ends up staying, we just add a little water to whatever is on the stove to make it go around." She added with a wink and a chuckle.

Soups, breads and a huge box of cookies given to us before we left Sault Sainte-Marie is what we lived on for the next 3-½ days and none of it was boring. Each meal was full of variety accompanied by butter melted on oven fresh breads. As the wind blew hard against the windows, the warmth from the oven and stove made the house smell as comforting as it felt. To this day, a winter storm and bowl of soup feels like a huge hug.

Be warned: Chili is a territorial food.

"Real chili doesn't have beans in it." Twanged my Texas friend.

Satisfy Gratify It wasn't the first time I'd heard that comment when I dished up my mild, hearty plenty of beans and ground beef chili. Where you come from depends on what you call chili, how it's made, what ends up in it or stays out of it. I know it's known as "the food of forgiveness and reconciliation" but I've seen the choice of chili cause a bigger heated difference of opinion argument than politics. So, I listen and learn which way they really like their favorite chili as they chow down and usually ask for seconds of my chili.

Chili can have one or many types of beans or no beans at all. It can have any degree of spiciness provided by spices, sauces, peppers, hot sauces or a combination. Other recipes call for ground meat, shredded meat or no meat. I know some who only have chili with game meat in it. A newer version called white chili doesn't have the tomato base, the same seasonings or beans. Chili can be served with shredded cheese, bread, saltine crackers, corn chips, cornbread, fritters, corn or flour tortillas, pretzels, tamales, peanut butter sandwiches, plain or grilled cheese sandwiches and more.

Nebraska chili is served with cinnamon rolls, in Missouri some add pickle juice, in Tennessee some prefer vinegar sprinkled in and in other states they like it served in a cup with Fritos and sour cream known as Frito Pie. An old-fashioned chili parlor in downtown St. Louis features a "slinger": two hamburger patties topped with melted American cheese and two eggs, then smothered in chili, topped with cheese. Louisville-style chili is spicier than Cincinnati—style but in general, it is not as spicy as Texas-style. So I serve my chili, then next time I fix and serve chili the way my guest likes it. Some are very grateful because they haven't had it "their way" for a long time. A satisfied guest becomes a gratified friend.

ASPARAGUS POTATO SOUP

A simple chicken broth can be made by placing 4 chicken wings in a pot of water, bring to a simmer, uncovered, simmer gently for about an hour. Remove bones and skin before using.

1-14 ½-ounce can chicken broth
3 cups peeled, chopped potatoes
⅓ cup chopped onions
8 ounces chopped asparagus spears

1 teaspoon salt
3 cups evaporated milk
1 cup water
2 cups shredded Cheddar cheese

In large stock pan, heat chicken broth, potatoes, onions, asparagus and salt. Cook until potatoes are tender. Add milk, water and cheese; stir and heat until cheese is melted.

BEAN AND BACON SOUP

This was always my favorite store soup and to finally figure out a way to make it at home. This is the best snuggling on a cold rainy night soup I have ever found.

2 cups navy beans
6 slices uncooked bacon, diced
3 small carrots, minced
3 stalks celery, minced
1 onion, minced
½ teaspoon thyme

2-4 garlic cloves, minced
1 (4 ounce) can tomato paste
1 dash dried red pepper flakes
6-8 cups water
1 teaspoon wine vinegar
3 drops liquid smoke salt and pepper

Soak beans overnight and discard water. Place bacon, carrots, celery, onion, theme, cloves, tomato paste, pepper flakes and water in large kettle. Simmer until beans are tender-around 3 hours. Puree 2 cups of soup and return to pot. Add wine vinegar and liquid smoke. Mix well, Salt and pepper to your desire.

BEEF VEGETABLE SOUP

All this recipe needs is homemade bread and cookies for dessert to have a perfect meal.

2 pounds beef stew meat or
    boneless beef chuck cut into
    1-inch cubes
1 teaspoon salt
1 teaspoon black pepper
1 teaspoon garlic powder
1 package onion soup mix
1 cup sliced celery
1 cup sliced carrots
¼ cup chopped mushrooms

¼ cup chopped onions
1 ½ cans beef broth
1 ½ cups water
1 ½ cups red wine
1 (16-ounce) bag frozen mixed
    vegetables
1-14 ½-ounce can diced tomatoes
2 cups potatoes peels and cubed
1 cup frozen green beans
1 cup frozen corn

In slow cooker, place mushrooms, onion and meat on top. Mix together salt, pepper, garlic, soup mix, broth, water and wine. Pour mixture over meat and vegetables. Cook on low setting for 5 hours. Then, stir well breaking up meat. Add carrots, celery, beans, mixed vegetables, tomatoes, corn, potatoes and more water if needed. Cook on low setting for another 4 hours or on high for 2 hours.

BEST CHICKEN NOODLE SOUP

Yes, chicken noodle soup is soothing to the sick, does it heal?—some believe it does—personally I believe a little homemade chicken noodle soup never hurts.

2 pound boneless skinless chicken
¼ cup grated carrot
¼ cup finely diced celery
8 cups chicken broth
8 cups water

4 cups egg noodles
1 teaspoon salt
½ teaspoon black pepper
1 teaspoon poultry seasoning

Place broth and water in large pot and add chicken, carrots, celery, salt, pepper and poultry seasoning. Boil until chicken is fully cooked. Remove chicken from broth. Chop into small pieces, and return meat to pot. Add egg noodles and cook until tender.

BROCCOLI SOUP

Any homemade cream soup is better than can. Broccoli is even more hearty, nutritious and delicious when made from scratch The green color makes it a nice spring soup to serve. Everyone loves this soup, including kids.

2 tablespoons butter	3 tablespoons butter
1 sweet onion, chopped	3 tablespoons all-purpose flour
2 stalk celery, chopped	2 cups evaporated milk
3 cups chicken broth	ground black pepper to taste
8 cups broccoli—stem, leaves and	
all chopped	

Melt 2 tablespoons butter in medium sized stockpot and sauté onion and celery until tender. Add chopped broccoli and broth, cover and simmer for 20 minutes. Mash broccoli mixture, but don't use a hand mixer to smash the broccoli. Use a potato masher and don't go nuts mashing it. Larger pieces of broccoli really make this soup exceptional, return soup to heat. In small saucepan, over medium-heat melt 3 tablespoons butter, stir in flour and add milk. Stir until thick and bubbly, and add to soup. Season with pepper and serve. Fry up a few pieces of bacon and crumble it in the soup or top with grated parmesan or shredded cheddar cheese to add more versatility to this soup.

CHEESY BROCCOLI CAULIFLOWER SOUP

A California deli got me hooked on this wonderful soup, it's even better in the middle of a snowstorm.

1 head broccoli chopped	2 tablespoons olive oil for sautéing
1 head cauliflower chopped	water to cover vegetables—if needed
3 potatoes, roughly chopped	3 cups chicken broth
4 carrots, finely chopped	salt and pepper to taste
3 celery minced	1 can evaporated milk
1 large onion, minced	2-3 cups shredded Cheddar Cheese
1 tablespoon minced garlic	1/2 cup gouda cheese

In a large stockpot, heat olive oil over medium heat. sauté onions, celery and carrots for about 3 minutes. Add remaining vegetables, garlic, broth and add enough water to cover. Season with salt and pepper to taste. Bring to a boil, then cover and reduce heat to a simmer. Simmer about 30 minutes or so, until vegetables are tender. Add evaporated milk and cheese, stirring constantly until cheese is melted. Remove 1/4 of soup to large bowl, use hand blender and puree. Return puree to soup pot and mix well. Serve with croutons, or extra cheese, or bacon, or ham.

CINCINNATI CHILI

There are several things that make this chili different than any other and Cincinnatians eat more than two million pounds of it every year. The meat is cooked differently; it has a thinner consistency and has ingredients including cinnamon, chocolate, allspice and Worcestershire sauce. tl originated from a Greek stew and served the Cincinnati way, includes a side order of oyster crackers.

2 cups water	⅛ teaspoon ground cloves
2 pound very lean ground beef	1 tablespoon Worcestershire Sauce
chuck or use 1 pound beef and	6 ounces can tomato paste
mix with 1 pound ground turkey	1 ounce unsweetened baking
2 teaspoons minced garlic	chocolate chopped into pieces
2 tablespoons chili powder	3 cubes beef bouillon
1 teaspoon ground allspice	2 bay leaves
2 teaspoon ground cinnamon	1 tablespoons red wine vinegar
1 tablespoon paprika	Dash each of salt and black pepper

Place raw meat in stockpot and cook on low heat for 5 minutes, then add water and slow boil using spatula to break up the meat until there are no clumps and well broken up. Continue to cook until meat has no pink left. Add the rest of the ingredients, mix well and continue to simmer for 45-60 minutes. Remove bay leaves and serve as follows:

A "two-way" is served on spaghetti—which most Cincinnatians would never order
A "three-way" add on shredded cheddar cheese
A "four-way" add on chopped onions
A "five-way" or "the works" add on kidney beans
"Wet" is for extra chili over spaghetti.
"Inverted" is to place cheese under chili so it melts.

CREAM SOUPS

This recipe makes enough to equal a can of condensed soup and 2 cans of water for other recipes.

2 tablespoons butter
1 ½ cups chopped celery
⅓ cup chopped onions
1 teaspoon salt divided
1 cup water
3 cups evaporated milk divided
3 tablespoons flour
⅛ teaspoon white pepper

Cream of Chicken:
1 cup cooked, chopped chicken
1 cube chicken bouillon
1 cup chicken broth
Cream of Broccoli:
2 cups cooked, mashed broccoli
Cream of Mushroom:
1 ½ cups chopped mushrooms

In large soup pot, add butter, celery, onions, ½ teaspoon of salt and water. Bring to boil and cook for 15 minutes until tender. Do not drain. Stir in 2 ½ cups of milk to pot, In small container combine rest of milk, flour, salt and white pepper. Stir flour mixture until smooth; add to pot. Over medium heat cook and stir until soup is bubbly. Puree soup and serve or use for other recipes.

Cream of Chicken: Omit celery, salt and water. Replace with chicken, bouillon and broth.
Cream of Broccoli: Omit celery and replace with broccoli
Cream of Mushroom: Omit celery and replace with mushrooms

CROCK POT BEAN SOUP

Beans can be eaten raw, sprouted or cooked, ground into flour, curdled into tofu, fermented into soya sauce, tempi and miso. They are excellent in soups and salads. Beans are intricately woven into the fabric of human history. The first 'permanent cultures' evolved when hunter-gatherers and nomadic people began tilling the earth and developing systems of agriculture, and beans were among the first cultivated crops.

2 15-ounce cans kidney beans
1 16-ounce can navy beans
1 15-ounce can black beans
1 15-ounce can pinto beans
1 cup frozen green peas
1 cup frozen lima beans
1 cup chopped onions
1 cup chopped celery
4 teaspoons minced garlic
1 teaspoon dried thyme
½ teaspoon black pepper

1 cup chopped green bell peppers
1 cup chopped mushrooms
⅓ cup cooked crisp bacon crumbled
1 cup instant potato flakes
2 cups water
Sausage:
Omit bacon
Add 1 cup smoked Polish sausages
    or cubed ham

Rinse and drain all cans of beans. Place all beans and rest of ingredients in crockpot. Stir and cover. Cook on low setting for 4 hours or high for 2 hours. If desired, top individual servings with shredded cheese.

FRENCH ONION SOUP

For a simple healthy beef broth—take beef bones and a pot of water; bring to a simmer, uncovered, very gently for a few hours. Remove bones and fat before using.

3 pounds white or Vidalia onions
    sliced thinly
6 tablespoons butter
2 tablespoons canola oil
1 tablespoon minced garlic
1 tablespoon sugar
7-8 cups beef broth

2 teaspoons ground thyme
3 bay leaves whole
1 teaspoon black pepper
1 ½ cups dry white wine
1 loaf French bread sliced thick
1 cup mix mozzarella and Parmesan
    cheese

In large stock pot, heat butter and oil until hot but not burning. Add and cook onions on low heat for 45 minutes, stir every 5 minutes or until onion are deep brown, tender and cooked down. Don't hurry this important caramelizing process. Meanwhile put equal amounts of cheese mixture on each slice of bread and place on a baking sheet. Broil on medium oven just until cheese is bubbly, do not allow to burn. Set aside. Add garlic and sugar to onions and cook additional 10 minutes. Sprinkle flour over top and stir, making a roux. Add

1 cup of beef broth at a time, stirring constantly on low, scraping bottom of pot to deglaze all bits, until soup is thickened. Add thyme, bay leaves, pepper and simmer on low for 30 minutes. Stir frequently; do not allow soup to burn. Turn off heat and add wine then let it sit. Remove bay leaves. Before serving, place slice of bread with cheese on bottom of bowl and pour ladle or two of hot soup over top.

GAZPACHO

Gazpacho is a cold Spanish tomato-based raw vegetable soup, I never tried cold soup. but after living in some pretty warm states, I missed my comforting tomato soup and tried my hand at the cold version. Surprising me, it was very satisfying and the flavors increase dramatically when made a day ahead and refrigerated overnight.

2 ½ pounds tomatoes chopped	¼ cup olive oil
2 cucumbers chopped	2 teaspoons honey
2 sweet red peppers chopped	½ teaspoon ground cumin
1 onion chopped	1 teaspoon salt
1 tablespoon minced garlic	Black pepper
¼ cup balsamic vinegar	

Combine all ingredients in large bowl. Blend small batches in blender until smooth. Combine all of mixture in large bowl when smooth and stir well. Cover and refrigerate several hours or overnight. Serve chilled, with dollop of yogurt stirred in and/or a dollop of sour cream on top.

GROUND BEEF VEGETABLE SOUP

1 pound browned ground beef	1 28-ounce can diced tomatoes
2 cups sliced carrots	3 cups beef broth
2 cups sliced celery	3 teaspoons instant beef bouillon
2-3 diced potatoes	2 teaspoons Worcestershire sauce
1 pound frozen green beans thawed	½ tablespoon sugar
1 pound frozen green peas thawed	2 tablespoons minced onions
1 16-ounce bag frozen corn thawed	1 can cream of mushroom soup

Place cooked meat in bottom of slow cooker and add vegetables. In large bowl, stir together broth, bouillon, Worcestershire sauce, sugar, mince onions and soup. Pour on top of vegetables and meat in slow cooker. Cover. Cook on low 7-8 hours or on high 4 hours. Serve with freshly baked bread for wonderfully easy and fulfilling autumn meal.

GUMBO

Gumbo comes in many forms depending on the cook and what's handy. It can feature any combination of meat, poultry, game, fish or shellfish. Shrimp and crawfish are popular, as are sausage and chicken.

3 boneless skinless chicken breasts
Salt and black pepper
¼ cup olive oil
1 pound smoked sausages ¼ inch slices
½ cup flour
5 tablespoons margarine
1 chopped onion
2 tablespoons minced garlic
1 chopped green bell pepper

3 stalks chopped celery
¼ cup Worcestershire sauce
4 cups hot water
1 can stewed tomatoes and juice
4 cubes chicken bouillon
2 cups sliced okra
4 sliced green onions white and green parts
½ pound cooked small shrimp
¼ dried parsley flakes

Season chicken with salt and pepper. Heat oil in heavy bottomed Dutch oven over medium-high heat. Cook chicken until browned on both sides and remove. Add sausage and cook until browned; remove. Sprinkle flour over oil and add 2 tablespoons of margarine, cook over medium heat, stirring constantly, until brown, about 10 minutes. Let mixture cool. Return Dutch oven to low heat and melt remaining margarine, Add onion, garlic, green pepper and celery, then cook 10 minutes. Add Worcestershire, salt and pepper. Cook, while stirring frequently, for 10 minutes. Add water and bouillon cubes, whisking constantly. Add chicken and sausage. Bring to boil, reduce heat, cover, and simmer for 45 minutes. Stir in tomatoes and okra. Cover and simmer for 1 hour. Just before serving add green onions, shrimp and parsley.

HAM AND BROCCOLI SOUP

This is a great way to use leftover ham after the holidays.

4 cups chicken broth

1 large bunch fresh broccoli
   chopped

½ cup diced onions

½ teaspoon salt

¼ teaspoon black pepper

¼ cup flour

⅓ cup diced ham

½ cup heavy cream

1 bay leaf

Pinch of shredded Cheddar cheese

Combine chicken broth, broccoli, onion, bay leaf, salt and pepper in large saucepan over high heat. When broth comes to boil, turn down heat and simmer, covered for 30 minutes. Remove bay leaf and discard. Let broth cool; transfer ½ of broth to blender and mix on low speed for 30 seconds. Pour blended mixture back into saucepan and place over medium/low heat. Add flour and whisk until all lumps are dissolved. Add ham and cream. Mix well and continue to simmer for 10-15 minutes or until soup is desired thickness. Serve with shredded cheese sprinkled on top.

HEARTY CHICKEN SOUP

3 cups cubed chicken

½ cup chopped onions

2 tablespoons olive oil

2 teaspoons poultry seasoning

6 cups water

2 cups frozen corn thawed

2 cups frozen green peas thawed

1 cup frozen green beans thawed

1 32-ounce box chicken broth

4 cubes chicken bouillon

1 bag egg noodles

In large skillet cook chicken and onions in olive oil until onions are tender. Reduce heat to simmer. Add poultry seasoning and water to skillet; simmer for 30 minutes or until chicken is completely cooked. Pour entire skillet contents into slow cooker. Add vegetables, chicken broth and bouillon cubes. Stir well, cover and cook on high 4-6 hours or on low 6-8 hours. Add noodles during last 2 hours of cooking.

HEARTY HAM AND BEAN SOUP

This is a tweaked version of my mom's recipe for this winter weekend family favorite. Everyone had to remember to stir it frequently since she didn't have the luxury of using a slow cooker at that time.

1 cup dry navy beans	4 cups fresh water
4 cups water	1 large finely chopped onion
1-1 ½ pounds meaty ham bones	1 teaspoon dried thyme crushed
1 ½ cups cubed, peeled potatoes	½ teaspoon black pepper
1 ½ cups sliced celery	

Rinse beans. In large saucepan combine beans and 4 cups of water. Bring to boiling; reduce heat. Simmer for 2 minutes. Remove from heat. Cover and let stand for 1 hour. Drain, discard water and rinse beans. In 4-quart slow cooker combine ham, potatoes, celery, onion, thyme and pepper. Stir in beans and fresh water. Cover and cook on low setting for 8-10 hours. Discard bay leaf. Remove meat and coarsely chop, discard bone. Return meat to slow cooker, cover and cook on high heat setting for 5-10 minutes more.

LENTIL SOUP FOR NEW YEARS

My first lentil soup was on midnight 1988 with my mother-in-law in Baltimore. She was continuing a long family traditions and she was right, it was a blessed year.

1 cup green lentils	1 8-ounce can tomato sauce
3 cups water	1 tablespoon Italian seasoning
1 onion diced	¼ cup apple cider vinegar
2 teaspoons minced garlic	1 teaspoon black pepper
1 large potato diced	½ teaspoon sugar
1 carrot diced	6 cubes chicken bouillon
1 stalk celery diced	5 cups water
½ cup olive oil	

Place sorted lentils in heavy pot and add first 3 cups of water, bring to boil and boil for 5 minutes. Discard water and return lentils to pot; add all remaining ingredients and stir. Bring to boil on high heat, reduce heat to simmer and cook for 30 minutes.

MARVELOUS WHITE CHILI

White chili is made with white meat chicken or turkey and white beans. Some variations include barley or hominy. It has many variations just like regular chili. Some even put chili powder in it.

1 15-ounce can garbanzo beans un-drained	2 tablespoons minced onions
1 15-ounce can northern beans un-drained	1 diced red bell pepper
1 15-ounce can pinto beans	1 tablespoon minced garlic
2 16-ounce bags frozen corn thawed	1 tablespoon ground cumin
2 cups shredded cooked chicken	½ teaspoon salt
	½ teaspoon dried oregano
	2 14 ½-ounce cans chicken broth

Combine all ingredients in slow cooker. Cover. Cook on low 8-10 hours or on high 4-5 hours. Serve with warmed tortilla chips with melted cheddar cheese on top.

MATZO BALL SOUP

Also called matzah, matza and matzoh, this Jewish dumpling soup is traditionally served at Passover. Butter should not be used in traditional Jewish cooking since Kosher law forbids eating meat and dairy together. Matzo meal was made by hand until 150 years ago.

2 eggs	1 teaspoon salt
2 tablespoons oils	1 ½ quarts water
2 tablespoons water	1 32-ounce box chicken broth
½ cup matzo meal or finely crushed matzo	

Beat eggs, oil and 2 tablespoon water together. Add matzo meal and salt. Mix well. Cover, refrigerate for 20 minutes. Bring water to boil in saucepan. Wet hands and roll matzo mixture into 1 inch balls. Drop into boiling water and cook for 20 minutes or until they float to the top. Remove from water. Pour chicken broth into slow cooker. Add balls. Cover and cook on high 2-3 hours or on low 5-6 hours.

NEW ENGLAND CLAM CHOWDER

My first bowl of clam chowder had me hooked for life. It was the first time I had clams too. Refining this recipe over the years has been bowls and bowls of creamy pleasure.

1 tablespoon olive oil

2 onions chopped

3 cups potatoes finely chopped

2 cups clam juice

1 teaspoon dried celery flakes

1 ½ teaspoons dried thyme

2 tablespoons butter

2 tablespoons flour

2 cups whole milk

2 tablespoons cornstarch

1 pound frozen, chopped clams
    thawed, with liquid

½ teaspoon salt

½ teaspoon black pepper

In large pot, heat olive oil over medium heat. Add onions and cook until tender, about 5 minutes. Add potatoes and clam juice. Bring to boil; lower heat and simmer until potatoes are tender, 5-7 minutes. Stir in thyme, parsley and keep warm over very low heat. In small saucepan, melt butter over medium heat. Whisk in flour and cook for 1 minute, whisk in 1 cup of milk until thickened. Whisk cornstarch into second cup of milk; add into hot milk mixture and whisk to combine. Cook stirring often until thickened and steaming, about 3 minutes. Stir milk mixture into potato broth pot; add clams and liquid. Bring to simmer and cook for 5 minutes, add salt, pepper and serve.

PASTA VEGETABLE SOUP

8 cups chicken broth

1 quart water

6 cups chicken bouillon

¼ teaspoon black pepper

2 bay leaves

1 tablespoon minced garlic

3 stalks celery thinly sliced

1 sweet onion thinly sliced

1 large red bell pepper chopped

2 carrots thinly sliced

6 mushrooms thinly sliced

1 package frozen perogies or ravioli

Place all ingredients except pasta, in large soup pot and simmer gently for 1-2 hours adding water if needed. Bring soup to boil 15 minutes before serving and add perogies or ravioli, boil gently until pasta rises to top and serve.

PUMPKIN SOUP

Pumpkins are considered to be a fruit and are 90 percent water. They're loaded with antioxidant beta-carotene, which has been shown to help improve immune function and can reduce the risk of diseases such as cancer and heart disease.

½ cup chopped onions	¼ teaspoon nutmeg
3 tablespoons butter	¼ teaspoon black pepper
2 cups mashed cooked pumpkin	3 cups chicken broth
1 teaspoon salt	½ cup half and half
1 tablespoon sugar	

If using new pumpkin, scoop out seeds and strands. Cut pumpkin top to bottom in half. Place both halves on sprayed baking sheet, cut side down. Sprinkle a few drops of water on sheet. Bake in 350° oven for 30-60 minutes depending on pumpkin size. When done, the skin darkens and pumpkin begins to collapse. Fork or knife will go in easily when done. Remove from oven, cool 20 minutes. Scoop pumpkin flesh away from skin. Discard skin and mash or puree pumpkin. Gently brown onions with butter in a pan. Add pumpkin, salt, sugar, nutmeg and pepper. Slowly add chicken broth and heat thoroughly, but do not boil. To serve, pour into a tureen and add cream.

SPLIT PEA SOUP

This is my sister-in-law Lenora's favorite soup and making it the best possible was nothing but fun.

1 pound dried split peas sorted, rinsed	6 cups water
	1 bay leaf
2 peeled and diced potatoes	¼ teaspoon salt
1 chopped onion	3 diced carrots
1 teaspoon minced garlic	3 diced celery
2 ham hocks	½ teaspoon dried thyme
2 teaspoons instant vegetables bouillon	¼ teaspoon black pepper
2 cups chicken broth	

Combine and mix well: peas, potatoes, onion, garlic, ham, bouillon, broth, water, bay leaf and salt in slow cooker. Cover and cook on high for 2 hours. Remove cover and stir in carrots, celery and thyme. Cover and cook on high for 2 hours; Remove ham bones and bay leaf from slow cooker; discard. Puree batches in blender until completely smooth. Stir in pepper.

SWEET POTATO SOUP

Sweet potatoes are a Native American plant that was the main source of nourishment for early homesteaders and for soldiers during the Revolutionary War. These tuberous roots are among the most nutritious foods in the vegetable kingdom.

4 sweet potatoes	2 tablespoons half and half
8 cups water	2 teaspoons salt
⅓ cup butter	⅛ teaspoon black pepper
⅓ cup tomato sauce	Dash dried thyme

Bake potatoes in 400° oven for 45 minutes. Cool potatoes and peel away skin. Mash potatoes for 20 seconds, don't mash them until smooth. Spoon mashed potatoes into large saucepan and add remaining ingredients. Stir and heat to boiling over medium/high heat. Reduce heat and simmer for 50-60 minutes.

TACO SOUP

Taco soup is a modern American soup usually consisting of similar ingredients to those used inside a taco: ground beef, tomatoes, corn, beans and a packet of taco seasoning.

1 pound ground beef	1 15 ½-ounce can kidney beans undrained
1 large onion chopped	
1 14 ½-ounce can diced tomatoes	1 15-ounce can black beans undrained
1 package taco seasoning mix	
1 cup tomato juice	1 16-ounce jar picante sauce
1 15 ½-ounce can pinto beans	Bag corn or tortilla chips
1 16-ounce bag whole kernel corn thawed	Sour cream
	Shredded Cheddar cheese

Brown meat and onions in skillet; drain. Place in slow cooker. Combine tomatoes, seasoning mix, juice, beans and picante sauce in slow cooker. Mix well. Cover and cook on low 4-6 hours. Serve with chips, sour cream and cheese as toppings.

THANKSGIVING CHILI

This fun to serve in a cleaned out pumpkin that has been baked in the oven. Just pour the soup in the warm baked whole pumpkin before serving and serve it from the pumpkin at the table.

1 cup chopped onions	2 teaspoons chili powder
1 cup chopped yellow bell pepper	2 cans black beans drained, rinsed
3 cloves minced garlic	3 cups cooked chopped turkey
2 tablespoons oil	1 15-ounce can pumpkin
2 teaspoons dried oregano	1 14 ½-ounce can diced tomatoes
2 teaspoons ground cumin	3 cups chicken broth

Sauté onions, pepper and garlic in oil until soft. Stir in oregano, cumin and chili powder. Cook 1 minute. Transfer to slow cooker. Add remaining ingredients. Cover. Cook on low 7-8 hours.

THE JUNCTION CHILI

This won first place in the "1993 Montana Western Days" chili contest and for good reason. Make it spicy or leave it mild.

1 pound ground beef	1 teaspoon black pepper
¼ pound ground pork or ground turkey	2 28-ounce cans diced tomatoes with juice
1 large onion chopped	3 cans kidney beans rinsed and drained
1 chopped green pepper	
1 tablespoon garlic powder	2 15-ounce cans chili beans
1 tablespoon paprika	1 teaspoon cayenne pepper
3 tablespoons chili powder	(optional)
1 teaspoon salt	1 tablespoon hot sauce (optional)

Brown meat in skillet and then place in slow cooker. Add onions, pepper and all seasonings, mix well and cook until onions and pepper are beginning to soften. Stir in tomatoes and beans. Cover and cook on low for 4-6 hours. This can be served with chips, crackers, shredded cheese on top or over hot dogs or nachos.

THICK BEAN SOUP

Beans have been used throughout the world for thousands of years. They come in hundreds of shapes sizes and colors, are versatile and amazingly convenient because they can be dried and stored for years. Soaking beans for a couple of hours brings them back to life, activating enzymes, proteins, minerals and vitamins.

8 strips bacon diced	1 teaspoon garlic powder
2 thinly sliced onions	1-28-ounce can baked beans
¾ cup brown sugar	2 cans kidney beans rinsed and
¼ cup molasses	drained
½ cup cider vinegar	1 can pinto beans rinsed and drained
1 teaspoon salt	1 16-ounce bag lima beans
½ teaspoon black pepper	1 can black beans rinsed and drained
1 teaspoon dry mustard	1 10 ½-ounce can chicken broth

Cook bacon in skillet until crisp. Remove to paper towels. Drain and reserve 2 tablespoons of drippings. Sauté onions in drippings until tender. Add brown sugar, molasses, vinegar, salt, pepper, mustard, garlic powder and broth to skillet. Bring to boil. Combine beans in slow cooker. Add onion mixture and bacon. Mix well. Cover and cook on high 3-4 hours.

TOMATO SOUP

Tomato soup is commonly used as an ingredient in more complex dishes and it may be served hot or cold. It can be made from chunks of tomato or with a puree. The canned version is one of the leading soups listed as a comfort food.

1 stalk celery finely diced	1/8 teaspoon black pepper
1 small onion finely diced	1 cup tomato juice or spicy tomato
3 tablespoons butter or margarine	juice
2 cups milk	1 can diced tomatoes
1/8 teaspoon salt	1/8 teaspoon baking soda

In large saucepan, sauté celery, onion and 1 tablespoon of butter for 1-2 minutes. Stir in milk, add rest of butter, tomatoes, salt and pepper. Heat on low until butter melts. In second saucepan heat tomato juice on low. When both pans of liquids are heated through, add baking soda into warm tomato juice. Immediately pour tomato mixture into milk mixture. Stir and continue to heat a few minutes before serving.

SIMPLE ONE BEAN SOUP

Beans are rich in nutrients, low in calories and a good source of protein, vitamins, minerals and fiber. This old fashioned recipe is cooked the new way.

2-1/2 cups dried navy beans	1 cup sliced carrots
3 quarts water	28 oz. can tomato juice
8 slices bacon	2 tsp. salt
3 onions, chopped	1/2 tsp. pepper
2 cups diced, peeled potatoes	1 bay leaf

Combine beans and 3 quarts water in large pot. Bring to a boil and boil for 2 minutes. Cover and let stand for 1 hour. Meanwhile, cook bacon until crisp in large stockpot. Remove bacon to paper towels to drain and crumble. Add chopped onions to bacon drippings. Cook and stir until onions are tender. (Precooking beans, bacon, and onion as directed is necessary, otherwise the beans would never get tender because of the acid in the tomatoes.) Combine all ingredients in 4-quart crockpot. Cover and cook 10-12 hours on low. Remove bay leaf before serving.

GAME MEAT

Our Montana move meant we joined the "wild west" and one of the favorite activities: hunting,—many in the area count on it for winter meat. New friends were avid hunters and assured Joe they never came home empty handed. After multiple attempts all Joe came home with was a broken truck. One day at the end of the hunting season Joe proudly walked into the house and announced, "I bagged my elk." Excitedly we went to the garage expecting to see an elk carcass, but found instead a huge garbage bag full of skinned meat chunks.

TAMING THE BEAST The Department of Fish and Game auctions off the confiscated illegal kills every year. Joe went there and heard the story about a guy who was arrested in the middle of processing his elk. A neighbor turned him in for killing the elk on private property. He shot it legal and the elk ran onto private property to die, which is where the hunter retrieved it.

Not allowed to buy his meat or the incredibly huge antlers, Joe outbid everyone and sold the rack to the hunter. A friend cut steaks, roasts and ground the rest, which we shared with friends and used all year long for meals. It was delicious meat and easy to fix and yes, I snapped a photo of my husband proudly holding the garbage bag of elk meat which is labeled in our scrapbook, "Joe bagged his first elk."

DON'T ASK -JUST EAT

The next year, he ended up at the auction again. This time another illegal hunter before being caught, had cut up the meat into roasts, steaks, stew chunks and ground meat, wrapped it and labeled each package. Joe bought it and we simply piled it into the freezers and again the meat was great.

Living now in the "northern wilderness" of Alaska, we've enjoyed lots of delicious red meats. Most people have only experienced chewy gamey-tasting wild meat. That's a shame, because marinades, sauces and rubs help take any "wild" taste out of game meat and tenderizes even the toughest cut from animals older than 2 years old. Unless the meat is bad to begin with, there is a recipe to make it delicious.

In my travel years, people were very generous in sharing the local "dishes" they hunted in their area. Just like hunting in Alaska, what is plentiful is hunted and eaten to offset the high cost of food not local to their area. Some Americans tend to be queasy about game meats on their plates. Rabbits, we think Bugs bunny; moose of course we imagine Bullwinkle; squirrels are Bullwinkle's sidekick Rocky; venison, elk or caribou brings images of poor motherless Bambi and our love of red nosed Rudolph causes hesitation in enjoying reindeer sausage.

We were served beaver, raccoon, frog, goat, duck, goose, ostrich, possum, quail, wild turkey, snake, mutton, alligator, rabbit, squirrel, turtle, elk, deer, antelope, emu, ostrich, bison and pheasant.

In Alaska there is an abundance of game meat and poultry and an important addition to many tables, so we get a chance to fixed it many ways. At special events in villages, tastes of musk ox, whale meat, seal, sea lion and wild birds are available and generously served to newcomers.

People everywhere are thrilled to serve you the dishes of their culture, region and family history when you travel. It's an honor for them to share a part of themselves and all a part of the adventure. People become more receptive when they know you're wiling to try the gift they offer and what they eat regularly.

If wild meat and wild poultry aren't your meal of choice, feel free to substitute your favorite red meat or poultry; the ingredients and recipes are very versatile, easily adjusted and still delicious.

ANTELOPE STEAK

This was one of the best steaks I've ever had.

3 antelope round steaks ¾ inch thick	¼ teaspoon garlic salt
2 teaspoons salt	Flour
¼ cup vinegar	3 tablespoons canola oil
1 teaspoon minced garlic	1 can cream of chicken soup
Dash black pepper	

Place antelope steaks in shallow pan and cover with water. Add salt, vinegar, bay leaf, and garlic and soak for 3 hour or overnight. Drain steaks and sprinkle with pepper and garlic salt. Dredge with flour. Brown on both sides in oil in lightly greased skillet and cover. Cook over low heat for 45 minutes or until tender, turning occasionally. Add soup and 1 soup can of water and cover. Simmer for 15-20 minutes. Gravy may be served over rice or potatoes. Mushroom soup may be substituted for chicken soup.

BAKED GOOSE

1 goose	¾ cup red wine vinegar
1 teaspoon salt	½ cup peanut oil
1 teaspoon black pepper	¾ cup cooking sherry
1 teaspoon cinnamon	1-3 teaspoons flour more if needed

Sprinkle salt, pepper, and cinnamon over entire goose. Rub into skin. Combine vinegar, oil and sherry. Pour over goose with breast down. Bake in 450° oven for 40 minutes with top on roasting pan. Take top off; broil 8 minutes. Turn goose breast side up and broil 8 minutes. SAUCE: Pour off oil and discard, whisk into drippings enough flour to make very thin sauce, heat to boiling. Pour over thinly sliced goose.

BEAR MEATLOAF

2 pounds ground bear meat	1 cup minced onions
½ cup milk	1 ½ teaspoons dry mustard
2 eggs	1 cup dry bread crumbs
Salt and black pepper	½ chopped green bell pepper
¼ teaspoon dried thyme	1 can mushrooms
¼ teaspoon dried oregano	Ketchup
¾ cup tomato sauce	

Mix all of ingredients except ketchup, in large bowl until well combined. Form loaf and place in sprayed casserole dish. Bake in 350º for 45 minutes. Pour ketchup over top of loaf and cook another 15 minutes.

BEAR STEW

If using bear meat, drain off the fat after cooking, bear meat is usually a very fatty meat.

5 pounds bear meat cut in 1-inch cubes	4 bay leaves
	2 pounds fresh sliced mushrooms
¼ cup flour	5 sliced carrots
1 tablespoon Italian seasoning	1 cubed turnips
4 tablespoons butter	5 sliced parsnips
2 tablespoons corn oil	2-3 quarts water
1 diced onion	
1 cup beef broth	

Put flour with seasonings in plastic bag, add cubed meat and shake until bear meat is coated. Heat oil and butter in skillet and brown coated meat. Drain off grease from meat. In large Dutch oven add 2 quarts of water, bear meat and rest of ingredients. Cook in 325º oven about. 2-3 hours adding water if necessary checking every 30 minutes. Remove bay leaves from stew before serving.

BEAVER STEW

3 pounds beaver, cut in 1-inch cubes
Bacon grease
2 cups flour
1 teaspoon salt
1 teaspoon black pepper

2 diced onions
½ pound sliced carrots
6 potatoes cut in 1-inch cubes
2 stalks diced celery

Combine flour, salt and pepper in 2-quart closable plastic bag and shake until mixed. Add beaver cubes and shake until well coated. Melt enough bacon grease in bottom skillet to about ½ inch depth. Sauté onions and floured beaver in bacon grease, adding more grease as needed. Place sautéed cubes and onions in 4-quart pot with enough water to cover. Add water to skillet to remove remainder of bacon grease and flour. Add this pan gravy to stew. Add carrots and celery to stew and simmer until beaver is somewhat tender (about 30 minutes). Taste broth and add additional salt or pepper to taste. Add potatoes and enough water to just cover meat and vegetables. Simmer until potatoes are done (about 30 minutes).

BLACK BEAR ROAST

Bear meat is very greasy, so when roasting you should always cook on a rack about 2 inches above the bottom of your pan and place about 1 inch of water in the bottom of the pan. Marinating is very important

4 pounds boneless bear roast or
    steaks
Marinade:
1 cup red wine
½ cup olive oil
1 chopped onion
2 tablespoons minced garlic

2 sliced carrots
1 teaspoon dried tarragon
Salt and black pepper
Gravy:
½ cup flour
1 ½ cups water
1 teaspoon celery salt

Combine all ingredients in roaster pan and mix well. Place roast or steaks in roaster, cover and refrigerate overnight, turning often. Remove from marinade 2 hours prior to cooking to allow meat to rest and reach room temperature. Strain marinade and reserve liquid for gravy. Place roast on rack about 2 inches above bottom roaster pan and place about 1 inch of water in bottom of pan.

Cover and cook in 350° oven for 1 ½ hours, turn roast over and cook another 1 ½ hours. Remove roast from pan and let rest before slicing. In meantime, skim large amount of grease from pan drippings. Pour what is left in saucepan. Over medium heat bring it to boil. Add marinade liquid. In separate bowl, stir until smooth flour, water and celery salt. Stir gravy flour mixture into saucepan and stir constantly until thickens. Remove from heat. Carve roast into ¼ inch slices and pour gravy over meat to serve.

BRAISED ANTELOPE ROAST

The braising liquid never drowns the food. Instead, there is just enough liquid to help break down the toughness; to penetrate and season; and to make the foundation for a flavorful sauce.

4 pounds antelope roast	2 cups water
1 teaspoon salt	1 tablespoon red wine vinegar
1 teaspoon black pepper	6 red potatoes
1 tablespoon flour	6 carrots cut in 3 pieces
3 tablespoons olive oil	

Mix together salt, pepper and flour; rub over entire roast. In skillet, heat oil and sauté in roast until browned on all sides. Add water and vinegar; reduce heat to simmer. Cover and simmer for 3 to 4 hours. Potatoes and carrots should be added last half hour of cooking. Place around roast and cover again,

BUFFALO STEAK

To enjoy that great bison taste best, serve these steaks with minimal condiments. Substitute bison for red meat in conventional recipes and prepared by grilling, roasting, broiling, stir-frying, or pan-frying. The main concern is to keep this low fat, delicious meat from becoming dry. It is helpful to cook bison meat at a lower temperature than other forms of red meat. Because it's leaner, it will cook through more quickly. Plan for faster cooking times when preparing bison.

½ cup sliced sweet onions

1 teaspoon sea salt

½ tablespoon black pepper

2 pounds chopped bison steak

Vegetable oil

4 tablespoons butter room
temperature

2 tablespoons minced garlic

2 teaspoons dried tarragon

¼ teaspoon dried thyme

Steaks are 1-inch to 1 ½-inch are best for grilling. A thin cut is likely to get dried out. Have steaks at room temperature before grilling. Season with salt and pepper steaks when you remove them from refrigerator. Lightly oil the grilling rack before putting steaks on (it keeps meat from sticking and cracking while keeping the natural juices in). Mix together butter, garlic, tarragon and thyme. Spread on top of steaks before placing on grill, buttered side up. Preheat grill to 600° to 800° and keep it at this temperature for 30 to 45 minutes before putting steaks on. Only flip once after five minutes of grilling. Use tongs or a spatula (A fork allows juices to spill out). Grill onion slices brushed with oil and serve on top of the steaks.

CABBAGE BEAR STEW

1 pound ground bear meat

2 medium onions thinly chopped

1 ½ cups cabbage coarsely chopped

½ cup celery diced

1 16-ounce can stewed tomatoes

1 can kidney beans Do not drain

1 can beer or 1 cup water

1 teaspoon salt

¼ teaspoon black pepper

2 teaspoons chili powder

Dumplings:

1 ½ cups flour

¾ cup milk

2 teaspoons baking powder

¾ teaspoon salt

3 tablespoons shortening

Brown meat and drain fat off. Add onion, cabbage and celery. Cook and stir until vegetables are lightly browned. Stir in tomatoes, beans with liquid, water/beer and seasonings. Simmer 30 minutes. Make dumplings by mixing dry ingredients and cut in shortening and add milk. Stir until just mixed. Drop dough by spoonfuls onto simmering stew. Cook uncovered 10 minutes; cover and cook additional 10 minutes.

CRANBERRY MEATBALLS

2 pounds venison, elk, moose or
   caribou
2 eggs beaten
1 cup ground cornflakes
½ cup ketchup
2 tablespoons soy sauce
1 tablespoon parsley flakes
1 tablespoon onion powder

½ teaspoon onion salt
¼ teaspoon black pepper
Sauce:
1 can whole cranberry sauce
1 cup ketchup
3 tablespoons brown sugar
1 tablespoon lemon juice

Combine cranberry, ketchup, brown sugar and lemon juice in a saucepan.
Heat and stir frequently until cranberry sauce is melted; set aside. Combine
meat with eggs, cornflakes, ketchup, soy sauce and spices in large bowl and
mix well. Make 1 inch balls, about 70. Place on well sprayed rimmed cooking
sheet. Bake in 350º oven for 20-25 minutes or until done. Watch carefully,
game meat has less oil and will easily burn. Pour sauce over meatballs and
put them back in warm but turned off oven to keep warm.

DUCK AND CRANBERRY SAUCE

*This is the sort of dish that would have been on a fine feast table in the
1600's*

5 pound duck
2 ½ teaspoons salt
2 teaspoons black pepper divided
1 onion quartered
3 stalks diced celery
¼ cup parsley flakes
3 onions thinly sliced
Sauce:

2 cups red wine
⅓ cup minced parsley leaves
1 teaspoon ground ginger
¼ cup chopped raisins
½ teaspoon ground mace
¼ cup chopped cranberries
1 tablespoon sugar
4 tablespoons chilled butter cut into
   4 pieces

Rinse duck inside and out and rinse any giblets included. Place duck and giblets
(except liver) in pot large enough to accommodate them, with 2 teaspoons of
salt, 1 ½ teaspoon pepper, onion quarters, parsley and celery. Cover with cold
water and bring to simmer over high heat. Reduce heat so broth stays at very

low simmer. Skim off froth, cover and simmer for 45 minutes. Preheat oven to 400º. Arrange sliced onions in 13 x 9-inch roasting pan. Carefully remove duck from broth; reserve broth. Season duck inside and out with remaining ½ teaspoon salt and ½ teaspoon pepper; place duck on top of onions. Roast duck for 25 minutes. Remove from oven, place duck on carving board; cover loosely with aluminum foil. While the duck is resting, make sauce. Strain 1 cup of reserved broth; place in saucepan with onions from roasting pan, wine, parsley, ginger, raisins and mace. Boil over medium-high heat until mixture is reduced by two-thirds and has syrupy consistency. After resting 10 minutes, carve duck into serving pieces. Place meat on heated platter; cover loosely with foil. Add juices given off during carving to sauce and stir in cranberries and sugar. Simmer for 30 seconds; remove from heat. Swirl in butter, tablespoon at a time, until sauce is silky. Serve duck immediately, accompanied by sauce.

EASY MOOSE ROAST

6 slices bacon	2 sliced onions
4 pounds moose rump roast	2 chopped carrots
1 tablespoon dry mustard	2 stalks chopped celery
2 teaspoons salt	2 cans diced or stewed tomatoes
1 teaspoon black pepper	

Wrap bacon slices around roast. Refrigerate overnight or at least 10 hours. Remove and discard bacon. Rub roast thoroughly with dry mustard. Season with salt and pepper. Place roast in roasting pan, surround it with onions, carrots and celery. Pour entire can of tomatoes over vegetables. Cover and bake in 350º oven for 2 ½ hours. Let rest before carving. Serve with vegetables and juice.

ELK MEDALLIONS

Lean and flavorful, elk meat is lower in fat than beef, pork, chicken and even some seafood according to experts and is a healthy, attractive alternative. Elk is a red meat which looks a lot like beef but is not marbled like other red meats. When preparing elk, there is less shrinkage. Because of the lower fat content, a higher percentage of protein and nutrients are present in the meat.

1 ½ pounds elk medallions	1 packet onion soup mix
1 ½ cups cream of mushroom soup	1 tablespoon olive oil
1 ½ cups beef broth	

Place elk meat in bottom of crockpot. Drizzle with olive oil. Mix soup, broth and dry onion mix together and pour over elk meat in slow cooker. Cook on high for 6-7 hrs. The elk comes out really tender and tasty and with its own gravy Serve over noodles, potatoes, or rice.

ELK IN A BAG

This recipe can be used for venison, bison, venison, caribou and moose roast. With less fat and extra protein in these game meats, they are a great value and a fantastic heart-healthy alternative to other red meats. Any of them can be substituted for red meat in all your conventional recipes and prepared by grilling, roasting, broiling, stir-frying, or pan-frying. The main concern is to keep it from becoming dry by cooking at a lower temperature and expect the cooking time to be shorter.

4 pounds roast 4 inches thick	1 quartered onion
1 tablespoon flour	2 bay leaves
1 cup red wine	1 sliced carrot
1 packet onion soup mix	1 tablespoon olive oil
Salt and black pepper	

Preheat oven to 325°. Shake flour in small size (10x16") brown-in-bag and place in 2 inch deep roasting pan. Pour wine into bag and stir until flour is well mixed. Rub meat with dry onion mix. Place meat in bag and drizzle olive oil over roast. Put onion, carrots and bay leaves around roast. Close bag with twist tie and make 6 half-inch slits in top. Cook for 2 to 2 ½ hours. Remove roast to slicing board and let meat rest 10 minutes before slicing. In meantime, remove bay leaves from juices, place juices and mixture in blender or use hand blender in pot and blend until smooth, Serve over slices of meat.

FRIED FROG LEGS

Frog legs taste different than chicken. They have a taste all their own—more like wild rabbit but slightly fishy and chewier. If you like seafood, you'd probably like them.

Frog legs	1 egg beaten
1 tablespoon salt	Round buttery cracker crumbs
2 quarts water	Vegetable oil

Wash and soak frog legs in salt water for 2 hours. Pat dry. Dip in beaten egg and roll in cracker crumbs. In a skillet, heat vegetable oil almost to boiling point. Add frog leg; turn until golden brown on both sides. Drain on paper towels. Serve hot.

FRIED RABBIT

Believe me, they're delicious with a unique "chicken-type" but subtle game taste.

1 rabbit cut into serving size pieces	4 tablespoons butter
1 cup flour	4 tablespoons corn oil or vegetable oil
¼ teaspoon black pepper	1 teaspoon vinegar
1 teaspoon salt	1 chopped onion
¼ cup water	

Combine flour, salt and pepper in a pie plate. Pat dry rabbit pieces and roll rabbit in flour mixture. Heat butter and oil in large skillet until sizzles. Brown floured pieces, turning to brown both sides. Reduce heat to simmer and add water, onion, and vinegar. Cover and simmer until tender. Remove cover last 10 minutes to brown.

GAME STEAK MARINADE

I've used this even on beef and some poultry meats.

½ cup vegetable oil
1 teaspoon Worcestershire sauce
½ cup ketchup
3 cloves crushed garlic

2 tablespoons soy sauce
¼ teaspoon dry mustard
½ cup red wine
1 teaspoon lemon juice

Blend all ingredients in blender. Prick venison, elk, bison, caribou or moose steak with fork. Pour marinade over steaks. Marinate 3-4 hours before cooking, turn once or twice. Grill or Broil steaks. Discard marinade

GRILLED BUFFALO BURGERS

These instructions work well for any "meat" ground up for a beautiful burger.

⅓ cup finely chopped green onions
2 teaspoons Worcestershire sauce
1 teaspoon dry mustard
1 teaspoon sea salt

½ teaspoon black pepper
½ teaspoon garlic powder
2 pounds ground bison
Vegetable oil

In medium sized bowl, combine onions, Worcestershire sauce, mustard, salt, garlic powder and pepper. Add ground bison and blend with seasonings; shape into 6 patties. Place patties in single layer on small cookie sheet or tray. Cover loosely with plastic wrap and refrigerate for 1 hour. Pre-heat barbecue to medium-high. Just before cooking, brush grill clean with a wire brush. Quickly grease grill with rag or paper towel soaked in some vegetable oil. Except when burgers are being flipped, the barbecue lid should be closed during cooking. Grill burgers for 3 minutes on one side without disturbing. Flip burgers over and cook opposite side for another 3 minutes. Continue cooking on same side without flipping for another 6-7 minutes but reduce heat to medium/medium-low. To finish, flip and cook opposite side for final 6-7 minutes for burger between medium-well and well-done. Don't over cook them, they will dry out quickly.

JERKY

Indians and early settlers dried meat primarily using salt, whatever spices they had and sun drying. North American Pioneers would first dry meat by hanging it outside of their covered wagon 2-3 day. Another method was to build a scaffold over a slow fire and smoke the strips. Any kind of meat makes it a favorite with my nephew Eric and husband Joe. Today we even use poultry and try different flavorings.

3 pounds boned beef or venison or elk	2 tablespoons popcorn salt
⅛ teaspoon salt	3 tablespoons water
2 tablespoons liquid smoke	¾ tablespoon seasoned pepper

Slice meat into ¼" thick strips about 5" long. Remove all fat. Combine liquid smoke, water and seasonings. Brush on strips and place (layer on layer) in a large bowl. Put a weighted plate on top of bowl and let stand in place overnight. Remove meat and dry it. Place strips across oven racks—edges may touch; don't overlap. Allow room for air to circulate. Racks should be no closer than 4" from top and bottom heat sources. Dry meat in oven for about 11 hours at 150°. Remove and cool completely. Store in an airtight container.

MOOSE STEAK

6 slices of bacon	2 tablespoons olive oil
2 pounds moose steak	1 cup chopped mushrooms
½ cup finely chopped onions	½ cup sour cream
2 tablespoons butter	2 tablespoons flour

Wrap each steak in bacon slices. Wrap in plastic and refrigerate 10-24 hours. Remove bacon and discard. In large skillet, melt butter and heat oil. Cook onion until tender. Sear steaks on both sides in onion mixture. Reduce heat to simmer. Simmer for 30 minutes. Remove steak to plate. Stir flour in sour cream. Add mushrooms and cream into skillet, deglazing and mixing all ingredients well. Return steak to skillet, cover and continue to simmer for 20 minutes.

PHEASANT (PARTRIDGE OR QUAIL) ROASTED

Most game poultry can be cooked this way and each kind has a significant distinguishing change in taste from chicken just like turkey doesn't taste like chicken.

1 pheasant	**1 chopped onion**
1 quart boiling water	**4 strips bacon**
1 cup chopped celery	**1 cup chicken broth**
Salt and black pepper	

Clean pheasant. Place in bowl and pour boiling water over it and into cavity. Drain water and discard. Place bird in sprayed baking dish. Place celery and onion inside bird; do not sew up or truss. Rub with salt and pepper; place bacon across breast. Add broth for basting and roast in 350° oven for 2 hours or until tender.

RACCOON OR OPOSSUM PATTIES

These meats need to be specially cleaned if the animal is not purchased from a meat market or professional butcher.

1 cup bread crumbs	**2 eggs beaten**
½ cup diced onions	**¼ cup bacon grease or melted butter**
1 teaspoon salt	**Vegetable oil**
1 teaspoon black pepper	**Currant jelly**

Remove meat from bones and grind. In bowl, combine breadcrumbs, onion, salt, pepper, 1 egg and bacon grease or butter; mix thoroughly. Place crumb mixture into pie plate. Place other beaten egg in small bowl. Form ground meat into patties; dip into egg; cover in breadcrumbs. Fry in hot vegetable oil in skillet until brown. Place browned patties in slow cooker. Cover tops of patties with currant jelly; cook on low for 1 hour.

RATTLESNAKE AND BEANS

This recipe can substitute rattlesnake meat with chicken, quail, dove, pork or rabbit. Which means the beans are good no matter what meat or fowl is used.

4 cups kidney beans drained and
    rinsed
4 cups pinto beans drained and
    rinsed
2 14 ½-ounce cans stewed tomatoes
1 4-ounce can dice jalapeno chilies
1 chopped red onion

Dash salt
2 teaspoons minced garlic
1 pound ground beef
½ pound rattlesnake meat, cut in
    chunks
Broken tortilla chip

Put drained and rinsed beans into large pot; add tomatoes, jalapenos, onion, salt and garlic. Bring mixture to boil, stir and reduce heat to simmer. Simmer for 20 minutes. Place ground beef in skillet, cook and crumble meat. Place beef in pot with beans. Place rattlesnake (or other meat) in same skillet with beef fat and fry meat until cooked. Place meat in pot; stir ingredients well. Simmer 10 minutes to heat thoroughly. Place broken tortilla chips in bottom of bowl and spoon over chips.

SLOW COOKER VENISON ROAST

3-4 pounds venison roast
¼ cup vinegar
2 cloves minced garlic
2 tablespoons salt
Sauce:
1 cup chopped onions
1 15-ounce can tomato sauce

1 tablespoon dry mustard
1 package brown gravy mix
½ teaspoon garlic powder
½ teaspoon salt
¼ cup water
½ cup chopped celery
½ cup chopped green bell peppers

Place venison in deep bowl. Combine vinegar, garlic and salt. Pour over venison. Add enough cold water to cover venison. Cover and refrigerate for 8-24 hours. Rinse and drain venison. Place in slow cooker. Combine remaining ingredients; pour over venison. Cover with lid. Cook on low 10-12 hours.

Surround yourself with and fill your days sharing what you have to give—because the moments, the people, the food and even your gift
Unlike photographs, will not last and may never be again.

SPICY GAME ROAST

A surprisingly simple recipe of unrelated spices that combine for an outstanding taste.

**4 pounds venison, moose or elk
    roast
1 packet onion soup mix
½ teaspoon cayenne pepper**

**½ teaspoon cinnamon
½ cup instant coffee crystals**

Rinse tenderloin with cold water and pat dry with paper towels. Set aside. Combine remaining ingredients and rub into tenderloin. Wrap in plastic wrap and refrigerate for 2 hours. Remove roast from refrigerator, unwrap and discard plastic wrap. Place roast on piece of heavy aluminum foil. Bring edges of foil together and seal tightly. Place in shallow roasting pan and bake in 425° oven for 2 to 2 ½ hours. The juice collected inside foil can be thickened for gravy.

SQUIRREL IN A CROCKPOT

This recipe can be used for rabbit, poultry or pork meat, but the squirrel is marvelous.

**4-6 squirrels, cut into halves
¼ cup soy sauce
½ cup chicken broth
¼ cup brown sugar
3 tablespoons lime juice
¼ teaspoon garlic powder**

**¼ teaspoon ground ginger
½ teaspoon black pepper
Gravy:
1 tablespoon flour or
1 teaspoon cornstarch mixed in 1
    cup water**

Place meat halves or pieces in crockpot. Mix soy sauce, water, sugar, juice, garlic, ginger and pepper in small bowl and pour over meat. Cover and cook on low heat for 7-8 hours. Remove meat to platter. To thicken gravy, use either flour or cornstarch mixed with water. Cook on high until thickened.

TURTLE SOUP

Turtle taste very good and isn't really like chicken. Each part taste different, I think the tail and legs are best. Soup is how most how most people eat it; in Louisiana it's served smothered in gravy; in Ohio they deep-fried it like chicken.

1 pound turtle meat	1 chopped green bell pepper
6 cups water	1 cup barley
1 teaspoon salt	2 tablespoons Worcestershire sauce
1 cup tomato soup	2 tablespoons lemon juice
1 chopped onion	½ cup lemon juice
1 stalk chopped celery	½ cup red wine

Pour water into large stockpot on stove and add salt. To salted water, add turtle meat, tomato soup and vegetables; cook on low heat for 1 hour. Add barley; stir and cook 30 minutes, stir occasionally. Reduce heat to simmer; add Worcestershire sauce, lemon juice and wine. Simmer for 10 minutes; serve hot.

People go to cookouts for a lot of reasons: business, celebrations, family obligations and socialization. We eat, we laugh, and we connect. The food doesn't have to be spectacular or expensive, just edible.

Then there are cookouts that we go to because the food is "to die for fabulous". Our family friend Steve has a knock out sauce he puts on things he grills. He could probably put it on shoe leather and we'd eat it. Hopefully someday he will bottle it and sell it; for now, we can only enjoy it at his house. That's what good sauces, dressings and gravies should do: distinguish one person's chicken, seafood, ribs or steak from another, just  like the restaurants do. He has that sauce mixture down to a science and any time Steve has grilling on his menu, we get a thrilling meal on ours.

VENISON, ELK OR MOOSE BURGERS

These burgers can be grilled or broiled or panfried. The key is to keep them from getting dry. Just cook until pink is gone and still has juices left in the meat whichever way you fix them, so watch closely as they cook and use tongs, not a fork to turn them.

½ pound 75% lean ground beef
½ pound ground moose, elk or
  venison
2 tablespoons Worcestershire sauce
2 tablespoons liquid smoke

2 teaspoons garlic powder
2 tablespoons olive oil
Salt and black pepper

In medium bowl, lightly mix together meat, Worcestershire sauce, liquid smoke and garlic powder. Form into 6 patties ¼ inch thick, handling meat as little as possible. Brush both sides of each patty with some oil and season with seasoned salt.

Grill: Place patties on grill grate 4 to 6 inches from heat over grey-hot coals and cook for about 5 minutes per side until well done.

Broil: Place patties 5 to 7 inches from heat until cooked through.

Pan Fry: Preheat nonstick frying pan. The pan is correct temperature when drop of water dances on surface rather than sticking to it. Place patties in pan and cook for 2-3 minutes. Flip patties and cook for another minute.

WILD BIRD CASSEROLE

This can be used for quail, dove, pheasant or any other wild bird or poultry.

12-18 bird breasts
1 diced onion
1 tablespoon olive oil
1 cup cream of mushroom soup
½ cup sherry

Pinch dried oregano
Pinch dried rosemary
Salt and black pepper
1 cup sour cream

Place breasts meaty side down in 15x12 inch baking dish. Do not over-crowd. Sauté onions with oil in skillet. Mix onion, sherry, herbs, salt and pepper in skillet; pour over bird breasts. Cover baking dish lightly with foil. Bake in 325° oven for 1 hour, turning occasionally. Stir sour cream in juices. Bake about 20 minutes longer.

Fruitcake made with chopped candied fruit or dried fruit, nuts and spices and soaked in spirits, is ridiculed relentlessly. However, if made correctly, you will find it has been wrongly accused of being tasteless.

Typical American fruitcakes are rich in fruit, nuts and flavorful. Mail-order fruitcakes in America began in 1913 and included lots of nuts, which is where the expression "nutty as a fruitcake" was derived in 1935. Most American mass-produced fruitcakes are alcohol-free, but traditional recipes are saturated with liqueurs or brandy and covered in powdered sugar, both of which prevent mold. With knowledge and several old recipes in hand, I took on the challenge and fine-tuned a few special ones. My Joe eagerly anticipates and devours them every year for the holidays.

The keys to a perfect one are moistness and taste—and they do taste good when multiple flavors are combined. I don't stick with just the candied fruit; I also use dried fruit, which gives a different texture and characteristic. I sometimes dry my own fruit in the oven, just chop it up and add to the batter. If you don't use liqueur than use the substitutions I have listed for the liqueur and let it sit in a refrigerator for at least a week before cutting and enjoying.—REALLY!

CAKES

Married only a short time, I really wanted to make things my husband liked to eat. The idea of having someone to cook for started me on my massive collection of cookbooks. I eagerly absorbed the science, the history and the language of cuisine. It was challenging and fun to find ways to make dishes and discover ways to construct a meal. His support and enthusiasm infused me with a love for planning and preparing food that has blossomed into a way of life.

Love on a Plate Then he asked me to make his favorite cake for Christmas, a fruitcake. I was sure Joe was just trying to be funny. No way could he be serious about wanting a tasteless brick of cake for Christmas. That's what I had been told. I gave out simple fruitcakes one year when I first started baking and was quickly informed what many people thought of fruitcakes: a joke, a ridiculed gift given out of obligation or as a gag.

Ten years later, Joe assured me that wasn't true for everyone. I had a lot to learn about real fruitcakes, good fruitcakes and he was right. Taking advantage of living where some of the best fruitcakes in the world are made; I studied the experts. Since then I've made a lot of different fruitcakes that my husband loves. Made correctly, fruitcakes are flavorful and moist and not hard to make. But I don't eat them. They just aren't something I ever acquired a taste for no matter how many different ways I made them.

However I still make several different kinds for Joe for Christmas *Picture Book Perfect* every year, because he loves them. In fact I've learned to make several things for him that I can't stand to eat: scrapple, liver and onions and spam anything, to name a few. But I make them all for the same reason, because he loves them and I love him. And I get a great deal of joy watching him eat something I only fix because he likes it.

No matter where we live, word always gets around that I bake cakes. I'm cautiously asked to make the first cake, after that, people seek me out and ask for specific cakes. I've gotten requests for some pretty fancy ones. I don't decorate cakes; if you want a decorated cake, call my sister Sharon. She likes doing it and has done some impressive ones. If you want a Chocolate-Crunch-Glazed-Cherry-Filled-Dream Cake—I'm your baker. People have wanted a cake they heard about or an old family favorite or one they read about or "wanted all their life". Some people just give me ideas from what they like and I create something. I love baking complicated cakes with elaborate fillings and interesting icings. I do use cake mixes to make other things, but not just a cake.

Memories can be stirred by songs, noises or smells, for me if someone says, Lemon Meringue Coconut Cake, my mind goes back to the person and all the good feelings surrounding the cake I made for them. I've made cakes for so many people and occasions that there are some I've only made once and once was enough. When I see a picture of a cake or hear a name of a cake, I picture certain people, places, occasions, relatives, families, celebrations and cities; just like a picture book.

Unfortunately I don't have actual photos of most of the people in my past. A camera just wasn't around or available most of the time. But I have the cake recipe and the pictures they stir up in my mind and in my heart.

Serving Up Memoriable Moments

ANGEL FOOD CAKE

This cake may be extra work but it really is worth it to make a cake everyone remembers and loves. Angel food cake became popular in the U.S. following the invention of the hand-crank egg-beater in the 19th century. It may have been called angel cake because of its white color and airy lightness: said to be the "food of the angels"—even though it takes "a devil amount of time" to make it.

1 ½ cups egg whites (10-12 large eggs)	1 ½ tablespoons cream of tartar
	2 teaspoons real vanilla
1 ½ cups sifted powdered sugar	1 cup sugar
1 cup sifted flour	

In extra large mixing bowl, allow egg whites to stand at room temperature for 30 minutes. Meanwhile sift powdered sugar and flour together 3 times; set aside. Add cream of tartar and vanilla to egg whites. Beat with electric mixer on medium speed until soft peaks form (tips curl). Gradually add sugar, about 2 tablespoons at a time, beating until stiff peaks form (tips stand straight). Sift about ¼ of sugar flour over beaten egg whites; fold in gently. Repeat folding in remaining flour mixture by fourths. Pour into ungreased 10 inch tube pan. Gently cut through batter with narrow metal spatula or knife to remove large air pockets. Bake on lowest rack in 350° oven for 40-45 minutes or until top springs back when lightly touched. Immediately invert cake (leave in pan), on long neck bottle to cool. Cool thoroughly. Turn cake upright in pan; using narrow metal spatula, loosen sides of cake from pan. Press spatula against pan, draw it around pan in continuous motion, not sawing motions. Remove cake. A glaze over the top will add just a touch of flavor to this special cake.

EASIER ANGEL FOOD CAKE

I know the original recipe can sound difficult to do, so after some searching, I found this really old way to make this wonderful cake—believe me, the bought ones just don't compare to doing this one at home.

1 cup sugar	½ teaspoon salt
1 ⅓ cups flour	⅔ cup scalded milk
½ teaspoon cream of tartar	1 teaspoon vanilla or almond extract
1 tablespoon baking powder	3 egg whites

Sift and mix together sugar, flour, cream of tartar, baking powder and salt four times. Add hot milk slowly to flour mixture beating continuously, then add extract of choice and mix in well. Whip egg whites until they are light. Fold whipped whites into milk and flour batter. When well combined, pour into ungreased tube cake pan. Bake in 300° oven for 45 minutes. Remove from oven, turn upside down on bottle neck to cool When completely cool remove from pan and glaze if desired.

APPLESAUCE CAKE

This is a really moist everyday cake, one day I put an orange icing on it for a special occasion and everyone swore it was a totally different cake.

4 cups flour	1 tablespoon cinnamon
1 ½ teaspoons baking soda	2 cups sugar
4 teaspoons baking powder	1 cup shortening
½ teaspoon salt	2 eggs
1 teaspoon cloves	3 cups applesauce
1 teaspoon allspice	1 cup nuts chopped
1 teaspoon nutmeg	2 cups raisins

Mix together flour, baking soda and powder and salt, set aside. Cream sugar and shortening together; add eggs and mix well. Add spices and applesauce to sugar mixture and mix well. Add flour mixture until blended; fold in nuts and raisins. Put batter in well sprayed or greased Bundt pan or angel food cake pan. Bake in 350° oven for 40-50 minutes. Remove from oven and cool on wire rack for 10 minutes before removing from pan on to wire rack. Cool completely before cutting.

AWESOME WACKY CAKE

This cake is made without milk or eggs and is moist, dark and delicious. A brain-child of the depression era when ingenious cooks developed a cake that could be made without expensive and scarce ingredients.

3 cups flour	2 teaspoons vanilla extract
2 cups sugar	2 tablespoons cider vinegar
½ cup unsweetened cocoa	¾ cup canola oil
2 teaspoons baking soda	2 cups water
1 teaspoon salt	

In large mixing bowl, combine flour, sugar, cocoa, soda and salt. Make three wells in flour mixture. In one put vanilla; in another vinegar, and in third oil. Pour cold water over mixture and stir until moistened. Pour into 13x9 inch baking pan. Bake in 350° oven for 25 to 30 minutes, or until it springs back when touched lightly.

BANANA NUT CAKE

This type of cake was my "requested birthday cake" for several years even when it came from a box or was store bought. It's so easy to make and taste so superior, scratch is a must now.

3 mashed bananas	¼ cup evaporated milk
1 ¼ cups sugar	1 ½ cups flour
½ teaspoon salt	1 teaspoon baking soda
½ cup canola oil	½ cup chopped walnuts
1 egg	1 teaspoon vanilla extract

Mix together in order given. Pour into lightly greased and floured oblong or small loaf pans. Bake in 350° oven for 30 to 35 minutes. This recipe can also be used to make banana nut muffins

CARROT CAKE

Carrot cake or Passion Cake, is a sweet cake with grated carrot mixed into the batter. The carrot softens in the cooking process and the cake usually has a soft, dense texture. The carrots themselves enhance the flavor, texture and appearance of the cake.

1 ¼ cups canola oil	2 teaspoons cinnamon
2 cups sugar	1 teaspoon vanilla extract
4 eggs	3 cups peeled and grated carrots
2 cups flour	1 cup chopped walnuts or pecans
2 teaspoons baking soda	1 cup raisins
2 teaspoons baking powder	1 cup coconut
½ teaspoon salt	

Beat oil and sugar together. Add eggs one at time. In another bowl, blend flour, baking soda, baking powder, salt and cinnamon. Add nuts and raisins to flour mixture, coating them well. Add carrots and coconut to sugar mixture; add flour mixture. Place batter in sprayed 13 x 9 baking pan. Bake in 350º oven for 45 minutes or until wooden pick comes out clean. Frost with icing when cool.

CARROT SPICE CAKE

Deceptively named, carrot cake more closely resembles a quick bread in construction: wet ingredients are mixed together, dry ingredients are mixed together and the wet is then added to the dry. Final consistency is usually denser than a traditional cake and has a coarser crumb. Many carrot cake recipes include optional ingredients, such as nuts, raisins, pineapple or coconut.

2 ½ cups flour	½ teaspoon salt
1 ¼ teaspoons baking powder	3 cups peeled, shredded carrots
1 teaspoon baking soda	1 ½ cups sugar
1 ¼ teaspoons cinnamon	½ cup brown sugar
½ teaspoon nutmeg	4 eggs
⅛ teaspoon cloves	1 ½ cups canola oil
⅛ teaspoon allspice	1 cup chopped walnuts (optional)

Whisk together flour, baking powder, baking soda, cinnamon, nutmeg, cloves, allspice and salt in large bowl; set aside. Beat sugars and eggs until thoroughly combined. With mixer on very low, slowly add oil in steady stream. When oil is all in, increase speed of mixer to high and beat until mixture is light in color. Stir in carrots by hand and fold in dry ingredients until no streaks of flour remain. Pour into sprayed 13x9 inch baking pan. Bake in 350° oven for 35-40 minutes until toothpick inserted in center comes out clean. Rotate pan halfway through baking time. Cool cake completely in pan on wire rack, about 2 hours before frosting with cream cheese frosting. Chopped nuts can be spread over cake after frosted.

CHARMING CINNAMON "SORRY" CAKE

This cake came about because I really messed up a pie I made, so I threw together this cake from left over stuff I had around to say I was sorry for the pie disaster. You can imagine my surprise and panic when this cake got RAVE reviews; people actually called and left messages on my answering machine telling me how much they liked it. Of course, I hadn't written down what I put in it. It took a while, but I finally figured out the ingredients and portions! You'll never have to say sorry for serving this dessert.

2 ½ cups flour	1 3 ½-ounce box instant vanilla
2 ½ teaspoons baking powder	pudding
½ teaspoon salt	**Crumb Mix:**
1 ¾ cups sugar	1 cup brown sugar
1 ½ teaspoons vanilla extract	1 tablespoon cinnamon
3 eggs	½ cup sugar
½ cup canola oil	**Glaze:**
1 cup evaporated milk	1 cup powdered sugar
⅓ cup sour cream	2 tablespoons lemon juice

Blend together flour, baking powder and salt, set aside. Make crumb mix by stirring together cinnamon, brown sugar and sugar; set aside. With electric mixer beat together sugar and oil. Add eggs one at a time and beat well after each. Add milk, sour cream and pudding. Beat for 2 minutes, add vanilla. Put half of batter in sprayed tube pan. Sprinkle evenly ½ of crumb mix over batter. Carefully place rest of batter on top of crumb mix, sprinkle second half of crumb mix over top of cake. Bake in 325° oven for 50-55 minutes. Check frequently after 50 minutes, the center must come out clean when checked, but don't over bake. Let cool 15 minutes in pan, remove from pan and let cool completely before drizzling with glaze: mix powdered sugar and lemon juice.

CHOCOLATE CHERRY CAKE

Anyone who loves chocolate covered cherries will cherish this gooey cake.

1 box devil's food cake mix
1 ½ cups evaporated milk
⅓ cup canola oil
3 eggs
1 teaspoon almond extract
1 bottle pitted dark sweet cherries
    chopped

Glaze:
¼ cup margarine softened
¼ cup unsweetened cocoa
5 tablespoons boiling water
½ teaspoon vanilla extract
2 3/3 cups powdered sugar
1 tablespoon drained cherry liquid

Beat together cake mix, milk, oil, eggs and almond extract. Drain juice from cherries and reserve juice for glaze. Fold in chopped cherries. Pour batter into sprayed Bundt pan. Bake 350° oven for 40-45 minutes. Combine sugar and cocoa, mix in butter. Add boiling water until dissolved. Add extract. Beat in powdered sugar in slowly until smooth. Add cherry liquid to make glaze consistency to drizzle. Spoon over cooled cake and let it run down outside and inside cake.

CHOCOLATE SAUERKRAUT CAKE

This was used as an April Fool's cake in the 1960's. The vinegar in older German and Polish chocolate cake recipes was used to moisten them. The sauerkraut also adds a coconut-like texture, the results always surprises those who have never had a sauerkraut cake.

2 cups flour
¾ cup cocoa powder
1 teaspoon baking powder
1 teaspoon baking soda
¼ teaspoon salt
1 cup water
3 egg, room temperature
1 teaspon vanilla extract
12 tablespoons butter, softened
1 ½ cups sugar

1 ½ cups sauerkraut, rinsed and
    drained
½ cup chopped peacans.
Filling and Frosting:
2 cups semisweet chocolate chips,
    melted
⅔ cup maonnaise
⅔ cup shredded coconut
⅔ cup chopped pecans

Whisk flour, cocoa, baking powder, baking soda and salt in medium bowl. Whisk water, eggs and vanilla in another bowl. With an electric mixer on medium high speed, beat butter and sugar together until fluffy, about 2 minutes. Add flour mixture and water mixture alternating in 2 batches., beat after each addition until combined. Fold in sauerkraut and pecans with rubber spatula. Divide the batter evenly among 3 sprayed 9-inch cake pans. Bake in 350° oven 25-30 minutes, rotating and switching pan positions halfway though baking. Cool cake in pan for 10 minutes, then turn on to racks to cool completely. Frosting: Whisk melted chips and mayonnaise in bowl and reserve 2 cups. To the frosting remaining in bowl, add ⅓ cup coconut and ⅓ cup pecans—this is your filling. Spread half the filling on one cake layer; repeat with second layer and spread top and sides of cake with the reserved frosting. Press remaining coconut and pecans into the sides and top of cake. Cover and refrigerate until ready to serve.

CHOCOLATE DEPOSIT CAKE

1 box non-instant chocolate pudding mix	2 cups semisweet chocolate chips
2 ⅓ cups milk	1 cup chopped nuts (optional)
1 box devil's food cake mix	1 cup flaked coconut (optional)
	1 can candied cherries (optional)

Lightly spray one 9 x 13 inch baking pan. Combine chocolate pudding and milk in a saucepan; cook over medium heat until thick, stirring frequently. Remove pan from heat and add in dry cake mix. Mix together and pour into pan. Evenly spread chocolate chips and any optional toppings, over top of cake. Bake in 350° oven for 40 to 45 minutes. Let cake cool and serve.

CHRISTMAS SPICE CAKE

2 cups cake flour	½ cup cold butter
1 ½ cups sugar	1 ½ cups unsweetened applesauce
1 ½ teaspoons baking soda	2 eggs unbeaten
1 ½ teaspoons salt	1 ½ cups raisins
2 tablespoons unsweetened cocoa	¾ cup mixed candied fruit
½ teaspoon ground cloves	¾ cup chopped nuts—mix walnuts,
½ teaspoon ground cinnamon	pecans and almonds
½ teaspoon ground nutmeg	½ cup flavored or plain rum
½ teaspoon ground allspice	

In large mixing bowl, combine flour, sugar, baking soda, salt, cocoa and spices. Cut cold butter into cubes and drop into dry ingredients; add applesauce. Beat with electric mixer until blended. Add eggs and beat until smooth and creamy. Gently stir in raisins, fruit and nuts. Pour batter evenly between two large sprayed loaf pans. Bake in 350° oven for 1 hour and 30 minutes. The cakes will look pretty brown. Using toothpick won't work to check doneness. Place loaf pans in cooling racks. When completely cooled, glaze each loaf with ¼ cup of rum. Cover both tightly with foil and refrigerate for 1 to 2 weeks before serving.

COCONUT CAKE

This was a favorite birthday choice and continues to be one of my family favorites for a special occasion. I like mine refrigerated before serving. Just cover it and place in refrigerator. It will keep longer this way as well. Coconut has such a distinct flavor. There is a lot of confusion about the difference between coconut water, milk and cream. Coconut water is the liquid that comes straight out of a cracked, green, coconut. Coconut milk is a thick liquid made from grated coconut meat. Coconut cream is almost solid cream obtained by standing coconut milk overnight and letting the cream rise to the top

1 cup butter	⅔ cup sour cream
2 cups sugar	½ cup flaked coconut
4 eggs	**Frosting:**
3 cups flour	1 ½ cups sugar
1 tablespoon baking powder	1 tablespoon corn syrup
⅓ teaspoon salt	⅛ teaspoon salt
1 cup coconut milk	⅓ cup water
1 teaspoon coconut extract	2 egg whites
Filling:	1 ½ teaspoons vanilla extract
½ cup sugar	Flaked coconut

Spray 3 round cake pans. Using electric mixer, cream butter until fluffy. Add sugar and continue to cream well for 6 to 8 minutes. Add eggs, 1 at a time, beating well after each addition. Add flour and milk alternately to creamed mixture, beginning and ending with flour. Add vanilla and continue to beat until just mixed. Divide batter equally among prepared pans. Level batter in each pan by holding pan 3 or 4 inches above counter, then dropping it flat onto counter. Do this several times to release air bubbles and assure you of a more level cake. Bake in 350 oven for 25 to 30 minutes or until done. Cool in pans 5 to 10 minutes. Invert cakes onto cooling racks. Cool completely before filling and frosting. While cake is baking, prepare filling. Stir together sugar, sour cream and coconut in bowl until well blended. Invert first layer onto cake plate. Spread ½ of filling mixture on cake layer. Top with second layer spread rest of filling mixture over cake, Top with last layer. Frosting: Place sugar, corn syrup, salt, water, and egg whites in the top of a double boiler. Beat with handheld electric mixer for 1 minute. Place pan over boiling water, being sure boiling water does not touch bottom of top pan. (If this happens, it could cause your frosting to become grainy). Beat constantly on high speed with electric mixer for 7 minutes. Beat in vanilla. Frost top and sides of cake. Sprinkle top and sides of cakes with additional coconut.

COKE CAKE

The famous soda cake. The acidity of soda equals that of lemons or vinegar and helps to stabilize baked goods. It also seems to help use its flavorings to make this a really different kind of chocolate cake and smooth chocolate frosting. Soda pop is now an ingredient in dozens of recipes.

2 cups sugar	2 eggs
2 cups flour	1 teaspoon vanilla extract
1 ½ cups miniature marshmallows	Frosting:
½ cup butter	½ cup butter
½ cup vegetable oil	3 tablespoons unsweetened cocoa
3 tablespoons unsweetened cocoa	6 tablespoons cola soda pop
1 cup cola soda pop	1 box powdered sugar
1 teaspoon baking soda	1 teaspoon vanilla extract
½ cup buttermilk	1 cup chopped pecans

Combine butter, cocoa and cola in a saucepan. Bring to a boil and pour over powdered sugar, blending well. Add vanilla extract and pecans. Spread over hot cake. When cool, cut into squares and serve. In bowl, sift together sugar and flour; add marshmallows. In saucepan, mix butter, oil, cocoa and cola. Bring to boil and pour over dry ingredients; blend well. Dissolve baking soda in buttermilk just before adding to batter along with eggs and vanilla extract, mixing well. Pour into well sprayed 9x13-inch pan and bake in 350° oven for 35 to 45 minutes. Remove from oven and frost immediately.

CRUMB CAKE

This bakery cake was a special treat we would get when I was young and from scratch version taste just like I remembered it.

1 ½ cups flour
1 tablespoon baking powder
1 cup sugar
½ teaspoon salt
1 tablespoon shortening
1 egg well beaten
1 teaspoon vanilla extract

½ cup evaporated milk
Crumb Topping:
3 sticks butter
3 cups flour
1 ½ cups sugar
Pinch salt

Sift together dry ingredients. Stir in shortening; add egg, vanilla and milk. Put into sprayed 13x9 inch pan; set aside. CRUMBS: Mix dry ingredients. Add butter, mix well with hands. Sprinkle crumbs onto top of cake. Bake in 350° oven for 30 minutes or until done. When cake is cooled, sprinkle confectioners' sugar (using sifter) onto top of cake.

CUPCAKES—BETTER THAN A MIX

3 cups cake flour
1 teaspoon baking powder
½ teaspoon baking soda
1 teaspoon salt
1 ⅓ cups sugar

1 ¼ cups buttermilk
2 teaspoons vanilla extract
4 eggs room temperature
¾ cup melted butter cooled.

Whisk flour, baking powder, baking soda and salt in bowl until combined. Whisk eggs and vanilla in large bowl until blended. Whisking constantly slowly add sugar into eggs. Gradually whisk in melted butter; add buttermilk. Add ⅓ of dry ingredients using whisk to gently combine; repeat twice with remaining dry ingredients. Gently stir batter with whisk until most lumps are gone. Do not over mix. Fill cupcake liners about ⅔ full, use ice cream scoop to save time and make even cupcakes. Bake in 350° oven for 18-22 minutes or until inserted wood pick comes out clean. Cool in tins for 5 minutes; remove and cool completely before frosting.

DEVIL'S FOOD CAKE

This is a very old recipe: tried and true. No new fancy anything, just an old-fashioned, but easy-to-make devil's food cake recipe. Its chocolately pound cake like texture can be frosted with any Chocolate, Fudge or as many of us prefer Vanilla Buttercream Frosting. A glaze poured over the top will work as well. The aroma of this cake baking will fill your house with an incredible chocolate aroma.

½ cup butter	2 ¼ cups flour
3 ounces unsweetened baking chocolate	1 ½ teaspoons baking soda
	¼ teaspoon salt
2 cups sugar	¼ cup buttermilk
2 eggs	1 teaspoon vanilla extract
1 cup boiling water	

In a small pan melt butter with unsweetened chocolate. Set aside to cool slightly. Cream together sugar and eggs until light in color. Add chocolate mixture to eggs and temper mixture by beating well Add boiled water when it is still warm and blend well. Mixture will be very liquid. Mix together flour, baking soda, and salt. Add mixture to chocolate mixture and blend well. Stir buttermilk into chocolate batter. Pour into sprayed 9 x 13 or 2 round cake pans. Bake in 350° oven for 30 minutes or until toothpick inserted in center comes out clean.

DEVILS POUND CAKE

4 eggs beaten	1 box instant chocolate pudding mix
1 cup sour cream	Glaze:
¾ cup vegetable oil	½ cup semisweet chocolate chips
½ cup sugar	2 tablespoons melted butter
¾ cup evaporated milk	1 tablespoon corn syrup
1 box devil's food cake mix	

Combine eggs, sour cream, oil, sugar, milk, cake mix and pudding mix. Beat with electric mixer on medium speed for 2 minutes and on high for 2 minutes. Pour into sprayed tube or Bundt pan. Bake in 325° oven for 50-60 minutes or until toothpick inserted in center comes out clan, but don't over bake. Cool in pan for 10 minutes, invert onto wire rack and let cool completely. Melt chocolate chips in microwavable boil, carefully, 15 minutes at a time on high and stiring in between. When melted, add butter and corn syrup, mix well. Drizzle glaze over cake, let cool before slicing.

DUMP CAKE

This is the original dump cake recipe; designed for kids to make. The basic recipe is one box cake mix; one can acidic fruit; one can pie filling and 1 & ½ sticks of butter or margarine, sliced. Basically you toss all the ingredients into a greased cake pan. The result is something in between a cake and a cobbler, There are many variations to this dessert now. The idea is the cake is just as easy as "dumping ingredients in a pan." One of my personal favorites is a spice cake mix with apple pie filling & mandarin oranges. Another tasty combo is chocolate cake with cherry filling & crushed pineapples.

1 21-ounce can cherry pie filling   ½ cup chopped walnuts

1 15-ounce can crushed pineapple   2 sticks cold butter cut in 12 slices

1 box yellow cake mix

In 9x13 inch baking dish, dump un-drained pineapple and spread out evenly. Using spoon, dump globs of cherry pie filling evenly on top of pineapple. Sprinkle dry cake mix evenly over cherries and pineapple. Place butter slices evenly over cake mix, don't overlap butter. Sprinkle nuts on top; place in 350° oven and bake for 1 hour. Use heavy mitts to remove from oven, pan will be very hot. Serve with spoon

EASY, GREAT FRUITCAKE REALLY!

2 ½ cups flour   1 cup coarsely chopped pecans

1 teaspoon baking soda   1 teaspoon cinnamon

2 eggs slightly beaten   ¼ teaspoon cloves

1 29-ounce can mincemeat   ¼ teaspoon nutmeg

1 14-ounce can sweetened   ¼ teaspoon allspice
    condensed milk

2 cups mixed candied fruit

In medium bowl, combine flour, baking soda and spices; set aside. In large bowl, stir together eggs, mincemeat, milk, fruit and nuts. Stir in dry ingredients until moistened. Fill 4 sprayed foil loaf pans. Fill each pan to ⅔ full; place on baking sheet. Bake in 300° oven for 35-40 minutes or until wooden pick inserted near center comes out clean. Cool pans on wire racks for 15 minutes. Remove from pans and cool completely. Wrap in plastic wrap and in foil.

EGGLESS CHOCOLATE CAKE

1 ½ cups cake flour
1 cup sugar
3 tablespoons unsweetened cocoa
¾ teaspoon baking powder
¾ teaspoon baking soda
½ teaspoon salt
1 cup water

⅓ cup vegetable oil
1 tablespoon white vinegar
1 teaspoon vanilla extract
Frosting:
½ cup unsweetened cocoa
1 14-ounce can sweetened
    condensed milk
2 tablespoons butter

Sift flour, sugar, cocoa, baking powder, baking soda and salt together. Make well in center and add water, oil, vinegar and vanilla. Beat until smooth and pour batter into sprayed 8 x 8 inch square pan. Bake in 350° oven for 30 minutes. Combine cocoa powder, milk and butter in double boiler and cook until thick. Spread mixture over top of slightly cooled cake. Cool completely before serving.

FARMERS RHUBARB LEMON CAKE

5 cups rhubarb
2 tablespoons tapioca
2 cups sugar

1 box yellow (lemon) cake mix
1 3-ounce box strawberry gelatin

Slice rhubarb into thin slices. Mix tapioca, sugar and gelatin. Mix in rhubarb and cover well. Place rhubarb mixture evenly in bottom of sprayed 13 x 9 inch baking dish. Mix cake together according directions on package. Pour batter over top of rhubarb. Bake in 350° oven for 40-50 minutes.

FUDGE CAKE

1 box devil's food cake mix	2 cups sugar
3 eggs	6 tablespoons unsweetened cocoa
½ cup vegetable oil	1 cup whipping cream
1 cup evaporated milk	½ teaspoon instant coffee
¼ cup butter	2 ½ teaspoons vanilla extract

Beat with electric mixer cake mix, eggs, oil and milk for 4 minutes. Pour batter into sprayed 13 x 9 inch baking pan. Bake in 350° oven for 30 minutes or until cake center comes out clean using a wooden pick. Remove from oven and while hot, poke holes over entire cake with fork. In saucepan, combine butter, sugar, cocoa, cream and instant coffee. Stir over medium heat until full boil starts. Cook at full bowl for 2 minutes. Stir in vanilla. Pour while hot over warm cake.

FUDGE CHOCOLATE LAYER CAKE

If you want an absolutely rich, luscious indulgence, this is it.

¾ cup butter	2 eggs
2 ounces unsweetened baking	Filling:
chocolate	5 tablespoons unsweetened cocoa
2 cups sugar	1 cup powdered sugar
2 ¼ cups flour	Frosting:
¼ cup unsweetened cocoa	¾ cup whipping cream
2 teaspoons baking soda	1 ½ cups semisweet chocolate chips
1 teaspoon salt	
1 ¾ cups buttermilk	

Place butter and baking chocolate in microwavable bowl and microwave 1-2 minutes until melted. In large bowl, combine flour, sugar, cocoa, baking soda and salt. Add melted chocolate mixture, buttermilk and eggs. Beat on low speed 1 minute. Increase speed to high and beat until light and fluffy, about 4 minutes. Pour ½ batter into sprayed tube pan. Mix cocoa and powdered sugar together and spread over batter in pan. Carefully pour remainder of cake batter on top of filling. Bake in 350° oven for 40-45 minutes. Cool in pan 5 minutes; invert onto wire rack. Cool before frosting. Place whipping cream in saucepan and over medium heat, bring just to boil; remove from heat and stir in chocolate chips; mix until frosting is smooth and starts to thicken. Frost cooled cake.

FUN CRUMB CAKE

2 cups flour
2 cups brown sugar
½ cup butter
1 well beaten egg
½ cup additional flour

2 teaspoons baking powder
1 ½ teaspoons cinnamon
¾ cup milk
Powdered sugar

In mixing bowl, combine sifted flour, brown sugar and butter until crumbly. Set aside ½ cup of crumb mixture for topping. To crumb mixture in mixing bowl add beaten egg, additional flour, baking powder, cinnamon, and milk. Blend well with electric mixer on low speed. Spread batter evenly in sprayed 8-inch square pan. Sprinkle reserved crumbs over batter and bake in 350° oven for 35 to 40 minutes, or until wooden pick inserted in center comes out clean. Cool and dust with powdered sugar before cutting.

FUZZY NAVEL CUPCAKES

2 sticks butter softened
2 cups sugar
4 eggs
2 tablespoons vegetable oil
2 ¾ cups flour
2 ½ teaspoons baking powder
½ teaspoon baking soda
1 teaspoon salt
¾ cup evaporated milk
¼ cup orange juice concentrate

½ teaspoon orange extract
2 tablespoons grated orange peel
Frosting:
1 stick butter softened
2 ½-3 cups powdered sugar
¼ cup peach schnapps
1 drop yellow food coloring
Dash salt
½ cup large, multicolored sugar
   crystals
24 orange wedge candies

Using electric mixer, beat butter and sugar until creamy. Gradually beat in the eggs and oil. Scrape bowl and mix well again. In medium bowl, whisk together flour, baking powder, baking soda and salt. In large measuring cup, stir together milk, orange juice and orange extract. On low speed, mix in ⅓ of wet mixture to butter mixture; add ⅓ of flour mixture. Repeat; ending with flour mixture. Mix in orange peel. Line 2 cupcake pans with liners; spray entire pan with non stick spray. Fill each cup ¾ full with batter. Bake in 350° oven about 25 minutes or until cupcakes spring back when gently touched. With electric mixer, beat butter until creamy. Beat in 1 cup of powdered sugar. Beat in peach schnapps, food coloring and salt until smooth and creamy. Beat in remaining powdered sugar, little at a time until soft enough to spread. Spread frosting on cupcakes. Place sugar crystals in bowl. Lay each frosted cupcake on its side in bowl and gently rotate to form a rim of sugar. Top each cupcake with an orange wedge.

GALLERY COFFEE CAKE

1 cup butter softened	⅓ cup evaporated milk
¾ cup firmly packed brown sugar	Topping:
½ cup sugar	1 cup flour
2 eggs	1 cup packed brown sugar
1 ½ teaspoons vanilla extract	½ cup butter softened
2 cups flour	1 ½ teaspoons cinnamon
1 teaspoon baking powder	½ cup chopped pecans or walnuts
¼ teaspoon salt	(optional)

In large bowl, cream together butter and sugars with mixer until smooth and fluffy. Add eggs and vanilla, mix well. In separate bowl combine flour, baking powder and salt. Add dry mix to moist in small amounts, mixing well; add milk and mix well. Spoon batter into sprayed 13x9 inch baking pan. Combine flour, sugar, butter and cinnamon until consistency of moist sand. Add nuts. Sprinkle crumb topping over batter completely covering batter. Bake in 325° oven for 50 minutes or until edges just begin to turn light brown. Cool before cutting. A simple Glaze: 1 cup powdered sugar, dash vanilla extract and enough milk to make a thin consistency and use fork to drizzle over cake before serving.

GERMAN CHOCOLATE CAKE

This cake is now a regular item in bakeries across the country and a box mix on grocery shelves. It was a family favorite and requested for many birthday parties in my house. Buttermilk chocolate cakes had been popular in the south (where pecans are plentiful), for over 70 years, when this cake recipe appeared in the 1950's. German chocolate is similar to a milk chocolate and sweeter than regular baking chocolate. Store bought versions are frosted with chocolate icing on the sides.

4 ounces chopped fine semi-sweet baking chocolate	1 cup sugar
¼ cup Dutch-processed sifted unsweetened cocoa	⅔ cup brown sugar
	¾ teaspoon salt
½ cup boiling water	4 eggs room temperature
2 cups flour	1 teaspoon vanilla extract
¾ teaspoon baking soda	¾ cup sour cream room temperature
1 ½ sticks softened butter	Frost with traditional Coconut Pecan Frosting

Combine chocolate and cocoa in small bowl; pour boiling water in bowl and let stand to melt chocolate, about 2 minutes. Whisk until smooth, set aside to cool. Sift together flour and baking soda, set aside. With electric mixer, beat butter, sugar and salt until light and fluffy. On medium speed, add one egg at a time, beating after each addition. Beat in vanilla. On low speed, add chocolate; increase speed and beat until smooth. On low speed, add dry ingredients alternating with sour cream. Begin and end with dry ingredients, beat after each addition only enough to barely combine. By hand make sure batter is all mixed and divide between 2 sprayed 9 inch round pans. Bake in 350° oven for about 30 minutes, or until wood pick comes out clean. Cool completely before adding Coconut Pecan frosting. Place ½ on top of first cake; place second cake on top and spread frosting on top only of cake. Leave the sides unfrosted for the traditional look.

A diary is where you keep tract of the moments in your life. My cookbook is my diary

GLOW LEMON POUND CAKE

Lemon has such a refreshing, light taste. It just reminds people of spring and things waking up from the long winter.

½ cup softened butter	3 cups cake flour
3 cups sugar	1 cup milk
5 eggs	2 teaspoons lemon extract

In large bowl, using electric mixer, combine butter and sugar until creamy. Add eggs, 1 at a time, beating well after each addition. Add flour and milk, alternately beginning with flour. Stir in lemon extract. Spoon batter into sprayed Bundt pan. Place pan in COLD oven. Turn oven on to 325°. Bake cake for 1 hour, increase oven temperature to 350° and bake 30 minutes more. DO NOT open oven door entire time cake is baking. Remove cake from oven. Cool cake in pan for 10 minutes and turn out on to wire rack to cool.

GRANNY'S NUT CAKE

Granny used one bowl and never measured any of the ingredients, but the cake was always great. This was eventually iced with milk chocolate icing and requested by grandpa for any occasion. It took a lot of experimenting to finally find the right combination and decide to just use shortening like she did instead of the butter or margarine we use for yellow cakes these days.

2 cups flour	1 cup milk
1 ½ cups sugar	1 teaspoon vanilla extract
1 tablespoon baking powder	2 eggs unbeaten
1 teaspoon salt	1 cup coarsely chopped walnuts
½ cup shortening	

Combine in large bowl, flour, sugar, baking powder and salt; mix well. Add shortening, ¾ cup milk and vanilla; beat 2 minutes at high speed with electric mixer. Add ¼ cup milk and eggs; beat 2 minutes longer. Stir in walnuts. Pour batter into sprayed 13x9 inch pan or 2 sprayed cake pans. Bake for 25 minutes, or until cake tests done. Cake will bounce back when lightly touched with finger. Cool cake 5 to 10 minutes in pan on wire racks, then remove cake from pans and cool completely.

LEMON COCONUT CAKE

Nothing says Spring more than lemon and coconut.

1 cup butter softened	2 cups sour cream
2 cups sugar	1 cup boiling water
2 teaspoons lemon extract	1 3-ounce box instant lemon gelatin
2 tablespoons lemon juice	Frosting:
4 eggs	3 tablespoons butter softened
3 cups flour	3 cups powdered sugar
2 teaspoons baking powder	2 teaspoons coconut extract
1 teaspoon baking soda	2-4 tablespoons milk
1 teaspoon salt	1 cup shredded coconut

In large bowl, cream butter and sugar until fluffy. Blend in lemon extract and juice. Add eggs, one at a time, beating well after each addition. Combine flour, baking powder, baking soda and salt in separate bowl. Add flour mixture alternating with sour cream, beating after each addition just enough to keep batter smooth. Place in sprayed tube pan, bake in 350° oven for 70 minutes or until cake test done. Remove from oven, cool for 10 minutes, remove from pan to cool completely. Place cake on aluminum foil. Fold foil edges up around cake. Poke holes in top of cake with handle of wooden spoon. Dissolve lemon gelatin in boiling water; when dissolved, slowly pour over top of cake. Let cake set for 15 minutes. Frosting: Beat butter until fluffy; add in coconut extract and 2 tablespoons of milk; gradually add powdered sugar. Add more milk if needed, but mixture should be stiff. Place icing in microwave and heat for 20 seconds. Stir well and slowly pour over top of cake, let it run down the sides. Sprinkle coconut on top of cake. Let stand until glaze is set, before serving.

LOW-FAT APPLE CAKE

1 cup flour	4 apples chopped
1 cup sugar	Egg substitute to equal 2 eggs
2 teaspoons baking powder	2 teaspoons vanilla extract
1 teaspoon cinnamon	½ cup chopped walnuts (optional)
¼ teaspoon salt	½ cup raisins (optional)

Combine flour, sugar, baking powder, cinnamon and salt. Add apples: stir lightly to coat. If you are using raisin and/or nuts add now. Combine egg substitute and vanilla; add to apple mixture and stir until just moistened. Spoon mixture into sprayed slow cooker. Cover with lid. Cook on high 2 ½ to 3 hours. Serve warm with whipped topping or ice cream on top. Sprinkle cinnamon on top. You can save raisins and walnuts and place either or both on top before serving.

LOW-FAT CHOCOLATE CUPCAKES

1 cup sugar	⅓ cup shortening
⅓ cup unsweetened applesauce	2 tablespoons powdered sugar
¼ cup egg substitute	¼ teaspoon salt
1 teaspoon vanilla extract	1 teaspoon hot water
1 ¼ cups cake flour	¼ teaspoon vanilla extract
½ cup unsweetened cocoa	Frosting:
1 teaspoon baking soda	1 cup sugar
½ teaspoon salt	⅓ cup unsweetened cocoa
½ cup buttermilk	¼ teaspoon salt
½ cup evaporated milk	⅓ cup very hot water
Filling:	1 teaspoon vanilla extract
2 cups marshmallow crème	1 ½ cups powdered sugar

Beat together sugar, applesauce, egg and vanilla for one minute in bowl. In separate bowl combine flour, cocoa, baking soda and salt using whisk until all cocoa lumps are broken up. Add dry ingredients to wet ingredients, mix together. Add both milks, beat until smooth. Spoon batter into sprayed 12 cup muffin tin. Bake in 350° oven for 20-24 minutes. Turn cupcakes onto cooling racks. As cupcakes cool, prepare filling. Combine salt with water; microwave for 10-20 seconds, stir until salt is dissolved. Beat marshmallow with shortening using mixer, until smooth and fluffy. Add sugar, salt water and vanilla; beat well. When cakes are cool, use toothpick to poke hole in each cupcake. Swirl toothpick inside to make room for filling. Fill each cake with about 2 teaspoons of filling. Frosting: Combine sugar, cocoa and salt in deep microwave bowl. Add hot water and vanilla, stirring until ingredients are well mixed. Cover bowl loosely with plastic wrap. Microwave at half-power for 2 minutes. Stir carefully to dissolve sugar. Tightly replace wrap; microwave on full-power for 30 seconds at a time for 2 minutes; don't let it boil over. Mixture will be bubbly, remove mixture from microwave and poke holes in wrap so steam will escape.

Let mixture stand for 15 minutes. Carefully uncover bowl. Stir in powdered sugar ½ cup at time until thoroughly mixed. Use about 2 teaspoons to frost each cupcake.

LOYAL RUM POUND CAKE

Even people who don't drink rum really love this cake and request it for parties.

2 sticks butter

2 cups sugar

2 cups flour

1 tablespoon lemon juice

1 teaspoon vanilla extract

5 eggs

12 ounces candied cherries

12 ounces candied pineapple chunks

2 tablespoons candied orange peels

1 pound pecans and walnuts mix

Chop nuts and mix together. Chop cherries, pineapple and orange peels. Cream together butter and sugar; beat until fluffy. Stir in flour just until moist. Stir in lemon juice and vanilla; add one egg at a time, beating well after each addition. Stir in fruit and nuts. Pour batter into sprayed tube or Bundt pan. Bake in 350° oven for 60-70 minutes, until center comes out clean. Cool in pan for 10 minutes before removing to wire rack to cool before slicing.

LUCIOUS YOGURT COFFEE CAKE

This recipe taught me to never even think about throwing away what I saw as a failed cake. I was trying to find a way to use some vanilla yogurt a guest had purchased but not eaten before going home. I used the vanilla yogurt and left out the vanilla extract. It worked and everyone loved the gooey middle.

1 cup butter

2 cups sugar

2 eggs

½ cup vanilla yogurt

½ cup sour cream

2 cups cake flour

1 teaspoon baking powder

¼ teaspoon salt

¼ cup sugar

1 cup chopped pecans

1 teaspoon cinnamon

Mix sugar, pecans and cinnamon and set aside. Cream butter and sugar with an electric mixer. Add eggs one at a time and blend. Add yogurt and sour cream.

Blend until smooth. Sift together flour, baking powder and salt; gradually add to batter. Pour half batter into sprayed tube pan and sprinkle with half topping mix. Pour in rest of batter. Sprinkle rest of topping mix over batter. Bake in 350° oven for 50 minutes, remove from oven; don't turn off oven—let cake cool and set for 15 minutes, return it to hot oven and bake another 15 minutes.

MARDI GRAS CAKE

The tradition is really a rich, sweet, yeast bread not a cake. The decoration is traditional Mardi Gras colors: green, representing faith, gold symbolizing power, and purple denoting justice. Some more modern versions have fancier fillings not in the original. This is a very old and basic recipe, traditional in all its glory, just like I was served in Mississippi on Fat Tuesday, many years ago.

1 cup milk	1 cup brown sugar
¼ cup butter	1 tablespoon cinnamon
2 ½ teaspoons yeast	⅔ cup chopped pecans
⅔ cup warm water	½ cup flour
½ cup sugar	½ cup raisins
2 eggs	½ cup melted butter
1 ½ teaspoons salt	1 cup powdered sugar
½ teaspoon nutmeg	1-2 tablespoons water
5 ½ cups flour	Food coloring or use colored sprinkles
Filling:	

Scald milk, remove from heat and stir in butter. Allow mixture to cool to room temperature. In large bowl, dissolve yeast in warm water with 1 tablespoon of white sugar. Let stand until creamy, about 10 minutes. When yeast mixture is bubbling, add cooled milk mixture. Whisk in eggs. Stir in remaining white sugar, salt and nutmeg. Beat flour into milk/egg mixture 1 cup at a time. When dough has pulled together, turn it out onto lightly floured surface and knead until smooth and elastic, about 8 to 10 minutes. Lightly oil large bowl, place dough in bowl and turn to coat with oil. Cover with damp cloth or plastic wrap and let rise in warm place until doubled in volume, about 2 hours. When risen, punch down and divide dough in half. Spray 2 cookie sheets or line with parchment paper. Filling: Combine brown sugar, cinnamon, pecans, flour and raisins. Pour melted butter over cinnamon mixture and mix until crumbly. Roll dough halves out into large rectangles (approximately 10x16 inches). Sprinkle filling evenly over dough and roll up each half tightly like jelly roll, beginning at wide side. Bring ends of each roll together to form 2 oval shaped rings. Place each ring on prepared cookie sheet. With scissors make cuts ⅓ of way through rings at 1 inch intervals. let rise in warm spot until doubled in size, about 45 minutes. Bake in 375° oven for 30 minutes. Make frosting ahead of time with powdered sugar blended with 1 to 2 tablespoons of water. Divide frosting in 3 bowls, color one bowl green, one gold and one purple. Frost cake while warm using 3 colors.

MIAMI FLORIDA CAKE

1 box yellow (lemon) cake mix	1 ½ cups toasted coconut
3 eggs	¼ cup orange juice
⅓ cup canola oil	1 cup sour cream
1 cup evaporated milk	2 cups coconut
1 3-ounce box instant orange gelatin	16 ounces frozen whipped topping
¼ cup water	Bottle maraschino cherries drained
2 cups sugar	

Mix cake mix with eggs, oil and milk. Beat slowly to moisten beat with electric mixer at medium speed for about 3 minutes until smooth. Reserve ¾ of batter: pour remainder in well sprayed Bundt pan. Stir gelatin powder and water into reserved batter. Drop by spoonfuls over top of lemon batter. Using a knife, swirl orange batter into lemon batter to create marble effect. Bake in 350° oven for 30-35 minutes, until wooden pick inserted comes out clean. When cool, split into 3 layers using serrated knife or dental floss. Mix sugar, toasted coconut, orange juice and sour cream together with electric mixer. Divide in half and spread between 2 layers; cover cake with whipped topping and sprinkle coconut on top and sides. Place cherries on top of cake in whatever pattern you like. Refrigerate for 24 hours before cutting.

NEW YEARS HONEY CAKE

It's a traditional dessert for Jewish holidays; the hope is that it will usher in a sweet new year.

4 tablespoons vegetable oil	3 cups flour
4 eggs	2 teaspoons baking powder
1 cup very strong coffee	1 teaspoon baking soda
1 cup honey	2 tablespoons cinnamon
1 cup sugar	1 ½ cups floured dried apricot

Whisk together coffee, oil and honey. Whisk in eggs and sugar. Combine in mixing bowl flour, baking powder, baking soda and cinnamon. Beat in wet mixture into dry ingredients. After lightly coating apricots with flour, stir into batter. It will be thin. Pour batter into large sprayed tube pan. Bake in 325° oven for 1 hour or until toothpick comes out clean.

NUTTY BUTTER LOAVES

½ cup brown sugar	3 eggs
⅓ cup butter softened	⅔ cup evaporated milk
1 cup finely chopped, toasted	½ cup softened butter
walnuts	1 cup powdered sugar
½ cup flour	¼ teaspoon vanilla or almond extract
Cake:	1-2 tablespoons milk
1 box Butter Recipe cake mix	

Spray 2 large loaf pans and set aside. Combine brown sugar, and butter in large bowl. Beat at medium speed with mixer until light and fluffy. Stir in nuts and flour. Blend well; divide and press evenly into prepared pan. Combine cake mix, milk, butter and eggs in mixing bowl. Beat with mixer on medium spread for 4 minutes. Pour into pans. Bake in 350° oven for 45-50 minutes, until wooden pick comes out clean. Cool pans for 10 minutes; invert onto cooling racks with crust side up. Cool completely before frosting with glaze. Mix powdered sugar, extract and milk to form glaze.

PECAN COFFEE CAKE

2 cups flour	½ cup buttermilk
½ cup sugar	¼ cup chopped pecans
2 teaspoons baking powder	Topping: ½ cup brown sugar
¾ teaspoon salt	2 teaspoons cinnamon
½ teaspoon baking soda	2 tablespoons melted butter
⅓ cup shortening	½ cup chopped pecans
1 beaten egg	

Sift together flour, sugar, baking powder, salt, and soda. Cut in shortening until mixture resembles coarse meal. Combine egg and buttermilk; stir into the flour mixture. Fold in chopped pecans. Spread into a sprayed 8-inch round or square cake pan. Sprinkle with topping and bake in 350° oven for 30 minutes. Combine topping ingredients; sprinkle over coffee cake batter just before baking.

PERFECT POUND CAKE

*A traditional American pound cake would contain one pound each of flour, butter, eggs, and sugar—which is where the name came from and would sometimes feel just as heavy to carry. This cake is a popular staple at picnics, barbecues, family gatherings and potlucks. American pound cakes are lighter but often contain an abundance of butter to provide a rich taste. **Do not preheat oven on this recipe!***

2 sticks butter room temp	3 cups cake flour
½ cup shortening	¼ teaspoon salt
3 cups sugar	1 teaspoon baking powder
5 eggs	1 teaspoon vanilla extract
1 cup evaporated milk	1 teaspoon lemon extract

Do Not Preheat Oven for this recipe. Cream butter, shortening and sugar until light and fluffy. Add eggs one at a time, beating well after each addition. Sift dry ingredients together. Add vanilla and lemon extract to milk. Add dry ingredients to sugar and egg mixture, alternating with liquid, beating just enough to blend, until all ingredients are combined. Beat batter on medium speed for 5 minutes. Place in sprayed tube pan and place into COLD oven. Bake until a cake tester inserted in the middle comes out clean, about 70-80 minutes. Cool for 20 minutes before removing from pan. Exchange vanilla extract with Peppermint, Mint, Banana, or Coconut Extract to give it a hint of a different flavor

PINEAPPLE UPSIDE DOWN CAKE

So where did people get the idea of putting fruit at the bottom of a cake pan? Well this technique has been around since the Middle Ages. Traditionally made with apples, cherries and other seasonal fruit upside down cakes were often made in cast-iron skillets on top of the stove. The use of pineapple and an oven was due to twentieth century technologies and need for convenience. It didn't take long for the recipes to work their way into the American homes and to be served as a "company dessert", one I've had in many states.

½ cup margarine	⅔ cup butter
⅔ cup brown sugar	1 ¾ cups sugar
2 tablespoons water	2 eggs
1 20-ounce can pineapple tidbits	1 ½ teaspoons vanilla extract
2 ½ cups flour	1 ½ cups pineapple juice and milk
½ teaspoon salt	1 jar maraschino cherries drained
2 ½ teaspoons baking powder	

Melt margarine in 13 x 9 baking pan. Add brown sugar and water and mix well, spreading evenly over bottom of pan. Drain pineapple from can and reserve juice. Spread pineapple evenly on bottom of pan, set aside. Blend flour, salt and baking powder together in bowl and set aside. Cream together butter, sugar; add eggs and vanilla. Measure reserved pineapple juice; add enough milk to equal 1 ½ cups liquid. Add flour mixture alternating with milk mixture. Beat with mixer for 3-4 minutes until light and fluffy. Spoon batter on top of pineapple in pan. Bake in 350° oven for 30-35 minutes. Cool in pan on wire rack for 5 minutes, loosen sides with knife and invert on to plate. Place cherries on top.

ST. LOUIS GOOEY BUTTER CAKE

This was a dessert we drooled over in the bakery. When a recipe for this got into my hands in the 1970's, I was finally able to make it more often and share it with those who had never had this "heaven in a pan" cake. People request this more often than my cinnamon desserts. Nothing compares to it.

1 box cake mix Yellow or White	1 8-ounce package cream cheese
1 egg	2 eggs
1 stick (8 Tablespoons) margarine	1 stick (8 Tablespoons) butter melted
melted	1 teaspoon vanilla extract
Filling	3 ¾ cups powdered sugar

Mix together cake mix, egg and margarine. Press dough evenly into bottom of 13x9 inch baking pan. Smooth out top and set pan aside. Beat room temperature cream cheese until fluffy. Add eggs, vanilla and melted butter and mix well. Beat for 1 minute. Slowly add powdered sugar while beating on low. Pour filling onto crust and spread out evenly. Bake in 350° oven for 45-50 minutes or until well browned but center still jiggles when you shake pan. Remove from oven and cool on wire rack for 30 minutes. Sprinkle top with additional powdered sugar; when completely cool, cut into squares.

SEVEN-UP CAKE

Although this cake first came about in 1929, it became named the 7UP cake in1936. 7UP cakes became very popular in the 1950's but used cake mixes. This one from scratch is worth the extra effort. You can use any lemon lime soda including Mountain Dew and get the same great taste.

3 cups flour	½ cup shortening
½ teaspoon salt	3 cups sugar
¾ cup 7UP	**Glaze:**
5 eggs at room temperature	1 cup powdered sugar
2 teaspoons grated lemon zest	4 teaspoons lemon juice
1 teaspoon vanilla extract	1 teaspoon water
2 sticks butter softened	

Whisk flour and salt in bowl. Whisk 7UP, eggs, lemon zest and vanilla in a large bowl. With an electric mixer on medium, beat butter, shortening and sugar together until fluffy, about 2 minutes. Reduce speed to low and add flour mixtur3e and 7UP mixture alternately in two batches, beating after each addition until combined. Scrape batter into sprayed large tube or Bundt pan. Bake in 325° oven for about 1 hour or until toothpick inserted in center come out clean. Cool cake in pan for 10 minutes, then turn out onto a rack to cool completely for at least 1 hour. Whisk powdered sugar, lemon juice and water in small bowl and drizzle over cooled cake.

STRAWBERRY RHUBARB CAKE

This is excellent with an orange glaze on top: orange juice mixed in with enough powdered sugar to form thin glaze, glaze after cooled.

5 cups rhubarb—½ inch chunks	1 teaspoon vanilla extract
2 cups strawberries sliced	1 ¼ cups flour
1 ⅓ cups sugar divided	1 teaspoon baking powder
⅓ cup butter softened	½ teaspoon baking soda
1 egg	⅛ teaspoon salt
2 teaspoons grated orange peel	¾ cup buttermilk

Place rhubarb and strawberries into bowl. Stir in ⅔ cup of sugar until fruit is coated. Pour into sprayed 9-inch square baking pan and spread out to cover bottom. In medium bowl, beat remaining sugar with butter until light and fluffy, about 3 minutes. Mix in egg, orange peel and vanilla. Combine flour, baking powder, baking soda and salt; stir into batter, alternating with buttermilk. Pour batter over fruit in dish. Bake in 350° oven until a toothpick inserted into center comes out clean, about 55 minutes.

TENNESSEE STACK CAKE

This Appalachian specialty is known by various names, including apple stack cake, pioneer stack cake, and washday stack cake. Be sure to let the cake set at least 24 hours: the moisture from the filling transforms the texture of the cookie-like layers into a tender apple-flavored cake

3 6-ounce packages dried apples
1 cup brown sugar
1 1/2 teaspoons ground cinnamon
1/2 teaspoon ground cloves
1/2 teaspoon allspice

6 cups flour
1 tablespoon baking powder
1 teaspoon baking soda
1/4 teaspoon salt
1 cup shortening
1 cup butter
2 cups sugar
2 eggs
1/2 cup buttermilk
1 teaspoon vanilla extract

1 cup whipping cream or powdered sugar

Place apples in saucepan; add water to cover. Bring to boil; cover, reduce heat, and simmer 30 minutes or until tender. Drain; mash apples. Stir in brown sugar, cinnamon, cloves, and allspice. Set aside. In medium bowl, whisk together flour, baking powder, baking soda and salt; set aside. In large mixing bowl, beat shortening, butter and sugar together on medium with electric mixer until light and fluffy. Add eggs and mix well. Add buttermilk and vanilla extract; mix well. Add milk and molasses; mix well. Stir in flour mixture, mixing until mixture forms stiff dough. Divide dough into 8 equal portions; cover and chill for 1 hour. Pat each portion of dough into 8-inch circle on well-greased baking sheets (if you don't have enough baking sheets to do all 8 at one time, be sure to cool pans before using again). Bake in 350° oven for 10 minutes or until golden. Carefully remove layers to wire racks and let cool completely. Stack layers, spreading even amounts of reserved apple mixture between layers. Cover with plastic wrap and chill for 24 hours. Whip cream until stiff peaks form and spread whipped cream over top of cake before serving or dust with powdered sugar over top.

SALADS

The first salad my brother Paul ate was on a camping trip our family took to Colorado. It was just torn up iceberg lettuce with oil and vinegar mixed in it. There's something about food around a campfire that makes it special. That was over 30 years ago and to this day, that's all a salad is to him and all it needs to be.

A Sage once said:
It takes four people to make a Salad.

Salads have come a long way through the years and salad recipes have evolved into much more than just lettuce with dressing for most people. Salads can be cool or cold, warm or hot, and served as a side dish or the main meal. Different salads have uniquely different flavors and textures along with a wide array of ingredients. The ingredients you choose depends a lot on what you have available locally in your area. With all the traveling, I found that just about anything could be called a salad or mixed into one. Dressings are the same way. Lots of different kinds, types and flavors and dependant on individual taste buds.

It's natural to think of a salad as a healthy lunch or dinner alternative to any other entree. But if you aren't careful about your selections and what you pour over it, you can end up eating more fats, calories, preservatives and carbohydrates in a salad than in a huge fast food cheesy, multi-leveled sandwich.

One of the ways I watch all of those excesses by making my own dressings. I can control the amounts and type of ingredients and make them fresh so they don't have the undesirable sugars, salts and chemicals. The new flavored vinegars and vinaigrettes are easy to make at home and a delicious,

Meals Made From Pieces

221

easy way to keep salads crisp, wholesome and diverse. Croutons made from stale bread also have fewer calories from fats and salts than what is added to the store bought versions.

Salads are fabulous to have for guest, especially an unknown number being expected. I set out a huge bowl of several lettuces and bowls of toppings that each person can add to their own salad. You don't have to buy a lot of expensive things to make a magnificent salad "buffet". Some grated cheeses, chopped or diced meats or poultry, sunflower seeds and different types of beans add the protein to the meal. Sometimes I have the guest bring the "add-in" ingredients to set out and their favorite dressing. It's a fun way to find out what people like and good conversation starters when you chat about salad preferences. You can feed a crowd for very little expense and I make the homemade croutons and rolls to serve a good size meal. This is the ideal feast to have during summer months and on game nights. I set out a plate of cookies or brownies for dessert or snack and no one ever goes away hungry. In fact they indulged in the desserts because they haven't eaten a heavy meal.

I like to have salads during the week so I can add leftover meats and poultry cut up over the top. Salad potlucks where the whole meal, including dessert, is some type of salad are unique an everyone bringing something makes the job easier for me. Not only does this provide more diversity to the meal and adds new foods to my repertoire; it's another chance to share recipes and stories about people's lives.

A BETTER TACO SALAD

Taco salad recipes have become more popular as tortillas have become a regular in our homes. Readily available, they are made with either flour or corn meal. This healthy taco salad recipe is an easy, quick and healthy alternative to expensive fast food choices.

1 pound lean ground beef
1 chopped onion
1 chopped green bell pepper
1 cup tomato sauce
1 tablespoon vinegar
1 teaspoon dry mustard
½ teaspoon crushed red pepper flakes

½ teaspoon dried basil
1 tablespoon water
1 package flour tortillas or corn
4 cups shredded lettuce
1 pint halved cherry tomatoes
1 can drained and rinsed kidney beans
1 shredded carrot
¼ cup grated Parmesan cheese

Cook beef, onion, and ¼ cup of green pepper till beef is brown; drain. Add next 7 ingredients. Bring to boil; reduce heat. Simmer 15 minutes. Warm foil-wrapped tortillas in 350° oven for 10 minutes. Spray 4 10-ounce casseroles with nonstick spray coating; press 1 tortilla into each. Bake in 350° oven for 15 minute, Place a tortilla on each plate. Spoon beef mixture into tortillas. Divide lettuce among 4 plates. Top with remaining green pepper, tomatoes, beans, carrot and cheese.

BLT SALAD

Who needs the bread when you can eat your bacon, tomato and mayonnaise like this!

½ head iceberg lettuce
½ head red leaf lettuce
4 sliced tomatoes
1 cup sliced red onions
1 ½ cups cooked crisp, crumbled
    bacon
½ cup chopped toasted cashew nuts
Creamy Bacon Dressing:
4 tablespoons mayonnaise

½ cup canola oil
1 tablespoon balsamic vinegar
1 tablespoon lemon juice
2 tablespoons minced shallots
½ teaspoon hot sauce
¼ cup finely chopped crispy bacon
1 ½ tablespoons chopped basil
Salt and black pepper

Creamy Bacon Dressing: First prepare dressing by combining all ingredients in a bowl and whisk until smooth. Assemble salad by tossing iceberg lettuce with tomatoes, onion, bacon, half the cashews, and the dressing. Sprinkle remaining cashews over top of salad and serve.

BEANS BEAN SALAD

*Robert Burton wrote **"The Anatomy of Melancholy"** in 1621 and listed 64 remedies for gas produced from eating beans. Some of them must have worked because they remain one of the largest crops grown and nutritious foods eaten around the world to this day.*

2 cans green beans drained
1 can yellow wax beans drained
1 can kidney beans drained and
    rinsed
1 can garbanzo beans drained and
    rinsed
1 can black beans drained and
    rinsed
1 chopped green bell pepper
1 large onion chopped
½ teaspoon celery seeds
1 cup chopped celery

Dressing:
½ cup apple cider vinegar
¼ cup canola oil
½ teaspoon black pepper
¼ teaspoon salt
1 teaspoon sugar
2 teaspoons honey
1 clove minced garlic

Combine all of the beans, green pepper, celery seed, celery and onion in a very large bowl. Dressing: Combine vinegar, pepper, sugar, garlic and salt in a blender, when mixed well. Add honey—if you decide you like your salad sweeter, add more honey. Put blender on low and slowly drizzle in oil until well blended. Pour over bean mixture. Cover and refrigerate overnight, stirring several times.

BROCCOLI-CAULIFLOWER SALAD

This salad became a favorite after I had it with garden fresh cauliflower and broccoli in North Carolina.

1 head cauliflower	½ teaspoon celery seeds
2 large stalk broccoli	Dressing:
1 small onion diced	1 cup mayonnaise
1 cup raisins (optional)	1 tablespoon apple cider vinegar
6 slices cooked and crumbled bacon	1 tablespoon sugar or artificial
1 cup sliced mushrooms	sweetener

Divide cauliflower and broccoli into bite sized flowerets; some tender stalks of the broccoli can also be used. Combine mayonnaise, sugar and vinegar. Add the dressing and onions, raisins, bacon, celery seeds and mushrooms to the broccoli and cauliflower. Refrigerate sealed tightly day ahead of being served.

CAESAR SALAD

Up until the 1920s and 1930s salads were more commonly served as side dishes composed of greens with a simple dressing of salt and vinegar and oil. Caesar and Cobb salads were the first commonly served, and widely known, as main course salads, both in restaurants and entertaining at home.

1 head Romaine lettuce	1 egg
¾ cup olive oil	2 teaspoons lemon juice
3 tablespoons red wine vinegar	Black pepper
1 teaspoon Worcestershire sauce	¼ cup grated Parmesan cheese
½ teaspoon salt	1 ½ cups garlic croutons
¼ tablespoon dry mustard	2 ounces can anchovy fillets
2 teaspoons minced garlic	

Clean lettuce and wrap in paper towels to absorb moisture. Refrigerate until crisp, at least 1 hour or more. In a bowl combine oil, vinegar, Worcestershire sauce, salt, mustard, garlic and lemon juice. Whisk until well blended. Coddle egg by heating 3 cups of water to boiling. Drop in egg (still in shell) and let stand for 1 minute. Remove egg from water and let cool. Once cooled crack open and whisk egg into dressing. Whisk until thoroughly blended. Mash desired amount of anchovies and whisk them into the dressing. To assemble, place torn lettuce leaves in a large bowl. Pour dressing over the top and toss lightly. Add grated cheese, croutons and freshly ground pepper, toss. Serve immediately

CAFE SALAD WITH GRAPES

Some newer combinations I first tasted in California with fresh grapes, this makes a great summer meal.

4 cups cooked chicken breasts	1 tablespoon Dijon style mustard
1 cup red seedless grapes cut in half	⅓ cup tarragon vinegar
½ cup toasted slivered almonds	⅔ cup olive oil
1 teaspoon minced onions	Salt and black pepper

Dice chicken, toss with grapes and almonds in large bowl. In separate bowl, combine onions, mustard, tarragon vinegar, oil, salt and pepper; whisk vigorously. Add to chicken mixture and toss well. It will keep in fridge for up to three days.

CARROT RAISIN SALAD

Nutritious, crunchy, healthy and delicious is this carrot raisin salad with pineapple chunks in a mouthful—way to get your necessary veggies and fruit for the day since I first tasted the flavors in Southern California in the "Carrot Capitol of the World."

2 tablespoons raisins	2 tablespoons pineapple juice
1 tablespoon cider vinegar	unsweetened
1 cup shredded carrots	Dash ground cinnamon
½ cup pineapple chunks drained	Dash ground nutmeg

Combine raisins and vinegar in a medium bowl; let stand 15 minutes. Add carrot and pineapple tidbits; stir well. Combine pineapple juice, cinnamon, and nutmeg; pour over carrot mixture, and toss well.

CHEF SALAD

Chef salads consist of hard-cooked eggs, strips of ham, roast beef, turkey, and/or chicken, and cheese, all of which are placed upon a bed of tossed salad greens. The dressing traditionally is Thousand Island, but today it's served with a dressing of choice. The Chef Salad has a fairly tarnished image in the dining community. While some high-end restaurants still feature Chef Salad, its inclusion on fast food menus has caused it to be made with less choice meats and lettuces. Made right it's a great entree and meal.

1 peeled, chopped cucumber
1 head red leaf lettuce
1 head Romaine lettuce
1 head iceberg lettuce
½ cup sliced radishes
1 cup thinly sliced celery
1 cup shredded carrots
1 pint halved cherry tomatoes
3 sliced hard boiled eggs
8 ounces ¼ inch slices ham
8 ounces ¼ inch slices deli turkeys

8 ounces shredded sharp cheddar
   cheese
8 ounces shredded Swiss cheese
¼ cup cooked crumbled bacon
4 cups garlic croutons
Dressing: 6 tablespoons olive oil
3 tablespoons red wine vinegar
2 teaspoons minced onions
1 teaspoon minced garlic
½ teaspoon dried thyme
¼ teaspoon salt
⅛ teaspoon black pepper

Whisk dressing ingredients together in small bowl. Tear lettuces into bite size pieces. Toss lettuce, cucumber, radishes, celery, carrots and tomatoes in large bowl. Arrange eggs, ham, turkey, bacon and cheeses on top, sprinkle with croutons. Serve with dressing.

CHICKEN LAYERED SALAD

3 cups shredded lettuce
2 cups shredded spinach
½ cup sliced radishes
2 cups cooked cubed chicken
½ cup chopped celery
1 cup shredded sharp cheddar
   cheese

⅔ cup mayonnaise
½ teaspoon Worcestershire sauce
¼ teaspoon dry mustard
2 tablespoons sliced green onions

In salad bowl, layer ingredients in following order; half of the lettuce and spinach, then radishes, chicken, celery, top with remaining lettuce, spinach and finally top with cheese. Combine mayonnaise, Worcestershire sauce and dry mustard. Spread evenly over top of salad. Cover and chill several hours or overnight. Garnish with sliced green onions. Toss just before serving.

COBB SALAD

This Cobb salad recipe is true to its historical roots. Cobb salad was named after its creator, Bob Cobb who owned the famous restaurant "The Brown Derby" in Hollywood California. Along with the Caesar Salad it was used as the main meal.

½ cup iceberg lettuce
½ bunch watercress
1 bunch endive
½ head Romaine lettuce
2 tablespoons minced chives
2 diced tomatoes

1 whole boneless skinless chicken
     breast cooked, diced
8 slices cooked diced bacon
1 peeled and diced avocado
1 hard boiled egg diced
½ cup Roquefort cheese crumbled
French salad dressing

Chop lettuce, watercress, endive and romaine in very fine pieces. Mix in large wide bowl. Add chives. Arrange tomatoes, chicken, bacon, avocado and eggs in narrow strips or wedges across top of greens. Sprinkle with cheese. Chill. At serving time, shake dressing well. At table, pour ½ cup dressing over salad and toss. Pass remaining dressing at table.

COLESLAW

Around since 1794 this salad made of raw cabbage and sometimes carrots, has many variations, which include things like red cabbage, pineapple and apple. It's mixed with a dressing based either on vinegar or mayonnaise; various seasoning may be added. The dressing is allowed to settle on the blended ingredients usually for several hours.

8 cups very finely chopped cabbage	¼ cup milk
¼ cup finely shredded carrots	½ cup mayonnaise
2 tablespoons minced onions	¼ cup buttermilk
⅓ cup sugar	1 ½ tablespoons white vinegar
½ teaspoon salt	2 ½ tablespoons lemon juice
⅛ teaspoon black pepper	

Combine cabbage, carrots and onion in large bowl. Combine sugar, salt, pepper, milk, mayonnaise, buttermilk, vinegar and lemon juice in blender and beat until smooth. Pour over cabbage mix and stir well. Cover and refrigerate for at least 2 hours before serving.

SUCCATOSH (CORN AND LIMA BEAN) SALAD

My favorite two vegetables put in a salad—perfection!

1 16-ounce bag frozen lima beans	½ cup olive oil
1 16-ounce bag frozen corn	¼ cup cider vinegar
1 cup chopped red onions	1 tablespoon mustard
1 green bell pepper	½ teaspoon salt
1 red bell pepper	½ teaspoon black pepper

In large saucepan, bring 2 cups water to boil, add lima beans and bring back to boil. Reduce heat and cook until tender, about 20 minutes. Watch water and add more if necessary. Don't overcook; they should still be firm. Remove beans from water and set aside in large bowl. Use same water and boil corn and cook until tender, 10 minutes. Drain and set aside to cool. Whisk together olive oil, vinegar and mustard. In bowl, combine all vegetables and toss. Add about half dressing, toss and taste. Add more dressing to taste. Adjust seasoning with salt and pepper.

CRANBERRY SALAD

I like this one after the holidays with leftover turkey meals.

1 3-ounce box raspberry gelatin
1 cup boiling water
½ cup cold water
½ cup orange juice
1 16-ounce can whole cranberry
   sauce

1 diced apple
1 8-ounce can pineapple chunks
1 stalk celery diced
½ cup chopped walnuts
Dash apple pie spice

Mix boiling water into gelatin in an 8-inch baking dish at least 2 minutes until completely dissolved. Mix in cold water and orange juice. Stir in cranberries, apple, pineapple, celery, walnuts and spice into gelatin mixture. Refrigerate overnight.

CRANBERRY SPINACH SALAD

This was a favorite holiday tradition with a family in the Northeast and taste great with poultry.

1 package salad spinach
½ cup dried cranberries
Slices red onion
4 slices cooked crisp crumbled bacon

½ cup honey
½ cup lime juice
2 tablespoons Dijon style mustard

Wash and clean spinach; divide evenly among 4 salad plates. Top each with 2 tablespoons dried cranberries and onion slices. Combine bacon, honey, lime juice and mustard in a small glass mixing bowl using a wire whisk. Heat in the microwave on HIGH for 1 minute or until warm; pour over salad.

CREAMY CUCUMBER SALAD

I grew up with this delicious summer treat when all the cucumbers started ripening in the garden.

3 cucumbers	1 minced shallot
½ teaspoon salt	½ teaspoon celery seeds
2 ½ tablespoons cider vinegar	1 tablespoon chopped chives
1 teaspoon sugar	¼ cup chopped fresh dill
1 cup sour cream	Black pepper

Peel the cucumbers; cut into thin slices and place in a large bowl. Sprinkle cucumber with salt, ½ tablespoon vinegar and ¼ teaspoon sugar. Gently toss. Let stand 30 minutes. Drain, gently pressing out liquid with the back of a spoon. Pat dry with paper towels. Meanwhile, place sour cream in a medium bowl and whisk until light. Whisk in the shallot, remaining 2 tablespoons vinegar, ¾ teaspoon sugar, celery seed, chives and salt to taste. Layer ⅓ of the cucumber slices in bottom of a small serving dish. Spoon ⅓ of sour cream mixture on top; sprinkle with ⅓ of dill. Continue to layer until all ingredients are used up. Sprinkle top with pepper to taste. Chill well.

CUCUMBER ONION SALAD

This was one we also enjoyed during the summer, what a German vinegar dressing treatment.

3 thinly sliced cucumbers	1 cup water
1 sweet onion thinly sliced	½ teaspoon sugar
1 cup white vinegar	Salt and black pepper
¼ cup canola oil	

The cucumbers may be scored or part of the skin can be peeled for better absorption of the juice. Layer cucumbers with onion in large bowl. In a separate bowl, mix remaining ingredients, stirring until sugar has dissolved. Taste and adjust sugar for sweetness, adding more sugar, if needed. Pour over vegetables and toss lightly. Cover and chill for 2-4 hours before serving.

EDAMAME SALAD

Edamame is a preparation of baby soybeans in the pod commonly found in Japan, China and Korea. The pods are boiled in water together with condiments such as salt, and served whole. Outside East Asia, the dish was most often found in Japanese and some Chinese restaurants, but has become popular in the US now as a healthy food choice and snack.

6 thinly sliced radishes

3 cups frozen, shelled edamame
   soybeans

2 cups frozen corn thawed

¼ cup finely chopped onions

1 tablespoon olive oil

1 tablespoon wasabi powder

1 teaspoon minced garlic

¼ cup chopped cilantro

½ cup white wine vinegar

Cook edamame and corn as directed on packages but omit salt from being added to either. Cool both under running cold water; drain well. Toss corn, soybeans, radishes, cilantro and onions together in a large bowl. Whisk together vinegar, oil, wasabi and garlic. Pour over salad mixture and toss. Chill and serve.

FETA CHEESE VEGETABLE SALAD

This salad recipe is perfect for when the garden is in season! fell in love with Greek food in Baltimore and continue to love incorporating the unique flavors in everyday dishes.

½ cup chopped walnuts

1 pint halved cherry tomatoes

1 bunch fresh sliced basil

1 bunch sliced green onions

1 peeled, sliced avocado

1 8-ounce package crumbled feta
   cheese

1 teaspoon chopped sun-dried tomatoes

½ cup pitted and chopped kalamata
   olives

1 diced red bell pepper

1 teaspoon garlic salt

1 tablespoon balsamic vinegar

1 tablespoon olive oil

Place walnuts in a small skillet over medium heat; cook, stirring constantly, until golden brown. In a bowl, gently mix walnuts, tomatoes, basil, onions, avocado, cheese, tomatoes, olives, and pepper. Season with garlic salt, and drizzle with vinegar and olive oil; allow to sit about 15 minutes and toss again just before serving.

FRUITY COLE SLAW

1 head cabbage sliced
2 teaspoons mayonnaise
2 teaspoons lemon juice
2 teaspoons cider vinegar
2 teaspoons honey Dijon style
    mustard

1 red delicious apple peeled and
    diced
1 cup pineapple chunks drained
1 cup raisins

Combine mayonnaise, lemon juice, vinegar and mustard and mix well. Place cabbage, apple, pineapple chunks and raisins in bowl. Pour dressing over cabbage mixture and toss. Chill before serving.

GREEN SPINACH SALAD

Spinach is excellent for cleansing, purifying and restoring balance to our digestive system and has long been linked to prosperity. People are eating more of it today than ever before.

Dressing:
½ cup vinegar
½ cup canola oil
½ cup honey
⅓ cup ketchup
1 teaspoon salt

Salad:
2 packages raw spinach
2 cups sliced water chestnuts
4 hard boiled eggs diced
1 red onion sliced
½ pound bacon fried and crumbled

Combine salad ingredients. Mix dressing ingredients together and pour over salad

GREEK SALAD

True Greek salad is made of sliced or chopped tomatoes with a few slices of cucumber, red onion, feta cheese, and kalamata olives, seasoned with salt, black pepper, oregano, and basil and dressed with olive oil. Common additions include bell peppers, capers, anchovies, and sardines. Lettuce and vinegar are sometimes included and in Detroit they add beets. So find what you like it yours and dive in!

1 red sweet onion chopped	Black olives
1 cucumber sliced	Fresh spinach
2 cups feta cheese crumbled	Dressing:
3 tomatoes cut in wedges	¾ cup olive oil
1 hardboiled egg sliced	⅓ cup red wine vinegar
1 green bell pepper sliced	1 ½ teaspoons crushed oregano
4 radishes sliced	1 teaspoon sea salt
Romaine and iceberg lettuce	¼ teaspoon black pepper

Tear up lettuces and spinach in bowl and mix in remaining ingredients. Pour dressing over salad and serve chilled. Dressing: Whisk together in a bowl olive oil, red wine vinegar, oregano, salt, and pepper, place in a tightly covered jar and shake to combine.

GULF WILTED SPINACH SALAD

Spinach is sold loose, bunches, in prepackaged bags, canned, or frozen. Fresh spinach looses much of its nutritional value with storage of more than a few days.

2 bunches fresh spinach rinsed and dried	½ teaspoon black pepper
	Pinch salt
1 pound bacon cut into ½ inch pieces	Dressing:
	¼ cup sugar
2 cups chopped red onions	¼ cup cider vinegar
5 hardboiled eggs quartered lengthwise	¼ cup white vinegar

Place bacon in large, deep skillet. Cook over medium high heat until evenly brown. Drain it, crumble, and set aside, reserving approximately ½ cup of drippings in skillet. In large bowl, toss together spinach and onions. Heat reserved drippings over low heat. In small bowl, whisk together sugar, white vinegar and cider vinegar. Add to warm grease and whisk for about a minute, until thickened. Season with salt and pepper. Pour at once over spinach, add crumbled bacon and toss to coat. Garnish with chopped egg.

HAUPIA AND TROPICAL FRUIT SALAD

Haupia is a traditional coconut milk-based Hawaiian dessert often found at luaus and local gatherings. Since World War II, it has become popular as a topping for white cake, especially at weddings. Although technically considered a pudding, the consistency of haupia closely approximates gelatin desserts and is usually served in blocks like gelatin.

1 mango	Mint leaves chopped
½ papaya	¾ cup coconut milk
2 kiwi fruits	¾ cup water
½ cup pineapple juice	⅔ cup cornstarch
½ cup honey	⅔ cup sugar
2 tablespoons lemon juice	2 teaspoons vanilla extract

Peel and cut fruit into 1-inch cubes and place in large mixing bowl. In separate bowl, mix pineapple juice, honey, lemon juice and mint. Refrigerate until you are ready to serve. In medium saucepan, combine coconut milk, water and place over medium heat. Add tablespoon or two of water to cornstarch, stir to make paste; add mixture to coconut milk, stirring constantly. Add sugar and vanilla to mixture and continue to cook over medium heat until thickened. When mixture coats back of a spoon, reduce heat to simmer and continue to cook for another 20 minutes, stirring often to avoid any lumps or scorching. Pour mixture into 8-inch square pan and chill until set, at least 4 hours. When ready to serve, cut haupia into squares. Put square on plate, add tropical fruit salad, and pour pineapple juice mixture on top.

LAYERED SALAD

During the 1970's and 1980's you couldn't go to a potluck without one of these on the table. Everyone had their favorite ingredients in it and little changes in the dressing. I still love it and it does travel well.

1 head iceberg lettuce torn into pieces	1 cup sliced water chestnuts
½ pound fresh spinach torn in to pieces	1 pound crumbled cooked bacon
1 cup diced celery	2 cups salad dressing
½ cup chopped onions	1 cup sour cream
2 cups frozen green peas do not cook	2 tablespoons sugar
	2 cups grated Cheddar cheese

Do not toss. Layer ingredients in a 9 x 13 inch dish: Layer above ingredients in order given: lettuce, spinach, celery, onions, thawed peas, chestnuts and bacon. Combine salad dressing, sour cream and sugar and whisk together until smooth. Cover top of ingredients completely. Cover tightly and refrigerate overnight. Top with grated cheese before serving.

OKTOBERFEST GERMAN COLE SLAW

I will never forget the taste of this salad at the annual festival in the German community in Missouri. It complimented beautifully the bratwurst, roast poultry, beer, pumpernickel bread and wiener schnitzel.

2 heads shredded cabbage	2 cups white vinegar
4 stalks chopped celery	1 cup water
4 shredded carrots	1 teaspoon celery seeds
2 chopped green bell peppers	1 teaspoon mustard seeds
2 cups sugar	Salt and black pepper

Place cabbage and celery in a large bowl; whisk together other ingredients until well-blended. Mix together other ingredients, except salt, in a medium saucepan and bring to a boil. Pour mixture over vegetables and mix well. Add salt to taste. Cover and refrigerate for at least three hours.

If the preparation of a recipe is done with love, the meal
can be shared without reservation no matter how
the food turns out.

ORANGE PINEAPPLE SALAD

This is a great salad for spring and summer, refreshing and colorful.

1 3-ounce box sugar free instant orange gelatin	¼ cup orange juice
1 ½ cups boiling water	1 tablespoon lemon juice
1 3-ounce package cream cheese	½ cup crushed pineapple drained

Dissolve gelatin in water; gradually add to softened cream cheese, blending
until smooth. Add orange juice and lemon juice mixing well. Chill until slightly
thickened. Blend in pineapple. Pour into mold and chill until firm. Unmold on
lettuce on serving plate.

PEA SALAD

*In early times, peas were grown mostly for their dry seeds. By the 1600s
and 1700s it had become popular to eat peas "green", that is, while they are
immature and right after they are picked. The popularity of green peas spread
to North America and Thomas Jefferson grew peas on his estate. With the
invention of canning and freezing of foods, green peas became available
year-round, and not just in the spring.*

1 16-ounce bag frozen green peas thawed	2 tablespoons cooked crumbled bacon
1 8-ounce can water chestnuts chopped	2 tablespoons thousand island dressing
1 finely chopped onion	½ cup mayonnaise
2 hardboiled eggs chopped	Salt and black pepper
2 teaspoons diced pimiento	

Combine salad dressing, mayonnaise, salt and pepper in small bowl. Mix all ingredients in a large bowl, pour dressing over ingredient, toss, cover and chill.

SHIRAZI SALAD

This is a traditional dish that all Persians have had in their lifetime. It's an easy recipe that is great for the end of summer when cucumbers, tomatoes and onions are abundant and fresh-simple and delicious.

2 large tomatoes, diced

2 medium cucumbers, peeled and
    diced

1 large onion, diced

1 tablespoon lemon juice

½ teaspoon salt

In a medium serving dish, toss the
    tomatoes, cucumbers

SQUASH SALAD

If starting with raw pine nuts, toast them first. Heat a small skillet on medium high heat. Add the pine nuts. Stir gently as the nuts start to brown. When slightly browned, remove from heat and cool.

2 zucchini thinly sliced

2 yellow summer squash thinly sliced

3 tablespoons olive oil

1 tablespoon lemon juice

¼ teaspoon sea salt

Black pepper

¼ cup pine nuts roasted

1 cup grated Parmesan cheese

Place squash in bowl. Combine oil and lemon juice in small bowl and whisk together. Whisk in salt and pepper and pour dressing over squash. Add pine nuts and toss all together, gently, but thoroughly. Let mixture stand for at least 10 minutes to soften squash and develop the flavors. Transfer salad to serving dish or to four individual salad plates. Garnish with cheese

SWEET AND SOUR PASTA SALAD

What a surprise this salad is, very fresh with just the right blend of sweet and sour.

1 package tricolor spiral pasta	Dressing:
1 sweet onion chopped	1 cup sugar
1 chopped tomato	⅓ cup vinegar
1 peeled and chopped cucumber	1 tablespoon dry mustard
1 chopped green bell pepper	1 teaspoon salt
2 tablespoons chopped fresh parsley	1 teaspoon garlic powder
½ teaspoon black pepper	

Cook pasta according to directions to al dente. Drain and rinse with cold water, set aside. Dressing: Whisk together dressing ingredients in a saucepan. Over medium heat, cook for 10 minutes and sugar is dissolved. Pour over salad and toss to coat. Cover and refrigerate for 2 hours before serving.

TOMATO BASIL PASTA SALAD

Snap peas, also known as sugarsnap peas are edible round pods that differ from snow peas with flat pods. Snap peas are nutritious and filling, yet not as high in total carbohydrates and fats as normal peas.

5 cups bow tie pasta	¼ teaspoon black pepper
½ cup olive oil	2 cups chopped basil
¼ cup balsamic vinegar	3 chopped tomatoes
2 teaspoons Dijon style mustard	½ cup toasted pine nuts
1 teaspoon salt	1 cup shredded mozzarella cheese

Cook pasta according to package directions to al dente. Drain and cool. In a small mixing bowl, whisk together oil, balsamic vinegar, Dijon-style mustard, salt and pepper. In a large mixing bowl, combine pasta, basil and tomatoes. Pour vinaigrette over top and toss together. Cover and chill at least 1 hour. Add pine nuts and cheese just before serving, tossing again to combine.

TOMATO CAJUN CHICKEN SALAD

I'm not able to eat many of the new hot spiced Cajun seasoned dishes this one is a perfect balance.

1 ½ tablespoons lemon juice	½ cup plain yogurt
6 teaspoons minced garlic	3 cups cubed, cooked chicken
½ teaspoon dried thyme	1 cup thinly sliced green onions
¼ teaspoon salt	½ cup diced green bell peppers
¼ teaspoon black pepper	½ cup diced celery
⅛ teaspoon cayenne pepper	3 cups diced tomatoes

Combine lemon juice and next five ingredients. Beat in yogurt. Gently fold chicken and next 3 ingredients into dressing. Chill. Just before serving, fold in tomatoes.

TOMATO SNAP PEAS SALAD

Snap peas, also known as sugarsnap peas are edible round pods that differ from snow peas with flat pods. Snap peas are nutritious and filling, yet not as high in total carbohydrates and fats as normal peas.

1 tablespoon olive oil	1 teaspoon sugar
½ pound snap peas ends snapped off	1 tablespoon minced garlic
2 cups grape or cherry tomatoes cut in half	1 tablespoon lemon juice
	Salt and black pepper

Heat oil in skillet over medium heat until just shimmering. Add peas and cook, stirring until crisps but tender, about 2-3 minutes. Put peas in medium serving bowl. In skillet place tomatoes, sugar and garlic; cook for no more than a minute. Add lemon juice, toss well then add mixture to peas in serving dish. Toss to combine, season with salt and pepper.

TUNA LETTUCE SALAD

During the summer months, nothing hits the spot for a meal like this one.

1 head chopped iceberg lettuce	1 tablespoon Italian seasoning
1 bunch chopped red leaf lettuce	1 tablespoon minced garlic
2 medium tomatoes diced	1 teaspoon each of salt and black
1 cucumber diced	pepper
1 green bell pepper diced	**Dressing:**
1 medium sweet or red onion diced	½ cup apple cider vinegar
⅓ cup bacon bits	¼ cup olive oil
2 teaspoons celery flakes	¼ cup canola oil
2 cans water packed tuna drained	

Mix all vegetables, bacon bits, celery flakes, Italian seasoning, garlic, salt and pepper together in large bowl. Mix in flaked tuna. Combine dressing ingredients together in bottle and shake well. Pour over salad, toss and serve.

TUNA MACARONI SALAD

This is a classic salad and family favorite. Tuna is a popular fish due to its convenience and distinct flavor. It's high in protein, B12, Niacin and omega 3 fatty acids, which helps lower blood pressure and cholesterol, improves brain function and eases arthritis pain.

8 ounces elbow macaroni	¼ cup chopped green onions
1 cup mayonnaise	1 teaspoon salt
½ cup Italian salad dressing	⅛ teaspoon black pepper
1 tablespoon mustard	2 cans water packed tuna drained
2 cups thin sliced cucumbers	and flaked
1 ½ cups diced tomatoes	1 hard boiled egg chopped
½ cup diced green bell peppers	Chopped parsley

Cook macaroni as label directs. Drain; rinse with cold water. In large bowl combine mayonnaise, Italian dressing and mustard; mix well. Add cucumber, tomato, green pepper, green onion, salt, pepper, tuna, and macaroni; toss to mix well. Refrigerate, covered, until well chilled—about 4 hours. Just before serving garnish with hard-cooked egg and parsley.

TUNA SALAD

Some people would never think of using eggs in their tuna salad, but I like it. I also substitute cubed chicken and turkey for the tuna. If you like yours without eggs, don't use them and cut back on the dressing.

3 hard boiled eggs chopped
½ cup diced onions
½ cup diced celery
2 tablespoons mayonnaise or salad
   dressing
2 tablespoons dill pickle relish

1 tablespoon sweet pickle relish
2 teaspoons mustard
2 cups water packed tuna drained
Dash white peppers
1 teaspoon hot sauce (optional)
Lettuce leaves

Combine eggs and dill relishes. Add the rest of the ingredients, except tuna and mix well; add tuna. If the mixture is dry, add some more mayonnaise. Cover and chill for at least an hour. Serve either on the lettuce leaves or roll tuna salad in leaves for a treat; spread on bread and make sandwiches; place on bed of green bell pepper slices or bed of quartered tomato.

WALDORF SALAD

A Waldorf salad consist of apple, celery, walnuts, mayonnaise or a mayonnaise-based dressing and traditionally served on lettuce. Dried fruit is often added usually chopped dates or raisins. Some newer versions include dried cranberries, apricots, pineapple chunks, carrots, almond slices and sunflower seeds. Another dish to "create your own".

4 medium red apples chopped
½ cup chopped celery
1 cup red seedless grapes cut in
   halves
½ cup raisins

1 teaspoon lemon juice
⅓ cup salad dressing or mayonnaise
8 lettuce leaves, washed and dried
¼ cup chopped walnuts

In a large bowl, combine apples, raisins and grapes. Mix together lemon juice and salad dressing and mix in with fruit. Cover and refrigerate 1 hour before serving. Arrange lettuce on individual plates. Spoon apple mixture onto lettuce and sprinkle nuts on top.

Whatever you do, if you keep this one purpose or goal in mind: "Everything Always Done With Love"—it will turn out awesome.

WONDERFUL VINEGAR COLE SLAW

Some of the best and oldest coleslaw recipes are created with a vinegar based dressing.

3 pounds grated cabbage	¾ cup white vinegar
1 diced green bell pepper	1 cup olive oil
1 diced red bell pepper	½ cup sugar
1 diced yellow bell pepper	2 tablespoons cider vinegar
1 diced onion	1 tablespoon salt

Combine all vegetables in large bowl. Mix other ingredients together in saucepan. Heat over medium heat until hot. Pour mixture over vegetables. Mix well and refrigerate for at least three hours. Serve cold.

To measure a substance with the consistency of peanut butter or shortening, first spray the measuring cup with non-stick spray before filling with shortening then use a spatula to pack it into a dry measure. Then, use the spatula to scoop it out again.

EQUALS SEQUALS

1/32 teaspoon =	Smidgen
1/16 teaspoon =	Pinch = 50 drops
⅛ teaspoon =	Dash = 0.5 milliliter
¼ teaspoon =	Tad = 1 milliliter
½ teaspoon =	2 milliliters
1 teaspoon =	5 milliliters = ⅓ tablespoon
1 tablespoon =	3 teaspoons = ½ fluid ounce = 15 milliliters
2 tablespoons =	1 ounce = 30 milliliters = ⅛ cup
1 jigger =	1 ½ ounce = 3 tablespoons
¼ cup =	4 tablespoons = 2 ounces
⅜ cup =	¼ cup plus 2 tablespoons = 3 ounces
⅓ cup =	5 tablespoons Plus 1 teaspoon = 2 ⅔ ounces
½ cup =	8 tablespoon = 120 milliliters = 4 ounces
5/8 cup =	½ cup plus 2 tablespoons = 5 ounces
⅔ cup =	10 tablespoons Plus 2 teaspoons = 160 milliliters
¾ cup =	12 tablespoons = 180 milliliters = 6 ounces
7/8 cup =	¾ cup plus 2 tablespoons = 7 ounces
1 cup =	16 tablespoons = 48 teaspoons = 240 milliliters
½ pint liquid =	1 cup = 8 fluid ounces
1 pint =	2 cups = 16 fluid ounces
1 pint of water =	Weighs 1 pound
1 quart =	4 cups = 32 ounces = 1 liter
½ gallon =	8 cups = 4 pints = 2 quarts
1 gallon =	16 cups = 8 pints = 4 quarts
1 liter =	4 cups plus 3 tablespoons
1 ounce (dry) =	2 tablespoons = 6 teaspoons
1 pound =	16 ounces = 2 fluid cups
8 quarts =	1 peck = 2 gallons
8 gallons =	4 pecks = a bushel
Dollop =	Solid: picks up just a spoonful = liquid dash

Another method for measuring large quantities of margarine, shortening or butter the displacement measurement: Take a large liquid measuring vessel such as a 2 cups measuring glass, fill it with cold water to 1 cup level. Scoop the food you want to measure into the water. Add the amount you until the water rises to the level of 2 cups. Pour off the water and the amount left in the measuring glass is 1 cup for your recipe.

My KITCHEN'S TAPESTRY of TRADITIONS

Here you will find several pieces of information and shortcuts I've collected over the years and use regularly; substitution for an ingredient I would have sworn was in my pantry or refrigerator; hints and actions I've sewn into my cooking techniques; a habit, a helpful clue or two as part of my recipes. Let's say they are the collection of fabric notes, finally put in one place and offered to help make your kitchen experience easier and fun.

Unless specifically instructed not do so, always preheat your oven

---

Sweetened Condensed Milk
6 cups whole milk 4-½ cups sugar
1 stick of butter 1-tablespoon vanilla
Mix together in saucepan; cook over medium heat for 1 hour. Stir occasionally.
Cool. This will give you 4 ½ cups that can Be stored in a refrigerator for several weeks.

BANANAS GETTING OLD?
Leave them unpeeled, place in a Ziploc bag and put them in the freezer. When you want to make some banana bread or muffins, Take what you need out of the freezer, cut he peeling off with a knife—Never throw away another over ripe banana again.

Bread crumbs:
Use crushed corn or wheat flakes, or Dry cereal or Potato flakes

Chili Powder:
3-tablespoon paprika
1 tablespoon ground cumin
2-tablespoon oregano
1-teaspoon cayenne pepper
½ teaspoon garlic powder

Sprayed pans means using the non-stick sprays. I've been spraying baking pans and dishes for 10 years or more, I've never had a problem with anything sticking, but some prefer the old fashioned way. So you can grease the pan with butter, margarine or shortening if you prefer, if it's an item to be baked, you will need to flour the surface after greasing it to keep baked items such as cakes, cupcakes, quick breads and muffins from sticking.

Prefer honey to sugar in baked goods
—For 1 cup of sugar, replace that with 1 cup honey but reduce other liquids in recipe by ¼ cup and reduce baking temperature by 25 degrees.

Let any roast: beef, pork, lamb or poultry to sit a while before carving. This allows juices to retreat into the meat. If you carve too soon, much of the juices will spill over into the carving board and affect the flavor and moistness

Apple Pie Spice:
½ teaspoon cinnamon,
¼ teaspoon nutmeg,
⅛-teaspoon cardamom

For Nuts being used in a baked item such as cakes, muffins, cupcakes: heat them first in oven then keep them from settling to the bottom of baked goods.

For juicier hamburgers, add ½ cup cold water to 1 pound ground beef

		Add an apple to the potato bag to keep potatoes from budding	Allspice: ½ teaspoon cinnamon ½ teaspoon cloves
No honey around: For 1 cup honey, use 1¼ cup sugar and ¼ cup of water	Do not mix salads in metal bowls, use wooden, glass or china	Need mayonnaise For salad or dressing: For 1 cup—use 1 cup pureed cottage cheese Or 1-cup plain yogurt	Corn Meal Mix: 1 cup cornmeal 1 cup flour ½ teaspoon salt 4 teaspoon baking powder
Milk: For 1 cup milk—use ½ cup of evaporated milk and ½ cup water or prepare liquid 1 cup of non fat dry milk and add 2½ teaspoons butter or margarine	When working with bread dough, don't flour your hands, coat them with olive oil to stop sticking	Don't throw away stale bread: cut into cubes and bake for croutons or place in blender and make breadcrumbs. To make Italian bread crumbs: add 1 tablespoon Italian seasoning.	Italian Seasoning: 1-teaspoon oregano 1 teaspoon marjoram 1 teaspoon thyme 1-teaspoon basil 1-teaspoon rosemary 1-teaspoon sage 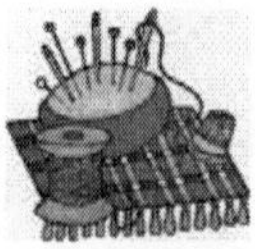
Eggs— Sizes should be large or extra large, I never use anything smaller	When sautéing, always heat pan before putting in the fat. It will reduce sticking	Pumpkin Piece Spice: ½ teaspoon cinnamon, ¼ teaspoon ginger ⅛-teaspoon allspice ⅛-teaspoon nutmeg	No eggs in the house to bake with- Use 2 tablespoons corn oil plus 1 tablespoon water

SUBSTITUTES FOR LIQUEUR IN RECIPES

Amaretto 2 tablespoons—use ½ teaspoon almond flavored extract plus water, milk; white grape juice or apple juice added to the specified amount for liquid	Bourbon or Sherry 2 tablespoons—use 2 teaspoons vanilla extract plus water, milk; white grape juice or apple juice added to the specified amount for liquid	Brandy or Rum 2 tablespoons—use 1 teaspoon brandy or rum extract plus water, milk; white grape juice or apple juice added to the specified amount for liquid	Orange Flavored Liqueur 2 tablespoons—Use 2 tablespoon orange juice concentrate or 2 tablespoons orange juice or ½ teaspoon of orange extract	Coffee or Chocolate Flavored Liqueur 2 tablespoons—use 1 teaspoon chocolate extract plus 1-teaspoon instant coffee in 2 tablespoons water.	Brandy, Port Wine, Rum, Sherry or Fruit Flavored Liqueur ¼ cup—Use equal amount of orange juice or apple juice plus 1 teaspoon of corresponding flavored extract or vanilla extract.
Red Wine—use equal amount of red grape juice or cranberry juice			White Wine—use equal amount white grape juice or apple juice.		
With electric ovens, always keep the door ajar when using the broiler					

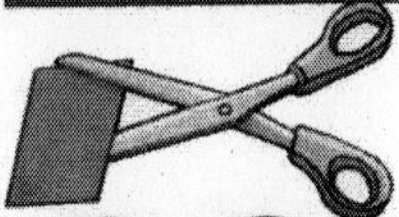

¼ cup butter	½ stick = 4 tablespoons	
½ cup butter	1 stick = 8 tablespoons	
1 cup butter = ½ pound	2 sticks = 16 tablespoons	
2 cups butter = 1 pound	4 sticks = 1 pound	
1 square chocolate	4 tablespoons cocoa plus 1 tablespoon butter	
1 cup grated cheese	4 ounces	
4 cups chopped nuts	1 pound	
⅓ cup uncooked rice	1 pound	
1 cup uncooked rice	3½ cups cooked rice	
2 cups white sugar	1 pound	
2¼ cup brown sugar	1 pound	
3½ cups powdered sugar	1 pound	
1 pound ground meat	2 cups	
1 tablespoon fresh herb	1 teaspoon dried herb	
1 clove garlic	1 teaspoon minced = ¼ teaspoon powder	
1 head garlic	8-15 cloves	
1 teaspoon garlic salt	⅛ teaspoon garlic powder plus 7/8 teaspoon salt	
1 tablespoon crystallized ginger	1 teaspoon ground ginger or 1 tablespoon chopped fresh ginger	1 inch piece ginger
1 whole nutmeg	2 teaspoon chopped nutmeg	
1 tablespoon onion powder	1 medium onion chopped or 4 teaspoons dried onions	¼ cup chopped onion
1 bunch green onions	5 to 8 green onions	1 cup sliced
¼ ounce pack yeast	2¼ teaspoon yeast	2 ounce cake
3 cups yogurt	1 cup yogurt "cheese"	
1 pound zucchini	3 medium zucchinis	1 cup sliced
1 teaspoon baking powder	¼ teaspoon baking soda plus ½ teaspoon cream of tartar	
1 tablespoon cornstarch	2 teaspoons quick cooking tapioca	2 tablespoons flour
1 cup breadcrumbs	¾ cup cracker crumbs	
½ cup brown sugar	½ cup sugar plus 2 tablespoons molasses	
1 cup powdered sugar	1 cup sugar plus 1 teaspoon cornstarch	
1 cup sour milk	1 cup milk plus 1 tablespoon vinegar	Let see for 5 minutes
1 cup buttermilk	1 cup milk plus 1 tablespoon lemon juice	Let see for 5 minutes
1 teaspoon dry mustard	1 tablespoon prepared mustard	
1 cup self-rising flour	1 cup flour, ½ teaspoon salt, 1 teaspoon baking powder	
1 cup heavy cream	⅔ cup milk plus ½ tablespoon butter	
1 cup whipped cream	⅔ cup evaporated milk whipped	

Herbs consist of fresh leaves and stems or crumbled or powdered dried leaves. *Spices* consist of many other parts of the plants—seeds, stems, roots, and berries, which have been dried—and can be whole, ground or powdered.

PIES

Everyone loves Pie. But people don't like to make pies and settle for overpriced store bought ones. The wrong image has circulated that a flaky crust or high-quality filling is hard to accomplish or must take massive amounts of time—neither need be true. Pies are the best way to indulge in all the outstanding fruits, nuts and vegetables bursting full of antioxidants and nutrients. With ways of sweetening them naturally, don't settle for just any store pie; the difference is indescribable and much more economical. Fact is pies are one of the few ways some people eat fruit at all. Practice makes perfect and makes you lots of friends.

 I also learned by watching and listening to others. The most unusual places gave me tips and recommendations on not only the crust but also the ingredients. Find and visit wineries, bakeries, specialty shops, holiday gift booths, state and county fairs, festivals, home shows, cooking contest, farmer's markets,

FIND YOUR PIE

roadside diners—information is abundant in these settings. They have people selling jams, syrups, jellies, preserves and candies made from fresh fruits, vegetables and nuts. These folk have a vast amount of knowledge about using pie filling items; cooking and mixing them. Just reading the simple ingredients of their products will give you an idea of how they sweeten them or flavors they mix together. People love to talk about their specialty products; they handle them for profit; perfecting their wares and their wisdom, what they can tell yocannot be found in a book.

I finally learned how to make the best cherry pie filling from a small café in a little Washington town. She was excited that I knew about other fillings and enjoyed hers the best. Even if they don't give you their specific recipe, compliment the baker or cook, taste and listen closely; the secret is within those words and deep down in our hearts, we all want to share in the goodness of life and what nature provides.

Other places to find data on different fillings: people who grow those fillings. In my travels, I've devoured cherries, apples, oranges, peaches, grapes, strawberries, cranberries, grapefruits, lemons, other berries, all kinds of nuts and more right out of the backyards of ordinary people. First taste it right off the tree or bush to experience the real flavor, then you know what you're trying to create.

Next, ask the owner of the yards, like my rhubarb, they can tell you ways of using that "excess" they sometimes take for granted. Next, look around your area. In that same rhubarb backyard, I had a wall of raspberry bushes that tasted magnificent in so many things, if I picked them before the ducks and birds ate them. Huckleberries are plentiful in some areas just take a talkative group to scare away the bears.

Don't be afraid to mix flavors, especially the too sweet with the too sour and use honey, molasses, raw sugar and brown sugar to add more natural sugars that have their own healthier benefits.

Definitely ask people to taste your experiments. It may not be flawless but I've never found anyone who wouldn't at least try a pie. And no matter

If You Bake It They Will Eat It

how it turned out, they'll look forward to your next effort.

Everyone likes sweet goodies. It's a safe subject to start a conversation over. Now days, so many subjects are off limits, lots of superstition when you ask questions; but not with recipes and food. My collage of information forms a beautiful picture of the generous, giving and fun people I've learned from and who benevolently encouraged me.

APPLE CRANBERRY PIE

The combination of apple and cranberry is really popular and they compliment each other well.

5 cups thinly slice, peeled apples	2 tablespoons butter
2 cups fresh cranberries	1 teaspoon apple pie spice
1 tablespoon lemon juice	1 egg lightly beaten
1 cup sugar	1 tablespoon milk
2 tablespoons cornstarch	1- Pastry for double crust pie

Place bottom pastry in a 9-inch pie plate; top with a thin layer of apples. Combine cranberries and remaining apples in a large bowl; sprinkle with lemon juice. Add sugar, apple pie spice and cornstarch and toss gently. Spoon into pie shell; dot with butter. Top with a lattice crust; seal edges. Combine egg and milk; brush over lattice top and pie edges. Bake in 375° oven for 50 minutes or until filling is bubbly and apples are tender. Sprinkle with additional sugar. Serve warm or at room temperature.

APRICOT PIE

2 eggs beaten	¼ cup butter
2 cups dried apricot	2 tablespoons cream
Water to cover apricots	1 9-inch unbaked refrigerated
¾ cup sugar	piecrust

Wash apricots, then cover with water and simmer for 40 minutes or until tender. Beat apricots until smooth; then allow to cool. In an electric mixer bowl, cream butter and sugar. Separate egg yolks from egg whites; whip egg whites until they form stiff peaks, set aside. Add to butter mixture, beaten egg yolks, cream, and apricots; blend well. Fold in beaten egg whites. Pour into unbaked pastry shell. Bake in 400° oven for 15-25 minutes, until done.

BANANA CHOCOLATE CREAM PIE

3 sliced bananas divided
2 egg yolk beaten
1 graham cracker piecrust
2 cups milk
¾ cup sugar
¼ cup cornstarch

⅓ cup unsweetened cocoa
1 teaspoon vanilla extract
¼ teaspoon salt
1 cup ground up milk chocolate
    chips
½ cup whipped cream

In top of double boiler, mix sugar, cornstarch, ¼ cup of cocoa and salt. Blend in ½ cup of milk and egg yolks; stir until smooth. Stir in remaining milk. Cook cocoa mixture over boiling water, constantly stirring, until thickened about 5-6 minutes. Remove from heat, stir in vanilla and allow to cool slightly. Arrange half of the slices of banana in bottom of piecrust. Spoon half of chocolate mixture over top of bananas. Layer remaining bananas and top with rest of chocolate mixture. Top pie with ground up chips. Place in refrigerator for 15-20 minutes. Beat cream with an electric mixer at high speed until soft peaks form. Top each serving with whipped cream.

BEST GRAPE PIE

When they stopped making my favorite grape pop tarts, I had to find a substitute.

Pastry for two crust pie
1 large jar grape jam
1 cup quick cooking oats
1 cup brown sugar

½ cup flour
½ cup butter
1- Pastry for two crust pie

Spray 9x13 inch baking dish and cover bottom and 1 inch up side of dish with unbaked crust. Spread grape jam over evenly over crust. Combine oats, brown sugar and flour; cut in butter until crumbly. Sprinkle over filling. Bake in 425° oven for 15-25 minutes until golden brown. Cool on a wire rack.

BIRD'S NEST PIE

Bird Nest Pudding was very popular in England so being served the pie in Vermont was a new one for me.

4 peeled, sliced apples	1 egg
2 cups flour	Topping:
1 cup sugar	¼ cup sugar
½ teaspoon baking soda	½ teaspoon cinnamon
½ teaspoon cream of tartar	¼ teaspoon nutmeg
1 cup sour milk	½ cup flaked coconut

Divide apples evenly between two sprayed 9-inch pie plates; set aside. In a mixing bowl, combine flour, sugar, baking soda, cream of tartar, sour milk and egg; mix well. Divide batter and pour over apples. Bake in 350° oven for 25-30 minutes or until pies are lightly browned and test done. Invert onto serving plates (so apples are on the top). Combine all topping ingredients; sprinkle over apples. Serve warm.

CHERRY CHEESE PIE

1 9-inch graham cracker piecrust	½ cup lemon juice
8 ounces cream cheese softened	1 teaspoon vanilla extract
1 14-ounce can sweetened	1 can cherry pie filling
condensed milk	

In medium bowl, beat cream cheese until light and fluffy. Add milk. Blend thoroughly. Stir in lemon juice and vanilla. Pour into crust. Let stand for 2-3 hours in refrigerator. Top with chilled pie filling before serving.

COCONUT CREAM PIE

A cream pie is a type of pie filled with a rich custard or pudding that is made from milk, cream, flour, and eggs. It can come in many forms, including vanilla, lemon, lime, banana, coconut, and chocolate. Making it from scratch, this flavorful pie will surprise your tastebuds if you've only eaten store bought ones.

1 9-inch baked pie shells	1 cup flaked coconut
1 cup sugar	Meringue:
½ cup flour	4 egg whites
¼ teaspoon salt	½ teaspoon cream of tartar
3 cups milk	½ cup sugar
4 egg yolk	½ cup flaked coconut
3 tablespoons butter	1 teaspoon vanilla extract
1 ½ teaspoons vanilla extract	

In a saucepan, combine sugar, flour and salt. Stir in milk. Over medium heat, cook, stirring constantly until thickened and bubbly. Reduce heat to low and cook stirring constantly for 2 more minutes. Remove from heat. Beat egg yolks slightly in separate bowl, take 1 cup of hot mixture and slowly stir into yolks. Pour yolk mixture into saucepan and bring to a gentle boil. Cook and stir for 2 minutes. Remove from heat. Stir in butter and vanilla. Stir in coconut. Pour the mixture in pie shell. Meringue: Beat egg whites with vanilla and cream of tartar until stiff peaks form. Gradually add sugar while continuing to beat. Spread over hot filling, sealing edges of crust. Sprinkle coconut over top. Bake in 350° oven for 12-15 minutes or until meringue is golden. Cool on wire rack. Then cover and refrigerate until completely cooled.

COCONUT PIE

1 cup sugar	1 cup sweetened flaked coconut
4 tablespoons cornstarch	¼ cup butter softened
3 egg yolk	1 teaspoon vanilla extract
2 cups milk	1 9-inch unbaked refrigerated piecrust

Combine sugar and cornstarch in a small bowl. In a large mixing bowl, beat egg yolks until light. Add sugar mixture. Stir in milk, coconut, butter and vanilla;

mix well. Pour in unbaked piecrust and bake in 325° oven for 1 hour or until the center is set.

COLD FAMILY REUNION PIE

No this isn't the review of a bad reunion, this pie is a no bake and refreshing to eat.

1 14-ounce can sweetened condensed milk	1 20-ounce can crush pineapple drained
½ cup lemon juice	1 (11-ounce) can mandarin oranges drained
1 12-ounce container frozen whipped topping thawed	1 21-ounce can cherry pie filling
	2 9-inchs graham cracker piecrust

In medium bowl, combine condensed milk and lemon juice. Fold in whipped topping. In separate bowl, mix together pineapple, oranges and cherry pie filling. Gently fold mixture into condensed milk mixture. Divide mixture evenly and pour into piecrusts. Cover and refrigerate overnight.

COLONIAL CRANBERRY PIE

This no crust pie could've been on the tables of long ago, it was passed down so many generations in the family who gave it to me, they didn't know how far back it went. This one is from the heart of cranberry country.

2 cups chopped cranberries	¾ cup melted butter
½ cup sugar	1 cup sugar
½ cup chopped walnuts	1 cup flour
Topping:	1 teaspoon almond extract
2 eggs	Butter for pie plate

Generously butter 9 inch pie plate. Place cranberries in pie plate; toss sugar and walnuts and sprinkle over berries. Mix together eggs, butter, sugar, flour and almond extract until smooth. Pour topping over cranberry mixture and bake in 350° oven for 40 minutes.

CRANBERRY NUT PIE

In the 1800's people began farming cranberries, at first by picking them by hand. Eventually came a revolutionary idea called wet harvesting where the bog is flooded with water and the cranberries float to the surface and easily scooped up.

2 cups cranberries	½ cup butter melted
½ cup chopped walnuts	2 eggs
½ cup brown sugar	1 teaspoon grated orange rinds
1 cup flour	Vanilla ice cream
1 cup sugar	

Grease a 9-inch pie plate. Spread cranberries and nuts on the plate and sprinkle with brown sugar. In a bowl, with electric mixer, beat flour, sugar, butter, eggs and orange rind until mixture is smooth. Pour mixture over cranberries and nuts. Bake in 325° oven for 1 hour and 15 minutes. Let cool before cutting and serving with ice cream.

CREAMY APPLE PIE

If you like apple pie, try this one, easy and just different enough to be a nice winter dessert.

2 large apples peeled and chopped	1 unbaked pie shell
1 egg	Topping:
¾ cup sugar	⅓ cup flour
½ teaspoon vanilla extract	¼ cup butter
2 tablespoons flour	⅓ cup sugar
⅛ teaspoon salt	1 teaspoon cinnamon
1 cup sour cream	

Mix egg, sugar, vanilla, flour, salt and sour cream together. Add apples and coat them well. Place apple mixture in unbaked shell. Bake in 350° oven for 30 minutes. While baking; make topping: Mix flour, butter, sugar and cinnamon together, Remove from oven and crumble topping and sprinkle over pie. Place back in oven and bake until top begins to brown.

CRUMB TOP APPLE PIE

Among the really good pie apples are Jonathan, Stayman-Winesap, Cox's Orange Pippin, and Jonagold, all of which provide a good mix of sweetness and tartness. Other sweet choices are Braeburn, Fuji, Mutsu, Pink Lady, Suncrisp, Rome Beauty, and Empire. Good tart baking apples include Idared, Macoun, Newton Pippin, and Northern Spy.

1 9-inch deep dish pie crust	1 cup sugar divided
6 cups apples peeled, cored, thinly	¼ cup brown sugar
sliced	¾ cup flour
1 teaspoon cinnamon	6 tablespoons butter
1 teaspoon apple pie spice	

Mix ½ cup sugar and ¾ teaspoon of cinnamon. Take 1 tablespoon of flour and spread evenly over bottom of unbaked crust. Arrange 2 cups of apples in crust, sprinkle ½ apples mixture over apples. Bake in 400° oven for 35 to 40 minutes, or until apples are soft and top is lightly browned.

DOUBLE BERRY PIE

Berries, more than any other food, are associated with a remarkably long list of health benefits. What a wonderful way to eat healthy and enjoy the labor of your berry picking.

¾ cup sugar	1 ½ cups blackberries fresh or
⅓ cup flour	frozen
½ teaspoon cinnamon	1 tablespoon lemon juice
4 cups blueberries fresh or frozen	2 tablespoons butter

Place one crust in a 9-inch pie dish. Mix sugar, flour, and cinnamon in large bowl. Stir in berries to coat. Turn filling into pastry lined pan. Sprinkle with lemon juice, dot with butter. Cover with top crust; cut slits in the top. Seal and flute. Bake in 425° oven for 35 to 45 minutes. Cover edges with foil to prevent burning, and remove foil for last 12 minutes of baking. Cool on wire rack before serving.

FLORIDA KEY LIME PIE

Key West, Florida, is famous for its fabulous key lime pie, one of America's best-loved regional dishes. Every restaurant in the Florida Keys, and especially in the city of Key West, serves this wonderful pie. There seems to be a key lime pie for every palate, with numerous versions made throughout the region since it's considered the official pie of the Florida Keys.

5 egg yolk beaten

1 14-ounce can sweetened condensed milk

½ cup lime juice

1 9-inch graham cracker pie crust

Combine egg yolks, milk and lime juice; mix well. Pour into graham cracker shell. Bake in 375° oven for 15 minutes; allow to cool. Top with whipped topping and lime slices.

FRIED PIES

My mom made the best apricot fried pies. She cooked the apricots all day, the smell filled the house with a sweet aroma of anticipation. We all gathered around the kitchen table that evening when she made the crust and fried those pockets of gooey goodness.

2 cups flour

½ cup shortening

1 teaspoon salt

½ cup cold water

Apple:

3 apples peeled, diced

⅓ cup sugar

½ teaspoon cinnamon

¼ teaspoon apple pie spice

Apricot:

1 bag dried apricot

4 cups water

Berry:

4 cups frozen or fresh strawberries blueberries,

Huckleberries, raspberries or mixed berries

½ cup sugar

Vegetable oil for frying pies

Stir together fruit, sugar and spices in a saucepan cook on low heat. Cook until soft, mash with fork to form until thick preserve like. Sift flour and salt together. Cut in shortening. Add water and mix with fork until forms dough. Roll out dough to about ⅛ inch thick on a floured board. Cut with large cookie cutter (6 inches in diameter). In each round, place 1 heaping tablespoon fruit. Moisten edges with cold water, fold and press edge with fork. Heat oil in large skillet on medium-high heat. Fry pies, few at a time, 2 to 3 minutes on each side; cook until golden brown. Drain on paper towels.

HEATH BAR PIE

Any candy bar can change this pie into a favorite and often requested indulgence. Or you can change the ice cream flavor or even the pudding flavor and create a masterpiece.

1 graham cracker piecrust
⅓ cup caramel ice cream topping
1 ½ cups milk
1 3 ½-ounce package instant vanilla
   pudding mix

1 8-ounce container frozen whipped
   topping thawed
6 bars chocolate-covered toffee
   candy bars chopped

Beat together in bowl milk and pudding mix for 2 minutes, let stand for 5 minutes. Stir in whipped topping and chopped candy bars. Spoon into crust. Freeze for 4 hours or until set. Before serving, let stand for 15 minutes so pie can easily be cut. Store any leftovers in refrigerator.

LEMON MERINGUE PIE

Lemon flavored custards, puddings and pies have been enjoyed since Medieval times. While Renaissance European cooks used whisked egg-whites in several dishes, it was not until the 17th century that they perfected meringue. Lemon meringue pie, as we know it today, is a 19th century product.

1 baked pie shell
5 egg yolk beaten slightly
2 cups water
1 ½ cups sugar
½ cup cornstarch
½ cup lemon juice
2 tablespoons butter

1 tablespoon grated lemon peels
Pinch salt
Meringue:
5 egg whites
½ teaspoon cream of tartar
½ cup sugar

In a suitably sized saucepan, blend cornstarch, sugar and salt; then gradually stir in water. Cook over medium heat, stirring frequently. Bring to boil and boil for 60 seconds. Gently stir half of mixture into egg yolks; then stir yolk mixture into saucepan. Cook over a low heat, constantly stirring for another 2 minutes. Remove from the heat and add butter, lemon juice and grated lemon peel. Allow to cool slightly, then pour into baked pastry shell. Beat egg whites and cream of tartar until they turn foamy. Gradually add half a cup of sugar. Continue to beat until meringue forms hard, glossy peaks. Swirl meringue onto pie filling with a spoon. Bake in 350° oven for 20 minutes.

MAGNOLIA OR BUTTERMILK PIE

This pie is a traditional Southern treat—and very sweet: here are 3 versions to try until you find the sweetness level you like.

1 cup sugar
2 tablespoons flour
½ cup butter melted
3 eggs
1 cup buttermilk
1 teaspoon vanilla extract
¼ teaspoon lemon extract

1 9-inch unbaked refrigerated
    piecrust
For less sweet version:
Use 1 more egg
For even less sweet version:
Also use ½ cup more of buttermilk

Beat eggs slightly and add sugar and flour. Then add melted butter and mix well. Add buttermilk, lemon and vanilla and mix. Dust unbaked pie shell with a little bit of flour. Pour batter into shell, and then sprinkle a little more flour on top. Bake in 325° oven until the custard is set, approximately 1 hour.

Cooking through time.....

MAINE PUMPKIN PIE

The Native Americans brought pumpkins as gifts to the first settlers, and taught them the many used for the pumpkin. This developed into pumpkin pie about 50 years after the first Thanksgiving.

1 15-ounce can pumpkin
1 14-ounce can sweetened
   condensed milk
2 eggs
½ teaspoon cinnamon

1 ½ teaspoons pumpkin pie spice
⅛ teaspoon ground allspice
½ teaspoon salt
1 9-inch unbaked pie shell

Combine pumpkin, milk, eggs, spices and salt. Mix well. Pour into pie shell. Bake in 425° oven for 15 minutes, then reduce oven heat to 350° and continue to bake 35-40 minutes or until knife insert 1-inch from edge comes out clean. Set on wire rack and cool completely before serving.

MAPLE WALNUT PIE

1 9-inch unbaked refrigerated
   piecrust
½ cup brown sugar
2 tablespoons flour
1 ¼ cups maple syrup

3 tablespoons butter
¼ teaspoon salt
3 eggs
1 ½ teaspoons maple extract
1 cup walnuts halves

In a saucepan, mix brown sugar and flour. Add maple syrup, butter and salt. Heat until butter melts, stirring constantly. In a medium bowl, beat eggs with maple flavoring. Stir in sugar mixture. Pour into unbaked pie shell and sprinkle with walnuts. Bake in 375° oven for 40 to 45 minutes, or until filling is set.

NUTTY CARAMEL APPLE PIE

Pastry for double crust pie
4 Granny Smith apples peeled,
   cored, sliced
1 tablespoon lemon juice
¾ cup brown sugar divided

1 tablespoon melted butter
1 tablespoon corn syrup
½ cup chopped pecans
3 tablespoons flour
1 teaspoon cinnamon

On a lightly floured surface, roll out piecrusts, and set aside. In a large bowl, toss apples with lemon juice; set aside. Combine ¼ cup brown sugar, butter and corn syrup; spread in bottom of a 9-inch pie dish (glass or ceramic works best). Sprinkle with chopped pecans. Cover with one piecrust. In a small bowl, mix together ½ cup brown sugar, flour, and cinnamon. Arrange half of apples in pastry lined plate. Sprinkle with half brown sugar mixture. Repeat layers. Cover with remaining piecrust, fold top edge under, and crimp. Cut a few slits in top to vent steam. Bake in 425° oven for 50 to 60 minutes, or until golden brown. Let stand 5 minutes. Loosen edge of pie, and carefully invert pie onto a serving dish. Serve warm.

NUTTY CARROT PIE

1 9-inch unbaked refrigerated
   piecrust
½ cup brown sugar
¼ cup melted butter
1 ½ cups chopped walnuts
4 cups carrots cut in chunks

2 eggs
1 14-ounce can sweetened
   condensed milk
1 teaspoon pumpkin pie spice
¼ teaspoon allspice
Pinch salt

Topping: In a medium bowl combine brown sugar, melted butter, and chopped walnuts.

Mix well and set aside. Carrot Custard: Steam carrots until tender. Drain and cool. Place cooled carrots in a blender or food processor and add eggs, condensed milk, pumpkin pie spice, allspice and salt. Blend until smooth. Pour carrot mixture into pie shell. Sprinkle with walnut topping. Bake in 375° oven for 45 minutes or until toothpick inserted in center comes out clean.

PEANUT BUTTER PIE

When their cotton crops were decimated by boll weevils, Southern farmers took to growing peanuts on the advice of George Washington Carver, in the 1800s.

1 8-ounce package cream cheese softened	**¾ cup frozen whipped topping thawed**
½ cup sugar	**10 peanut butter cups divided**
⅓ cup creamy peanut butter	**1 9-inch chocolate cookie crumb piecrust**

In a small mixing bowl, beat cream cheese, sugar and peanut butter until smooth and light. Fold in whipped topping. Coarsely chop half of peanut butter cups; stir in to cream cheese mixture. Spoon into crust. Quarter remaining peanut butter cups; arrange over top. Refrigerate for at least 4 hours before cutting. Refrigerate leftovers.

PECAN PIE

No recipes dated earlier than 1925 can be found for this pie and well-known cookbooks did not include it before 1940. It's popular to serve at holiday meals and is also considered a specialty of Southern U.S. cuisine.

4 eggs	**2 cups corn syrup**
½ cup butter melted	**1 cup chopped pecans**
1 teaspoon vanilla extract	**1 cup whole pecans**
2 ½ tablespoons flour	**1 9-inch unbaked deep dish pie shells**
1 teaspoon salt	
1 ⅓ cups sugar	

Beat eggs in large bowl, add each ingredient, beat after each addition: butter, vanilla, flour, salt, sugar and syrup. Line unbaked pie shell with whole pecans. Stir in chopped pecans into batter and pour into pie crust. Bake in 350° oven for 40-45 minutes.

PINEAPPLE PIE

I know it sounds strange, but this one is so good and fun to include at tropical theme get-togethers.

1 cup sugar

3 tablespoons flour

½ teaspoon salt

2 egg yolk

¼ cup water

1 8-ounce can crushed pineapple

1 tablespoon butter

3 tablespoons lemon juice

1 tablespoon grated lemon peels

1 9-inch baked pie shells

In a medium bowl, mix together sugar, flour, salt and egg yolks. Bring water and pineapple to a boil in a medium saucepan. Stir in sugar mixture and mix well. Cook over medium heat until thickened; stirring constantly. Remove from heat and stir in butter, lemon juice and lemon zest to saucepan. Then spoon entire mixture into pie shell. Cover and refrigerate pie until ready to be served.

PLUM COBBLER

Plums are now the second most cultivated fruit in the world, second only to apples. They date back in writing to 479 B.C and early American colonists found wild plums growing along the east coast.

14 plums pitted and halved

½ cup brown sugar

½ cup sugar

½ teaspoon cardamom

Pinch salt

2 tablespoons quick cooking tapioca

2 tablespoons lemon juice

1 tablespoon butter

Pastry for one crust pie

Spray well a 9-inch baking dish and fill about three-quarters full with the plums, placed cut side down. In a separate bowl, combine sugars, cardamom, salt and tapioca. Sprinkle over plums and shake the dish slightly so that the sugar will sift down through the fruit. Sprinkle with the lemon juice and dot with butter. Place crust over top of fruit, fold in the sides to cover but keeping crust within the sides of dish. Bake in 375° oven for 20 minutes or until crust is brown and filling bubbly.

RAISIN CREAM PIE

Raisins and dried fruits are simple, wholesome foods, grown by nature and "made" basically the same way for thousands of years—long before artificial, frozen, canned, or processed foods.

2 cups raisins	1 8-ounce package cream cheese
1 cup sugar	softened
½ teaspoon cinnamon	½ cup powdered sugar
¼ teaspoon cloves	4 cups frozen whipped topping
1 cup sour cream	thawed
2 eggs	1 9-inch baked pie shells
1 tablespoon butter	

Combine raisins, sugar, spices, sour cream, eggs, and butter in a saucepan. Bring mixture to a boil, and reduce heat. Cook until thick, stirring constantly. Set aside to cool. With electric mixer, blend cream cheese and powdered sugar together. Fold in 2 cups whipped topping. Spread half of cream cheese mixture on bottom of baked and cooled pie shell. Cover with cooled raisin mixture, and top with remaining cream cheese mixture. Spread additional whipped topping on top of pie. Refrigerate.

REAL WHISKEY PIE

This Kentucky family recipe amazed all of us and they gladly shared the recipe.

1 ½ cups sugar	1 cup semisweet chocolate chips
1 cup flour	1 cup chopped pecans
3 eggs	1 9-inch unbaked refrigerated
1 stick butter melted	piecrust
3 fluid ounces whiskey	

In a small saucepan, melt butter over low heat. Beat in eggs. In a medium bowl, sift together sugar and flour; blend in egg mixture, beat until smooth. Stir in whiskey, chips, and pecans. Pour into 9-inch pie shell, bake in 275° oven 15 minutes. Raise the ovens temperature to 300° and bake an additional 30 minutes, or until the center is set but soft. Cool before cutting.

RHUBARB CRUMBLE PIE

Rhubarb is a very old plant. Its medicinal uses and horticulture have been recorded in history since ancient China. This is an exceptional way to enjoy it that I first tasted in Arkansas.

1 cup flour	3 cups diced rhubarb
¼ teaspoon salt	¼ teaspoon cinnamon
1 cup rolled oats	½ teaspoon orange extract
1 cup sugar divided	1 tablespoon water
⅓ cup shortening	1 tablespoon butter

In a medium bowl, sift together the flour and salt; stir in oats and ½ cup sugar. Cut in shortening until mixture is crumbly. Pat half of the mixture into a 9 inch pie pan; set aside remaining half for the topping. Arrange rhubarb in pie shell. Sprinkle ½ cup sugar, cinnamon, extract and water over rhubarb, then dot with butter. Spread remaining oat mixture over filling. Bake in 350° oven 40 minutes until rhubarb is tender.

ROBUST STRAWBERRY PIE

When I saw a piled high strawberry pie in a California restaurant in 1980, I promised myself I would eventually find a way to create the same mouth watering treat at home.

1 9-inch baked pie shells	3 tablespoons cornstarch
1 cup water	2 tablespoons corn syrup
1 cup sugar	6 cups strawberries

In large saucepan, mix together water, sugar, cornstarch, corn syrup. Over medium high heat bring mixture to a boil. Continue to cook until the mixture begins to thicken. Remove from heat and allow to cool. Once cooled, pour strawberries into baked pie shell. Chill, then serve.

SHOO FLY PIE

It's a traditional Pennsylvania Dutch dessert so sweet it attracted flies that had to be "shoo-ed away" and used only the limited ingredients available to them at the time.

2 unbaked pie shells	Filling:
Crumbs:	1 ½ cups molasses
3 cups flour	1 ½ cups hot water
1 cup brown sugar	1 teaspoon baking soda
½ cup shortening	½ cup brown sugar
½ teaspoon baking soda	3 eggs beaten

Combine flour, brown sugar, shortening and baking soda in a bowl. Remove 1 ½ cups from crumb mixture, place in large bowl and add to it the fillings: molasses, water, baking soda, brown sugar and eggs. Beat well. Divide batter into unbaked pie shells. Top with crumb mixture. Bake in 425° oven for 10 minutes, turn oven heat down to 350° and continue to cook for another 45 minutes. Remove from oven and cool before serving.

SWEET POTATO PIE

Don't assume this will taste like "pumpkin" pie even if it has many of the same flavorings; there is a major difference and stands on its own as a traditional pie well known in the southern states.

1 pound sweet potatoes (not yams)	Dash salt
½ cup butter softened	½ teaspoon cinnamon
1 cup sugar	⅛ teaspoon cloves
½ cup milk	1 teaspoon vanilla extract
2 eggs	1 9-inch unbaked refrigerated
½ teaspoon nutmeg	piecrust

Boil sweet potato whole in skin for 40 to 50 minutes, or until done. Run cold water over sweet potato, and remove skin. Break apart sweet potato in a bowl. Add butter and mix well with mixer. Stir in sugar, milk, eggs, nutmeg, salt, cinnamon, cloves and vanilla. Beat on medium speed until mixture is smooth.

Pour filling into an unbaked piecrust. Bake in 350° oven for 55 to 60 minutes, or until knife inserted in center comes out clean. Pie will puff up like a soufflé, and then will sink down as it cools.

THREE BERRY PIE

This is helpful to make after you've picked berries and don't have enough for one specific pie or have small left over packages in the freezer or canned on the shelf. Plus the different berry combinations create such delicate changes in the taste—all winners.

1 cup strawberries halved	Pastry for 9-inch double crust pie
½ cup sugar	Substitute:
3 tablespoons cornstarch	2 cups huckleberries
2 cups raspberries	2 cups raspberries
1 ½ cups fresh blueberries	2 cups blackberries

In a large mixing bowl, stir together sugar and cornstarch. Add strawberries, raspberries, and blueberries; gently toss until berries are coated. When using frozen fruit allow fruit mixture to stand for 15 to 30 minutes, or until fruit is partially thawed. Line pie plate with half of the pastry. Stir berry mixture and transfer to crust lined pie plate. Top with second crust, seal the edges. To prevent overbrowning, cover edge of pie with foil. Bake in 375° oven for 25 minutes when using fresh fruit, 50 minutes for frozen fruit. Remove foil. Bake for an additional 20 to 30 minutes, or until top is golden. Cool on a wire rack.

VINEGAR PIE

I know it sounds bad, but Kansas Pioneers living in sod houses made this pie in the winter when the dried fruits were depleted and has lasted the test of time. It's really a custard type of pie with raisins, but you will be shocked how good it is.

5 eggs	½ teaspoon cinnamon
2 tablespoons flour	½ teaspoon nutmeg
1 cup sugar	1 cup sour cream
3 tablespoons melted butter cooled	Whipped cream
3 tablespoons cider vinegar	1 9-inch unbaked refrigerated
1 teaspoon vanilla extract	piecrust
½ cup raisins	

Beat eggs with a whisk in a large mixing bowl. Add flour, sugar, butter, vinegar, vanilla, raisins, cinnamon, nutmeg and sour cream. Stir just until mixed. Add filling to unbaked crust and bake in 300° oven until top is golden, about 1 hour. There will be tiny bubbles on the surface, but filling should not wiggle when pan is shaken. Serve warm, or refrigerate and serve cold. Top with whipped cream if desired.

WALNUT TOLL HOUSE PIE

Need a familiar taste, but more formal to serve than cookies, this will be the one. Ruth Wakefield would be surprised how far her basic cookie recipe has gone.

1 9-inch unbaked refrigerated	½ cup flour
piecrust	1 cup melted butter
2 eggs	1 cup semisweet chocolate chips
½ cup sugar	1 cup chopped walnuts
½ cup brown sugar	

In large mixing bowl, beat eggs until foamy. Beat in sugars until ingredients are thoroughly combined, add flour. Stir well. Blend in melted butter. Stir chips and walnuts into mixture. Pour mixture into pie shell. Bake in 325° oven for 1 hour. Serve warm with whipped cream or ice cream, if desired.

CRUST OR BUST

 The original purpose of a pastry shell was to serve as a storage container and serving vessel, and was too hard to  actually eat. The first pies were called "coffins" with the crusts or pastry being tall, straight-sided with sealed-on floors and lids. Open-crust pastry—no tops—were known as "traps." These pies held assorted meats and sauces and were baked more like a modern casserole with no pan because the crust itself was the pan, tough and inedible.

Unlike today, making pie crust or pastry was taken for granted by the majority of early cookbooks, so recipes are not usually included. It wasn't until the 16th century that  cookbooks include pastry ingredients and instructions. This was because cookbooks began being produced for the general homemaker and not just for professional cooks.

The bakers to the Egyptians pharaohs incorporated nuts, honey, and fruits in bread dough, a primitive form of pastry. It's believed the Greeks actually originated pie pastry. The pies during this period were made by a flour-water paste wrapped around meat; this served to cook the meat and seal in the juices.

 English women were baking pies long before the settlers came to America. The pie was an English specialty that was unrivaled in other European cuisines. Two popular early examples were shepherd's pie and cottage pie.

The Pilgrims brought their favorite family pie recipes with them to America. The colonist and their pies adapted ingredients and techniques available to them in the New World. At first, they baked pie with berries and fruits

271

pointed out to them by the Native Americans. Colonial women used round and shallow pans literally to cut corners and stretch the ingredients.

Pioneer women often served pies with every meal, thus firmly making pies a unique part of American culture and a chosen dish to share during celebrations and gatherings. As settlers moved westward, American regional pies developed and continually adapted to changing conditions and ingredients.

There are many ways to prepare a crust for a pie. Try the simplest first and work your way up to the difficult. In the meantime while you are experimenting with fillings, just buy the crust you need. That way you can concentrate on one expertise at a time. Eventually you will find that making your own crust, all kinds, is cost effective and more flavorful than any store bought one.

GRAHAM CRACKER CRUST

The simple graham cracker crust can be used for a variety of recipes. It can be the base of a quiche or any elegant or simple cheesecake. No fear, just three simple ingredients. I don't put sugar in mine, I find the crackers are sufficiently sweet, especially if you use the honey grahams or cinnamon graham crackers.

8-10 whole graham crackers
¼ cup sugar (optional)
1/3 cup margarine or butter, melted

Place the graham crackers into a plastic bag and use a rolling pin, or a food processor or food grinder to make fine crumbs. Pour the crumbs into a bowl and add sugar and melted margarine. Stir well. Pour the mix into a pie pan and use your hands or the back of a large spoon to press the mixture into the bottom and sides of the pie pan. Place in refrigerator and chill for 1 hour before using. If you need a pre-bake pie crust, bake in 375° oven for 7-8 minutes. Cool before filling.

COOKIE CRUST

These ingredients can be used to make a quick and delicious pie crust and this recipe is very versatile. Don't limit yourself—use wafer cookies, sandwich crème filled cookies—all flavors, gingersnaps, cereal, toasted breads, shortbread cookies, whatever you like: The only thing you have to worry about is what to fill it with.

1 ½ cups fine crumbs
½ cups butter, melted

Take cookie crumbs and stir in melted butter. Line pie plate with mixture, pressing firmly into place. Chill for 20 minutes or bake at 350° for 10 minutes. Makes 1 pie shell, 9-inch. Reserve some crumbs to sprinkle over the top of your pie to give it a pretty finished appearance

COCONUT CRUST

This is a great crust I discovered several years ago and use now for lots of custard pies and any pie that I just want to throw together using the instant pudding pie mixes for a last minute treat.

2 cups shredded coconut
½ cup coconut milk or cream or
    evaporated milk
dash of salt

¼ cup white sugar or sweetener
    equivalent
12 tablespoons butter, melted

Spray 9-inch pie pan with cooking spray. Combine all ingredients in a bowl. Transfer to pan and press firmly into bottom and up the sides of pan. Bake in 375° oven for about 20 minutes or until lightly brown. Sometimes I use the broiler for the last few minutes to brown the inside. Let cool before filling with non bake filling.

ALMOND OR NUT CRUST

I discovered this type of crust when I was researching low carbohydrate treats for Joe. Now I use it when I want something special and nutty to compliment a simple filling.

1 ½ cup almond flour or crushed
    almond, walnuts, macadamia,
    pecan or peanuts

¼ cup white sugar or sweetener
    equivalent
6 tablespoons butter or margarine,
    melted

The most important thing to remember if you use regular nuts for the base instead of almond flour, chop them to a very fine powder in a food processor or food grinder. Mix together ingredients in a bowl. Place in well sprayed 9-inch pie pan and press against the bottom and sides. Place in refrigerator until ready if you need an unbaked crust to fill or if you need a baked crust, place in 350° oven for 10-15 minutes until lightly browned.

SIMPLE PIE CRUST

This is the one I first learned from my mom. It makes a great crust every time and is easy to follow, no worry over having to work in the solid oils like shortening, butter and lard.

2 ¼ cups flour   1/3 cup Very COLD milk
1 ½ teaspoon salt   ½ cup plus 1 tablespoon vegetable
                                    or olive oil

Mix flour and salt together. Make a well in center of dry ingredients. In a small bowl first measure and pour oil then add COLD milk and DO NOT STIR. Add wet ingredients all at once to flour. Stir with fork until combined. Do not over mix. Shape into 2 flat balls. Wrap in plastic wrap. Refrigerate for 15 minutes. Roll out on very lightly floured surface. Avoid working with dough too much or it will cause it to be tough. Transfer it to your pan. Makes 1 double crust for a 9-inch pie or 2 single-crust 9-inch.pies.

STANDARD RELIABLE PIE CRUST

This recipe makes enough dough for two crusts—one for the bottom of the pie and one for the top. This is the most reliable and easy recipe using shortening I have found and used. It's simple: Use shortening for a flaky texture and butter for a delicious flavor. Follow it exactly and there will be no failure. Then put it in your family recipe box.

2 ½ cups all purpose flour   ½ cup (1 stick) chilled unsalted
1 ½ tablespoons sugar   butter, cut into 1/2-inch pieces
1 ¼ teaspoons salt   6 tablespoons (or more) ice water
2/3 cup solid vegetable shortening, 2 teaspoons apple cider vinegar
    frozen, then cut into 1/2-inch
    pieces

Blend flour, sugar and salt in processor. Add shortening and butter and cut in using on/off turns until mixture resembles coarse meal. Transfer mixture to bowl. Mix 6 tablespoons ice water and vinegar in small bowl; pour over flour mixture. Stir with fork until moist clumps form, adding more ice water by teaspoonfuls if dough is dry. Gather dough into 2 balls; flatten each into disk. Wrap each in plastic and chill 30 minutes. (Can be prepared ahead and refrigerated up to 2 days or frozen up to 1 month. If frozen, thaw overnight in refrigerator. Soften slightly at room temperature before using.)

TRADITIONAL PIE CRUST

If you're a purist and want the traditional, here it is. This one I've used many times and works good, just make sure you read about working with pie dough. If you prefer and would like to use lard—which also contributes flavor and flakiness to pie crust—substitute 2 tbsp. lard for 2 tbsp. of the shortening. Try to get good-quality lard from a butcher shop; it's generally much better than ordinary grocery-store lard.

2 ½ cups flour	7 tablespoons very cold butter, cut
1 tablespoon sugar	into small pieces
1 ½ teaspoons salt	7 tablespoons very cold shortening,
	cut into pieces

Mix flour, sugar, and salt in a large bowl. Drop in butter and shortening. Using a fork, a pastry cutter, or two knives, work butter and shortening into the flour mixture until it resembles cornmeal with some small pea-size pieces. (don't use your hands, the heat from your hands melts the butter too much). Using a fork, quickly stir in 1/2 cup ice water (mixture will not hold together). Turn dough and crumbs onto a clean surface. Knead just until dough starts to hold together but some bits still fall away, 5 to 10 times. Divide dough in half and pat each half into a 6-inch disk. Wrap each disk in plastic wrap and refrigerate at least 20 minutes and up to overnight. Roll it out, and transfer it to your pan. Makes 1 double crust for a 9-inch pie or 2 single-crust 9-inch.pies.

~ Let the Good Times Roll ~

THINGS TO REMEMBER ABOUT FLOUR CRUST:

Make Pie Crust Without Fear:

Even experienced cooks can find it intimidating to make pie pastry.

The following tips will help you turn out a terrific crust with ease. Keep the dough cold and the butter chunky.

For a flaky crust, keep the butter from melting before baking. Those bits of butter, which should be roughly pea-size, are meant to melt in the oven, giving off steam that creates flaky pockets. If the dough is softening too much as you're working with it, put it in the refrigerator for 15 minutes. As you roll out the dough, you should see veins of butter running through it.

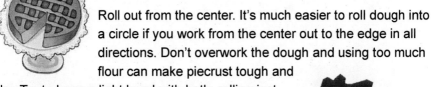

Roll out from the center. It's much easier to roll dough into a circle if you work from the center out to the edge in all directions. Don't overwork the dough and using too much flour can make piecrust tough and dry. Try to keep a light hand with both, rolling just enough to reach your desired size and using only enough flour to keep the dough from sticking to the counter.

Use a piecrust bag available in any cooking store or section. This tool takes the strain out of rolling by providing a nonstick round frame for the dough as you roll it out, allowing you to use less flour and avoid shaggy edges.

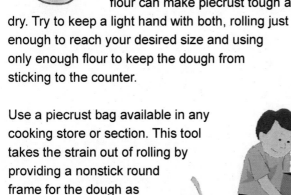

SNICKS & SNACKS

Joe and I are both nurses and we agree the best medicine for any illness is laughter. Humor is a love saving element in our marriage. We love to laugh,to share a joke, to make others laugh and know it keeps you younger and healthier. Laughter puts things in perspective and breaks the tension. Humor clarifies, shakes our emotions loose and keeps us sane. Our view of anything is clearer with a smile.

CARNIVAL CRAVINGS That being said, when we wanted to buy a business, the fast food place in the mall jumped out at us. It already served carnival type food and was located at a strategic corner of the small 30-store mall. It was called "The Junction" and Joe quickly came up with the winning slogan, "Where Food and People Meet."

My sister Sharon joined us in our quest. We wanted people coming to the counter, chatting, laughing and moving on, to return another day. The goal was they'd take that little moment and change their day and pass it along. We hoped lives could be made a little better and positively influence our new hometown.

We knew the right food was crucial and agreed on foods found at carnivals, fairs and rodeos. People look forward to going to these events for the rides and shows, but part of the fun is the food. With excellent food, courteous customer service, genuine smiles, affordable prices, we encouraged people to stop, snack and chat. We all made a point to be little positive sparks—to be a part of an optimistic domino affect. We worked hard tinkering with simple recipes that would be enjoyed by all ages and something someone would choose to splurge on.

The snacks and quick lunch foods worked marvelously. We had a small sitting area, but the majority of the patrons would use the counter. Some people came by just to chat or chuckle or tell us a joke, share their woes or just to say hi. We heard many stories about memorable treats from the past

It helped that we had the best popcorn in town. People came to our place just for the popcorn and when we were slow, we'd pop a fresh batch, letting the incredible scent travel down the length of the mall, always causing a sudden rush. We'd be selling bags for the next hour as the smell lingered. A popular reporter from the small local newspaper loved our popcorn and would come by to find out what stories we'd heard "going around town" before he wrote his weekly column. If it was an important issue, we'd heard all the opinions on it

Our slushies, ice cream, soft pretzels, hot dogs, nachos, desserts were the best. We had the only licorice, peppermint, pumpkin, huckleberry and gingerbread ice cream in town.

When there were special event weekends in the mall like singing groups, bands, charity booths, automobiles, contest and advertisers; they would set up at our corner because of all the traffic. Joe performed with local bands, we got involved in the community theaters; obtained jobs; participated in town activities; the kids had a place to hang out and learn early job skills; we made life long friends and contacts. My sister Sharon's family still lives in the town that's grown to a small city. It was a place we paused, received and gave back and then moved on. Stories, experiences and recollections captured and imbedded in so many lives—all at the intersection of "The Junction".

LAUGHTER RELIEVES LONESOME: SOMETIMES CURES IT

****

BUTTERSCOTCH HAYSTACKS

These are favorites in every state and great decoration on the table for a harvest time party.

1 ⅔ cups butterscotch chips	2 5-ounce cans chow mien noodles
¾ cup peanut butter	3 ½ cups miniature marshmallows

Line cookie sheet with wax paper. Microwave chips in large, uncovered bowl on medium-high power for 1 minute; stir. If necessary, microwave additional 10 to 15 second intervals, stirring just until chips are melted. Stir in peanut butter until well blended. Add chow mien noodles and marshmallows; toss until all ingredients are coated. Drop by rounded tablespoons onto prepared trays. Refrigerate until ready to serve.

CARAMEL APPLES

Caramel apples are usually consumed as treats at Autumn festivals and celebrations. Candy apples are made with a red candy syrup coating.

2 14-ounce packages caramels	8 sheets waxed paper
¼ cup water	Sugar
8 medium apples	Margarine
8 sticks	

Combine caramels and water in slow cooker. Stir frequently while caramels melt. Take margarine and grease shiny side of each waxed paper sheet. Wash apples and dry. Insert a stick into stem end of each apple. Once caramels are melted dip each apple into hot caramel. Turn apple to coat entire surface. Hold apple above cooker and scrape off excess of caramel from bottom of apple. Dip bottom of caramel coated apple in sugar to keep it from sticking. Place apple on buttered waxed paper and cool.

CARAMEL POPCORN

This was too scrumptious not to find a way to make at home.

7 quarts plain popped popcorn	½ teaspoon baking soda
2 cups brown sugar	1 teaspoon vanilla extract
1 cup butter	Caramel Nut:
½ cup corn syrup	2 cups dry roasted nuts
1 teaspoon salt	

Place popped popcorn into two shallow greased baking pans; use roasting pans, jelly roll pans, or disposable roasting pans. Add peanuts to popped corn if using. Set aside. Preheat oven to 250°. Combine brown sugar, corn syrup, butter and salt in saucepan. Bring to boil over medium heat, stirring enough to blend. Once mixture begins to boil, boil for 5 minutes while stirring constantly. Remove from heat and stir in baking soda and vanilla. Mixture will be light and foamy. Immediately pour over popcorn in pans and stir to coat. Don't worry too much at this point about getting all of corn coated. Bake for 1 hour, remove pans; give each a good stir every 15 minutes. Line counter top with waxed paper. Dump corn out onto waxed paper and separate pieces. Allow to cool completely, store in airtight containers or resealable bags.

CHEESE AND BEAN DIP

This can be used for super nachos, in a taco salad or in burritos.

1-16-ounce can refried beans	1 cup sour cream
1 cup finely chopped onions	1 3-ounce package cream cheese
1 cup finely chopped green bell	cubed
peppers	1 packet taco seasoning mix
1 14 ½-ounce can diced tomatoes	Large bag tortilla chips
2 cups shredded Cheddar cheese	

Combine all ingredients except chips in slow cooker. Cover with lid. Cook on high 2 hours. Stir 2-3 times during cooking. Bring cooker to table and serve with chips, keep setting on warm and stir as needed.

CINNAMON SWEET TREATS

My siblings and I remember Mom's special crust and prayed for leftover scraps of crust to be turned into this quickly eaten confection. Finally mom started making extra dough just to make the treat.

3 tablespoons butter	PIE CRUST:
2 cups sugar	2 ¼ cups flour
3 tablespoons milk	1 ½ teaspoon salt
2 teaspoons vanilla extract	1/3 cup Very COLD milk
Cinnamon	½ cup plus 1 tablespoon vegetable
	or olive oil

Cream butter and sugar together. Add milk and vanilla, mix well; should be consistency of frosting; set aside. Mix flour and salt together. Make well in center of dry ingredients. Pour COLD milk and oil in a small bowl. DO NOT STIR. Add wet ingredients all at once to flour. Stir with fork until combined. Do not over mix. Shape into 2 flat balls. Wrap in plastic wrap. Refrigerate for 15 minutes. Roll out on very lightly floured surface. Avoid working with dough too much or it will cause it to be tough. In cookie sheet with sides, cover bottom and sides with rolled out dough. Spread butter mixture evenly over crust surface. Sprinkle generously with ground cinnamon over top. Bake in 425° oven for 10 minutes. Remove from oven, let cool in pan before cutting into pieces.

COOKIES AND CREAM FUDGE

My friend loved fudge and Oreos since she was little; this just seemed like the right birthday combination for her.

3 cups sugar	½ cup finely crushed chocolate
¾ cup butter	sandwich cookies
⅔ cup evaporated milk	1 teaspoon vanilla extract
2 cups white chocolate chips	1 cup crumbled chocolate sandwich
1 7-ounce jar marshmallow crème	cookies

Line 9-inch-square baking pan with foil. Combine sugar, butter and milk in medium, heavy-duty saucepan. Bring to full rolling boil, stirring constantly for 3 minutes. Remove from heat. Stir in chips, marshmallow crème, finely

crushed cookies and vanilla extract. Pour into prepared pan. Sprinkle
crumbled cookies on top. Gently swirl cookies into fudge using a knife.
Refrigerate until firm.

CREAMY SALSA DIP

*This is simple and so versatile with all the oodles of flavored salsas available,
the idea inspired by my dear friend in Montana.*

2 cups salsa   1 ½ teaspoons horseradish
1 8-ounce package cream cheese   2 or 3 boxes of crackers

Place block of softened cream cheese onto plate or shallow bowl, wide side
down. Mix Horseradish (which can be optional) into salsa and pour over cream
cheese. Serve with crackers.

CRUNCHY NO BAKE TREATS

You really can't go wrong with peanut butter and chocolate anything.

4 cups cheerio type cereal   1 cup sugar
2 cups dry roasted peanuts   1 teaspoon vanilla extract
1 cup corn syrup   1 cup semisweet chocolate chips
1 ½ cups creamy peanut butter   1 cup white chocolate chips
2 cups crispy rice cereal

In large bowl, combine cereal, peanuts and chips; set aside. In saucepan,
boil corn syrup and sugar stirring frequently. Remove from heat; stir in peanut
butter and vanilla. Pour over cereal mixture and toss to coat evenly. Spread
into a greased 15x10 pan, cool. Cut into bars.

EASY CHEX MIX

This has been around since the 1970's and can be made so many ways—just change the seasonings.

8 cups Chex cereal mix wheat, rice
   and corn
6 cups from the following: bagel chips,
   snack crackers, goldfish crackers,
   pretzel, Cheerios, any nuts
6 tablespoons melted butter

2 tablespoons Worcestershire sauce
1 teaspoon Montreal Chicken
   Seasoning
½ teaspoon garlic powder
½ teaspoon onion salt
½ teaspoon onion powder

Combine cereals, pretzels, crackers and nuts in slow cooker. Combine butter and seasonings. Pour over dry mixture. Toss until well mixed. Cover with lid and cook on low 2 hours, stirring every 30 minutes.

FILIPINO FRIED EGG ROLLS

I always loved egg rolls, once I tasted these from a nurse friend in Juneau, none anywhere compare.

½ pound ground pork
½ cup finely chopped green onions
1 egg
1 tablespoon soy sauce
½ pound finely chopped shrimp

½ cup chopped water chestnuts
1 teaspoon black pepper
1 teaspoon salt
1 package egg rolls wrappers
½ cup vegetable oil

Combine pork, onions, egg, soy sauce, shrimp, chestnuts, pepper and salt. Mix well; place one level tablespoon of mixture on each egg roll wrapper. Seal with few drops of water. Deep fry in hot oil and drain on paper towel. Serve with mustard sauces or sweet and sour sauce.

FRIDAY NIGHT NACHO DIP

2 pounds cooked ground beef
1 pound cooked ground pork or
   sausage
1 16-ounce jar salsa
1 package taco seasoning mix

1 2-pound box Velveeta cheese
   cubed
1 10 ¾-ounce can cream of
   mushroom soup
1 chopped onion

Combine meats, salsa and seasoning mix in slow cooker. Cover and cook on high 1 hour. Stir in cheese, soup and onions. Cover and cook on low 3-4 hours, until cheese and soup are melted, stir occasionally. Serve dip warm from slow cooker with chips, tortilla chips, pita wedges, bread sticks, corn chips or party rye bread. On the side serve with chopped tomatoes, salsa, warm refried beans and sour cream.

FRIED COKE

Believe it or not, both Texas and North Carolina State Fair claim the origin of this new carnival sensation. These are easy to make and will give you a real sugar rush, but then that's why we eat at carnivals and fairs. Here's the most passed around recipe, everyone should try them once.

2 cups flour
1 teaspoon baking powder
2 eggs slightly beaten

1 ½ cups Coke soda pop
½ teaspoon salt
Oil for frying

In medium bowl, mix together flour and baking powder. Mix in eggs and cola and stir until smooth batter forms. Preheat oil in skillet or deep fryer to 375°. Pour batter into fryer and cook up a mass of doughy strands. Fry up for about a minute on each side and drain on paper towels. Stuff into a cup, sprinkle with powdered sugar and pour Cola syrup over it. Top with whipped cream, sprinkle of cinnamon and a maraschino cherry. Serve while still warm and top with

FRY BREAD

This fried dough is known by different names in various parts of the country. In Arizona it's Fry Bread; in New Mexico Sopaipillas; in Washington they are known as Elephant Ears; other regions call them Beaver Tails, Whale Tails, Tiger Ears, Pizza Frita, Frying Saucers and Doughboys. Whatever the name, they're loved everywhere and usually only available at circus, festivals or fairs, unless you know someone who likes to make them at home.

4 cups flour	4 tablespoons shortening
1 teaspoon salt	1 ⅓ cups cold water
1 tablespoon baking powder	

Whisk baking powder, salt and flour together. Cut in shortening. Add water gradually until a soft dough. Dough will be little sticky. Flour hands and knead about 5 minutes until smooth and no longer sticky. Divide into 8 pieces. Cover each piece of dough with plastic wrap. Working with one piece at a time, flatten until ½ inch thick and size of lunch plate. Heat 2-3 inches shortening or vegetable oil in deep skillet. Fry dough in oil; turn with tongs to brown on both sides. Drain on paper towels. Keep warm in 200° oven while cooking the rest of dough pieces. Serve plain, sprinkled with sugar; cinnamon; honey; powdered sugar; cinnamon sugar; maple syrup; chocolate sauce; fruit sauce; whipped cream or split open and fill with chili, cheese, salsa or tomato sauce; or garlic butter or put it on top and fold up the sides like a taco to eat.

FUDGE

The goal for perfect fudge is creamy and rich and this one works great for anyone—with any level of cooking skills.

1 ½ cups sugar	1 jar marshmallow crème
⅔ cup evaporated milk	1 ½ cups semisweet chocolate chips
2 tablespoons butter	½ cup chopped nuts
¼ teaspoon salt	1 teaspoon vanilla extract
2 cups miniature marshmallows	

Line 8-inch-square baking pan with foil. Combine sugar, milk, butter and salt in medium saucepan. Bring to full rolling boil over medium heat, stirring constantly. Boil, stirring constantly, for 4 to 5 minutes. Remove from heat. Stir in marshmallows, chips, nuts and vanilla extract. Stir vigorously for 1 minute or until marshmallows are melted. Pour into prepared baking pan; refrigerate for 2 hours or until firm. Lift from pan; remove foil. Cut into pieces. Milk Chocolate Fudge: Substitute 1 ¾ cups milk chocolate chips Butterscotch Fudge: Substitute 1 ⅔ cups butterscotch chips. Chocolate Peanut Fudge: Substitute 1 ⅔ cups peanut butter and use milk chocolate chips and peanuts for nuts.

FUNNEL CAKES

This a regional specialty food originally associated with the Pennsylvania Dutch region. Funnel cakes are popular around the US at ballparks, fairs and festivals. It always seems there is a line waiting for these at the stands and the same thing happens at home too.

4 cups flour	2 ½ cups milk
¼ cup sugar	3 eggs
2 tablespoons brown sugar	1 ½ teaspoons vanilla extract
2 teaspoons baking powder	Vegetable oil for frying
1 teaspoon salt	Powdered sugar

In medium bowl, combine flour, sugars, baking powder and salt. Stir with whisk until thoroughly combined. Pour milk into measuring cup and add eggs. Whisk with fork until combined. Pour milk and egg mixture into dry ingredients and whisk thoroughly until you have smooth batter. Add ½ inch of oil to large, heavy skillet or deep pot and heat to 350° (use deep-fat thermometer or cubes of bread to test: if bread turns golden brown in 30 seconds, oil is right temperature). Fill funnel with batter, holding thumb over opening. Drizzle batter out in spiral, starting from center of pan. Hold funnel as close to pan to minimize splatter. Let cake cook until golden brown, about 45 seconds to minute, flip with tongs and brown other side. Drain on paper towels. Sift powdered sugar over cake and serve hot.

GARLIC PITA CHIPS

These are great with a tuna, egg or chicken salad or crumbled over a lettuce type salad.

3 tablespoons butter	6 pita bread
½ cup olive oil	Italian seasoning
8 teaspoons minced garlic	Parmesan cheese

Melt butter in small saucepan. Add olive oil and garlic to melted butter and sauté over low heat for 10 minutes. Take care not to brown butter or garlic. Discard garlic pieces. Split pita breads to make two rounds. Cut each round in half. With rough inner side up, lay pita slices on baking sheet. Brush entire surface with garlic butter mixture. If desired, sprinkle with little Italian seasoning. Bake in 350° oven for 10 minutes. If desired, sprinkle with Parmesan cheese. Place about 4 inches from broiler and broil for about 1 minute, until nicely browned. Remove from oven and place on paper towels to drain. Break into smaller chip-size pieces. Serve with your favorite dip.

HIKERS GRANOLA BARS

It has been said to me that if lost in the woods, one could live off these for several days.

½ cup softened butter or margarine	2 cups semi-sweet chocolate,
1 ½ cups packed brown sugar	butterscotch, white or milk
1 ½ cups sugar	chocolate chips or mix
4 eggs	1 cup flaked coconut
2 teaspoons vanilla extract	1 cup chopped nuts walnuts,
1 teaspoon water	pecans, almonds, peanuts or
4 cups old fashion oats	combination
3 cups flour	1 cup chopped dried fruits (optional)
2 teaspoons salt	1 cup mixed candied fruit (optional)

In mixing bowl cream butter and sugars. Add eggs, one at a time, beating well after each. Beat in vanilla and water. Combine in small bowl oats, flour and salt; gradually add to creamed mixture; stir in raisins, chips, coconut, nuts and fruit, if desired. Press batter into sprayed 15x10 baking pan. Bake in 350° oven for 22-27 minutes or until golden brown. Cool on wire rack. Cut into bars when cooled. Dust top with combination of ¼ cup cornstarch and ¼ cup powdered sugar if you want more sweetness. For special occasions, drizzle chocolate or vanilla icing before cutting into bars. They pack best for camping trips if you leave them plain.

HOLIDAY NUTS

These are always a hit at parties or wrapped up in holiday plastic bags and given as gifts or as a parting gift to guest.

1 cup sugar	4 tablespoons melted butter
1 teaspoon salt	1 cup pecans halves
2 teaspoons cinnamon	1 cup walnuts halves
1 egg white	1 cup peanuts
1 tablespoon water	

Line rimmed baking sheet with foil and spray foil well with nonstick spray; set aside. In small bowl, stir together sugar, salt and cinnamon; set aside. In medium bowl, whisk egg white and water until foamy. Add nuts to bowl and stir until coated. Pour in sugar mixture and melted butter; stir well to combine. Spread nut mixture in even layer on prepared baking sheet and bake in 300° oven for 25 minutes, sitting occasionally. Remove from oven and cool completely.

INDOOR BANANA BOAT

A banana boat is a traditional campfire treat consisting of a banana filled with marshmallow and chocolate wrapped in aluminum foil and cooked in an open fire.

4 bananas	Miniature marshmallow
Semisweet chocolate chips	Caramel ice cream topping (optional)

Peel banana down one side keep peel attached on other end and slice exposed banana in half lengthwise, but do not slice through to peel on other side. Place marshmallows and chips into wedge and cover with peel and aluminum foil. Put into coals for about 5 minutes. Or place on grill for about 5 minutes. Or this can be done in oven as well. Set oven to 350°; place bananas wrapped in foil on baking sheet and heat in oven for 5-10 minutes. If you want to use caramel sauce, place it over banana before covering with peel and wrapping in foil.

INDOOR S'MORES

A s'more is a roasted marshmallow and a slab of chocolate sandwiched between two pieces of graham cracker. It's a campfire institution and an absolute on the cook's menu in the US and Canada. The recipe makes it possible to enjoy these popular gooey messes in the winter and stormy weather.

1 cup graham cracker crumbs	¼ teaspoon salt
6 tablespoons melted butter	2 teaspoons vanilla extract
1 teaspoon sugar	2 cups miniature marshmallows
1 cup softened butter	1 ⅔ cups powdered sugar
2 cups sugar	⅓ cup unsweetened cocoa
½ cup unsweetened cocoa	½ cup butter
4 eggs	⅓ cup evaporated milk
1 ½ cups flour	

Mix together crumbs, melted butter and sugar, firmly pat crumbs into 8-inch baking pan lined with foil and sprayed with cooking spray. Bake in 350° oven until firm and lightly browned, 8-10 minutes. In a large bowl, combine softened butter, sugar and cocoa until well combined; stir in eggs. Add vanilla, salt and flour. Pour batter over baked graham cracker crust, make sure batter covers the crust into the edges. Bake in 350° oven for 20 minutes. Remove pan from oven and place an even single layer of mini marshmallows over brownie. Return to oven and bake for 3 minutes; Make frosting now: Mix together powdered sugar, butter, cocoa and milk until smooth and creamy. Remove pan from oven and immediately frost. Cool completely before cutting. Lift out with foil. Coat knife with cooking spray to prevent sticking to knife when cutting squares.

IRISH POTATO CANDY

No one wants to eat this German/Irish confection when you tell them it's made with potatoes. So let them try it first, then tell them and watch their faces drop. "Irish Potato Candy" is a traditional Philadelphia treat not Irish but Scottish in origin and doesn't contain any potato, but is a cocoa powder and cinnamon covering a coconut nougat center made to look like a potato

1 large potato	1 teaspoon vanilla extract
½ teaspoon salt	Peanut butter
2 pounds powdered sugar	

Cook peeled, cut up potato in salted water. When tender, drain and mash. Mix powdered sugar into potato a little at a time; potato mix will liquefy at first. Keep adding sugar until dough is pastry consistency and dry enough to roll out. Sprinkle wax paper with powdered sugar. Take baseball size ball of mixture and roll out with rolling pin. Remove paper and spread with peanut butter and roll up like jellyroll. Wrap rolls in plastic wrap and chill for several hours. Slice ½ to 1-inch thickness, let set out to dry out before storing in refrigerator in covered container.

CHILI BEAN DIP

2 15-ounce cans chili con carne with beans	1 2-pound box Velveeta cheese cubed
1 finely chopped onion	Spicy:
1 finely chopped green bell pepper	1-2 teaspoons hot sauce

Combine all ingredients in slow cooker. Cover. Cook on high 2 hours, stirring 3-4 times during cooking. Serve warm from cooker on warm with chips or vegetables.

CHOCO-NUT TREATS

A sophisticated version of a chocolate chip cookie for those fancier parties.

¾ cup softened butter
¾ cup sugar
1 ½ teaspoons vanilla extract
1 egg
1 teaspoon salt
2 cups flour

½ cup semi-sweet mini chocolate
    chips
Chocolate Coating
1 tablespoon butter
1 ½ cups semisweet chocolate chips
1 ¼ cups chopped nuts

Line two large cookie sheets with parchment paper. In large bowl, combine butter, sugar and vanilla. Beat well with electric hand mixer. Add egg, salt, flour, mini chocolate chips and chopped walnuts. Use hands, shape 1 tablespoon of dough into 2-inch-long log or 1-inch round balls. Bake in 350° oven for 10 to 12 minutes, or until lightly browned. Place on rack to cool completely before frosting. For chocolate coating, melt chocolate chips and butter in double boiler. No double boiler: fill small, deep pan with water and bring to low boil. Place glass bowl over simmering water, but not touching it. Place chocolate and butter bowl. As soon as chocolate begins to melt, remove pan from heat and stir with spoon until smooth and silky. Meanwhile, place chopped nuts in small bowl. For easy cleanup, place sheet of parchment paper under cookie rack before dipping cookies in chocolate. Dip top of cookie in chocolate; dip in chocolate sprinkles or chopped nuts until completely covered. Place on rack and dry completely before storing in airtight tin or plastic container. Place waxed paper or parchment paper between layers to protect chocolate and sprinkles. Properly stored, cookies should last seven to 10 days.

CHRISTMAS SPICED NUTS

One Christmas season I tasted nuts at a small mall shop and fell in love with these. I worked on replicating them for several years and now enjoy giving them as gifts to those who have never experienced the taste.

¼ cup vegetable oil
2 teaspoons chili powder
½ teaspoon ground cumin
½ teaspoon ground turmeric

Pinch cayenne pepper
3 cups nuts any variety or mixture
½ teaspoon salt

Combine oil and spices in large skillet. Heat over low heat until oil is quite hot. Remove pan from heat. Add nuts to oil; stir until well coated. Spread nuts onto paper towel lined cookie sheet. Bake in 300° oven for 10 minutes. Sprinkle with salt. Keeps a month in airtight container. May also be frozen.

Not everybody enjoys sharing their kitchen space. When you find someone you can work side by side, preparing your favorite dishes and then sharing the results with each other, you taste the successes, the mistakes and only remember the wonderful camaraderie.

MIDNIGHT MOVIE SLICES

These are a nice treat at the end of the movie after you have been eating all the salty treats during the movie.

1 box white (vanilla) cake mix	**¼ cup brown sugar**
1 ¼ cups evaporated milk	**¼ cup sugar**
3 eggs	**¼ cup corn syrup**
½ cup canola oil	**1 teaspoon vanilla extract**
1 cup raisins	**Dash salt**
2 tablespoons cinnamon	

Beat in bowl, cake mix, milk, eggs and oil for 5 minutes. Pour half of batter into sprayed tube pan. Mix together in small bowl, raisins, cinnamon and sugars. Sprinkle entire mixture evenly over batter in pan. Top with rest of batter. Bake in 350° oven for 40-50 minutes. When done, cool completely, remove from pan and drizzle with glaze. Mix corn syrup, vanilla and salt until smooth; drizzle over cooled ring before slicing.

MILE HIGH SNOW ICE CREAM

Remember those days of snow angels, snowmen and snowball fights? Back to the "good old days" with some memories and a sweet treat too. Always make sure you've had snow falling a while before you collect it for ice cream so you know it's clean and free from contamination.

1 gallon snow	1 tablespoon vanilla extract
1 cup sugar	2 cups milk

When it starts to snow, place large, clean bowl outside to collect flakes. When full, stir in sugar and vanilla to taste; stir in just enough milk for desired consistency. Serve at once. You can experiment with other extracts like almond, mint and other flavors. Or you can use orange, lime or lemon extracts for a "sherbet". To make ice cream even creamier add ½ of mashed banana or mashed mango or other fruit you enjoy for another way to flavor this delicious concoction.

MILION DOLLAR YUMMY CUPS

Whenever I want to have a "finger food only" party or get together, these are easy and a change from cookies or bar cookies. They are almost like having a pie dessert, but easier to serve.

2 sticks butter	1 cup honey
8 ounces cream cheese	2 teaspoons vanilla extract
2 ½ cups almond flour	6 beaten eggs
Filling:	2 ¼ cups chopped pecans
¾ cup butter	2 ¼ cups chopped walnuts
2 cups brown sugar	

Soften cream cheese and butter to room temperature. Mix together well with almond flour; form into small balls. Press thumb into middle of each ball forming it into a shell or cup. Melt butter over low heat and mix in sugar and honey. Do not let it boil. When smooth and blended well, add vanilla and eggs and blend completely. Add nuts. Keep mixture warm and spoon into dough shells. Bake in 350° oven for 30 minutes or until lightly brown.

Making someone something they love to eat is a way to say I care ~ a way to give pleasure in a world too full of hard times and lonely places.

MONKEY BREAD

This is also called Hungarian coffee cake, golden crown, pinch-me cake and bubble loaf. A sticky, gooey pastry served as a breakfast treat, the bread is named for the act of people pulling at the bread being reminiscent of monkey behavior. First appearing in the 1950s, serve it hot so the baked segments can be torn away with fingers and eaten by hand.

4 12-ounce tubes refrigerated biscuits
2 tablespoons cinnamon
⅔ cup butter

1 cup brown sugar
1 cup sugar
Optional Additions:
½ cup pecans, walnuts, raisins, or coconut

Cut each biscuit into 4 pieces. Pour sugar and cinnamon into a plastic bag and mix. Add biscuit pieces, several at a time; shake to coat well. Place pieces in buttered tube or Bundt pan until all are used. [Sprinkle layers with nuts, raisins or coconut if using at this time.] Bring brown sugar and butter to a boil in saucepan. Cool 10 minutes, then pour over top of biscuits. Bake in 350° oven for 45 minutes. Allow to cool 15 minutes before removing from pan. Turn upside down to serve.

MONKEY TAILS

These are a carnival treat made of frozen bananas on a stick dipped in chocolate and rolled in peanuts. These are too simple to make to wait for a hot day at the fair.

3 bananas

6 wooden ice cream sticks

1 cup frozen apple juice concentrate
    thawed

½ cup chopped nuts, crispy rice
    cereal, coconut or granola

Chocolate Sauce:

1 cup semisweet chocolate chips

2 tablespoons vegetable oil

Peanut Butter Sauce:

½ cup creamy peanut butter

2 tablespoons honey

½ cup milk

Peel bananas. Cut in half crosswise to make "short" bananas. Push wooden stick into cut end of each banana half. Dip banana in apple juice. Place banana halves on cookie sheet. Cover with waxed paper and place in freezer for 1 to 2 hours or until bananas are frozen solid. While bananas are in freezer, decide if you will dip bananas in chocolate sauce or peanut butter sauce. Or you can dip bananas in peanut butter sauce and then chocolate sauce for double dipper. Prepare whichever sauce you want. Chocolate Tails: Place chocolate chips and oil in a 1-cup glass measuring cup. Microwave for 2 minutes. Remove from microwave oven and stir to blend chocolate and oil. Dip frozen bananas in sauce. Peanut Butter Tails: Place peanut butter and honey in a 1-cup glass measuring cup. Microwave for 1 minute. Stir. Microwave 30 seconds longer. Remove from microwave oven. Slowly stir in milk, about 2 tablespoons at a time, until mixture is smooth and creamy. Dip frozen bananas in sauce. Remove frozen bananas from freezer. Dip in sauce. If you wish, roll bananas in nuts, cereal, coconut or granola while sauce is still soft. Return bananas to the freezer for about 5 minutes to firm up the coating, then eat!

NACHOS

Nachos are not traditional Mexican food, but many assume so. This dish can be made in so many varieties just by adding your favorite extras to enjoy this crunchy, cheesy snack.

Tortilla chips	**1 diced tomato**
3 cups refried beans	**1 chopped onion**
3 cups grated Cheddar cheese	**Guacamole**
4 jalapeno chilies sliced	**Sour cream**
Salsa	**Black olives chopped**

Arrange layer of tortilla chips along bottom of wide, shallow baking pan. It will make things easier if this baking pan also can be used as a serving pan. The layer of tortilla chips can be a couple layers thick. Drop teaspoonfuls of refried beans over chips. Sprinkle grated cheese over top of chips and beans. Bake in 350° oven for 10 minutes, or until cheese is melted. Serve with any combination of ingredients or place chilies, salsa, tomato, onion, guacamole, sour cream and olives in separate bowls and let each person dress up their own.

NEAT SNACK SWEETS

Often I dip one side of these in melted dark, milk or white chocolate or in melted almond bark during the holidays.

2 cups peanut butter	**2 eggs**
2 cups sugar	

Blend all three ingredients. Roll into balls and flatten on ungreased cookie sheet with fork dipped in sugar. Bake in 350° oven for 10 minutes. Serve plain or dipped.

NICE PEANUT BALLS FOR CHOCOLATE FONDUE

You will find lots of uses for this delicious little ball of goodness.

2 cups powdered sugar	¾ cup crushed graham crackers
¾ cup peanut butter	1 stick margarine

Make peanut balls ahead of time. In microwave bowl, melt margarine, Remove from microwave; stir in peanut butter until completely mixed. In bowl, mix together powdered sugar and cracker crumbs, pour in butter mixture and mix together very well. Roll balls of dough into walnut size balls. Place on sprayed waxed paper in a baking sheet and stick long toothpicks in each ball. Place baking sheet in refrigerator until firm. Remove when ready to serve.

OLD FASHIONED POPCORN & MORE

I have always loved the popcorn from the stove over any of the popcorn machines; making it was all part of the fun we had as kids.

½ cup popcorn kernels	2 tablespoons butter
1 tablespoon corn oil	Salt

Add oil to heavy-lidded or electric skillet over high heat. Oil is hot enough when single drop of water added to pan sizzles. If oil starts to smoke, it's too hot. When oil is hot, cover bottom of pan with thin layer of popcorn kernels and cover pot with tight-fitting lid. As soon as popcorn begins popping, run pan back and forth across burner. When popping slows, remove pan from heat (keeping lid on) and wait for popping to subside. Pour popcorn into large bowl and discard imperfect kernels. To save time, use same pan for melting butter. Top warm popcorn with butter and salt and toss gently with a wooden spoon. Add peanuts: plain, roasted or honey roasted. Add M&Ms for a touch of color and a mouth-watering mixture of salty and sweet. Sprinkle Parmesan Cheese Sprinkle the warm popcorn with brown sugar. Add some cinnamon to spice things up even more. Looking for a little extra kick, try adding Cajun seasoning. For a milder kick, add Greek seasoning.

RANCH DRESSING AND DIP

Nothing compares to making your own Ranch dressing.

½ cup mayonnaise
½ cup buttermilk
½ teaspoon dried parsley flakes
¼ teaspoon black pepper
¼ teaspoon Accent

¼ teaspoon salt
⅛ teaspoon garlic powder
⅛ teaspoon onion powder
Dash dried thyme

Combine all ingredients in medium bowl and whisk until smooth. Cover and chill for several hours before serving.

ROCKY SNACK "GRANOLA"

You can add other kinds of dried fruit like cranberry or apricots or yogurt covered nuts to add a totally different sensation.

2 cups peanuts
1 cup shelled sunflower seeds
2 cups raisins
½ cup chopped walnuts
½ cup chopped pecans

1 cup semisweet chocolate chips
   (optional)
1 cup sweetened flaked coconut
   (optional)

Mix all ingredients in large zip lock bag and enjoy.

SNACK CAKES

You'll be surprised how much better these taste and lot less chemicals in the product.

Vanilla Cake:	**3 eggs**
4 egg whites	**Filling:**
16-ounce box pound cake mix	**4 teaspoons very hot water**
⅔ cup water	**½ teaspoon salt**
Chocolate Cake:	**4 cups marshmallow crème**
1 box devil's food cake mix	**1 cup shortening**
1 ⅓ cups evaporated milk	**⅔ cup powdered sugar**
½ cup oils	**1 teaspoon vanilla extract**

Beat egg whites until stiff. In separate bowl combine dry cake mix with water and beat until thoroughly blended. Fold egg whites into cake batter and slowly combine until completely mixed. Divide batter even in sprayed 12 cup muffin pan. Bake in 325° oven for 30 minutes or until cake is golden brown and toothpick to center comes out clean. Remove from pan and cool on wire rack. Combine mix, milk, oil and eggs and beat with mixer until smooth and fluffy. Divide batter evenly in sprayed 12 cup muffin pan. Bake 350° oven for 15-17 minutes or until toothpick in center comes out clean. Remove from pan and cool on wire rack. Combine hot water with salt in small bowl and stir until salt is dissolved. Let mixture cool. Combine marshmallow, shortening, sugar and vanilla well with mixer on high speed until fluffy. Add salt mix to it and mix well. When cakes are cool, use a pastry bag with a small tip to squeeze some filling into each cake. Careful not to overfill.

SO GOOD TORTILLA CHIPS

Tasty tortilla chips made at home are superior store bought chips. Not only are they relatively inexpensive, but also a breeze to make. These chips can be cooled and stored in an airtight container for two days They're worth the extra work and all kinds of seasonings can be sprinkled on.

1 11-ounce package corn tortillas	**Baked:**
Cut each tortilla into 8 chip sized	**1 tablespoon canola oil**
wedges	**3 tablespoons lime juice**
Fried:	**1 teaspoon ground cumin**
Canola oil	**1 teaspoon chili powder**
Salt	**1 teaspoon salt**

Fried Chips: Heat oil in 10-inch skillet to 375°. Drop triangles in hot oil, 8 at a time. Fry, turning chips once or twice, until they stop sizzling and turn golden brown, about 2 minutes. Remove with tongs or slotted spoon and drain on wire rack set over shallow pan; sprinkle with salt immediately. Baked Chips: Preheat oven to 350°. Arrange wedges in single layer on cookie sheet. In a mist bottle, combine oil and lime juice; mix well and spray each tortilla wedge until slightly moist. Combine cumin, chili powder and salt in small bowl and sprinkle on chips. Bake for about 7 minutes. Rotate pan and bake for another 8 minutes or until chips are crisp, but not too brown.

SOFT CINNAMON RAISIN PRETZELS

I developed this recipe when we owned the food place. Warmed up in the microwave, they make a great snack or breakfast.

4 teaspoons yeast	**1 tablespoon cinnamon**
1 teaspoon sugar	**1 tablespoon canola oil**
1 ¼ cups warm water	**½ cup baking soda**
5 cups flour	**4 cups hot water**
¼ cup brown sugar	**½ cup melted sweet butter**
¼ cup sugar	**1 cup sugar mixed with**
1 ½ teaspoons salt	**1 teaspoon cinnamon**
1 cup chopped raisins	

In small bowl, dissolve yeast and 1 teaspoon sugar in warm water. Let stand until creamy, about 10 minutes. In large bowl, mix together flour, sugar and brown sugar, salt, raisins and cinnamon. Make well in center; add oil and yeast mixture. Mix and form into dough. If mixture is dry, add one or two tablespoons of water. Knead dough until smooth, about 7-8 minutes. Lightly oil large bowl, place dough in bowl and turn to coat with oil. Cover with plastic wrap and let rise in warm place until doubled in size, about 1 hour. In large bowl, dissolve baking soda in hot water. Turn dough out onto lightly floured surface and divide into 12 equal pieces. Roll each piece into rope and twist into pretzel shape. Once dough is shaped, dip each pretzel into baking soda solution. Place on sprayed baking sheet. Let dough rise for another 30 minutes. Bake in 450° oven for 8 minutes or until browned. Brush with sweet butter and dip in cinnamon sugar mix.

TOASTED SOUTHWEST EGGROLLS

With everyone leaning toward southwest spices these days; food places are rapidly coming out with Cajun, Mexican, spicy, Texan, volcano this and pepper that to satisfy the millions. With our taste buds exploding with these new flavors, it's no wonder so many of us go home and immediately experiment to bring our favorite restaurant choices to our own tables. Here's how we like them at my house from some that are circulating.

2 tablespoons vegetable oil
1 skinless, boneless chicken breast
    half
2 tablespoons minced green onion
2 tablespoons minced red bell
    pepper
⅓ cup frozen corn kernels
¼ cup black beans, rinsed and
    drained
2 tablespoons frozen chopped
    spinach, thawed and drained
2 tablespoons diced jalapeno
    peppers
½ tablespoon minced fresh parsley
½ teaspoon ground cumin

¾ cup shredded Monterey Jack
    cheese
5 (6 inch) flour tortillas
1 quart oil for deep frying
Avocado-Ranch Dipping Sauce:
¼ cup smashed, fresh avocado
¼ cup mayonnaise
¼ cup sour cream
1 tablespoon buttermilk
1 ½ teaspoons white vinegar
⅛ teaspoon salt
⅛ teaspoon dried parsley
⅛ teaspoon onion powder dash
    dried dill weed dash garlic
    powder dash pepper

½ teaspoon chili powder   Garnish:
⅓ teaspoon salt   2 tablespoons (chopped tomato
1 pinch ground cayenne pepper   1 tablespoon chopped onion

Sprinkle chicken breast with salt and pepper and grill 4-5 minutes per side, or until done; set aside, when cool, dice chicken. Sauté red pepper and onion in oil until soft, about 2-3 minutes. Add chicken to pan. Add corn, black beans, spinach, jalapeno peppers, parsley, cumin, chili powder, salt, and cayenne pepper to pan. Cook for 4 minutes, distributing spinach evenly. Remove from heat and add cheese; stir until cheese melts. Wrap tortillas in a moist cloth and microwave on high temperature for 1 ½ minutes or until hot. Working on flat surface, divide filling evenly among the tortillas, spooning it into the center of each. Fold in ends of tortilla, then roll up side closest to you—be sure to roll tightly. Set aside, with fold side down. Put egg rolls on a plate, cover and freeze from 4 hours to 24 hours. Preheat 4-6 cups of oil to 375 degrees. (using an electric skillet is a great way to do this, because you can control the temp of the oil better.) Fry egg rolls for 12-15 minutes and drain on paper towels or a rack. To make dipping sauce, just combine all of sauce ingredients and mix in a bowl, then garnish with the chopped tomato and onion. To serve, slice each egg roll on diagonal.

TOASTED PUMPKIN SEEDS

Also flavor them with garlic powder, cayenne pepper, seasoning salt or other seasoning blends.

1 ½ cups pumpkins seeds   Salt to taste
2 teaspoons butter or olive oil

Clean off major chunks of pumpkin off seeds, some strings or pulp is fine to vleave. Toss seeds in bowl with melted butter or oil and seasoning of choice. Spread seeds in single layer on baking sheet. Bake in 400° oven for 45 minutes or until golden brown.

TOFFEE

Toffee comes in so many ways, this one meets the test: easy and delicious.

1 ¼ cups butter divided
40 soda crackers
1 cup brown sugar
1 14-ounce can sweetened
    condensed milk

1 ½ cups semisweet chocolate chips
¾ cup finely chopped walnuts

Line 15 x 10-inch jelly-roll pan with heavy-duty foil. Melt ¼ cup butter in medium saucepan. Pour into prepared jellyroll pan. Arrange crackers over butter, breaking crackers to fit empty spaces. Melt remaining butter in same saucepan; add sugar. Bring to a boil over medium heat. Reduce heat to low; cook, stirring occasionally, for 2 minutes. Remove from heat; stir in sweetened condensed milk. Pour over crackers. Bake in 425° oven for 10 to 12 minutes or until mixture is bubbly and slightly darkened. Remove from oven; cool for 1 minute. Sprinkle with morsels. Let stand for 5 minutes or until morsels are shiny; spread evenly. Sprinkle with nuts; press into chocolate. Cool in pan on wire rack for 30 minutes. Refrigerate for about 30 minutes or until chocolate is set. Remove foil; cut into pieces.

We stop, sit down and spend precious time with one another. The reason: to eat, But when we also laugh We give of ourselves more freely and generously around that food.

MUFFINS & BISCUITS

Many have generously invited me to visit behind the doors of food factories and participate in the Annual Festivals of all kinds of foods. I can't think of a state anywhere without remembering the charity, kindness and openness of so many towns, groups, communities and individuals. Giving, gracious and friendly persons everywhere.

Besides potlucks, I sought out chances to work on my new cooking skills and justify my experimenting. So I volunteered to bake things: bake sales, church auctions: school carnivals, birthday parties, snacks for sports events; classroom functions, school meetings, celebrations, sleepovers; anniversaries, and camp outs. I would take things to soup kitchens, food banks, volunteer organizations; homeless shelters, church meetings, rehabilitation facilities and my work. Any excuse to test out a new recipe.

I've spent years studying what ingredients work together, how **Muffin** to mix and match things, seeking cohesive flavors and **Stuffin** discover new techniques. In the process I visited food factories from potato chips to jerky and attended the Annual Festival of just about every **Lovin** kind of food items.

No Panic, These adventures were fabulous and another thing happened: I gained a reputation as a charitable person. I made friends and associates in many places and immensely **Pantry Plenty** enjoyed my way of being benevolent.

Sometimes I'd get very little notice of someone needing a contribution, so I'd keep my pantry full to have things on hand and not caught off guard. The times I didn't have a certain ingredient, did teach me to improvise. It took awhile but I began to trust my instincts, added to my knowledge and experiment without the panic.

These days, I still make sure there's something in my pantry to make a muffin that would work in any situation. Whether you need a bread, dessert, appetizer, entrée or vegetable you can make a muffin. They're quick to grab and eat; everyone loves having an individual one; easily transported and speedy clean up. I can also control the ingredients that go into the product and attempt to make healthier alternatives.

My recent physical limitations prevent me from my much-treasured job as a nurse and away from the people I love to visit. However, my pantry stays full and I can still send donations into the community. The conveniences of electric graters, blenders and food processors allow short and uncomplicated preparation. Muffins can stretch less expensive ingredients to serve a crowd. Doubling the recipe to make enough for several groups or to keep a few at home for your family is never a trouble. I can easily use my too ripe fruits and vegetables, which add moisture effortlessly.

If you really like the tops of muffins, take the topping and put it in the middle as a filling, The texture will change a little, but you can have an incredibly delicious center to bite into along with the crunch on top. Hopefully you are inspired to go get that muffin tin out of storage and find someone who could use a warm delicious muffin or biscuit from your kitchen.

Baking Heaven

A BETTER MUFFIN

American style muffins are a quick bread made in individual molds. The molds are necessary due to the mixture being a batter rather than dough. Muffins were originally leavened with potash which produces carbon dioxide gas in the batter. When baking powder was developed around 1857 it put an end to the use of potash.

¾ cup low-fat milk
1 cup low-fat yogurt
½ cup brown sugar
3 egg whites
¾ cup unsweetened applesauce
2 cups whole wheat flour

½ cup rolled oats
½ cup oat bran
3 teaspoons baking powder
2 teaspoons cinnamon
⅔ cup raisins
½ cup chopped dried apricot

Beat in large bowl, egg whites lightly; add milk, yogurt, brown sugar and applesauce. Combine flour, oats, bran, baking powder, cinnamon, raisins and apricots in a separate bowl. Add dry mix to wet mix until combined; don't over mix. Spoon into muffin tins and bake in 350° oven for about 20 minutes or until cooked.

APPLE RAISIN MUFFINS

These are great no matter what kind of apples are used.

2 cups grated apples
½ cup brown sugar
½ cup vegetable oil
2 eggs
1 teaspoon vanilla extract
¾ milk
2 cups chopped raisins
1 cup chopped walnuts

2 teaspoons lemon juice
2 cups flaky bran cold cereal
3 cups flour
½ teaspoon baking soda
2 ½ teaspoons baking powder
¼ teaspoon salt
2 teaspoons cinnamon
2 teaspoons apple pie spice

Combine well apples, sugar, oil, eggs, vanilla, milk, raisins, walnuts and lemon juice in large bowl. In another bowl, combine cereal, flour, baking soda, baking powder, salt and spices. Mix dry ingredients into wet ingredients and stir just until all ingredients are moistened. Spoon into sprayed and papered muffin tins. Bake in 400° oven for 20-25 minutes.

BACON CORN BISCUIT

Quick and easy, these were the number one compliment with most of our winter soups.

2 ¾ cups biscuit baking mix
⅓ cup yellow cornmeal
4 slices cooked and diced bacon

½ teaspoon black pepper
¾ cup milk

Combine all ingredients in bowl until dough forms. Knead sprinkled with baking mix on surface until dough holds together. Roll dough ½ inch thick, cut with 2 inch round cutter. Place biscuits on ungreased baking sheet. Bake in 450° oven for 10-12 minutes until golden brown.

BAKED POLENTA CRISP

Polenta is a dish made from boiled cornmeal and was considered a peasant food. Since the late 20th century, polenta has become a premium product. Polenta dishes are on the menu in many high-end restaurants, and in supermarkets at high prices. Many current polenta recipes have given new life to an essentially bland and common food.

2 cups milk
2 cups water
1 ½ cups polenta

1 teaspoon sea salt
½ cup grated Parmesan cheese
½ cup olive oil

Bring milk and water just to a boil in large saucepan. Slowly stream in polenta while stirring constantly. Stir in salt and turn down heat a bit if needed (you don't want the polenta to scorch). Continue stirring until polenta thickens up. Stir in cheese. Remove from heat and spread out ½-inch thick onto baking sheet using spatula. Chill in refrigerator for at least an hour, or overnight. Cut into wide-cut "fry" shapes. Rub each fry with a bit of olive oil and sprinkle with some salt. Bake in 450° oven, middle rack for 20 minutes or until golden and crispy. Flip fries once after ten minutes. Or cut polenta slab into small cubes and pan-fry them in oil until you've got a crunchy crouton—perfect for salads and soups. Or cut into cookie-sized rounds, layer them in casserole with pasta sauce, cheese and bake.

BAKING MIX

This is a homemade version of the commercial biscuit baking mix. Use this mixture any time a recipe calls for store biscuit baking mix as an ingredient.

6 cups flour	1 tablespoon salt
3 tablespoons baking powder	1 ¼ cups butter flavored shortening
½ cup dry milk powder	

Mix together flour, baking powder, milk powder and salt in a large bowl. Cut in shortening with pastry blender until mixture resembles coarse corn meal. Store in a container with tight-fitting lid. For Buttermilk Mix, add 9 tablespoons dry buttermilk powder to the basic mix.

BANANA BRAN MUFFINS

A great way to get your fiber and potassium at the same time and use up those "stale" cereals.

1 ½ cups flour	½ cup sugar
1 cup all bran cereal, no flakes	2 tablespoons water
½ teaspoon baking powder	½ cup chopped nuts
½ teaspoon baking soda	Topping:
½ teaspoon salt	⅓ cup brown sugar
1 ½ cups mashed bananas	2 tablespoons flour
1 egg beaten	¼ teaspoon cinnamon
1 tablespoon vanilla extract	1 tablespoon butter
¼ cup shortening	

Blend together in large bowl, flour, cereal, baking powder, baking soda and salt. Set aside. In separate bowl beat banana, egg, vanilla, shortening, sugar and water until smooth. Make a well in center of dry ingredients; add liquids stirring just until all combined. Fold in nuts. It will be thick. Place batter in sprayed muffin cups, filing each ¾ full. Mix together topping ingredients until well combined. Sprinkle over each muffin. Bake in 400° oven until brown about 20 minutes.

BEER SAUSAGE BISCUITS

Food preferences and ingredients in various regions of the country often determine what type of biscuit is favored. People in the North enjoy tall, tender flaky biscuits; in the South they like biscuits with a soft, tender crumb.

2 pounds cooked and crumbled pork sausages	1 teaspoon crushed caraway seeds
	¼ cup chopped green onions
4 cups biscuit baking mix	12 ounces beer

Combine in large bowl, sausage, dry baking mix, crushed seeds and onions. Stir in beer just until moistened. Fill sprayed muffins cups. Bake in 400° oven for 20 minutes. Cool for 5 minutes before removing from muffin tin. Remove from tins carefully and serve warm with soup or egg dish.

BEGINNERS ZUCCHINI MUFFINS

Muffin recipes first began to appear in print in the mid 18th century and quickly caught on. By the 19th century muffin men walked the streets of England at tea time to sell there muffins.

2 eggs	1 ½ cups flour
1 cup shredded zucchini	1 teaspoon baking soda
1 cup sugar	½ teaspoon salt
½ cup canola oil	¼ teaspoon baking powder
½ cup chopped walnuts	

Mix together oil, sugar and eggs. Add shredded zucchini. Combine in another bowl, flour, baking powder, baking soda and salt. Stir dry ingredients into wet ingredients just until combined. Fold in chopped walnuts. Lightly spray muffin tin; fill two-thirds full with batter. Bake in 375° oven for 25 minutes.

BERRY BRAN MUFFINS

Three states in the United States of America have adopted official muffins: Minnesota, Massachusetts and New York.

2 cups wheat bran	⅓ cup canola oil
1 cup oat bran	⅓ cup molasses
1 cup whole wheat flour	⅓ cup honey
2 teaspoons baking soda	1 teaspoon vanilla extract
1 teaspoon baking powder	2 cups frozen
½ teaspoon salt	or fresh blueberries
2 eggs	or 2 cups frozen strawberries
⅔ cup milk	or 2 cups frozen mixed berries
⅔ cup yogurt	or 2 cups frozen blackberries

Spray muffin pan or line with paper liners. Combine wheat bran, oat bran, flour, baking soda, baking powder and salt in large bowl and set aside. Combine eggs, milk, yogurt, canola oil, molasses and honey in small bowl and mix well. (Note: you can use all honey or all molasses instead) Pour wet ingredients into dry ingredients and mix with rubber spatula just until combined. Gently fold fresh or frozen berries into batter. There is no need to defrost frozen berries, but do quickly rinse off any ice with cold water. Generously fill muffin cups with batter. Bake in 375° oven until toothpick inserted in center comes out clean, about 20 to 25 minutes. Cool muffins in pan for 10 to 15 minutes, carefully remove from pan and serve warm, or let cool on a wire rack.

BERRY SCONES

Traditional English scones could include raisins or currants, but are often plain, relying on jam, preserves, lemon curd or honey for added flavor. Fancy scones usually with dried fruit such as cranberries and dates, nuts, orange rind, chocolate morsels and other flavorings and "fresh" fruit scones—are best enjoyed without butter and jam

1 ¾ cups flour
4 teaspoons baking powder
½ teaspoon baking soda
½ cup sugar
½ teaspoon salt
½ cup butter

½ cup milk
½ cup sour cream
1 egg beaten
1 ½ cups frozen blackberries, raspberries
Mixed berries, huckleberries or blueberries

Sift flour, baking powder, baking soda, sugar and salt into large bowl. Cut in butter using a pastry blender or rubbing between your fingers into pea sized lumps. Mix together milk and sour cream in a measuring cup, add egg. Pour all at once into dry ingredients; stir gently until well blended. Fold in berries. Overworking the dough results in terrible scones! With floured hands, pat scone dough into balls 2 to 3 inches diameter, depending on what size you want. Place onto greased baking sheet and flatten lightly. Let scones barely touch each other. Whisk together another egg and 1 tablespoon of milk. Brush tops of scones with egg wash. Let them rest for about 10 minutes. Bake for 10 to 15 minutes in 400° oven, until tops are golden brown, not deep brown. Break each scone apart, or slice in half. Serve with butter and a selection of jams—or plain.

BRAN MUFFINS

You can't go wrong with a good bran muffin for breakfast or even as a snack.

1 ½ cups wheat bran
1 cup buttermilk
⅓ cup canola oil
1 egg
⅔ cup brown sugar
½ teaspoon vanilla extract

1 cup flour
1 teaspoon baking soda
1 teaspoon baking powder
½ teaspoon salt
½ cup raisins

Mix together wheat bran and buttermilk; let stand for 10 minutes. Beat together oil, egg, sugar and vanilla and add to buttermilk/bran mixture. Sift together flour, baking soda, baking powder and salt. Stir flour mixture into buttermilk mixture, until just blended. Fold in raisins and spoon batter into sprayed paper lined muffin tins. Bake in 375° oven for 15 to 20 minutes, or until a toothpick inserted into the center of a muffin comes out clean.

CARROT MUFFINS

Carrots can be eaten in a variety of ways: the simplest way is raw, chopped and boiled, fried or steamed, in salads, soups and stews, but the most unexpected was when I started using them in baking for carrot cakes, breads and muffins.

2 eggs	1 ½ cups flour
1 cup grated carrots	1 teaspoon baking powder
1 cup sugar	½ teaspoon baking soda
½ cup canola oil	½ teaspoon cinnamon
¼ cup orange liqueur	½ teaspoon nutmeg
¼ cup raisins	⅛ teaspoon allspice
½ cup chopped pecans	¼ teaspoon salt

Prepare muffin tins with paper liners and spray whole tin. Heat orange liqueur to just boiling. Add raisins and remove from heat. Set aside and allow to soak Combine in large mixing bowl, grated carrots, sugar, oil and eggs. Combine in separate bowl flour, baking powder, baking soda, spices and salt. Mix dry ingredients in to wet ingredients and mix just until blended. Drain raisins and fold in chopped pecans and raisins. Fill muffin tins two-thirds full. Bake in 350° oven for 40 minutes.

CINNAMON OATMEAL SCONES

Originally, scones were made with oats, shaped into a large round, scored into wedges and griddle-baked over an open fire. With the advent of oven baking, the round of dough was cut into triangles and the scones were baked individually. Today's scones are quick breads, similar to American biscuits.

1 ½ cups quick rolled oats—toasted	½ teaspoon salt
¼ cup evaporated milk	¼ teaspoon cinnamon
¼ cup heavy cream	10 tablespoons cold butter cut into
1 large egg	½ inch cubes
1 ½ cups flour	Topping:
⅓ cup sugar	1 tablespoon sugar
2 teaspoons baking powder	1 teaspoon cinnamon

Whisk milk, cream and egg until well mixed; remove 1 tablespoon to small bowl for glazing at end. Mix flour, sugar, baking powder and salt until combined, cut cold butter into dry ingredients until resembles coarse cornmeal. Take 2 tablespoons of toasted oats and place in small bowl. Add rest of toasted oats to batter and stir. Pour liquid ingredients into dry ingredients and combine with rubber spatula. Dough will be very chunky. With hands, gently knead dough in bowl until all dry bits are incorporated and dough forms cohesive ball. Turn dough onto work surface dust with the oats and add 2 tablespoons of reserved toasted oats. Gently pat into 7-inch disk. Cut dough into 8 wedges, place on sprayed baking sheet. Mix together sugar and cinnamon, brush tops with egg and milk wash, and sprinkle cinnamon sugar. Bake in 450° oven 12-14 minutes or until golden brown. Cool on baking sheet on wire rack for 5 minutes; remove scones to cooling rack and cool for 30 minutes before serving.

CORN FRITTERS

Fritters are small cakes made with a primary ingredient, mixed with batter and fried, are found in many American cuisines. "Corn fritters" are eaten with southern type foods and fish.

3 cups vegetable oil for frying	2 eggs slightly beaten
3 cups flour	½ cup evaporated milk
2 teaspoons baking powder	1 tablespoon melted shortening
2 teaspoons salt	2 cans whole kernel corn drained
1 teaspoon sugar	1 ½ cups cream-style corn

In deep-fryer or on stove top in deep skillet, preheat oil to 375°. In large bowl combine flour, baking powder and salt. Stir together eggs, milk and shortening; fold ingredient into flour mixture until thoroughly mixed. Stir in drained corn and cream style corn, mix well. Dip spoon into heated oil, then take a 2 tablespoon sized scoop of fritter mixture and carefully drop into oil. Turn fritter over when first side is browned. Fritters should be cooked through and browned in 4 to 5 minutes. Remove with a skimmer and drain on brown paper bag or paper towels.

CRANBERRY MUFFINS

Lingonberries are known as 'lowbush' cranberries or partridge berries in North America from Alaska to the Atlantic coast of Canada and can be substituted in any cranberry recipe. Lingonberry jam is a staple food in Scandinavian cuisine and homes.

1 ½ cups flour	1 cup fresh or frozen cranberries
1 tablespoon baking powder	1 cup milk
Pinch salt	¼ cup melted butter
½ cup sugar	1 egg

Mix together all of dry ingredients in large bowl. Combine milk, melted butter and egg in small bowl. Add liquid mixture to dry mixture; stir until moistened. Fold in cranberries. Fill sprayed muffin cups almost full. Bake in 375° oven for 25 minutes.

CREAMY POLENTA

This polenta is light, fluffy and creamy; it could almost be a dessert. Polenta is made from coarsely ground cornmeal and is a staple of Northern Italy.

4 cups water	4 tablespoons butter
Salt	1 cup cream cheese
1 cup yellow polenta	

Heat water lightly seasoned with salt to a boil over high heat, about 5 minutes. Quickly whisk in polenta until fully combined. Reduce heat to low simmer, add butter and allow polenta to cook, stirring occasionally, for 30 minutes. Stir in cream cheese and salt to taste. If preparing in advance, cool, cover and refrigerate. Reheat in microwave, about 5 minutes on high, just before serving. Stir vigorously after reheating to fluff.

DARK ZUCCHINI BREAD

3 eggs	1 teaspoon baking soda
1 cup canola oil	1 teaspoon salt
1 ¾ cups sugar	2 teaspoons cinnamon
2 cups grated zucchini	1 tablespoon vanilla extract
2 cups flour	1 cup chopped nuts

In a large bowl, beat eggs until light and fluffy. Stir in sugar, oil and zucchini. In separate bowl, sift together dry ingredients and blend into egg mixture. Add vanilla. Fold in nuts. Pour batter evenly in 2 sprayed loaf pans. Bake in 350° oven for 1 hour.

DELICIOUS FLAXSEED MUFFINS

Ground flaxseed can go rancid at room temperature in as little as one week. Refrigeration and storage in sealed containers will keep ground flax from becoming rancid for longer. One tablespoon of ground flax seeds and three tablespoons of water may serve as a replacement for one egg in baking by binding the other ingredients together. Ground flax seeds can also be mixed in with oatmeal, yogurt, water, or any other food item where a nutty flavor.

3 cups ground flaxseed	2 tablespoons canola oil
1 ¼ cups flour	1 tablespoon baking powder
1 cup skim milk	2 eggs
½ cup molasses	

Whisk together ground flax seed, flour and baking powder. In separate bowl, stir together remaining wet ingredients. Stir this mixture into dry ingredients until just moistened. Pour into sprayed muffin tins. Bake in 350° oven for 20 minutes or until done.

DROP BISCUITS AND SAUSAGE GRAVY

Biscuits and gravy is a popular breakfast dish among people of the Southern US. Buttermilk biscuits are covered in thick "country" or "white" gravy made from the drippings of cooked pork sausage and flavored with black pepper. In some parts of the South it's known as sawmill gravy.

Biscuits:
2 cups flour
2 teaspoons baking powder
½ teaspoon baking soda
1 teaspoon sugar
¾ teaspoon salt
1 cup cold buttermilk

8 tablespoons melted and cooled butter
Gravy:
1 pound pork sausages
2 tablespoons black pepper
4-6 tablespoons flour
4 cups milk

Biscuits: Whisk flour, baking powder, baking soda, sugar and salt in large bowl. Combine buttermilk and butter in medium bowl, stirring until butter forms small clumps. Add milk mixture to dry ingredients and stir with rubber spatula until just combined and batter pulls away from sides of bowl. Using greased or sprayed ¼ cup measurer, scoop level amounts of batter and drop onto sprayed baking sheet. Bake in 475° oven for 12-14 minutes or until golden brown.

SAUSAGE GRAVY: Fry sausage into small pieces. As soon as sausage is completely brown, turn to medium heat. Remove sausage to plate. Add black pepper. Add flour by the tablespoon, stirring constantly. Let flour turn BROWN before adding another tablespoon (if you don't, your gravy will taste like flour). After you have added enough flour to make gravy as thick as you like, add milk and stir with whisk. Whisk until smooth and hot; add sausage, stir. Put sausage gravy on open-face biscuits.

ENGLISH MUFFINS

These are found on breakfast menus of fast food restaurants worldwide. Most often toasted then topped with butter and/or jam; they're also used in breakfast sandwiches with a meat (bacon, ham, or sausage), an egg (fried, scrambled, poached or steam-poached) and cheese. They're also an ingredient in the traditional New York brunch dish,

Eggs Benedict	2 tablespoons vegetable oil
2 cups flour	1 tablespoon yeast
1 cup warm water	1 teaspoon salt
1 cup whole wheat flour	Cornmeal

In mixing bowl, mix warm water, vegetable oil, yeast and salt. Beat in flour, followed by whole wheat flour; mix thoroughly. Use more vegetable oil and cover entire dough surface and allow to rise for 30-40 minutes. Knead dough until soft; cut into six pieces and roll each piece in cornmeal. Form each ball into muffins, four inches in diameter. Place on cookie sheet and bake in 350° oven for 15 minutes.

EVERYDAY MUFFINS

Minnesota has adopted the blueberry muffin as the official state muffin. Massachusetts in 1986 adopted the Corn Muffin as the official state muffin. Then in 1987 New York took on the Apple Muffin as its official muffin of choice.

1 ¾ cups flour	Berry Muffin:
⅓ cup sugar	¾ cup fresh or frozen berries
2 teaspoons baking powder	½ teaspoon lemon juice
¼ teaspoon salt	Raisin Muffin:
1 beaten egg	1 cup raisins
¾ cup evaporated milk	¼ teaspoon allspice
¼ cup canola oil	

Spray a muffin tin and line with baking cups. In medium bowl combine flour, sugar, baking powder and salt. Make well in center of dry mixture; set aside. In another bowl, combine egg, milk and oil. Add egg mixture all at once to dry mixture. Stir just until moistened. Spoon batter into cups filling ⅔ full. Bake in 400° oven for 20 minutes or until golden. Cook in muffin tins on wire rack for 5 minutes. Remove from muffins cups.

FLAKY BISCUITS

Mixing ingredients is crucial in producing an excellent biscuit. Mix dough by hand using either a pastry blender, two knives or just your fingertips. Mixing by hand helps to prevent over mixing of the dough. Adding cream of tartar keeps the biscuit very white during the baking process and the topping will encourage the outside to become golden brown and delicious.

2 ½ cups flour	1 egg lightly beaten
1 tablespoon baking powder	⅛ teaspoon cream of tartar
½ teaspoon salt	Topping:
1 tablespoon sugar	1 egg lightly beaten
½ cup butter cut in pieces	1 tablespoon milk
¾ cup milk	

Line baking sheet with parchment paper. In large mixing bowl, whisk together flour, baking powder, salt, cream of tartar and sugar. Cut butter into dry ingredients until mixture resembles coarse crumbs. Add milk, egg and stir until just combined. The texture should be sticky, moist and lumpy. Place dough on lightly floured surface and knead dough gently until it comes together and is smooth dough. Roll out dough to about ½ inch thickness. Cut out biscuits with a lightly floured cutter of your choice. Place on baking sheet and brush tops with egg and milk mixture. Bake in 400° oven for about 10-15 minutes or until tops are golden brown. Remove from oven and place on wire rack. Serve warm with butter and honey.

FLAVORFUL OATMEAL MUFFINS

The 1970s and 1980s led to significant changes in this simple food. The decline in home-baking and rise in health food concerns, specialty food shops and gourmet coffees contributed to the creation of a new muffin trend. New recipes sprang up overnight and continue to show up everywhere.

2 cups old fashion oatmeal	2 tablespoons brown sugar
1 packet instant brown sugar	2 eggs
oatmeal	3 tablespoons shortening
⅔ cup sour milk	1 ½ teaspoons baking soda
1 cup flour	½ teaspoon salt
½ cup sugar	1 cup raisins

Soak old fashion oatmeal in sour milk overnight. Next day, preheat oven to 425°. Take oatmeal and milk mixture, add instant oatmeal, sugars, eggs, shortening and mix well. Mix together flour, baking soda, salt and raisins. Mix dry ingredients into wet ingredients and mix to combine, do not over mix. Spoon into lightly greased or sprayed muffin tins, two-thirds full. Bake for 20-25 minutes or until toothpick inserted in middle comes out clean.

FRUIT LOVERS MUFFINS

Muffin paper cups are used to line the bottoms of muffin pans to facilitate the easy removal of the finished pastry from the muffin tin. The advantage is easier removal and cleanup, more precise form, and moister muffins; however, using them will prevent a crust.

1 ¾ cups flour	⅓ cup raisins
⅓ cup sugar	¼ cup canola oil
2 teaspoons baking powder	¾ cup evaporated milk
¼ teaspoon salt	½ teaspoon vanilla extract
½ teaspoon allspice	¼ cup orange juice
⅓ cup chopped dried apricots	2 beaten eggs
⅓ cup dried cranberries	

In large bowl, combine flour, sugar, baking powder, salt and allspice. Add apricots, cranberries and raisins coating well. Stir together oil, milk, vanilla, orange juice and beaten eggs. Stir into dry mixture just until moistened. Batter will be lumpy. Spoon batter into cups of sprayed muffin tin. Bake in 400° oven for 18-20 minutes. Cool muffins in tin on wire rack for 5 minutes then remove cupcakes to cool on wire rack.

FRUITY SCONES

The original scone was round and flat, usually the size of a small plate, made with unleavened oats and baked on a griddle, then cut into triangle-like quadrants for serving. Today many would call the large round cake a bannock, and call the quadrants scones. In Scotland, the words are often used interchangeably.

1 cup sour cream	¼ teaspoon cream of tartar
1 teaspoon baking soda	1 teaspoon salt
1 cup room temperature butter	1 cup raisins, candied fruit, chopped
¾ cup sugar	dates, chopped dried apricot
1 egg	and/or cranberries,
1 teaspoon vanilla extract	Semisweet chocolate chips or any
4 cups flour	flavored chips
2 teaspoons baking powder	

In small bowl, blend sour cream and baking soda, and set aside. Lightly grease large baking sheet. In bowl, mix together flour, sugar, baking powder, cream of tartar and salt. In large bowl mix butter with sugar. Beat vanilla into egg. Add to butter mixture. Add flour mixture to butter mixture and combine, do not over mix. Stir sour cream with baking soda into batter, again, do not over mix. Mix in raisins, candied fruit, chips or other dried fruit. Divide and form into 16 balls and press by hand into flat circle and place 2 inches apart on baking sheet. Cut each circle into 12 wedges. Bake in 350° oven for 12 to 15 minutes until golden brown on bottom. The key to keeping them from drying out or being tough is not to over mix or over handle.

HUSH PUPPIES

Hush puppies are a southern American food consisting of thick cornmeal batter deep fried or baked in a sphere, oblong or ring shape. A distinctly Southern food, they are now available on the menus of fried-fish fast food restaurants everywhere. The name is often attributed to those who fry corn meal and feed it to their dogs to hush the puppies. Recipes vary from state to state, some include onion seasoning, chopped onions, beer or jalapeños. Fried properly, the hushpuppy will be moist and yellow or white on the inside, while crunchy and medium to dark brown on the outside.

2 ½ cups cornmeal	1 tablespoon baking powder
1 teaspoon baking soda	1 egg beaten
1 teaspoon salt	2 cups buttermilk
2 tablespoons sugar	Vegetable oil
2 tablespoons flour	

Mix cornmeal, soda, salt, sugar, flour, and baking powder in a bowl. In measuring cup, whisk egg into milk. Combine milk mixture into dry ingredients. Batter should hold its shape when picked up with a spoon. If batter is too soft, add more cornmeal until firm. Drop 3-4 at a time by tablespoons into oil heated to 350° in a deep skillet. Fry until gold brown, about 3 minutes, turning several times. Drain on paper towels.

HEAVENLY MUFFINS

There are many varieties and flavors of muffins made with ingredients such as sweet spices, blueberries, chocolate, flavored chips, cucumbers, huckleberries, raspberry, cinnamon, pumpkin, dates, savory spices, nuts, lemon, banana, orange, peach, fresh herbs, strawberry, boysenberry, almonds, carrot and much so much more baked into the muffin.

2 eggs	Topping:
3 cups flour	1 cup melted butter
1 cup milk	1 cup sugar
1 cup sugar	1 tablespoon cinnamon
1 teaspoon salt	
½ teaspoon nutmeg	

5 tablespoons butter

5 tablespoons shortening

3 teaspoons baking powder

Spray 12 muffin tin very well with nonstick cooking spray. Cream together butter, shortening and sugar. Beat in the eggs, salt, nutmeg and baking powder. Stir in flour and milk alternately until mixture is just combined. Fill muffin cups to top. Bake in 350° oven for about 20 minutes. Allow to cool for a few minutes. Mix together sugar and cinnamon for topping. With each muffin, dip in melted butter then roll each muffin in cinnamon sugar blend. Let cool before serving

HONEY BRAN MUFFINS

Delicious, healthy muffins in no time and experiment by stirring in fruits or nuts or chips.

2 cups wheat bran	⅔ cup milk
1 cup oat bran	⅔ cup yogurt
1 cup whole wheat flour	⅓ cup canola oil
2 teaspoons baking soda	⅓ cup molasses
1 teaspoon baking powder	⅓ cup honey
½ teaspoon salt	1 teaspoon vanilla extract
2 eggs	

Combine wheat bran, oat bran, flour, baking soda, baking powder, and salt in a large bowl and set aside. Combine eggs, milk, yogurt, canola oil, molasses, and honey in a small bowl and mix well. (Note: you can use all honey or all molasses instead). Pour wet ingredients into dry ingredients and mix with a rubber spatula just until combined. Generously fill sprayed or paper lined muffin cups with batter. Bake in 375° oven until a toothpick inserted in the center comes out clean, about 20 to 25 minutes. Cool muffins in pan for 10 to 15 minutes, then carefully remove from pan and serve warm, or let cool on a wire rack. Store muffins in an airtight container for up to 3 days or freeze.

Blueberry Banana Bran Muffins: Follow Basic Bran Muffin recipe, but stir 3 mashed very ripe banana. Gently fold 1-½ cups fresh or frozen blueberries into batter. Baking time may need to be increased to 25 to 28 minutes.

Cranberry Orange Bran Muffins: Follow Basic Bran Muffin recipe, but replace milk with ⅔ cup orange juice and omit the vanilla extract. Stir 1 cup dried cranberries to finished batter.

HUMPBACK CHEDDAR DROP BISCUITS

We were snacking on these when we saw our first group humpback whales and dolphins. The original biscuit was a flat cake put back in the oven after being removed from it's tin, hence the French name "twice-baked". This very hard, dry biscuit was the staple for sailors and soldiers for centuries.

3 cups biscuit baking mix

1 tablespoon chopped fresh chives

¾ cup shredded sharp cheddar cheese

1 tablespoon chopped green onions

¾ cup evaporated milk

Combine all ingredients in bowl until forms dough and well combined. Drop by spoonfuls onto ungreased baking sheet. Bake in 450° oven for 8-10 minutes or until golden brown.

IRISH COFFEE MUFFINS

A simple way to enjoy the taste without the headache, for breakfast, coffee break or dessert.

1 egg beaten

2 cups flour

½ cup sugar

½ cup melted butter

½ cup heavy cream

¼ cup coffee liqueur

¼ cup Irish whiskey

1 tablespoon baking powder

½ teaspoon salt

Combine together flour, baking powder and salt. Stir together egg, sugar, butter, cream, liqueur and whiskey in separate bowl. Mix dry ingredients into wet ingredients, just until moistened. Fill paper-lined and sprayed muffin tins full. Bake in 400° oven for 20 minutes.

IRRESISTIBLE CRUMB TOPPING

This can be used to top pies, muffins, coffee cake, plain cakes or as a filling for cakes.

1 cup brown sugar	¼ cup butter diced
1 cup flour	1 tablespoon ground cinnamon (optional)

In a medium bowl, mix together the sugar and flour. Mix in butter with a fork or stand mixer just until the topping is crumbly. Top your pie, cake or muffins before baking.

LEMON EGG BISCUITS

These cookies are light, cakey and refreshingly citrusy. Feathery, light biscuits originated in Southern plantation kitchens but, now are popular throughout the United States

6 cups flour	½ cup milk
1 ½ cups sugar	Lemon Icing:
3 tablespoons baking powder	2 ½ cups powdered sugar
1 teaspoon salt	2 tablespoons lemon extract
6 eggs	Few drop milk
4 tablespoons lemon extract	Colored sprinkles
1 cup canola oil	

Line four large cookie sheets with parchment paper. In a large bowl, mix flour, sugar, baking powder and salt. In a small bowl, lightly whisk eggs, lemon extract, oil and milk. Add wet ingredients to dry ingredients. Using rubber spatula, mix until dough starts to form. Using hands, lightly squeeze and knead dough. If it seems a bit dry, add 1 teaspoon of milk at a time until it reaches desired consistency. Dough should be somewhat sticky and elastic. Scoop 1 tablespoon of dough and roll between palms until a smooth ball forms. Place balls on parchment-lined baking sheet 2 inches apart. Bake cookies in 325° oven for 15 to 20 minutes, or until lightly browned on bottoms. Tops will be white but cooked through. Transfer to rack and cool completely before frosting.

To make icing, whisk powdered sugar and lemon extract in small bowl. Add few drops of milk and continue whisking until icing is smooth and opaque and clings to back of spoon. Taste and add more lemon extract, if desired. Dip top of biscuit in icing, place on rack. Decorate with sprinkles. Allow to dry completely before storing in airtight tin or plastic container. Place waxed paper between layers to protect icing.

MILE HIGH BISCUITS

A perfect biscuit, should have a golden brown crusty top and bottom and when you split it in half it should be soft and flaky and moist.

2 cups flour	**½ teaspoon baking soda**
1 tablespoon baking powder	**4 tablespoons cold butter**
1 tablespoon sugar	**1 ½ cups cold buttermilk**
1 teaspoon salt	

In large bowl, combine flour, baking powder, sugar, soda, and salt. Cut in butter until you have pieces size of small peas. Make well in center of dry ingredients; pour in buttermilk. With wooden spoon, gently blend dry ingredients into buttermilk, just until mixture is clumping together. If necessary, add few more teaspoons of buttermilk. Transfer dough to lightly floured board. Pat out in circle about 8 inches in diameter and ½-inch thick. Using biscuit cutter, cut out and place on ungreased baking sheet. Bake in 450° oven on center oven rack for about 10 to 12 minutes, until tops are browned.

PUMPKIN MUFFINS

In colonial times, Native Americans roasted long strips of pumpkin in an open fire. Colonists sliced off pumpkin tops; removed seeds and filled the insides with milk, spices and honey. This was baked in hot ashes and is the origin of pumpkin pie.

2 eggs	1 teaspoon salt
1 cup brown sugar	1 teaspoon cinnamon
1 cup milk	1 teaspoon nutmeg
1 cup canned pumpkins	1 teaspoon pumpkin pie spice
½ cup unsweetened applesauce	¼ teaspoon cloves
2 tablespoons sugar	¼ teaspoon allspice
3 cups flour	¼ teaspoon ginger
4 teaspoons baking powder	

In a large bowl, combine sugars, eggs, milk, pumpkin and applesauce mix well. Mix together flour, baking powder, salt and spices in separate bowl. Mix dry ingredients into wet ingredients and stir to combine, do not over mix. Spoon into lightly greased or sprayed muffin tins almost to top. Bake at 325° for about 25 minutes.

RAISIN BRAN MUFFINS

This is very old recipe and loved by so many. It has some variations along the way, but was good from the start, so not too many changes were ever needed.

4 ½ cups All Bran Cereal (no flakes)	2 ¼ cups sugar
1 ⅓ cups boiling water	3 ¾ teaspoons baking soda
3 cups buttermilk	¾ teaspoon salt
4 eggs	1 cup raisins
¾ cup canola oil	1 cup chopped walnuts (optional)
3 ¾ cups flour	

Combine and stir well All Bran and boiling water. Let stand. In another bowl, combine buttermilk, eggs and oil; add sugar. Combine and sift together flour, baking soda and salt. Combine All Bran mixture and liquid ingredients. Add flour mixture and stir just until flour is incorporated (Do NOT over mix or muffins will not have the right texture. Fold in raisins or nuts if desired. Bake in 400° oven in greased muffin pan for 18-20 minutes. To test for doneness, insert a toothpick. If it comes out clean, your muffins are done.

SHORTCAKE BISCUITS

These can be eaten as biscuits or used with fruit and whipped topping to make Shortcake desserts

3 cups flour	3 tablespoons sugar
4 teaspoons baking powder	2 eggs
¾ teaspoon salt	½ cup milk
¼ teaspoon cream of tartar	¾ cup shortening

Sift together in large bowl, flour, baking powder, salt, tartar and sugar. In a separate bowl, beat eggs with milk and set aside. Mix shortening with dry ingredients cutting in until makes coarse crumbs. Add milk and eggs; knead for a few minutes on board. Roll ¾ inch thick. Cut in to rounds with glass or biscuit cutter; place on sprayed cookie sheet and bake in 450° oven for 10 to 15 minutes.

SWEET BACON BISCUIT

If you want crusty biscuits, cool them uncovered. If a softer crust is desired, then wrap the hot biscuits in a clean dish towel.

1 pound bacon cut into ½ inch pieces	¾ cup buttermilk
2 ½ cups biscuit baking mix	¼ cup maple syrup
	Additional maple syrup

Cook bacon over medium heat until cooked but not crispy, remove to paper towel to remove excess fat. In large bowl, stir in biscuit baking mix, bacon, buttermilk and maple syrup just until dough is well combined. Don't overwork the dough. Refrigerate dough until chilled. Drop by spoonfuls onto ungreased cookie sheet. Bake for 20 minutes in 350° oven. Remove tray from oven; quickly drizzle 1 additional teaspoon maple syrup over each biscuit. Place tray back in oven for 3 more minutes.

ZUCCHINI BREAD

This is more of a muffin texture and can be made into muffins instead of a loaf.

3 eggs	3 cups flour
2 cups sugar	1 teaspoon cinnamon
1 cup canola oil	1 teaspoon baking soda
2 cups grated zucchini	¼ teaspoon baking powder
½ cup sour cream	1 cup white chocolate chips

Beat together eggs, sugar, and oil. Blend in grated zucchini; add sour cream. Mix together in separate bowl, flour, baking powder, soda, and cinnamon. Stir in chips. Pour batter into 2 sprayed loaf pans. Bake in 350° oven for 80 minutes. Cool on wire rack.

Avoid Common Mistakes Making Muffins

If a muffin turns out hard that means there is too much flour and not enough liquid in the batter. Or, the batter may have been stirred too long and too hard. If muffins are tough and soggy, with peaks in the center, the batter was probably over-mixed, which toughens it. A muffin that rises and then falls flat in the center does not have enough flour. Sometimes eggs are so large that they increase the ratio of liquid ingredients, so you may need to increase the flour by about ¼ cup. If muffins are coarse-textured, it may mean not enough stirring and baking at too low a temperature.

BASIC OLD FASHIONED BISCUIT

If you want crusty biscuits, cool them uncovered. If a softer crust is desired, then wrap the hot biscuits in a clean dish towel.

2 cups self-rising flour	**½ teaspoon baking soda**
1 cup canola oil	**(if buttermilk is used)**
1 cup milk or buttermilk	**self-rising flour**

In large bowl, add flour and make a well in the center for mixing. Add oil to the well. Stir the well as you add buttermilk mixing in more and more flour until all flour is mixed in and dough is sticky, gummy and on the verge of being "too wet". You may need less that 1 cup for this. Turn out the dough onto a floured surface and with flour on your hands make into a very soft dough, sprinkling a little extra self-rising flour over it all as needed until no longer sticky. Try not to work the dough at all or anymore than necessary for it to be consistent throughout. Pat out dough to ½-inch thickness. Cut with floured 2 ½-inch round cutter. Place on greased cookie sheet. Bake in 450° oven for 12 to 14 minutes or until golden brown. Brush with melted butter. Serve warm.

POULTRY

I didn't realize it at the time but growing up in a Methodist Church immersed me in an atmosphere of cooking for others with their potluck dinners. What a perfect example of the parable about the loaves and fishes; no one ever went hungry. Most churches and organizations had potlucks, it just seemed that we United Methodist had perfected the whole process. An important part of that bounty was having plenty of the dish everyone counted on being there: fried chicken.

I liked being at our church potlucks, people were happy. Everyone helped and made sure the group was getting fed. The women of the church were in charge and they took the responsibility of serving very seriously. It was their gift; even cleaning tables, doing dishes and handing out covered leftovers for others to take home. They got an occasional applause, compliments and thanks, but that isn't why they did it. For them, this was a way to serve God. Feeding the body so the spirit could be fed. One of those giving hearts was a wonderful lady Peg G. who gave me my first and most used cookbook when I got married. She and those wonderful Stephan Memorial United Methodist Church women taught me this wisdom years ago, "How can a hungry child or adult be expected to listen to you tell them how much you love them? Their growling stomach is always speaking louder. Quiet the hungry tummy and then you can speak to their heart."

Blessed Are They That Cook

There are dishes that cooks are famous for and are obligated to bring to every potluck. They are known and loved for their expertise and ability to cook something that's made best by them. I wanted to make a dish of such high quality that everyone asked me to bring it to all the potlucks. It took awhile, but once I started fixing potluck dishes I had my chosen dish perfected and ready for potluck history.

Turkey was inexpensive and plenty to feed a crowd. It was something that most people only ate once or twice a year for the holidays. It wasn't any harder to cook than a roast and always made my house smell wonderful. I found my signature dish and never took any leftovers home. How appropriate it is to bring the symbol of the first Thanksgiving on a plate to a potluck, both excellent representations of sharing, giving and fellowship.

Since those days, more people eat turkey during the year; it can be fixed in so many ways and is now recognized as being much healthier to eat. Turkey is a well loved meat in our family. My brother Hugh has the perfect personality to spend the time and the patience one needs to smoke an incredibly wonderful bird. Smoked turkey leftovers make an absolutely incredible soup base, so the goodness goes on for days.

I believe every guy should have a special meal he can fix when called upon to do so. I can always count on my brother Paul to make his roasted turkey breast impeccably, no leftovers there. Even animals know how good poultry is for us. I drive my poor dog crazy when that roasting turkey smell overwhelmingly fills the house. Even at 16 years old, he will pace his painful hips through the kitchen hoping something will drop his way during the carving process. Hugh, Paul, Marlowe and I know, you can't go wrong with poultry.

BARBECUED CHICKEN BREAST

4 whole chicken breasts halved	2 tablespoons Worcestershire sauce
Marinade:	2 tablespoons Dijon style mustard
4 cups cold water	3 tablespoons molasses
½ cup salt	2 tablespoons maple syrup
1 tablespoon garlic salt	3 tablespoons cider vinegar
2 tablespoons chili powder	2 teaspoons chili powder
Sauce:	1 tablespoon garlic powder
1 cup ketchup	1 teaspoon black pepper
2 tablespoons finely grated onions	

Place chicken in bowl with salts and chili powder mixed with water. Let chicken soak in brine for 30 minutes. Remove chicken and discard brine. Pat dry chicken. Preheat grill. Mix all sauce ingredients together in saucepan and heat until boiling; set aside ¾ of sauce to use when serving. Place chicken on grill, baste with remaining sauce frequently. Grill about 5 minutes on one side; turn and grill another 5-10 minutes until chicken juices run clear. Don't overcook. Serve with reserved sauce.

BLUE CHEESE STUFFING FOR POULTRY

The popularity of blue cheese has grown so much in the last few years, it's being used on everything: as a veggie dip, on top of steaks, in salads, in and on top of hamburgers—why not poultry.

¼ cup butter	¾ cup crumbled American blue
½ cup chopped celery	cheese
1 cup sliced mushrooms	1 tablespoon poultry seasoning
1 cup chopped onions	½ teaspoon sugar or artificial
4 cups croutons	sweetener
¼ cup chopped parsley	⅛ teaspoon black pepper
1 can sliced water chestnuts	Chicken broth

Melt butter in skillet, add celery, mushrooms and onion; sauté. In large bowl, combine croutons, parsley, chestnuts, cheese, seasoning, sugar and pepper. Add celery mixture and toss lightly to blend well. Add enough broth to dampen ingredients; mix well. Place in sprayed casserole dish and bake covered in 325° oven for 20 minutes; uncover and cook for 10 more minutes.

BRINE A TURKEY

This process can be used for whole chickens and when cooking chicken thighs or breast. Cut back on amount of ingredients, size of container and time in brine. Brining poultry before cooking can make an incredible difference in the moisture and juiciness. Try it once and you will brine all your poultry.

4 quarts water	2 tablespoons black pepper
3 ½ cups kosher or sea salt	8 cloves garlic
4 cups sugar	2 tablespoons poultry seasoning

Wash and dry cooler which is large enough to hold turkey and brine. Combine ingredients in a non-aluminum pan. Bring to boil, stir occasionally until all sugar and salt are dissolved. Allow brine to cool. Pour into cooler. Add 2-3 quarts of ice to bring temperature of brine up to 35°. Remove giblets, neck, etc from inside turkey; wash turkey well, inside and out. Rub inside of turkey liberally with additional salt. Submerge turkey entirely. (Recipe can be doubled or halved if needed) Keep the turkey cold- at or below 35°. Add ice as needed or place cooler in cold place. Check temperature to make sure it doesn't go above 40°. Keep in brine for 24 hours. Remove turkey from brine, discard brine; rinse thoroughly with cold water. Pat dry with clean towel; rub turkey with combination of melted butter and olive oil. Sprinkle with salt and pepper and roast.

CAJUN CHICKEN SALAD

1 head chopped iceberg lettuce	2 tablespoons soy sauce
½ cup each shredded carrots,	½ tablespoon Worcestershire sauce
cheddar cheese and mozzarella	¼ cup mayonnaise
cheese	¼ cup Dijon style mustard
½ cup chopped red cabbage	1 tablespoon mustard
1 hard-boiled egg diced	¼ cup honey
1 large tomato diced	1 tablespoon white vinegar
2 chicken breasts fillets	⅛ teaspoon paprika
1 cup water	4 teaspoons Cajun seasoning
3 tablespoons lime juice	½ tablespoon butter

Whisk mayonnaise, mustards, honey, vinegar and paprika together until well combined. Cover and refrigerate until salad is ready. Combine water, lime juice, soy sauce and Worcestershire sauce; add chicken, cover bowl and refrigerate several hours or overnight. Remove chicken from marinade and discard. Sprinkle a teaspoon of Cajun seasoning over one side of each fillet. Cover entire surface of chicken. Melt butter in large skillet over medium/high heat. Sauté chicken for 4 minutes on side with spices. Sprinkle teaspoon of remaining seasoning over top of chicken. Flip chicken over, cook 4 minutes or until done. Remove from skillet and let stand for 5 minutes; slice crosswise ½ inch thick pieces. Toss lettuce, cheese, cabbage, egg and tomato together; spread sliced chicken over salad and serve with dressing.

CHICKEN BEAN ALFREDO

I developed this recipe during Joe's low carb days and it is still one of our favorites.

1 stick butter or margarine	1 teaspoon black pepper
1 8-ounce package cream cheese	1 teaspoon lemon juice
½ cup Parmesan cheese	4 boneless, skinless chicken breasts
½ cup evaporated milk	1 tablespoon olive oil
1 teaspoon garlic powder	1 16-ounce bag frozen green beans

In skillet brown both sides of chicken breasts in olive oil. Place breast in sprayed 13 x 9 baking dish. Let skillet cool down. Melt butter on low heat, scraping bottom of skillet with wooden spoon. Don't let butter brown. When melted, cut softened cream cheese into small chunks and add to butter; whisk until mixture is smooth. Add Parmesan cheese, stir in milk and continue to whisk smooth; add garlic, pepper and lemon juice; stir well. Place frozen green beans on top of chicken breast in baking dish. Pour sauce over beans and chicken. Cover with aluminum foil. Bake in 350° oven for 25 minutes. Remove foil and bake another 5 minutes until sauce is bubbly.

CHICKEN BROCCOLI CASSEROLE

There was a time in the 1980's when every potluck I attended had some variation of this dish.

2 cans cream of chicken soup

1 16-ounce bag frozen chopped
   broccoli

1 cup skim milk

¼ cup cooked mushrooms

1 tablespoon Montreal Chicken
   Seasoning

4 chicken breasts halves

4 cups al dente cooked egg noodles

½ cup grated Parmesan cheese

In large bowl, mix together chicken soup, broccoli, milk and mushrooms. Spread chicken seasoning over each breast and broil until juices run clear. Remove breast from oven, cut into cubes and add to bowl. Stir in noodles and place well combined mixture into sprayed 13x9 baking dish. Top with Parmesan cheese. Bake in 400° oven for 30 minutes or—until heated through.

CHICKEN JAMBALAYA

I look at this as a Louisiana chicken soup, a great Mardi Gras dish to serve.

½ cup chopped celery

½ cup chopped onions

½ cup chopped green bell peppers

3 tablespoons butter

2-14 ½-ounce can tomatoes cut up
   do not discard juice from can

2 cups chicken broth

1 cup long grain rice uncooked

1 teaspoon dried basil

1 teaspoon dried thyme

1 teaspoon garlic powder

1 teaspoon black pepper

½ teaspoon hot pepper sauce

1 bay leaf

2 cups cooked, cubed chicken

In skillet cook celery, onion and bell pepper with butter until vegetables are tender. Stir in tomatoes and juice, broth, uncooked rice, basil, thyme, garlic powder, pepper, hot sauce and bay leaf. Bring to boil; reduce heat. Cover and simmer about 20 minutes or until rice is tender. Stir in chicken and heat through. Discard bay leaf before serving.

CHICKEN LO MEIN VEGETABLE

I love doing Chinese at home, most restaurants use too much sugar, salt and thickeners for me.

3 boneless, skinless chicken breasts	⅓ cup chicken broth
½ pound snow peas	1 tablespoon soy sauce
1 cup julienne style cut carrots	2 teaspoons minced garlic
1 ½ cups cooked spaghetti	2 teaspoons finely chopped fresh
2 teaspoons cornstarch	ginger
1 teaspoon sugar	1-2 tablespoons canola oil
2 teaspoons water	

Cut chicken into small strips. In large saucepan, fill with water and heat to boiling. Add snow peas, carrots and pasta. Boil for 5 minutes or until pasta is al dente; remove pan from heat and drain. In medium bowl mix together cornstarch, sugar and water; add broth, soy sauce, garlic and ginger to cornstarch mixture. Heat oil in large nonstick skillet or wok. Add chicken and stir-fry about 2 minutes or until chicken is white. Stir in broth mixture and vegetables with pasta, continue to cook another 2 minutes.

CHICKEN POT PIE

Use piecrust or biscuits to top, either will this compliment this filling. There are so many ways to fill a chicken pot pie and getting just the right balance has included short cuts and substitutions, this balance seems to gratify my guest the most.

4 carrots, peeled and cut into pieces	⅓ cup flour
1 stalk sliced celery	2 ½ cups chicken broth
1 10-ounce package frozen peas	⅔ cup milk
1 4-ounce can sliced mushrooms	½ teaspoon salt
drained	½ teaspoon black pepper
1 large onion, chopped	½ teaspoon poultry seasoning
2 cups chicken cook, cube	2 crust refrigerated piecrust or 1 can
¼ cup butter	refrigerated biscuits

Use 3 quart casserole dish, place crust into bottom of dish to cover entire bottom and sides; leave some half inch extra dough around edge to fold over top crust before baking. Steam carrots and celery for 5 minutes. Add frozen peas, onions and mushrooms; continue to steam for an additional 10-12 minutes or until carrots are tender. In a separate saucepan, melt butter over medium heat, remove from heat, add flour, whisk together until smooth. Add chicken broth and milk; continue stirring over high heat until mixture boils. Cook for an additional minute or until thick, reduce heat to low. Add chicken chunks, salt, poultry seasoning and pepper to sauce. Stir steamed vegetables in to sauce and simmer mixture over low heat for 4-5 minutes. Spoon filling into casserole dish and carefully cover dish with dough. Fold edge of dough over edge of top dough edge. Brush beaten egg on dough. Cut slits in top crust. Bake on cookie sheet in 425° oven for 30-45 minutes or until top crust is light brown. Or place this filling in sprayed 9x13 baking dish and top with biscuits. Bake in 450° oven for 10-15 minutes, or until chicken mixture is hot and biscuits are well browned.

CHICKEN THREE WAYS

Wanting to put more poultry in our diet and not become bored with the flavor but not having a lot of time to cook, this kept us on the right healthy track.

4 boneless, skinless chicken breasts halves	1 cup fresh water
	RANCH:
4 cups cold water	2 packets ranch salad dressing mix
½ cup table salt	TACO:
½ of chosen seasoning	2 packets taco seasoning mix
1 tablespoon butter	PESTO:
2 tablespoons olive oil	1 cup pesto with basil

Place chicken halves in large bowl with table salt and ½ of whichever seasoning you choose. (1 packet of ranch or taco mix or ½ cup of pesto) mixed with 4 cups of water. Let chicken soak in this seasoned brine for 30 minute; discard water. Heat butter and oil in large skillet on medium high heat. Sprinkle in other ½ of seasoning. Sauté each side of chicken breast in skillet. Reduce heat, pour in fresh water, cover skillet and simmer for 15 minutes. Remove breast, cook liquid on medium heat, scraping skillet bottom with wooden spoon to loosen browned bits until slightly thickened, about 5 minutes. Serve over breast.

CHICKEN AND DUMPLINGS

Chicken and Dumplings-the ultimate comfort food was first introduced in the early 17th century and is a popular soul food dish. When we were kids, my mother made it by simply adding store biscuit dough. For light and fluffy dumplings, the trick: No peeking into the pan while they are cooking. The dumplings need to cook in the steam generated by the simmering stew.

3 pounds chicken pieces	2 cups flour
8 cups chicken broth	1 tablespoon baking powder
2 bay leaves	¾ teaspoon salt
1 teaspoon poultry seasoning	½ cup cold butter
¾ cup frozen green peas	½ cup milk
Dumplings:	

In large wide pot, simmer chicken pieces in broth until chicken is tender, 30 minutes or more. Remove chicken and set it aside. When chicken is cool enough to handle, skin and bone chicken and shred or cut it into bite-sized pieces. Skim chicken fat off surface of broth. In large bowl, thoroughly mix flour, baking powder and salt. Using food processor, pastry blender, or two knives, cut in butter until size of very small peas and distributed throughout dry ingredients. Add milk and knead 8 to 10 times. If dough seems too sticky, add a little more flour. Roll dough out to ⅛-inch thickness and cut into 1-inch squares. Bring broth to a rolling boil, drop in dumplings, cover pot and reduce heat to simmer. Cook for 10 minutes or until dumplings are cooked. Overcooking will cause dumplings to fall apart. To serve, place the chicken pieces in a bowl and ladle hot broth and dumplings over the chicken. {For a major short cut, use can biscuits, cut in half and dredge in flour before placing in pot}

CORDON BLEU

Chicken cordon bleu as a dish is clearly an American recipe innovation first appearing on menus in the early 1960s. It was considered a trendy dish and served at high-class restaurants, becoming a mainstay in all types of American restaurants in the latter half of the 20th century. The type of cheese used can vary from mozzarella to Gruyere to Swiss, according to the chef's choice.

6 boneless skinless chicken breasts
6 thin slice ham
6 slices Swiss cheese
1 cup sliced fresh mushrooms
¼ cup butter or margarine
1 teaspoon minced garlic

1 medium onion chopped
1 10 ¾-ounce can cream of celery
   soup
½ teaspoon black pepper
½ cup evaporated milk

Pound each breast until flat. Place one slice of ham and one slice of cheese on top of each breast. Fold and roll each one, secure with wooden toothpicks. Place rolled breast in sprayed 13 x 9 inch baking dish. Sauté mushrooms, garlic and onions in margarine in large skillet. Remove from heat, stir in soup, pepper and milk. Mix well and pour over breast in baking dish. Bake in 400° oven for 40-45 minutes. Let stand 5 minutes before serving.

CRUNCHY CHICKEN CASSEROLE

This supper is simple and it makes a great dish to pack along to a potluck.

2 cups cooked and cubed chicken
½ cup diced onions
½ cup diced green bell peppers
1 cup thinly sliced celery
½ cup toasted slivered almonds

2 teaspoons lemon juice
½ teaspoon salt
½ cup shredded cheese
1 cup toasted croutons

Combine chicken, onions, peppers, celery, almonds, lemon juice and salt. Place lightly into sprayed baking dish. Sprinkle with cheese and croutons. Bake in 450° oven for 20 minutes or until bubbly.

EASY ROAST TURKEY

There is a huge difference between the wild and domesticated turkey. The wild bird is fast, its eyesight and hearing are sharp. Although unattractive looking, the male has an iridescent plumage. In the US all states boast large inventories except Alaska. Pelee Island, the most southerly landmass in Canada, has sizeable wild turkey population attracting hundreds of turkey hunters. Commercial turkey is completely different. It is specifically bred for its huge breast and tender meat. It cannot fly at all or even run: it's too heavy and cannot mate due to the size of its breasts. This turkey meat is naturally dry; because the bird does not have a chance to create a fat layer that actually provides taste. For this reason carcasses are injected with vegetable oil solutions, water and salt to render it "self basting" an insult to the wild turkey.

4 tablespoons softened butter	**6-7 pounds bone in, skin on turkeys**
¾ teaspoon salt	**breast**
¼ teaspoon black pepper	**1 cup water**

Mix butter, salt and pepper in bowl with rubber spatula until combined. Work butter mixture under skin of breast and over top of breast skin. Spray rack and roasting pan, place turkey with skin side up on rack. Pour water into roasting pan. Place turkey in 425° oven; roast for 30 minutes. Reduce oven heat to 325°; continue to roast turkey until thickest part registers 160° on instant thermometer, about 1 hour. Remove from oven and transfer to carving board, let rest for 20 minutes before slicing.

GROUND TURKEY SAUSAGE

This is a trick I learned back in the early 1970's when I first joined a diet club. I use it to replace regular pork sausage in any kind of recipe—once you cook it, the taste and texture is equal to pork sausage.

1 pound ground turkey meat	**¼ teaspoon tarragon**
½ tablespoon Worcestershire sauce	**¼ teaspoon Thyme**
¼ teaspoon Hickory Smoke	**½ teaspoon black pepper**
Liquid—no more	**1 teaspoon salt**
¼ teaspoon sage	**1 teaspoon garlic powder**

Mix all ingredients and let set for 1 hour to blend flavors. Form into small to medium patties or links or cook breaking up for ground meat. Use 2 tablespoons of vegetable or olive oil or spray Pam in frying pan for less calories. Fry until brown.

KUNG PAO CHICKEN WITH PEANUTS

The original Chinese version includes Sichuan peppercorns that in 1968 was illegal to import because they were potential carriers of a tree disease that can harm citrus crops. The ban's been lifted but in the 37-year ban, a distinct American version doesn't incorporate Sichuan peppercorns. This is my husband's favorite Chinese food choice; learning to make it at home was a necessity.

1 pound skinless, boneless chicken breasts cut in chunks	1 teaspoon white vinegar
2 tablespoons white wine divided	2 teaspoons brown sugar
2 tablespoons soy sauce divided	4 chopped green onions
2 tablespoons sesame oil divided	1 tablespoon minced garlic
2 tablespoons cornstarch dissolved in 2 tablespoon water	1 can water chestnuts
	1 tablespoon peanut butter
1 ounce hot chili paste	½ cup chopped peanuts

Combine 1tablespoon wine, 1 tablespoon soy sauce, 1 tablespoon oil and 1 tablespoon cornstarch/water mixture and mix together. Place chicken pieces in glass dish or bowl and add marinade; toss to coat. Cover dish and place in refrigerator for about 30 minutes. In small bowl combine 1 tablespoon wine, 1 tablespoon soy sauce, 1 tablespoon oil, 1 tablespoon cornstarch/water mixture, chili paste, vinegar and sugar. Mix together; add green onion, garlic, water chestnuts, peanut butter and peanuts. In skillet, heat sauce slowly until aromatic. Meanwhile, remove chicken from marinade and sauté in large skillet until meat is white and juices run clear. When sauce is aromatic, add chicken to it and let simmer together until sauce thickens.

Food is like a Scrapbook

- Full of memories of things done and happy times
- Reminder of moments spent with special people
- Part of capturing and celebrating choice events
- A way to travel to unique and exciting place

MOJITO CHICKEN

I just had to come up with something to celebrate my favorite new drink and it's all my sister-in-law Dee's fault. She served me my first Mojito—it was fabulous. I can't find anyone making them as good, so the closest I could come was put the essence in a recipe.

4 pounds chicken cut in 8 pieces	¼ cup olive oil
4 tablespoons canola oil	¼ cup sugar
1 teaspoon paprika	½ cup rum
2 tablespoons garlic powder	**Glaze:**
2 tablespoons onion powder	½ cup rum
1 tablespoon ground cumin	½ cup chicken broth
½ cup chopped mint leaves	1 tablespoon brown sugar
2 tablespoons kosher salt	3 tablespoons cold water
½ teaspoon ground cinnamon	1 tablespoon cornstarch
½ cup orange juice	¼ cup chopped mint leaves
½ cup lime juice	Salt and black pepper
¼ cup white wine vinegar	

Combine paprika, garlic powder, onion powder, cumin, mint, salt and cinnamon in a bowl; rub over all chicken pieces. Place chicken in zip loc bag and refrigerate for 30 minutes. In very large bowl, combine orange juice, lime juice, vinegar, olive oil, sugar and rum; mix well. Add chicken, coat well with marinade and refrigerate for 1 hour in bowl. Remove chicken from marinade; shake off excess. In large skillet, heat canola oil over medium high heat and sear each piece of chicken on both sides. When chicken is golden brown, add ½ cup of marinade in skillet; place skillet in 300° oven for 25-30 minutes. Remove from oven. Brush chicken with glaze. Place chicken under broiler for 5-6 minutes. Remove from broiler and serve with more glaze. Glaze: In medium saucepan, combine rum, chicken broth and brown sugar. Over high heat, cook until reduces by ⅓. In a small mixing bowl, whisk together water and cornstarch. When rum mixture is reduced, add cornstarch mixture slowly to simmering liquid and whisk for 3 minutes.When glaze is at desired thickness, add mint leaves and transfer to small bowl. Season with salt and pepper, to taste.

ONE POT CHICKEN

This will fill your house with such a wonderful aroma and the dish is incredible.

6 potatoes quartered	1 teaspoon ground cloves
1 large onion sliced	1 tablespoon garlic salt
4 carrots cubed	½ teaspoon celery seeds
5 pounds chicken thighs and breast	1 teaspoon oregano
1 tablespoon onion powder	1 teaspoon rosemary
1 teaspoon black pepper	½ cup chicken broth

In bottom of slow cooker, layer potatoes, sliced onions and carrots. Remove skin from chicken pieces, rinse and pat chicken dry. In bowl mix together onion powder, pepper, cloves and garlic salt. Place chicken in cooker over vegetables. Spoon seasonings over chicken. Sprinkle oregano and rosemary over top. Pour broth over chicken. Cover and cook on low for 6 hours.

OUTSTANDING TURKEY GYRO BURGERS

I serve these on simple buns, French or Italian breads, focaccia loaf, in pita pockets, taco shells, and tortillas or wrapped in lettuce leaves with cucumber sauce, blue cheese or ranch dressing, Greek salad or even shredded cheeses can make it a special dinner to serve to guest.

1 pound ground turkey	1 teaspoon dried cumin
2 ounces cream cheese	1 teaspoon dried oregano
1 egg	½ teaspoon black pepper
1 teaspoon minced garlic	½ teaspoon salt

Combine all ingredients in large bowl, mix until all blended well. Shape into oblong or round patties. Broil patties or grill until no longer pink.

OVEN FRIED CHICKEN

My sister Sharon first oven fried her chicken and it was so much easier, crunchy crisp and delicious. I may have changed some ingredients and some preparation, but she started me on my oven frying journey.

1 pound chicken, cut into 8 pieces or	½ teaspoon black pepper
6 chicken breasts or 8 thighs	1 teaspoon salt
1 stick melted butter	½ teaspoon onion powder
½ teaspoon garlic powder	1 ½ cups dried breadcrumbs
½ teaspoon paprika	4 quarts cold water
¼ teaspoon poultry seasoning	2 cups kosher salt

Dissolve salt in cold water; submerge chicken in brine and refrigerate for 30 minutes. Rinse chicken under running water, pat dry and discard water. Microwave butter until melted in small shallow dish. Fill plastic bag with garlic powder, paprika, poultry seasoning, pepper, salt, onion powder and breadcrumbs. Shake each piece of chicken in plastic bag until all are coated well. Place pieces in sprayed 9x13 baking dish. Bake in 350° oven for 25 minutes, turn all pieces over and bake another 25 minutes or until golden brown and cooked through.

PARMESAN CHICKEN

This popular and famous dish started out in Italy in the 1600's as veal parmigiana—no cheese or tomato anywhere on it. Many cooks and hundreds of years later most recipes put both on top and replaced the veal with more available chicken.

4 boneless, skinless chicken breasts	1 beaten egg
1 cup dry breadcrumbs	½ cup milk
½ cup grated Parmesan cheese	¼ cup olive oil
1 teaspoon dried oregano	4 ounces shredded mozzarella cheese
1 teaspoon garlic powder	½ cup salt
½ teaspoon paprika	2 tablespoons poultry seasoning
¼ teaspoon black pepper	2 cups hot tap water
¼ teaspoon poultry seasoning	1 ½ quarts cold tap water

Combine salt, poultry seasoning and hot water into stockpot. Let stand 10 minutes; add cold water, stir and submerge chicken; refrigerate 1 hour. Remove chicken from brine, pat chicken dry; discard brine. Mix breadcrumbs, cheese and spices in paper bag. In small bowl combine egg and milk. Dip chicken in egg mixture and shake in bread mixture; shake until coated thoroughly. Place oil in 13x9 baking dish; arrange chicken so pieces don't touch. Spray chicken with olive oil baking spray. Place dish in 375° oven and bake for 45-55 minutes or until chicken is tender and no longer pink. Do not turn chicken pieces while baking. Do not over bake, check frequently after 30 minutes of baking. Serve each breast on a warm plate on top of spaghetti noodles and sauce. Place 1 ounce of cheese on each breast, spread a spoonful hot spaghetti sauce on top of cheese and sprinkle top with more Parmesan cheese.

PEAR BBQ CHICKEN

Sounds strange but try it, it's great for a summertime grill party or picnic, one I got from time in Oregon.

1 large can pears in light juice	¼ teaspoon hot sauce
½ cup finely chopped onions	4 boneless, skinless chicken breasts
1 tablespoon Worcestershire sauce	cut into chunks
½ tablespoon lemon juice	1 tablespoon olive oil

Combine can of pears including juice, onions, Worcestershire sauce, lemon juice, and hot sauce in heavy-bottomed saucepan on medium heat. Bring to boil, reduce heat and simmer until slightly thickened. Stir frequently. When sauce has thickened slightly, process in food processor or blender until smooth. Sauté chicken pieces in hot skillet with olive oil. As soon as chicken loses pink color, reduce heat to simmer, pour in BBQ sauce coating all chicken pieces. Simmer sauce until thick and serve chicken and sauce over rice. Peaches can be substituted for pears.

PEACH CHICKEN AND RICE

Cultivated peaches are divided into clingstones and freestones, depending on whether the flesh sticks to the stone or not. Peaches with white flesh typically are very sweet with little acidity, while yellow-fleshed peaches have an acidic tang coupled with sweetness. Either one makes this a light summer dish.

1 halved chicken breast	¼ cup peaches juice from can
1 ½ tablespoons flour	2 tablespoons orange marmalade
1 teaspoon salt	2 ¼ teaspoons vinegar
1 teaspoon black pepper	2 ¼ teaspoons brown sugar
2 ¼ teaspoons butter	½ teaspoon dried basil
2 ¼ teaspoons canola oil	¼ teaspoon nutmeg
¼ cup orange juice	4 ounces peach nectar

Shake chicken pieces in plastic bag with flour, salt and pepper; Brown chicken in butter and oil in skillet. Place browned chicken in sprayed 3-quart casserole dish. Combine juices, marmalade, vinegar, sugar, basil and nutmeg. Pour mixture over chicken. Cover and bake in 375° oven for 1 hour and 15 minutes. Baste every 15 minutes. Place peaches between chicken pieces, baste well again and bake uncovered for 15 more minutes.

RED WINE CHICKEN (COQ AU VIN)

Much popular in the past, the red wine can make a rich meal of the simple ingredients and easy preparation.

2 tablespoons flour	2 cups sliced mushrooms
⅛ teaspoon salt	1 cup red wine
⅛ teaspoon black pepper	1 cup chicken broth
4 chicken breasts halved	2 teaspoons minced garlic
2 tablespoons minced onions	1 bay leaf
¼ cup canola oil	1 teaspoon thyme
12 small white onions	

Shake chicken pieces in plastic bag with flour, salt and pepper. Brown chicken with onion, in skillet with canola oil. Place browned chicken in casserole dish. Sauté onions and mushrooms in skillet until lightly browned. Add wine, broth, garlic, bay leaf and thyme. When liquid starts to boil, stir well and pour over chicken in casserole dish. Cover and bake in 350° oven for 35-40 minutes. Before serving, discard bay leaf.

SAUSAGE TURKEY DRESSING

1 pound ground turkey	1 cup chopped mushrooms
½ pound pork sausage	¼ cup chopped parsley
8 cups dried bread cubes	½ teaspoon black pepper
½ cup butter	2 teaspoons salt
2 teaspoons minced garlic	2 teaspoons poultry seasoning
2 cups chopped celery	1 cup chicken broth
1 cup chopped onions	

Sauté ground turkey and sausage until light brown; remove sausage to bowl. Add to fat in skillet, stir in bread cubes. Remove bread to bowl with pork. Heat butter in same skillet, sauté garlic, celery, onion, mushroom and parsley until tender. Add salt, pepper and poultry seasoning; add chicken broth, heat through, add to bread cubes and meat. Toss and place in sprayed baking dish and bake in 325° oven for 20 minutes covered; bake uncovered for 10 minutes more.

SIMPLE ROASTED CHICKEN

Roasted chicken once was a common specialty just for Sunday dinner, with leftovers used for soups and stews during the week. Store delis now make them available for any weekday dining. This easy to make meal will cost you less and give you more control over the spices when made at home.

3 pounds chicken	½ teaspoon dried parsley
1 teaspoon salt	½ teaspoon dried oregano
¼ teaspoon black pepper	½ teaspoon dried sage
½ teaspoon paprika	1 lemon sliced
½ teaspoon dried thyme	2 tablespoons butter

Rub chicken inside and out with salt, pepper and herbs. At cavity end, loosen skin from breast and stuff 2 slices lemon and 1 tablespoon of butter on each side of breast. Place remaining lemon directly in chicken cavity; transfer to roasting pan. Roast in 400° oven for 45 minutes, basting occasionally. Transfer chicken to cutting board and allow to sit 10 minutes before carving. Remove fat from drippings and serve with juice.

SLOW COOK HERBED CHICKEN

Fill your kitchen with the wonderful aroma of this meal and the whole family will want to sit down to eat.

4 whole chicken breasts halved	1 teaspoon ground ginger
1 cup chicken broth	½ teaspoon dried oregano
¾ cup evaporated milk	½ cup chopped onions
¼ cup soy sauce	¼ teaspoon dried rosemary
¼ cup olive oil	½ teaspoon dried sage
¼ cup red wine vinegar	¼ teaspoon dried basil crushed
½ cup water	½ teaspoon dried thyme
1 teaspoon minced garlic	

Place chicken in slow cooker. Combine remaining ingredients and pour over chicken. Cover with lid and cook on low 2-2 ½ hours. Uncover and cook 15 minutes more.

SPICE RUBBED TURKEY BREAST

A roasted turkey breast is a great alternative to a whole turkey. For one thing, it cooks in about an hour, as compared with up to five hours for a whole bird. But more importantly, by roasting the breast by itself ensures that it comes out moist and juicy.

1 cup salt	1 ½ teaspoons ground allspice
16 cups cold water	1 teaspoon dry mustard
5-6 pounds frozen turkey	1 ½ tablespoons paprika
breast—thawed	1 tablespoon ground ginger
¾ teaspoon olive oil	1 ½ teaspoons dried thyme
Spice Rub:	½ teaspoon black pepper
2 ¼ teaspoons ground coriander	½ teaspoon cinnamon
1 ½ teaspoons ground cumin	

Dissolve salt in water and add turkey breast. Refrigerate for 4 hours. Remove turkey from brine and rinse under cool running water. Pat dry inside and out with paper towels; place turkey skin side up on flat wire rack over rimmed baking sheet. Refrigerate, uncovered for 30 minutes. Combine all spice rub seasonings in a bowl. In a separate bowl mix olive oil and 1 tablespoon of spice rub mixture and set aside. Remove turkey from refrigerator and wipe any water on baking sheet. Carefully separate skin from breast meat and rub oil/spice mixture directly onto breast meat. Rub 1 tablespoon to back side of breast and along wings. Apply remaining spice rub to skin on top of breast. Press and pat to make spice adhere. Re-apply any spice that falls off. Tuck wings behind back; turn turkey so breast side is down, re-apply any spice rub that has fallen off. Roast in 400° oven for 30 minutes. Remove from oven and rotate turkey to breast side up; roast until thickest part of breast registers 165°, 25-30 minutes longer. Transfer turkey to carving board. Let rest 15-20 minutes before carving.

SWEET MUSTARD CHICKEN

2 pounds skinned chicken breasts	⅓ cup Dijon style mustard
⅓ cup mustard	1 tablespoon dried dill
¾ cup red wine vinegar	2 tablespoons orange marmalade
2 tablespoons olive oil	⅓ cup honey
½ teaspoon black pepper	

Combine mustard, vinegar, oil and black pepper in plastic zip loc bag; add chicken. Refrigerate for 6-8 hours, turning occasionally. Remove chicken and discard marinate. Mix together honey, marmalade, dill and Dijon style mustard. in small bowl. Brush sauce on both sides of chicken, coat well. Place on grill, turn often, glazing as needed until cooked thoroughly.

TERIYAKI CHICKEN SLOW COOKED

Teriyaki is a cooking technique used in Japanese cuisine in which foods are broiled or grilled in a sweet soy sauce marinade. The sweet sauce seems to have caught on in the US in the last few years and is applied to just about any kind of food.

2 skinless chicken breasts cubed

4 skinless chicken thighs cubed

½ cup soy sauce

2 tablespoons brown sugar

2 tablespoons grated ginger

2 cloves minced garlic

1 8-ounce can crushed pineapple

Wash and dry chicken; place in slow cooker. Combine remaining ingredients; pour over chicken. Cover and cook on high 1 hour. Reduce heat to low and cook 6-7 hours. Serve over cooked rice.

TURKEY ENCHILADAS

An enchilada is one of the Mexican dishes enjoyed by Mexicans and non-Mexicans. It's one of the most popular dishes that can be bought from a street vendor in Mexico. Originally, an enchilada was made from a tortilla dipped in chili sauce and stuffed with cheese and beans or chicken and beef, sometimes with spinach. Today, numerous versions of enchiladas are served in restaurants around the world.

2 cups cooked and chopped turkey

1 cup finely chopped green bell
   pepper

1 8-ounce package cream cheese
   cubed

2 teaspoons ground cumin

1 small finely chopped onion

1 bottle salsa

1 package flour tortillas

1 pound grated cheese—your favorite

Sour cream

In large saucepan, stir together turkey, peppers, cream cheese, cumin, onion and ½ cup of salsa on low heat until cream cheese is melted. Spoon equal amounts of turkey mixture down center of each tortilla. Roll tortilla up and place seam side down on lightly sprayed 13 x 9 baking dish. Sprinkle cheese over rolled tortillas. Cover with aluminum foil and bake in 350° oven for 20 minutes or until heated through. Remove foil and pour rest of salsa over tortillas. Serve with sour cream.

TURKEY FLORENTINE

Florentine of Florence, Italy meant egg, meat and fish dishes that usually contained spinach and a creamy-style sauce. Modern definition of Florentine developed in France in the early or mid-19th century when Spinach began turning up in fancier dishes that mostly likely already had a cream sauce. I think it's a fancy way to say spinach is in the dish or hide the fact that spinach is in the dish these days.

1 ½ tablespoons butter
½ cube chicken bouillon
½ cup diced cooked turkey
2 ½ tablespoons mushrooms
    drained
2 teaspoons flour
5 ½ tablespoons milk

2 ½ tablespoons shredded Cheddar
    cheese
½ teaspoon salt
1 ½ teaspoons sherry
1 teaspoon nutmeg
3 ⅓ ounces frozen chopped spinach
    cooked and drained well

Melt ½ of butter in skillet crush bouillon cube in hot butter. Add turkey cubes and heat stirring for 2-3 minutes. Remove turkey; place mushrooms in skillet with butter; sauté for 2-3 minutes. Place mushrooms with turkey and keep them warm. In same skillet, melt remaining butter and blend in flour. Gradually add milk, stirring until sauce is smooth and thick. Add cheese, salt, sherry and nutmeg, stirring until cheese is melted. Spread spinach over bottom of sprayed 9x13 baking dish. Cover with turkey and mushroom mixture. Pour sauce over all and bake in 350° oven for 30 minutes or until heated and bubbly.

BREADS

Growing up we only had store bought sliced breads. The first time I smelled fresh baked bread filling a house, I was hooked on it. As soon as possible I started making my own breads. There's nothing that compares to the taste and texture. But it does take extra time, although the improved quality is totally worth it. I fix a stew or hearty soup and with the bread, we have a complete meal. I'm also able to fix desserts from the same dough. Using the baked loaves makes economical meals like eggs and toast or French toast exceptional.

In fact it gives the meal an informal special friendly family mood. Fresh bread invites conversation; makes a more cozier atmosphere. Guest appreciate the extra work involved making the meal extraordinary. No one ever feels like they're being fed an more economical meal when homemade bread is served.

Then one day Joe bought me a home bread machine. The machines themselves only require the baker to put the ingredients in and set the cycle; the machine does the rest from beginning to end: producing a fully cooked and ready to eat loaf of bread. It also could be stopped at the dough stage, which I prefer, and baked in the oven. Nearly any flavor of bread can now be made at home because of these wonderful machines. That's not all; I make pizza dough, rolls, soft pretzels, sourdough, holiday breads and any recipe that calls for yeast dough or requires kneading.

How many of us can resist those wonderful cinnamon roles or soft pretzels as their smell waffles down the mall walkways and leads us right to their counters. Well, if you watch the workers for a little while, you will notice that the process really isn't hard and doesn't take that long. Bread is quite easy to make at home, and you only need a few staple ingredients to make a simple loaf.

I also like the idea of controlling the ingredients: increasing the fiber, using less sugar, minimal amount preservatives, heartier grain and adding flavorings, nuts or dried fruit. All of that improves the flavor and texture and makes ingesting more of the important nutrients our bodies need.

Give Us Our Daily Bread

Besides being economical, bread making can increase your confidence in the kitchen. When you can master a loaf of bread, you feel like you can attempt just about anything. Once you learn to pull off the different bread types, you can wrap up your bread items and give them out as a hostess gift or for Christmas presents or be the hit at any potluck. Some of the quick breads are actually quite simple and also make a great impression and is always a welcomed gift.

Bread has been important throughout history and in many households bread is still served with every meal. Bread has a long history for a reason. It's a healthy and nutritious food that fills the stomach as well as the soul. Whether you do it by hand or a machine try some of the recipes and discover the magic that's in fresh baked bread. Best of all, it simply makes fabulously amazing toast for a snack or as a special breakfast.

Bringing Home The Harvest

BANANA CRUMB MUFFINS

This one was a wonderful Winter morning shared with friends in Nebraska.

1 ½ cups flour	1 lightly beaten egg
1 teaspoon baking soda	⅓ cup melted butter
1 teaspoon baking powder	⅓ cup brown sugar
½ teaspoon salt	2 tablespoons flour
3 mashed bananas	⅛ teaspoon cinnamon
¾ cup sugar	1 tablespoon butter

Spray muffin tin. In large bowl, mix together flour, baking soda, baking powder and salt. In another bowl, beat together bananas, sugar, egg and melted butter. Stir banana mixture into flour mixture just until moistened. Spoon batter into prepared muffin cups. In small bowl, mix together brown sugar, 2 tablespoons flour and cinnamon. Cut in 1 tablespoon butter until mixture resembles coarse cornmeal. Sprinkle topping over muffins. Bake in 375° oven for 18 to 20 minutes, until toothpick inserted into center of muffin comes out clean.

BEER BATTER WAFFLES

In 14th-century England, wafers were sold by street vendors called waferers. In medieval Europe, vendors were permitted to sell them outside of churches. Competition eventually became so heated, and at times violent, that King Charles IX of France imposed a regulation on waferer sales, requiring vendors to maintain a distance of at least 12 feet from one another. The modern waffle is a leavened form of this waferer, which is what the beer does in this recipe.

2 cups self-rising flour	2 eggs separated
12 ounces beer	1 tablespoon honey
½ cup melted butter	1 teaspoon vanilla extract
¼ cup milk	

Preheat waffle iron according to manufacturer's instructions. Combine flour, beer, butter, milk, egg yolks, honey, and vanilla in large bowl; stir until mixture is smooth. In separate bowl, beat egg whites until stiff peaks form. Gently fold egg whites into batter. Spray preheated waffle iron with non-stick cooking spray. Ladle batter into waffle iron. Cook waffles until golden and crisp. Serve immediately.

BEER PIZZA DOUGH AND PIZZA TOPPINGS

TOPPING IDEAS. Alfredo Sauce, minced garlic, cilantro, tomatoes and cooked chicken; Caramelized onions and roasted garlic; Mozzarella cheese, Camembert, Romano and Feta (for a really, really cheesy pizza!); Equal parts of basil pesto and olive oil mixed together with Parmesan or Romano cheese; Roughly chopped sundried tomatoes, sliced black olives. Mozzarella cheese, salt and black pepper; Mozzarella cheese, shredded chicken and sliced avocado; Pineapple chunks, canadian bacon; Cooked chicken, minced garlic, tomatoes, onions, mozzarella cheese, parmesan cheese; Alfredo sauce, pesto, cooked chicken, any white cheese or; Cranberry jelly, shredded chicken, sliced Brie—Nothing is off limits to try on your pizza. Everywhere I've been, people put what they like and find new family favorites.

12 ounces flat beer	1 tablespoon yeast
3 tablespoons butter	Italian Crust: add to machine
3 tablespoons sugar	2 ¼ teaspoons Italian seasoning
1 ½ teaspoons salt	6 tablespoons Parmesan cheese
3 ¾ cups flour	

Put beer, butter, sugar, salt, flour and yeast in bread machine in order recommended by manufacturer. Select Dough setting and press Start. Remove dough from bread machine when cycle is complete. Press dough to cover a prepared pizza pan: Sprayed and cornmeal spread over pan bottom. Brush top of dough lightly with olive oil. Cover and let stand 15 minutes. Preheat oven to 450°. Spread sauce and toppings on top of dough. Bake until crust is lightly brown and crispy on the outside, about 24 minutes.

BREAD MACHINE: BACON BREAD

Bread is one of the oldest prepared foods, dating back to the Neolithic era. The development of leavened bread can probably also be traced to prehistoric times.

¾ cup flat beer

½ cup water

¼ cup chopped green onions

2 tablespoons mustard

1 tablespoon butter softened

3 ¼ cups bread flour

1 tablespoon sugar

¾ teaspoon salt

1 ¾ teaspoons yeast

⅓ cup crumbled cooked bacon

Add ingredients to machine according to manufacturers directions. Select Basic White cycle. Add bacon at the beep. Makes one (1 ½ pound) loaf.

BREAD MACHINE: CINNAMON ROLLS

No one will ever know where the true origin of cinnamon rolls come from, after all, cinnamon and bread are very ancient foods. Cinnamon was once so highly-prized that wars were fought over it.

Dough:

1 cup warm milk

1 teaspoon vanilla extract

⅓ cup butter room temp

2 eggs room temp, beaten

1 teaspoon salt

½ cup sugar

4 ½ cups flour

2 ½ teaspoons yeast

Filling:

½ cup butter softened

1 cup brown sugar

5 tablespoons ground cinnamon

Frosting:

3 tablespoons shortening

3 tablespoons butter

1 ½ cups powdered sugar

1 ½ teaspoons vanilla extract

⅛ teaspoon salt

Add all dough ingredients in bread machine according to manufacturers instructions for dough setting. Check dough; it should form elastic ball. If too moist, add additional flour a tablespoon at a time and if dry, add warm water a tablespoon at a time. It should be slightly tacky to touch. Turn dough out on lightly sprayed surface. Form into oval, cover with plastic wrap; rest for 10 minutes. Butter 9x13 baking pan; set aside. Roll dough into 15x24-inch rectangle. Filling: Brush butter on dough with rubber spatula. In bowl, combine brown sugar and cinnamon. Sprinkle filling over butter on dough. Starting with long edge, roll up dough; pinch seams to seal. NOTE: Rolling log too tightly will result in cinnamon rolls whose centers pop up above rest of them as they bake. Use serrated knife, saw gently to cut 1 ½ inch thick rolls. Place in pan, flatten them only slightly. Rolls should not touch each other before rising and baking. Covered rolls with plastic wrap and refrigerate overnight or freeze for 1 month. Before baking, thaw completely and rise in warm place if frozen. If refrigerated, bake upon removing from refrigerator. Cover and let rise in warm place for approximately 45 to 60 minutes or until doubled in size—after rising, rolls should be touching each other and sides of pan. Bake in 350° oven for 20 to 25 minutes until light golden brown. Remove from oven and let cool slightly. Spread frosting over rolls while still warm. Frosting: In medium bowl, combine shortening and butter until creamy. Add sugar and vanilla extract until well mixed and creamy. Refrigerate frosting until ready to use and bring to room temperature before spreading.

BREAD MACHINE: COOL POTATO BREAD

1 cup milk	½ cup instant potato flakes
½ cup water	2 tablespoons sugar
2 tablespoons butter	2 teaspoons salt
4 cups bread flour	3 teaspoons yeast

Place ingredients in bread machine pan in order suggested by manufacturer. Select Basic bread cycle and start machine. Makes 2 pound loaf.

BREAD MACHINE: DELICIOUS RAISIN BREAD

Raisins are high in certain antioxidants and comparable to prunes and apricots in this regard. Mix them with a little cinnamon and who can resist

1 cup milk	3 ¼ cups flour
1 egg	2 tablespoons yeast
3 tablespoon honey	¾ cup raisins
2 teaspoons vanilla extract	½ teaspoon cinnamon
4 tablespoons butter	

Place ingredients in bread machine according to manufacturers instructions—raisins are an add in. Set machine for sweet bread cycle with light crust.

BREAD MACHINE: DILL ONION BREAD

This bread is great around Spring when you have corned beef, ham and pork roast leftovers.

¾ cup cottage cheese	3 tablespoons sugar
¾ cup sour cream	3 tablespoons dried onions
¼ cup water	2 teaspoons dill seeds
1 ½ tablespoons butter	¼ teaspoon baking soda
1 egg	2 ½ teaspoons yeast
3 ⅓ cups bread flour	

Place ingredients in bread machine pan in order suggested by manufacturer. Select Basic bread cycle and start machine. Makes one (1 ½ pound) loaf.

BREAD MACHINE: DINNER ROLLS

Bread is a staple food prepared by baking a dough of flour and water. It may be leavened or unleavened.

¾ cup milk	¼ cup sugar
6 tablespoons butter softened	1 teaspoon salt
1 egg beaten	1 ½ teaspoons yeast
3 cups bread flour	Melted butter

Measure ingredients into bread machine in order recommended by manufacturer. Select dough or manual setting. When cycle is completed, remove dough from machine and either shape as desired, or wrap in plastic wrap and place in refrigerator for up to 24 hours. If refrigerated, let set out for about 45 minutes to an hour before using. The easiest shape to make is to just divide the dough into equal parts and roll into balls in your hand. Place on lightly greased baking sheet. Cover shaped dough with damp cloth and let rise in a warm place for 20 minutes or until doubled in size. Bake in 400ˣ oven for 15 to 20 minutes; brush tops with butter or margarine.

BREAD MACHINE: FLAXSEED BREAD

1 ½ teaspoons dry active yeast	½ teaspoon salt
⅓ cup water	1 cup flaxseed meal
3 tablespoons honey	1 ¼ cups whole wheat flour
1 tablespoon canola oil	1 ¾ cups bread flour

Place all ingredients in bread machine according to manufacturers directions. Set on "Dough" setting. When ready, take dough and add flour if dough is sticky and knead another 5 minutes until dough is smooth and elastic. Shape dough into sprayed loaf pan and cover and let rise in warm place until doubled in bulk about 1 hour. Bake in 350° oven for 40-45 minutes or until loaf is browned on top and sounds hollow when tapped.

BREAD MACHINE: FULL RAISIN BREAD

Raisins are dried grapes. They are created in many regions of the world.

1 ½ cups buttermilk	1 cup quick or old fashioned oats
1 egg beaten	2 tablespoons brown sugar
2 tablespoons butter melted	½ cup raisins
1 ½ teaspoons salt	⅓ cup sunflower seeds
1 ½ cups bread flour	2 tablespoons wheat germ
1 ½ cups whole wheat flour	3 teaspoons quick rising yeast

Place ingredients in bread machine pan according to manufacturer's directions or as listed above. Select white bread and light crust settings. Remove bread from pan to wire rack. Cool completely before slicing. Makes 1 ½ pound loaf.

BREAD MACHINE: GARLIC BREAD

This is often made into a baguette or Italian bread: A modern variation on the recipe tops the garlic bread with a variety of cheeses, often mozzarella, cheddar or feta. A light layer of freshly-grated parmesan on top of the mozzarella adds an extra boost of flavor.

3 tablespoons dry milk powder	1 ½ teaspoons yeast
1 ½ teaspoons sugar	1 cup water
½ tablespoon garlic powder	1 egg
3 cups flour	2 tablespoons melted butter
½ teaspoon salt	4 cloves garlic

Place all ingredients into bread machine as directed by manufacturer, except for garlic cloves. Place settings of machine for dough. Place separated garlic cloves in dough for last knead cycle. When dough is ready, remove from machine, knead a few times and shape into loaf. Sprinkle cornmeal on a sprayed or greased cookie sheet and place dough loaf on top of cornmeal. Cover with cloth and place in warm spot to rise. When double in size, remove cloth and place in 375° oven for 40-50 minutes or until loaf sounds hollow when lightly tapped. Remove from oven and let cool on wire rack before cutting.

BREAD MACHINE: HAWAIIAN MACADAMIA NUT BREAD

In the world of nuts and berries, macadamia nuts are almost as precious as gold. These delicious, exotic nuts with a rich flavor and oil are considered delicacies and served as dessert nuts. They are popular gifts at holiday times and are prized as souvenirs from Hawaii. This is a good recipe to stretch out the treat.

¾ cup water	2 ¼ cups flour
2 eggs	3 tablespoons dry milk powder
1 ½ tablespoons butter	1 ½ teaspoons yeast
3 tablespoons sugar	1 cup macadamia nuts chopped
½ teaspoon salt	

Place ingedients in bread machine according to manufacturers directions. Set on "Dough" setting. When ready, take dough and shape into loaf and place on sprayed cookie sheet. Cover and let rise for 15 minutes. Uncover and place in 375° oven for 30-40 minutes or until bread sounds hollow when tapped on top with fingers. Remove from oven and cool on wire rack.

BREAD MACHINE: MAPLE OAT BREAD

Maple syrup is a sweetener made from the sap of maple trees. Being used as an ingredient in baking, making candy, preparing desserts and a sugar source and flavoring agent in making beer has increased its usage and popularity. It was first collected and used by Native Americans and later enjoyed and very popular among the European settlers.

1 ¾ cups milk

½ cup maple syrup

3 tablespoons vegetable oil

1 egg

3 cups bread flour

1 ½ cups oats

1 ½ teaspoons salt

1 ¾ teaspoons yeast

Place ingredients in the bread machine pan in the order suggested by the manufacturer. Select Basic bread cycle and start machine. Makes 2 pound loaf.

BREAD MACHINE: MOZZERELLA TOMATO BREAD

Once this bread is baked, I slice it and put a good bruschetta on top or salsa.

1 cup warm water

½ cup shredded mozzarella cheese

and chopped

2 tablespoons olive oil

3 cups bread flour

1 ½ tablespoons sugar

1 teaspoon garlic powder

½ tablespoon salt

2 ¾ teaspoons yeast

Place ingredients in the bread machine pan in the order suggested by the manufacturer. Select Basic bread cycle, and start machine. Makes one (1 ½ pound) loaf.

BREAD MACHINE: PESTO BREAD

Historically, pesto is prepared in a marble mortar with a wooden pestle. The leaves are placed in the mortar with garlic and coarse salt, and crushed to a creamy consistency. The pine nuts are added and crushed together with the other ingredients.

1 egg	3 cups bread flour
¼ cup white wine	1 tablespoon sugar
1 teaspoon minced garlic	1 tablespoon salt
3 tablespoons olive oil	2 ½ teaspoons yeast
½ cup pesto sauce	½ cup pine nuts
⅓ cup water	

Place all ingredients except pine nuts in machine according to manufacturers directions. Set for sweet bread and press start. When beeper sounds, add pine nuts. Makes one (1 ½ pound) loaf.

BREAD MACHINE: SOURDOUGH BEER BREAD

1 ⅓C sourdough bread STARTER	3 cups bread flour
¼ cup water	1 ½ teaspoons salt
½ cup flat beer	1 tablespoon sugar
2 tablespoons canola oil	1 ½ teaspoons yeast

Place ingredients in bread machine pan in order suggested by manufacturer. Select Basic bread cycle and start machine. Makes one (2 pound) loaf. To flatten beer, pour it into small saucepan and heat it to simmer and allow to cool.

BREAD MACHINE: SOURDOUGH BREAD

1 ½ cups Sourdough Starter	2 ½ teaspoons salt
1 egg	3 tablespoons sugar
1 tablespoon water	4 ¾ cups bread flour
1 cup warm milk	1 packet yeast
2 tablespoons butter softened	

In bread machine, place ingredients as recommended by our machine manufacturer. Place on "dough" setting. When ready, take dough out and divide into 2 equal pieces. Shape into 2 loaves, place on sprayed cookie sheet. Brush tops with beaten egg or beaten egg whites. Sprinkle top with sesame seeds or caraway seeds, if desired. Use sharp knife to make 3-4 diagonal cuts on top of loaves. Bake in 375° oven for 35-40 minutes or until bread sounds hollow when tapped. Cool on wire rack.

BREAD MACHINE: WHOLE WHEAT BRAN BREAD

Bread that has stiffened or dried past its prime is said to be stale. Modern bread is sometimes wrapped in paper or plastic film, or stored in an airtight container such as a breadbox to keep it fresh longer. Bread that is kept in warm, moist environments is prone to the growth of mold. Bread kept at low temperatures in a refrigerator, will develop mold growth more slowly than bread kept at room temperature. Unwrapped bread kept in a refrigerator will turn stale quickly due to the low humidity of the air.

1 ⅛ cups water	1 cup whole wheat flour
2 tablespoons canola oil	¼ cup bran
2 tablespoons honey	¾ teaspoon salt
1 ½ cups bread flour	1 ½ teaspoons yeast

Place ingredients in bread machine pan in order suggested by manufacturer. Select Whole Wheat bread cycle and start machine. Makes one (1 pound) loaf.

BUDDIES CORNY CORNBREAD

1 cup flour	2 eggs
1 tablespoon baking powder	1 cup milk
½ teaspoon salt	1 11-ounce can corn
1 cup cornmeal	2 tablespoons sugar (optional)
¼ cup melted shortening	

Mix all dry ingredients together in bowl. Make a well in middle of dry mixture. Mix all the wet ingredients together in a bowl, dump wet ingredients into dry ingredients. Add corn and stir until all ingredients are moistened. Put into 8 or 9 inch sprayed or greased pie pan. Bake in preheated 425° oven for 20-25 minutes or until a wooden toothpick come out clean. Remove from oven and cool on wire rack. Serve with butter, honey or honey butter

CHEESY CORNBREAD

1 can whole corn undrained
1 can cream-style corn
2 eggs beaten
2 packages corn bread and muffin mix
½ cup melted butter

1 cup chopped onions
½ cup chopped green bell peppers
1 tablespoon canola oil
1 cup shredded Cheddar cheese

In skillet, heat oil and sauté onions and green peppers until tender; set aside. In large bowl, combine corn, cream corn, eggs, corn bread mix; mix well. Add butter stir in cooked vegetables. Pour batter into sprayed 9x13 baking dish. Top with cheese. Bake in 375° oven for 45 minutes.

CHOCOLATE BABKA

Eastern European babka is one version of leavened egg breads that are available around the world. This desert, a cross between cake and sweet bread, is often baked for Easter

1 cup milk
5 tablespoons butter
¼ cup warm water
2 ½ teaspoons yeast
6 tablespoons sugar

1 teaspoon salt
5 ½ cups flour
Vegetable oil
1 ½ cups semisweet chocolate chips
¼ cup unsweetened cocoa

Pour milk into small pan, heat on medium and cook until just about ready to boil. It will start to form bubbles around edges. When it does, remove from heat; stir in butter. Put water in large bowl, sprinkle yeast over it; stir in 1 tablespoon of sugar. After sitting few minutes, it will start to thicken up and emit yeasty smell. Wait until milk is cool enough to touch without burning. Use electric mixer; pour milk into yeast bowl, add rest of sugar and salt; mix with wooden spoon; add 5 cups of flour, one cup at a time. Mix until dough ball forms. Pull ball out and knead for several minutes until solid and smooth. Wipe oil around interior of bowl, and place dough ball in, rolling it around until all covered in oil. Cover it and let sit out for about 2 hours. Take chunk of butter and heavily grease a bundt pan. Really make it thick. Take chocolate chips and chop them up in blender or food processor; mix in cocoa. Pour about ⅓ of chocolate mix in bundt pan. Use fingers or tilt pan to bring chocolate as far up sides as possible. Punch down dough few times. Toss it back into mixer with ½ cup flour, or onto work surface with flour; knead into nice ball, about 5 minutes by hand, or minute in mixer. Return dough to floured board. Pull it out into an oval shape, about 16x9 inches. Pour remaining chocolate on top, pressing it in leaving about ½ inch around edge. Roll it up and pinch edges shut. Place in pan, push it gently down and make sure it presses against chocolate. Cover and wait 1 hour more. Bake in 375° oven, for 30 to 40 minutes, until it sounds hollow when tapped. Put plate on top of babka, flip whole thing over so babka is right-side up on plate. Wait 45 minutes before cutting into, but it is meant to be served warm, use microwave for about 20 seconds if it's not warm, you want chocolate inside melted.

CHOCOLATE BANANA BREAD

A marvelous combination; not only do they taste great when combined, but both bananas and dark chocolate contain health benefits. Choose a dark chocolate that is labeled at least 70% Dark.

2 cups flour	1 egg
1 tablespoon baking powder	⅓ cup milk
½ teaspoon salt	¼ cup canola oil
1 cup sugar	¾ cup semisweet chocolate chips
1 cup mashed ripe bananas	

Combine flour, baking powder, salt, sugar and salt in large bowl. Mix together bananas, egg, milk and oil. Pour banana mixture into flour mixture just until ingredients are moistened. Stir in chips. Pour batter into sprayed loaf pan. Bake in 350° oven for 60 minutes or until toothpick in the center comes out clean. Remove from oven to cooling rack. Cool in pan for 10 minutes. Loosen sides, remove from pan. Cool completely.

CHOSEN ONION SAUSAGE STUFFING

½ pound pork sausages	1 teaspoon poultry seasoning
3 sticks diced celery	½ teaspoon black pepper
8 cups bread crumbs	3 cups chicken broth
1 diced onion	⅔ cup melted butter
1 teaspoon sage	

In large skillet over medium heat, crumble sausage. Add onion and celery and cook, stirring occasionally until sausage is brown. In a large bowl, place cubed stuffing. Add sausage mixture. Sprinkle with poultry seasoning. Pour broth and butter over top and toss to combine. Spoon mixture into 9x13 inch baking dish; cover. Bake in 350° oven for 45 minutes.

CINNAMON BABKA

Babka is a polish sweet bread, usually made with cinnamon and nuts. Traditional babka has some type of fruit filling, especially raisins, and is glazed with a fruit-flavored icing, sometimes with rum added.

½ cup butter softened	¾ cup raisins soak overnight in rum
½ cup sugar	½ cup chopped nuts
4 eggs	Topping:
1 egg yolk	2 tablespoons sugar
5 teaspoons yeast	¼ teaspoon cinnamon
¼ cup warm water	2 tablespoons butter
1 cup milk	1 egg white
1 teaspoon vanilla extract	1 tablespoon water
1 teaspoon salt	2 tablespoons flour
4 ½ cups flour	

In large mixing bowl, cream butter and sugar until smooth. In separate bowl, beat eggs and egg yolk until creamy. Mix yeast in warm water. When mixture thickens, add to eggs with milk, vanilla and salt. Add yeast mixture to butter/ sugar mixture and mix well. Slowly add flour until soft dough is formed. Stir in raisins and nuts until distributed. Turn dough onto floured work surface; knead until dough is no longer sticky. Cover dough and allow to rise in warm place until it doubles. Butter two 2-quart pans and shape dough into it. [or use 7 mini loaf pans and bake for 20-25 minutes]. Allow dough to rise again for about 1 hour. Beat egg white with 1 tablespoon water; use to brush top of Babka. Mix flour, sugar, cinnamon and butter, sprinkle on Babka. Bake in 350° oven for 40-50 minutes or until cake tester comes out clean. Cool in pan on wire rack 15 minutes in pan on wire rack before removing. Cool completely on wire rack.

ENGLISH MUFFIN BREAD

2 teaspoons salt	2 ¼ teaspoons yeast
1 tablespoon sugar	2 cups warm milk
5 cups flour divided	½ cup warm water
¼ teaspoon baking soda	

In large mixing bowl, combine salt, sugar, 2 cups of flour, baking soda and yeast. Add warm milk and water; beat on low speed of electric mixer for 30 seconds. Beat on high for 3 minutes. Stir in remaining flour, batter will be stiff. Do Not Knead. Spray 2 loaf pans and sprinkle with cornmeal. Spoon batter into pans and top with cornmeal. Cover and let rise 45 minutes. Bake in 375° oven for 35 minutes or until golden brown. Remove from pans immediately and cool on wire rack.

FOCACCIA

Plain focaccia can be topped with a light sprinkling of salt and pepper. Other toppings may include browned onions, minced garlic, goat cheese, pesto, Parmesan Cheese, Cheddar Cheese, Italian Seasoning, sage, bacon, potatoes, rosemary, sun-dried tomatoes, Gorgonzola cheese, olives, or any combination.

1 cup water	2 teaspoons salt
3 tablespoons olive oil	5 teaspoons Italian seasoning
3 cups flour	2 ¼ teaspoons yeast

Place all ingredients into pan of bread machine. Program for Dough or Manual, and press Start. At end of cycle, remove dough from machine and punch it down. Roll it out to form rectangle; transfer to cookie sheet; pat dough into pan. Make indentations in dough with fingertips, about an inch apart; drizzle sparingly with olive oil. Top with choice of toppings. Allow focaccia rise for 30 minutes to an hour. Bake the focaccia in the preheated 450 oven for 15 to 20 minutes, or until lightly browned. Drizzle with extra-virgin olive oil; serve. If using small (1-pound) bread machine, remove dough from machine at end of second kneading cycle; transfer to lightly greased bowl to rise for 1 to 1 ½ hours.

FRENCH TOAST

"French toast" can be found in print in the US as early as 1871. The Oxford English Dictionary cites usages of "French toast" in English as early as 1660 (toasted bread with wine, orange juice, and sugar), and cites an egg-based recipe of the same name from 1882. It likely dates back to medieval times and may have been a logical "invention", akin to battering and frying any food.

3 eggs

1cup milk   1 ½ tablespoons vegetable oil

1 teaspoon vanilla extract   12 slices stale bread any kind

⅛ teaspoon salt   Baked French Toast:

½ teaspoon cinnamon   8 slices hot dog or hamburger buns

1 tablespoon powdered sugar   Melted butter

In large shallow dish (pie plate works good), whisk together eggs, milk, sugar, salt and cinnamon. Heat enough oil to cover bottom of large skillet over high heat until hot. Dip each side of bread in mixture, one at a time. Transfer soaked bread to skillet. Reduce heat to medium. Cook 2-3 minutes per side, until nicely browned. Once all cooked, heat oven to 200°, place large wire rack on cookie sheet and place browned french toast on rack in single layer, uncovered. This will keep the toast warm and keep it from getting soggy for up to 15 minutes, so everyone can sit down and eat at the same time. Baked French: Let buns soak 1-2 minutes per side. Place on generously oiled baking sheet. Bake in 500° oven 5-6 minutes until underside is golden brown. Flip over all slices; brush with melted butter. Bake additional 4-5 minutes or until golden brown and no uncooked egg mixture remains. Top with preserves, fruit compote, maple syrup or fruit syrup.

FRESH JUNCTION SOFT PRETZELS

Cities in the US like Philadelphia, Chicago, and New York are famous for their soft pretzels and the state of Pennsylvania is a core area for hard pretzel history and production. Southeastern Pennsylvania, with its large German population, is considered the birthplace of the American pretzel industry and many pretzel bakers are still located in the area. Cut one in half horizontally and use it to make a sandwich, it doesn't get better than that.

1 package yeast	5 cups flour
⅛ cup warm water	Coarse salt
⅓ cup brown sugar	1 stick melted butter
1 ⅓ cups warm water	

Dissolve yeast in ⅛ cup water. Mix in brown sugar and let set for 10 minutes. Add rest of water. Add flour, cup at at time until a smooth ball forms. Kneed until dough is elastic and not sticky to touch. Let dough rest for an hour. Punch it down. Break off pieces of dough depending on how big you want pretzels to be. Roll dough into pencil shapes and twist into pretzel. Prepare your cooking sheet by spraying with non stick spray, sprinkle with coarse salt. In large saucepan, bring to boil 8 cups of water and ¼ cup baking soda. Place pretzels in boiling water for 15 seconds. Remove and place on cookie sheet. Bake in 500° oven with rack in highest position possible. Bake 8-10 minutes depending on how hard you like the crust. Remove from cookie sheet onto wax paper to cool. Brush with melted butter. Serve plain or with melted cheese or mustard.

GOLDEN HONEY PAN ROLLS

1 cup evaporated milk	2 ¼ teaspoons yeast
1 egg	Glaze:
1 egg yolk	⅓ cup sugar
½ cup canola oil	2 tablespoons melted butter
2 tablespoons honey	1 tablespoon honey
1 ½ teaspoons salt	1 egg white
3 ½ cups bread flour	

Place ingredients in bread machine in order suggested by manufacturer. Select dough setting, check dough 10 minutes after mixing is started; add

1-2 tablespoons water or flour if needed. When completed, turn dough on to lightly floured surface. Punch down and cover. Let it rest for 10 minutes. Divide into 24 pieces; shape each into ball. Place 12 balls each in 2 sprayed 8 inch baking pans. Cover and let rise in warm place until doubled, about 30 minutes. Combine glaze ingredients and drizzle over dough. Bake in 350° oven for 20-25 minutes or until golden brown. Brush with additional honey as they cool.

SOURDOUGH—REPLENISH MIX

Mix this batter the night before to put in any refrigerated Sourdough Starter the day you use it for a recipe.

1 cup Sourdough Starter Mix	**1 ½ cups water**
2 cups flour	

Mix together starter mix, flour and water in NON METAL BOWL and with NON METAL SPOON. Batter should be moist but very thick. It will thin out during fermentation. Cover and set in warm place. Next day, beat Replenish mix into your Starter Mix from refrigerator until well blended. Take from this stock what you need for recipe you are using.

GOOEY CINNAMON ROLLS

The ultimate comfort food brought to us by English and German immigrants. In the 18th century the Philadelphia cinnamon roll was born: brown sugar, honey, cinnamon, and raisins. Americans have been adding and putting individual touches on this wonderful roll ever since. Add nuts inside or out, use an orange or cream cheese frosting, add raisins to the dough, the filling or even the icing if you like.

Dough:	**Filling:**
½ cup warm water	2 cups brown sugar
½ cup melted butter	5 tablespoons cinnamon
1 small box instant vanilla pudding	⅔ cup butter melted
2 cups warm milk	**Vanilla Icing:**
2 eggs room temperature	3 cups powdered sugar
2 tablespoons sugar	1 teaspoon vanilla extract

1 teaspoon salt	1 teaspoon almond extract
8 cups flour	¼ teaspoon salt
5 teaspoons yeast	2-6 tablespoons milk

Dissolve yeast in warm milk in large bowl. Add sugar, butter salt, eggs, and flour, mix well. Knead the dough into large ball, using hands dusted lightly with flour. Put in bowl, cover and let rise in warm place about 1 hour or until the dough has doubled in size. Roll dough out on lightly floured surface, until 21 inches long by 16 inches wide and ¼ thick. To make filling, combine brown sugar and cinnamon in bowl. Spread softened butter over surface of dough, sprinkle brown sugar/cinnamon evenly over surface. Working carefully, from long edge, roll dough down to bottom edge. Cut dough into 1 ¾ inch slices, and place in lightly greased baking pan. Bake in 400° oven for 10 minutes or until light golden brown. While rolls are baking combine icing ingredients.

HEARTY ITALIAN BREADSTICKS

3 cups flour	¼ cup warm water
1 tablespoon sugar	1 cup lukewarm water
1 teaspoon salt	Melted butter
¼ cup butter softened	Parmesan cheese
2 ½ teaspoons yeast	Coarse salt

Combine flour, sugar and salt in bowl. Cut in butter until crumbly. Dissolve yeast in warm water. Add yeast mixture and 1 cup lukewarm water to flour mixture, mixing well. Let rise for 45 minutes. Punch dough down. Divide into 4 portions. Roll each piece into 12-inch rope. Cut each rope into 12-14 pieces. Roll as thin as pencil. Place on greased baking sheet. Let rise for 20-30 minutes. Bake at 400° for 15 minutes or until golden brown. Immediately brush with butter and sprinkle Parmesan Cheese or Coarse Salt.

HEAVENLY BUNS: STICKY OR CINNAMON

This recipe is from mid 1880's and all the tweaking over the years hasn't made it better than the original. The difference between Cinnamon Rolls and Buns is the sticky topping that is put in the bottom of the pan to coat the rolls when they are turned out to cool. No need for an icing on these. If you are in a hurry, then use a store bought cinnamon roll dough and put the topping in the pan before baking them.

1 cup warm water	1 ¼ cups brown sugar
4 teaspoons yeast	¾ cup soft butter
⅔ sugar	¼ cup honey
½ cup room temperature butter	¼ cup corn syrup
½ cup dry milk powder	¼ cup water
1 ½ teaspoons salt	2 cups pecans halves
2 eggs	Filling:
4 ½ cups flour	5 teaspoons sugar
Glaze:	5 teaspoons cinnamon

Mix ¼ cup warm water, yeast and pinch of sugar in small bowl. Let stand until foamy, about 8 minutes. Using electric mixer, beat remaining sugar, butter, milk powder, and salt in large bowl until well blended. Beat in eggs 1 at a time. Mix in remaining ¾ cup warm water and yeast mixture, then 3 cups flour, 1 cup at a time. Using rubber spatula, mix in 1 cup flour, scraping down sides of bowl frequently—dough will be soft and sticky. Sprinkle ¼ cup flour onto work surface and knead until smooth and elastic, adding more flour if sticky, about 8 minutes. Butter another large bowl. Add dough; turn to coat. Cover bowl with plastic wrap and let dough rise in warm area until doubled, about 2 ½ hours. Glaze: Butter two 10-inch round cake pans with 2-inch high sides. Beat brown sugar, ½ cup butter, honey, corn syrup, and ¼ cup water in medium bowl to blend. Spread half of glaze in bottom of each prepared pan. Sprinkle 1 cup pecans over each. Punch down dough. Divide dough in half. Roll each dough piece out on floured work surface to 12x9-inch rectangle. Brush any excess flour off dough. Spread remaining butter over dough rectangles, dividing equally. Mix sugar and cinnamon in small bowl. Sprinkle cinnamon sugar over rectangles. Starting at long side, tightly roll up each rectangle into log. Cut each log into 12 rounds. Place 12 rounds, cut side down, in each prepared pan, spacing evenly. Cover with plastic wrap. This can be made day ahead and refrigerate. Let buns rise in warm area until almost doubled, about 1 hour (or 1 hour 25 minutes if refrigerated). Bake in 375° oven buns until deep golden brown, about 30 minutes. Run small knife around pan sides to loosen sticky buns. Turn hot buns out onto platter. Cool about 30 minutes and serve.

HEIRLOOM PANCAKES OR WAFFLES

Pancakes and Waffles are one of the easiest, and cheapest, entree recipes on earth. As long as you can measure and stir and can use a spatula, you can make fluffy, delicious pancakes for four people for about a dollar, when you add blueberries, or bananas, or cornmeal, the cost will go up, but it's still one of the most inexpensive meals around.

2 cups flour	1 ½ cups milk
3 tablespoons sugar	½ cup evaporated milk
1 ½ teaspoons baking powder	2 eggs
1 teaspoon baking soda	3 tablespoons canola oil
½ teaspoon salt	Solid shortening

In large bowl combine flour, sugar, baking powder, baking soda and salt. Stir with wire whisk until combined. In small bowl, combine both milks, eggs and oil; beat until smooth. Add to flour mixture; stir just until combined. Cover batter and let stand for 10 minutes. Heat a griddle to 350°. Lightly rub griddle with a bit of shortening. When drop of water sizzles dropped onto griddle, use ¼ cup measure to pour four circles of batter onto griddle. Cook until edges look dry and bubbles just begin to burst, about 2-4 minutes. Turn pancakes and cook for 1-2 minutes on second side just until golden.

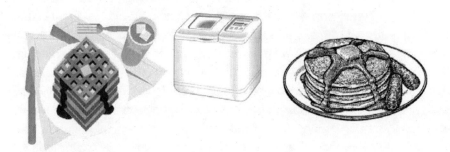

HOT CROSS BUNS

A hot cross bun is a type of sweet-spiced bun made with currants or raisins and leavened with yeast.

4 teaspoons yeast	1 teaspoon grated lemon peels
1 cup warm milk	1 egg with 1 tablespoon cold water
1 ½ teaspoons salt	Pastry Cream:
¼ cup honey	1 cup milk
1 bread flour	1 teaspoon vanilla extract
1 teaspoon cinnamon	2 tablespoons cornstarch
½ teaspoon ground nutmeg	½ cup sugar
¼ teaspoon ground cloves	Pinch salt
2 tablespoons soft butter	1 egg
½ cup raisins	

In bowl of mixer, dissolve yeast in warm milk. Stir in salt and honey. In another bowl, combine flour with spices. Mix into yeast and milk mixture, using dough hook at low speed. Alternatively, stir gently with wooden spoon until fully combined. Mix in soft butter. Knead at medium speed for 8 to 10 minutes, adding additional bread flour if dough is sticky and tacky rather than smooth and soft. Do not over knead dough. Place dough, covered with plastic, in warm place and let rise until doubled in volume, about 1 hour. Meanwhile, make pastry cream. In heavy-bottomed saucepan, bring milk and vanilla to boil. Keeping an eye on milk, mix cornstarch, sugar and salt in bowl with whisk. Add egg and mix until smooth. Slowly add about ⅓ of hot milk to egg mixture while whisking. Pour tempered egg mix back into remaining milk. Place over medium heat and cook, stirring constantly, until mixture comes to boil and thickens. Pour custard in bowl and cover surface directly with plastic. When cool, store in refrigerator, if making later. Knead in raisins and lemon peel by hand, kneading until dough is smooth. Let dough rest, covered for 10 minutes. Divide dough into three equal pieces. Roll pieces into 6-inch ropes and cut each rope into six equal pieces. Form small pieces into tight round buns. Place approximately 1 ½ inches apart on sheet pans lined with parchment. Using sharp knife cut cross on top of buns just deep enough to penetrate skin. Let buns rise, covered, until slightly less than doubled in volume. Brush buns with egg wash. Place pastry cream pastry bag fitted with No. 3 plain tip, or cut a hole in corner of zip loc bag for makeshift pastry bag. Pipe cross of pastry cream in opened cut on top of each bun. Bake for approximately 20 minutes or until golden brown. Let cool slightly.

LOW FAT BREAD MACHINE BRAN BREAD

3 cups bread flour

1 cup wheat bran

2 teaspoons active yeast

1 teaspoon salt

4 tablespoons soft pitted prunes, minced

2 egg whites

1 cup whole grain flour

1 ⅓ cups water

1 cup raisins

All ingredients should be at room temperature. Add all ingredients, except raisins, in order specified for your bread machine manufacturer. Set on standard setting, medium or normal baking cycle. Add raisins at the end of the first kneading cycle.

MULTIPLE USE BREAD DOUGH

Fresh bread is prized for its taste, aroma, freshness and texture. Retaining its freshness is important to keep it appetizing. Serve all breads with flavored butters and make something simple a real treat.

1 ½ cups evaporated milk

2 eggs

4 tablespoons butter or margarine

1 ⅓ tablespoons brown sugar

½ teaspoon salt

4 cups bread flour

2 teaspoons yeast

Onion Bread:

Omit salt and add

1 package onion soup mix

½ cup diced caramelized onions

Garlic Bread:

1 tablespoon garlic powder

1 tablespoon minced garlic

Cinnamon Raisin:

1 tablespoon cinnamon

1 cup raisins

Plain Bread: Place all ingredients in bread machine according to directions from manufacturer. Place on "Dough" setting. When ready, divide dough into 2 equal parts, form into loaf and place in 2 sprayed loaf pans. Bake in 375° oven for 40-45 minutes, until bread sounds hollow when tapped on top. Remove from pan and cool on wire rack before slicing. Onion Bread: Omit salt from Plain bread recipe, add onion mix with rest of original ingredients. When machine signals adding extra ingredients, add onions. Garlic Bread: Add garlic powder to rest of original ingredients. When machine signals adding extra ingredients, add minced garlic. Cinnamon Bread: Add cinnamon to rest of original ingredients. When machine signals adding extra ingredients, add raisins.

NEVER FAIL PIZZA DOUGH

Dough can be made ahead of time, place it in an oiled plastic bag, seal, refrigerate for up to two days.

1 ⅜ cups lukewarm water	1 teaspoon salt
3 tablespoons olive oil	4 cups flour
2 ½ teaspoons yeast	

Place ingredients in bread machine pan in order recommended by manufacturer. Select Dough Cycle and press Start. During cycles first kneading, use spatula to scrape down sides of pan, if necessary, to help combine ingredients. When dough cycle is complete, gently deflate dough and allow it to rest for 10 minutes before using in recipe. By Hand: Place water, oil, yeast and salt in bowl and stir to dissolve yeast. Stir in flour and knead on a lightly floured work surface to form a smooth and elastic dough, about 8 to 10 minutes. Place dough in a large bowl that has been coated with oil, turning dough once in bowl to coat with oil; cover bowl with plastic wrap and set it in warm place to rise for an hour, or until it doubles in volume. Gently deflate dough and allow it to rest for 10 minutes before using in recipe. To Bake: Preheat oven to 425. If using a pizza stone, place it in oven to heat. Pat dough into an oiled 12 x 15-inch jelly roll pan, 2 (10 to 12-inch) pizza pans, or 1 (14 to 16-inch) pizza pan. Brush top of pizza dough with olive oil; top with desired sauce and toppings. Bake for 15 to 18 minutes or until crust is golden. For crispier bottom crust, carefully slide pizza off pan (not the jelly roll pan) onto oven rack or pizza stone, if using, after about first 12 minutes and finish baking. While pizza is continuing to bake, sprinkle empty pizza pans with little cornmeal—this helps absorb any moisture that can cause crust to become soggy. Allow pizza to sit 2 to 3 minutes for easier slicing.

NEW YORK STYLE BAGELS

Toppings: sesame seeds, poppy seeds, minced fresh garlic, minced fresh onion, caraway seeds, coarse salt. Storage Suggestion: To store in freezer, first slice cooled bagels, place a small piece of plastic between the bagel halves and place in a plastic self-sealing freezer bag. When you're ready for a bagel, they will come apart easily, ready to toast without having to pry apart or thaw.

1 ½ cups lukewarm water plus	2 teaspoons salt
2 tablespoons lukewarm water	4 ½ to 5 cups bread flour
1 tablespoon yeast	Kettle Water:
1 tablespoon sugar	2 tablespoons malt syrup or powder
1 tablespoon vegetable oil	1 teaspoon salt
2 teaspoons malt syrup or powder	

Place ingredients for dough into bread pan in order recommended by bread machine manufacturer. Select Dough Cycle and press Start. During cycle's first kneading check to see if more flour or a few drops of water is needed to form a stiff dough ball (use a spatula to scrape down sides of pan, if necessary, to help combine ingredients). Once first kneading cycle is finished, remove dough and divide into 8 sections, forming each section into 10-inch long strips. Roll ends together to seal and make a ring. Place on a lightly floured surface, cover, and let bagels rest 15 to 20 minutes, rising about halfway and becoming slightly puffy. Meanwhile, fill large cooking pot or Dutch oven three quarters full with water. Add malt syrup and salt. Bring water to boil. Preheat oven to 450°. Line two large baking sheets with baking parchment. Set aside. Line two other baking sheets with kitchen towel, set near stove. Reduce boiling water to immer and cook 2 bagels at a time (do not crowd pot). Simmer bagels for about 45 seconds on one side, turn and cook other side for another 45 seconds and drain bagels on towel-lined baking sheet. Carefully place bagels on parchment-lined baking sheets. Bake bagels plain or sprinkled with topping. Place in the hot oven, immediately reduce heat to 425°, and bake about 17 to 25 minutes. When almost baked, turn bagels over (a pair of tongs do the job easily). If you have a baking stone, finish bagels on the stone directly. Transfer bagels to wire rack to cool completely before storing.

OLD FASHIONED BUTTERMILK PANCAKES

Buttermilk Pancakes are so easy and inexpensive. This recipe is perfect; top with powdered sugar and fruit or maple syrup.

1 ½ cups flour	1 ¼ cups buttermilk
2 teaspoons baking powder	2 tablespoons butter
1 teaspoon baking soda	1 egg
½ teaspoon salt	Solid shortening
2 tablespoons sugar	

Sift dry ingredients into large bowl. In small saucepan, combine buttermilk and butter; heat over low heat just until butter starts to melt; stir and remove from heat. Quickly beat egg into buttermilk mixture; pour over dry ingredients. Stir with whisk just until batter is blended. A few lumps are okay. Let batter stand for 10 minutes. Heat griddle to 350° or heat over. Rub with a little shortening and pour batter by ¼ cup measures onto griddle. Cook on first side until edges look dry and bubbles just begin to burst, about 2-3 minutes. Carefully flip over and cook for 1-2 minutes on second side. Serve immediately.

OLD TIMERS ALASKAN STYLE SOURDOUGH STARTER

The sourdough tradition was carried into Alaska and the western Canadian territories during the Klondike Gold Rush. Conventional leavening such as yeast and baking soda were much less reliable in the conditions faced by the prospectors. Sourdough starter needed to be kept warm to survive, miners and settlers carried a pouch of starter around their neck or on a belt and were often fiercely guarded. Old hands came to be called "sourdoughs", a term that is still applied to any Alaskan old-timer.

2 large potatoes quartered	2 tablespoons sugar
4 cups water	Cool water
2 cups flour	

Boil potatoes in water until potatoes start to fall apart. Drain water off and remove skin from potatoes. In glass or plastic mixing bowl, mash potatoes with plastic or wood utensils. Add flour, sugar and small amounts of water until able to whip into smooth, creamy batter. Cover and set in warm place for several days; check and stir daily. When fermented—batter will have lots of bubbles—then you have a sourdough starter. Loosely cover in non metal container and store in refrigerator.

POULTRY STUFFING

This is the stuffing I grew up eating. No frills, just moist and a compliment to the turkey. I remember granny preparing her broth by cooking the liver and organ meats in water. Then she would cut up the cooked meats and put them in the dressing. It wasn't until I started to travel that I came across the multitude of dressings families consider traditional for their celebrations. This is a basic dressing anyone can add their own favorite herbs, spices, dried fruits and choice of bread.

½ cup butter

1 chopped onion

2 cups diced celery

2 cups chicken broth

1 loaf bread cut up

1 teaspoon poultry seasoning

¼ teaspoon salt

½ teaspoon black pepper

¼ teaspoon sage

Pinch thyme

Pinch marjoram

Melt butter in saucepan. Saute onion in melted butter until soft, but not brown. Add celery and stir well. Add broth mixture. Bring to boil. Cover and simmer for 10 minutes. Place bread cubes into large mixing bowl. Add poultry seasoning, salt, pepper, sage, thyme and marjoram. Add onion and celery mixture. Combine thoroughly. If still too dry, add more chicken broth. Makes enough to stuff a 10 to 15 pound turkey. ✐To bake dressing out of turkey, place in buttered baking dish; bake in 350° oven for 45 minutes or until top is lightly browned. More broth may be needed for this method to keep it from drying out.

SLOW COOKER STUFFING

Much easier and keeps the kitchen cool, so you can have stuffing in the warmer months. This way also frees up space in your oven with those big dinners.

12 cups dried bread cubes	4 cups chicken broth
¼ cup dried parsley	2 cups finely chopped celery
2 eggs beaten	1 cup finely chopped onions
1 teaspoon salt	1 cup butter melted
½ teaspoon black pepper	1 8-ounce can sliced mushrooms
1 teaspoon ground sage	drained
2 teaspoons ground poultry seasoning	

Sauté celery, onion and butter in skillet until cooked. Stir in mushrooms. Combine bread cubes and parsley in slow cooker. Add skillet contents, eggs, seasoning and chicken broth; stir mixture well. Cover with lid and cook on high for 1 hour or low for 2 hours, stir occasionally. 1 loaf of bread (20 ounces) can be used. Cut up into cubes, on baking sheet and place in 300° oven for 10-15 minutes to dry out bread. Turn with spatula every 5 minutes. Don't let the bread get brown, just dried out.

SOURDOUGH BREAD

This no-knead bread is no fuss to make and delicious, too, which I first learned when I helped cook in a camp. It has a crisp crust and distinctive sourdough flavor from the 'starter' yeast mixture you stir up in advance. I was surprised how fast and easy a sourdough could be made.

2 ½ teaspoons yeast	2 tablespoons butter melted
3 ½ cups warm water divided	2 tablespoons sugar
7 cups flour divided	2 teaspoons salt
¼ cup dry milk powder	

In 4-qt. non-metallic bowl, dissolve yeast in 2 cups warm water; let stand for 5 minutes. Stir in 2 cups of flour until smooth. Cover loosely with a clean towel. Let stand in a warm place to ferment for 48 hours; stir several times daily. The mixture will become bubbly and rise, have a "yeasty" sour aroma and a transparent yellow liquid will form on the top. Stir in milk powder, butter, sugar, salt, remaining water and enough remaining flour to form a soft dough. Do not knead. Cover and let rise in warm place until doubled, about 1-½ hours. Turn onto floured surface; punch dough down. Do not knead. Divide in half. Shape each into a round loaf. Heavily grease baking sheets and sprinkle with cornmeal. Place dough on prepared pans. Cover and let rise until doubled, about 30 minutes. With a sharp knife, make three diagonal slashes across tops of loaves. Bake in 350° oven for 10 minutes. Brush loaves with cold water; bake 35-40 minutes longer or until golden brown.

SOURDOUGH BREAD—YEAST STARTER

The sourdough tradition was carried into Alaska and the western Canadian territories during the Klondike Gold Rush. Conventional leavening such as yeast and baking soda were much less reliable in the conditions faced by the prospectors.

1 packet yeast	1 tablespoon white vinegar
2 ⅓ cups warm water	1 teaspoon salt
2 tablespoons sugar	2 cups flour

Use only glass or plastic bowls and wood or plastic utensils when working with Sourdough Starter. NO Metal bowls or utensils. Dissolve yeast in ¼ cup of warm water. Let it bubble. Add rest of water, sugar, vinegar and salt, mix well. Add flour to make creamy batter. Place in 1 gallon glass or ceramic container, cover lightly and let sit. Once fermented, stir until creamy. Store in refrigerator, lightly covered until needed for recipe. The night before using Starter Mix: Mix up Replenish Mix (see recipe) and follow instructions. Stir in Replenish Mix until well mixed. Remove amount needed for recipe

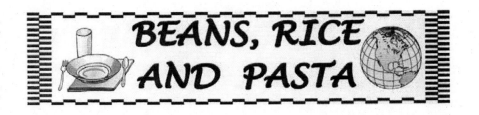

Living the life of a missionary, the meals we made for ourselves usually contained lots of pasta or rice or beans. We ate more than our share of peanut butter sandwiches, macaroni and cheese, spaghetti, tuna casserole, bean soup and chili—mostly starches made to fill us up.

FRACTIONS of RATIONS

It made us grateful to finally get back out on tour, so we could be in a host home and eat hearty again. But those scrap meals had their own significance. We were people involved in something more important than ourselves: more important than the meal. The faces, the conversations, the events and actions around us were more important than the food. We were people joined by a purpose and goal, it was more than the needs of our body, and we were doing something for our souls, for each other and for the world. The meal wasn't important, the person sharing it with you was. We sacrificed a little nutritionally, but none of us starved. In fact thinking back to those days, still fills me up.

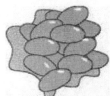

These days I use healthier fiber laden rice, beans and pasta. They still stretch a meal further, but the emphasis is no longer a total cost issue. Now we want them to provide high quality protein, more fiber and not spike our blood sugars.

Our information and facts about nutrition and a healthy diet has evolved in the last 50 years. Cookbooks from the 1950's and 60's are incredibly out of date with their amount of sugar, fat and starch in the recipes and leave us astonished. The mere mention of their excessive use of lard, shortening and bacon fat makes us gasp and clogs arteries about it. But they had their reasons for using those items.

The fresh and frozen vegetables and fruits available now to most of us was unheard of by our grandparents. They were excited to finally get those canned peaches, pineapple, pears, beans, tomatoes and milk with no concern for the heavy laden salt water and sugar-loaded juices they contained. They were just glad to have things available on a daily basis and to be freed from the years of creative shortcuts and burdensome wartime shortages. This allowed them to developed well-rounded meals enjoying new dishes making the interest in home cooking soar. The bake-offs, cook-offs, explosion of cookbooks, television shows and magazine recipes had begun.

Ration Correction

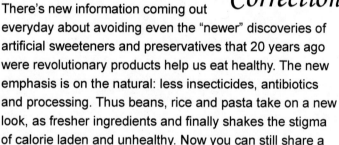

We've become educated about the accumulative affect of what we eat and how it's prepared and grown; moving us away from the high salt and fat contents. There's new information coming out everyday about avoiding even the "newer" discoveries of artificial sweeteners and preservatives that 20 years ago were revolutionary products help us eat healthy. The new emphasis is on the natural: less insecticides, antibiotics and processing. Thus beans, rice and pasta take on a new look, as fresher ingredients and finally shakes the stigma of calorie laden and unhealthy. Now you can still share a frugal meal and moment with a friend but fill up the improved way.

Comfort Food For Every Mood

BBQ BAKED BEANS

No one seems to know when we started putting BBQ in our baked beans, I grew up on them this way. I can't imagine a summer without them.

2 16-ounce cans pork and beans	1 teaspoon hickory smoke
1 15-ounce can kidney beans rinse, drain	½ teaspoon regular mustard
2 14-ounce bottles barbecue sauce	Water as needed
1 can beer	
⅓ cup molasses	

Combine all ingredients into large sprayed baking dish. Bake uncovered in 300° oven about 2 ½ hours, stir occasionally and if necessary, add additional water.

BAKED BEANS

Canned baked beans were among the first convenience foods. Canned salt pork and beans with stewed tomatoes was supplied to the US Army during the American Civil War in the 1860s.

4-11-ounce can pork and beans	2 tablespoons molasses
1 15-ounce can kidney beans	1 teaspoon dry mustard
1 large onion chopped	1 cup ketchup
¾ cup firmly packed brown sugar	

Combine all ingredients together in 13x9 inch baking pan. Bake uncovered in 350° oven for 2 hours

BEANS AND FRANKS

In New England baked beans usually are sweetened with maple syrup, and are traditionally cooked with salt pork in a bean pot in a brick oven for a full day. In southern states along the eastern seaboard of the US, the beans become tangier.

4 cups raw dried navy beans	½ cup brown sugar
10 cups hot water	2 cups ketchup
3 teaspoons salt	3 cups water
1 tablespoon molasses	¼ pound bacon slices raw
2 teaspoons mustard	1 pound package beef hot dogs

Place beans into slow cooker. Add hot water, cover; cook on High for 2 hours. Test beans, they should be soft; drain. Put remaining ingredients into slow cooker; stir gently. Cover and cook on Low for 8 to 10 hours or on High for 4 to 5 hours. About 1 hour before serving, cut hot dogs into 1-inch chunks and stir into beans. Continue to cook on low for 1 hour.

BLACK EYED PEAS

The planting of black-eyed pea crops was promoted by George Washington Carver because, as a legume, it adds nitrogen to the soil; has high nutritional value and is an excellent source of calcium. A staple in the Southern diet for over 300 years, black-eyed peas have long been associated with good luck and prosperity when eaten on New Years Day.

1 pound black-eyed peas	½ teaspoon red pepper flakes
½ pound salt pork or thick bacon diced	½ teaspoon black pepper
	1 teaspoon dried thyme
1 cup chopped onions	¼ teaspoon dried oregano
1 diced carrot	2 teaspoons salt
4 teaspoons minced garlic	Dash hot sauce

Rinse peas and pick over for bad or discolored peas and small stones; transfer to medium saucepan. Cover with water and bring to a boil. Reduce heat to a simmer and continue cooking for 5 minutes; set aside. Put the meat in a large stockpot and cook over medium heat for about 5 minutes, until fat is rendered.

Add the onion, diced carrot, and garlic. Cook, stirring, until tender, about 6 to 8 minutes. Add peas and enough water to cover by 2 inches. Add pepper flakes, black pepper, thyme, and oregano. Bring to a boil; reduce heat to medium and simmer, covered, for about 1 hour. Uncover and cook for 30 to 45 minutes longer, or until peas are tender. Add more water as needed to keep them moist. When the peas are tender stir in the salt and hot sauce.

BOSTON BAKED BEANS

Beans slow-baked in molasses has been a favorite Boston dish since colonial days, when the city was "awash in molasses" due to its rum-producing. The Great Molasses Flood of 1919, occurred when a tank holding molasses for rum production exploded. Boston Baked Beans continue to be one of New England's most-loved traditional dishes. This one was given to me by a family who had relatives in that "flood".

2 cups navy beans	¼ teaspoon black pepper
½ pound bacon	¼ teaspoon dry mustard
1 finely diced onion	½ cup ketchup
3 tablespoons molasses	1 tablespoon Worcestershire sauce
2 teaspoons salt	¼ cup brown sugar

Soak beans overnight in cold water. Simmer beans in same water until tender, about 1 to 2 hours. Drain and reserve liquid. Arrange beans in 2-quart bean pot or casserole dish by placing a portion of beans in bottom of dish and layering with bacon and onion. In saucepan, combine molasses, salt, pepper, dry mustard, ketchup, Worcestershire sauce and brown sugar. Bring mixture to boil and pour over beans. Pour in just enough of reserved bean water to cover beans. Cover dish with lid or aluminum foil. Bake in 325° oven for 3 to 4 hours until beans are tender. Remove lid about halfway through cooking and add more liquid if necessary to prevent beans from getting too dry.

COWBOY BEANS

This is a very old recipe found in a very old book. I've since seen it printed in many places, which is a good sign that people like it enough to keep passing it along. It's been the hit at every western and cowboy party we've been to, "once good, always good".

1 15-ounce can kidney beans	1 cup chopped onions
1 15-ounce can pinto beans	1 teaspoon minced garlic
1 15-ounce can butter beans	2 teaspoons mustard
1 15-ounce can pork and beans	1 cup ketchup
1 15-ounce can navy beans	½ bottle French salad dressing
1 pound ground pork sausage	

In skillet, cook sausage, onion and garlic until sausage is browned and onions are tender, drain off fat. Rinse and drain all of the beans. Combine all ingredients in slow cooker; stir. Cook on Low 4-6 hours.

HOPPIN' JOHN

This dish is traditionally a high point of New Years Day, when a shiny dime is buried among the black-eyed peas before serving. Whoever gets the coin in his or her portion is assured good luck throughout the year. At the stroke of midnight on New Years Eve, many southern families toast each other with Champagne and a bowl of Hoppin' John.

2 cups dried black-eyed peas	4 cups chicken broth
Cold water	2 cups uncooked long-grain white rice
1 pound meaty ham hocks or bacon	Dash black pepper
1 chopped onion	Dash salt
½ teaspoon crushed red pepper flakes	

Sort, soak, rinse, and drain dried black-eyed peas. Place black-eyed peas in large soup pot over medium-high heat and cover with cold water; bring to boil. Remove from heat; cover and let stand 1 to 2 hours. Drain and rinse beans. Using same large soup pot, over medium-high heat, add soaked black-eyed peas, bacon or ham hock, onion, and red pepper. Add water or chicken broth; bring to boil. Reduce heat to medium-low and cook for 1 ½ to 2 hours or until peas are tender (do not boil; beans will burst). Remove bacon or ham hock and cut into bite-size pieces. Return meat to pot. Stir in rice, cover, and cook 20 to 25 minutes or until rice is tender and liquid is absorbed. Remove from heat and season to taste with salt and pepper.

RED BEANS AND RICE

Red beans and rice was traditionally cooked in Louisiana on Monday while the laundry was being done; the beans and a ham bone could be left to simmer on the stove while the wash dried on the line.

1 pound dried red beans	1 bay leaf
3 tablespoons vegetable oil	½ teaspoon dried thyme
3 chopped onions	1 pound sweet Italian sausages cut
3 chopped green bell peppers	in bite size pieces
3 tablespoons minced garlic	1 pound kielbasa cut in bite size pieces
6 stalks chopped celery	1 teaspoon hot pepper sauce
¼ pound chopped smoked sausages	Salt and black pepper
1 smoked ham hocks	Cooked rice

Soak beans overnight. Drain, rinse and set aside. In deep skillet, heat oil and sauté onions, peppers, garlic and celery. Add beans, ham hock, bay leaf and thyme. Add water to cover (plus a little). Cover and cook over low-medium heat for two hours, or until beans are soft but not mushy. Remove bay leaf. Add smoked sausage, Italian sausage and kielbasa for last 30-45 minutes. Season with pepper sauce, salt and pepper to taste. Serve over rice.

REFRIED BEANS

Refried beans is a dish of cooked and mashed beans and is a traditional staple of Mexican and Tex-Mex cuisine. Refried beans are traditionally prepared with pinto beans, but many other varieties of bean can be used, such as black or red beans.

2 quarts water	1 teaspoon salt
1 diced onion	⅓ cup canola oil
2 cups pinto beans washed, picked over	½ teaspoon black pepper

Bring water to boil in a medium saucepan. Add beans, reduce heat to simmer, cover and cook, skimming occasionally, approximately 1 ½ hours. To test for doneness, taste 3 or 4 of smaller beans. They should be cooked through and creamy inside. Mash, along with liquid in pot, with potato masher or back of wooden spoon until creamy. Heat canola oil in medium saucepan over medium-high heat. Sauté onions with salt and pepper until golden brown, about 10 minutes. Add mashed beans and continue cooking, stirring occasionally, until liquid evaporates and beans form mass that pulls away from sides and bottom of pan, about 10 minutes. Serve immediately. Refried beans can be kept in refrigerator 3 or 4 days and reheated in covered casserole in 350° oven.

*BAKED SPAGHETTI

This tasty dish makes a good family feast during those chilly winter months and holds the heat really well out of the oven.

1 pound package spaghetti	2 eggs
1 pound ground beef	⅓ cup grated Parmesan cheese
1 chopped onion	3 tablespoons butter melted
3 ½ cups meatless spaghetti sauce	2 cups small curd cottage cheese
½ teaspoon seasoned salt	4 cups shredded mozzarella cheese

Cook spaghetti according to package directions to al dente. Meanwhile, in a large skillet, cook beef and onion over medium heat until meat is no longer pink; drain. Stir in the spaghetti sauce and seasoned salt; set aside. In a large bowl, whisk the eggs, Parmesan cheese and butter. Drain spaghetti; add to egg mixture and toss to coat. Place half of the spaghetti mixture in a greased 13 x 9 inch baking dish. Top with half of the cottage cheese, meat sauce and mozzarella cheese. Repeat layers. Cover and bake in 350° oven for 40 minutes. Uncover; bake 20-25 minutes longer or until cheese is melted.

*CREAMY FETTUCCINE ALFREDO

Fettuccine Alfredo has become ubiquitous in Italian-American restaurants in the US. Additions like cut up meats or poultry and vegetables make it a complete meal. There are differing recipes to decrease the fat content and ones that use fancier more expensive cheeses.

8 ounces dry fettuccini pasta	½ cup margarine
¼ cup diced sweet onions	1 ½ tablespoons lemon juice
1 tablespoon	½ cup milk
butter	1 teaspoon garlic powder
2 3-ounce packages cream cheese	½ teaspoon dried basil
¾ cup grated Parmesan cheese	

Bring large pot of lightly salted water to boil. Add pasta and cook for 8 to 10 minutes or until al dente; drain. In small microwavable bowl, place butter and onions. Microwave just until onions are soft. In medium saucepan, combine cooked onions, cream cheese, Parmesan, margarine, lemon juice, milk, garlic powder and basil. Stir over low heat until smooth and creamy, 10 to 15 minutes. Toss sauce with pasta and serve in warmed bowls or plates.

*FRIED CABBAGE NOODLES

This is an extremely old recipe and is a quick treat.

1 head cabbage	Butter
1 box noodles	

Cut up head of cabbage and sauté in butter in skillet. Reduce heat and continue to cook slowly. Meanwhile, in large pot of salted boiling water, prepare 1 box of elbow macaroni according to al dent. Once noodles are done and the cabbage is soft, drain noodles and mix with buttered cabbage. Cover and let simmer on low for about 15 minutes.

*HOMEMADE EGG NOODLES

This recipe explains how to make the basic dough for egg noodles by hand. Using this recipe, you can cut the dough into a variety of sizes and shapes to prepare cannelloni, tortellini, ravioli, tagliarini, fettuccine, tagliatelle and lasagna. Follow the manufacturer instructions when using pasta maker.

2 cups flour	Topping:
½ teaspoon salt	Melted butter
2 eggs	Crisp fried onion
1 tablespoon olive oil	Grated sharp cheddar cheese
1 tablespoon water	

Pour flour into large mixing bowl or in heap on pastry board, make well in center of flour and in it put eggs, oil and salt. Mix together with fork or your fingers until dough can be gathered into rough ball. Moisten any remaining dry bits of flour with drops of water and press them into ball. Knead dough on floured board, working in a little extra flour if dough seems sticky. After about 10 minutes, dough should be smooth, shiny and elastic. Wrap it in wax paper and let dough rest for at least 10 minutes before rolling it. Divide dough into 2 balls. Place 1 ball on floured board or pastry cloth and flatten it with palm of hand into oblong about 1 inch thick. Dust top lightly with flour. Using heavy rolling pin, start at one end of oblong and roll it out lengthwise away from yourself to within an inch or so of farthest edge. Turn dough crosswise and roll across its width. Repeat, turning and rolling dough, until it is paper thin. If at any time dough begins to stick, lift it carefully and sprinkle more flour under it. To make tortellini and ravioli, follow the cutting directions in those recipes. To make tagliarini, fettuccine, tagliatelle and lasagna, dust rolled dough lightly with flour and let it rest for about 10 minutes. Gently roll dough into jelly-roll shape. With long sharp knife, slice roll crosswise into even strips—⅛ inch wide for tagliarini, ¼ inch wide for fettuccine or tagliatelle, and 1-½ to 2 inches wide for lasagna. Unroll strips and set them aside on wax paper. In same fashion, roll, shape, and slice second half of dough.

Homemade egg noodles may be cooked at once or covered tightly with plastic wrap and kept in refrigerator for as long as 24 hours. Cook them in 6 to 8 quarts of rapidly boiling salted water for 5 to 10 minutes, or until just tender (al dente). To test, lift out strand and taste it.

*LASAGNA FOR ALL

Although the dish is generally believed to have originated in Italy, the word "lasagna" comes from the Greek. The Romans borrowed the word meaning "cooking pot". The Italians used the word to refer to the dish in which lasagna is made. It wasn't long before the name of the food took on the name of the serving dish. The recipe was featured in the first cookbook ever written in England, leading to an urban legend that the dish originated in the British Isles.

Meat Sauce:
1 pound ground beef
1 pound ground turkey
1 tablespoon Worcestershire sauce
1 teaspoon sage
1 large onion chopped
2 cloves garlic minced
1 14 ½-ounce can tomatoes
1 8-ounce can tomato sauce
1 6-ounce can tomato paste
2 teaspoons dried basil crushed
1 teaspoon dried oregano crushed

¼ teaspoon black pepper
1 teaspoon salt
1 box No-boil lasagna noodles
Cheese Filling:
1 beaten egg
1 16-ounce container cottage cheese
   small curd
½ cup grated Parmesan cheese
1 tablespoon fresh parsley
12 ounces shredded cheese
   mozzarella, provolone and
   cheddar mix

Cook ground meat, Worcestershire sauce, sage, onion and garlic until meat is no longer pink; drain fat. Stir in rest of sauce ingredients. Bring to a boil, reduce to simmer and cover pan. Simmer for 15 minutes, stirring occasionally. Combine egg, cheeses and parsley in separate bowl until well mixed. Spray or grease large rectangular baking dish, layer starting with sauce, then noodles, then cheese filling, meat sauce, repeat layers and top with noodles, sauce. Sprinkle with additional parmesan cheese or shredded cheese. Bake in 375° oven for 30-45 minutes. Remove from oven and let stand for 15 minutes before cutting to serve.

*LIGHT SHRIMP FETTUCCINE

1 pound fettuccini pasta
2 tablespoons olive oil
1 cup chopped sweet onions
2 teaspoons minced garlic
½ cup white wine
1 8-ounce bottle clam juice

½ teaspoon salt
1 pound shelled and deveined
   shrimp
1 bag spinach
½ cup fresh parsley chopped

Cook pasta to al dente. In large skillet, heat oil on medium. When hot, add onion and garlic and cook for 10 minutes or until golden and tender, stir often. Add wine and increase heat and cook for 1 minute. Stir in clam juice and salt. Heat mixture to boiling. Stir in shrimp and cook 2-3 minutes. Drain pasta and add to skillet. Add spinach and parsley and toss to coat. Serve.

*MACARONI AND CHEESE

Macaroni and cheese was created to be a casserole. The main ingredients are cooked elbow macaroni and a cheese sauce, usually cheddar. The cheese sauce is generally either made in the fashion of Mornay sauce, or as a custard base with added cheese. Extra ingredients, like ground beef, ketchup, jalapeños, sliced hot dogs, ham, bacon, tuna, tomatoes, and other vegetables are sometimes incorporated into the dish.

1 8-ounce package elbow macaroni
1 cup shredded sharp cheddar
   cheese
1 ½ cups small curd cottage cheese
1 cup sour cream

¼ cup grated Parmesan cheese
Salt and black pepper
1 cup dry bread crumbs
¼ cup melted butter

Bring large pot of lightly salted water to boil, add pasta and cook until done; drain. In 9x13 inch baking dish, stir together macaroni, shredded Cheddar cheese, cottage cheese, sour cream, Parmesan cheese, salt and pepper. In small bowl, mix together bread crumbs and melted butter. Sprinkle topping over macaroni mixture. Bake in 350° oven for 30 to 35 minutes, or until top is golden.

*MANICOTTI

Manicotti is one of the oldest shapes of pasta that is still prepared today much like it was originally made. In ancient times, pasta dough was prepared, cut into large rectangles, filled with flavorful stuffing's, then rolled and baked in the oven. Manicotti is large hollow pasta tubes, approximately 3-4 inches long and 1 inch in diameter. This elegant shaped pasta is typically stuffed with a cheese mixture and baked in flavorful sauces.

4 cups mild salsa	1 egg beaten
3 cups diced tomatoes	2 tablespoons chopped chives
½ cup diced bacon	⅛ teaspoon black pepper
2 ¼ cups ricotta cheese	12 manicotti shells
1 cup grated Parmesan cheese	

In large bowl, mix together salsa and tomatoes. In saucepan, fry bacon over high heat until crisp and brown. Remove from heat, drain fat and let cool down. Add to pan ricotta cheese, ½ cup of parmesan cheese, egg, chives and pepper. Using teaspoon stuff mixture into manicotti shells. Manicotti does not have to be precooked, there is enough liquid to tenderize. Spray 13x9 inch baking pan. Pour half of tomato mixture into bottom of dish, spreading to cover bottom. Arrange manicotti over sauce in one layer. Cover with remaining tomato mixture. Sprinkle with remaining Parmesan. Bake in 350° oven for 1 hour or until sauce is bubbly and manicotti is tender.

*PASTA PRIMAVERA

Pasta primavera is an Italian-American dish that consists of pasta and fresh vegetables. A meat such as chicken, sausage or shrimp is sometimes added, but the focus of primavera is the vegetables themselves. The dish may contain almost any kind of vegetable, but cooks tend to stick to firm, crisp vegetables.

1 1-pound package penna rigate
    pasta
4 quarts water
1 sliced summer squash
1 sliced zucchini
1 small red onion chopped
1 cup chopped carrots
1 cup chopped broccoli
½ green bell pepper sliced
½ red bell pepper sliced
Salt and black pepper
Sauce:
2 15-ounce cans tomato sauce

1 can diced tomatoes
1 ½ cups water
½ cup diced onions
1 tablespoon minced garlic
1 diced tomato
1 tablespoon dried parsley
1 tablespoon brown sugar
2 teaspoons lemon juice
2 teaspoons red wine vinegar
1 teaspoon dried basil
1 teaspoon dried oregano
½ teaspoon salt
¼ teaspoon black pepper

Sauce: Combine all ingredients in saucepan over high heat. Bring sauce to boil; reduce heat to low and simmer for 1 to 1 ½ hours or until sauce thickens. Bring water to boil. Dump pasta into water, stir and cook for 11-15 minutes, until al dente; drain. Steam vegetables over boiling water for 8-10 minutes or until tender. Salt and pepper vegetables to taste. Serve in bowls with pasta layer first, layer vegetables over pasta and top with sauce.

*PASTA SAUCE

Use this on most any pasta or in any recipe that calls for a pasta sauce.

¼ pound mushrooms
2-29-ounce can tomato sauce
1 can diced tomatoes
3 tablespoons sugar or splenda
2 tablespoons olive oil
2 tablespoons dried minced onion
2 tablespoons grated Romano
    cheese

1 tablespoon grated Parmesan
    cheese
2 teaspoons dried basil
1 teaspoon dried parsley
1 teaspoon garlic powder
½ teaspoon black pepper
1 bay leaf

Combine all ingredients in saucepan over medium heat. Bring to boil then reduce heat and simmer for 15-20 minutes, stirring often. Remove bay leaf before using.

*PAYDAY ST. LOUIS TOASTED RAVIOLI

Authentic St. Louis Style unique and deliciously toasted ravioli that can be found on the menu of any restaurant in St. Louis. When I traveled, I was shocked that no one had even HEARD of these wonderful treats. Please don't be tempted to buy the premade kind. This isn't hard and you will be rewarded.

¼ cup evaporated milk	1 package frozen cheese ravioli,
2 eggs	thawed
1 ½ cups dry bread crumbs	3 cups canola oil for frying
1 ½ tablespoons Italian seasoning	2 tablespoons grated Parmesan
1 teaspoon garlic salt	cheese
	4 cups spaghetti sauce

Combine milk and egg in small bowl. Place breadcrumbs, Italian seasoning and salt in shallow bowl. Dip ravioli in milk mixture and coat with breadcrumbs. In large saucepan, heat marinara sauce over medium heat until bubbling. Reduce heat to simmer. In large heavy pan, pour oil to depth of 2 inches. Heat oil over medium heat until small amount of breading sizzles and turns brown. Fry ravioli, a few at a time, 1 minute on each side or until golden. Drain on paper towels. Sprinkle with Parmesan cheese and serve immediately with hot marinara sauce.

*PENNSYLVANIA PIEROGIES

Pierogies are a dish consisting of boiled dumplings of unleavened dough stuffed with varying ingredients. I learned how to make the real thing in a mining town in Pennsylvania. They are found in Canada and the US, having been popularized primarily by Slavic immigrants. They are particularly common in areas with large Slavic-derived populations, such as Chicago, western Massachusetts, Minneapolis, Detroit, northern Ohio, western and northeastern Pennsylvania.

Filling:

8-10 potatoes

6 tablespoons butter

1 finely chopped onion

4 cups shredded Cheddar cheese

½ teaspoon salt

¼ teaspoon black pepper

4-6 strips cooked crumbled bacon
(Optional)

Dough:

2 eggs

2 tablespoons vegetable oil

6-7 cups flour

1 ½ teaspoons salt

2 ¼ cups cooled potatoes water

Peel and cube potatoes, place in large saucepan and cover with water. Boil until tender, drain, reserving water for dough. Sauté onions in skillet with butter until tender; set aside to cool down. Mash potatoes, add onions and butter mixture. Add cheese, salt and pepper and bacon if using.

Dough: Combine water, eggs, oil and mix well. In separate larger bowl, combine flour and salt. Make a well in center of flour mixture. Pour egg mixture into well and stir until smooth. Turn dough out onto lightly floured surface and knead 5-6 times. Place dough in sprayed bowl, turning dough once. Cover and let rest for at least 20 minutes and up to 2 hours. On lightly floured surface, roll dough into 1/6 inch thickness. Cut out circles with floured glass rim or biscuit cutter. Fill each circle half with 1 teaspoon of potato mixture. Pinch edges together, seal seams. Place on baking sheets lined with waxed paper. Freeze. Once frozen, place in large zipper style plastic bags to store. To cook: Bring large pot of water to boil. Cook frozen pierogies in batch of 6-8; they are done when they float to top. Drain well in colander. Melt butter in large skillet and over medium heat fry boiled pierogies, turning once to brown on both sides. Serve with sour cream, more cheese, meat entree or with salad.

*PIEROGI BAKE

I had to find an easy way to make my favorites and this was it.

1 pound ground beef

1 large chopped onion

1 package frozen perogies

1 (16-ounce) bag frozen mixed
     vegetables

1 pint sour cream

6 tablespoons margarine

2 cups shredded Cheddar cheese

Melt 3 tablespoons of margarine in 13 x 9 inch baking dish in 350° oven. Remove dish and place frozen vegetables over bottom of dish, evenly distributing the margarine with the vegetables. Place frozen pierogi over vegetables, don't overlap pierogies. Cook the onions with the rest of the margarine and pour them evenly over pierogies. Cook ground beef until no longer pink, drain fat and spread over the onions. Spread shredded cheese on top. Cover with aluminum foil. Cover with foil and bake in oven for 30 minutes. Serve with sour cream.

*SLOW COOKER LASAGNA

In finding an easier way to fix this dish, the slow cooker really made the difference.

1 pound cooked ground beef	1 egg
¼ cup minced onions	¼ cup Parmesan cheese
4-5 cups spaghetti sauce	8-10 uncooked lasagna noodles
3 cups small curd cottage cheese	2-3 cups shredded mozzarella
1 10-ounce box chopped spinach	cheese
thawed and liquid pressed out	

Combine beef, onions and sauce. In another bowl combine egg, cottage cheese, spinach and parmesan cheese. Layer half of ground beef mixture then 4-5 dry noodles, ½ of cottage cheese mixture and ½ of mozzarella cheese in slow cooker, then repeat layers. Cover with lid. Cook on high 4-5 hours or on low 6-8 hours.

*SWEET-SOUR PASTA SALAD

1 package tricolor spiral pasta	Dressing:
2 cups finely chopped sweet onions	1 ½ cups sugar or artificial
2 cups diced tomatoes	sweetener
2 cups chopped cucumbers	½ cup cider vinegar
1 cup chopped green bell peppers	1 tablespoon dry mustard
2 tablespoons chopped fresh parsley	1 teaspoon salt
	1 teaspoon garlic powder

Cook pasta according to directions. Drain, rinse with cold water. Place pasta in large bowl. Stir into pasta, onions, tomatoes, cucumbers, pepper and parsley. In saucepan, mix together sugar, vinegar, mustard, salt and garlic powder. Cook over medium low heat for 10 minutes or until sugar is dissolved. Pour over salad and toss to coat. Cover and refrigerate for 2 hours before serving.

^BASIC RICE PUDDING

Rice puddings are found in nearly every area of the world. Recipes can greatly vary even within a single country. Different types of pudding vary depending on preparation methods and ingredients selected.

½ cup rice	1 teaspoon salt
1 ½ cups boiling water	¼ teaspoon nutmeg
2 eggs	2 cups milk
½ cup sugar	¼ cup raisins
1 tablespoon rum	

Measure out raisins and soak them in teacup with 1 tablespoon of rum (hot water may be used). Select long or short grain rice (do not use Minute Rice). Wash rice thoroughly until water runs clear in cold running water; drain. Sprinkle rice into boiling water. Cover and cook gently over low heat until all water has been absorbed and rice is tender, about 20 minutes. In medium large bowl, beat eggs using fork. Stir in sugar, salt and nutmeg, milk, cooked rice and raisins rum mixture. Transfer mixture to buttered 1 quart ovenproof baking dish. Cover container securely; bake in 250° oven for 1-½ hours, or until it is firm and grains of rice are very soft. Serve warm or cold.

Generally, honey is bottled in its familiar liquid form. However, honey is sold in other forms, and can be subjected to a variety of processing methods. Honey has a higher sweetening power than sugar so use less honey than sugar when you want to substitute it in the recipes. Start by substituting up to half of the sugar called for. When baking with honey always: reduce

any liquid called for by ¼ cup for each cup of honey used, add ½ teaspoon baking soda for each cup of honey used and reduce the oven temperature by 25 degrees to prevent over browning.

^BEST RICE CAKES

This is an incredible recipe shared with me by a superb Filipino nurse—both sweet and memorable.

3 cups coconut milk	1 cup brown sugar divided
2 cups sweet rice	¼ cup cream of coconut
1 teaspoon salt	2 tablespoons anise seeds

Bring coconut milk to boil in saucepan. Add sweet rice and salt and turn heat down to medium. Cook over medium heat until mixture is dry; stir constantly to keep from burning. When dry, reduce heat to low. Add ¼ cup of brown sugar. Stir well. When combined, pour into well greased or sprayed round cake pan. Top with cream of coconut and rest of brown sugar. Sprinkle with anise seeds. Bake in 350° oven for 20 minutes.

^CHICKEN CARROT FRIED RICE

1 pound skinless boneless chicken breasts	½ onion sliced
	2 tablespoons olive oil divided
4 tablespoons soy sauce divided	3 shredded carrots
2 cups chopped broccoli	2 cups cooked rice
2 teaspoons minced garlic	¼ teaspoon black pepper

Cut breast into cube pieces. In bowl combine chicken cubes, 1 tablespoon soy sauce and garlic, stir well and set aside. In large skillet stir fry broccoli and onion in 1 tablespoon oil for 5 minutes. Add carrots, fry 4 minutes longer or until crisp tender. Remove from skillet and set aside. In same skillet, stir fry chicken in 1 tablespoon of oil, until no longer pink. Add rice, pepper, vegetables and remaining soy sauce. Heat through and serve.

^FRIED RICE

My co-worker, dear friend and fellow nurse in St. Louis introduced me to this dish in 1977. I tried the dish everywhere I traveled to find someplace that did it just as good. Since I couldn't find any, I make my own.

3 cups cooked rice	2 ounces diced, cooked chicken,
¼ cup crumbled cooked bacon	pork, shrimp or ham
3 eggs	1 medium onion chopped
¼ teaspoon black pepper	2 tablespoons soy sauce
3 tablespoons oils	½ cup shredded cabbage
2 teaspoons ginger	¼ cup chopped fresh parsley

Scramble eggs and chop into rice size pieces. In large skillet, stir in oil, pepper, ginger, onion and cabbage; cook for 5 minutes. Add bacon and choice of meat. Stir well and heat for 1 minute. Add eggs and rice. Stir well until everything is coated and heated through.

^RICE PILAF

This dish is rice or cracked wheat browned in oil, and then cooked in a seasoned broth. Depending on the local cuisine, it may also contain a variety of meat and vegetables. Pilaf and similar dishes are common to Middle Eastern, Central and South Asian, East African, Latin American, and Caribbean.

½ cup chopped onions	¾ cup long grain rice
½ cup fresh sliced mushrooms	1 ½ teaspoons instant chicken or
¼ cup chopped celery	beef bouillon
1 teaspoon minced garlic	⅛ teaspoon black pepper
1 tablespoon butter	2 slices crisp crumbled bacon
1 ½ cups water	

In saucepan cook onion, mushrooms, celery and garlic in melted butter until tender but not brown. Stir in water, rice and bouillon and pepper. Bring to boil, reduce heat. Cover and simmer about 15 minutes or until rice is tender and liquid is absorbed. Stir in bacon.

RISOTTO

A rich and creamy, traditional Italian rice dish; one of the most common ways of cooking rice in Italy.

½ pound rice	2 cups chicken broth
1 onion	Salt and black pepper
4 tablespoons vegetable oil	Nutmeg
¼ cup grated Parmesan cheese	½ teaspoon saffron
1 cup tomato sauce	

Wash rice in several courses of water, drain and dry. Peel and chop onion. Melt vegetable shortening in skillet; when hot add onion, fry over gentle fire until light color; add rice; shake pan over fire for a few minutes, so as to fry rice a little. Add seasoning, salt, pepper, nutmeg, and saffron; moisten with little stock, and add more as rice begins to swell. When stock is used up, gradually add sauce. When rice is tender mix in grated cheese. It is then ready to serve. In preparing this dish remember that rice should be well done, and should be neither too dry nor too moist.

^SPANISH RICE

Spanish rice is a popular dish in the Southwest of the US, where it often features liberal portions of grilled and stewed vegetables. Spanish rice cooked in South America tends to be more standardized, often with just enough tomato and chili to provide the characteristic reddish orange color and a smoky, garlic and onion taste. It's frequently served as a side dish alongside Mexican Cuisine.

½ cup chopped onions	1 teaspoon sugar
½ cup chopped green bell peppers	1 teaspoon chili powder
1 teaspoon minced garlic	Dash hot pepper sauce
1 tablespoon canola oil	½ cup shredded Cheddar cheese
1 28-ounce can diced tomatoes	⅛ teaspoon black pepper
¾ cup long grain rice	1 cup water

In large skillet cook onion, pepper and garlic in oil until tender. Stir in undrained tomatoes, rice, sugar, chili powder, pepper sauce, pepper and water. Bring to boil; reduce heat. Cover; simmer for 20-25 minutes until rice is tender and liquid absorbed. Sprinkle cheese on top before serving.

^VERMICELLI VEGETABLES

1 box Rice A Roni—chicken and
   Broccoli
1 bag frozen mixed vegetables for
   stir fry

1 bag frozen broccoli
3 tablespoons margarine
2 ¼ cups water

In large skillet, combine rice mix and 1 tablespoon of margarine. Sauté over medium heat until vermicelli is golden brown, stir frequently. Slowly stir in 2 cups of water and special seasoning from Rice mix, bring to boil. In 13 x 9 inch microwavable baking dish, place both bags of vegetables and ¼ cup water. Microwave for 5 minutes on high. Stir vegetables and add 2 other tablespoons margarine. Microwave another 3 minutes. Stir in rice mixture into baking dish with vegetables. Combine well. Microwave on high for 15 minutes, until rice is tender. Let stand for 5 minutes before serving.

Johnny Appleseed Grace Song:

Oh the Lord is good to me
And so I thank the Lord
For giving me the things I need
the sun, and the rain and the apple seed
The Lord is good to me, Amen.

APPETIZERS

When I first lived in California in the mid 1980's, I didn't have much personal interaction with the people I worked with; our days were extremely long and busy with little time to socialize. There were no friends in town to spend relaxing time with for an evening. My weekends were spent traveling for performances and workshops. With very little money at the time, I had few options for down time fun.

No Muss No Fuss

One Monday a coworker and I wanted to watch Monday night football but neither of us had a TV. Sports bars were just beginning to pop up, never having been to one, we opted to try one out. It was everything advertised: several big TV screens, free food, and half price drinks.

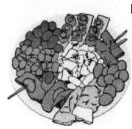

Nursing our 2 drinks and filling up on great food while we watched the game, we talked sports to like minded strangers—what a blast to have an evening free of anything intense or deep.

Every Monday night we found a different sports bar where we could watch football games. Besides the needed relief of stress, I was introduced to the world of hors d'oeuvres. We never left hungry sampling all the different flavors and versions of old favorites. It was cheap, no clean up, entertaining and social without the headaches; I was very sorry to see the football season end that year. But it left an impression about no muss entertaining and no fuss socializing.

After Joe and I got married, we regularly had people over for game nights, bible study, sports events, movie viewing and organization meetings. I

Entertainment Treatment

learned that if I served appetizers, I didn't miss any of the fun. I prepared the food ahead of time and just finished them off or heated them up before the guest arrived. No worry about allergies or someone not liking what I fixed, there were lots of choices and they could eat as much as they wanted. If they wanted to start with dessert, that was fine, it was all out for them to decide.

Such an atmosphere allowed people to freely move about and encouraged conversations. If someone wanted to bring some food, there was no pressure to fit a certain theme or dinner plan. For inexperienced cooks, appetizers are fundamentally easier to make without all the usual pressures. There's no difficult timing of dish preparation with a big fancy meal or spending a lots of money. When the evening was done, clean up was a breeze as I packed up leftovers especially for those who lived alone or didn't like to cook. That always sent them home wanting to come back again.

APPETIZER TREE

This is a great way to serve deli meat, cheeses and fruits when you are short on table space. Instead of a huge platter, this one goes up and can also do double duty as your table centerpiece, saving more space.

1 fresh pineapple—not too ripe	Cooked ham in ½ inch squares
Block cheeses, cut into	Any fruit cut in ½ inch squares
½ inch squares	Any cooked meats in ½ inch squares
Sausage or pepperoni in	
½ inch squares	

Select a pineapple that stands upright without any supports. Slice off green top; cut away outer skin, carve into desired shape. Begin at bottom of pineapple, use toothpicks to attach cheeses, meat and fruit in decorative pattern. Modify colors of food to fit party theme. Serve with dipping sauces for fruit and meats. When the party is over, you have a pineapple to cut up and enjoy the next day.

BACON WRAPPED SCALLOP

The popularity of scallops skyrocketed with new equipment in 1965 enabling deepwater mollusks to be processed. They're so rich, sweet and tender that a little goes a long way.

6 very large scallops	1 teaspoon ground ginger
¼ cup balsamic vinegar	12 slices bacon halved
1 tablespoon brown sugar	1 can sliced water chestnuts drained
1 tablespoon minced garlic	

Spray heavily slotted broiler pan and preheat pan in 450° oven. Pat scallops dry and quarter them. Combine vinegar, sugar, garlic and ginger. Stir in scallops and marinate for 10 minutes. Arrange bacon slices in single layer. On each half slice of bacon, place 2 chestnut slices and one piece of scallop. Sandwich scallop between chestnut slices and wrap with bacon; secure each with toothpick. Place on heated broiler pan. Bake in 450° oven 10 minutes, turning once, serve warm.

BEST QUESADILLA TRIANGLES

Exactly what constitutes a quesadilla varies from region to region and between the U.S. and Mexico and is not universally agreed upon by chefs. However, it is generally agreed that the quesadilla is cooked after being filled or stuffed with cheese. In fact the word comes from Spanish, and literally means "little cheesy thing"

2-10 inch flour tortilla	2 teaspoons diced onions
2 tablespoons butter softened	¼ pound cook, crumble sausages or
⅓ cup shredded Monterey Jack cheese	3 slices crisp, crumbled bacon
⅓ cup shredded Cheddar cheese	¼ teaspoon finely chopped fresh cilantro
½ medium tomato chopped	Dash salt

Heat large frying pan over medium heat. Spread half of butter on one side of each tortilla. Put one tortilla, butter side down, in hot pan. Spread cheeses evenly onto center of tortilla in pan. Leave margin of inch or so all way around. Sprinkle tomato, onion, meat, cilantro and salt over top. Top off quesadilla with remaining tortilla, buttered side facing up. When bottom tortilla has browned, after 45-90 seconds, flip quesadilla over and grill other side for same time. Remove quesadilla from pan, and using sharp knife or pizza cutter; cut quesadilla 3 times through middle like pizza, creating 6 equal sizes. Serve hot with sour cream, guacamole and salsa.

BLACK BEAN DIP

In writings from the 1800's, gold prospectors to Alaska ate meals consisting mainly of beans and gave the "dried beans" the name "Alaskan strawberries".

1 can black beans drained	¼ teaspoon sugar or Splenda
1 small onions chopped	¼ teaspoon salt
1 green bell pepper chopped	¼ teaspoon black pepper
1 teaspoon minced garlic	¼ teaspoon hot sauce
1 ¼ tablespoons red wine vinegar	Cheese Dip:
1 ¼ tablespoons olive oil	⅓ cup shredded Cheddar cheese

Blenderize all ingredients together. For warm dip, place mixture in casserole dish, cover and place in 350° oven for 10-15 minutes, until heated through. Cheese Dip: Stir in Cheddar cheese to casserole dish before heating; heat until cheese is melted.

BREADSTICKS, PARTY PIZZA AND POCKETS DOUGH

This can used to make any size pizzas, calzone, breadsticks and pizza pockets.

⅔ cup water

2 cups flour

1 tablespoon olive oil

¼ teaspoon salt

1 teaspoon yeast rapid-rising

Flavored Crust:

2 teaspoons garlic powder (optional)

1 tablespoon Parmesan cheese

(optional)

Put all ingredients in bread machine according to manufactures directions and place on "dough" setting. Pizzas: Sprinkle small amount of cornmeal on bottom of large cookie sheet with sides. Pat dough on top of cornmeal; make small appetizer size, individual size or one big one. Calzone: Roll out dough in 10" circle. Place 1-2 cups fillings in center of dough. Fold over and crimp shut. Place on greased cookie sheet. After 15 minutes cooking, brush with melted butter. Cook for 25 minutes in 375° oven or until golden brown. Breadsticks: Divide dough into 12 pieces and shape into pencil shape lengths or roll out into rectangle or circle and cut with knife or pizza cutter into strips. Place on sprayed cookie sheet; brush with melted butter; sprinkle with garlic powder or Parmesan or mozzarella cheese. Bake in 450° oven until brown. Pizza Pockets: Same as Calzone, just smaller circles and bake less time

BRUSCHETTA—COOKED

Bruschetta is usually served as a snack or appetizer. Variations may include toppings of spicy red pepper, tomato, vegetables, beans, cured meat, and/ or cheese and whether it's cooked or not. The most popular involves basil, mozzarella, and tomato.

4 tablespoons olive oil

½ diced red bell pepper

1 cup finely chopped sweet onions

1 tablespoon minced garlic

2 cups chopped tomatoes

1 teaspoon dried basil

1 teaspoon dried oregano

⅛ teaspoon black pepper

1 tablespoon balsamic vinegar

½ teaspoon salt

12 slices (1-inch thick) French or

Italian bread

3 tablespoons olive oil

1 large peeled garlic clove

½ cup grated Parmesan cheese

1 cup pitted, ripe olives chopped

(optional)

Broil bread slices until golden brown on both sides. Brush both sides with oil and rub with garlic clove. Heat 3 tablespoons oil, bell peppers, onions and ¼ teaspoon salt in skillet over medium high heat, stir occasionally until vegetables are brown about edges, 10-12 minutes. Reduce heat to medium; make clearing in middle of skillet and add remaining oil and mash in garlic, cook for 30 seconds. Stir vegetables into garlic; reduce heat to low and stir in tomatoes and seasonings. Cover and cook until moisture has evaporated. Take skillet off heat, stir in vinegar and rest of salt. Divide mixture evenly among bread slices and top with Parmesan cheese. Return slices to ungreased baking sheet. Bake in oven for 2-3 minutes more until cheese starts to melt. If desired place chopped olive on top and serve warm.

BRUSCHETTA—UNCOOKED TOPPING

Bruschetta is a food whose origin dates to at least the 15th century from central Italy. My first really great ones were on an Italian cruise ship and I think my sister-in-law Lenora and I could have eaten just these for the whole meal. Talk about a certain food bringing back the grandest of memories—every time I fix these I see myself on that ship.

2 cups coarsely diced tomatoes	1 clove garlic peeled and halved
1 teaspoon minced garlic	½ cup fresh grated Parmesan cheese
1 cup chopped sweet onions	12 slices Italian or French bread
2 tablespoons chopped oregano	1-inch thick
2 teaspoons chopped basil	4 tablespoons olive oil
4 teaspoons chopped parsley	¼ teaspoon black pepper

Rub cut side of garlic over one side of each slice of bread. Place bread, garlic side down on ungreased baking sheet. Bake in 350° oven for 5 minutes on each side or until lightly browned. In bowl combine tomatoes, minced garlic, onion, oil, oregano, basil, pepper and parsley. Spoon tomato mixture on each piece of bread on the side rubbed with garlic. Sprinkle with Parmesan cheese and serve.

BUFFALO CHICKEN WINGS

This spicy appetizer was created in the 1960s is also called "hot wings" became wildly popular across the US and are served as appetizers in many restaurants and bars. They continue to be served with celery and bleu cheese dressing just like at the Anchor Bar in Buffalo, New York where they were created and equally first-rate served with Ranch or Roquefort dressing and a salad or carrot sticks to help "cut the heat".

4 pounds chicken wings	1 tablespoon white wine vinegar
1 teaspoon black pepper	**Less Spicy:**
4 cups vegetable oil	1 tablespoon Tabasco hot sauce and
4 tablespoons margarine	4 tablespoon ketchup
5 tablespoons Tabasco Hot Sauce	

Chop off wing tip of each chicken wing and discard it. Chop wing in half, cutting at joint, to make 2 pieces; season with salt and pepper. In deep skillet, heat oil over high heat until it starts to sizzle. Add half of chicken wings and cook; until golden and crisp, stir and shake occasionally. When done, remove them to paper towel to drain. Cook remaining wings same way. Place wings on warm serving tray. Melt margarine over medium heat in separate saucepan. Add hot sauce and vinegar. Mix well, remove from flame and immediately pour sauce over top of wings and serve.

CHEESE FONDUE

Fondue is a Swiss dish shared at the table in a pot over a small burner. Forks are used to dip bits of food into the warm sauce. While cheese fondue is the most widely known, there are other pot and dipping ingredients. Fondue etiquette can be both helpful and fun. Most often, allowing one's tongue or lips to touch the dipping fork will be thought of as rude. With meat fondues use a dinner fork to take meat off the dipping fork. After a dipped morsel has been tasted it should never be returned to the pot.

4 cups shredded Swiss cheese
4 cups shredded Gruyere cheese
2 tablespoons cornstarch
1 teaspoon minced garlic
4 cups white wine

3 tablespoons kirsch liqueur (cherry brandy)
Dash nutmeg
2 loafs French bread cut in 2 inch chunks

In large bowl, combine cheeses and cornstarch; set aside. Place in large pot garlic and wine; heat over medium heat until tiny bubbles begin to form at edges. Reduce heat to very low. Add cheese mixture by handfuls, stirring constantly with wooden spoon, continue stirring 10-15 minutes or until cheese is melted. Stir in kirsch and nutmeg. Transfer cheese mixture to fondue warmer; set in center of table along with bowl of bread chunks. Bread should be cut day before, left uncovered at room temperature to firm up.

CHEESY RYE BREAD

This is another recipe my sister Sharon made first, I have no idea where she got her original recipe, but it has been a hit at numerous parties for over 20 years.

1 loaf party rye bread
½ pound ground pork sausage
½ pound ground turkey
1 large box Velveeta cheese cubed

1 cup finely chopped onions (optional)
1 teaspoon hot sauce (optional)
¼ teaspoon garlic powder

Spread bread slices in single layer on cookie sheet. Brown meats until pink is all gone, add onions, sauce and garlic powder. Stir well, add cheese and stir until melted. Spread meat mixture on each slice of bread and place on ungreased cookie sheet. Before ready to serve place cookie sheet under broiler on high until cheese warms and bubbles.

CRAB DIP

I started out using imitation crab in my dip until I had the real thing. Whether I use Chesapeake Bay blue crab, snow crab from North Atlantic or North Pacific oceans or gulf coast rock crab or any of our fresh Alaskan crabs: Dungeness, King, Tanner or Opilio—this is requested constantly.

½ cup milk	⅛ teaspoon black pepper
2 8-ounce packages cream cheese	½ teaspoon dry mustard
1 8-ounce container sour cream	½ teaspoon Old Bay Seasoning
1 finely chopped green bell pepper	1 teaspoon salt
1 finely chopped onion	1 pound crab meat
1 cup finely chopped celery	

Combine milk, cheese, sour cream in slow cooker until smooth. Add vegetables, seasonings, crab meat and mix well; cover. Cook on low 3-4 hours, stirring every 30 minutes. Serve warm from cooker with any type of crackers, cut raw vegetables, bread crisps, pretzels or chips.

CRESCENT WRAPPED APPETIZERS

When my friend Paula first introduced me to this kind of appetizer, it didn't take long for me to tinker and take a crack at flavor combinations. This is a good "last minute" fix.

2 cans refrigerated crescent rolls	1 pound kielbasa or Polish sausage
1 8-ounce round brie cheese	rope
	1 egg beaten

Use one can of rolls for cheese and one for sausage rope. Open and stretch dough firmly around cheese and sausage rope pressing perforations to seal evenly. Cover both completely with dough, brush with beaten egg. Bake both on cookie sheet in 350° oven for 20-25 minutes or until golden brown. Cool 15 minutes. Serve Brie whole with crackers and knife. Cut sausage rope into 1-inch rounds to serve on plate with mustard to dip.

DELI WITH DIPPING SAUCE

This is a great dip for raw, fried or grilled vegetables. It can also be used for the appetizer tree.

1 pound ham cubed	1 cup mayonnaise
1 pound cooked turkeys cubed	4 teaspoons ketchup
1 pound block cheese cubed	⅓ cup creamy horseradish
2 cups cherry tomatoes	½ teaspoon paprika
1 stalk celery sliced into 2 inch pieces	½ teaspoon salt
1 pound cooked beef roast, cubed	2 teaspoons onion powder
1 bag baby carrots	¼ teaspoon dried oregano
2 green bell peppers cut into wedges	⅛ teaspoon black pepper
Dip:	⅛ teaspoon cayenne pepper

For dip: combine all ingredients, cover and refrigerate at least 1 hour before serving. Arrange meats and vegetables on platter with toothpicks and leave place for bowl of dip in center or on both sides of platter.

DILL DIP FOR VEGGIES

Dill Folklore: To the Greeks the presence of dill was an indication of prosperity. In the 8th century, Charlemagne used it at banquets to relieve hiccups and in the Middle Ages it was used in a love potion so be cautious when serving it.

1 cup sour cream	1 teaspoon salt
1 cup mayonnaise	½ teaspoon dill weed
2 teaspoons lemon juice	1 teaspoon dry mustard
1 tablespoon grated onions	

Blend all ingredients together. Allow to sit in refrigerator for several hours before using.

FRUIT DIP

This will get them eating their daily servings of fresh fruits.

1 cup sour cream	Bunch of grapes—any kind
1 cup milk	Bowl of melon balls
1 3-ounce package instant vanilla	Bowl of strawberries
pudding	Bowl of bananas chunks
Bowl of drained pineapple chunks	Bowl of sliced apples

Mix sour cream and milk well, add pudding mix. Let it sit at least 1 hour before serving.

GARLIC BREAD

Garlic bread typically consists of bread topped with garlic and olive oil or butter, either grilled or broiled. It is often used as a simple accompaniment to pasta and other Italian dishes. Bread can be spread with garlic butter 8 hours ahead and chilled, wrapped in foil; let stand at room temperature 30 minutes before baking. I also use leftover bread the next day for open face sandwiche

1 loaf Italian, French or sourdough	1 tablespoon finely chop fresh
bread	parsley
3-6 tablespoons olive oil or butter	½ cup grated Cheddar cheese
½ cup cream cheese	½ teaspoon paprika
Mixable Items:	½ teaspoon black pepper
2 teaspoons minced garlic	¼ cup mozzarella cheese
1 teaspoon Italian seasoning	1 tablespoon garlic powder
½ cup grated Parmesan cheese	1 tablespoon chopped fresh herbs
1 tablespoon finely chop fresh basil	¼ cup grated other cheeses
	1 teaspoon cayenne pepper

Bread is sliced diagonally towards bottom, but kept in one piece. Spread top of each slice with plain butter, oil or with butter and oil mixtures—see suggestions. Wrap loaf in foil and bake in 350° oven for 15 minutes. Open foil and bake 5 minutes more. Alternatively, bread can be cut into individual 1-inch slices. Place slices on large baking sheet; covered with butter or oil and other ingredients individually. Grill or Broil at 475° oven until the cheese melts and begins to brown. Suggested ways of preparing butter and oil mixtures:

- Combine cream cheese with garlic and herbs.
- Mash garlic into a paste with salt, stir in butter or oil in bowl until smooth; add parsley;
- Combine butter, garlic and herbs in a small microwave dish. Microwave on high for 1-2 minutes, until butter is barely melted. Remove from microwave and stir in Italian seasoning, paprika and Parmesan cheese.

GREAT STUFFED MUSHROOMS

My husband could make a meal of these and never got enough in the appetizers sizes when eating out, the solution: making a home version and they do make a nice meal for all you mushroom lovers. You can take the filling and stuff four prepared Portobello mushroom caps for a spectacular entrée.

24 large mushrooms	**½ cup soft bread crumbs**
5 tablespoons butter	**1 egg**
2 tablespoons minced onions	**½ teaspoon dill weed**
1 teaspoon lemon juice	**¾ cup Monterey Jack cheese**
8 ounces crab meat or shrimp,	**½ cup white wine or chicken broth**
or mix of Shrimp and crab or	
sausage and ham.	

Remove stems from mushrooms and chop them finely. Fry stems and onions in 2 tablespoons butter over medium heat until onions are tender. Remove from heat and add lemon juice, crabmeat, breadcrumbs, egg, dill weed and ¼ cup cheese. Melt 3 tablespoons butter in 9x13 baking dish. Turn and coat mushrooms. Fill cavities with stem mixture. Sprinkle with remaining cheese over mushrooms and pour wine or broth into bottom of pan. Bake uncovered in 400° oven for 15-20 minutes.

HAM AND CHEESE SPIRALS

These are quick to make and any leftover deli meats after a party can be used or slice thin the leftovers from those holiday meals to make these a "day after" tradition.

4 ounces softened cream cheese	1 cup whipping cream
1 cup shredded Swiss cheese or any kind	2 tablespoons Dijon style mustard
	2 tablespoons mustard
4-8 inch flour tortilla	3 tablespoons horseradish
3 tablespoons mustard	Honey Mustard:
1 tablespoon honey	½ cup sour cream
¾ pound thinly sliced ham, beef or turkey	½ cup mayonnaise
	2 tablespoons mustard
Mustard Sauce:	1 tablespoon honey

Combine cream cheese and Swiss cheese. In another bowl combine mustard and honey. Spread cheese mixture evenly over tortillas; place meat slices evenly over cheese mixture; spread honey mustard mix on meat. Roll up each tortilla. Wrap each roll in plastic wrap; chill for 1 hour. Remove plastic wrap; slice each roll into six ¾-inch pieces. Serve with both Mustard Sauces for dipping. Mustard Sauce: Beat whipping cream until it forms soft peak. Fold in horseradish and mustards. Cover and store in refrigerator for up to 24 hours. Honey Mustard Sauce: Beat together sour cream, mayonnaise, mustard and honey. Cover and refrigerate several hours before serving.

HOLIDAY CLAM DIPS: TRADITIONAL AND SPICY

This the kind of dip I never have any leftover and first enjoyed in Rhode Island many moons ago.

3 8-ounce packages cream cheese	1 packet onion soup mix
½ cup dried onions flakes	¼ cup milk
1 tablespoon garlic powder	Spicy:
32 ounces sour cream	1 package taco seasoning mix
1 can clams chopped	1 jar salsa
Traditional:	

Blend softened cream cheese, onion flakes, garlic powder and sour cream together. Beat in onion soup mix and milk; or taco seasoning and salsa. Add clams; for thinner dip add clam juice until desired consistency. Serve with crackers, chips or vegetables.

HUMMUS

With a long and sometimes controversial history outside the US, Americans have only one issue with it: how many ways they can enjoy this versatile and unique dip. Garnishes include chopped tomato, cucumber, cilantro, parsley, sautéed mushrooms, whole chickpeas, olive oil, hard-boiled eggs, paprika, cooked beans, olives and pickles.

1 15 ½-ounce can chickpeas or	2 teaspoons cumin
garbanzo beans	1 tablespoon minced garlic
¼ cup liquid from can of beans	½ teaspoon salt
¼ cup lemon juice	2 tablespoons olive oil

Drain chickpeas and set aside liquid from can. Combine remaining ingredients in blender or food processor. Add ¼ cup of liquid from chickpeas. Blend for 3-5 minutes on low until thoroughly mixed and smooth. Place in serving bowl; serve immediately with fresh, warm or toasted pita bread, pita chips and vegetables or cover and refrigerate. If you like it spicier: add 1 teaspoon cayenne pepper

LAYERED BEAN DIP

First tasted this one at a party in Nevada in the 1980's and given this recipe to everyone I know.

1 can refried beans	2 packages taco seasoning mix
1 14-ounce container avocado dip	2 cups shredded Cheddar cheese
2 cups finely chopped onions	Sliced olives (optional)
2 cups sour cream	Sliced pepper (optional)
2 cups mayonnaise	

Spread beans over bottom 13x9 baking dish. Spread avocado dip over beans. Spread chopped onions on top. Mix together sour cream, mayonnaise and taco seasoning; spread on top. Sprinkle cheese over top and add olive and pepper slices if desired. Serve with veggie sticks, corn or tortilla chips.

MEATBALLS

This one has that little spice to it that makes everyone crave more, I got this in Utah.

1 pound lean ground turkey	**1 egg**
⅓ cup finely diced onions	**⅓ cup grated Parmesan cheese**
1 teaspoon minced garlic	**2 teaspoons soy sauce**
2 teaspoons Italian seasoning	**3 tablespoons ketchup**
⅓ cup bread crumbs	

In medium bowl, mix all ingredients until well combined. Using tablespoon, roll to make small ball shapes. Repeat until all meat mixture is made into balls. Place meatballs on aluminum foil lined cookie sheet and bake in 375° oven until meat is no longer pink, approximately 8-10 minutes. Serve on platter with toothpicks.

PARTY SMOKIES SIX WAYS

Since my teens these little smokies seem to please year after year and while they are not on any health food list, I think everyone looks for them at holiday parties to splurge on. Serve right out of the crockpot by setting to low heat and warm for an hour or two. Stir now and then to make sure all the sausages are evenly coated.

1 16-ounce package little smokies sausages	**—1 bottle hickory barbecue sauce**
—1 pound bacon	**—1 can of chili sauce**
—1 cup brown sugar	**—1 small jar of grape jelly**

1. Cut bacon into thirds; wrap each strip around each sausage. Place wrapped smokies on wooden skewers, several to a skewer. Arrange skewers on baking sheet; bake in 350° oven until bacon is crisp 2. Sprinkle bacon wrapped smokies liberally with brown sugar; bake until bacon is crisp and brown sugar melted. Always remove them from skewers, carefully. 3 Simply place plain smokies in small amount water in slow cooker; heat on low for 1 hour before serving. 4. Place plain smokies and bottle of barbecue sauce in slow cooker on low, cover and heat for an hour before serving. 5.Cook the sausages as in number one, but instead of brown sugar, place smokies in crockpot and cover with barbecue sauce, heat through before serving. 6. In a saucepan, heat and stir chili sauce and grape jelly until it's mixed well and warm. Add the sausages. Let heat for about 30 minutes on low heat before serving.

PARTY VEGETABLE DIP

1 cup mayonnaise	1 teaspoon salt
1 cup sour cream	1 teaspoon black pepper
2 tablespoons minced onions	1 tablespoon fresh minced parsley
2 tablespoons minced garlic	1 tablespoon Dijon style mustard

Blend and refrigerate a few hours before serving

POTSTICKERS

The legend is these dumplings were accidently burnt on the bottom by a Chinese cook. Voila, a chef covering a mistake becomes a sensation. The filled dumplings are pan-fried on one side and then steamed in broth or water. Properly made, the potstickers are crisp and browned on the bottom, sticking lightly to the pan, but easy to remove with a spatula.

½ pound ground pork	1 ½ teaspoons kosher salt
2 tablespoons dried minced onion	½ teaspoon black pepper
1 egg	35 small wonton wrappers
2 teaspoons ketchup	Water to seal wontons
1 teaspoon mustard	Vegetable oil
2 teaspoons Worcestershire sauce	1 ⅓ cups chicken broth divided
1 teaspoon brown sugar	

Combine pork, onions, egg, ketchup, mustard, Worcestershire sauce, sugar, salt and pepper in medium bowl. Set aside. Remove 1 wonton wrapper from package, covering others with damp cloth. Brush 2 wrapper edges lightly with water. Place ½ rounded teaspoon of pork mixture in center of wrapper. Fold over, seal edges and shape as desired. Set on sheet pan and cover with damp cloth. Repeat procedure until all of filling is gone. Heat 12-inch skillet over medium heat. Brush with vegetable oil once hot. Add 8 to 10 potstickers at a time to pan and cook for 2 minutes, without touching. Once 2 minutes are up, gently add ⅓ cup chicken broth to pan, turn heat down to low, cover and cook for another 2 minutes. Remove to heatproof platter and place in 200° oven. Clean the pan in between batches by pouring in water and allowing pan to deglaze. Repeat until all are cooked. Serve immediately

REUBEN APPETIZER

The Reuben Sandwich is unquestionably one of New York's greatest contributions to the world of eating and is found in restaurants in all of the major cities of North America—and one of our favorites, so I wanted a way to enjoy it more often.

1 cup thousand island salad dressing	1 jar sauerkraut drain, dried,
1 12-ounce package Swiss cheese	chopped
½ pound thinly sliced corned beef	1-2 loaves sliced party rye bread

Combine all ingredients except bread in slow cooker. Cover and cook on low 3-4 hours, or until cheese is melted. Serve hot on rye bread.

SALMON DIP

I grew up on and loved canned salmon. Little did I know I would also one day enjoy the different varieties, fresh and even catch my own. Using different salmon will totally change the way this turns out—all impressive.

4 cups smoked, freshly cooked or canned salmon	1 3-ounce package cream cheese
1 tablespoon mustard	2 tablespoons diced onions
2 teaspoons tarragon	1 teaspoon minced garlic
¼ cup salad dressing	Dash salt
1 cup sour cream	Dash black pepper

Mix all ingredients together until very well combined. Refrigerate covered for 3-4 hours before serving with crackers or chips.

SPAM DIP

It's become part of so many jokes and urban legends about supposed mystery meat; it's now part of pop culture and folklore. The largest consumer of Spam internationally is the United Kingdom and South Korea. In the US, residents of Hawaii are the number one consumers of it followed by those in Alaska. In Hawaii, Spam is so popular it is sometimes dubbed "The Hawaiian Steak".

1 8-ounce package cream cheese	2 tablespoons chopped cilantro
½ cup grated Cheddar cheese	1 can spam grated
1 cup finely chopped green bell peppers	½ cup chopped celery
2 tablespoons Worcestershire sauce	⅓ cup chopped onions

Beat cream cheese, SPAM and Worcestershire sauce with mixer on medium until smooth. Stir in rest of ingredients, cover and chill for 1 hour. Serve with crackers, chips and vegetables.

Most people have something they deem a special comfort food. That would be anything that reminds us of reassuring, soothing, calming, consoling moments in our lives. It usually invokes feelings of nostalgia, safety, security, and encouragement and provides a solace of the mind and spirit. Sometimes those are childhood moments; for others it's a more recent occurrence when they felt confident from within. Studies have made a list of the current top 25 American comfort foods:

==

1. Apple Pie
2. Baked Beans
3. Banana Pudding
4. Beef Stew
5. Pot Roast
6. Chicken and Dumplings
7. Chicken Pot Pie
8. Chicken Soup
9. Chili
10. Chocolate Chip Cookies
11. Corn on the Cob
12. Fried Chicken
13. Gelatin
14. Green Bean Casserole
15. Hot Dogs
16. Ice Cream
17. Macaroni and Cheese
18. Mashed Potatoes
19. Meatloaf
20. Potato Salad
21. Pumpkin Pie
22. Shepherds Pie
23. Spaghetti
24. Tomato Soup
25. Tuna Casserole

==

My husband loves liver and onions, SPAM, cheese and scrapple. Even though they aren't on the "current list", they bring him great comfort. I was shocked just plain chocolate or brownies weren't included in the top 25. I've included recipes from most of the list or something that includes the food item. They're food we all relish eating alone or proudly sharing with others, but "Comfort Food" isn't usually an item we associate eating with others. It's a food we use to get in contact with a part of ourselves.

This is a perfect time for me to finally get my current collection together to pass along the wonderful things enjoyed over the years. Now my nieces, nephews and friends can make their own favorites and add on to the list. I hope they receive at least half of the praise, fun and joy that I have doing it—and every recipe shared brings them closer to the kind of world God would smile on.

The "First Thanksgiving" Menu

The following items were most likely on the table of the 1621 harvest festival celebrated by the colonists or Pilgrims, to thank God for saving their lives after the long voyage in the Mayflower and the years of draught at Plymouth. They celebrated with the Wampanoag tribe: Chief Massasoit and his extended family, about 90 people came for dinner and stayed for three whole days. Only four married Colonists ladies were left after the grueling time of famine who did all the cooking while soldiers killed enough fowl to feed the village for a week. The Native Indians supplemented by contributing five deer and other supplies.

The rest of the menu is what historians have assumed was available in plenty. They do know there was no hams because pigs had not been butchered yet. White and sweet potatoes or yams were not a common crop. Corn was kept dry at this point, so no corn on the cob dripping with butter. And the pumpkin was probably just stewed pumpkin as well as the cranberry sauce was not possible since there was no sugar.

Chicken hens were brought from England, but not a common food source except for the eggs they were still laying. No cows were aboard the Mayflower but they may have used goat milk to make cheese.

They probably feasted on the abundance of coastal seafood like Cod, eel, clams and lobster. The wild fowl would have included turkey, goose, duck, crane, swan, partridge and eagles. Besides the venison, seal was eaten as a plentiful meat source. Other items to work with were wheat flour, pumpkins, peas, parsnip, leeks, currants, beans, onions, lettuce, radishes, carrots, plums, grapes, walnuts, chestnuts, olive oil and acorns.

APRICOT LAMB SHANKS

Lamb shank is cut from the arm of shoulder, contains leg bone and part of round shoulder bone, and is covered by a thin layer of fat and fell (a thin, paper-like covering).

6 pounds lamb shanks trimmed	1 tablespoon minced garlic
½ cup olive oil	½ teaspoon cardamom
2 sliced onions	5 cups chicken broth
15 baby carrots chopped	Salt and black pepper
2 cups dried apricots	

Sprinkle lamb with salt and pepper. In Dutch oven, heat oil over medium-high heat and brown lamb on all sides. Set lamb aside on jellyroll pan to catch drips. Spoon off any visible fat. Sauté onions and carrots for about 5 minutes over medium heat in the same pan you used to brown the shanks. Add fruit, garlic and cardamom to the pan, stirring, and cook for about two minutes. Add stock and bring to a boil. Pour stock, vegetables and fruit into slow cooker and carefully place shanks on top. Set slow cooker for 8 hours on low. Take out shanks to cool on cutting board and spoon fat off top of pot. If desired, shred meat off bones with two forks; it should come off very easily and place meat back in pot with the sauce. Discard the bones. Turn pot back on low on warm until ready to serve.

BRAISED LAMB SHANKS

Braising is a combination cooking method using both moist and dry heat; typically the food is first seared at a high temperature and finished in a covered pot with a liquid for flavor.

4 (1 pound each) well trimmed lamb shank	4 cups red wine
2 tablespoons olive oil	4 cups chicken broth
2 chopped onions	1 14 ½-ounce can crushed tomatoes
1 chopped carrot	4 strips bacon
1 rib celery chopped	5 cups canned northern beans drained
1 tablespoon minced garlic	Salt and black pepper
1 tablespoon chopped fresh rosemary	

In heavy skillet brown lamb shanks on all sides in olive oil; remove to ovenproof casserole; set aside. Add carrot, celery and half of onions to same skillet and brown. Stir in garlic and rosemary. Cook 2 minutes. Add red wine, chicken broth and crushed tomatoes; heat to boiling. Spoon mixture over lamb; cover and bake in 350° oven for 2 hours or until 155° at thickest part. To serve, fry bacon until crisp. Drain; set aside. Add rest of chopped onions to same pan. Stir in beans; heat through. Stir in crumbled bacon; salt and pepper to taste. Divide and spoon onto platter or individual serving plates. Arrange shanks on top. Skim fat from vegetable mixture, discard fat and spoon vegetables over all. Serve.

GLAZED LAMB ROAST

Compared to other meats, lamb contains very little marbling (fat in the meat). Since lamb fat is on the edges of the meat, it is easily trimmed off, which means fewer calories, only 175 in an average 3-ounce serving. Try it, most of my guest who hadn't, ended up loving it. It makes a great company meal.

4 pounds boneless leg or lamb roast-trimmed	1 tablespoon minced garlic
¼ cup chopped onions	½ teaspoon salt
2 tablespoons chopped fresh parsley	½ teaspoon black pepper
2 teaspoons ground thyme	½ cup honey
1 teaspoon ground rosemary	3 tablespoons lemon juice
1 teaspoon dried sage	Garlic salt

Combine onion, parsley, herbs, garlic, salt and pepper. In separate bowl, combine honey and lemon juice. Place lamb on flat surface, meat side up. Season with garlic salt. Brush lamb with honey mixture. Sprinkle onion mixture over lamb. Roll and tie meat up. Brush rolled roast with honey mixture. Bake on roasting rack in oiled roasting pan in 350° oven for at least one hour for medium rare meat. Cook up to 30 more minutes depending on how well done you want the meat to be. During baking time, brush meat with honey mixture every 15 minutes; when honey mixture is gone, brush with pan drippings. Let roast stand 10 minutes before carving. Add ½ cup water to roasting pan to deglaze, thicken with flour or cornstarch to serve a gravy with lamb slices.

GREEK GYRO

Gyro is a Greek dish with seasoned meat; lamb, beef and pork, tomato, onion, and tzatziki sauce and served with pita bread. Gyros may also refer to the sandwich with the same ingredients.

1 pound ground lamb	½ teaspoon black pepper
½ pound ground beef 20% fat	Tzatziki Sauce:
¾ cup shredded onions	2 cups yogurt
1 tablespoon minced garlic	1 cucumber peeled, deseeded and
1 teaspoon sea salt	grated drained of extra liquid
¾ teaspoon dried marjoram	2 teaspoons minced garlic
¾ teaspoon dried rosemary	

Mix all ingredients together in large bowl, cover and refrigerator for 2 hours. Remove from refrigerator and blend in food processor for 1 minute. This will help give it more gyro feel to your palate. Form into meatloaf shape. Place on sprayed rimmed cookie sheet and bake in 325° oven for 45-60 minutes. It should be a bit dry. Slice into very thinly slices to make gyro. Place on plate with quartered and warmed pita bread. Add sliced tomato, sliced onions and tzatziki sauce. Tzatziki Sauce: Combine all 3 ingredients, cover and refrigerate for at least 2 hours before using.

GREEK SHISH KEBAB

Kebab refers to a variety of meat dishes consisting of grilled or broiled meats on a skewer or stick; most common lamb and beef, goat, chicken, fish, or shellfish. Now kebab ingredients include vegetables and fruit.

⅓ cup olive oil	2 pounds lean boneless lamb
3 tablespoons lemon juice	shoulder trimmed of fat, cut into
½ cup finely chopped onion	2-inch cubes
2 bay leaves	1 red onion cut into 1-inch pieces
2 teaspoons ground oregano	1 green bell pepper cut into 2-inch
½ teaspoon black pepper	pieces
	½ pound whole mushrooms

In a large nonmetallic bowl, stir together oil, lemon juice, chopped onion, bay leaves, oregano and pepper. Add lamb; stir to coat. Cover and refrigerate for at least 4 hours or overnight; stirring several times. Lift meat from marinade and drain briefly. Add red onion, bell pepper and mushrooms to marinade; turn to coat, then lift out reserving marinade. Thread meat cubes alternately with the vegetables on six skewers. Place skewers on a lightly greased grill 4 to 6 inches about a solid bed of medium-hot coals. Cook, turning and basting frequently with reserved marinade, until meat and vegetables are well browned but meat is still pink in the center, about 12 to 15 minutes (cut to test).

GRILLED LAMB CHOPS WITH POMEGRANATE

Pomegranates have grown in popularity; have wonderful health benefits; add color and taste.

1 cup pomegranate juice	4 thick loin lamb chops
1 ½ teaspoons minced garlic	2 teaspoons olive oil
1 teaspoon black pepper	¼ cup pomegranate seeds
¼ cup finely chopped fresh mint leaves	Mint leaves

Combine pomegranate juice, garlic, pepper and chopped mint in glass bowl; mix well. Add chops and turn several times to coat well. Refrigerate 8 to 12 hours, turning occasionally. Remove chops from marinade; drain and set aside. Pour marinade into small saucepan. Heat to boiling and simmer 20 minutes or until reduced to ⅓ cup. Brush chops with reduced marinade and oil. Broil or grill chops about 3 inches from heat, brushing once or twice with marinade. Cook to preferred doneness, about 5 to 6 minutes each side for medium rare, 7 to 8 minutes for medium and 9 to 10 minutes for well done. Garnish each chop with pomegranate seeds and mint leaves

IRISH LAMB STEW

This stew is a traditional Irish dish made from lamb or mutton; as well as potatoes, onions and parsley. It's a nice change from beef stew and good for a spring meal. My first taste was in New Mexico.

2 tablespoons olive oil	3 cups sliced carrots
2 pounds boneless lamb cut into	1 peeled and sliced turnips
chunks	1 pound sliced leeks divided
3 cups chicken broth	3 peeled and cubed potatoes
5 ½ cups water	¼ cup flour
1 teaspoon salt	½ cup chopped fresh parsley
½ teaspoon black pepper	

In a heated skillet add oil and lamb, cook for about 5 minutes, turning often, until lamb is browned. Transfer lamb to a large stockpot and add chicken broth and 5 cups water, salt and pepper; mix well and simmer slowly for 20 minutes. Add carrots, turnips and white part of leeks; simmer gently for 1 hour. Add potatoes and continue to simmer for another 30 minutes. Whisk flour with remaining ½ cup water and pour into soup mixture. Add green part of leeks along with parsley; simmer for 10 minutes. Remove from heat and serve hot.

LAMB CHOPS WITH MANGO SALSA

Mangoes account for approximately fifty percent of all tropical fruits produced worldwide and is the national fruit of India, Pakistan and the Philippines

4 thick loin lamb chops	2 tablespoons chopped cilantro
Salt and black pepper	½ teaspoon red pepper flakes
Mango Salsa:	Salt and black pepper
2 peeled, pitted mangos cut in	¼ cup lime juice
chunks	
1 red onion diced	

Season lamb chops with salt and pepper; set aside. In medium bowl, combine salsa ingredients. Grill lamb chops 4 to 6 inches from medium hot coals. For best flavor and texture, lamb chops should be cooked medium to medium rare, 3 to 5 minutes on each side on a covered grill. Remove from heat and serve with salsa. Or broil lamb chops by placing on broil pan 3 to 4 inches away from heat source. Turn chops once during cooking, until desired doneness is reached.

LAMB LEG WITH CUMIN

Lamb is one of the most popular meats all over the world except in the US. That is slowly changing as people try it and enjoy the delicate flavor and easy preparation.

6 pounds leg of lamb trim fat	**2 peeled sweet potatoes cut in**
5 tablespoons olive oil	**halves**
4 tablespoons ground cumin	**2 teaspoons cornstarch**
1 tablespoon garlic salt	**2 tablespoons cold water**
3 peeled potatoes cut in quarters	

Thoroughly rinse lamb under cold tap and dry it with paper towels. Lay lamb in roasting pan. Make 3 to 4 deep cuts in each side of lamb. In small bowl add olive oil, cumin and garlic salt; mix well. Insert into cuts and spoon rest all over lamb. Cover with aluminum foil and stand for at least 2 hours. The longer meat stands, the stronger the flavor will be. Bake in 425° oven for 30 minutes; lower oven temperature to 350°. Sprinkle potatoes and sweet potatoes with salt. Arrange potatoes beside meat. Continue to cook for another hour or until meat is tender and cooked. When meat is cooked, slice meat and serve with potatoes. Make gravy with juices left in roasting pan by adding mixture of cornstarch and cold water plus some boiling water until a thick consistency is reached.

LAMB SHANKS WITH VEGETABLES

Lamb is often sorted into three kinds of meat: forequarter, loin, and hindquarter. The forequarter includes the neck, shoulder, front legs, and the ribs up to the shoulder blade. The hindquarter includes the rear legs and hip. The loin includes the ribs between the two.

1 tablespoon olive oil

2 pounds lamb shanks cut in to 1 ½-inch pieces

¼ cup flour

1 chopped onion

7 peeled garlic cloves

2 teaspoons minced ginger

1 pound peeled potatoes cut in 1-inch chunks

½ pound peeled turnips cut in ½-inch chunks

3 peeled carrots sliced thick

1 cup chicken broth

½ cup white wine

¾ teaspoon rosemary crumbled

1 teaspoon grated lemon peels

½ teaspoon black pepper

Heat oil in ovenproof Dutch oven or pan over medium-high heat. Dredge lamb in flour. Working in batches, add lamb to oil; sauté until browned well browned, about 5 minutes. Remove lamb to bowl as it browns. Lower heat, add onion, garlic and ginger to pan; cook, stirring occasionally, until onion has softened. Add potatoes, turnips, carrots, broth, white wine, rosemary, lemon rind, pepper and browned lamb. Bring to boiling; cover and remove from heat. Bake in 350° oven for 1 hour or until meat in fork-tender.

MEDITERRANEAN SANDWICH

A Greek community festival had these sandwiches and I have wowed many a guest with them since.

2 tablespoons olive oil

1 pound ground lamb

½ cup minced onions

1 ¼ teaspoons grated lemon peels

¾ teaspoon oregano

¾ teaspoon garlic powder

1 teaspoon salt

1 teaspoon black pepper

¼ cup plus 1 tablespoon lemon juice

1 cup water

6 ounces plain yogurt

3 ounces feta cheese crumbled

6 pita bread

Heat olive oil in large skillet over medium-high heat. Stir in lamb, and cook until it begins to crumble. Add onions; continue cooking until lamb has browned and onions soften, about 5 minutes. Drain off any excess fat, reduce heat to medium-low, stir in 1 teaspoon lemon peel, ½ teaspoon dried oregano, ½ teaspoon garlic powder, ½ teaspoon salt and ½ teaspoon black pepper. Stir lemon juice into water; pour ¼ cup of this mixture into lamb. Cook until liquid mostly evaporates; stir in another ¼ cup, and cook again until mostly evaporated. Continue adding liquid ¼ cup at a time until all is used; about 30 minutes in all. Meat should look moist, but not sitting in liquid. While meat cooks, make feta sauce by placing yogurt, feta cheese, 1 tablespoon lemon juice, ¼ teaspoon dried oregano, ¼ teaspoon garlic powder, and ¼ teaspoon lemon peel into blender. Puree until smooth; season with rest of salt and pepper. Set aside. Spoon lamb mixture onto warmed pita bread. Top with feta sauce to serve.

MINTED LEG OF LAMB

Many folks served lamb with mint jelly, an old custom originally used to disguise mutton's strong flavor. The hint of mint is preferred today over the overly sweet jelly. Don't overcook your meat; just to a rosy-pink, medium-rare doneness will bring out the quality of today's choice lamb.

½ cup mint jelly	3 cloves garlic sliced
2 tablespoons white wine	½ teaspoon salt
1 teaspoon Dijon style mustard	½ black pepper
7 pounds leg of lamb	

Mint Glaze: Place jelly, wine, mustard and pinch of black pepper in small food processor or blender; cover; process until smooth. Cut slits all over lamb with tip of sharp knife; insert garlic slices. Season with salt and pepper; place lamb in shallow roasting pan. Bake in 425° oven uncovered, on center rack for 1 hour. Remove from oven; reduce temperature to 375°. Brush about ½ cup Mint Glaze over lamb; return to oven and bake additional 40 to 45 minutes. Remove from oven; insert instant-read meat thermometer into the thickest part of meat (temperature should read 155°—for medium.) Brush remaining glaze over lamb. Loosely cover; let stand for 15 minutes before carving.

"MUTTON" SOUP

Lamb, hogget, and mutton are the meat of domestic sheep. The meat of an animal in its first year is lamb; that of an older sheep is hogget and later mutton.

8 loin lamb chops	½ teaspoon dried thyme
1 teaspoon salt	½ teaspoon dried rosemary
1 teaspoon black pepper	1 pound peeled, diced potatoes
2 tablespoons olive oil	2 cups shredded cabbage
2 cups water	1 chopped onion
1 teaspoon black pepper	2 cups sliced celery
1 tablespoon chopped parsley	1 16-ounce bag frozen green peas
1 bay leaf	

Season lamb chops with salt and pepper. Heat oil in a saucepan and brown both sides of lamb chops. Remove lamb and place in Dutch oven. Pour off any fat and deglaze saucepan by adding water. Pour water over lamb in Dutch oven and bring to a boil. Enclosed in cheesecloth bag, add chopped parsley, bay leaf, thyme, and rosemary to the boiling water. Cover and reduce heat to simmer for 15 minutes. Add potatoes, cabbage, onion and celery. Simmer for 20 minutes or until meat and vegetables are tender; add peas. Add more water if needed; simmer for 10 minutes.

ORANGE LAMB AND NOODLES

Citrus is just the delicate taste to combine with lamb meat.

1 tablespoon olive oil	1 sliced carrot
2 teaspoons minced garlic	1 sliced red bell pepper
1 pound lamb 1-inch strips	1 rib sliced celery
3 ounces ramen noodles plus	¼ cup sweet and sour sauce
seasoning	½ cup mandarin orange segments
1 cup water	¼ cup chopped almonds
1 sliced zucchini	

Heat oil and garlic on medium-high heat in large skillet or wok. Add lamb and stir-fry about 3 minutes, or until no longer pink; remove from skillet and set aside. Break up ramen noodles and add noodles, water, flavor packet, zucchini, carrot, red bell pepper, and celery to skillet. Bring to boil, reduce heat, cover, and simmer for 3 to 5 minutes, or until vegetables are tender-crisp. Stir in cooked lamb, sweet and sour sauce and orange sections. Heat through; top with almonds.

PASTA AND LAMB DINNER

1 pound sliced lamb	¼ teaspoon black pepper
1 tablespoon olive oil	½ teaspoon dried basil
½ cup finely chopped onions	½ teaspoon dried oregano
1 teaspoon minced garlic	8 ounces mostaccioli pasta
3 cups tomato juice	16 ounce bag frozen mixed
¼ teaspoon salt	vegetables thawed

Heat oil in large saucepan over medium heat until drop of water sizzles in oil. Add lamb and cook, stirring frequently until no longer pink. Add onion and garlic; sauté for 5 minutes, but do not brown. Add tomato juice, salt, pepper, basil and oregano; simmer covered for 10 minutes. Add mostaccioli and continue to cook for approximately 10 minutes or until pasta is almost cooked. Stir in mixed vegetables and simmer for 15 minutes, or until vegetables are tender-crisp.

ROASTED LAMB SALAD

This was a great way to enjoy the leftover Easter Dinner of Lamb roast when I was in Colorado.

3 tablespoons red wine vinegar	⅛ teaspoon black pepper
2 teaspoons brown mustard	2 pounds bag mixed lettuce
4 tablespoons olive oil	1 pound roasted lamb sliced
1 teaspoon thyme	¼ cup grated Parmesan cheese
¼ teaspoon salt	

In a bowl, whisk together red wine vinegar and brown mustard. Add olive oil, thyme, salt and pepper. Toss with shredded lettuce and arrange on serving plates. Divide thinly sliced, cooked lamb on top. Sprinkle with grated Parmesan cheese.

SHEPHERDS PIE—ENGLISH STYLE

The term "shepherd's pie" didn't appear until the 1870s and used when cottage pie is made with mutton or lamb, with the suggested origin being that shepherds are concerned with sheep and not cattle, however this may be an example of folk etymology.

1 onion diced	1 tablespoon flour
1 tablespoon olive oil	3 tablespoons tomato sauce
1 pound ground lamb	¼ teaspoon salt
½ teaspoon minced garlic	¼ teaspoon black pepper
1 large carrot diced	2 large russet potatoes
1 cube beef bouillon ground	½ cup butter
1 cup diced tomatoes	

Place olive oil in large skillet. On medium heat, cook onion, garlic and carrot until soft. Add lamb and bouillon cube and cook until lamb is brown and crumbly. Stir in tomatoes, tomato puree and flour. Leave to simmer, stirring occasionally about 15 minutes. Peel and chop potatoes; boil in small amount salted water until soft. Drain potatoes, mash with salt, pepper and butter. Put meat mixture into a deep dish and top with mashed potatoes. Place dish under broiler until brown and crispy. Top with melted cheese if desired.

SIMPLE BROILED LAMB CHOPS

Lamb chops are cut from the rib, loin, and shoulder areas. Shoulder chops are usually considered inferior to loin chops; both kinds of chop are usually grilled.

2 ½ pounds loin lamb chops	2 teaspoons ground marjoram
2 teaspoons minced garlic	¼ teaspoon black pepper
1 tablespoon olive oil	

Trim fat from lamb meat; rub with garlic. Brush with olive oil; sprinkle with marjoram and pepper. Place chops on unheated rack of broiler pan. Broil 4 to 5-inches from heat for 5 minutes, or until done

SUNDAY LEG OF LAMB

1 tablespoon minced garlic	½ teaspoon black pepper
1 tablespoon paprika	6 pounds leg of lamb
2 teaspoons salt	1 18-ounce jar orange marmalade
1 ½ teaspoons dried rosemary	

Combine garlic, paprika, salt, rosemary and pepper in a small bowl; mix well and set aside. Trim fat from lamb; make 12 deep slits on outside of lamb; rub spice mixture into slits and over entire surface of lamb; place on a rack in roasting pan. Insert meat thermometer, making sure it does not touch fat or bone. Bake, uncovered, in 350° oven for 45 minutes; baste with orange marmalade. Bake additional 1 hour and 10 minutes or until meat thermometer registers 160°, basting frequently with orange marmalade. Let stand 15 minutes before serving.

TURKISH LAMB ROLL

The cuisine of Turkey is a melting pot of recipes from Greece, Armenia, Bulgaria, Syria and Iraq, stretching as far as the border of China, from Muslims and Jews, Byzantines and Kurds, Arabs and Persians. It's a shame the rest of life can't find the peace and harmony achieved in the kitchen.

1 tablespoon grated orange peel	¼ teaspoon garlic powder
1 tablespoon cinnamon	½ teaspoon white pepper
1 ½ teaspoons ground cardamom	1 sheet frozen puff pastry shells
2 pounds ground lamb	thawed
¼ cup water	1 16-ounce can whole cranberry sauce
1 teaspoon dried dill	Sour cream
1 teaspoon onion powder	

In large cup, combine orange peel, cinnamon and cardamom. Place lamb, water, dill, onion powder, garlic powder and pepper in large bowl. Sprinkle orange mixture over lamb. With clean hands, mix well to combine. Spray loaf pan. Place pastry sheet in loaf pan covering bottom, allowing edges to hang over sides. Spoon lamb mixture in pan; smooth with knife. Spread ½ of cranberry sauce over top. Bring up hanging pastry sheet to cover. Pinch to seal. With sharp knife, make cuts for steam to escape. Bake in 375° oven for 1 hour. Let cool in pan for 10 minutes before removing to serve and slice. Serve with remaining cranberry sauce and sour cream.

WESTERN LAMB STEW

Forequarter meat of sheep, as of other mammals, includes more connective tissue than some other cuts, and if not from a young lamb) is best cooked slowly using either a moist method such as braising or stewing or by slow roasting.

1 tablespoon canola oil	1 8-ounce can tomato sauce
1 teaspoon minced garlic	1 package taco seasoning mix
1 pound boneless lamb roast,	1 10-ounce bag frozen corn
Cut in ½-inch cubes	1 diced red bell pepper
2 cups beef broth	1 ½ cups instant rice

Heat oil in deep skillet; sauté garlic and lamb, cooking until no longer pink. Drain any excess fat; discard fat. Return skillet to heat; add broth, tomato sauce and taco seasoning mix. Bring to boil, reduce heat, cover and simmer for 5 minutes. Remove cover, add corn and peppers. Bring to boil; stir in instant rice. Remove from heat; cover. Allow to stand for five minutes or until moisture is absorbed and rice is tender. Serve immediately.

The Gift Of Food

Caring	Consolation	Faith
Cheerfulness	Sharing Sorrow	
Thankfulness	Hope	Harvest the Love
Tradition	Friendship	
Memories	Celebration	
Companionship	Congratulatory	
Nourishment	Love	
Laughter	Forgiveness	
Fun	Trust	
Compliment	Confidence	
Healing	Reliance	
Congratulations	Independence	Patriotism
Affection	Assurance	Honor

POTATOES

When traveling and living in host homes across the country our meals were fixed by people who'd never met us or knew anything about us. They fixed things that were family favorites or special foods of their region and culture or something served only on a holiday. We were introduced to a lot of dishes and foods I'd never seen or heard before.Tasting the unknown was a way of life.

Cuisine I always breathed a sigh of relief when the meal included a potato dish. I blame my German and Irish ancestry; genetically it's impossible for me to hate anything made with potatoes, including raw. What a comfort to know there was a dish I'd love no matter what else was on the table. It also reminded a weary homesick traveler of the family she missed.

Comfort The potato has a long history as the most versatile vegetable and staple food in the world. Plain boiled, mashed, baked, fried, chipped, or stewed, there are hundreds of ways to combine them with other ingredients; as well as being used to brew alcoholic beverages. Since potatoes where found to be cheap, plentiful and able to be raised in a wide variety of climates and locales, they've been an important field crop and on most tables at every meal for years.

They conjure up images of farms and homesteads, alone on the prairies, hundreds of miles from the nearest neighbor. I think of the West being settled, which reminds me of watching westerns on television with my grandpa. The lone rider approaches a ranch, tired and hungry, asking to stay in the barn; the stranger's invited to share whatever was cooking on the stove and it's gratefully accepted. They welcomed him in their home for much needed socializing and news exchange. They both received nourishment in many ways and strangers became friends, services were traded, relationships created and communities born.

As a guest in homes, we became a part of their history, of the ages, a part of something more than just a meal. History is full people sharing food—for thousands of years—along the way important decisions made, businesses begun, marriages started. People gathering to celebrate, create, weep and build or to just fill their stomachs; taking in enough fuel to survive another day.

These days anything can and is put on, in, or around potatoes. I learned from my West coast friends to dip my French fries in ranch dressing. My European friends preferred brown gravy on theirs, in Texas tomato based salsas and sauces were used on fried potatoes, such as my husband's choice of Tabasco sauce on his hash browns.

For best results, choose **Cook And They Will Come** potatoes by how you'll be using them. The russet, or Idaho, is best for frying or baking, while the similar long white can be boiled, baked or fried. Round red and round white have less starch and more moisture, making them best for boiling. They can also be roasted or fried. New potatoes are firm and waxy; they're excellent boiled or roasted, and hold their shape well in salads.

BACON SPUDS

4 slices bacon	½ teaspoon each of salt and black
2 medium onions chopped	pepper
2 teaspoons minced garlic	4 Russet potatoes unpeeled, cut
	lengthwise into 8 wedges each

Cook bacon in roasting pan until crisp. Remove bacon, drain and crumble. Pour bacon fat into small bowl, if not at least ¼ cup, add vegetable oil. Add garlic and onions to fat. Place potatoes, skin side down, in roasting pan and pour fat mixture over potatoes. Sprinkle with salt and pepper. Bake in 425° oven for 45 minutes until lightly brown and tender. Sprinkle with crumbled bacon and serve.

BAKED SWEET POTATO FOR 2 MEALS

Columbus brought the sweet potato to the New World from the island of St. Thomas. At that time, potato referred to the sweet potato, and not the white potato as it does nowadays. The white potato didn't arrive in the North America from South America until the late 17th century, more than a hundred years later.

10 large size sweet potatoes or yams	2 eggs, beaten
⅔ cup butter melted	½ cup evaporated milk
Dash each of black pepper and salt	Topping:
Second Day:	⅓ cup chopped pecans
1 tablespoon molasses	2 teaspoons margarine melted
2 tablespoons brown sugar	2 tablespoons flour
1 tablespoon orange juice	¼ cup brown sugar

Scrub and prick potatoes with fork. Wrap each in aluminum foil and arrange in slow cooker. Cover. Cook on low 6-8 hours or high 4-5 hours. Remove from foil and mash potatoes with butter. Take mashed potatoes, cover and place in refrigerator. The next day, combine mashed potatoes, molasses and brown sugar. Beat in orange juice, eggs and milk until smooth. Place mixture into sprayed slow cooker. Combine Topping ingredients: pecans, butter, flour and brown sugar together and spread over potatoes. Cover with lid, set on high and cook for 3-4 hours.

BOARDWALK FRIES

For nostalgic Americans, boardwalks are the stuff of summer dreams, mixing memories of salt water taffy at sunset, white-knuckled wooden rollercoaster rides. My first visit to one was in late summer of 1987, while strolling along the Boardwalk of Ocean City, Maryland, enjoying the sights and smells of the ocean. From the first taste of the specially made French fries, none have compared to them. Since we had no boardwalk fries in the western states I lived in or in Alaska now, these come as close as I could create to the real thing.

2 pounds russet potatoes	2 teaspoons onion powder
¼ cup Old Bay seasoning	Mix of peanut and vegetable oil for
1 ½ tablespoons sea salt	frying
2 teaspoons black pepper	Malt vinegar
2 teaspoons paprika	

In small bowl, mix together Old Bay, salt, pepper and paprika. Wash and dry potatoes. Do not peel potatoes. Cut potatoes in long, uniformly shaped sticks. Place sticks in large bowl cold salt water with ice in it. Leave in water for 30 minutes. Remove from water; discard water and use paper towels to thoroughly dry potato sticks before frying. Fry in hot oil (about 325°) to desired doneness (dark & well done is the way they do them at the stands on the boardwalk). Remove fries to paper towels and generously season right away. Serve with plenty of malt vinegar.

CHEDDAR BACON POTATOES

There is just something about potatoes, bacon and cheese.

¼ pound bacon	½ teaspoon chopped parsley
2 thinly sliced onions	(optional)
6-8 thinly sliced potatoes peeled or	½ teaspoon black pepper
unpeeled	½ teaspoon garlic salt or plain salt
½ pound thinly sliced Cheddar	¼ cup butter
cheese	1 ½ cups sour cream

Cook bacon until crisp, drain on paper towels and when cool, crumble. Layer half of bacon, onions, potatoes, parsley and cheese in sprayed slow cooker. Season with ½ of salt and pepper. Dot with butter. Repeat layers of bacon, onions, potatoes and cheese. Top with sour cream. Cover with lid. Cook on low 8-10 hours or on high 3-4 hours or until potatoes are soft.

CHEESE SCALLOPED POTATOES

Scalloped Potatoes in their simplest form consist of potatoes, sliced thinly, and layered with milk or cream.

2 tablespoons butter	5 peeled russet potatoes ⅛ inch
1 cup minced onions	slices
2 teaspoons minced garlic	1 cup chicken broth
¼ teaspoon dried thyme	1 cup evaporated milk
1 ¼ teaspoons salt	2 bay leaves
½ teaspoon black pepper	1 cup shredded Cheddar cheese

Melt butter in large deep skillet over medium heat until foaming subsides. Add onion and stir occasionally while cooking about 4 minutes until soft and lightly brown. Add garlic, thyme, salt and pepper; cook about 30 seconds. Add potatoes, broth, milk and bay leaves and bring to a simmer about 10 minutes until potatoes are almost tender. Discard bay leaves. Transfer mixture to 8-inch square baking dish. Sprinkle with cheese and bake in 425° oven until milk is bubbling around edges and golden brown, about 15 minutes. Remove from oven and cool 10 minutes before serving.

COMPANY POTATO BAKE

This is the one I like to take to potlucks, it travels well and serves a crowd.

3 medium russet potatoes	½ cup sliced green onions
2 tablespoons margarine or butter	1 tablespoon minced garlic
2-4 tablespoons milk	½ cup sour cream
½-1 teaspoon salt	½ cup shredded cheese
¼-½ teaspoon black pepper	

Peel and quarter potatoes, cook, covered in small amount boiling water for 20 minutes. Drain. Mash with butter, salt, pepper and sour cream. Add onions and garlic. Gradually add milk to make light and fluffy. Do not over beat. Place in sprayed casserole dish, top with cheese. Cover and chill for 24 hours. Bake in 350° oven for 40-45 minutes and serve.

COTTAGE FRIED POTATOES

Home fries or cottage fries are a type of basic potato made by pan or skillet frying—diced, chunked, wedged or sliced potatoes (sometimes unpeeled)—that have been par-cooked by boiling, baking, steaming, or microwaving.

3 tablespoons margarine	1 teaspoon garlic salt
1 tablespoon vegetable oil	1 teaspoon black pepper
3 large potatoes cut up, unpeeled or peeled	1 small chopped onion

Melt margarine in large skillet, layer potatoes and sprinkle with salt and pepper. Cook, covered, over medium heat for 8 minutes (this is the par-cooking: steamed). Add onion, cook uncovered for 8-10 minutes turning frequently until potatoes are tender and browned.

DELICIOUS YAM CHOWDER

I love yams and this delicious soup just makes a warm and cozy meal in Autumn chill. Yam or sweet potato—Many people use these terms interchangeably both in conversation and in cooking, but they are really two different vegetables. The true yam is a tropical vine and is not even distantly related to the sweet potato and a popular vegetable in Latin American and Caribbean. You can use sweet potato in this recipe but generally yams are sweeter than sweet potato so the soup will taste different, but still delicious.

½ pound bacon cut in ½-inch pieces	3 14 ½-ounce cans chicken broth
½ diced sweet red pepper	3 cans chipotle chili minced
½ diced green bell pepper	2 15-ounce cans corn drained
½ diced onion	1 cup low-fat milk
2 peeled yams cut in 1-inch cubes	½ teaspoon salt

Cook bacon in large stockpot over medium heat until it begins to crisp. Spoon off bacon fat, except for a thin coating. Add peppers and onion to bacon and continue cooking, stir frequently, until vegetables are tender. Add sweet potatoes, chicken broth, and chipotles and simmer, covered, 15 minutes or until potatoes are tender. Stir in corn, milk, and salt; heat through

FRENCH FRIES

Whether you eat them plain, with ketchup, ranch dressing or brown gravy—nothing compares to fries.

4 peeled russet potatoes cut into	**2 quarts peanut oil**
¼-inch thick strips	**Salt and black pepper**

Rinse cut potatoes in large bowl with lots of cold running water until water becomes clear. Cover with water by 1-inch and cover with ice. Refrigerate at least 30 minutes and up to 2 days. In 5-quart pot or Dutch oven fitted with candy or deep-frying thermometer, or in an electric deep fryer, heat oil over medium-low heat until thermometer registers 325°. Make sure there is at least 3-inches of space between top of oil and top of pan—fries will bubble up when added. Drain ice water from cut fries and wrap potato pieces in a clean dishcloth and thoroughly pat dry. Increase heat to medium-high and add fries, a handful at a time, to hot oil. Fry, stirring occasionally, until potatoes are soft and limp and begin to turn a blond color, about 6 to 8 minutes. Using skimmer or slotted spoon, carefully remove fries from oil and set aside on paper towels. Let rest for at least 10 minutes or up to 2 hours.

When ready to serve fries, reheat oil to 350°. Transfer blanched potatoes to hot oil and fry again, stirring frequently, until golden brown and puffed, about 1 minute. Transfer to paper lined platter and sprinkle with salt and pepper, to taste. Serve immediately.

GERMAN POTATO SALAD

Early settlers in America noticed that the German Immigrants made a salad that was warm, had bacon and onions and a nice sweet and tart dressing, so they called it Hot German potato salad. It's very popular to use left over roasted or boiled potatoes.

6 cups peeled diced potatoes	1 teaspoon salt
¼ pound bacon	¼ teaspoon black pepper
1 diced onion	1 teaspoon celery flakes
½ cup cider vinegar	2 teaspoons mustard
¼ cup water	1 teaspoon paprika
1 ½ tablespoons sugar	

Place potatoes in large saucepan. Add enough water to cover. Bring to boil over high heat. Reduce heat and simmer, uncovered, 20 to 30 minutes or until potatoes are fork—tender; drain. Let potatoes cool. Peel potatoes and cut into ¼-inch pieces; set aside. Cook bacon in medium skillet over medium heat until crisp. Remove with slotted spoon. Crumble into small bowl; set aside. Cook and stir onion in 3 tablespoons bacon drippings until tender. Combine vinegar, water, sugar, salt, pepper, celery flakes and mustard in large bowl. Add potatoes and bacon; toss until well coated. Garnish with parsley and paprika. Serve hot or cold.

LATKES

These are potato pancakes: shallow-fried grated potato and egg, often flavored with grated onion. Potato pancakes are sometimes made from mashed potatoes to produce pancake-shaped croquettes. These are eaten especially for Hanukkah.

6 potatoes	1 teaspoon salt
1 onion	2 tablespoons sour cream
½ cup pancake, waffle mix	2 eggs
½ cup canola oil	½ teaspoon black pepper

Peel potatoes and grate into bowl. Pour off extra liquid. Peel onion and grate into potatoes. Add eggs, pancake mix, sour cream, salt and pepper. Mix well. Heat oil until it sizzles. Drop a tablespoon of batter at a time into hot oil. Flatten with pancake turner. When bottoms are brown turn them over. When done remove and drain on paper towel lined plate. Serve with applesauce, sour cream or plain.

MASHED SWEET POTATOES

Popular in the South, there are two types: the paler-skinned has a thin, light yellow skin with pale yellow flesh which is not sweet and has a dry, crumbly texture similar to a white baking potato. The darker-skinned has a thicker, dark orange to reddish skin with a vivid orange, sweet flesh and a moist texture.

3 pounds sweet potatoes peeled, cut in chunks	¼ teaspoon white peppers
	4 tablespoons sour cream
½ teaspoon salt	4 tablespoons butter

Boil potatoes until tender, drain, return pot to stove top over medium heat. Set flame to medium-low and mash gently with a potato masher. Add salt, pepper, sour cream, and butter and fold together until thoroughly combined. Remove from heat and keep warm, covered, until ready to serve.

MOJITO SWEET POTATOES

My two favorites, Mojito and sweet potatoes, a very nice addition to a Spring or Summer meal.

4 sweet potatoes peeled and sliced	2 ounces rum
Salt	¼ cup orange juice
¼ cup butter	¼ cup lime juice
2 tablespoons sugar	¼ cup chopped mint leaves

Place potatoes in small pot and cover with water. Bring the water to boil and salt. Cook potatoes until tender 15 minutes. Drain potatoes and return to hot pot and mash with butter, sugar, rum, orange juice, lime juice and mint. Season Mojito Mash with salt to taste.

OVEN ROASTED POTATOES

Easy to fix and always a big crowd pleaser, these can be served with a multitude of gravies, sauces, dips or just plain.

4 russet potatoes peeled, cut into wedges	2 teaspoons garlic salt
5 tablespoons olive oil	2 teaspoons black pepper
1 tablespoon onion powder	2 teaspoons paprika

Place potatoes in a bowl and cover with hot tap water; soak 10 minutes. Drain potatoes and spread on paper towels, thoroughly pat dry. Rinse and wipe out bowl. Return potatoes to bowl. Combine oil and seasonings. Drizzle over potatoes, tossing to coat. Arrange potatoes in single layer on sprayed rimmed cookie sheet. Cover tightly with foil. Bake in 475° oven for 5 minutes. Remove foil and continue to bake for 15-20 minutes. Rotate baking sheet every 10 minutes. Flip each wedge, keeping potatoes in single layer. Continue baking until potatoes are golden and crisp, 10-15 minutes. Transfer potatoes to drain on paper towels. Season with additional salt and pepper if desired.

POTATO BREAD

The potato makes a really nice fluffy bread dough that can be used for all occasions.

1 small potato shredded	1 egg beaten
½ cup orange juice concentrate	3 cups flour
¼ cup water	½ cup sugar
⅓ cup orange marmalade	2 teaspoons baking powder
¼ cup vegetable oil	¼ teaspoon salt

Cook shredded potato in just enough water to cover it, for 10 minutes Cool and drain. Combine cooled potato with orange juice concentrate, water, marmalade, oil and egg. In large bowl, sift together flour, sugar, baking powder and salt. Add liquid ingredients and stir just until combined. Spoon batter into 3 greased or sprayed mini loaf pans and bake in 350° oven for 30-35 minutes or until tester comes out clean. Cool in pans for 10 minutes; remove from pan and let cool. Or spoon into sprayed muffin tins and baked for 20-25 minutes to make Potato Rolls

POTATO CASSEROLE

2 pounds frozen hash brown
  potatoes, thawed
1 pint sour cream
1 can cream of chicken soup
½ cup margarine, melted
1 12-ounce package shredded
  Cheddar cheese
½ teaspoon black pepper

1 teaspoon salt
1 finely chopped onion
¼ cup chopped mushrooms
  (optional)
Topping:
2 cups crushed cornflakes
¼ cup melted butter

Mix sour cream, soup, margarine, cheese, salt, onions and mushrooms into thawed hash browns. Pour into sprayed 9x13 baking pan. Mix cornflakes and melted butter together and top potato mixture. Bake in 350° oven for 45 minutes.

POTATO KUGEL

Many think of kugel as a dessert and there are plenty of those recipes. It can be a savory side dish or entrée. A Jewish kugel casserole wouldn't contain meat, since mixing meat with milk and eggs isn't Kosher.

6 cups peeled baking potatoes
1 onion
2 eggs
1 teaspoon salt

6 tablespoons melted butter
2 tablespoons matzah meal or flour
¼ teaspoon black pepper
2 tablespoons butter

Grate potatoes and onion. Place in colander and drain well, squeezing out excess moisture. In large bowl, whisk eggs, salt, melted butter and matzah meal or flour. Stir in potatoes until well combined. To Bake: Place 2 tablespoons butter in 9 x 13 baking dish. Melt in oven or microwave. Tilt dish to coat evenly. Pour potato mixture into dish and spread evenly. Bake, uncovered, in 400° oven for 15 minutes. Reduce oven temperature to 375° and continue baking for 45 more minutes or until top is crisp. Cut into squares.

POTATO PANCAKES

Fried food is traditionally eaten on Hanukkah in commemoration of the oil that miraculously burned for eight days when the Maccabees purified and rededicated the holy Temple in Jerusalem. These fried potato "pancake" or patties are the favorite choice for the holiday.

5 potatoes	¼ cup flour
2 egg	¼ cup chopped onions
1 teaspoon salt	1 tablespoon butter
½ teaspoon black pepper	1 tablespoon olive oil

Peel potatoes, cut up and grate them into bowl. Add eggs, salt and pepper to taste and enough flour to thicken to good pancake batter; add onion. Cook in skillet with butter and oil, turning over once. Good for breakfast or as side dish with dinner.

POTATO SALAD ALWAYS PERFECT

Potato salad is often served with barbecue, roasts, fried chicken, hamburgers, sandwiches and hot dogs. It's generally considered casual fare, and is typically served at picnics, outdoor barbecues, and other casual meals and events. Easily made in large quantities; prepared in advance and refrigerated until needed; and requires only inexpensive ingredients.

2 pounds potatoes cooked and cubed (peeled or unpeeled)	3 hard boiled eggs chopped
	¼ cup finely chopped dill pickles
1 ½ cups mayonnaise	⅓ cup sweet pickle relish
1 tablespoon mustard	½ teaspoon salt
2 stalks chopped celery	½ teaspoon black pepper
1 small chopped onion	½ teaspoon celery seeds
2 tablespoons minced garlic	Paprika

Mix together mayonnaise, mustard, garlic, salt and celery seeds, Set aside. Combine potatoes, celery, onion, bell pepper, eggs, pickle and relish. Stir in mayonnaise dressing. Sprinkle paprika on top. Cover, chill for 6-24 hours before serving.

POTATOES AU GRATIN

The creamy cheese sauce and tender potatoes in this classic French dish combine to make a deliciously addictive experience. Gratin is a culinary technique in food preparation in which an ingredient is baked or broiled to form a golden crust on top.

3 cups cooked diced potatoes	1 cup shredded Cheddar cheese
6 tablespoons butter	½ teaspoon salt
3 tablespoons flour	⅛ teaspoon white peppers
1 ½ cups milk	1 cup soft bread crumbs

Place potatoes in shallow, broiler proof baking dish. In saucepan over medium-low heat, melt butter. Remove 3 tablespoons of butter to cup or bowl; set aside. To remaining 3 tablespoons of butter in saucepan, add flour. Stir to blend well; gradually stir in milk. Continue cooking, stirring constantly, until sauce is thick and smooth. Add cheese and continue stirring until cheese is melted. Pour sauce over potatoes in baking dish; mix gently. Place bread crumbs in a bowl; drizzle with remaining 3 tablespoons melted butter; toss to coat. Sprinkle bread crumbs evenly over potatoes. Bake in 400° oven for about 15 minutes to heat through, then broil until golden brown.

SCALLOPED PARSNIPS AND YAMS

These days, the potato has pretty much taken the place of the parsnip as a source of starch in our diets. In days of old, before potatoes were deemed edible, the parsnip was prized not only for its long storage life, but also for its sweet, nutty taste and nutritional value. Parsnips can be eaten raw as well as cooked.

½ pound parsnips peeled, sliced ¼ inch thick	¼ teaspoon salt
	¼ teaspoon dried oregano
½ pound yams peeled and sliced	½ cup chicken broth
Sauce:	½ cup milk
¼ cup chopped onions	Topping:
2 tablespoons butter	¼ cup fine dry bread crumbs
2 tablespoons flour	1 tablespoon butter melted

Cook yams covered in small amount of boiling water for 8 minutes, add parsnips and cook an additional 8 minutes; drain. For sauce, cook onion in butter in skillet until tender; stir in flour, salt and oregano. Add broth and milk all at once. Cook and stir until thick and bubbly. Stir in parsnips, yams and transfer to 1-quart casserole dish. Combine bread crumbs and melted butter, sprinkle over casserole. Bake uncovered in 350° oven for 15 minutes.

SCALLOPED POTATOES

Scalloped simply means a sliced ingredient cooked in milk or cream sauce. There are many ways to make delicious scalloped potatoes, this one is an old one I got from an Irish family in Illinois.

4 cups thinly sliced potatoes peeled or unpeeled	1 ½ cups milk
	1 ½ teaspoons salt
1 large onion thinly sliced	½ teaspoon black pepper
4 teaspoons flour	1 tablespoon dried parsley
3 tablespoons margarine	¼ cup chopped fresh chives

Place 1 cup potatoes in sprayed casserole dish. Sprinkle with 1 teaspoon flour. Place ¼ of onions over floured potatoes. Continue to layer potato slices, flour and onions for 4 layers and all potatoes, flour and onions are used. Heat in saucepan milk and margarine. When margarine melted, add salt, pepper and parsley. Pour mixture over potatoes. Cover casserole dish and bake in 350° oven for 1 hour. Remove cover and continue to bake 30 more minutes or until brown on top. Sprinkle top with chives and serve.

SWEET POTATO BAKE

In Colonial days sweet potatoes were an item of trade and were shipped from the Carolinas out to northern cities. The potato was an essential food for all the colonies in the days before modern means of preservation.

3 ½ pounds sweet potatoes or yams	¼ teaspoon ground cinnamon
½ cup orange juice	¼ teaspoon ground ginger
¼ cup brown sugar	2 tablespoons butter

Peel and slice potatoes and place slices evenly in sprayed 9x13 baking dish. Mix together juice, sugar, cinnamon and ginger. Pour over potatoes. Dot with butter. Bake, uncovered, in 350° oven for 35-45 minutes.

SWEET POTATO CAKE

2 ¾ cups pecans halves	1 tablespoon cinnamon
⅓ cup brown sugar	2 teaspoons ground allspice
2 tablespoons pumpkin pie spice	2 teaspoons vanilla extract
5 tablespoons butter melted	3 tablespoons rum
Cake:	Frosting:
2 pounds sweet potatoes	6 egg yolk
4 eggs	¾ cup sugar
2 cups sugar	½ cup corn syrup
1 cup canola oil	1 pound butter room temperature
2 cups cake flour	1 tablespoon vanilla extract
2 teaspoons salt	⅛ teaspoon salt

Place pecans on baking sheet and toast in 350° oven for 10 minutes. Combine brown sugar and pumpkin pie spice in medium bowl. Stir in melted butter; add toasted pecans and stir to coat, spread evenly on baking sheet; return to oven for 8 minutes. Leave oven on but lower temperature to 325°. Remove from oven, cool completely; chop pecans and set aside. Microwave potatoes on high until tender. Cool, peel, and mash. Spray 13x9 pan and set aside. In bowl with electric mixer beat eggs and sugar together on medium speed until light and fluffy, 4 minutes. Add canola oil; beat until combined. Add potatoes and mix until combined. Sift together cake flour, baking powder, salt, cinnamon and allspice; mix dry ingredients into sweet potato mixture. Mix in vanilla and rum. Fold in 1¼ cup of chopped pecans. Place batter in pan; bake until toothpick inserted into center comes out clean, 45 to 55 minutes. Let pan cool on wire rack 10 minutes. Invert cake onto rack; cool completely. Make frosting while cake is baking: Beat egg yolks in clean bowl with electric mixer on medium-high until very thick, about 5 minutes. Combine sugar with syrup in small saucepan, set over medium-high heat, stirring constantly until mixture comes to full boil. Scrape mixture into small glass bowl. With mixer on high speed, pour few tablespoons of sugar mixture into yolks and beat for a few seconds. Repeat until all of syrup has been added. Beat until bowl has cooled to room temperature. On medium speed add butter, 2 tablespoons at a time, beating well after each addition. Frosting will begin to come together after all of butter is combined; it will curdled first, then it will come together. Scrape bowl and beat in vanilla and salt. Mix in 1 cup of pecans. Frost cooled cake. Sprinkle remaining toasted pecans on top of cake. Chill for 1 hour.

SWEET POTATO HASHBROWNS

In 1543 Spanish explorers found sweet potatoes growing in "Indian gardens" in what became Louisiana. They were also cultivated in the Carolina area of North America before the European colonization.

2 tablespoons olive oil	1 cup diced green bell peppers
2 tablespoons butter	¼ cup diced celery
4 cups shredded sweet potatoes 　　or yams	Dash salt and black pepper
1 cup diced onions	

Add oil and butter to large skillet. Add potatoes, onion and bell pepper and celery; stir well and pat down. Cook over medium heat for 3-4 minutes without stirring. Stir in salt and pepper and cook until potatoes are tender, about 10 to 12 minutes.

SWEET POTATO OVEN FRIES

In spite of all the nostalgia and history of the nutritious sweet potato, it has slowly lost it's prominent position on the dinner tables of North America, even at Thanksgiving. But the new trend to use sweet potatoes in white potato recipes created a resurgence of it's popularity and sweet potato fries are on a lot of restaurant menus.

2 peeled or unpeeled sweet potatoes 　　cut into 4 inch long and ½-inch 　　thick fries	1 teaspoon paprika
	½ teaspoon chili powder
	Coarse ground salt and black pepper
2 tablespoons olive oil	

Preheat oven to 450°. Line baking sheet with aluminum foil and set aside. Place potatoes in large bowl and toss with olive oil until potatoes are coated. Add paprika, chili powder, salt, and pepper; toss to distribute evenly. Arrange coated fries in single layer on prepared pan. Bake for 20 minutes on lower rack until sweet potatoes soften. Transfer pan to upper rack of oven and bake 10 minutes longer, until fries are crispy.

SWEET POTATO OR YAM BISCUITS

Yams will make this biscuit a little sweeter than using sweet potato: both are scrumptious and make a great biscuit sandwich with leftover holiday ham, roasted or smoked turkey or lamb.

5 cups flour	½ teaspoon ground allspice
1 cup brown sugar	1 cup solid frozen shortening
2 tablespoons baking powder	2 cups mashed and cooled sweet
1 ½ teaspoons cinnamon	potatoes
1 teaspoon salt	1 cup heavy cream
1 teaspoon ground ginger	½ cup chopped pecans

In large mixing bowl, stir together flour, brown sugar, baking powder, cinnamon, salt, ginger and allspice. Add shortening and cut in until crumbly. In another bowl combine potatoes, cream and pecans. Make well in dry ingredients and add potato-cream mixture; mix to combine well. Turn dough out onto lightly floured surface. Roll out dough to 1 ½-inches thick. Cut out with 2-inch floured biscuit cutter. Place biscuits 1-inch apart on ungreased baking sheet. Bake in 425° oven for 5 minutes, then turn down temperature to 375° and bake for another 10 to 15 minutes until golden brown. Serve warm or let cool on a wire rack until room temperature.

TWICE BAKED POTATO

In 1995, the potato was the first vegetable grown in space and is the world's 4th most important food crop after rice, wheat and corn. The potato is grown in more countries than any crop but corn and grown in all 50 states and in about 125 countries throughout the world. These are an easy side dish or light meal and take a little extra time, but well worth the effort and very popular in most restaurants.

4 large baking potatoes	½ teaspoon salt
8 slices bacon	½ teaspoon black pepper
1 cup sour cream	1 cup shredded Cheddar cheese
½ cup milk	divided
4 tablespoons butter	8 green onions sliced, divided

Bake potatoes in 350° oven for 1 hour. Meanwhile, place bacon in a large, deep skillet. Cook over medium high heat until evenly brown. Drain, crumble and set aside. When potatoes are done allow them to cool for 10 minutes. Slice potatoes in half lengthwise and scoop flesh into large bowl; save skins. To potato flesh add sour cream, milk, butter, salt, pepper, ½ cup cheese and ½ of onions. Mix with hand mixer until well blended and creamy. Spoon mixture into potato skins. Top each with remaining cheese, onions and bacon. Bake for another 15 minutes.

TWICE BAKED POTATO CASSEROLE

Wrapping the potato in aluminum foil before cooking in a standard oven will help to retain moisture, while leaving it unwrapped will create a crispy skin. When cooking over an open fire or in coals of a barbecue it may require wrapping in foil to prevent burning of the skin.

6 unpeeled potatoes baked	2 cups shredded mozzarella cheese
¼ teaspoon salt	2 cups shredded sharp cheddar
¼ teaspoon black pepper	cheese
1 pound cooked, crumbled bacon	2 cups chopped green onions
3 cups sour cream	

Cut baked potatoes into 1-inch cubes. Place half of them in sprayed 13x9 baking dish. Sprinkle with half salt, pepper and bacon. Top with half of sour cream and cheeses. Repeat layers. Bake uncovered in 350° oven for 20 minutes or until cheese is melted.

SWEET TOOTH

As desserts go, brownies were a breeze, a delicious reliable choice. But they didn't stay that way. One day I took a pan of freshly made chocolate treats into work and the first person to cut into them exclaimed, "Oh no, you didn't cook these enough."

Another person cut a piece, and retorted, "Are you kidding? These are perfect, just like the gooey ones in the mall."

Another voice piped up, "I like the ones you fixed last time that had the frosting and tasted like a cake."

VARIETY SOCIETY

That entire 12-hour work shift was filled with debates and suggestions on the "perfect" brownie. Everyone had an opinion about his or her favorite type of brownie. The commercial mixes and bakeries creating signature confections had turned the simple little old brownie into an extravagant indulgence with a multitude of choices.

The earliest brownie recipe produced a relatively mild and cakey brownie. The name "brownie" first appeared in the 1896, but this was in reference to molasses cakes, not true brownies of today. The evolution of the brownie now has developed into 3 basic types of recipes: Fudgy, Classic and Cake. The difference comes from the ratio of ingredients not how you bake them. From these three variations, additions are made and added to step up into making what I call the "luxury brownies".

Which ever you prefer, remember chocolate desserts such as brownies should be removed promptly from the oven to retain the best chocolate taste. This is because the compounds that give chocolate its flavor are highly volatile and easily lost. The smell of brownies cooking is an indication that flavor and aroma are being released. They'll continue to cook for a few minutes from residual heat; so it's best to remove them from the oven when a toothpick test still shows a few moist crumbs, no matter which kind you choose to make.

When we opened our food place in the mall, we needed a unique sweet treat but it couldn't be a brownie or cookie because there was a cookie store already. I started to think beyond just the recipes and concentrate on what was the most popular and current taste bud exploding flavors. What would please a crowd?

I knew people loved cake but it's not a "fast food" item. We needed something unusual and I remembered our friend Claire in Baltimore introducing me to something called Dirt Cake. A few tests and trials later, we had our own "Junction Dirt Cake". We put it in a clear 6-ounce cup for single servings and the 8 different layers could be admired. With gummy worms and a plastic flower, they were a big sensation.

The second successful hit came from a 1981 holiday homemade candy I ate in Ohio: something close to a peanut butter cup, but a 100% improvement over any commercial product. In fact, the taste was so superior; I never ate another store bought peanut butter cup. From my experimenting with different ingredients and combinations came "The Junction Peanut Butter Squares". They're easy to make, to store, and to eat profitable. People proclaim they're addicted to them; continue to be instant winners and are requested for meetings and parties to this day.

When All Else Fails - Ask The Cook

ALMOND JOY BARS

1 envelope gelatin	1 ¼ cups flaked coconut
1 ¼ cups cold water divided	1 cup chopped almonds
3 cups cooked rice	1 cup semisweet chocolate chips
1 14-ounce can sweetened	3 tablespoons softened butter
condensed milk	

In small bowl, combine ¼ cup cold water and gelatin; set aside. Combine 1 cup water, rice and sweetened condensed milk in 2-quart saucepan. Cook over medium heat until thick and creamy 5 to 7 minutes, stirring frequently; stir in gelatin. Remove from heat; stir in coconut and almonds. Pour rice mixture into a sprayed 9-inch baking pan; smooth top. Combine chocolate chips and butter in small saucepan. Cook over low heat until blended; stir constantly. Spread chocolate over rice mixture. Chill until firm, about 2 hours. To serve, run knife around sides of pan; remove sides

BAKLAVA

I first had this in the Greek community in Baltimore and after making it realized it's not really difficult and worth the extra time to make it at home. Just try this unique dessert at home. Our Greek friends in Alaska prefer mine so much, they stopped purchasing theirs from the wholesale store—"because it just wasn't the same". It's a great dish to make for special occasions.

1 stick butter—for the pan	1 cup water
1 box frozen phyllo pastry leaves	1 cup sugar
1 pound chopped nuts	1 teaspoon vanilla extract
1 cup butter—for the pastry	½ cup honey
1 teaspoon cinnamon	

Generously butter bottoms and sides of 13 x 9 pan. Toss nuts with cinnamon and set aside. Carefully unroll pastry dough. Cut whole stack in half to fit pan. Cover phyllo with damp cloth to keep from drying out as you work. Place 2 sheets of dough in pan, butter thoroughly. Repeat until you have 8 sheets layered. Sprinkle 2-3 tablespoons of nut mixture on top. Add on top 2 sheets of dough, butter, nuts: layering as you go. The top layer should be about 6-8 sheets deep. Using sharp knife cut into diamond shapes all the way to bottom pan. Bake for about 50 minutes until golden and crisp. Make sauce while baklava is baking. Boil sugar and water until sugar is melted. Add vanilla and honey. Simmer for about 20 minutes. Remove baklava from oven and immediately spoon sauce over it. Let cool. Store uncovered, it gets soggy if wrapped up.

BANANA BARS

This sweet, potassium rich fruit is perfect to cook into all types of dough. Those who think they like banana flavored baked goods, find they love these over any breads or muffins. They are surprisingly popular.

½ cup margarine	¼ teaspoon salt
1 ½ cups sugar	1 ½ cups bananas well ripe
2 eggs	Frosting:
1 cup sour cream	1 8-ounce package cream cheese
1 teaspoon vanilla extract	½ cup butter softened
2 cups flour	2 teaspoons vanilla extract
1 teaspoon baking soda	4 cups powdered sugar

In mixing bowl, cream butter and sugar; add eggs, sour cream and vanilla. Combine flour, baking soda and salt in separate bowl; gradually add to the creamed mixture. Stir in banana., Spread into sprayed 15x10 baking pan. Bake in 350° oven for 20-25 minutes or until toothpick inserted near center comes out clean; cool completely. For frosting: Beat in mixing bowl cream cheese, butter and vanilla. Gradually beat in enough powdered sugar to achieve desired consistency to frost. Frost bars and store in refrigerator

BLONDE BROWNIES OR BLONDIES

Blondies are a rich sweet, non-chocolate variation of the traditional chocolate brownie. They may contain white or dark chocolate chips, but the dominant flavor of a blondie is butterscotch, not chocolate and may also contain walnuts or pecans.

1 ½ cups brown sugar
¾ cup melted butter cooled
2 eggs lightly beaten
4 teaspoons vanilla extract
1 ½ cups flour

1 teaspoon baking powder
½ teaspoon salt
1 cup white chocolate chips or
    butterscotch chips
1 cup chopped nuts

In saucepan heat brown sugar and butter over medium heat until sugar is dissolved, stirring constantly. Cool slightly. Using wooden spoon, stir in eggs, one at a time, add vanilla. Mix flour and baking powder in separate bowl. Stir into sugar mixture just until ingredients are moist. Stir in chips and nuts. Spread into sprayed 13 x 9 baking pan. Bake in 350° oven for 20-30 minutes. Cool slightly in pan before cutting.

CAKE BROWNIES

These flavorful chocolate brownies are fluffier than regular brownies and should be iced with frosting.

1 cup butter softened
1 cup sugar
4 eggs
1 tablespoon vanilla extract
1 cup flour
1 teaspoon baking powder
¼ teaspoon salt
6 tablespoons unsweetened cocoa

½ cup chopped pecans or walnuts
Frosting:
¼ cup butter
4 tablespoons unsweetened cocoa
3 ½ cups powdered sugar
½ teaspoon vanilla extract
5-6 tablespoons hot evaporated milk

In mixing bowl, combine butter and sugar; beat until light and fluffy. Add eggs one at a time, beating after each addition. Stir in vanilla. In another bowl, combine flour, baking powder, salt, and cocoa. Add dry mixture to first mixture, stirring until blended. Fold in nuts. Spread in sprayed 13x9 baking pan. Bake in 350° oven for 20 to 25 minutes, Start checking at 20 minutes. Brownies are done when toothpick inserted into center comes out with no wet batter, it may have a few crumbs which is fine. Don't over bake or undercook Cool in pan on rack. Frosting: Melt butter in saucepan over low heat; stir in cocoa until smooth. Sift powdered sugar; add to cocoa mixture along with vanilla and enough hot milk to make mixture soft and spreadable. Spoon evenly over brownies and spread to cover thoroughly.

CARROT CAKE SQUARES

With an abundance of carrots, who can resist getting your vegetable servings like this.

3 large eggs	½ teaspoon allspice
½ cup unsweetened applesauce	¼ teaspoon salt
¾ cup brown sugar	1 ¾ cups flour
½ cup canola oil	2 cups grated carrots
1 teaspoon vanilla extract	½ cup raisins
2 teaspoons baking powder	½ cup chopped walnuts or pecans
2 teaspoons cinnamon	

Line 13 x 9 baking dish with foil, make foil extend over ends of pan; spray foil with nonstick spray and set aside. In large bowl, beat eggs, applesauce, brown sugar, oil, vanilla, baking powder, cinnamon, allspice and salt with electric mixer until combined. On low speed, beat in flour until blended. Stir in grated carrots, raisins and nuts. Spread in pan; bake 22-24 minutes, until wooden pick inserted in center comes out clean. Cool in pan on wire rack. Spread cream cheese frosting over carrot bars. Cut into squares.

CHEESE DANISH

Danish is a pastry with ingredients including generous amounts of butter. A yeast dough is rolled out thinly, coated with butter, and then folded into numerous layers. The rolling, buttering, folding, and chilling is repeated several times to create a dough which is fluffy, buttery and flaky. The store crescent dough replaces all that work. Many so-called Danish pastries are not made this way.

2 tubes refrigerated crescent rolls	1 cup sugar
2 8-ounce packages cream cheese	1 teaspoon vanilla extract
softened	1 egg

Lightly grease 9 x 13 pan. Separate 1 can crescent rolls. Press triangles together in a single layer on bottom of pan. With electric mixer, combine cream cheese, sugar, vanilla and egg. Spread in pan. For the top layer use last can of crescents. Be sure edges are pinched together. Brush milk over dough. Sprinkle with sugar. Bake in 350° oven for 30 minutes.

CHEESE STRUDEL

The oldest Strudel recipe is from 1696, handwritten at the Viennese City Library. A strudel is a type of sweet layered pastry with a filling inside, that gained popularity in the 18th century

Filling:
⅓ cup sugar
2 teaspoons cornstarch
1 egg white beaten
1 teaspoon vanilla extract
½ teaspoon grated lemon peels
1 cup ricotta cheese

½ cup raisins
Strudel:
1 tablespoon canola oil
½ cup melted butter
2 tablespoons dry breadcrumbs
8 sheets frozen phyllo pastry leaves

In small bowl, combine sugar, cornstarch, egg white, vanilla and lemon zest; stir gently until combined. With rubber spatula, gently fold in ricotta cheese just until combined. Gently fold in raisins. Set aside. Strudel: Lightly oil large baking sheet. In small bowl, combine oil and butter. Unroll phyllo onto a clean, dry surface; cover with wax paper and a slightly damp tea towel to prevent dough from drying out. Lay one sheet of phyllo on baking sheet. Sprinkle with ½ teaspoon of butter mixture and spread it thin with pastry brush. (Not all the dough will be covered.) Sprinkle with ½ teaspoon breadcrumbs. Repeat with 7 more sheets of phyllo; align each sheet over previous ones. Over eighth layer, sprinkle all remaining breadcrumbs; reserve remaining 1 ½ teaspoons butter mixture. Gently spoon cheese filling in a long, 12-by-2-inch mound along one long edge of phyllo layers, leaving 2-inch border between mound and edges of phyllo. Fold up long edge and loosely roll up strudel. (Do not roll too tightly; filling will expand during baking.) Set strudel seam-side down on baking sheet. Fold and tuck open ends securely but not tightly beneath roll. Brush strudel with remaining butter mixture. With sharp paring knife, make four short (1-inch) diagonal slashes along top of strudel to allow steam to escape. Bake in 350° oven for 35 to 40 minutes, or until phyllo is golden brown. Carefully transfer strudel to a wire rack and let cool completely. Just before serving, dust with powdered sugar.

CHOCOLATE COCONUT SURPRISE

This was a special dessert I created for my husband on his low carb diet, I used sugar free puddings and instead of milk: half and half. It ended up a favorite of my whole work area. They called it sinfully good. It seems chocolate and coconut can be combined in many ways and always be a hit.

1 5-ounce box instant vanilla pudding	1 cup chopped walnuts
1 5-ounce box instant chocolate pudding mix	1 can coconut milk
	3 cups coconut divided
	4-5 cups half and half or milk divided

Pour coconut milk into large measuring cup and add enough milk to equal 3 cups. Pour mixture into large mixing bowl; add vanilla pudding mix and beat with electric mixer until smooth, about 5 minutes. Stir in 2 cups of coconut. Place mixture into large casserole type dish or bowl. Sprinkle chopped nuts evenly over top of pudding. In same mixing bowl, place chocolate pudding mix and 3 cups milk. Beat with electric mixer until smooth, about 5 minutes. Carefully place chocolate pudding over nut layer, spread out evenly. Sprinkle remaining coconut on top. Chill for at least 4 hours before serving.

CHOCOLATE FONDUE

Dessert fondue recipes began appearing in the 1960s. Slices of fruit or pastry are dipped in a pot of melted chocolate. Other dessert fondues can include coconut, honey, caramel and marshmallow.

1 tablespoon butter	Plate of cubed angel food cake,
16-1-ounce square chocolate bar	strawberries,
30 large marinated artichoke hearts	Pineapple, bananas, apples,
1 ⅓ cups milk	oranges,
	Any size pretzels, mini size cookies

Grease slow cooker generously with butter. Turn cooker on high for 10 minutes. Add chocolate, marshmallows and ⅓ cup milk; cover. Turn to low and stir after 30 minutes; continue cooking for 30 more minutes, or until melted and smooth. Gradually add remaining milk. Cover; cook on low 2-4 hours. Bring cooker to table, along with dipping plate and fondue sticks or long toothpicks.

CHOICE RHUBARB DESSERT

The term rhubarb has also come to mean a "quarrel" or "heated discussion." This comes from theatrical direction, believe it or not. Stage and movie directors would have actors repeat "rhubarb" and various other phrases over and over to simulate background conversations or mutterings of a surly crowd.

1 cup sugar	4 cups chopped rhubarb
1 cup water	1 small box instant strawberry
1 box white (vanilla) cake mix	gelatin

Place rhubarb evenly over bottom sprayed 13x9 baking dish. Sprinkle with sugar, sprinkle gelatin on top. Sprinkle dry cake mix over top of gelatin. Over this carefully pour water. Bake in 350° oven for 45 minutes. Serve with whipped cream or ice cream or alone.

CHRISTMAS STOLLEN

A Stollen is a loaf shaped bread sprinkled with powdered sugar. The cake is usually made with chopped candied fruit and/or dried fruit, nuts and spices. Stollen is a traditional German bread usually eaten during the Christmas season. Many households make it to give as gifts. It's nothing like a cake; sliced and toasted, it makes a wonderful holiday breakfast or fireside treat with some Wassail or hot cider.

1 ½ cups milk	½ cup sliced candied cherries
½ cup sugar	2 ½ to 3 cups flour
1 ½ teaspoons salt	Melted butter
¾ cup butter	Icing:
1 tablespoon yeast	1 ½ cups powdered sugar
1 tablespoon sugar	½ teaspoon vanilla extract
2 eggs	¼ teaspoon almond extract
2 egg yolks	Cream
3 cups sifted flour	Candied cherries
½ teaspoon ground cardamom	Citron
½ cup raisins	Blanched almonds
½ cup finely chopped citron	

Scald milk; add ½ cup sugar, salt and butter; mix well. Cool to lukewarm. In separate bowl, stir together yeast and 1 tablespoon sugar until liquid. Stir yeast into lukewarm milk. Add eggs and egg yolks to milk mixture; beat well. Add flour and beat well; cover. Let rise in warm place until doubles, about 1 ½ hours. Add cardamom, raisins, citron, cherries and enough flour until dough pulls away from sides of bowl and is no longer sticky to touch. Place dough on lightly floured board; knead until smooth and satiny. Place in lightly greased bowl. Cover; let rise 1 ½ hours or until doubled. Divide dough into thirds to make 3 stollen loaves. Roll each on floured board into 8x10 oval. Spread with melted butter. Press down center, fold over lengthwise. Place on sprayed cookie sheet, brush with melted butter. Let rise until double in size, about 45 minutes. Bake in 350° oven for 30 minutes. When cool, frost with icing and decorate with cherries, citron and almonds. Icing: Combine sugar and extracts; add cream until smooth and spreadable.

CINNAMON NUT STREUSEL

A streusel has a crumb like topping for coffee cakes and rich breads, consisting of flour, sugar, butter, cinnamon, and sometimes chopped nutmeats.

Batter: 1 ½ cup flour
1 tablespoon plus 2 teaspoons
   baking powder
1 ¼ teaspoons salt
½ cup shortening
1 ½ cups milk
2 eggs
Filling: ½ cup brown sugar
½ cup chopped nuts

2 teaspoons cinnamon
Streusel: ½ cup flour
1 cup sugar
¼ cup firm butter
Glaze:
2 cups powdered sugar
1 teaspoon vanilla extract
¼ cup softened butter
¼ to ½ cup water

Mix flour, baking powder, salt, shortening, milk and eggs until moistened. Beat vigorously for ½ minute. Butter 2 9-inch round or square pans. Spread 1 ½ cup batter in each pan. Filling: Mix brown sugar, nuts and cinnamon together; sprinkle half over the batter in each pan. Divide remaining batter evenly and spread gently over the filling in each pan. (Do not worry if it does not cover filling entirely.) Streusel topping: combine flour, sugar and butter and mix until crumbly. Sprinkle half on top of each pan. Bake in 375° oven for 30 to 35 minutes. Glaze by mixing sugar, butter, vanilla and water; adding 2 tablespoons at a time until glaze is spreading consistency. Drizzle glaze on slightly cooled cakes.

CLASSIC BROWNIE

This brownie is not like the gooey fudge kind, nor is it cake like—but just right in between. This is the batter that works best to create a gourmet brownie adding your favorite candy bar or pieces or specialty "icing". Don't be afraid to try small batches with cream cheese in the batter or in the frosting or all the variety flavored chips, coconut or other dried fruits too to find your "Super Duper Special Brownie"

1 ½ sticks butter	1 cup chopped walnuts (optional)
2 ¼ cups sugar	½ teaspoon salt
4 eggs	¾ teaspoon baking powder
1 ¼ cups cake flour	1 tablespoon vanilla extract
6 ounces unsweetened baking chocolate	

Combine together flour, baking powder and salt; set aside. Finely chop chocolate squares. In microwave heat butter and chocolate in microwave bowl on high for 45 seconds, stir and heat for 30 seconds more. Stir again and if necessary repeat in 15 second increments until completely melted. When chocolate is cool, add eggs one at a time, whisk after each addition. Whisk in vanilla. Fold in dry ingredients, ⅓ amount at a time, until completely smooth. Stir in walnuts. Spread in sprayed 13 x 9 baking pan. Bake in 325° oven 30 minutes or until done. Start checking at 20 minutes. Brownies are done when toothpick inserted into center comes out with no wet batter, it may have a few crumbs which is fine. Don't over bake or undercook; cool in pan on wire rack and let cool completely before cutting.

The Bakers Quilt:
Every recipe is a patch added to the quilt.
Each square has a story.
Each bit has a textured memory of places.
Each scrap is an incident and a friend.
Fabric sections of happenings,
Pieced together
Becoming a warm memory
Of astonishing adventures
And multi-layered life.

COCONUT LIME MOJITO BARS

Since being introduced to "Mojito" drinks by my brother Hugh's wife, Dee, I've been working the taste into all kinds of dishes. With this newest dessert, My goal is by the time they come visit, I can serve them a complete Mojito meal: appetizer- entrée-side dish-dessert-snack-beverage. We will "MOJITO OUT"

1 cup butter softened	½ cup butter softened
2 cups sugar	2 ½ cups powdered sugar
4 large eggs	2 tablespoons rum
2 tablespoons vegetable oil	2 tablespoons lime juice
2 ¾ cups flour	½ teaspoon rum extract
2 ½ teaspoons baking powder	2 tablespoons grated limes peel
½ teaspoon baking soda	½ teaspoon salt
1 teaspoon salt	1 drop green food coloring
1 cup coconut milk	½ cup large multicolored sugar
¼ cup shredded coconut	crystals
½ teaspoon coconut extract	24 lime wedge candies diced up
Frosting:	

Using electric mixer, beat butter and sugar until creamy. Gradually beat in eggs and oil. Scrape bowl and mix well. In medium bowl, whisk together flour, baking powder, baking soda and salt. In large measuring cup, stir together coconut milk and coconut extract. On low speed, mix in ⅓ of wet mixture to butter mixture; add ⅓ of flour mixture. Repeat ending with flour mixture. Stir in shredded coconut. Spray large rimmed cookie sheet. Pour batter evenly in pan. Bake in 350° oven about 25 minutes or until cakes spring back when gently touched. With electric mixer, beat butter until creamy. Beat in 1 cup of powdered sugar. Beat in rum, rum extract, grated lime peel, food coloring and salt until smooth and creamy. Beat in remaining powdered sugar a little at a time until soft enough to spread. Spread frosting on cooled cake. Sprinkle top with sugar crystals and place wedges over top.

COLOSSAL CHEESECAKE

Cheesecake never seems to be a dessert anyone can turn down. Cheesecake is a large family of sweet, cheese-based tarts generally made with soft cheeses and ingredients such as sugar, eggs, flour and liquids often mixed in. Typically, the filling covers a crust, which may be pastry, cookie, graham cracker or shortbread

1 ½ cups fine graham cracker crumbs	1 cup sugar
½ cup butter softened	2 tablespoons butter softened
Filling:	1 teaspoon vanilla extract
2-8-ounce package cream cheese	Topping:
1 cup sour cream	¾ cup sour cream
2 tablespoons cornstarch	¼ cup powdered sugar

Combine crumbs and butter; mix well. Press mixture firmly into ungreased 9-inch pie plate. Press flat onto bottom only. Bake 8 minutes in 375° oven, or until slightly brown. Remove crust from oven and turn oven temperature down to 350°. Combine cream cheese, sour cream, cornstarch and sugar with mixer until sugar has dissolved. Add butter and vanilla and blend until smooth; don't over mix. Pour filling over crust. Bake 30-35 minutes or until knife inserted 1-inch from edge comes out clean. Remove from oven and cool for 1 hour. Mix sour cream and sugar; spread mixture over top of cooled cheesecake. Chill until ready to eat.

COOKER BREAD PUDDING

Puddings of all types were very popular in England most likely originating there in the late 1600s. Homes contained no ovens to bake, so dishes had to be made in a pot over a fire. Bread pudding is a comfortable dessert beloved by many, especially in New Orleans, where you will find a huge number of variations; all basically bread, eggs, milk, sugar and flavoring.

8 slices cubed bread	¼ cup sugar
2 cups milk	1 teaspoon cinnamon
2 eggs	1 teaspoon vanilla extract

Place bread in slow cooker. Whisk together milk, eggs, sugar, cinnamon and vanilla.

Pour over bread. Cover with lid and cook on high 2-2 ½ hours, or until mixture is set. Serve with warmed honey, fruit syrups, fruit preserves or maple syrup drizzled over top.

CREME FILLED DONUTS

A doughnut is a sweet, deep-fried piece of dough or batter. The two most common types are the ring doughnut (which can be made of a cake dough or a yeast dough) and the filled doughnut—injected with jam, jelly, cream, custard, or other sweet filling.

1 can refrigerated biscuits	¼ teaspoon salt
Vegetable oil	½ cup shortening
Powdered sugar	⅓ cup powdered sugar
Sugar	½ teaspoon vanilla extract
2 teaspoons very hot water	

Combine salt with hot water and stir until salt dissolved; let cool. Combine marshmallow, shortening, sugar and vanilla in bowl and mix well with electric mixer on high until fluffy. Add salt mixture to filling and combine. When donuts are cool, fill each one using pastry bag. While heating about 2 inches of vegetable oil to around 360° in a skillet, open biscuits. Cut each biscuit in half and place on waxed paper. Add biscuits to hot oil. They will brown quickly, be ready to turn with tongs or fork. When golden brown, remove and place on paper towels to drain. Roll donuts in powered sugar or regular sugar. Using pastry bag, insert a hole in side of each donut and squeeze tablespoon amount of filling into each donut.

OVEN DONUTS

Okay, baked aren't the same, but baked donuts can be just as delicious;just different and a little healthier. Don't over bake them, if anything, under bake them a bit—they will continue baking outside the oven for a few minutes. You want an interior that is moist and tender and be sure to cut big enough holes in the center—too small and they will bake entirely shut.

1 ⅓ cups scalded milk	⅓ cups warm water
⅓ cup sugar	2 eggs
⅓ cup brown sugar	5 cups flour
2 tablespoon shortening	1 teaspoon. lemon flavoring
1 teaspoon salt	⅛ teaspoon nutmeg
2 ¼ teaspoon yeast	

Stir sugars, shortening, and salt into hot milk. Dissolve yeast in warm water. Beat eggs and add; stir in flavoring. Add milk mixture alternately with flour and nutmeg. Cover bowl and let rise until double in size. Place on board lightly sprinkled with flour and roll until about ⅓-inch thick. Cut with donut cutter or biscuit cutter and then cut center hole out with smaller circle. Place on greased cookie sheet, then brush with melted butter. Bake about in 375° oven about 12 minutes—start checking around 8. While the donuts are baking, place butter in a medium bowl and cinnamon sugar in a separate bowl; or have a glaze mix ready to dip the tops of the donuts. Remove donuts from oven and let cool for just a minute or two. Dip each one in glaze mix or in melted butter and a quick toss in sugar bowl.

DAD'S OLD FASHIONED CHEESECAKE

My diabetic Dad would splurge on his favorite store bought cheesecake. It took me 20 years to finally get this right; just in time because I haven't seen it in any bakery or store for several years; the last time was 1992 in Baltimore. Don't expect the "normal cheesecake flavor or texture, try it and you may prefer it too.

3 8-ounce packages cream cheese	5 eggs or egg substitute to equal
1 cup sour cream	5 eggs
1 teaspoon lemon juice	2 cans refrigerated crescent rolls
1 ½ teaspoons vanilla extract	Raisins
1 ½ cups sugar	Cinnamon

Beat cream cheese, sour cream, sugar, lemon juice and vanilla until smooth. Add eggs one at time and beat well after each addition. Line bottom and halfway up sides of a 13 x 9 baking dish with crescent roll dough, pinch seams to seal. Pour filling and sprinkle with cinnamon. Bake in 350° oven for 35 minutes; it will not look done, but it is. Turn off oven; don't open oven door and let dish set in oven another 5 minutes. Remove from oven and immediately sprinkle raisins on top. Refrigerate for at least 4 hours before serving.

DING DONG BROWNIES

When I took this creation to work, our pharmacist exclaimed—"these are like ding dongs for adults"—thus a recipe is named. Seems others have agreed through the years.

1 ¼ cups sugar	¼ instant coffee
¼ cup margarine	2 boxes instant cheesecake flavor
½ cup unsweetened cocoa	pudding
2 eggs	12-ounce container frozen whipped
1 ½ cups flour	topping
1 teaspoon baking powder	2 cups chopped chocolate sandwich
¼ teaspoon baking soda	cookies
1 teaspoon vanilla extract	¼ cup grated semisweet chocolate
1 cup milk	chips
Filling:	¼ teaspoon cinnamon
1 cup milk	

Place sugar, margarine, cocoa, eggs, flour, baking powder, baking soda, vanilla and milk in mixing bowl and beat until batter is smooth. Pour into sprayed 13x9 baking dish. Bake in 350° oven for 25-30 minutes. Remove and cool completely in pan. Stir coffee into milk until dissolved. Mix in pudding mix and half of thawed whipped topping with whisk until smooth. Fold in chopped cookies. Spread over cooled brownie crust. Use remaining whipped topping to spread over filling. Sprinkle grated chocolate and cinnamon over topping. Refrigerate 30 minutes at least before serving.

FROSTED WHOOPIE PIES

A whoopie pie, sometimes called a gob, black-and-white or bob is traditional to the Pennsylvania Dutch culture and New England. Made of two small, chocolate cakes with a sweet, creamy frosting sandwiched between them; it's common to see them being sold at roadside farm stands. These were considered a special treat because they were originally made from leftover batter. According to Amish legend, when children would find these treats in their lunch bags, they would shout "Whoopie!"

½ cup shortening	¼ teaspoon salt
1 cup brown sugar	2 cups marshmallow crème
1 egg	½ cup shortening
½ cup baking cocoa	⅓ cup powdered sugar
2 cups flour	½ teaspoon vanilla extract
1 ½ teaspoons baking soda	Frosting:
½ teaspoon baking powder	1 cup powdered sugar
½ teaspoon salt	¼ cup chocolate syrup
1 teaspoon vanilla extract	2 tablespoons shortening
1 cup milk	½ teaspoon vanilla extract
Filling:	Dash salt
2 teaspoons very hot water	

Cream together shortening, sugar and egg. In separate bowl, mix cocoa, flour, baking powder, baking soda and salt. In separate bowl, mix milk and vanilla. Add dry ingredients to shortening mixture alternating with milk mixture. Beat until smooth. Drop ¼ cup batter on to sprayed baking sheets to make 18 cakes. Spread batter into 4-inch circles, leave 2 inches between each cake. Bake in 350° oven for 15 minutes or until they are firm to touch. Remove from oven, cool on wire rack. Filling: Combine hot water with salt in small bowl and stir until salt is dissolved. Let mixture cool. Combine marshmallow, shortening, sugar and vanilla well with mixer on high speed until fluffy. Add salt and mix well. Frosting: combine ingredients with mixer until smooth. Spread filling over 9 cookies and top with remaining cookies. Frost tops.

FUDGIE CHEESECAKE

Fudge AND Cheesecake? Together?—This has to be the dessert they serve in heaven.

⅓ cup unsweetened cocoa
⅓ cup butter melted
1 cup vanilla wafers crumbs
½ cup powdered sugar
Filling:
1 14-ounce can sweetened
    condensed milk

3 8-ounce packages cream cheese
    softened
2 teaspoons vanilla extract
4 eggs
2 cups semisweet chocolate chips

Melt chips in microwave: set aside to cool. Combine cocoa, butter, vanilla wafers and sugar; press into bottom of sprayed 9-inch springform pan and set aside. Beat with electric mixer cream cheese, milk and vanilla until smooth. Add cooled chocolate and mix until well blended and smooth. Add eggs, beating on low speed just until combined. Pour over crust. Place pan on baking sheet. Bake in 325° oven for 40-45 minutes or until center is almost set. Cool on wire rack for 10 minutes. Carefully run knife around edge of pan to loosen. Cool 1 hour longer. Refrigerate overnight before serving.

I'm continually amazed and thankful for the friends and fun in my life because of my love for cooking and using it to bring periods of happiness to the lives of those around me.

FUDGY BROWNIES

Yeah, this is my ooey, gooey, lick your finger, no icing needed recipe.

1 cup butter	1 cup flour
4 1-ounce squares unsweetened	1 teaspoon vanilla extract
baking chocolate	½ teaspoon salt
2 cups sugar	1 cup walnuts (optional)
4 eggs	

Grease or spray 9x13 baking pan. In 3-quart saucepan over very low heat, melt butter and chocolate, stirring mixture constantly. Remove from heat; stir sugar into chocolate. Allow mixture to cool slightly. Beat in eggs one at a time, mixing well after each; stir in vanilla. Combine flour and salt; stir into chocolate mixture. Fold in walnuts if using. Spread batter evenly into prepared pan. Bake in 350° oven 30 to 35 minutes. Start checking at 20 minutes. Brownies are done when toothpick inserted into center come out with no wet batter, it may have crumbs, which is fine. Don't over bake or undercook. Cool in pan on wire rack for 5 minutes, then dump out on to a flat surface and let cool completely before cutting.

GERMAN TEXAS BROWNIES

Yeah, this is the well circulated Texas Brownie with my own touch for a special birthday setting when a German Chocolate Cake just wasn't practical—it was a major success.

2 cups flour	1 ½ cups flaked coconut
2 cups sugar	Frosting:
1 stick butter or margarine	1 stick butter
½ cup shortening	2 tablespoons dark unsweetened
1 teaspoon baking soda	cocoa
2 eggs	¼ cup milk
¼ cup dark unsweetened cocoa	1 teaspoon vanilla extract
½ cup buttermilk	Dash salt
1 teaspoon vanilla extract	3 ½ cups powdered sugar
1 cup strongly brewed coffee	1 cup chopped, toasted pecans

In large bowl mix flour and sugar. In microwavable bowl, melt butter, shortening, coffee and cocoa on high for 2 minutes. Pour melted liquid over flour mixture and stir well. Add buttermilk, eggs, baking soda and vanilla; beat well. Pour into sprayed 17 x 11 pan. Bake in 400° oven for 20 minutes or until done in center. While brownies are baking, prepare frosting. In microwavable bowl mix butter, cocoa and milk on high for 2 minutes. With electric mixer, add powdered sugar, salt and vanilla. Stir in pecans and immediately pour over hot brownies when removed from oven. Let cool and cut into squares.

HUNGARIAN NUT TORTE

A torte is a cake made with many eggs and usually ground nuts or even bread crumbs instead of or in addition to flour, The cake is layered, filling placed between layers, icing on the top and sides of the torte

12 eggs separated	¼ teaspoon salt
1 cup sugar	½ cup cups milk
¾ cup ground nuts	3 ½ cup powdered sugar
2 teaspoons baking powder	Frosting:
⅔ cup breadcrumbs or cake flour	¼ cup butter
1 teaspoon vanilla extract	2 1-ounce squares unsweetened
Filling:	chocolate
4 1-ounce squares German	1 ¾ cups powdered sugar
chocolate	½ teaspoon vanilla extract
¼ cup butter	⅓ cup milk
1 teaspoon vanilla	

Separate eggs; beat yolks with sugar 15 minutes until thick and lemony. Add nuts, breadcrumbs or flour, baking powder and vanilla; set aside. Whip egg white until stiff peaks form. Fold stiffly beaten egg whites into egg yolk batter. Pour even amount of batter into 3 sprayed round cake pans. Bake 25 minutes in 350° oven. Remove from pan and cool on wire rack. Filling: In small saucepan, combine chocolate squares and butter. Cook over low heat, stirring constantly until baking bars melt and mixture is smooth. Transfer to large mixer bowl; cool to room temperature. Add vanilla and salt. Beat in powdered sugar alternately with milk; beat until smooth. Frosting: Melt chocolate and butter in the microwave. In large bowl, combine powdered sugar, vanilla and ½ of the milk. Blend in melted chocolate mixture. Add remaining milk, a little at a time, until desired consistency is achieved. With a serrated knife, slice each cake layer into 2 layers. for total of 6 layers. Place filling over each layer just to the edge as you stack them. Once top layer is placed on, pour warm frosting over cake, make sure sides are completely covered, use a knife to "frost" if needed—frosting will thicken as it cools. If you desire, more ground nuts can be places on the sides or top of cake. Refrigerate.

I LOVE MY JUNCTION PEANUT BUTTER SQUARES

Here they are—the prize winners that you will be asked to bring over and over again.

1 ½ cups graham cracker crumbs	2 sticks (1 cup) butter
1 pound powdered sugar	12 ounces semisweet chocolate
1 ½ cups peanut butter	chips

Combine graham cracker crumbs and sugar in large bowl. Melt butter in a medium microwavable bowl. Stir in peanut butter to butter until combined and smooth. Pour peanut butter mixture into crackers mixture. Mix together until smooth and completely combined. Press mixture into 13x9 dish. Melt chocolate chips and spread over top. Chill for at least 2 hours before cutting and serving.

JUNCTION DIRT CAKE

Playing with a new recipe in 1990, this was a big hit at our food place in the mall. After tweaking it a little, we served this in clear cups so the layers could be admired. Serve it in a pot and set on the table to serve with a large spoon and everyone thinks it's the centerpiece, not the dessert. This is a great way to serve individual cake servings for a birthday party, large celebration or shower.

1 package chocolate sandwich cookies	1 large container frozen whipped topping
2 8-ounce packages cream cheese softened	4 cups milk
2 cups powdered sugar	2 small box chocolate instant pudding mix
	1 box devil's food cake mix

Bake cake according to directions on cake box; bake in sprayed 13x9 baking dish. Cool thoroughly. Crush cookies and thaw out whipped topping. Mix together cream cheese and powdered sugar; fold in whipped topping, set aside. In electric mixing bowl, beat milk and pudding mix until smooth and well blended. Assemble dessert in either 2-quart casserole dish; large new clean foil lined flowerpot; or individual serving small flower pots or 6-8 ounce disposable cups. Whichever container you choose, layer starting with chocolate cake, then cream cheese mixture, then chocolate pudding, then sprinkle crushed cookies. Repeat layers. End with cookie topping. You can add gummy worms, spider and such. Also add plastic flowers, cover stems with plastic wrap before sticking into top of dessert.

Use a White, Yellow, Lemon Cake instead; Vanilla, Mint or Peanut Butter Sandwich Cookies instead; and Lemon or Fruit Pie Fillings or other flavored puddings to make "Dirt" of your choice.

KOLACHE

In Chicago, the Czech community calls them kolachky, signifying a small size. Kolachky is a generic Slavic term for "cakes" or "wheel" depending on the translator. The small, pillows of dough with a bit of sweet topping, cheese or fruit or poppy seed, is Czech in origin or a more modern twist of chocolate filling. They made there way to Texas in 1840's and evolved into many different types including sausage filled. Making them with the bread machine helps me to continue to share them with company.

1 ¼ cups warm water	1 teaspoon salt
½ cup butter, softened	3 7/8 cups bread flour
1 egg	2 teaspoons active dry yeast
1 egg yolk	4 cups pie, poppy, fruit or cheese
⅓ cup milk powder	filling
¼ cup instant mashed potato flakes	¼ cup butter, melted
¼ cup white sugar	

Place water, butter, egg, egg yolk, milk powder, potato flakes, sugar, salt, flour and yeast in bread machine pan in the order recommended by the manufacturer. Select Dough cycle; press Start. Check dough after 5 minutes of mixing, add 1-2 tablespoons of water if necessary. When cycle is complete, spoon out dough and roll into walnut size balls. Place them 2 inches apart on lightly sprayed cookie sheet. Cover and let rise until doubled in size, about 1 hour. Flatten balls just slightly with palm of your hand and make a depression in the center with our thumb. Brush the edges with another egg yolk and additional tablespoon of oil mixed together. Use your thumb and forefinger to spread the dough and make a deep, round hole. The indention must be firm and deep or the filling will cook out while rising or when in the oven. Fill each depression with 1 tablespoon with filling of choice.

You can use canned *Fruit pie fillings*, I make my own: 2 cups frozen blueberries or apples or cherries, mixed-berries, peaches stirred in with 1/4 cup sugar, 1/2 cup water and 1-2 tablespoons cornstarch in a saucepan. Bring it to a boil and simmer until thick.

Cheese filling: Mix together so it's spreadable: 2 cups cottage cheese, 1/2 cup sugar, 1 teaspoon lemon extract, 2 tablespoons butter, pinch of salt, 1 egg yolk and 1/2 cup raisins.

Poppy seed filling: Mix together 1 pound ground poppy seeds, 8-ounce jar apple jelly, ½ cup honey and 1/2 cup melted butter

Prune or Apricot filling: In a saucepan add 2 cups dried fruit with 1/3 cup water—remove pits from prunes, add 1/2 teaspoon cinnamon and 2 tablespoons sugar. Cover and cook until fruit is softened, 5-7 minutes then puree until smooth.

KRINGLE

The Scandinavian or Dutch pastry called Kringle (pronounced kring-la) which arrived with Catholic monks in the 13th century, developed into several kinds of sweet, salty or filled giant oval shaped pastries. The fillings include marzipan remonce or marzipan and raisins, sprinkled with coarse sugar, nut flakes or iced. Norwegian Kringle is more of the original sweet bread pretzel the monks made, nothing like this popular Danish pastry.

2 cups flour	1 teaspoon cardamom
½ teaspoon salt	¼ cup soft butter
1 Tablespoon sugar	2 cups powdered sugar
1cup butter, room temp	2 tablespoons evaporated milk
2 ¼ teaspoons yeast	1 cup raisins
¼ cup warm water	Topping:
¼ cup cold milk	¼ cup white sugar
1 egg, beaten	½ cup chopped almonds
Filling:	

Add yeast to warm water and set aside. Sift flour with salt and sugar; blend in butter, add yeast water. Mix milk to beaten egg; add to flour mix and stir with fork to dampen the flour. Cover and refrigerate overnight. Prepare filling before shaping kringle. Filling: Add cardamom and butter, stir in powdered sugar; add milk mix well and stir in raisins; set aside. Topping: Mix together sugar and almonds in small bowl; set aside. Divide dough into 2 parts; keep one in fridge while preparing the other. Roll dough to an 18x16 rectangle. Spread 3" lengthwise center strip with filling. Fold over one side of dough then the other to cover filling completely. Place on baking sheet in pretzel shape taking both ends and fold toward the middle section, don't overlap dough, it will look like an oval. Brush top with additional beaten egg, sprinkle with topping. Cover and let rise 1 hour or until dough is no longer cold and dent remains when touched Bake in 325° oven for 25 minutes.

Store those onions, tomatoes and potatoes on the shelf of your pantry. Refrigerating tomatoes gives them a waxy taste, potatoes taste sweet and onions lose their pungency. Once you cut onions, wrap them up and store them in the refrigerator. Other items not to put in the refrigerator are ketchup, olive oil and butter.

LEMON PIE BARS

These are close to the lemon squares you could find at any bake sale in the 1970's and are still welcome at any picnic or potluck today. These taste a touch more like lemon pie.

1 box yellow or white (vanilla) cake mix	3 tablespoons cornstarch
1 stick margarine melted	2 tablespoons margarine
1 egg	Dash salt
Filling:	⅓ cup lemon juice
3 eggs	1 ½ cups water
1 ½ cups sugar	1 6-ounce box lemon gelatin
3 tablespoons flour	

Mix together ingredients and press batter evenly into bottom of 13x9 baking dish. Bake in 400° oven until top is just slightly brown, about 5-10 minutes. In saucepan over medium heat combine eggs, sugar, flour cornstarch, margarine, salt, water and lemon juice until bubbly and starting to thicken. Reduce heat to low heat and stir in lemon gelatin powder and cook for 2 minutes. Pour mixture over crust. Bake additional 10-15 minutes or until top is set. Cool on wire rack before cutting.

LEMON SQUARES

My sister Sharon loved this treat, this is the one you are more likely to see at all the bake sales.

2 cups flour	1 teaspoon baking powder
1/2 cup confectioners' sugar	1/4 teaspoon salt
2 sticks butter	4 eggs, well beaten
2 cups sugar	1 heaping tablespoon grated lemon rind
1 tablespoon flour	1/4 cup lemon juice

Sift flour and powdered sugar together. Cut in butter until well blended. Press mixture in 9x13 pan. Bake about 25 minutes in 300° oven until lightly browned. Combine remaining ingredients and spread on top of baked crust. Bake in 350° oven for 25 to 30 minutes. Sprinkle with powdered sugar.

NEW YORK CHEESECAKE

New York cheesecake is the pure, unadulterated cheesecake with no fancy ingredients added either to the cheesecake or placed on top. Here's an easy version of an old favorite.

15 graham crackers crumbs	4 eggs
2 tablespoons melted butter	1 cup sour cream
4 8-ounce packages cream cheese	1 tablespoon vanilla extract
1 ½ cups sugar	¼ cup flour
¾ cup cream or half and half	

Grease 9-inch springform pan. In medium bowl, mix graham cracker crumbs with melted butter. Press onto bottom of springform pan. In large bowl, mix cream cheese with sugar until smooth. Blend in cream, then mix in eggs one at a time, mixing just enough to combine. Mix in sour cream, vanilla and flour until smooth. Pour filling into prepared crust. Bake in 350° oven for 1 hour. Turn the oven off, and let cake cool in oven with the door closed for 5 to 6 hours; this prevents cracking. Chill in refrigerator until serving.

PAGACHE (POLISH PIIZZA)

This was a wonderful recipe given to me when I was in the coal-mining country of gorgeous rural West Virginia. She let me help stretch the dough while she spread out the filling and peeled potatoes while telling me about her memories of how her aunts had to let the dough rise near a woodstove. I have adapted it for my own use taking advantage of the bread machine.

1 cup warm water	1 pounds baking potatoes
1 tablespoon olive oil	2 cups shredded sharp Cheddar
½ teaspoon sugar	cheese
3 ½-4 cups flour	3 tablespoons butter
2 ¼ teaspoons dry yeast	Dash of pepper
Dash of salt	

Place in bread machine water, olive oil, sugar, flour and yeast in order of recommended bread machine manufacturer; place setting on dough cycle. In the meantime, peel and cut potatoes into 1-inch chunks. Cover potatoes with 1-inch of water in a large saucepan; bring to simmer over medium heat. Reduce heat and simmer until potatoes are tender about 15 minutes. Drain and mash until potatoes are smooth. Stir in cheese, 2 tablespoons of butter, salt and pepper. On lightly floured surface, roll dough into large rectangle about 12x6. Spread potato filling on only half of the dough and fold other half of dough over filling. It should look like a 6x6 book. Pinch the edges to seal and transfer to sprayed 8-inch baking pan. Prick the top of dough several time with fork and bake in 400° oven until golden brown about 30 minutes, The top should feel firm to touch. If you press lightly on the top and the dough yields, it needs more time to bake. Turn pagache onto cooling rack; melt remaining butter in microwave and brush top. Sprinkle with additional ½ teaspoon salt. Let cool 10 minutes, cut into 2-inch strips to serve.

PECAN BARS

These are so close to a real pecan pie, no fork needed and so much easier to transport for the holiday parties.

8 tablespoons butter melted	1 ½ cups corn syrup
1 box yellow or white (vanilla) cake mix	½ cup brown sugar
	1 teaspoon vanilla extract
2 cups chopped pecans	4 eggs

Blend dry cake mix, butter and 1 egg until combined. Measure out ⅔ cup of batter and reserve. Pat rest into bottom of sprayed 13 x 9 baking dish. Bake in 350° oven for 15 minutes, remove from oven and cool. Leave oven on 350°. Place reserved crust mix, corn syrup, sugar, 3 eggs and vanilla in bowl and beat with electric mixer until blended about 3 minutes. Fold in pecans. Pour on top of crust. Bake 40-50 minutes. Edges should be browned, center will still be soft. Remove from oven. Cool for 30 minutes before cutting.

"I give you every seed-bearing plant on the face of the whole earth and every tree that has fruit with seed in it. They will be yours for food. And to all the beasts of the earth and all the birds of the air and all the creatures that move on the ground—everything that has the breath of life in it—I give every green plant for food." ~ Genesis 1:29-30

GRANNY'S CHEESECAKE

American dairymen achieved a technological breakthrough in 1872 that ushered in the Modern Age of cheesecakes. Since then hundreds of types have been created. But this one is a family favorite for generations and considered the best. I've NEVER seen it anywhere else and everyone I serve it to, agrees they have never had it before.

3 ½ cups graham cracker crumbs or ground vanilla wafers	1 cup sugar
	1 teaspoon lemon extract
1 stick butter melted	1 teaspoon lemon juice
1 3-ounce box instant lemon gelatin	1 20-ounce can crushed pineapple
1 cup boiling water	(well drained)
3 8-ounce package cream cheese	1 12-ounce can evaporated milk

Place can of milk, mixing bowl and beaters in the refrigerator to get very cold. Mix together 3 cups graham cracker crumbs and butter together. Press evenly into bottom 13x9 pan. Reserve ½ cup of crumbs for topping. Dissolve gelatin in boiling water and set aside to cool. Beat together cheese, sugar and lemon juice and extract. Add cooled gelatin and drained pineapple. Whip cold milk in cold dish with electric mixer using cold beaters. Fold whipped milk into cheese mixture until well combined. Pour mixture on top of crust. Sprinkle plain reserved crumbs over top. Refrigerate for at least 4 hours before serving.

RICH CHOCOLATE MOUSSE

Most people think a good mousse is difficult to make, I've never had anyone complain about this easy one.

8 squares semi-sweet baking chocolate	3 egg yolks
2 tablespoons powdered sugar	1 8-ounce container frozen whipped topping
3 tablespoons strong hot coffee	

Thaw out whipped topping. In top of double boiler over simmering water; melt chocolate. Remove top pan from heat; stir in sugar and coffee. Add one yolk at a time, stirring each time until smooth. Place top pan over double boiler with boiling water. Cook and stir for 3-4 minutes. Fold in 3 cups of whipped topping. Spoon into dishes and top with remaining topping.

RUGELACH

Rugelach means "creeping vine," because of the rolled-up shape. The different fillings can include raisins, walnuts, cinnamon, chocolate, marzipan, poppy seed, or apricot preserves which are rolled up inside.

2 sticks butter	1 tablespoon cinnamon
1 8-ounce cream cheese	½ cup sugar
⅓ cup sour cream	1 cup finely chopped walnuts
2 cups flour	½ cup raisins chopped
¼ teaspoon salt	½ cup apricot preserves

Cream together butter and cream cheese. Gradually add sour cream, salt and flour, blending until crumbly. Knead dough lightly. Divide dough in half, wrap both in plastic; Refrigerate dough for 90 minutes. Combine cinnamon, sugar, ½ of nuts and ½ of raisins; set aside. Remove dough from fridge 1 at a time; keep remaining dough in refrigerator until ready to use. Roll dough on floured board to about ⅛ inch thick circle. Spread sugar, cinnamon, walnuts and raisins over dough. Cut dough into 16 wedges (like a pizza) and roll up each section starting at large end to small end looking like a crescent roll. Repeat process with second dough, but spread apricot preserve over dough instead of cinnamon sugar—sprinkle remaining ½ of nuts and raisins. Place all completed rolls on ungreased cookie sheet and sprinkle with additional sugar. Bake in 350° for 15-18 minutes. Cool before serving.

SALTED PEANUT BARS

Who can resist the combination of peanuts and chocolate—it's an American Addiction.

3 ½ cups salted peanuts	Topping:
1 ½ cups flour	½ cup corn syrup
¾ cup brown sugar	2 tablespoons butter
½ teaspoon salt	1 tablespoon water
½ cup softened butter (not margarine)	1 ½ cups milk chocolate chips

Line 15 x 10 baking sheet with parchment paper. Combine all crust ingredients and press into bottom of pan. Bake in 350° oven for 10 minutes, do not over bake. Remove from oven and sprinkle peanuts evenly over crust. In saucepan, combine topping ingredients, bring to boil and cook, stirring constantly for 2 minutes, until smooth. Pour hot mixture over nuts and return to oven. Bake for 15 minutes more. Cool completely before cutting into bars.

Twice the Rice

I never figured a simple grain of rice could stir up such a story. I'd just started traveling when one evening I was served a plate filled with a wonderful chicken and plain rice on the side. I hadn't had rice since I left home, so excitedly I asked for the butter and sugar. All conversation came to a halt and our host asked why. I explained I'd never had rice for any meal but breakfast with butter and sugar on it. They all laughed and explained they never ate it for breakfast and put gravy on it when they served it with chicken. I tried it their way and liked it. Now I eat rice many different ways, even for breakfast with butter and sugar.

The point is, no matter who we are, what we believe, where we're from or where we're headed, we all have experiences with food. I've met wonderful people, spent incredible times, and have thousands of recollections from my travels. What I discovered the most and hope to convey in these pages—Where Food And People Meet there is LIFE.

TEXAS BROWNIES

Here is the tried and true recipe around for over 30 years, just in case someone out there doesn't have it.

2 cups flour
2 cups sugar
1/2 cup butter
1/2 cup shortening
1 cup coffee, strong brewed
1/4 cup unsweetened cocoa
1/2 cup buttermilk
2 eggs

1 teaspoon baking soda
1 teaspoon vanilla extract
Frosting—
1/2 cup butter
2 tablespoon cocoa
1/4 milk
1 1/2 cups powdered sugar
1 teaspoon vanilla extract

In a mixing bowl, combine flour and sugar. In a heavy saucepan over medium heat, combine butter, shortening, coffee and cocoa. Stir constantly until heated to a boil. Pour boiling mixture over flour and sugar. Add buttermilk, eggs, baking soda and vanilla. Mix well, using a wooden spoon or high speed mixer. Pour batter into sprayed 11x7 baking pan. Bake in 400° oven for about 20 minutes, or until done in center. Meanwhile, prepare the frosting combining butter, cocoa and milk in a saucepan over medium heat. Stir frequently until heated to a boil. Mix in powdered sugar and vanilla and stir until smooth. Pour warm frosting over brownies as soon as they come out of the oven. Cool and cut into squares.

What Happens In The Kitchen,
Should NEVER
Stay In The Kitchen.

SANDWICHES

My dad's bologna and onion sandwiches; grade school's peanut butter and jelly; hot dogs; fast food single hamburgers; and fried ham between to pieces of bread are all I knew about sandwiches. That changed when I began traveling and receiving sack lunches from people we stayed with the night before. Quickly it became clear that a sandwich meant many different things and it became apparent anything and everything could be put between two pieces of bread.

Bags and snacks we were given, would be in various sizes and shapes and we never could accurately guess what would be lying within those bulges. It was a moment of suspense when a brave soul would look into our gifted bag. Some of the largest bags had very little in them and the smallest were packed with enough goodies for snacking, lunching and splurging for several days.

You wouldn't believe what was in some of those lunches . . . . I didn't—thus began the days where, by faith or fate, I would choose to spend my lunchtime fasting. The fasting lunches were sporadic, motivated by the contents of a blessed sack lunch.

At all times, the food was gratefully accepted and happily consumed; I made it a point to try everything once. Every bag provided nourishment for our bodies and a reprieve to our finances: gifts from their kitchen, their hearts and their wallets. It may not have landed on my favorite list of foods, but we always thanked God for those so willing to show us they cared.

Sandwiches went by the wayside after I stopped traveling except for the usual fast food fare; then my husband and I moved to Alaska and worked at the same hospital. He worked the 12-hour day shift and I worked the 12-hour night shift. We didn't see much of each other those 3 days: just a quick kiss, a hug, a hi and goodbye. I wanted to make him at least one homemade meal in the 3 workdays. Simplicity was the priority: eaten while doing other tasks, utensils were out of the question, no heating before eating and travel smart.

Sandwiches were the key, as long as I kept them neat and not dripping with sauces. Thus began my discoveries into putting favorite foods between breads and things. I played with bread recipes adding flavors and found ways to put a "casserole" on a sandwich. It was my way of reminding him of my love and make him stop in his busy day to eat.

A Taste Of Heaven

BEER BRATWURST

Popular at tailgate and Super Bowl parties, beer brats are good year-round. It's hard to believe a few simple ingredients make this quick and tasty dish. Don't stop at bratwurst; use this method with hot dogs, Italian sausage, knockwurst, or just about any link sausage.

1 tablespoon olive oil divided	1 teaspoon mustard seeds
1 sweet onion sliced into thick rings	Salt and black pepper
6-8 bratwurst, kielbasa polish	12 ounces lager or dark beer
sausages knockwurst or hot dogs	6-8 hoagie buns
1 teaspoon caraway seeds	Mustard—hot, sweet, any kind

Place mustard and caraway seeds in small resealable plastic bag and crush with meat mallet or rolling pin. Melt butter in Dutch oven or large, heavy-bottomed pot with tight fitting lid over medium heat. When foaming subsides, add bratwurst and cook, turning, until browned on all sides, about 10 minutes. Remove to plate. Reduce heat to low, add onions and mustard and caraway seed mixture and season generously with salt and pepper. Cook, stirring occasionally, until onions have softened and beginning to brown, about 20 minutes. Pour in beer and place braised bratwurst nestling them in onions, turning once, until completely cooked through, about 20 minutes. Toast hoagie rolls and spread mustard on each. Place bratwurst in each bun and cover with onions.

BREAD MACHINE—ITALIAN CALZONE

Fillings can include other or only vegetables, or other cheeses, turkey, beef, sausages or other deli meats. Pizza sauce is served with calzones in the US, but not in Italy. Pizza sauce, marinara sauce, mustard sauce or salsa can also be placed inside the calzone. Some people put Ricotta cheese in their calzone and that is the difference between their calzone and Stromboli.

1 ¼ cups water	¼ pound sliced salami
2 teaspoons yeast	¼ pound sliced ham
1 ½ teaspoons sugar	¼ pound sliced Provolone or
3 cups bread flour	mozzarella cheese
1 teaspoon salt	1 thinly sliced tomato
1 teaspoon dry milk powder	2 tablespoons melted butter
1 teaspoon olive oil	

Place water, yeast, sugar, flour, salt, powdered milk and olive oil in pan of bread machine, in order suggested by manufacturer. Select Dough cycle. After cycle is completed, divide into four pieces; on lightly floured surface roll each into 10" circle. Divide salami, ham, cheese and tomato between 4 circles of dough, placing fillings over only half of dough circles. Fold over and crimp edges shut. Place on foiled and sprayed cookie sheet. Brush with melted butter after 15 minutes of cooking. Cook for total of 25-30 minutes in 375° oven or until golden brown. Remove from oven and cool for 5 minutes slice and serve.

BREAKFAST TO GO

Making our own on the go meals is so much healthier and the ingredients personalized. It can be made even healthier by using my ground turkey sausage recipe.

8 ounces breakfast sausage	4 pita bread
1 tablespoon minced onions	1 cup shredded American cheese
6 eggs beaten	Ketchup, salsa or hot sauce
Dash salt	(optional)
Dash black pepper	

Sauté crumbled sausage and onion for 3-4 minutes or until cooked. Pour beaten eggs into pan and scramble eggs with sausage, add salt and pepper. Cut 3 inch opening along edge of each pita bread; heat bread in microwave by wrapping in moist paper towels for 20-30 seconds. Divide cheese between 4 pita pockets; place in pocket, spoon ¼ of egg filling into each pocket and if desired add ketchup, salsa or hot sauce. Fold top closed and go.

BREAKFAST WRAP

My husband puts everything in wraps these days to avoid excessive carbohydrate consumption and enjoys the variety now available.

4 eggs slightly beaten	4 whole wheat pita bread
1 package frozen shredded hash brown potatoes thawed	4 slices ham
	4 slices Swiss cheese
¼ cup diced onions	Salt and black pepper

In bowl, thoroughly mix eggs, hash browns and chives together. Season with salt and pepper. Divide egg mixture; spread evenly on top of pitas. Lay slice of ham and cheese on top of each. Fold pita sandwich in half and wrap tightly in aluminum foil. Place on baking sheet and bake in 375° oven for 15 minutes. Open aluminum foil; bake for an additional 5 minutes. Pitas can be sliced after 10 minutes, or wrapped in foil.

CALIFORNIA CHILI CHEESE DOG

Pink's, a Hollywood landmark, has been selling the same all-beef, natural casing dog since 1939. Its chili cheese dog goes for $3.20 and the chili is a secret family recipe.

4 kosher all beef frankfurters	1 cup homemade chili no
4 white hot dog buns	beans—see recipe in SOUPS
1 finely diced onion	Mustard
8 slices American cheese	

Grill or boil hot dogs to desired doneness. Steam hot dog buns in bamboo steamer or on hot grill for 60 seconds. Spread two slices of cheese overlapping diagonally across the base of hot dog bun, and place hot dog on top of cheese. Drizzle mustard on dog and cover with chili and onion.

CAPTAIN'S CORNISH PASTIES

Tradition claims the pasty was originally made as lunch for Cornish tin miners who were unable to return to the surface to eat. The story goes that, covered in dirt from head to foot (including some arsenic often found with tin), they could hold the pasty by the folded crust and eat the rest without touching it, discarding the dirty pastry. Also the pasty's dense, folded pastry could stay warm for 8 to 10 hours and, when carried close to the body, could help the miners stay warm.

4 cups flour	1 cup coarsely chopped turnips
⅛ teaspoon salt	2 cups diced boneless beef round
1 ½ cups shortening chilled cut in	steaks
cubes	1 cup coarsely chopped onions
8-10 tablespoons ice water	2 cups finely diced potatoes
1 egg beaten	1 ½ teaspoons salt
Filling:	1 teaspoon black pepper

Pastry: Rub together flour and shortening to make coarse meal. Add 8 tablespoons ice water all at once. If dough crumbles, add more water. Form ball of dough, wrap in plastic wrap and refrigerate for one hour. Roll dough out ¼ inch thick, cut out 6 inch rounds. Re-roll scraps and cut into additional rounds. Filling: Make sure ingredients are cut into uniform size pieces. Combine ingredients in bowl to mix evenly. Put ¼ of mixture into center of rolled out pastry round. Moisten pasty edges, fold in half and crimp to seal. Place on sprayed baking sheet and brush lightly with egg wash. Bake in 400° oven for 15 minutes, reduce heat to 350° and continue to bake until golden brown. Serve hot or cold.

CELEBRATED DODGER DOG

One of the more simple things you can eat in Los Angeles. A California buddy says if the hot dog is good quality, don't mess it up with a lot of fixings.

8 foot-long hot dogs boiled or grilled	Mustard
8 foot-long hot dog buns steamed	Sweet pickle relish

Place cooked hot dogs in buns and top with mustard and relish.

CHEESY LOAF

This is a nice meal for those Friday Movie nights at home or Saturday game night.

1 pound ground beef, pork, turkey, or chicken or any combination	1 loaf bread dough
1 chopped onion	1 cup shredded mozzarella cheese
1 can mushrooms drained and chopped	1 cup shredded Cheddar cheese
	2 cups cooked broccoli cut up

Cook ground meat until thoroughly cooked and drain off grease. Roll out thawed bread dough onto ungreased cooking sheet into 14x12 rectangle. Spoon ground meat down center of dough. Top meat with onion, mushrooms, broccoli and cheeses. Fold long sides of dough over filling meeting in center. Press edges and ends to seal. Bake in 350° for 25-30 minutes or until gold brown. Remove from oven and let set for 5 minutes cut into crosswise slices.

CHICAGO ITALIAN BEEF SANDWICH

This sandwich can be found at most hot dog stands and small Italian-American restaurants throughout the city of Chicago and its suburbs. They are difficult to find outside the Chicago metropolitan area. In some cities outside of Illinois, however, Chicago expatriates have opened restaurants across the country serving Italian beef, Chicago-style hot dogs.

5 pounds beef rump roast	1 bay leaf
1 diced onion	1 teaspoon hot pepper sauce
2 cups beef broth	2 tablespoons Worcestershire sauce
2 teaspoons dried oregano	3 tablespoons minced garlic
1 teaspoon dried thyme	1 chopped green bell pepper
1 teaspoon dried marjoram	30 Italian rolls

Pat roast with salt and pepper and place on rack in roasting pan. Sprinkle onions over top. Roast in 300° oven until instant-read thermometer inserted into center of meat reads 140°. Remove roast to platter or cutting board, cover loosely with foil and let rest for half hour. Leave roasting juices in roasting pan and add all other ingredients except bread. On top of stove, simmer mixture for

15 to 20 minutes; add any juices collecting from resting beef. Slice beef thinly, arrange slices in dish. Strain juice mixture, pour over beef and refrigerate for 8 to 12 hours. Heat roast beef and sauce thoroughly. Put sliced beef on Italian bread or rolls and spoon sauce on top or serve it alongside for dipping. If desired, add cheese or sliced sweet bell peppers or hot giardinara (made from pickled Greek peppers, carrots, cauliflower, cucumbers, celery, turnips, red peppers, olives and onions.)

CHICAGO RED HOT

About 80% of the vendors in Chicago use Vienna Beef frankfurters. They're simmered using steam heat to between 170° and 180° internal temperature, but grilling or boiling work just fine for home cooking. Most delis in Chicago sell a dog with "the works," or "dragged through the garden,".

8 hot dogs grilled or cooked on griddle	Chopped white onion
	Diced fresh tomato
8 hot dog buns	8 pickle spears
Yellow mustard	Hot peppers
Sweet pickle relish	Celery salt

Place cooked hot dogs on buns and top with the remaining ingredients.

CINCINNATTI CONEY CHEESE

8 hot dogs	Cincinnati chili (see soups)
8 hot dog buns	1 cup grated mild Cheddar cheese
Mustard	Diced onion

Place grilled hot dogs on buns. Spread bottom half of each bun with a tablespoon of mustard. Top each hot dog with some of hot chili, a few tablespoons of cheese and onions.

CLASSIC BLT

The BLT is a popular variety of sandwich. Mayonnaise is the traditional condiment used but avocado can also be used and bacon fried in balsamic vinegar adds extra flavor.

12 slices bacon	Add 2 teaspoon chili powder and
8 slices bread	lime juice to mayonnaise
8 leafs iceberg lettuce	Add a slice of avocados
8 slices tomatoes	Add slices of pickles
8 tablespoons mayonnaise	Add slice any kind of cheese
Beyond Classic:	

Cook bacon until crispy, drain on paper towels. Toast 8 slices of bread. Spread 1 tablespoon mayo on each slice of toasted bread. Add 1 slice of lettuce to 4 pieces of mayo-spread toast. Add 2 slices of tomato on top of lettuce. Arrange 3 slices of bacon evenly on top of tomato. (Break bacon slices in half to fit, if needed.). Add 1 slice of lettuce on top of bacon. Put remaining 4 pieces of mayo-spread toast on top.

CLASSIC FANCY SANDWICH LOAF

This is a stacked party entree that looks like a cake. It was very popular in the mid 1900's. It makes sandwiches fancy enough for any party

1 loaf white or wheat bread	1 pound cream cheese—whipped

Take the loaf and cut it horizontally into 6 slices. Spread filling on each layer. Fill each layer with same or different or 2 or 3 different fillings and alternate the layers which will create a ribbon effect. Fillings to try: cheese whizz / egg salad / chicken salad / tuna salad / ham salad / deviled ham spread / tofu / peanut butter / jelly or jams / salmon spread / Spam spread. After layers are assembled ending with bread on top, coat entire loaf with cream cheese that has been whipped. Food Coloring can be used to tint cream cheese for more festive look or to match party theme or holiday. Garnish loaf with olives, lettuce, parsley, carrots curls, radish roses, cucumbers, parsley, grapes, cherry tomatoes or other festive vegetables and fruits. To serve, slice the "cake" like a loaf of bread and serve with a fork.

CLUB SANDWICH

A club sandwich or clubhouse is often cut into quarters. The traditional club ingredients are turkey, bacon, lettuce, and tomato. Chicken is sometimes substituted for turkey; honey mustard is a nice difference. Some versions also contain ham; any bread, meats and veggies, cheeses, condiment can be used to make this classic healthier.

12 slices bread	Kosher salt and black pepper
¾ cup mayonnaise	16 slices crispy cooked bacon
8 leafs Romaine lettuce	16 ounces sliced roasted turkeys
16 slices tomatoes	16 plastic cocktail swords

Toast both sides of bread. Cut lettuce leaves in half crosswise. To make a double-decker club: On clean work surface, arrange 3 bread slices in a row. Spread 1 tablespoon mayonnaise over 1 side of each bread slice. Place lettuce stack on top of first bread slice; top with 2 tomato slices and season with salt and pepper. Place 2 slices bacon over tomatoes and top with 2 ounces of turkey (without letting any hang over the sides). Season turkey with salt and pepper; repeat with second bread slice. Carefully place second layered bread slice on top of first layered bread, turkey side-up. Cover with third bread slice, mayonnaise side-down. Pin sandwiches layers together by piercing them with 4 frill picks or cocktail swords through top bread slice, in 4 places in diamond-like pattern, all the way to bottom bread slice. Repeat entire process with remaining ingredients to form 3 more sandwiches. Using a serrated knife cut each sandwich, diagonally, into 4 triangular pieces (each piece should be secured in center with pick or sword). Serve with potato chips and pickles.

CORN DOGS

Start with a good hot dog: all-beef, natural casings, kosher or kosher-style. You will need 10, 8-inch wooden skewers, a large (12-inch or larger) skillet with high sides, a deep—frying thermometer or an electric deep fryer, a sheet pan and a pair of tongs. Because the entire dog-on-stick is about 10 inches long, the traditional Dutch oven or electric deep fryer won't work for this recipe. The whole corn dog, including the stick, needs to fit into the frying pan of hot oil. My nephew Eric could live off these for days, if we had let him.

1 cup yellow cornmeal

1 cup flour

¼ teaspoon salt

⅛ teaspoon black pepper

¼ cup sugar

4 teaspoons baking powder

1 egg

1 cup milk

Vegetable oil for frying

2 16-ounce bags beef hot dogs

16 wooden skewers

In medium bowl, combine cornmeal, flour, salt, pepper, sugar and baking powder. Stir in eggs and milk. Preheat oil in a deep saucepan over medium heat. Insert wooden skewers into frankfurters. Roll frankfurters in batter until well coated. Fry 2 or 3 corn dogs at a time for 8 to 10 minutes, or until lightly browned. Drain on paper towels.

CUBANO

These panini-style sandwiches of citrus-braised pork, ham, salami and cheese are knock—down delicious.

Cooked citrus braised pork roast
   sliced
(see recipe in Pork)
2 10-inch loaves Italian breads
Mustard

Butter

8 slices Swiss cheese

8 thin slices cooked ham

8 thin slices Genoa salami

Dill pickle slices

Cut bread in half horizontally. Spread outsides of halves with butter; insides with yellow mustard; add ham, salami, braised pork, cheese and pickles. Heat grill pan, panini maker or griddle to medium heat. If a panini maker, press sandwich and cook until cheese melts. If using grill pan or griddle, press sandwich down with baking sheet and canned goods. Turn sandwich after about 7 minutes; cook until browned.

FRAJITA

A fajita is a generic term used in Tex-Mex cuisine referring to grilled meat served on a tortilla. Though originally only steak, all meats are used now. In restaurants, the meat is cooked with onions and bell peppers. Popular condiments are shredded lettuce, sour cream, guacamole, salsa, pico de gallo, cheese, and tomato.

¾ cup lime juice	Flour tortilla
2 teaspoons minced garlic	Sweet onion thinly sliced
¼ cup olive oil	Guacamole
¼ teaspoon salt	Salsa
¼ teaspoon black pepper	Sour cream
3 pounds beef skirt steak	

Combine lime juice, garlic and oil. Marinate meat in mixture for several hours. Grill, turning meat after few minutes and basting with marinade. Serve with warm flour or corn tortillas, onion, guacamole, salsa and sour cream.

FRANKIE'S PASTRAMI AND RYE—OPEN FACED

A good pastrami is God's smile on a bun according to my New York friends.

2 slices rye bread	2 tablespoons brown mustard
4 slices Swiss cheese	1 tomato thinly sliced
8 slices pastrami thinly sliced	

Spread each slice of bread with mustard. Layer sliced pastrami, Swiss cheese and tomato. Cover with remaining slice of bread. Microwave on high just until cheese begins to melt. Serve hot or warm. Garnish with pickles. Cut in half and serve.

FRENCH DIP

Finally a way to make a really good well packed French Dip without paying more than the rump roast cost. This is so easy and such a great sandwich, I don't ever order it in a restaurant anymore.

5 pounds beef rump roast	2 cans condensed French onion
1 tablespoon garlic powder	soup
1 can beef broth	6 French bread rolls sliced
2 cans beer	lengthwise

Trim excess fat from roast and place in slow cooker. Add beef broth, onion soup, beer and garlic powder. Cook on low setting for 8 hours. Remove liquid from slow cooker. Shred meat and leave in slow cooker on warm with lid on. Remove fat from juice; strain liquid into a saucepan and heat to reduce liquid. Place shredded meat on bottom half of roll and cover with top half of roll. Serve with ½ cup of liquid to dip.

GEORGIA SLAW DOG

Slaw has been a popular sandwich topping in the South for a long time. It makes your meal complete—all in one bun, just have plenty of napkins to wipe your chin.

8 hot dogs grilled or cooked on	¼ cup sugar
griddle	1 ½ teaspoons salt
8 hot dog buns	1 ½ teaspoons black pepper
Mustard or ketchup optional	2 tablespoons cider vinegar
White slaw:	⅔ cup mayonnaise
1 head cabbage cored, chopped fine	

Place cooked hot dogs on buns and top with lots of slaw. White Slaw: Mix all together in large bowl, starting with sugar and mayonnaise. Ingredient amounts may vary slightly depending on size of head of cabbage. Do not use too much mayonnaise or slaw will be too juicy.

GOOD OLD SUBMARINE

Depending on where you are in the US, these are also known as a Hero, Hoagie, Bomber, Grinder, Blimpie, Po' Boy, Poor Boy, Rocket, Torpedo, Cosmo, Dagwood, Spuckies, Zeppelin, Wedge and Italian Sandwiches.

1 pound honey ham	1 head torn lettuce
1 pound pepperoni	1 cup sliced dill pickles
1 pound Italian salami	Mayonnaise or Salad Dressing
2 sliced tomatoes	Regular or spiced mustard
1 pound sliced cheese	2 loafs French, Italian or sourdough
1 sliced onion	bread

Place ham, salami and pepperoni in oven to slightly bake for a couple of minutes. Horizontally slice bread loaves. Place meats over bottoms of loaves; layer onions, tomatoes, pickles and lettuce on top of meats. Spread mayonnaise and mustard on top slice; cut sandwich into servings.

GRILLED CHEESE—ALL AMERICAN

No matter what your childhood was like, region you grew up in or culture you lived in, this is one of the basic and most popular sandwiches in the US. This is the perfect sandwich—but we grow up, our taste evolve and we add extras: ham, turkey, beef, different cheeses and all kinds of vegetables, so make each person their favorite sandwich for any meal. But start with the right basics.

2 slices bread	2 slices American cheese
2 tablespoons butter divided	

Heat small skillet to medium high heat. Spread a thin layer of butter on one side of both bread slices; place one slice bread, buttered-side-down, in hot skillet. Immediately place both cheese slices on bread and cover with second bread slice, butter-side-up. When first side is browned, turn over and brown other side. Remove from heat and let cool 2 to 3 minutes before serving.

GRILLED PEANUT BUTTER SANDWICH

This sandwich has the advantage of not containing any perishable ingredients, so no required refrigeration in hot weather; great for lunch bags and popular with both adults and children. A high energy food; for more health benefits and variety add one of these ingredients: carrots, celery, honey, syrup, marshmallows, raisins, bananas, pickles, marshmallow fluff, vegemite, beans or dried fruit.

2 tablespoons peanut butter divided	1 sliced banana
2 slices bread	2 tablespoons butter divided

Heat skillet or griddle over medium heat and coat with cooking spray. Spread thin layer of butter on one side of both bread slices; on other side, spread 1 tablespoon of peanut butter onto one side of each slice of bread. Place banana slices onto peanut buttered side of one slice, top with other slice and press together firmly. Fry sandwich until golden brown on each side, about 2 minutes per side.

HOT DOG: NEW YORK STREET STYLE

There is no right or wrong way to make onion sauce, just as there's no right or wrong way to dress your dog. Adjust the recipe to add your favorite spices to the mix.

8 kosher hot dogs boiled	½ teaspoon cinnamon
8 hot dog buns	½ teaspoon chili powder
Spicy brown mustard	¼ cup ketchup
Onion Sauce	½ cup water
Cooked sauerkraut	1 teaspoon cayenne pepper
Onion Sauce:	½ teaspoon kosher salt
2 tablespoons vegetable oil	¼ teaspoon black pepper
2 onions sliced	

Place boiled hot dogs on buns. Spread bottom half of each bun with mustard and top each hot dog with onion sauce or sauerkraut or both. Hot Dog Onion Sauce—Heat oil in medium saucepan over medium heat. Add onions and cook until soft. Stir in cinnamon and chili powder and cook for 1 minute. Add ketchup, water, cayenne, salt and black pepper and bring to simmer. Cook mixture for 10-15 minutes or until thickened. Transfer to bowl and let cool to room temperature before serving. Can be refrigerated for up to 2 days, but bring to room temperature before serving.

KENTUCKY BBQ TURKEY SANDWICH

Barbecue has many regional variations, based on several factors: the type of meat; the sauce; the flavorings added; when they are added during preparation; the smoke; the equipment and the fuel used to cook the meat. Kentucky, barbecue has a long and rich tradition with a combination of hickory and oak being used.

2 cups cooked turkeys cut in cubes	**1 teaspoon hot pepper sauce**
⅔ cup white vinegar	**½ teaspoon salt**
⅔ cup ketchup	**¼ cup bourbon (optional)**
2 teaspoons Worcestershire sauce	**½ teaspoon lemon juice**
2 teaspoons black pepper	**4 hamburger buns split and toasted**

In medium saucepan, over high heat, combine vinegar, ketchup, Worcestershire sauce, pepper, hot sauce, salt, bourbon (if using) and lemon. Bring mixture to boil, reduce heat and simmer uncovered 30 to 35 minutes. Fold in turkey and cook 5 to 7 minutes until mixture is heated throughout. To serve, spoon hot barbecue mixture over bottom half of toasted burger buns, top with other half; or simply serve on the side to dip sandwich.

LEGENDARY SLOPPY JOE

The name "sloppy" refers to the obvious mess of meat and sauce on ones chin, fingers and other places if one attempts to eat it like a normal sandwich. This explains why it's sometimes served "open face" with fork and knife. I loved canned or dry package version which is all I had eaten until I made my own. I find the store bought bland and too sweet now; you may discover the same thing happens.

1 pound ground beef	1 tablespoon vinegar
1 chopped onion	1 teaspoon salt
1 chopped green bell pepper	¾ cup ketchup
2 tablespoons sugar	¼ cup water
1 tablespoon mustard	

In large skillet, brown beef and drain off fat. Add remaining ingredients; bring to boil. Reduce to simmer and cook for 1 hour. Serve on buns.

MONTANA PORK CHOP SANDWICH

The standard toppings for a Butte pork chop sandwich are onions, pickles and mustard, some people add lettuce and a tomato. There are no set rules for topping off a pork chop sandwich. People have come up with toppers that can be very creative including a fried egg, applesauce or slaw.

8 boneless pork loin chops	2 tablespoons paprika
½ tablespoon cinnamon	2 teaspoons garlic powder
½ teaspoon coriander	¼ teaspoon cayenne pepper
½ teaspoon nutmeg	2 cups flour
¼ teaspoon ginger	3 eggs
⅛ teaspoon allspice	2 cups bread crumbs
⅛ teaspoon cloves	Vegetable oil
2 tablespoons kosher salt	Kaiser roll

Preheat oil in heavy skillet over medium-high heat. Mix flour and spices together for dredge and place in pie pan. Place beaten eggs in second pie pan and place breadcrumbs in third pie pan. Place chops between two sheets of plastic wrap and pound until they are roughly ½" thick. Dredge chop in flour/spice mixture. Dip into beaten eggs, making sure both sides are well coated. Dredge in bread crumbs, thoroughly coating both sides. Place chop in pan, frying 3-4 minutes per side, until golden brown. Drain briefly on paper towels. Place on bun with condiments and garnishes: Mustard of any kind; onion slices; pickle slices; lettuce leaves; tomato slices; bean sprouts; and more.

All the world loves a sandwich. Whether the choice is a pastrami on rye, Cubano, muffuletta, Italian beef, Gyro, Submarine, Monte Cristo or simple PBJ, its foundation, the most important single element, is the bread. Great bread can elevate wonderful ingredients to even greater points of satisfaction.

MUFFULETTA

In the mid-19th century, an influx of Italian immigrants to New Orleans affected the city cuisine in many ways including the birth of the muffuletta sandwich. Ideally, the sandwich should be made an hour or more in advance and then tightly wrapped in plastic to enable the juices to soak the bread.

2 cups olives salad
1 loaf French bread cut horizontal
½ pound sliced hard salami
6 slices Swiss cheese
6 thin slice provolone cheese
Olives Salad:
1 quart jar mixed pickled vegetables
1 red sweet onion quartered
1 16-ounce jar pitted green olives
    drained

2-2 ¼-ounce can chopped ripe olives
    drained
¼ cup chopped pepperoncini pepper
2 tablespoons minced garlic
½ cup olive oil
1 ½ teaspoons dried parsley flakes
1 teaspoon dried oregano
1 teaspoon dried basil
½ teaspoon black pepper
1 jar roasted sweet red peppers
    drain, chop

Spread 1 cup Olive Salad evenly on bottom half of bread; layer with salami, ham, and cheeses, and spread with remaining Olive Salad. Cover with bread top. Cut crosswise into sandwiches. Olive Salad: Drain pickled vegetables, reserving ¼ cup liquid. Pulse pickled vegetables, onion, olives, pepper, garlic, olive oil, parsley, oregano, basil and pepper in a food processor until coarsely chopped. Stir in reserved vegetable liquid and roasted red peppers; cover and chill 8 hours. Chill leftover mixture up to 2 weeks. *Mixed pickled vegetables contain cauliflower, onion, carrot, pepper, and celery.*

NEBRASKA RUNZAS

This yeast dough bread pocket is extremely popular in Nebraska, The recipe was passed down from one generation to the next and one I made for an Alaskan friend who missed her home state sandwich.

1 1-pound loaf frozen bread dough thawed	1 cup shredded Swiss cheese OR
1 pound ground beef, pork, sausages, turkey or combination.	2 tablespoons Italian seasoning 1 small can diced tomato OR
½ head very finely chopped cabbage	1 cup shredded mozzarella cheese
2 large very finely chopped onions	¼ cup diced pepperoni
2 teaspoons salt	OR
2 teaspoons black pepper	1 cup finely chopped green bell
Other fillings:	peppers
1 cup chopped mushrooms	1 small can diced tomatoes

Brown ground beef in very large skillet until all pink is gone; drain. Add cabbage, onions, salt and pepper to skillet and cook until moisture is almost completely evaporated. Remove from heat. Cut dough into 15 equal ball size pieces. Take ball of dough, roll out flat into circle, place spoonful of meat mixture onto dough. Wrap dough around meat and place ball on to sprayed cookie sheet with bread seam facing down. Repeat with each ball size of dough. Cover cookie sheet with kitchen towel, place in warm place and let meat filled bread mounds rise for 30 minutes. Bake 375° oven for 20-30 minutes or until golden brown. To use additional fillings, place in skillet with cabbage, onion, salt and pepper and cook until liquid is evaporated.

Many of these recipes are very old and like the taste in food, they have evolved. Some have recently been tweaked to take into consideration the current constraints on our time, energy, economics and availability of ingredients. Having read hundreds of cookbooks, ancient and modern, I find the evolution of food is obvious and will continue; however, the need people have for meal sharing and companionship, not so much

PATTY MELT

Some say this sandwich was developed in ancient times to fuel the Greek army during the Trojan War. There are a lot of different "melts" out there, but this is the original and when made right, more satisfying than any regular hamburger.

2 tablespoons butter softened	1 tablespoon olive oil
4 slices rye bread	1 red onion sliced into rings
Salt and black pepper	3 slices Swiss cheese divided
1 ½ pounds ground beef divided	

Melt butter in large cast-iron skillet and toast rye bread slices. Remove bread to plate. Salt, pepper and grill burgers in skillet; cook to medium. Put olive oil in skillet and cook onions until caramelized. Melt cheese slices over each burger. Assemble patty melt by placing cheeseburgers over one slice each rye toast, top with caramelized onions and remaining slice of rye toast. Slice diagonally.

PEPPER JACK HAM SANDWICH

This hits the spot with the new "pepper jack cheese" trend that my husband loves so much.

1 loaf Italian or French bread sliced horizontally	1 jar sliced dill pickles Kosher style
	¼ cup Dijon style mustard
½ pound sliced ham	2 tablespoons horseradish
½ pound sliced pepper jack cheese	1 teaspoon black pepper

Open up loaf of bread, place on large piece of aluminum foil on cookie sheet. Spread cheese on both sides of bread. Place pan under broiler on high. Leave in just until cheese begins to soften. Take loaf halves out of oven, place ham slices on top of cheese. Spread mustard on one side of bread and spread horseradish on other side of loaf on top of ham. Return cookie sheet under broiler for 5 minutes, just until things begin to sizzle. Remove from oven, sprinkle black pepper top half of loaf and place pickles on bottom half of loaf. Carefully using foil, place top of loaf onto bottom. Wrap sandwich in warm aluminum foil. Leave wrapped until ready to serve. This makes a great way to transport it to a picnic or gathering.

PERFECT STROMBOLI

This dish is similar to a calzone found in pizzerias and named after the 1950 film. A Stromboli and a Calzone start off the same—both made with pizza dough. But, their shapes are different. The Calzone's dough starts off like a triangle. The Stromboli dough looks like a long rectangle. Some say it's as simple as a calzone is an inside-out pizza and a Stromboli is inside out sandwich.

1 loaf frozen white bread dough
  thawed
¼ pound thinly sliced turkey or ham
¼ pound thinly sliced salami
¼ pound thin sliced pepperoni
1 large sweet onion sliced
1 green bell pepper sliced
2 thinly sliced tomatoes
¼ pound sliced Provolone or
  mozzarella

¼ cup graded Romano or Parmesan
  cheese
1 cup thinly sliced mushrooms
1 tablespoon Italian seasoning
½ teaspoon garlic salt
¼ teaspoon black pepper
1 egg beaten
1 tablespoon sesame seeds

Spray large baking sheet (a pizza or bread stone, bake Stromboli directly on stone). Divide dough in half. On lightly floured surface, roll each dough half into rectangle about 10 x 8 inches. Arrange fillings over dough, finishing with sprinkling of Romano or Parmesan. Roll dough like a jelly roll. Pinch edges of seam and tuck ends under. Cut long diagonal slashes, about ½ inch deep, along top of loaf every 3 inches or so. Brush top of loaf with beaten egg, avoiding area in slashes. Sprinkle with sesame seeds. Bake in 375° oven about 30 minutes or until bread is golden brown. Cool slightly before cutting and serving, or if you prefer to eat Stromboli cold, cool completely on wire rack before wrapping and refrigerating.

PHILLY CHEESE STEAK

Nothing compares to the aroma and taste bud sensation of a cheese steak sub, it's one of the things our East Coast friends living in Alaska miss the most. So I try to bring them a little of that Philadelphia.

1 stick butter	½ cup sliced mushrooms
1 pound beef flank steaks sliced	½ cup sliced onions
thinly	4 French bread rolls
1 green bell pepper julienne	8 slices mozzarella cheese

Heat flat grill and melt 1tablespoon butter. Fry steak until browned, remove to plate. Grill green peppers in another tablespoon of butter. When tender, place on separate plate. Sauté mushrooms with tablespoon butter, set aside. Sauté onions in tablespoon of butter and set aside. Split each roll on 1 side lengthwise; butter each side and grill until warm. Place each roll on piece of foil. Place ¼ of steak on each roll. Take peppers, onions and mushrooms and divide evenly on 4 rolls on top of steak. Top each with 2 pieces of cheese. Wrap sandwich in foil. Remove foil when ready to serve.

REUBEN SUBMARINE

I get request for this submarine more often than any other. The combination is just the right mix for a satisfying sensation.

1 loaf sourdough bread	12 slices pepper jack cheese
1 pound sliced corned beef	½ cup thousand island salad
3 cups drained dry sauerkraut—see	dressing
recipe	1 tablespoon horseradish

Place sauerkraut in large strainer and press out all the excess liquid. Let drain for 5 minutes and then place sauerkraut on several layers of paper towels and press as much liquid out as possible. Set aside. Cut loaf of bread length-wise and place both pieces on foil, crust side down. Place 6 cheese slices on each side. Broil both halves under broiler until cheese just starts to melt around edges. Remove from broiler, spread out sauerkraut on top of cheese on bottom half of bread. Place corn beef slices over cheese on top half of bread. Broil both halves for 10 minutes. Remove from broiler. Mix together horseradish and dressing, spread mixture on top of corned beef. Using foil, fold 2 halves together. Wrap in foil. Leave in foil for 10-15 minutes before serving. Remove foil, slice and serve.

SIOUX CITY LOOSEMEAT SANDWICH

This is the famous Midwestern treat and does not contain tomato sauce, which many recipes include, but that makes it a Sloppy Joe. Once you make this, you can add other kinds of mustard, liquid smoke or Worcestershire sauce; but do try the original way once and you may not want to add anything else.

1 pound ground beef	1 tablespoon sugar
2 teaspoons salt	Water
1 finely chopped onion	1 teaspoon salt
1 tablespoon mustard	½ teaspoon black pepper
1 tablespoon vinegar	Hamburger bun

Place hamburger buns in slow cooker with cover on, turn on low to heat them up. In large skillet, break up beef really well while cooking, stir in salt and onions. Make sure meat is browned and cooked into small crumble. Drain off fat from meat and skillet. Add mustard, vinegar, sugar and enough water to barely cover meat in pan. Cook on simmer until water is all cooked out, about 15-20 minutes. When buns are warm, put yellow mustard on them, add some sliced dill pickle and place meat on bun and place top on sandwich.

SOURDOUGH PANINI

The loaf is cut horizontally, filled with salami, ham, meat, cheese or other food and served hot. A grilled panino is buttered on the outside and grilled in a press. If you are using a grill pan you will need something heavy to place on top to press it, a pot with a heavy bottle of water in it for the weight.

1 boneless skinless chicken breast	2 slices mozzarella cheese ½ inch
½ teaspoon Montreal chicken	thick
seasoning	1 tablespoon pesto sauces
2 slices sourdough bread 1 inch	1 tablespoon butter
thick	

Pound chicken breast to uniform thickness. Sprinkle both sides with grill seasoning. Grease pan with cooking spray. Grill chicken till cooked through. Slice chicken into 1 inch strips. Butter both slices of bread on one side. Spread Pesto on other side of one slice. Start with one slice bread; add chicken strips, mozzarella and top slice of bread with pesto on it. Press in hot skillet on both sides and enjoy!

SPECIAL TURKEY WRAP

Wraps are so popular right now as an alternative to eating bread. Try other flavors of tortillas for distinct flavor sensations.

1 flour tortilla	**1 red bell pepper sliced**
1 cup tomato sauce	**1 thinly sliced red onion**
1 cup salsa	**1 thinly sliced zucchini**
½ pound fresh spinach	**1 cup grated mozzarella cheese**
½ pound roasted turkeys thinly sliced	**1 cup grated Parmesan cheese**

Place tortilla on a sheet pan and brush with tomato sauce. Spoon salsa over sauce. Layer on spinach leaves, followed by the turkey breast, red pepper, onion and zucchini. Top with grated cheese. Heat in 350° oven just until cheese melts, about 5 minutes. Fold in the sides of tortilla. Roll tightly, starting with long end. Let cool for 5 minutes before cutting into 4 portions.

SPINACH TURKEY ROLL

These can also be used as an appetizer; which are generally not this healthy.

1 can refrigerated crescent rolls	**2 boxes frozen chopped spinach**
3 cups cooked turkeys cut into 1-inch cubes	**8 slices Swiss cheese**

Remove dough from can. Lay dough out on sprayed cookie sheet. Stretch to make 12x7 inch rectangle, pinch perforated openings together. Place turkey evenly down center of dough. Place 4 slices cheese across turkey.

Thaw spinach and drain very well. Top cheese with spinach, place last 4 slices of cheese over spinach. Pull sides of dough over mixture, braiding covering mixture. Bake 350° oven for 20-25 minutes or until golden brown.

Over the last years, I've gradually moved towards making more of my own food elements at home. There are several reasons for this: it helps the final dish taste better, it reduces preservative intake, it's more nutritious, and it's often substantially cheaper than what you find in the store. It takes time, but once you get used to it and find the shortcuts that work for you, most food preparation doesn't take much more time than going to the store, buying it, taking it home, popping it out of the package, and following the directions. I've also found involving the whole family somewhere in the process, teaches all members of the household to cook and prepare and is an excellent way to increase communication and discover more about each other.

SUMMER SQUASH JOES

This is a great way to enjoy those plentiful nutrition filled squash that are also easy on the pocketbook or from your own garden.

1 pound ground turkey	**1 teaspoon paprika**
¾ cup finely chopped onions	**1 teaspoon dried oregano**
1 finely chopped carrot	**Dash each of Kosher salt and black**
1 ½ cups diced summer squash	**pepper**
1 6-ounce can tomato paste	**3 ounces thinly sliced Cheddar**
1 ½ cups water	**cheese**
2 teaspoons minced garlic	**6 hamburger buns**
1 tablespoon chili powder	

Over medium high heat, cook turkey in skillet until brown. Add onion; cook 2 minutes. Add carrot; cook 2 more minutes. Add squash and cook 1 more minute. Stir in tomato paste and water until paste dissolves. Add garlic, chili powder, paprika and oregano; cook until mixture is thickened, 8-10 minutes. Divide cheese among bottom halves of buns. Transfer both halves of buns to broiler, open face and toast until cheese has melted and top buns are toasted. Remove buns from oven and fill each sandwich with squash mixture. Serve immediately.

TUNA MELT

2 6-ounce cans water-packed tuna drained	½ cup mayonnaise
	4 thick slice bread
1 stalk finely diced celery	1 cup shredded sharp cheddar
2 tablespoons minced fresh parsley	cheese
2 tablespoons sweet pickle relish	4 lemons wedges
1 teaspoon lemon juice	

Preheat broiler. In bowl, combine tuna, celery, parsley, pickle relish, lemon juice and mayonnaise. Toss with fork until well mixed. Place bread slices on broiler pan. Divide tuna mixture evenly among them, mound it slightly. Sprinkle cheese evenly over tuna mixture. Place under broiler and broil until tops just begin to bubble and are golden, 3 to 4 minutes. Watch carefully or cheese may brown too much. Serve immediately.

Not all hot dogs are alike. Just like barbecue, you will find hot dogs reflecting regional flavors, heritage and opinions of culinary correctness. A properly topped hot dog is one of those rare foods that can send us to paradise in a single bite: salty, sweet, sour, soft, crunchy and oozy all at once. Nothing taste better than one fixed just the way you prefer it.

There are many ways to enjoy chili including over your cooked potatoes or French fries with cheese as Chili cheese fries or over white rice or as Chili Mac: a dish of chili made with macaroni.

Chile Verde is a Mexican-American stew or sauce usually made from chunks of pork slow-cooked in chicken broth; tomatoes are rarely used. Coney Island chili sauce is thin and watery; many other restaurant chili sauces resemble gravy more than the typically thick chili con carne. Chili con carne is a spicy stew made from chili peppers, meat, garlic, onions, and cumin. The name "chili con carne" means "peppers with meat." Chili con carne is the official dish of Texas. Other hot dog chilies are thicker, but nearly all feature ground beef rather than any other cuts of beef.

St. Louis World's Fair of 1904

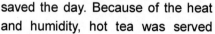

The Victorian-era Louisiana Purchase Exposition was combined with the Annual St. Louis Exposition, held since 1880, for this international celebration of the 1804 Louisiana Purchase: which was an event in American history having an importance secondary only to the Declaration of Independence.

Many of the best things in life are brought about because of necessity. German sausage or frankfurters (hot dogs) and beef patties (hamburgers) were served in a bun type bread to make it easier to eat as you strolled through the fair. Another vendor selling ice cream ran out of dishes and his fellow vendor selling waffles, rolled one up and saved the day. Because of the heat

and humidity, hot tea was served over ice, something many people had not seen before. Dr. Pepper, peanut butter and puffed wheat were used only medicinally until this fair. A new confection introduced as "fairy floss" was made popular and is now called Cotton Candy. Most of these probably weren't invented at the fair, but first introduced to mass audiences and popularized at the fair and continue to be American favorites today.

EGGS

As much as I love eggs equals how much my niece Heather disliked them in her teens. So, you can imagine my surprise when she ordered an omelet one day when she was about 13. When the dish came, she looked at this huge plate of eggs and disgustingly wanted to know what was she being served. I told her it was the Ham and Cheese Lovers Omelet she ordered. She loves ham and cheese and assumed she was getting a massive heaping of both with perhaps some bread thing around it. Luckily her uncle loves omelets and she ordered something else more familiar and edible to her.

When I was growing up, I didn't like any eggs except my dad's fluffy scrambled eggs he made on Saturday mornings. I wouldn't touch an egg fixed any other way until I stayed overnight at a school friend's house. My poor mom nearly dropped on the floor when I came home and announced I loved fried eggs.

Since then I will eat eggs anytime and fixed most any way, but it's one of those foods that when you order it, you have to find out what other people mean by soft boiled or over easy or sunny side up. Eggs are easy to fix and yet they can be hard to get the way you like them if someone else is preparing them.

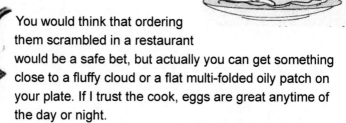

Amused & Confused

You would think that ordering them scrambled in a restaurant would be a safe bet, but actually you can get something close to a fluffy cloud or a flat multi-folded oily patch on your plate. If I trust the cook, eggs are great anytime of the day or night.

When Joe decided to go on an extreme low carbohydrate diet, eggs became an even bigger part of our daily meals. He loves omelets and I love quiche, it was perfect. Eggs are widely used in many types of dishes, both sweet and savory. They can be pickled, hard-boiled, soft-boiled, scrambled, fried and deviled. They can also be eaten raw, but that's not my preference or always safe. A boiled egg can be distinguished from a raw egg without breaking the shell by spinning it. A hard-boiled egg's contents are solid allowing it to spin freely, while the liquid contents of a raw egg cause it to stop spinning within approximately three rotations. A fact that comes in handy when you eat them like we do.

I've fixed a large variety of egg dishes for company meals, potlucks and lunches. A batch of deviled eggs can be a meal or snack. Crust-less quiches are allowed on a large number of diets. They provide an inexpensive meal for a family or to serve guest or a large crowd. Many simple salsas, sauces, gravies and toppings create a diverse way to include them in a week of meal planning. One of my favorites since I went to South Carolina is just stirring plain grits and scrambled eggs or fried eggs together—no need for toast or potatoes—add sliced tomatoes or cucumbers and the meal is complete.

Our friend Lonnie loves Angel Food Cake, so whenever I make that particular cake, it requires a large number of just the egg whites. Joe knows we will be having several egg meals and desserts until I use all the leftover yolks.

Viva La Egg

A REAL MANS QUICHE

*My Joe loves this dish I threw together for a meal one night. When friends chided him on how much he loves my quiches, he let them know about it and set them straight about the kidding he was getting about some of our favorite music choices: "**Real men** can eat quiche and listen to Barry Manilow."*

2 unbaked pie shells
2 teaspoons mustard
1 ½ cups shredded cheese
   mozzarella, Provolone, Cheddar,
   Swiss, American or mixed
½ cup chopped cooked bacon
1 cup chopped ham
1 tablespoon flour (to coat the meat
   and vegetables)

½ cup French onions dip or sour
   cream
½ tablespoon minced garlic
½ teaspoon black pepper
½ teaspoon cayenne pepper
¼ cup milk
8 eggs
½ cup mushrooms chopped
½ cup green bell peppers chopped

Spread piecrust in 13x9 baking dish. Cut as needed to cover bottom and sides of dish. Spread mustard over bottom of crust, layer cheese on top of mustard covering bottom of crust completely. Place ham, bacon mushroom and bell pepper in plastic bag with flour and shake to coat. Then lay them evenly on top of cheese. Mix together eggs, milk, peppers, dip or sour cream and garlic. Stir until well blended. Pour over items in baking dish. Bake 325° oven for 40-45 minutes. Let stand for 5 minutes before cutting to serve.

WEEKEND SCRAMBLED EGGS

Dad knew I loved his Saturday eggs and it took me awhile and more ingredients than he used to finally get the same great dish.

8 large eggs
½ teaspoon salt
½ teaspoon black pepper
¼ cup evaporated milk

¼ cup water
Pinch cream of tartar
1 tablespoon butter

In bowl, beat eggs, salt, pepper, milk and water with fork until streaks are gone and color is pure yellow. Meanwhile, heat butter in non-stick skillet over high heat, when butter foams, swirl to coat bottom and sides of pan. Before foam completely subsides, pour in eggs; reduce heat to low. Cover with lid and check on them after 5 minutes. With wooden spoon slowly push eggs from one side of pan to other, lifting and folding eggs as they form curds. Continue to cover and then move with spoon every 1-2 minutes until eggs are nicely clumped into single mound but remain shiny. Don't over cook. Serve immediately.

BACON OMELET

Optional Ingredients: diced onions, minced garlic, diced vegetables, diced tomato and just about anything else would like to try, just don't put too much of anything other than the bacon.

3 large eggs	3 strips crispy cooked bacon
2 tablespoons cold water	crumbled
1 tablespoon bacon fat from frying	Pinch each of salt and black pepper
bacon	¼ cup shredded cheese Swiss or
	Cheddar

Blend eggs with large fork, don't over mix, no beating or whisking. Gently add salt and pepper. Using 8-inch nonstick skillet over medium heat, melt bacon fat and swirl it around to coat base and sides of pan. Add eggs. After eggs begins to set around edges, about 25-30 seconds, with heat-safe spatula, carefully push cooked egg from side of skillet toward center so uncooked egg can reach bottom of hot skillet. Repeat 8-10 times around skillet, tilting as necessary, for about 1 to 1 ½ minutes. Cook until eggs begin to coagulate, but are still creamy on top. Sprinkle with cheese, bacon and any optional fillings evenly over half of egg. As cheese melts, fold unfilled half over filling. Continue to cook to golden color on bottom and gently slide omelet onto warm plate.

Bless us, O Lord,

and these thy gifts which we are about to receive from thy bounty, through Christ our Lord. Amen.

BAKED CUSTARD

Baked custard is a warm and comforting dessert and a quick breakfast that provides both your protein and calcium. Cooking them with a slow, gentle heat keeps the eggs soft and smooth.

5 eggs	¼ teaspoon salt
½ cup sugar	3 cups milk heated until very hot
2 teaspoons vanilla extract	Ground nutmeg or cinnamon

Adjust oven rack to center position. Lightly butter (or use non-fat vegetable spray) six custard cups and set them into large baking dish. If cooking custards in metal pan, cover bottom of pan with layer of newspaper to ensure even temperature on bottom. In large bowl, beat eggs slightly; add sugar, vanilla extract, salt and beat until dissolved. Mix in hot milk until blended. Pour egg mixture into prepared custard cups. Sprinkle with nutmeg or cinnamon. Bring water for water bath to a light simmer on top of stove; carefully pour hot water into baking pan to come half-way up sides of custard cups. The most common mistake people make in baking a custard is not putting enough water in hot-water bath. The water should come up to level of custard inside cups. You must protect your custard from heat. Bake in 350° oven for 25 to 30 minutes or until set around edges but still loose in center. The cooking time will depend largely on size of custard cup you are using, but begin checking at 20 minutes and check back regularly. When center of custard is just set, it will jiggle a little when shaken, that's when you can remove it from oven. Remove oven and immediately remove cups from water bath; cool on wire rack until room temperature. Cover with plastic wrap, and refrigerate at least 2 hours or up to 2 days.

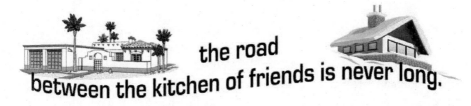

the road between the kitchen of friends is never long.

BAKED WESTERN OMELET

Baking the eggs this way, gives you the taste and texture of an omelet, but everyone eats at the same time, including the cook.

½ cup butter	1 ½ teaspoons sweet basil
6 tablespoons sour cream	6 eggs
¾ teaspoon dry mustard	¾ cup chopped ham
6 tablespoons shredded cheese	¾ cup chopped green bell peppers
¾ teaspoon onion powder	¾ cup chopped onions
¾ teaspoon salt	6 slices cheese
¾ teaspoon black pepper	¾ cup salsa

In 13x9 baking dish melt 3 tablespoon of butter. In bowl, combine sour cream, mustard, cheese, onion powder, salt, pepper, basil and remaining butter and eggs. Beat until frothy, stir in ham, peppers and onions, pour mixture into baking dish. Bake in 350° oven for 20-25 minutes until firm and beginning to brown. It will rise high in oven but will fall when taken out. Cut into squares and serve topped with slice of cheese and salsa.

BETTER EGGNOG BREAD

Eggnog is a sweetened dairy-based beverage made with milk, cream, sugar, beaten eggs (which gives it a frothy texture), and flavored with cinnamon and nutmeg; alcoholic versions also exist with addition of various liquors, such as brandy, rum, and whiskey. Eggnog is a popular drink throughout the US, and is usually associated with winter Celebrations, Christmas and New Year

¼ cup butter or margarine melted	2 teaspoons baking powder
¾ cup sugar	1 cup eggnog
2 eggs beaten	½ cup chopped pecans
1 teaspoon salt	½ cup raisins
2 ¼ cups flour	½ cup chopped candied cherries

In large bowl, combine butter, sugar and eggs. In separate bowl, combine flour, baking powder and salt; stir in to butter mixture alternately with eggnog. Mix only until dry ingredients are moistened. Fold in pecans, raisins and cherries;

spoon into sprayed loaf pan. Bake in 350° oven for 70 minutes or until bread test done. Cool on wire rack for 15 minutes; remove from pan and cool before slicing.

BREAKFAST BURRITO

Interest in Southwestern, New Mexican and Tex-Mex cuisine has popularized the breakfast burrito. An entire American breakfast can be wrapped inside a 15-inch flour tortilla. Southwestern breakfast burritos may include scrambled eggs, potatoes, onions, chorizo or bacon. Like other egg dishes, experiment with your favorite ingredients.

1 pound breakfast sausages	Sliced avocado
8 eggs	Sour Cream and salsa
Shredded cheese	4 flour tortillas

Fry sausage in skillet. Drain off fat and pat dry with paper towel. Break eggs in bowl and scramble with fork. Add eggs to skillet with sausage in it. Cook on medium heat until fluffy. Top with cheese. Heat flour tortillas in microwave on plate covered with paper towel. Fill each tortilla with adequate amount of egg/sausage mixture and garnish with sliced avocado, salsa & sour cream. Serve Hot.

BREAKFAST CASSEROLE

I was first served this type of breakfast in the early 1970's and loved it. Since then I've tasted lots of varieties and seen it fixed many different ways. This is my families way. It makes breakfast for a large amount of company an absolute breeze. We used it for big crowds on several Easter Sunrise Breakfast.

1 ½ pounds cooked bacon, pork sausages or cubed ham	2 cups milk
	1 teaspoon salt
1 4-ounce can mushrooms diced	1 teaspoon black pepper
10 slices bread crust removed	1 teaspoon dry mustard
2 cups grated Cheddar cheese	½ cup diced onions
8 eggs	½ cup diced green bell peppers

Brown bacon or sausage in skillet, drain on paper towel. Layer bread in bottom of 9 x 13 well-sprayed baking pan. Sprinkle sausage over bread. Add cheese. Sauté onion, pepper and mushrooms in 2 tablespoons of bacon or sausage fat. Sprinkle vegetables over cheese. Top with second layer of bread. Beat eggs, milk, salt, pepper and mustard. Pour slowly over casserole. Cover and refrigerate overnight. Bake in 350° oven for 50-60 minutes. Remove from oven and let set for 20-30 minutes before cutting.

BREAKFAST FRUIT STRATA

Strata is a brunch casserole dish, similar to a quiche, made from a mixture which mainly consists of bread or hash browns, eggs and cheese. It may also include vegetables or meat. The ingredients are combined in a casserole dish and baked.

½ cup butter divided

1 cup brown sugar divided

1 20-ounce can crushed pineapple

4 eggs

3 sourdough English muffins

½ cup quick cooking oats

2 tablespoons grated orange peel

In large bowl, beat together 6 tablespoons butter and ¾ cup brown sugar with electric mixer on medium speed until fluffy. Spread mixture over bottom of 9-inch deep dish pie pan. Drain juice off pineapple and reserve juice. Spread pineapple over brown sugar mixture; set aside. In another large bowl, whisk together eggs and reserved pineapple juice. Tear muffins into 1-inch pieces. Add pieces to eggs; press down to soak. Pour mixture over crushed pineapple. In small bowl, cut oatmeal, orange peel and remaining brown sugar into remaining butter until mixture crumbles. Sprinkle over pie. Bake in 375° oven for 40 minutes or until bubbly at sides. Serve warm.

COMPANY QUICHE LORRAINE

Most people think that quiche was invented by the French, but quiche actually originated in Germany; from the German 'Kuchen', meaning cake. The original 'quiche Lorraine' was an open pie with a filling of egg and cream custard with smoked bacon or pork pieces. It was only later that cheese was added.

¼ pound bacon strips	½ teaspoon salt
1 9" lightly baked pie shell	¼ teaspoon black pepper
½ cup chopped onions	1 cup shredded Swiss cheese
3 eggs	2 tablespoons butter
1 ½ cups sour cream	

Cook bacon until crisp; remove from skillet and crumble, scatter pieces evenly on bottom of pie shell. Sauté onion in bacon fat until soft, remove from skillet and spread on top bacon. Beat eggs, sour cream, salt and pepper together; add cheese and pour mixture into shell. Cut butter into tiny dots and scatter over top of egg filling. Place pie plate on cookie sheet and bake in 375° oven for 40 minutes or until set; check often. It is done when knife inserted into center comes out clean. Cool slightly before cutting on wire rack and serve warm.

CREME BRULEE

This dessert looks fabulous and is worth the effort. This popular dessert means "burnt cream," referring to the caramelized finish and can be served slightly warm or chilled. A hot water bath is used to cook custards and baked eggs in the oven without them curdling or cracking. Water baths allow the heat sensitive proteins in eggs to cook with a slow, gentle heat that keeps the eggs soft and smooth.

6 egg yolks chilled	1 ½ cups whipping cream chilled
6 tablespoons sugar	4 tablespoons sugar for topping

Butter six custard cups and set them into glass baking dish. If cooking custards in a metal pan, cover bottom of pan with a layer of newspaper to ensure even temperature on bottom. In large bowl, beat egg yolks until slightly thickened. Add sugar and mix until dissolved; mix in cream, pour mixture into prepared custard cups. Bring water for water bath to light simmer on top of stove; carefully pour hot water into baking pan to come half-way up sides of custard cups. NOTE: The most common mistake people make in baking a custard is not putting enough water in the hot-water bath. The water should come up to the level of the custard inside the cups. You must protect your custard from the heat. Bake in 275° oven for about 25 to 40 minutes or until set around edges but still loose in center. The cooking time will depend largely on size of custard cup, but begin checking at 25 minutes and check regularly. When center of custard is just set, it will jiggle a little when shaken, that's when you can remove it from oven. If using digital instant-read thermometer, inserted in centers, it should register 170° to 175°. Begin checking temperature about 5 minutes before recommended time. Remove from oven and leave in water bath until cooled to room temperature. Remove cups from water bath, cover with plastic wrap, and refrigerate at least 4 hours.

When ready to serve, uncover. If condensation has collected on custards, place paper towel on surface to soak up moisture. Sprinkle approximately 1 to 2 teaspoons of sugar over each crème Brulee. For best results, use small hand-held torch. Hold torch 4 to 5 inches from sugar, maintaining slow and even motion. Stop torching just before desired degree of doneness is reached, the sugar will continue to cook for a few seconds after flame has been removed. If you don't have a torch, place crème Brulees 6 inches below the broiler for 4 to 6 minutes or until sugar bubbles and turns golden brown. Refrigerate crème Brulee at least 10 minutes before serving. Serve within 1 hour or topping will deteriorate.

Life is a great big Cookbook.

Sample and collect as many of the wonderful recipes and events as possible. Savor the unique, the different and the familiar taste.
Try something unfamiliar now and then.
Introduce yourself to new techniques and directions.
Explore the textures and variations,
       the range of colors and smells

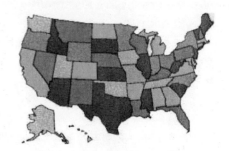

CRUSTLESS CHEESE QUICHE

Another low carb dish that made it to the regular meals list and even used for company.

6 ounces cooked, chopped ham, sausage, bacon, meat, poultry or seafood	½ cup shredded Monterey Jack cheese
	8 eggs
1 cup frozen chopped broccoli, chopped asparagus thawed or drained spinach	½ cup milk
	½ teaspoon salt
	½ teaspoon black pepper
½ cup shredded Swiss cheese	½ cup finely chopped onions
½ cup shredded Cheddar cheese	¼ cup finely chopped green bell peppers

Spray 13 x 9 baking dish. Arrange meat, vegetable, cheese, onions and peppers in layers evenly over bottom of dish. Blend together eggs, milk, salt and pepper and pour over ingredients in dish. Bake in 350° oven for 1 hour or until firm. Cover with foil if begins to brown before cooked through.

DEVILED EGGS

There are never leftovers when served as an appetizer, main entree or with a lunch salad. Deviled eggs are popular with all ages and are simple to make. One of the best aspects of deviled eggs, though, is that you can flavor them with just about anything you like. Choose a single variation or make several differently colored and flavored variations for a large gathering.

1 dozen eggs	¼ teaspoon salt
⅓ to ½ cup mayonnaise	¼ to 1 teaspoon sugar or Splenda
1 teaspoon dry mustard	¼ teaspoon black pepper

Place raw eggs in a single layer in a saucepan. Add enough cold water to cover eggs. Add enough salt to make the water taste salty. This can make eggs easy to peel later. Cover with lid. Heat until water boils. Don't remove the lid so water doesn't cool off too quickly. You want it to hover at a temperature close to but just below boiling. Remove pan from heat and leave eggs in the hot water for ten to fifteen minutes. It's important you don't time the ten minutes until water started boiling, which is right when you take it off the heat. If you set the timer before that, you will end up with soft-boiled eggs. Cool eggs under cold water. Peel shells off eggs and cut in half lengthwise. Remove yolks, place in bowl and mash with fork until lumps are out. Add mayonnaise, mustard, salt, pepper and sugar to mashed yolks. Mix well until yolk mixture is smooth. Spoon yolk mixture in each egg white half until all are filled. Sprinkle paprika or ground parsley on top of eggs.

Quick-and-easy method: Remove yolks and place in 1-quart plastic food-storage bag. Add filling ingredients. Press out air. Seal bag. Press and roll bag until yolk mixture is well blended. Push yolk mixture toward bottom corner of bag. Snip off about ½ inch of bag corner. Squeezing bag gently from the top, fill reserved whites with yolk mixture. Chill to blend flavors.

Variations: Add to egg yolk mixture 1 teaspoon to 2 tablespoons of any of following: minced parsley, chives, dill relish, sweet pickle relish, celery, pimientos, minced ham, crisp bacon, flaked lobster, flaked salmon, taco sauce, cooked spinach or carrots, spices, chopped nuts, herbs, hot sauces or crabmeat before filling egg whites

EGG FOO YUNG

Contrary to popular belief, Egg Foo Yung is only based on an authentic Chinese dish. **Fu Yung Egg Slices** *is an elaborate Shanghai recipe made with beaten egg whites and ham. From these dishes came the Egg Foo Yung many of us remember enjoying in Chinese-American restaurants throughout the 1950's and 1960's—a deep-fried pancake filled with eggs, vegetables and meat or seafood. Today, homemade Egg Foo Yung is normally pan-fried instead.*

6 eggs slightly beaten	1 tablespoon vegetable oil
1 cup cooked shrimp, pork, beef or	Sauce:
chicken	1 14 ½-ounce can chicken broth
1 cup bean sprouts	2 tablespoons cornstarch
¼ cup finely chopped green onions	2 teaspoons soy sauce

Mix eggs, meat, bean sprouts and onions together. In skillet heat oil and fry until eggs are cooked. Serve with sauce. Sauce: Combine broth, cornstarch and soy sauce in saucepan. Cook stirring constantly until thickened.

EGG SALAD SANDWICH

There is a challenge to properly hard boil an egg. The center needs to be set, stay moist and avoid the green/grey ring thing that surrounds the yolk. After removing from hot water, dunk eggs in a bowl of icy water stops the cooking process.

6 eggs	2 stalks chopped celery
2 tablespoons mayonnaise	½ cup chopped chives
Salt and black pepper	Lettuce
⅛ teaspoon lemon juice	8 slices whole wheat bread toasted

Place raw eggs in a single layer in a saucepan. Add enough cold water to cover eggs. Add enough salt to make the water taste salty. This can make eggs easy to peel later. Cover with lid. Heat until water boils. Don't remove the lid so water doesn't cool off too quickly. You want it to hover at a temperature close to but just below boiling. Remove pan from heat and leave eggs in the hot water for ten to fifteen minutes. It's important you don't time the ten minutes until water started boiling, which is right when you take it off the heat. If you set the timer before that, you will end up with soft-boiled eggs. Crack and peel each egg, place in medium mixing bowl. Add mayonnaise, couple pinches of salt and pepper, mash with fork. Don't overdo, leave egg mixture with some texture. Add more mayo to moisten mixture if needed, but add tiny amounts at a time. Stir in celery and chives. Add more salt and pepper if needed. To assemble each egg salad sandwich: place a bit of lettuce on piece of toast, top with egg salad mixture, top with second piece of toast.

EGGS BENEDICT

Many variations on the traditional eggs Benedict are available in restaurants.

Hollandaise Sauce:	Salt and black pepper
1 ½ tablespoons white wine vinegar	2 eggs
2 tablespoons butter melted	2 slices warm ham
1 egg yolk	1 large butter, toasted English muffin

Place vinegar in small pan and simmer until reduced by half. Place egg yolk and vinegar in small heatproof bowl and set it over pan of gently simmering water. Whisk egg yolk until mixture is thick enough to leave a ribbon trail when whisk is lifted. Gradually whisk in butter until mixture has thickened. Season to taste. Remove bowl from heat; set aside. Pour 2 inches of water in large frying pan and bring to gentle simmer. Carefully crack eggs into simmering water and simmer for 2-3 minutes or until eggs are poached to your liking. Place buttered muffin on plate, top with slices of ham, place poached egg on top of each. Spoon sauce over each and serve. Slices of toast or Bagels may be used instead of English muffins.

Seafood Benedict: crab, shrimp, lobster and/or baby scallops.

Eggs Blackstone: bacon and add tomato slice.

Eggs Florentine: substitute spinach for ham.

Salmon Benedict: replace with smoked salmon.

Pacific Northwest Eggs Benedict: Smoked Salmon for meat and Crab Cakes for English Muffin.

Artichoke Benedict: replaces English muffin with a hollowed artichoke.

Country Benedict: replace English muffin, ham, and hollandaise sauce with biscuit, sausage patties, and country gravy.

Irish Benedict: replaces ham with corned beef hash or Irish bacon

Eggs Chesapeake: replaces bacon with crab cake.

Dutch Benedict: replaces ham with scrapple. Popular eastern region of Pennsylvania.

Veggie Benedict: replaces ham with avocado and tomato.

Waffle Benedict: replaces muffins with waffle. It is commonly topped with maple syrup

Eggs Benedict Arnold: replaces muffin with biscuit and hollandaise with country gravy.

Eggs Pope Benedict: replaces pumpernickel bread for muffin and Bratwurst Sausage for ham.

FRIED EGG SANDWICH

An egg sandwich is made with some kind of egg filling: sliced boiled eggs, fried egg or scrambled egg. Popular in the US is an egg sandwich on a kaiser roll, bagel, or biscuit, with a breakfast meat and cheese making a breakfast sandwich.

2 teaspoons butter	Salt and black pepper
4 eggs	2 tablespoons mayonnaise
4 slices American cheese	2 tablespoons ketchup
8 slices toasted bread	

In large skillet, melt butter over medium high heat. Crack eggs in pan and cook to desired firmness. Just before eggs are cooked, place slice of cheese over each egg. After cheese has melted, place each egg on toast. Season eggs with salt and pepper. Spread ketchup and mayonnaise on remaining slices of bread and cover eggs with bread. Serve warm.

FRITTATA

A frittata is a type of Italian omelette that frequently features fillings of meats, cheeses, and vegetables. Like traditional French omelette, a frittata is prepared in a skillet. An omelette is cooked on a stovetop and served folded, a frittata is first partially cooked on a stovetop but then broiled to finish and served open-faced.

8 eggs	2 or 3 filling ingredients
2 tablespoons olive oil	3 tablespoons grated Parmesan
1 teaspoon minced garlic	cheese
2 tablespoons minced parsley	Salt and black pepper

Chop filling ingredients and sauté them with garlic and oil in 10 inch skillet on medium heat until tender. If you are using a filling like potatoes, put potatoes in first with a few tablespoons of water. Cover and steam for few minutes before uncovering and adding rest of filling ingredients. While filling ingredients are sautéing, mix eggs, Parmesan, herb, salt and pepper in bowl. When filling ingredients are soft, shake pan to distribute ingredients, pour on egg mixture and let it set for about one minute. When edges of eggs have set; place skillet in 400° oven and bake for 10-12 minutes. When frittata is fluffy but set, slide it onto a plate, cut into wedges and serve. Like many egg dishes, you can do a lot of experimenting with this and add what you like. In Naples, the frittata often contains spaghetti, macaroni, or another kind of pasta. Usually this pasta is left over from a meal and has sauce on it. A traditional peasant frittata might contain onions and Parmesan cheese—a simple meal for a farmer or laborer.

GREEK SPINACH AND FETA QUICHE

The bottom crust of quiche was originally made from bread dough, but that has long since evolved into a piecrust or puff pastry crust. This one forms a crust with the biscuit mix as it's baking to make this a very easy recipe for new quiche makers.

6 ounces fresh spinach	1 ⅓ cups milk
6 ounces crumbled feta cheese	3 eggs
¼ teaspoon dried basil	¾ biscuit baking mix
1 cup chopped onions	½ teaspoon salt
1 chopped tomato	¼ teaspoon black pepper

Steam spinach. Combine spinach, cheese, basil, onion and tomato and place in bottom of sprayed 10-inch pie pan. In medium bowl combine milk, eggs, biscuit mix, salt and pepper. Pour mixture over top of vegetable mixture. Bake in 400° oven for 25-35 minutes until puffed and set.

HAM AND SPINACH QUICHE

After World War II, Quiche became popular in England and later in the US. Today, one can find many varieties of quiche, from the original quiche Lorraine, to ones with broccoli, mushrooms, ham and/or seafood (primarily shellfish). Quiche can be served as an entrée, for lunch, breakfast or an evening snack.

½ cup finely diced cooked ham	3 eggs
1 9" lightly baked pie shell	1 ½ cups sour cream
1 10-ounce package frozen chopped	½ teaspoon salt
spinach, cooked, drained and	½ teaspoon black pepper
re-chopped	½ teaspoon nutmeg
¼ cup finely chopped onions	¼ cup shredded Swiss cheese
3 tablespoons butter	

Scatter ham evenly on bottom of pie shell. Cook spinach and onion in 2 tablespoons of butter stirring until all liquid has evaporated and spinach begins to stick to pan. Remove from heat. Beat eggs, sour cream, salt, pepper and nutmeg together. Add cheese. Add spinach and cheese and blend well. Pour mixture into shell. Cut remaining butter into tiny dots and scatter over top of egg filling. Place pie plate on cookie sheet and bake in 375° oven. Bake for 40 minutes or until set, check often. It is done when knife inserted into center comes out clean. Cool slightly before cutting on wire rack and serve warm.

HAWAIIAN LOCO MOCO

Loco Moco is a dish unique to Hawaiian cuisine. There are many variations, but the essential loco moco consists of white rice topped with a hamburger patty, a fried egg, and brown gravy. Variations may include bacon, ham, kalua pork, Portuguese sausage, teriyaki beef, teriyaki chicken, mahi-mahi, shrimp, oyster and other meats. It's a popular dish in Hawaii and a favorite of local fast food restaurants, but is almost completely unknown elsewhere, except for in Japan where it's very popular.

¼ pound ground beef	Gravy:
1 egg	¼ cup butter
Hot prepared gravy	¼ cup flour
Hot pepper sauce	1 ½ teaspoons Worcestershire sauce
Ketchup	2 cups beef broth
Soy sauce	Salt and black pepper
Cooked rice	

Form ground beef into patty. In frying pan over medium-high heat, cook patty; remove from heat and set aside. Fry egg (sunny-side up or over easy) in grease from ground beef. Assemble dish by putting bed of cooked rice in large bowl, top with hamburger patty, fried egg and ladle of hot gravy. Add hot pepper sauce, ketchup, or soy sauce according to your preference. Gravy: In saucepan, melt butter over medium-low heat. Add flour and cook, stirring, for 5 minutes, until mixture is golden-brown. Whisk in cup of cold beef broth and Worcestershire sauce. Bring to a simmer, whisking and reduce heat to low and simmer for 20 minutes, stirring occasionally. Season with salt and pepper.

OMELET: BASIC

An omelet is the easiest dish you can make. An omelet is the perfect breakfast, brunch, lunch and dinner. The dictionary defines omelet as beaten eggs cooked until set and folded over, often around a filling.

3 eggs	Pinch cream of tartar
½ tablespoon canola oil	Pinch salt and black pepper
½ tablespoon butter	Fillings: chopped vegetables, meat,
2 tablespoons cold water	cheese

Spread butter and oil on standard cooking pan. Let pan warm in medium heat. Pour eggs into bowl, add water, salt and mix ingredients all together. When pan is warm, pour egg mixture into pan. Tilt pan until mixture covers it. While you are waiting for eggs to set, prepare fillings. When sides of omelet start to look crispy, pour fillings into one half of omelet. Fold empty half of omelet onto other half. Let folded omelet cook for a few minutes, gently pour it into your plate.

OMELET: ULTIMATE

Making a basic omelet is easy. Omelet fillings can be anything vegetables, meat, seafood, cheese, herbs, pasta, bread or leftovers. Like so many other egg dished, enjoy creating your own specialty.

French:	**Farmers:**
Minced leek	Diced, uncooked potato
Shredded onion	Diced ham, onion, cheddar cheese
Diced mushrooms	**Cheese:**
Spanish:	Tomato, any kind of cheese and onions
Chopped baked potato	**Vegetarian:**
Chopped onion, tomato, beans and spinach	Green bell pepper, zucchini and fresh
Sweet: Strawberries, cream cheese and a	parsley
pinch of vanilla	**Toppings:**
Low Fat:	Salsa, hot sauce, ketchup
Use only egg white	Grated or shredded cheese
Olive oil instead of butter	**Italian:**
Low fat meats such as turkey and salmon	Onions, green pepper, olives, pepperoni,
Fresh vegetables, garlic and herb	sausage,
seasoning	Ham, cheese, tomato and pizza sauce

Some filling items need to be sautéed in olive oil before placing in omelet. Start with Basic Omelet Recipe and add your preferences. While you are waiting for eggs to set, prepare fillings. When sides of omelet start to look crispy, pour fillings into one half of omelet. Fold empty half of omelet onto other half. Let folded omelet to cook for a few minutes, gently pour it into your plate.

POACHED EGG ON POTATO AND SAUCE

A poached egg is an egg that has been cooked in water. No oil or fat is used in the preparation. Poached eggs are commonly used in Eggs Benedict and Eggs Florentine. The term, "poached egg" is also applied to a different method of preparation using an "egg poacher", where the egg is suspended in steam, rather than being poached in water. In India, the term "poached egg" often refers to a fried egg.

½ cup chopped onions	Sauce:
1 ½ grated potatoes	½ cup butter
½ teaspoon salt	2 egg yolk
¼ teaspoon black pepper	4 teaspoons lemon juice
2 slices chopped bacon	2 teaspoons Dijon style mustard
4 eggs	1 cup chopped basil
4 thick slices tomatoes	Salt and black pepper

Sauce: In small saucepan over medium heat, melt butter and keep it warm. In blender or food processor blend egg yolks, lemon juice, mustard and basil leaves for 5 seconds. With motor running add melted butter in stream and season with salt and pepper. In large bowl, combine onion, grated potatoes, salt, pepper and bacon. For each pancake, spread ½ cup of mixture on hot oiled grill or skillet, keeping pancakes two inches apart. Cook over low heat, undisturbed, for 20 minutes. Increase heat to medium and cook pancakes for additional 5 to 10 minutes or until undersides are browned. Turn pancakes and cook them another 10 minutes. Pancakes may be kept warm in preheated 250° oven for up to 30 minutes while you poach eggs. Poach eggs: Use pan that is at least 3 inches deep so there is enough water to cover eggs and they do not stick to the bottom of the pan. To prevent sticking, grease pan with a little oil before filling with water. Bring poaching liquid to boil and reduce to simmer before adding eggs (bubbles should not break the surface). Break each egg onto saucer or into small cups. Slip eggs carefully into simmering water. Let egg flow out. Immediately cover with lid and turn off heat. Set timer for exactly three minutes for medium-firm yolks. Adjust time up or down for runnier or firmer yolks. Cook 3 to 5 minutes, depending on firmness desired. Remove from water with slotted spoon; hold it over skillet briefly letting water clinging to drain off. To serve, arrange potato pancakes on heated serving plates, top each one with tomato slice and top each with hot poached egg. Spoon sauce over eggs.

BACON=BACON=BACON

In the twelfth century, a church in an English town promised a side of bacon to any married man who could swear before the congregation and God that he had not quarreled with his wife for a year and a day. A husband who could "bring home the bacon" was held in high esteem by the community for his character and tolerance. My husband Joe and my brothers Paul and Hugh probably can't meet that exact high criteria, but all are husbands dedicated and loyal to their families—and they do bring home the bacon. Literally.

They have a love for bacon that matches the commercial dog running around the house looking for his bacon snack. Every couple of months my family has a bacon-fest where several pounds of it are cooked and eaten anyway you like for the whole weekend.

Dont put all your eggs in one basket!

In this health-conscious day and age, you would think that bacon would be low on the list of preferred foods due to its fat content. Yet, bacon is solely responsible for giving a boost to the pork market. Bacon has become extremely popular as a sandwich ingredient and a favorite of chefs in fine dining establishments for enhancing a multitude of dishes. Bacon shortages have caused prices to rise, but it's still a bargain that can't be beat when it comes to adding flavor. Which is why you will always find dozens of recipes for bacon including desserts in my recipe box.

SEAFOOD

Seafood for me in St. Louis was going down to the shack by the river on Sunday and pick out the catfish caught that morning. At home it was cleaned, fried and then slowly eaten around the dinner table carefully picking the tiny bones out. Nothing compares to that taste from the bottom of the river or so I thought.

A crab fest in Baltimore means picking up a large paper sack of blue crabs freshly caught and steamed in a huge barrel. At home the bag is placed on a newspaper covered table. Each person is given instruments to crack open the shells and pull out the succulent meat. For the next 4-6 hours you sit around opening crabs and eating the meat while drinking your lemonade, beer or ice tea. When you get tired of opening crabs or a belly full, you watch some TV or play some games and return to the table to crack and eat more over and over again until all the crabs are gone. It's very caveman-like, casual and a long held tradition. You don't get seafood fresher, or so I thought.

Sitting on the dock, the fresh caught shrimp in the bucket is handed to us and we take it to the kitchen, where it's breaded, sautéed or boiled. We feast on pounds and pounds of hot and cold shrimp. No seafood meal could beat this one, or so I thought.

I've had stunning trout taken from the freshwater river and immediately cooked over our campfire; mouthwatering Maine lobster fresh plucked from the ocean and steamed at home; scrumptious freshly caught bay scallops sautéed to perfection; each better than the last and meals that are matchless, or so I thought.

Our move to Alaska made me think it all over again. Joe and Lonnie take the boat to throw out the crab pots and 3 hours later return with crabs of all kinds.  Paula and I steamed the legs of King, Dungeness, Tanners and snow species and had no need to dip in butter before eating.

During the salmon season we go to local streams and almost pick up a salmon with our hands, they are so thick traveling up stream. We fill the freezer, can some and smoke the rest—and the bits are used to make dog treats.

Halibut is caught and sold the same day down at the dock or by friends with boats. One halibut can be from 40 to 400 pounds and fill a freezer or two or three full of fillets.

The biggest discovery of all—the bright orange Alaska rockfish. It reminds me of my beloved catfish only the meat isn't as oily and has that magnificent flavor that is missing from the farm fed catfish restaurants serve now. I think this is heaven on earth, no—I know it is.

ALMOND HALIBUT

The Halibut is the largest of all flat fish, with an average weight of about 25-30 lb, but Halibuts as large as 734 lb have been reported as caught; the largest recently recorded was 465 lbs and 8 ft long. The Halibut is blackish-grey on the topside and off-white on the underbelly side. Halibut cheeks are most desired and called the "Steak of the sea"

½ cup flour	4 tablespoons butter cut into
4 halibut steaks ½-inch thick	4 pieces
Salt and black pepper	1 tablespoon chopped fresh parsley
2 tablespoons vegetable oil	2 tablespoons lemon juice
2 tablespoons butter cut into 2	¼ cup slivered almonds
pieces	Salt

Place flour in baking dish. Season both sides of each fillets generously with salt and pepper; let stand until fillets are glistening with moisture. Coat both sides of fillets with flour, shake off excess and place in single layer on baking sheet. Heat 1 tablespoon oil in nonstick skillet over high heat until shimmering; add 1 tablespoon butter; swirl to coat pan. Carefully place 2 fillets in skillet, reduce heat to medium; cook without moving fish until edges are opaque and bottom is golden brown, about 3 minutes. Gently flip fillets and cook on second side until thickest part of fillet easily separate into flakes, about 2 minutes longer. Transfer fillets to heated dinner plate. Place in 200° oven to keep warm. Wipe out skillet and repeat process to cook other 2 fillets. Heat butter in clean skillet over medium heat until melts. Add almonds to butter. Swirl pan constantly until butter is golden brown and has nutty aroma. Remove skillet from heat. Remove plates from oven and sprinkle halibut steak fillets with parsley. Add lemon juice to browned butter and almonds; season with salt. Spoon sauce over fish and serve immediately with lemon wedges.

BAKED COD AND SLAW

Cod is a popular fish with a mild flavor, low fat content and a dense white flesh that flakes easily. Cod livers are processed to make cod liver oil, a source of Vitamin A and D and omega-3 fatty acids.

2 pounds skinless boneless cod filets	1 red sweet onion thinly sliced
	1 diced green bell pepper
2 tablespoons olive oil	3 tablespoons cider vinegar
1 teaspoon lemon pepper seasoning	1 teaspoon onion salt
1 head cabbage core and thinly slice	1 teaspoon black pepper

In large bowl, toss together cabbage, onion, bell pepper, vinegar, salt and pepper. Place in well sprayed 9x13 baking dish. Brush fish on both sides with olive oil and sprinkle with lemon pepper seasoning. Place fish skin side down, on top of cabbage mixture. Bake in 450° oven for 25-30 minutes until thickest part is opaque.

BROILED ORANGE ROUGHY

The orange roughy is notable for its extraordinary lifespan—a recorded (disputed by commercial fishers but supported by scientists) maximum of 149 years—and importance to commercial deep trawl fishery. Actually a bright brick red in life, the orange roughy fades to a yellowish orange after death.

3 tablespoons lemon juice	4-each 4 ounces—orange roughy fillets (rock or cod can be
1 tablespoon Dijon style mustard	
1 tablespoon melted margarine	substituted)
1 teaspoon lemon pepper seasoning	4 lemons wedges

In small bowl mix together lemon juice, mustard, margarine and seasoning. Divide mixture in half. Place fish fillets on rack of broiler pan coated with cooking spray. Brush fillets with half lemon juice mixture. Broil 5 ½ inches from heat for 5 minutes or until fish flakes easily. Drizzle with remaining half of lemon juice mixture. Serve with lemon wedges.

BROILED ROCKFISH

Commercial harvesting of Shortraker rockfish in the Gulf of Alaska began in the early 1960's. Their body color is pink to orange-pink; fins are reddish, typically edged with black; dusky red bars may be present on back.

1 ⅓ pounds Rockfish fillets	1 teaspoon dried dill
1 tablespoon mayonnaise	¼ teaspoon salt
1 tablespoon lime juice	¼ teaspoon black pepper
2 tablespoons honey	⅓ cup bread crumbs
2 teaspoons Dijon style mustard	2 teaspoons margarine

Combine mayonnaise, lime juice, honey, mustard and dill. Spread over fillets and place on broiler pan. Sprinkle fillets with salt and pepper. Pat bread crumbs on top of fish and dot with margarine. Broil until fish flakes easily with fork.

CHEESY TUNA CASSEROLE

2 cups dried pasta	1 16-ounce bag frozen chopped
2 cans cream of mushroom soup	broccoli green beans or mixed
⅔ cup skim milk	vegetables
½ cup light mayonnaise	2 cups diced string cheese
1 teaspoon dry mustard	2 cans water packed tuna drained
¼ cup finely diced onions	1 cup grated Cheddar cheese

Cook pasta to al dente and drain. Mix soup, milk, mayonnaise, mustard, pepper and onion in large bowl. Stir in vegetables, cheese and gently fold in flaked tuna. Place in sprayed casserole dish. Top with grated cheddar cheese. Bake in 350° oven for 45 minutes.

COUNTRY FRIED CATFISH

Catfish are a diverse group of bony fish. Named for their prominent barbels, which resemble a cat's whiskers. Most catfish in the wild are bottom feeders. Catfish are of considerable commercial importance; which is why many of the larger species are farmed or fished for food. Restaurants mostly serve farm-fed catfish these days.

6 catfish filets 6-8 ounces each	½ cup flour
½ cup evaporated milk	1 cup cornmeal
1 tablespoon salt	1 package bacon
¼ teaspoon black pepper	

Clean, wash and dry fish. Combine milk, salt and pepper in bowl. In shallow dish, combine flour and cornmeal. Dip fish in milk mixture; roll in flour mixture. Fry bacon in heavy skillet until crisp. Remove bacon for another use. Leave bacon drippings in skillet. Fry fish in hot dripping for about 4 minutes. Turn carefully with spatula and fry for 4-6 minutes longer, or until fish flakes easily with fork and is browned. Drain on paper towel.

COZY TUNA CASSEROLE

1 onion chopped	2 cans fat free cream of celery soup
¼ cup finely diced mushrooms	1 cup skim milk
1 tablespoon olive oil	½ cup light mayonnaise
3 cans solid tuna water packed, drained	1 tablespoon Mrs Dash Seasoning
4 cups dry, non-egg noodles	1 bag frozen green peas or mix vegetables

Boil pasta to al dente. Sauté onions and mushrooms in olive oil. Add soup and milk and heat until smooth. Remove mixture from heat, stir in mayonnaise and seasoning. Mix all ingredients together and pour in sprayed casserole dish. Bake in 350° oven for 40 minutes.

CRAB ALFREDO

Substitute shrimp for crab meat and substitute frozen or fresh broccoli for asparagus or frozen spinach that has been thawed and dried well. Increase cooking time to 20 minutes covered with aluminum foil with asparagus.

1 stick butter	1 teaspoon black pepper
1 8-ounce package cream cheese	1 teaspoon lemon juice
½ cup grated Parmesan cheese	1 ½ pounds cooked crab meat
½ cup heavy cream	1 pound fresh or frozen asparagus
1 teaspoon garlic powder	spears

Place crab evenly in sprayed 13x9 baking dish. In skillet, melt butter on low heat. Don't let butter brown. When melted, add small chunks of softened cream cheese and add to butter; whisk until mixture is smooth. Add Parmesan cheese, stir in cream and continue to whisk smooth. Add garlic, pepper and lemon juice; stir well. Place frozen or fresh asparagus on top of crab meat in baking dish. Pour sauce over spears and crab. Cover with aluminum foil. Bake in 350° oven for 15 minutes. Remove foil and bake another 5 minutes until sauce is bubbly.

CRAB CAKES

About 850 species of crab are freshwater or (semi-)terrestrial species; they are found throughout the world's tropical and semi-tropical regions. They were previously thought to be a closely related group, but are now believed to represent at least two distinct lineages, one in the Old World and one in the New World.

⅓ cup mayonnaise	2 teaspoons Old Bay Seasoning
1 egg	1 pound cooked crabmeat
2 tablespoons finely chopped onions	2 cups finely chopped breadcrumbs
2 tablespoons chopped parsley	divided
2 tablespoons lemon juice	2 tablespoons butter divided
1 teaspoon Dijon style mustard	4 tablespoons vegetable oil divided
¼ teaspoon red pepper flakes	

Combine mayonnaise, egg, onion, parsley, lemon juice, mustard, pepper flakes and Old Bay seasoning. Fold in crabmeat and 1 cup of breadcrumbs, just until blended. Line cookie sheet with wax paper. Place remaining crumbs in large plate. Gently shape crab mixture into patties, about ⅓ cup. Coat each patty lightly with crumbs on plate; place each one on wax papered sheet. Refrigerate patties for 4 hours. Heat oven to 250°. Heat 1 tablespoon butter and 2 tablespoons oil in large skillet. Brown 4 crab cakes at a time until golden brown on both sides, about 4 minutes per side. Transfer to oven proof plate and place in oven to keep warm. Wipe out skillet and cook remaining cakes with remaining butter and oil. Serve with lemon, tartar sauce or more Old Bay seasoning.

CRAB FRITTERS

Fritters are small, sweet or savory, deep-fried cakes made by combining chopped food with a thick batter or by dipping pieces of food into a similar batter, These kind are very popular in the East and are quickly catching on by using different ingredients like this.

3 cups vegetable oil for frying	½ cup milk
1 cup flour	1 tablespoon melted shortening
1 teaspoon baking powder	1 cup crab meat
½ teaspoon salt	¼ cup Parmesan cheese
1 egg slightly beaten	

Heat oil in heavy pot or deep fryer to 365°. In medium bowl, combine flour, baking powder, salt and parmesan cheese. Beat together egg, milk and melted shortening; stir into flour mixture. Mix in crabmeat. Drop fritter batter by spoonfuls into hot oil and fry until golden. Drain on paper towels.

CRISP RED SNAPPER

The red snapper commonly inhabits waters from 30 to 200 feet but can be caught as deep as 300 feet or more on occasion. They stay relatively close to the bottom, and inhabit rocky bottoms, ledges, ridges, and artificial reefs, including offshore oil rigs and shipwrecks.

4 (8-ounce each) red snapper fillets skin on	2 teaspoons onion salt
	¾ cup cornmeal
2 teaspoons ground coriander	Vegetable oil
2 teaspoons black pepper	Lemon juice

Score skin of fish fillets by making few shallow cuts in skin so it will get crispy. Sprinkle each fillet with coriander, salt and pepper evenly over flesh side of fillets. Dust fillets on both sides with cornstarch. Heat large nonstick skillet over high heat with ⅛ inch deep oil. Add fish fillets, skin side down and cook for 3-4 minutes on each side, until crisp and firm. Sprinkle with lemon juice.

CRISPY PAN FRIED COD

Cod is moist and flaky when cooked and white in color. In the United Kingdom, Atlantic cod is one of the most common kinds of fish to be found in fish and chips, along with haddock and Pollock. In Alaska we also use our halibut and rockfish.

6 cod filets	2 teaspoons black pepper
⅓ cup flour	2 tablespoons butter
2 teaspoons salt	2 tablespoons olive oil

Rinse and pat fillets dry. Combine flour, salt and pepper in shallow dish. Coat fish on all sides with flour mixture, shake off excess and set fillets aside. In large nonstick skillet over medium-high heat, melt butter and olive oil until hot but not browned. Place fish in skillet. Cook 4 to 5 minutes on the first side and turn fillets over carefully. Continue cooking until flesh is firm and no longer opaque, about 5 more minutes.

FISH NUGGETS

Halibut, Rockfish or any firm white fish can be cut and used for this recipe.

Canola oil	1 cup pancake, waffle mix
3 pounds scrod or cod filets	1 cup bread crumbs
bite size pieces	¼ cup water
Lemon pepper seasoning	1 egg beaten
Garlic salt	

Heat ½ inch oil in large deep skillet over medium heat. Lightly sprinkle fish pieces with lemon pepper and garlic salt. Combine pancake mix and bread crumbs in plastic bag. Mix water and beaten egg in shallow dish. Dip fish in egg mixture and place in bag to coat. Fry in hot oil 7-8 minutes until golden brown, turning once. Drain well on paper towels, serve immediately.

FISH SAUTE

This can be used for any light dry meat fish or for shrimp

½ teaspoon dried oregano	1 tablespoon teriyaki sauce
1 teaspoon garlic powder	1 tablespoon butter
1 tablespoon diced onions	1 tablespoon olive oil
1 cup white wine	4 fish fillets bass, rockfish, lingcod,
1 tablespoon lemon juice	halibut

In skillet, heat butter and oil; add oregano, garlic and onion. Cook 1-2 minutes, quickly stir in ½ cup of white wine, lemon juice and teriyaki sauce. Place fish fillets and cook about 5 minutes on each side, depending on thickness of filet. Do not overcook fish. Remove fish to plate. Add another ½ cup white wine and deglaze pan with wooden spoon, heat sauce until thickened, about 1 minute and pour over fish and serve.

FOOL PROOF STUFFED TROUT

As a group, trout are somewhat bony, but the flesh is generally considered to be tasty. Additionally, they provide a good fight when caught with a hook and line, and are sought after recreationally. Because of their popularity, trout are often raised on fish farms and planted into heavily fished waters.

2 pounds boneless trout	½ cup plain yogurt
½ pound cooked, crumbled pork sausages	1 teaspoon garlic powder
	2 teaspoons chopped coriander
1 finely chopped green bell pepper	1 teaspoon onion salt
1 finely chopped onion	½ teaspoon black pepper
½ cup fresh bread crumbs	Large piece foil brushed with corn oil
4 tablespoons lemon juice	

Combine sausage, green pepper, onion, crumbs and lemon juice. Stuff fish with sausage mixture and place on lightly oiled foil. Seal ends to form a parcel and bake in 350° oven for 20-30 minutes or until fish feels firm and flesh is opaque. Combine yogurt, garlic powder, coriander, onion salt and pepper. Remove fish from foil and place on serving plate. Spoon sauce over fish and serve rest separately.

FRESH TUNA FLOWER

This is a favorite I came up when on a low fat diet in the early 1970's and no one guesses how good it is for them; they just love the taste combination. The presentation works great for showers and small summer parties.

4 large tomatoes	2 large green bell peppers
2-3 tablespoons mustard	2 cans water packed tuna drained
1 stalk diced celery	½ teaspoon salt
½ sweet onion finely chopped	¼ teaspoon black pepper
2 teaspoons sugar or artificial	2 teaspoons horseradish (optional)
sweetener	8 leafs lettuce

Mix tuna, celery, onion, sweetener and mustard together in bowl. Add horseradish, if using. Refrigerate for an hour. Remove top of each tomato; cut each ¾ way down into 6 wedges for each tomato. Place lettuce leaf on serving plate, place tomato on leaf. Using ice cream scoop to scoop tuna onto tomato, pressing down to open up wedges. Cut pepper into 6 wedges and cut each wide into 2 pieces to look like leaf. Place under wedges of tomato and serve.

FRIED ROCKFISH

One of best ways to serve freshly caught rockfish is with buttermilk, light breaded and shallow fried like these tasty fish nuggets. They end up crispy on the outside while moist and juicy on the inside. Many choose to fry fish in peanut oil and bacon grease for that extra-crispy coat and hint of smoke flavoring.

Peanut oil	Salt and black pepper
1 tablespoon bacon grease	1 cup buttermilk
1 cup yellow cornmeal	2 pounds rockfish fillet cut in 3-inch
1 cup flour	chunks

Preheat large fry pan, preferably cast iron, to medium-high. Add peanut oil and bacon grease up to 1 ½-inches deep. Mix together in shallow dish cornmeal, flour, salt and pepper. Pour buttermilk into another bowl. Add fish to buttermilk and let sit for at least 15 minutes or up to 2 hours in refrigerator. Then coat fish in cornmeal mixture, shaking off any excess. Once oil is hot, add fish, being careful not to crowd. Fry fish until golden, about 2 to 3 minutes per side, depending on thickness of filet. Remove fish to wire rack to drain. Sprinkle with additional salt. To keep fish warm, place in 200° oven. Serve with tartar sauce, lemon wedges and hot sauce.

GARLIC ORANGE SCALLOPS

Scallops are a popular type of shellfish in both Eastern and Western cooking. In Western cuisine, scallops are commonly sautéed in butter, or else breaded and deep fried. Scallops are commonly paired with light semi-dry white wines. In the U.S., when a scallop is prepared, usually only the adductor muscle is used; the other parts of the scallop surrounding the muscle are ordinarily discarded.

½ cup finely diced onions	¼ teaspoon cayenne pepper
2 tablespoons olive oil	¼ cup orange liqueur
¾ cup orange juice	10 large scallops rinse, dried
1 ¾ cups chicken broth	Salt and black pepper
⅔ cup white wine	

Brush scallops with olive oil and season with salt and pepper. Sear scallops in skillet to slightly under-cooked state, about 3 ½ minutes per side but watch them closely. Remove from pan, set aside. Cook onions in olive oil over medium-high heat until brown. Add orange juice, broth, wine and cayenne pepper. Cook over high heat to reduce. Add liqueur and deglaze pan. Add scallops to the thickened orange glaze, tossing to coat well until scallops are cooked to desired doneness.

GLAZED SALMON

Sport-fishermen from all around the world travel to the Alaska to catch trophy-size salmon. King, Sockeye, Coho, and Chum salmon are the most popular being bright, firm, and rich in flavor. Alaska is also the home to the legendary Copper River salmon and the Yukon River salmon—which are among the most sought-after, and tastiest, salmon in the world.

2 pounds salmon cut into 4 fillets

Butter melted

Salt pepper

Glaze:

⅔ cup water

1 cup pineapple juice

2 tablespoons pineapple tidbits

¼ cup teriyaki sauce

1 tablespoon soy sauce

1 ⅓ cups brown sugar

1 tablespoon minced garlic

1 teaspoon olive oil

3 tablespoons lemon juice

3 tablespoons minced onions

1 tablespoon whiskey

¼ teaspoon cayenne pepper

Brush entire surface of cleaned salmon fillets lightly with melted butter. Lightly salt and pepper both sides; place on hot grill or under broiler on high. Cook for 8-15 minutes depending on thickness of fillets by turning them 3-4 times during cooking. Be careful fish doesn't burn. Remove and spoon glaze over each fillet to serve. Combine water, pineapple juice, pineapple tidbits, teriyaki sauce, soy sauce and brown sugar in saucepan and heat over medium heat. Stir occasionally until mixture boils, reduce heat to simmer. Add remaining ingredients and let simmer 40-50 minutes or until glaze is reduced to syrup.

GOLDEN FISH CAKES

Alaska Pollock generally spawn in late winter and early spring on Southeast Bering Sea. The Alaskan Pollock fishery in the Bering Sea fishery is the largest single-species food fish fishery in the world

1 pound haddock, cod, Pollock or
    other white fish cook, flake

1 ½ cups soft bread crumbs

1 cup finely chopped onions

3 eggs

3 tablespoons water

2 tablespoons mayonnaise

1 ½ teaspoons dry mustard

¾ teaspoon salt

1 teaspoon parsley flakes

2 teaspoons Old Bay Seasoning

1 ½ cups Italian dry bread crumbs

Corn oil or vegetable oil

In large bowl, combine fish, bread crumbs, onions, eggs, water, mayonnaise, mustard, salt, parsley and Old Bay; mix well and shape into 12 patties. Coat patties with dry crumbs. Heat oil in skillet over, brown patties, about 4-5 minutes on each side. Serve with tarter sauce and lemon.

GRILLED ORANGE ROUGHY

1 ½ pounds orange roughy fillets	¾ cup lime juice
⅓ cup tequila	1 tablespoon minced garlic
⅓ cup orange juice	2 teaspoons vegetable oil

Place fish in glass dish large enough to hold fillets in single layer. Combine tequila, orange juice, lime juice, garlic and oil; pour over fish; rubbing all over. Cover and marinate for 1 hour at room temperature or for 3 hours in refrigerator, turning occasionally. Heat oiled grill to very hot. Remove fish from marinade, reserving marinade; pat fish dry. Place in well oiled fish cooking basket. Cook about 4 minutes on each side or until fish is opaque. Boil reserved marinade in saucepan 2-3 minutes and strain. Spoon over fish fillets when served.

HALIBUT FILLETS

When the Halibut is born the eyes are on both sides of its head, and it swims like a salmon. After about 6 months one eye will migrate to the other side of its head, making it look more like the flounder. This happens at the same time that the stationary eyed side begins to develop a blackish-grey pigment while the other side remains white. This disguises a halibut from above (blending with the ocean floor) and from below (blending into the light from the sky). The large size of the Halibut gives it the common title "Cow of the Sea".

2 pounds halibut steaks fillets	1 tablespoon lemon juice
2 tablespoons butter	Dash salt
½ cup Parmesan cheese	3 tablespoons chopped onions
2 tablespoons mayonnaise	Dash hot pepper sauce

Spread butter on aluminum foil, place fillets on buttered area. Place under broiler for 10 minutes or until fish is flaky—don't over cook. Mix together cheese, mayonnaise, lemon juice, salt, onions and sauce. Spread over top of fillets. Return to broiler until topping is bubbly and brown.

MUSTARD DILL BAKED SALMON

Every summer, millions of salmon return to Alaska's streams and rivers to spawn, where they are eagerly greeted by thousands of fishermen.

½ cup honey mustard dressing
1 10-ounce package baby carrots
2 tablespoons chopped dill

4 salmon fillets
¼ teaspoon salt
¼ teaspoon black pepper

Mix dressing and dill. Reserve 4 tablespoons for fish. Add carrots to remaining dressing and toss. Place carrots in sprayed 13x9 inch baking dish. Season each fillet with salt and pepper. Place salmon on top of carrots. Spoon 1 tablespoon of reserved dressing over each fillet of salmon. Bake in 450° oven 15-18 minutes or until salmon is cooked through.

NO BAKE TUNA AND PASTA

Grilled fresh tuna can be used if you like; this is a great summer meal for company.

½ pound penne pasta
6 teaspoons olive oil
½ cup bread crumbs
2 teaspoons onion salt
1 teaspoon black pepper
1 tablespoon minced garlic

1 pint grape or tomatoes halved
1 9-ounce box frozen green beans
  thawed
1 can kidney beans drain and rinse
2 cans water packed tuna drained
½ teaspoon lemon juice

In large saucepan boil pasta in salted water until al dente. Drain and reserve ¾ cup of pasta water. In large skillet, heat 2 tablespoons olive oil over medium high heat. Add bread crumbs and toast, stirring for 1-2 minutes. Transfer crumbs to bowl and season with salt and pepper. In same skillet, add remaining oil, garlic and cook over medium heat until golden, about 2 minutes. Stir in tomatoes and cook until soft, about 4 minutes. Add pasta water and heat to simmer. Stir in green beans, kidney beans and cook for about 4 minutes. Add pasta, tuna, lemon juice and toss. Top with toasted crumbs.

OVEN FRIED HADDOCK

Young Atlantic cod or haddock prepared in strips for cooking is called scrod. Most cooks use paprika just for chicken, but it really works well with the taste of this fish.

¾ cup milk
2 teaspoons salt
3 frozen haddock filets
¾ cup fine bread crumbs
¼ cup grated Parmesan cheese

¼ teaspoon dried thyme
¼ cup melted butter
1 teaspoon paprika
4 lemons wedges

Put milk in shallow bowl; stir in salt. In another shallow bowl, combine bread crumbs, Parmesan cheese, and dried thyme. Dip fish pieces in milk, in bread crumb mixture. Arrange haddock on well greased baking dish; drizzle evenly with butter. Bake haddock on top rack for 12 to 15 minutes. Fish should flake easily with fork. Sprinkle lightly with paprika and garnish with parsley and lemon. Place in 500° oven on rack placed near top of oven.

PAN FRIED SEASONED FISH

Make the following seasoning in larger quantities and use on any fish dish. It works well with chicken and pork too. Just place in an airtight container and it'll last several weeks on the shelf. To increase the amounts: a pinch is equal to 1/16 teaspoon.

1 pound fresh/frozen fish filets 1
    inch thick
1 beaten egg
2 tablespoons water
⅔ cup fine dry bread crumbs
Seasoning:
1 tablespoon celery salt
¼ teaspoon paprika
⅛ teaspoon black pepper

⅛ teaspoon cayenne pepper
Pinch ground dry mustard
Pinch mace
Pinch cinnamon
Pinch cardamom
Pinch allspice
Pinch ground cloves
Pinch ginger
Oil for frying

Combine seasoning ingredients in sealable container, mix well and store with spices. Makes about 4 teaspoons. Thaw fish, if frozen. Rinse fish and pat dry with paper towels. Cut into 4 serving size pieces. In shallow dish combine egg and water. In another dish mix crumbs and 1 ½ teaspoons of Seasoning mix. Dip fish into egg mixture; coat fish with crumb mixture. In large skillet heat oil and fry fish on 1 side until golden; turn carefully. Fry until second side is golden and flakes easily with fork. Drain on paper towels. Keep warm in 300° oven while frying remaining fish.

REAL TUNA BURGERS

2 pounds fresh tuna steak, cut in
    chunks
1 tablespoon minced garlic
3 tablespoons soy sauce
½ cup finely chopped onions

½ cup finely chopped red bell
    peppers
1 tablespoon Montreal Chicken
    seasoning
2 teaspoons vegetable oil
1 tablespoon olive oil

Place tuna in food processor and pulse until reaches consistency of ground beef. In large bowl, combine ground tuna, garlic, soy sauce, onion, bell pepper, grill seasoning and vegetable oil. Form into 4 large patties. Heat olive oil in large skillet over high heat. Add patties and cook for 4 minutes on each side.

SALMON LOAF AND CAKES

This how we usually eat our salmon in late winter or spring when the freezer is empty and the fishing hasn't started. This is the fresh stuff we canned the year before.

4 cups cooked/canned salmon
1 egg
½ cup finely chopped onions
¼ cup crushed pretzels
1 teaspoon dried basil

1 teaspoon dried dill
¼ cup salad dressing
½ teaspoon celery salt
¼ teaspoon black pepper
½ tablespoon lemon juice

Mix all ingredients in bowl until well combined. Shape and press into sprayed loaf pan. Bake in 350° oven for 30-35 minutes. Let stand 5 minutes before slicing and serving. Salmon Cakes: Combine all ingredients until well mixed. Form into patties. Dip each patty in bowl with 1 beaten egg in it; drag through bowl with cornmeal in it. Sauté in skillet with canola or olive oil until browned on both sides. Place on paper towel to drain.

SALMON WITH SAUCE

Typically, salmon are born in fresh water, migrate to the ocean, then return to fresh water to reproduce. However, there are rare species that can only survive in fresh water habitats. Folklore has it that the fish return to the exact spot where they were born to spawn; tracking studies have shown this to be true but the nature of how this memory works has long been debated.

4 pounds salmon fillets	1 teaspoon minced garlic
1 tablespoon minced garlic	1 tablespoon Worcestershire sauce
2 tablespoons ketchup	3 tablespoons soy sauce
Sauce:	2 tablespoons ketchup
½ cup butter	1 tablespoon dry mustard

Mix ketchup and garlic together and brush over fillets. Broil until done. Place Sauce ingredients in small saucepan and heat gently. Pour over baked salmon before serving.

SAUTEED GARLIC SHRIMP

While in biological terms shrimps and prawns belong to different suborders, they are very similar in appearance. In commercial farming and fisheries, the terms shrimp and prawn are often used interchangeably. However, recent aquaculture literature uses the term "prawn" only for the freshwater forms and "shrimp" for the marine.

2 pounds large shelled shrimp	4 tablespoons garlic butter
¾ cup white wine	Salt and black pepper

In a medium size skillet, heat garlic butter and add shrimp. Let cook for few minutes. Deglaze with white wine. Add seasoning and stir 30 seconds; increase heat and reduce mixture. Salt and pepper to taste

SCORE WITH STEAMED CLAMS

The word "clam" can be applied to freshwater mussels, and other freshwater bivalves, as well as marine bivalves. Numerous edible marine bivalve species live buried in sand or mud, and respire by means of siphons which reach to the surface. In the USA, these clams are collected by "digging for clams" or clam digging.

1 Vidalia onion	**3 tablespoons olive oil**
1 cup beer	**6 pounds steamer clams**

Over medium heat in large pan, olive oil. Chop onion into large chunks and sauté in oil until lightly cooked, about 5 minutes. Add beer and clams. Cover and cook until all clams are opened, about 10 to 15 minutes depending on how many you have in pan. Remove pan from heat, uncover and allow to cool touch before shucking.

SEARED ROCKFISH AND CREAM SAUCE

Simple preparation, a buttery texture, crispy crunch and creamy sauce could make anyone love this fish.

4 filets rockfish skin on	**2 cloves minced garlic**
Salt and black pepper	**⅓ cup sweet onions chopped**
1 teaspoon butter	**¼ cup olive oil**
1 tablespoon canola oil	**½ cup grated Parmesan cheese**
Sauce:	**Salt and black pepper**
¼ cup fresh shallots	**1 pint light cream**

In food processor, combine shallots, garlic and onion. On low speed, pour in olive oil in thin stream. Process for about 40 seconds, or until mixture begins to emulsify. Add Parmesan; blend for 1 minute. Heat cream in saucepan over low heat until simmering. Pour ½ of hot cream into processor and pulse for

20 seconds. Pour mixture back into cream and simmer for 5 minutes, or until thickened. Score outside skin of each piece of rockfish two or three times, careful not to cut too deeply. Pat fish dry with paper towel. Season both sides of fish with salt and pepper; set aside. Preheat skillet to medium-high; add butter and canola oil to skillet. Once pan is hot, place fish, skin-side down, in pan and sear until skin is crispy, about 3 to 4 minutes, depending on thickness of fish. Carefully turn fish over and continue to cook 2 to 3 minutes or until fish is done. Continue cooking fish in 350° oven if filets are extra thick Spoon ¼ cup of sauce onto large plate. Place rockfish filet on sauce, skin side up so it doesn't get soggy.

SHRIMP EGG ROLLS

Thank you Gina for finally helping me finally make a perfect egg roll.

1 cup chopped shrimp	12 egg rolls wrappers
1 cup chopped bean sprouts	Sauce:
1 cup shredded cabbage	4 ½ teaspoons cornstarch
1 cup chopped onions	½ cup sugar
½ cup grated carrots	1 cup pineapple juice
1 tablespoon canola oil	½ cup white vinegar
½ teaspoon black pepper	2 tablespoons ketchup
¼ teaspoon salt	1 teaspoon soy sauce

In skillet, stir fry shrimp bean sprouts, cabbage, onions and carrots in oil. Add pepper and salt, stir; set aside to cool. Position wrappers with long edge facing you, spoon ¼ cup of shrimp mix on bottom half of wrapper leaving enough to roll bottom of wrapper over filling toward center. Fold sides over filling toward center, moisten top edge and roll down over filling to create tight seal. When all wrappers and filling is used, heat more oil in skillet and fry egg rolls, a few at a time, about 4-5 minutes or until golden brown, turning often. Drain on paper towels and serve with sauce. Combine sauce ingredients in saucepan. Mix until smooth, place over medium heat and bring to a boil. Cook and stir for 1-2 minutes or until thickens.

STEAKS AND SCALLOP SAUCE

Who can resist a great Surf and turf or Surf 'n' Turf—a main course particularly common in British pubs and North American steakhouses which combines seafood and meat. The term is believed mostly to have originated along the Atlantic coast of North America and in 1967, however there's a claim that it was served in Seattle's Space Needle at the 1962 World's Fair.

5 tablespoons olive oil divided	1 medium chopped onion
4 beef tenderloin steaks	2 tablespoons minced garlic
3 cups small scallops	½ cup white wine
Salt and black pepper	2 tablespoons butter

Use 2 tablespoons oil to lightly coat each steak. Heat non stick skillet very hot; add meat and cook for 3-4 minutes on each side. Remove meat from pan. Let skillet cool down for minute. Use 2 tablespoons oil to coat scallops and season with salt and pepper. Heat skillet to hot; add scallops and cook about 2 minutes, stir well while cooking. Remove scallops to small bowl. Reduce heat to medium; add last tablespoon oil, onions, garlic and white wine. Stir scraping pan with wooden spoon and cook about 30 seconds to reduce sauce; add butter to pan to finish sauce. Remove from heat and stir in cooked scallops. Serve one steak covered with ¼ of the scallops and sauce.

Fishing for the Best

MAKING IT SPECIAL

With every single meal my grandpa ate at home, he had bread smothered in gravy. Breakfast, lunch and dinner. The meal always ended with one or two gravy soaked pieces of bread. So making gravy was one of the first things I learned by watching Granny. She taught me to make white, sausage and brown gravy from flour, later I learned how to make them with cornstarch.

This became a notable issue when my sister Sharon, 12 year old niece Heather and 8 year old nephew Eric, moved to Montana with us. They didn't like most homemade things I fixed or any of my experiments. They preferred the tried and true, no surprises packaged store bought foods. Any of my inventive culinary tricks and attempts to please their taste buds failed miserably. One day they came home from school raving about the cafeteria's processed turkey, gravy (made from powder) and fake mash potatoes—that pushed my competitive success button. I had them describe *exactly* what the meal looked like. I baked my turkey as usual, but this time I cut some meat into cubes like the schools, stirred them into *my simple* turkey gravy and served it poured over the top of a mound of *plain smoothly mashed potatoes*. No fussing this time, they gladly ate it all without a word until the end when both exclaimed it taste *almost* as good as the schools.

Shorcuts On Time, Not Taste

What a challenge the processed foods have made for the average cook. But all those chemicals, sugar and fat added to make them taste so good, really isn't a healthy way to eat on a regular basis. Besides they really do assault the taste buds and you never know what fresh produce and real meat taste like—the store bought stuff numbs your senses to the delicious taste of nature made flavors. That's why I make my own dressings, gravies condiments and sauces as much as possible. Once you get used to the fresher, natural taste, the store stuff all taste bland—you will decide it's worth the extra endeavor to make scratch.

You won't find anything fancy or complicated or full of ingredients you can't pronounce or things not found in your local stores. I cook from the heart, I make what people like, I don't cook to impress people, and I cook things to be enjoyed. I freely share what I know and look forward to eating what others have cooked as well. Each recipe gathered for this book was about foods made memorable because of the people involved. The food made the moment the people made the memory.

My physical limitations made it necessary to change many of my preparation techniques and even the recipes themselves. My emphasis includes less time involvement; making several meals from one main dish, and using what's in my pantry or refrigerator. I've made some simple and a few drastic changes to old favorites with less clean up, more nutrition and utilizing only certain prepackaged items.

Even if you never cook or bake any recipe, I hope you enjoy the stories and perhaps they'll remind you of a special moment or person in your life when you shared a treat, meal or drink. If this book makes you recall the warm fuzzy moments of the past then you might be inclined to enjoy each meal you're eating now with more appreciation for the one who made it and whom you're sharing it with. I believe more food has been prepared and consumed to relieve the hunger in our souls and spirits than physical hunger.

All of the information in this cookbook is offered as a stepping-stone and assistance to all who desire to fix something good to eat for themselves or others. This cookbook is an accumulation of years of food and people meeting because *where food and people are meeting—there is life.*

Meals, Moments, Memories

*APPLE CIDER—MUSTARD VINAIGRETTE

3 tablespoons apple cider vinegar
1 tablespoon white wine vinegar
1 tablespoon mustard
½ teaspoon garlic salt

1 teaspoon Mrs. Dash seasoning
½ teaspoon black pepper
½ cup olive oil

Whisk together vinegars, mustard, salt, seasoning and pepper in medium bowl. Slowly whisk in oil.

*BASIC ITALIAN DRESSING

¼ cup olive oil
¼ cup salad oil
½ cup apple cider vinegar
2 teaspoons minced garlic

1 teaspoon black pepper
1 teaspoon salt
2 tablespoons Italian seasoning

Place all except oil in a bowl. Mix well. Then slowly add oils while whisking mixture.

*BERRY VINAIGRETTE

Most restaurants are offering a berry flavored vinaigrette, mostly raspberry, but I use any combination including marionberries, strawberries, boysenberries, huckleberries, lingonberries and cranberries.

¾ cup canola oil
½ cup red wine vinegar
¼ cup white vinegar
3 tablespoons pureed any berries
    or combination

¼ cup seedless raspberry,
    strawberry, blackberry or berry
    jam
¼ teaspoon sea salt
¼ teaspoon ground black pepper

Place jam in a small microwave-safe bowl. Microwave, uncovered, on high for 10-15 seconds or until melted. Pour into a jar with a tight-fitting lid. Add oil, vinegars, fruit puree, salt and pepper; shake well. Serve with salad greens. Refrigerate any remaining vinaigrette.

*BLUE CHEESE DRESSING

My husband's favorite on salads, hamburgers, steaks, potatoes and veggies.

1 cup crumbled blue cheese	2 tablespoons sugar
½ cup low fat buttermilk	1 tablespoon minced garlic
½ cup reduced fat sour cream	½ teaspoon black pepper
¼ cup low fat mayonnaise	¼ teaspoon onion powder
1 teaspoon salt	2 tablespoons white wine vinegar

Mix all ingredients together and refrigerate covered.

*CITRUS SURPRISE VINAIGRETTE

With the small amount of alcohol that is in this dressing that actually ends up on the salad, no one will get tipsy from it, they just enjoy the taste "kick".

6 large lemons	¼ cup Citrus-flavored vodka or rum
½ cup olive oil	Sea Salt and Black pepper
1 teaspoon Dijon mustard	

Squeeze fresh lemons to yield about a cup of fresh lemon juice. Add olive oil, Dijon mustard, citrus-flavored vodka or rum. The flavored alcohols are sweetened, so this ingredient takes the place of the sugar that usually goes into this dressing. Add some salt and fresh ground black pepper to taste, whisk

*COOKED CAESAR SALAD DRESSING

The original recipe didn't have anchovies and it didn't use Parmesan Cheese—it used Romano.

½ cup canola, peanut or vegetable oil	¼ teaspoon dry mustard
	¼ teaspoon sugar
1 teaspoon minced garlic	⅛ teaspoon Worcestershire sauce
2 egg whites	
4 tablespoons lemon juice	

Grab a jar with tight fitting lid; pour oil and garlic into jar. Place jar in refrigerator for several hours or overnight. Remove garlic and set jar of oil aside. In small saucepan, cook remaining ingredients over low heat stirring continuously. When mixture begins to thicken, remove it from heat. Place saucepan over ice water for 1 minute to stop cooking. Let stand at room temperature for 5 minutes. Pour into blender and slowly add oil while on low speed. Cover and chill until use.

*CREAMY GARLIC DRESSING

This one can be made with the regular instead of low fat ingredients, but why add fat when it really doesn't make any taste different, just enjoy the garlic.

½ cup low fat mayonnaise

½ cup low fat sour cream

¼ cup low fat milk

4 teaspoons cider vinegar

1 teaspoon minced garlic

2 teaspoons garlic powder

½ teaspoon onion salt

1 teaspoon black pepper

1 teaspoon Italian seasoning

Combine all ingredients in medium bowl, whisk until smooth. Cover and refrigerate until ready to serve.

*GREEN GODDESS DRESSING

This creamy, herby dressing was invented at the historic Palace Hotel in San Francisco in the 1920's in honor of William Archer's hit play The Green Goddess. It enjoyed great success, especially in California, for decades and, in my opinion, is worth a second look.

1 cup mayonnaise

½ cup sour cream

¼ cup snipped fresh chives or
    minced scallions

¼ cup minced fresh parsley

1 tablespoon fresh lemon juice

1 tablespoon white wine vinegar

3 anchovy fillets, rinsed, patted dry,
    and minced

Salt and freshly ground pepper to
    taste

Stir all the ingredients together in a small bowl until well blended. Taste and adjust the seasonings. Use immediately or cover and refrigerate.

ALMOND BARK FROSTING

Using this frosting is such an awesome addition to any baked item. The different flavored liqueurs can compliment the item and make the subtle changes so you never need use a canned icing again.

12 ounces almond bark	**1 ½ cups softened butter**
½ cup any flavored liqueur	**½ cup powdered sugar**

In small saucepan, melt bark over low heat stirring constantly. Remove pan from heat and stir in liqueur. Cool for 30 minutes. In mixing bowl, combine butter and sugar with electric mixer until light and fluffy. Beat in cooled bark mixture until smooth.

BROILED COCONUT FROSTING

3 tablespoons melted butter	**2 tablespoons light cream**
5 tablespoons brown sugar	**½ cup flaked coconut**

Mix all ingredients. Spread on warm cake before removing cake from pan. Broil until sugar is melted and bubbles. This takes only a few minutes, and should be watched carefully, it can burn easily.

BUTTERCREAM FROSTINGS

I've used this basic frosting mix since it was taught to me many years ago. It's a variation of the butter cream icing used in France, but nothing beats the taste and is worth the time to make it. It can easily be adjusted to create many different types of frostings using the same basic cake recipe, add a different frosting and have a favorite for everyone without any extra work.

6 egg yolk	**½ cup corn syrup**
2 cups butter cut in pieces	**1 tablespoon vanilla extract**
¾ cup sugar	

In bowl beat with mixer egg yolks at medium-high speed until creamy and pale yellow, about 5 minutes. Using a bit of butter, lightly grease inside of heatproof measuring cup and position it alongside stove top. In a nonstick saucepan, combine sugar and corn syrup; place over medium-high heat and bring to full rolling boil without stirring. Immediately pour mixture into buttered measuring cup to halt the cooking. With mixer on high speed, slowly drizzle syrup into eggs in a steady stream. Avoid hitting beaters with syrup while pouring. Continue to beat until mixture is cooled completely. Add remaining butter, 1 piece at a time, and beat until incorporated before adding next piece. When all butter has been blended in, add vanilla and blend well. Use immediately, or cover and refrigerate for up to 1 week; return to room temperature and beat if necessary to achieve spreading consistency before using.

VARIATIONS Almond: Substitute 1 ½ teaspoons pure almond extract, for vanilla

Butterscotch: Substitute 1 cup firmly packed dark brown sugar for ¾ cup granulated sugar in syrup.

Chocolate: Melt 8 ounces finest-quality bittersweet (not unsweetened), semisweet, milk, or white chocolate. Cool slightly, add with vanilla.

Coconut:. Add 1 cup canned sweetened cream of coconut with vanilla.

Nut: Add 1 cup finely ground toasted nuts with vanilla.

Coffee: Combine 2 tablespoons instant espresso with just enough hot water to dissolve espresso. Cool to room temperature; add with vanilla.

Lemon: Add ¼ cup freshly squeezed lemon juice to sugar-corn syrup mixture and substitute ½ teaspoon pure lemon extract for vanilla.

Liqueur: Substitute amaretto, Cointreau, Kahlua, or other favorite liqueur for vanilla.

Maple: Substitute ½ cup maple syrup for ½ cup corn syrup. Substitute 2 teaspoons maple extract for vanilla.

Mint: Substitute 2 teaspoons pure mint extract for vanilla.

Mocha: Combine flavorings for Chocolate and Coffee variations and add with vanilla.

Orange: Substitute orange liqueur for vanilla and add 1 tablespoon minced orange zest.

Pineapple: Substitute 1 cup pureed canned pineapple for vanilla.

CARAMEL FROSTING

Homemade caramel is so much better than any store bought brand or candy pieces melted. It really doesn't take that much more time to make the real thing. This is the uncooked version. Caramel frosting is the perfect accompaniment to many desserts. While oatmeal cake or oatmeal bars go well with cream cheese frosting, they are also delicious when caramel frosting or icing is used. Add a few drops of hot water to make a thin frosting or icing, which can then be drizzled over granola bars or apple pie.

½ cup butter

2 cups brown sugar

¼ teaspoon vanilla extract

Heavy cream

Cream butter, add sugar gradually and mix very well. Add vanilla and only enough cream to obtain desired consistency

CLASSIC CARAMEL FROSTING

This frosting recipe must be heated on the stove. Make sure your saucepan is heavy-bottomed and large enough to hold all of the ingredients and still allow for stirring room. Stir with a rubber spatula or a flat-sided wooden spoon. While heating, stir constantly to prevent scorching.

⅓ cup brown sugar, tightly packed

2 tablespoons butter

2 tablespoons water

1 teaspoon vanilla

1 cup powdered sugar

2 tablespoons chopped pecans

Mix brown sugar and butter in heavy-bottomed saucepan. (Brown sugar should be packed so tightly in cup that when you dump it into saucepan it will retain its shape). Turn heat to medium-high and melt butter and sugar together, stirring constantly. Bring mixture to boil and continue boiling for one minute before removing it from heat. While mixture is still warm, add vanilla and then stir in powdered sugar until it reaches frosting consistency you desire.

CHOCOLATE BUTTERCREAM FROSTING

3 ¾ cups powdered sugar
½ cup unsweetened cocoa
¼ teaspoon salt

⅓ cup butter softened
¼ cup milk
1 teaspoon vanilla extract

In medium bowl, whisk together sugar, cocoa and salt. Set aside. Cream butter. Add milk and vanilla. Slowly add sugar mixture to butter mixture. Beat until creamy. If too thick, add more milk.

CHOCOLATE FUDGE FROSTING

½ cup butter
3 1-ounce squares unsweetened
   baking chocolate

1 pound powdered sugar
½ teaspoon vanilla extract
¾ cup milk

Melt chocolate and butter in microwave, or in top of double boiler. In large bowl, combine sugar, vanilla and ½ cup of milk. Blend in melted chocolate mixture. Add remaining milk, a little at a time, until desired consistency. Let stand until spreadable (frosting will thicken as it cools).

COCOA FROSTING

¼ softened butter
6 tablespoons boiling water
½ cup unsweetened cocoa

2 teaspoons vanilla extract
3 cups powdered sugar

In small bowl, stir together butter and water until butter is melted. Add cocoa and vanilla; beat until well blended. Gradually add powdered sugar, beating until smooth, creamy and spreading consistency. Add additional water, if necessary.

COCONUT PECAN FROSTING

This is the one everyone looks for on the German chocolate cake, but it's great on any kind of cake.

1 egg	¼ cup butter
⅔ cup evaporated milk	1 ⅓ cups flaked coconut
⅔ cup sugar	½ cup chopped pecans

In medium saucepan slightly beat egg. Stir in milk, sugar and butter. Cook and stir over medium heat about 12 minutes or until thick and bubbly. Remove from heat; stir in coconut and pecans. Cover and cool.

CREAM CHEESE FROSTING

This is the best cream cheese frosting you will ever find. It's really an old recipe, but tried and true—and if it works why mess with great results.

1 8-ounce package cold cream cheese	2 teaspoons vanilla extract
	Dash salt
5 tablespoons softened butter	4-4 ½ cups powdered sugar

Beat together cream cheese, butter, vanilla and salt until light and fluffy. Slowly add sugar to reach spreading consistency. Gradually add 2 cups powdered sugar that has been sifted after measuring. Continue to add more sifted powdered sugar until you reach a consistency and sweetness that fits your taste. No softening the cream cheese need, but the butter does need to be softened.

CREAM CHEESE GLAZE

1 3-ounce package cream cheese	2 cups powdered sugar
1 teaspoon vanilla extract	1-2 tablespoons milk

In a small bowl combine softened cream cheese and vanilla; beat with electric mixer on medium speed until light and fluffy. Gradually add powdered sugar and beat in enough milk to reach spreading consistently.

CUSTARD FILLING

In 1837, an English chemist introduced custard thickened with cornstarch. This became widely known as Bird's Custard, but it's not considered true custard because it's thickened with cornstarch. However, this is the main reason Bird's custard became popular; because there were no eggs used there was no risk for the mixture curdling.

1 tablespoon cornstarch	½ teaspoon vanilla extract
½ cup sugar	Chocolate:
1 cup scalded milk	Add 2 1-ounce squares unsweetened
2 egg yolk beaten	baking chocolate

Mix cornstarch and sugar, add the hot milk and pour gradually on beaten egg yolks. Cook in double boiler, stirring constantly until thickened. Cool and flavor with vanilla. Chocolate Custard: Add chocolate to double boiler before cooking. Cook and follow instructions for Vanilla Custard.

DECORATOR FROSTING

1 ½ cups shortening	2 teaspoons orange, vanilla, almond,
½ cup evaporated milk	rum or lemon extract
½ teaspoon salt	Drop of butter flavored extract
2 pounds powdered sugar	

Beat shortening at high speed for 5 minutes. On low speed, add milk and salt. Slowly add sugar and extracts. Beat on high until light and fluffy. Adjust liquid or flavorings if necessary. Makes enough for one 9-inch, two layer cake. This recipe may be cut in half for hand mixers or doubled for large mixers for icing cakes.

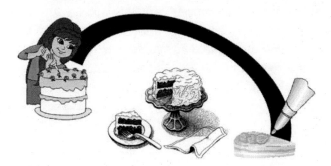

DELICIOUS PENUCHE FROSTING

Penuche (puh-NOO-chee) is a fudge-like candy made from a brown-sugar based **sugar syrup** that has been boiled to soft-ball stage and then whipped. Typical additions include butter or cream, and toasted nuts. In recent years, it's become common in the New England area to add maple syrup when making penuche fudge.

½ cup butter

1 cup brown sugar

¼ cup milk

3 ½ cups powdered sugar

In saucepan, melt butter; add brown sugar, bring to boil and lower heat to medium low; continue to boil for 2 minutes, stirring constantly. Add milk and bring to boil, stirring constantly. Cool to lukewarm. Gradually add sugar. Beat until thick enough to spread. If too thick, add a little hot water.

EASY FLAVORED FROSTING

½ cup shortening

½ cup butter softened

2 pounds powdered sugar

⅛ teaspoon salt

½ teaspoon vanilla extract

½ cup milk

Orange: 1 teaspoon orange extract

Peppermint: 1 teaspoon peppermint
      extract

Coffee: omit milk add ½ cup
      espresso

Lemon: 1 teaspoon lemon extract

Mint: 1 teaspoon crème de menthe
      extract

Maple: 1 teaspoon maple extract

Rum: 1 teaspoon rum extract

Almond: 1 teaspoon almond extract

Beat on medium speed shortening, butter, sugar, salt, vanilla and milk together until fluffy. If you want a simple vanilla flavor, this is it. If you want a stronger vanilla flavor, add another ½ teaspoon vanilla extract. For the other flavors, omit vanilla extract and use desired flavor. More extract flavors are available and if you want the color to match drop in some food coloring. For the coffee flavor, omit vanilla extract.

FUDGE FROSTING

Sometimes I simply use my fudge frosting in between the layers and top with another type of icing. It makes a nice chocolate surprise in the middle of any cake.

1 stick butter	1 teaspoon vanilla extract
3 tablespoons unsweetened cocoa	1 cup chopped nuts (optional)
1 pound powdered sugar	

In a saucepan, combine butter, cocoa, and milk; bring to a boil. Add sugar and vanilla; beat well until smooth. If frosting becomes too stiff, add 1 drop of water at a time to desired consistency.

GLAZES (ICING)

A glaze can add pizzazz to any plain cake and bring out a delicate taste mix.

BASIC: 1 cup powdered sugar	2 tablespoons softened butter
1 teaspoon vanilla extract	1 cup powdered sugar
ORANGE:	1 teaspoon vanilla extract
Omit milk; Add orange juice	Few drops milk
Omit vanilla; Add orange extract	FLAVOR LIQUEUR:
COCONUT:	Use ONLY ¼ teaspoon vanilla extract
Add ½ teaspoon coconut extract	Add 2 tablespoon any flavored
½ cup flaked coconut	liqueur
PEANUT BUTTER:	CREAM CHEESE:
Omit vanilla; add peanut butter	Omit butter; add 1 ounce cream
BASIC BUTTER:	cheese

CHOCOLATE: OMIT: vanilla ADD: 1 ounce square of chocolate (German, semi-sweet, milk chocolate or white chocolate) MOCHA: Omit milk Add drops of very strong coffee to Chocolate Glaze

MERINGUE FROSTING

Meringue is a type of dessert made from whipped egg whites and often flavored with vanilla and a small amount of almond or coconut extract. They are very light and airy and extremely sweet.

1 cup sugar	2 egg whites beaten stiffly
½ cup water	½ teaspoon flavored extract

Boil sugar and water over low heat until syrup spins a thread; pour very slowly onto stiffly beaten whites and beat until smooth and stiff enough to spread. Add flavoring. Spread on cake.

MOCHA FROSTING

In many parts of the world, mocha is understood as a coffee with a unique flavor that sets it aside from other coffee beans. Using the basic recipe of coffee and chocolate, a number of different types of mocha beverages have appeared in recent years. Swiss mocha will make use of rich Swiss chocolate in the recipe, while Suisse mocha often used referring to mocha drink that is made with a powered form of chocolate.

3 tablespoons hot strong coffee	½ teaspoon vanilla extract
3 tablespoons unsweetened cocoa	1 ⅓ cups powdered sugar

Add coffee to cocoa, stir until smooth, add vanilla and enough sugar to reach spreading consistency.

ORANGE FROSTING

⅓ cup margarine	1 teaspoon orange extract
¼ cup orange juice	Dash salt
1 teaspoon vanilla extract	4-4 ½ cups powdered sugar

Beat margarine in mixing bowl until fluffy. Add orange juice, extracts, salt and mix. Slowly add powdered sugar until icing is consistency desired.

SOUR CREAM CHEESE FROSTING

2 8-ounce packages cream cheese
   softened
10 tablespoons margarine softened
2 tablespoons sour cream

⅛ teaspoon salt
1 teaspoon vanilla extract
2 ½ cups powdered sugar

Beat together cream cheese, margarine and sour cream until light and fluffy. Add salt and vanilla mixing well; slowly beat in powdered sugar to desired consistency.

WARM BUTTERMILK FROSTING

1 cup granulated sugar
½ teaspoon baking soda
½ cup buttermilk

½ cup butter
1 tablespoon corn syrup
1 teaspoon vanilla extract

Combine sugar, baking soda, buttermilk, butter and corn syrup in saucepan. Bring to a boil, stirring boil about 5 minutes, remove from heat and add vanilla. Pour over hot cake.

WHIPPED CHOCOLATE FROSTING AND FILLING

2 1-ounce squares unsweetened
   baking chocolate
½ cup light cream

1 teaspoon vanilla extract
2 egg whites beaten stiff
1 ½-2 cups powdered sugar

Cook in double boiler, chocolate and cream over boiling water until smooth; cool, add vanilla. Take beaten whites and add sugar. Continue beating until stiff enough to cut. Combine the two mixtures, beat well.

WHIPPED CREAM FILLING

1 cup heavy cream	½ teaspoon vanilla extract
¼ cup powdered sugar	

Beat cream until it begins to thicken; add sugar gradually, add vanilla; beat until cream holds its shape when beater is raised.

*CREAMY ROQUEFORT DRESSING AND DIP

The cheese is white, tangy, crumbly and slightly moist, with distinctive veins of green mould. It has characteristic odor and flavor with a notable taste of butyric acid; the green veins provide a sharp tang. The overall flavor sensation begins slightly mild, then waxes sweet, then smoky, and fades to a salty finish.

½ cup crumbled Roquefort cheese	½ cup sour cream
1 tablespoon cream cheese—room	1 tablespoon lemon juice
temperature	1 tablespoon white wine vinegar
½ cup mayonnaise	

Cream together the Roquefort and cream cheese until smooth. Add the rest of the ingredients and mix well. Refrigerate for at least 2 hours.

*GARLIC VINAIGRETTE

Vinaigrette dressings can be simple to complex depending upon recipes. Generally the simplest forms, which can be used as a marinade or to top a variety of salads, are a combination of oil and vinegar. Other common ingredients for the basic vinaigrette include salt and pepper, and a number of different herbs, which depend on preference.

1 tablespoon balsamic vinegar	¼ teaspoon ground thyme
⅓ cup olive oil	½ teaspoon paprika
½ cup apple cider vinegar	¼ teaspoon black pepper
¼ teaspoon ground oregano	2 cloves minced garlic

Combine all ingredients, cover and shake well. Refrigerate.

*GRAPEFRUIT VINAIGRETTE

It's really easy to make simple vinaigrettes, and those who favor "Italian style" dressing may wonder why they bothered with buying bottled versions after making their own dressing at home.

1 ½ cups olive oil	⅔ teaspoon salt
¾ cup canola oil	1 teaspoon black pepper
1 tablespoon fresh chopped thyme	1 cup sweet pink or red grapefruit
2 ½ tablespoons Dijon style mustard	juice

In small pot over low heat, combine olive oil, canola oil and thyme. Heat oil just short of bubbling. Remove from heat and set aside for at least an hour. With electric mixer, combine mustard, salt, black pepper and 1 tablespoon of grapefruit juice. On slow setting drizzle in about ¼ cup of oil, then more grapefruit juice. Repeat in that order, tasting for balance as you go along, until oil and grapefruit juice are all mixed in. Add a little red-wine vinegar if it needs some acidity. Pour into airtight container. Refrigerate. Remove 15 minutes before using, and shake very well.

*HONEY MUSTARD DRESSING

Honey mustard has become a popular condiment, as the flavors of the two components are very complementary. It's used as topping on sandwiches and as a dip for chicken strips, fries, onion rings and other finger foods, as well as a glaze for grilled lamb and pork. Combined with vinegar and/or olive oil, it's offered in most dining places as a salad dressing. Peppers and spices are added to give it a distinct hot and spicy taste.

2 tablespoons olive oil	¼ teaspoon salt
1 tablespoon canola oil	⅛ teaspoon black pepper
1 tablespoon honey	1 teaspoon dried minced onion
2 teaspoons mustard	1 teaspoon garlic powder

Shake all ingredients in tightly covered container and refrigerate at least 1 hour before using.

*ITALIAN DRESSING

½ cup cider vinegar	½ tablespoon dried minced onion
½ teaspoon balsamic vinegar	½ tablespoon Italian seasoning
½ cup olive oil	¼ teaspoon celery salt
1 teaspoons minced garlic	¼ teaspoon black pepper

Mix all ingredient in a bottle or container with airtight lid. Shake vigorously before pouring on salad.

*LEMON CAESAR SALAD DRESSING

1 tablespoon minced garlic	2 tablespoons fresh lemon juice
¼ teaspoon coarse salt	1 tablespoon red wine vinegar
1 tablespoon anchovies rinsed, dried and minced	1 tablespoon Dijon style mustard
	½ cup olive oil
2 teaspoons finely grated lemon peels	Black pepper

Combine garlic, salt, anchovies, lemon peel and juice, vinegar and mustard. Whisk constantly while drizzling oil until thickened. Season with pepper and refrigerate.

*LEMON AND THYME DRESSING

1 ½ cups olive oil	⅔ teaspoon salt
¾ cup canola oil	1 teaspoon black pepper
1 ½ tablespoons dried thyme	4 tablespoons lemon juice
2 ½ tablespoons Dijon mustard	½ cup red wine vinegar

In medium pot over low heat, combine olive oil, canola oil and thyme. Heat oil to just short of bubbling. Remove from heat and set aside for at least an hour. Meanwhile, with a mixer, combine mustard, salt, pepper and 1 tablespoon lemon juice. Begin whisking on slow setting. Slowly drizzle in about ¼ cup of oil. Whisk in 1 tablespoon lemon juice. Repeat, alternating oil and lemon juice (taste for balance as you go along) until both are mixed in. Add a little red-wine vinegar if more acid is needed. Transfer to airtight container scraping in everything from bottom of bowl. Seal securely; refrigerate. Remove 15 minutes before using. Shake well. Store for a month or more.

*MANGO DRESSING

Native to southeast Asia and India, the mango is purportedly the most widely consumed fresh fruit in the world, with worldwide production exceeding 17 million metric tons a year. This dressing is ideal for fruit salads and on grilled fruits.

2 peeled, sliced mangos	½ teaspoon Dijon mustard
½ teaspoon grated ginger	Dash salt
½ cup mint leaves	Dash white pepper
4 teaspoons lime juice	6 tablespoons plain yogurt

In blender, combine mango, ginger, mint, lime, mustard, salt and pepper; puree until smooth. Add yogurt and puree until smooth and moderately sweet. Store in airtight container up to two weeks.

*MARVELOUS ROMANO DRESSING

Romano cheese is a type of cheese that is known for being very hard, salty and sharp. It's usually grated. This cheese is named after Rome itself, where it has been made for over two thousand years, originally in the region of Latium. It's one of the oldest Italian cheeses.

½ cup white vinegar	1 ¼ teaspoons salt
⅓ cup water	1 teaspoon lemon juice
⅓ cup olive oil	½ teaspoon minced garlic
¼ cup corn syrup	¼ teaspoon dried parsley flakes
3 tablespoons grated Romano cheese	⅛ teaspoon dried oregano
2 tablespoons egg substitute	Pinch of crushed red pepper flakes
	⅛ teaspoon onion powder

Combine all ingredients with mixer on medium speed or in blender on low speed for 30 seconds. Chill at least 1 hour; serve over mixed greens or use as marinade.

*OLD FASHIONED SALAD DRESSINGS

All great on any type of salad, burgers, chicken, steak, fish or made thicker as dips with vegetables.

French:
½ cup ketchup
½ cup canola oil
¼ cup white vinegar
2 tablespoons sugar
1 teaspoon dried minced onion
¼ teaspoon hot sauce

Creamy French:
½ cup mayonnaise
1 cup French salad dressing

Thousand Island:
1 cup mayonnaise
½ cup French salad dressing
¼ cup sweet pickle relish
¼ cup dill pickle relish

Ranch:
1 cup mayonnaise
½ cup sour cream
¼ cup buttermilk
1 tablespoon minced garlic
¼ teaspoon dill weed
1 tablespoon parsley flakes
1 tablespoon finely chopped red onions
½ teaspoon ground celery seeds
¼ teaspoon Accent Seasoning
¼ teaspoon black pepper
1 tablespoon dried chives

Mix ingredients for each dressing, beat until smooth. Cover and Refrigerate.

*RED WINE VINAIGRETTE

Choice of vinegar can really change the profile of dressings. While many people choose apple cider or red wine vinegar, a heartier dressing will result by using balsamic vinegar. There are wonderful vinegars made from raspberries, which can completely change the taste of vinaigrette dressing. Alternately, people can choose a much lighter acidic taste by using rice wine vinegar. It's worthwhile to explore the different types of vinegar available, to make subtle or huge difference.

⅔ cup olive oil
⅓ cup white vinegar
⅓ cup red wine vinegar
1 teaspoon sugar
½ teaspoon dried thyme
½ teaspoon dried oregano
1 teaspoon paprika
½ teaspoon dry mustard
1 teaspoon minced garlic

Mix ingredients together either by whisking or shaking in a screw top jar. Cover and refrigerate.

*SMOOTH AVOCADO DRESSING

Avocados are a commercially valuable crop whose trees and fruit are cultivated in tropical climates throughout the world producing a green-skinned, pear-shaped fruit that ripens after harvesting. They've grown in popularity since the 1970's.

1 peeled, pitted, cut up avocado	1 tablespoon honey
¼ cup mayonnaise	½ teaspoon chili powder
2 tablespoons chopped green chili	¼ teaspoon salt
peppers	1 teaspoon minced garlic
2 tablespoons lemon juice	

Place all ingredients in blender. Blend until smooth. Refrigerate.

*VINAIGRETTE

Other ways to change vinaigrettes is by adding spices or additional seasonings. The types of spices used can be as simple as a bit of chopped parsley, or they can be a complex blend of a variety of spices and herbs or other additions such as Parmesan cheese or chopped anchovies. Each addition will add its own flavor.

⅓ cup olive oil	Omit basil
⅓ cup cider vinegar	½ teaspoon dried oregano
1 teaspoon sugar	2 tablespoons Parmesan cheese
½ teaspoon dried basil	¼ teaspoon celery seeds
½ teaspoon paprika	1 teaspoon minced garlic
¼ teaspoon dry mustard	Garlic:
⅛ teaspoon black pepper	Omit basil and paprika
Italian:	Add 1 tablespoon minced garlic

Whisk together oil, vinegar, sugar, basil, paprika, mustard and pepper. Cover and refrigerate

BROWN GRAVY WITHOUT DRIPPINGS

Gravy is a sauce made often from the juices that run naturally from meat or vegetables during cooking. They are often thickened with a starch, starting with a roux made of flour or arrowroot. The liquids from cooked meat, the liquids from dissolved bouillon cubes/stock cubes, or stock are added gradually to the mixture, while continually stirring to ensure that it mixes properly and that the thickener doesn't clump.

½ cup peeled and chopped carrots	2 cups beef broth
½ cup chopped celery	1 bay leaf
¾ cup chopped onions	¼ teaspoon dried thyme
3 tablespoons butter	¼ teaspoon black pepper
¼ cup flour	¼ teaspoon salt
2 cups chicken broth	

Chop carrots, celery and onions (with food processor, electric chopper or wand chopper)—don't worry if the mix is mushy. Heat butter in saucepan over medium-high heat, add vegetables and cook, stirring frequently until softened and well browned. Reduce heat to medium, stir in flour and stir constantly until browned, about 5 minutes. Gradually add broths, whisking constantly. Bring to a boil. Reduce heat to low and add bay leaf and thyme. Simmer, stir occasionally, until thickened and reduced, about 20-25 minutes. Strain gravy through fine mesh strainer into clean saucepan, press on solids to extract as much liquid as possible. Discard solids. Use salt and pepper to taste and serve hot.

CARAMELIZED ONIONS

Caramelizing is the oxidation of sugar, a process used extensively for the nutty flavor and brown color.

2 large onions cut into ¾-inch chunks	2 tablespoons butter
Or sliced thinly or thin wedges	1 tablespoon canola oil

Heat butter and oil in medium skillet over medium heat until melted and hot but not burning. Reduce heat to low and add onions. Cook on low for 40-45 minutes, stirring every 5 minutes until onions are deep brown, tender and cooked down. Don't hurry the process or try to cook at high heat, the taste is definitely worth the effort.

CELEBRATION GARLIC BUTTER

Garlic was frowned upon by higher society cuisine in the US until the first quarter of the twentieth century, being found almost exclusively in ethnic dishes in working-class neighborhoods. But, by 1940, America had embraced garlic, finally recognizing its value as not only a minor seasoning, but as a major ingredient in recipes. Diner slang in the 1920's referred to garlic as Bronx vanilla, halitosis, and Italian perfume. Today, Americans consume more than 250 million pounds of garlic yearly.

1 pound butter cut in cubes	**½ cup chopped parsley**
5 cloves garlic	**3 tablespoons brandy**
3 shallots	

Mix all ingredients together until smooth. Cover and refrigerate.

COOKED MAYONNAISE

Raw eggs are an important ingredient in mayonnaise. If you are concerned about using raw eggs in your mayonnaise, try this method which heats the eggs just enough to kill bacteria. You can also use coddle or radiated eggs and skip the heating process.

2 egg yolk	**½ teaspoon salt**
2 tablespoons cider vinegar	**Pinch cayenne pepper**
2 tablespoons cold water	**1 cup canola, peanut, vegetable oil**
½ teaspoon sugar	**or pure olive oil—not extra virgin**
1 teaspoon dry mustard	**Large pan filled with very cold water**

Whisk together egg yolks, vinegar, water and sugar in small skillet; heat over very low heat, stirring and scraping bottom of pan constantly with a spatula. At first sign of thickening, remove pan from heat but continue stirring. Dip pan bottom in a large pan of cold water to stop cooking. Scrape into a blender, blend for a second or so, then let stand uncovered at least 5 minutes to cool.

Add dry mustard, salt, and cayenne. Cover and with blender running, drizzle oil in very slowly at first, down center hole into egg mixture. Transfer mayonnaise to a clean container and chill immediately. This will keep for at least 7 days refrigerated.

COOL GUACAMOLE

As Mexican foods became more common in the 1950s, home cooks began to come up with variations on the more-traditional recipes. Some versions of "creamy" guacamole, sometimes called avocado dip, included smoothing agents such as sour cream or mayonnaise, which some claim mask the pure avocado flavor while adding fat.

2 avocados

1 tablespoon lemon juice

2 tablespoons finely chopped onions

2 tablespoons olive oil

½ teaspoon salt

Cut avocados into halves. Remove seeds and scoop out pulp into small bowl. Use a fork to mash avocado. Stir in lemon juice, onion, salt, and olive oil. Cover bowl and refrigerate for 1 hour before serving.

DRY ONION SOUP MIX

The expensiveness of this wonderful mix is cut drastically by making it at home. It also has less preservatives and more punch of flavor.

¼ cup unsweetened iced tea mix

½ teaspoon black pepper

1 ½ cups dry minced onions

¼ cup onion powder

¼ cup dried parsley flakes

⅛ cup onion salt

3 tablespoons yeast

2 teaspoons ground celery seeds

1 tablespoon sugar

8 cubes beef bouillon ground up

Combine all ingredients, mix very well—do not use blender. Keep mixture in an airtight container or bag. To use: ¼ cup of mix equals amount in 1 envelope of commercial onion mix.

FLAVORED BUTTERS—SAVORY

Spice-flavored butters and oils instantly turn a simple plate of vegetables or a ho-hum bread, meat, poultry, fish or pasta into a gourmet dish. You'd think this delight would be harder to come by, but delicious butters and oils are very simple to make, keep for weeks in the refrigerator.

Garlic:

1 cup soft butter or margarine

2 teaspoons paprika

½ teaspoon black pepper

1 teaspoon garlic powder

1 tablespoon minced garlic

Italian Herb:

1 cup soft butter or margarine

1 teaspoon chives

1 teaspoon oregano

1 teaspoon garlic powder

1 tablespoon Italian seasoning

1 tablespoon lemon juice

¼ teaspoon salt

Mustard:

1 cup soft butter or margarine

¼ cup chopped fresh parsley

¼ cup Dijon style mustard

¼ teaspoon salt

Beat specific ingredients for your choice of butter well, refrigerate in covered container up to 3 weeks.

FLAVORED BUTTERS—SWEET

These will make any yeast bread, dessert bread, slices, toast, muffin or biscuit special. Use unsalted butter or natural margarine. You can always salt later, to taste, but for starters you don't want the salt competing with the other flavors.

Berry:

1 cup soft butter

½ cup any berry jam: raspberries,
    strawberry,

Huckleberries, blackberries,
    or blueberries

Almond:

1 cup soft butter

2 tablespoons finely chopped almonds

1 teaspoon almond extract

Honey:

1 cup soft butter

¼ cup honey

Orange:

1 cup soft butter

2 teaspoons grated orange peel

2 tablespoons orange juice

After beating well, Refrigerate in covered container for up to 3 weeks.

GRAVY WITH DRIPPINGS

Gravy is also commonly eaten with pork, chicken, lamb, turkey, beef, meatloaf, American style biscuits, Yorkshire pudding, stuffing and sandwiches. One Southern American variation is sausage gravy eaten with biscuits another is white gravy over chicken fried steak. In Australia, Canada and the northern parts of the UK, chips and gravy is seen as a popular dish. It's also common with traditional "Sunday Roast". Here are the two basic ways of making gravy from drippings, using cornstarch or flour. For each cup of gravy start with a tablespoon of drippings.

Gravy with cornstarch:
2 tablespoons drippings
2 tablespoons cornstarch
¼ cup water
About 2 cup broth, water, cream,
    milk or stock
Salt or Mrs Dash seasoning

Gravy with flour:
2-4 tablespoons drippings
1-2 tablespoons flour
1-2 cups water, milk, broth, cream or
    stock
Salt, Mrs Dash, herbs and black
    pepper

Cornstarch: Remove meat or poultry from pan; place pan on stove on medium high heat. Pour off all but 2 tablespoons of drippings in pan. Dissolve cornstarch in minimum amount of water needed to make thin paste—about ¼ cup. Pour into pan with drippings and use wire whisk or spatula to blend into drippings Stir with wire whisk until gravy begins to thicken. As it thickens, slowly add water, stock, broth, milk, cream or some combination to pan. Alternate stirring and adding liquid, maintaining consistency you want, for about 5 minutes. You will probably add about 2 cups of liquid all together. Season gravy with salt, Mrs Dash, pepper and/or herbs.

Flour: Remove meat from pan. Place pan on stove on medium high heat, pour off all but 2 tablespoons of drippings in pan. Into drippings in pan stir in 1 to 2 tablespoons of flour. Stir with wire whisk until flour has thickened and gravy is smooth. Continue to cook slowly to brown flour; stir constantly. Slowly add back some of previously removed drippings—remove some of fat beforehand if there is a lot of fat. In addition, add either water, milk, broth, stock or cream to gravy, enough to make 2 cups. Season gravy with salt, Mrs Dash, pepper and/or herbs.

KETCHUP

Ketchup, also spelled as catsup and called red sauce or Tommy sauce is a condiment, usually made from tomatoes. The primary ingredients in a typical modern ketchup are tomato concentrate, spirit vinegar, corn syrup, salt, spice, herb extracts and garlic powder. Allspice, cloves, cinnamon, onion, and other vegetables may be included.

1 28-ounce can whole tomatoes in purée	1 tablespoon tomato paste
	⅔ cup brown sugar
1 medium onion, chopped	½ cup cider vinegar
2 tablespoons olive oil	½ teaspoon salt

Purée tomatoes (with purée from can) in a blender until smooth. Cook onion in oil in a 4-quart heavy saucepan over moderate heat, stirring, until softened, about 8 minutes. Add puréed tomatoes, tomato paste, brown sugar, vinegar, and salt and simmer, uncovered, stirring occasionally, until very thick, about 1 hour—stir more frequently toward end of cooking to prevent scorching. Purée ketchup in 2 batches in blender until smooth—use caution when blending hot liquids. Chill, covered, at least 2 hours for flavors to develop. Ketchup can be chilled up to 3 weeks.

KETCHUP BY RHUBARB

Is there any way rhubarb can't be used? Haven't found any yet. It grows so well, with so little attention. Ben Franklin is credited for bringing rhubarb seeds to the North American east coast in 1772, yet the red stalks did not catch on until the early 1800s. In the late 1800's, rhubarb was brought to Alaska by the Russians and used as an effective counter-agent for scurvy. By the mid-1900s, its popularity was firmly entrenched in the New England states where it was used as pastry and pie fillings and also to make homemade wine.

4 cups diced rhubarb	3 14 ½-ounce cans diced tomatoes
3 chopped onions	2 teaspoons salt
1 cup white vinegar	1 teaspoon cinnamon
1 cup brown sugar	1 tablespoon pickling spices
1 cup sugar	

Combine all ingredients in large saucepan. Cook over medium high heat until boiling, reduce heat to low and cook until thick. Store in refrigerator.

KOOL FRESH SALSA

Salsa is the Spanish, Arabic, and Italian word that can refer to any type of sauce. Here it usually refers to the spicy, tomato or corn-based hot sauces typical of Mexican cuisine, particularly those used as dips. There are many other salsas; some are made with mint, pineapple, or mango

3 diced tomatoes	1 tablespoon cider vinegar
1 chopped sweet onion	1 tablespoon canola oil
½ cup diced celery	½ teaspoon dried coriander
¼ cup diced green bell peppers	2 tablespoons dried cilantro
½ teaspoon salt	¼ teaspoon black pepper
1 tablespoon apple juice	2 teaspoons minced garlic
⅓ teaspoon lime juice	

In small bowl, stir together tomatoes, onions, celery and bell peppers. In blender mix salt, juices, vinegar, oil, spices and garlic on high. Pour over vegetables. Cover and refrigerate for 2 hours before serving.

MAYONNAISE

Commercial mayonnaise contains preservatives and prevents anything mixed with it from going bad for a longer period of time. It's the protein (eggs, tuna, etc.) that begins to grow bacteria after two hours at room temperature. This recipe has no preservatives, so keep anything it's used with or for refrigerated. This is great to use when making homemade salad dressings.

2 egg yolks	Pinch cayenne pepper
¾ teaspoon salt	4-5 teaspoons lemon juice
½ teaspoon dry mustard	1 ½ cups olive oil
⅛ teaspoon sugar	4 teaspoons hot water

In Blender or Processor, place yolks, salt, mustard, sugar, pepper and 3 teaspoons lemon juice in blender cup or work bowl of food processor fitted with metal chopping blade and buzz 15 seconds (use low blender speed). With motor running, slowly drizzle in ¼ cup oil (use moderately high blender speed). As mixture begins to thicken, continue adding oil in fine steady stream, alternating with hot water and remaining lemon juice. Stop motor and scrape mixture down from sides of blender cup or work bowl as needed.

MILK GRAVY—ANYTIME

Besides milk gravy, common names include white, sawmill gravy, cream gravy and country gravy. A gravy soaked bread slice was eaten after every single meal by my grandpa, no matter the meal. Bacon, sausage or chicken drippings are used to start it. A thick creamy gravy is the result you want. Follow these simple rules: equal amounts of fat and flour; whisk constantly; add cold milk slowly to hot roux and medium heat only.

2 tablespoons meat drippings or shortening	1 teaspoon salt
	½ teaspoon black pepper
2 tablespoons butter	3 cups cold milk
4 tablespoons flour	

Remove meat with a slotted spoon and do NOT drain grease. Measure out 2 tablespoons of drippings, discard rest or save for more gravy later. If you have no drippings, start with melting shortening, over medium heat—don't brown or burn roux. Add butter and melt it. Cook for about 2-3 minutes. Add flour a little at a time constantly whisking. You must whisk roux and gravy constantly throughout. Now start adding cold milk a little at a time. When you reach the desired consistency add salt and pepper to taste.

PICANTE SAUCE

Picante sauce is usually a little more pureed than bottled salsa, but is chunkier than fresh red salsa.

1 tablespoon olive oil	3 tablespoons minced garlic
6 seeded and chopped jalapeño peppers	1 cup chopped onions
	9 cups canned diced tomatoes
2 chopped green bell peppers	3 tablespoons red wine vinegar
1 teaspoon celery flakes	4 tablespoons chopped cilantro
1 teaspoon sugar	Salt

In large pot, heat oil and add jalapenos, celery, sugar, peppers, garlic and onion. Sauté until everything is soft but not browned. Add tomatoes and cook until tomatoes are quite soft, about 5 minutes. Add remaining ingredients and cook for about 10 minutes more to give the flavors a chance to mix together and water to boil off. When sauce is as thick as you like it, add salt to taste if needed and let stand for at least one minute. Refrigerate and stir well before serving.

PINEAPPLE CHUTNEY

Chutney and relish are often used interchangeably as condiment terms. In general, chutneys have a chunky spreadable consistency much like a preserve; relishes are hardly cooked, use less sugar and are more crunchy to the bite.

2 20-ounce cans pineapple chunks	1 teaspoon cinnamon
2 fresh limes	1 teaspoon ground allspice
1 cup red wine vinegar	1 teaspoon salt
1 cup raisins	¼ teaspoon black pepper
1 tablespoon ground ginger	¼ teaspoon hot pepper sauce
1 finely chopped onion	½ cup honey
2 teaspoons minced garlic	

Reserve 2 cups of pineapple chunks without liquid. Pour rest of pineapples and juice in large saucepan. Grate limes and place zest in blender. Add juice of both limes to blender; add vinegar and blend until totally combined; add blended liquid to saucepan. Stir in raisins, ginger, onion, garlic, cinnamon, allspice, salt, pepper and pepper sauce to saucepan. Cook over high heat to boiling; gradually stir in honey. Reduce heat and simmer gently uncovered for 50-60 minutes stirring frequently until reduced to 6 cups; let cool. Add reserved pineapple to cooked mixture and serve.

WHITE SAUCE BASICS PLUS

A cooking controversy: What is the difference in a sauce and a gravy—To some it has to do with the addition of flour and cornstarch; to others it's served in a fancy or family restaurant; and some believe it starts with using meat drippings or pure fat like butter. Truth is the two words have been interchangeable for thousands of years: both are liquids which flavor foods.

2 tablespoons butter	¼ teaspoon salt
2 tablespoons flour	1 cup milk or cream

In small, heavy saucepan, melt butter over low heat; blend flour into butter; add salt.

Cook over low heat, stirring, for 4 to 5 minutes. Cooking for this length of time will minimize 'flour' taste. Slowly add 1 cup of milk or cream, stirring constantly. Continue cooking slowly until smooth and thickened.

Thin white sauce: use 1 tablespoon of butter and 1 tablespoon of flour. Thin sauce is used in cream soups.

Thick white sauce: use 3 tablespoons of butter and 3 tablespoons of flour. Thick sauce is used in soufflés.

Heavy sauce: use 4 tablespoons of butter and 4 tablespoons of flour. Heavy sauce is used as a binder for croquettes.

Some seasonings to add to sauce: Celery Salt, Nutmeg, Sherry, Lemon Juice, Onion Juice, Parsley, Chives or other fresh herbs.

Bechamel: to milk add 1 small onion studded with 3 cloves, a bay leaf and dash nutmeg

Veloute Sauce: Use fish stock instead of milk.

Momay Sauce: Add ½ cup Swiss or Gruyere Cheese to finished sauce and stir until melted.

Onion White Sauce: add 1 tablespoon minced onions to butter before adding flour Mustard White Sauce: Add 1-2 teaspoons mustard to finished sauce.

Brown Sauce: Cook flour until it urns a nice brown and use chicken or beef broth instead of milk.

Curry Sauce: 1-3 teaspoons curry powder.

I didn't know what a holiday was or whose birthday we were celebrating, I was just glad our family was all together again. I loved family gatherings. There were weddings, cookouts, picnics, birthdays, school functions and holidays.

My Aunt Teresa said that if weren't for the special occasions we'd never see each other. There was always plenty of delicious food and everyone was happy, talkative, joking and nothing bad ever happened while we were all together. No one was sad, fighting or disagreeing and I always learned something new about our family at each one.

Faith

Family

Feast

As we all get older the gatherings change, faces vary, more time passes between the visits and the "extending" of the family makes travel plans harder, but the sentiments never waver. Getting together is more important than ever before and in spite of healthier habits, we like to have our favorite family foods to help bring back the comfortable feelings, memories and thoughts of those no longer with us.

As our adult lives have become more involved, it just seems easier to "get together" over meals, combining the activity of eating with our socializing. The explosion of the restaurant industry has either exploited that or contributed to it. We meet each other over a meal to share our own information and exchange the latest news we know of others. The Internet can keep us informed but lacks the ability to give a hug, provide a reassuring look or manufacture a domino-effect laugh making everyone hurt from the amusement shared.

Caring about the Sharing

When Joe and I had our first dinner as a married couple, it was a wonderful steak dinner at an Aero Squadron restaurant. I'm not sure the steak was really that exceptional, but the company and atmosphere were memorable. Since then we've had every anniversary dinner at a steak place some where in the U.S.

Lots of folk have a special beef meal for celebrations. Meat from cows has been eaten since prehistoric time and now we eat the simple ground to the tough roast and primal steak cuts. We've learned to season the parts that have no flavor, tenderize the tough parts and cut the meat up just right to produce spectacular mouth watering steaks. In most states I visited, someone wanted to take me to the "best steak place in the country", and that place was always in their own town, city or county.

I think it has to do with the preparation. I've tasted tough, bland expensive cuts and the juiciest ground meat burgers, flavorful stews and spectacularly tender roast in everyday kitchens, opulent dining rooms, affluent restaurants, exclusive lodges, luxurious cabins and simple shacks. It seems to me that the chef is the key. When the preparer has a love for the food they are serving and wants to please the people they've invited to their table—restaurant or home—the caring attitude automatically infuses the meat and meal.

BASIC MEATLOAF

Meatloaf has been around since long before the advent of meat grinders. In the 1900s, meatloaf was not only a quick dish to prepare but also one that could easily be stretched with fillers. As a result, it has become one of America's comfort foods.

1 pound ground beef	1 egg lightly beaten
1 ¼ teaspoons salt	1 cup diced tomatoes
¼ teaspoon black pepper	½ cup quick cook oats
½ cup chopped onions	⅓ cup ketchup
½ cup finely chopped green bell	2 tablespoons brown sugar
peppers	1 tablespoon mustard

Mix beef, salt, pepper, onions, peppers, egg, tomatoes and oats together until combined. Shape into loaf and place in sprayed baking dish. Mix ketchup, brown sugar and mustard together; spread on top of loaf. Bake in 375° oven for 1 hour.

BEEF STROGANOFF

A Russian dish with sautéed pieces of beef served in a sour cream sauce, from its origins in 19th-century, it's become popular in much of Iran, Europe, North America, Australia, South Africa, Lebanon and Brazil, with considerable variations in the actual recipe.

2 pounds boneless beef sirloin	1 teaspoon salt
steaks	1 ½ cups sliced fresh mushrooms
1 large onion chopped	1 tablespoon flour
1 teaspoon minced garlic	1 can cream of mushroom soup
2 tablespoons butter or margarine	1 8-ounce container sour cream
1 14 ½-ounce can beef broth	1 ½ teaspoons lemon juice
1 teaspoon black pepper	Cooked egg noodle

Sauté onion and garlic in butter. Add meat after being cut into thin strips; brown meat. Add broth, pepper, salt, mushrooms, flour and soup; stir until well combined. Cover and cook on medium heat for 15 minutes. Stir in sour cream and cook, uncovered, 5 minutes. Stir in lemon juice, remove from heat and serve over cooked noodles.

BEEF SWISS STEAK SLOW COOKED

The name doesn't refer to Switzerland, but to the process of "swissing", which refers to fabric or other materials being pounded or run through rollers in order to soften it. The process is done to enable tougher and cheaper pieces of meat to be tenderized.

2 pounds beef cube steaks	1 package onion soup mix
1 teaspoon garlic powder	1-16-ounce can diced tomatoes
½ teaspoon black pepper	

Place steak in bottom of slow cooker. Mix rest of ingredients together and pour over steak in cooker. Cover. Cook on low 8 hours or on high for 3-4 hours.

BEEF TOMATO STIR FRY

Stir Fry, which is similar to Sautéing, is an Asian method of quick cooking food in a hot pan with a small amount of fat for a relatively short period of time. The goal being to brown the food while preserving the color, texture and flavor of the individual ingredients.

½ pound beef round steaks thinly sliced	1 onion cut in strips
¾ teaspoon dried ginger	2 ribs celery sliced
1 teaspoon minced garlic	½ cup water
4 teaspoons cornstarch divided	¼ cup ketchup
1 teaspoon soy sauce	3 tablespoons sugar
1 egg white	2 tablespoons water (for cornstarch)
1 tablespoon canola oil	4 tomatoes peeled, cut in wedges
1 green bell pepper cut in strips	3 cups cooked rice

Mix ginger, 1 teaspoon cornstarch, soy sauce and egg white together and toss with cut meat; set aside for 5 minutes. In large skillet or wok, heat oil and stir fry meat until no longer red; remove meat and set aside. Place peppers, onion, celery and water into skillet; cover and cook for 3 minutes. Stir in ketchup and sugar, cover and cook another 2 minutes. In small bowl, combine 3 teaspoons cornstarch and 2 tablespoons water; stir into beef and return meat to skillet. Cook until sauce is slightly thickened. Add tomatoes; heat through. Serve over cooked rice.

BEEF VEGETABLE STIR FRY

There are two techniques—Chao and Bao—that differ in the amount of heat used on the wok, the speed of cooking, and the amount of tossing of the ingredients. Both techniques use various seasonings, meats, vegetables, seafood, and staples such as cooking oil, garlic, soy sauce, vinegar, wine, salt, sugar, broth, and cornstarch. Because the stir fry is a fast and easy one-dish meal, it has grown in popularity in the US

1 pound beef sirloin steaks ¼-inch slices	½ pound broccoli florets cut into bite size pieces, stem peeled and cut on diagonal ⅛ inch thick slices
3 tablespoons soy sauce	2 cups julienned carrots
1 tablespoon lemon juice	2 cups julienned celery
½ cup beef broth	1 can water chestnuts sliced
1 teaspoon cornstarch	⅓ cup water
1 tablespoon brown sugar	1 large onion thinly sliced
2 tablespoons minced garlic	1 red bell pepper 1-inch chunks
1 tablespoon minced ginger	Toasted sesame seeds
3 ½ tablespoons canola oil divided	

Mix soy sauce with beef slices, cover with plastic wrap and refrigerate 30-60 minutes; drain beef and discard liquid. Whisk lemon juice, beef broth, cornstarch, brown sugar and ½ tablespoon oil in measuring cup. Combine garlic, ginger and ½ tablespoon oil in bowl. Heat ½ tablespoon oil in nonstick large skillet over high heat until smoking; add half of beef to skillet and cook for 1 minute. Stir beef and cook until browned, about 30 seconds; transfer beef to bowl. Heat another ½ tablespoon oil in skillet and cook remaining beef; place all beef on plate. Add 1 tablespoon oil to empty skillet, add broccoli, carrots, celery and cook 30 seconds; add water, cover pan and reduce heat to medium. Steam vegetables until tender crisp, about 2 minutes. Transfer vegetables to paper towels. Add remaining oil to skillet, increase heat to high and heat until smoking. Add bell pepper and onions; cook about 1 ½ minutes. Clear center of skillet and add garlic/ginger/oil mix to skillet. Mash mixture and stir in with peppers and onions. Return beef, vegetables and drained water chestnuts to skillet; toss to combine well. Whisk sauce to recombine and add to skillet. Cook stirring constantly until sauce is thickened and evenly distributed. Transfer to platter and sprinkle with sesame seeds.

BEEF YANKEE POT ROAST

YANKEE POT ROAST is a natural evolution of colonial-era 'New England Boiled Dinner,' a meal generally composed of the same ingredients. The difference? Cooking technique (boiling/stewing vs. roasting in a pot) and type of meat (corned beef vs. fresh rump or round). The hallmarks of classic New Englan) cuisine are frugality, sensibility, and simplicity. As such, Yankee pot roast fits the bill perfectly.

5 pounds beef chuck pot roast	1 cup diced carrots
1 tablespoon shortening	1 cup diced potatoes
Black pepper and salt	¼ cup sliced celery
¼ cup water	2 teaspoons dried parsley flakes
1 sliced onion	2 tablespoons flour
1 cup diced turnips	¼ cup cold water

In Dutch oven or heavy kettle, brown meat on all sides in hot shortening. Sprinkle with salt. Add water and sliced onion, cover and simmer for 3 to 4 hours. Add remaining ingredients; simmer for 30 minutes more, or until vegetables are done. Remove meat; Mix flour into cold water until smooth. Stir hot liquid while adding small amounts of flour water until thickened as desired. Season with salt and pepper to taste.

BEEF FOR 3 MEALS

One week my main meat will be beef, then chicken, then pork—each first preparation leads to 2 more meals for the week. Those busy Autumn and Spring school nights really made this kind of planning a necessity to keep up with everyone's schedules.

3 pounds beef chuck roast	¼ cup vinegar
1 large onion chopped	1 clove minced garlic
½ cup sliced mushrooms	1 teaspoon salt
1 cup beef broth	¼ teaspoon black pepper

Place meat in slow cooker. Top with onions and mushrooms. Combine broth, vinegar, garlic, salt and pepper. Pour over meat. Cover and cook on low 8-10 hours.

Meal #1 Beef Dip Sandwich: Drain and strain sauce. Shred meat. Serve meat on warmed rolls with sauce on side to dip. Meal #2 Shred meat and place over ½ cup mashed potatoes or baked potato on plate, spoon sauce over beef and potatoes. Meal #3 Drain sauce into blender. Transfer to saucepan and cook over medium heat until thickens. Shred meat; place on buttered toasted roll. Top with mozzarella cheese, broil until cheese melts; top with toasted roll.

BRAISED IRISH SHORT RIBS

One beautiful thing about braising is you can be creative about what you put in the pot. With the beer as the liquid instead of wine or stock, it taste a little nutty and malty. Other flavored and types of beer gives it a more delicate or robust flavor.

6 pounds beef short ribs	4 teaspoons minced garlic
Flour	1 bay leaf
4 tablespoons vegetable oil	½ teaspoon dried thyme
4 carrots cut in chunks	4 tablespoons tomato paste
2 stalks celery cut in chunks	2 bottles Stout beer
1 chopped onion	Salt and black pepper

Dredge short ribs in flour, coating lightly. Remove any excess flour from ribs. Heat oil in large Dutch oven over medium-high heat on stove. In batches, brown short ribs, a few minutes per side, making sure not to crowd them too closely in pan and allow ribs to develop a nice crust. Remove cooked ribs and all but 2 tablespoons of fat from pan. Add carrots, celery, onion, garlic, bay leaf and thyme and stir, making sure scrape any residue off the bottom of pot. Cook for several minutes, until vegetables start to get tender. Add salt and pepper to taste. Add beer and tomato paste to pot and stir mixture until combined. Return ribs back to pot; cover and place in 300° oven. Cook for 1 ½ to 2 hours, stirring occasionally, until meat is fork tender.

BROCCOLI BEEF DISH

The secret to this recipe is cooking the beef in 1 cup of oil to seal in the juices, and cooking the broccoli in water to make it crisp and tender.

½ cup water	1 pound thinly sliced beef round
¼ cup red wine	steaks
1 teaspoon sugar	1 bunch fresh broccoli cut in pieces
¼ cup vegetable oil	and blanched
1 tablespoon minced garlic	1 large onion sliced into thin wedges
3 tablespoons soy sauce	1 cup sliced fresh mushrooms
2 teaspoons cornstarch	

In medium bowl, mix together garlic, sugar, soy sauce and cornstarch. Add meat strips and toss to mix well. Let stand 5-10 minutes. In large skillet heat 2 tablespoons of oil. Remove meat from soy sauce mixture—saving mixture—add meat to hot skillet and sauté. Remove beef and set aside. Add remaining oil into skillet. Sauté blanched broccoli, onions and mushrooms for 5 minutes. To reserved soy sauce mixture, add water and wine; stir well. Pour mixture over vegetables; add meat and cover pan. Reduce heat to simmer; cook until broccoli is tender, about 5 minutes. Serve broccoli beef over cooked rice.

CALIFORNIA FLANK STEAK

This is one of the newer ways flank steak is being prepared; marinating tenderizes a tough piece of meat.

4 teaspoons minced garlic	1 teaspoon five spice powder
1 teaspoon salt	2 teaspoons salt
2 beef flank steaks 1 ½ pound each	2 teaspoons sugar
Rub:	1 teaspoon black pepper
1 tablespoon chili powder	1 teaspoon ground ginger

Rub garlic on both sides of steaks. Combine all rub ingredients in small bowl. Divide and pat onto both sides of steaks. Place steaks and rub in large resealable plastic storage bag and seal; marinate steaks in refrigerator 2 hours. Refrigerate up to 24 hours. Oil and heat grill. Grill steaks over medium-high heat, 9 minutes per side for medium-rare. Slice on 45° angle and thin slices.

CHICKEN FRIED STEAK

Chicken-fried first appeared in print in 1952. A long time favorite dish in the South, Midwest and Southwest, the coating is crispy and browned like good southern fried chicken. A milk gravy has to be served with the steak, along with mashed potatoes according to my Texas friend. He also insist the meal is not complete without corn on the cob and if you're really lucky a homemade buttermilk biscuit.

2 pounds beef cubed steaks	2 eggs
¾ cup flour	½ cup canola oil
½ teaspoon salt	2 cups saltine crackers crumbs,
½ teaspoon garlic powder	finely crushed
½ teaspoon black pepper	1 ½ cups evaporated milk

Mix flour with salt, garlic powder and pepper. Beat eggs. Heat oil in heavy skillet over medium high heat. Reserve 3 tablespoons of seasoned flour; set aside. Dredge steaks in remaining flour, dip in egg and into cracker crumbs. Add to hot oil. Brown steaks well, turning to brown both sides. Reduce heat to medium, cover skillet and cook for 15 to 20 minutes, turning occasionally, until steaks are cooked through and tender; steak should be well done, but not dry. Remove steaks from pan and drain on paper towels; keep warm. Pour off all but 3 tablespoons of fat in skillet. Whisk reserved seasoned flour into ½ cup of milk. Pour milk mixture into skillet and fat. Stir well with wooden spoon and scrape bottom of pan to loosen browned bits. Stir in remainder of milk. Cook, stirring constantly until thick and bubbly. Then cook 2-3 minutes longer. Serve gravy over each steak and on potatoes, whatever kind you fix.

CHOICE SPAGHETTI MEAT SAUCE

In the 1890s it was daring to go to an Italian restaurant and eat spaghetti. Pastas weren't new in this country. Thomas Jefferson brought several cases back from Paris in the 1780s and when he ran out he imported a piece of equipment for making macaroni (as all pastas were known then). Macaroni occasionally shows up on menus before the Civil War. Spaghetti became a staple restaurant dish during successive decades, in speakeasies of the 1920s, Depression dives and diners, and a variety of restaurants during the meatless months of World War II.

1 ½ pounds ground beef

2 onions chopped

1 cup finely chopped green bell peppers

1 pound mushrooms sliced

3 teaspoons minced garlic

1 teaspoon garlic powder

1 teaspoon onion powder

2 tablespoons Italian seasoning

½ teaspoon black pepper

½ teaspoon salt

¼ cup grated Parmesan cheese

⅛ cup Romano cheese

1-6-ounce can tomato paste

2-15-ounce can tomato sauce

2-14 ½-ounce can crushed tomatoes

1 pound cooked pasta

Brown beef and onion in skillet; reserve drippings and transfer meat to slow cooker. Sauté mushrooms, green pepper, onion and minced garlic until onions are transparent. Add skillet ingredients to slow cooker. Add remaining ingredients to cooker, except spaghetti and mix well. Cover with lid and cook on low for 5-6 hours. Spoon over pasta.

COASTAL GRILLED STEAK TIPS

2 pounds beef sirloin steaks tips, trim

⅓ cup soy sauce

⅓ cup vegetable oil

1 tablespoon minced garlic

1 tablespoon minced fresh ginger

2 tablespoons brown sugar

1 tablespoon orange juice concentrate

½ teaspoon red pepper flakes

1 tablespoon onion powder

Combine all ingredients except steak in blender. Pour into zip lock bag and place meat in bag, press out all air. Refrigerate 1 hour and flip bag after 30 minutes. Remove steak from marinade, pat dry. Grill, uncovered, until well-seared and dark brown on first side, about 4 minutes. Using tongs, flip steak and grill until second side is well-seared and thickest part of meat is slightly less done than desired. Transfer steak to cutting board, tent loosely with foil and let rest for 5 minutes. Slice steak very thinly on the bias and serve immediately.

COKE BRISKET

The Coca-Cola company has for a very long time promoted the soda as an substitute ingredient for things like Worcestershire sauce, wine, stock, Beer, juices or vinegars. The soda's ingredients include sugar, caramel, caffeine flavoring, carbonated water and what the company describes as "natural flavorings—a unique blend of spices and extracts. Over the years many recipes have been created and adapted to use coke: sauces, gelatin, cakes, frostings, brownies, meats, poultry and marinades. It does have a unique flavor and is fun to tell your guest is the secret ingredient.

4 pounds beef brisket	1 cup diced onions
2 tablespoons olive oil	1 cup diced celery
2 teaspoons paprika	1 cup tomato sauce
Kosher salt and black pepper	1 cup cola soda pop
4 teaspoons minced garlic	1 packet onion soup mix

Line a roasting pan with foil. Rub brisket on both sides with olive oil. Sprinkle both sides with paprika, salt and pepper. Place brisket in pan; top with garlic, onion and celery. Whisk together tomato sauce, cola and dry soup mix. Pour over top of vegetables on brisket. Cover with foil; roast in 350° oven 2 ½ to 3 hour, until very tender. Baste with pan juices every 30 minutes. Remove from oven; let rest 10 minutes. Slice against the grain and serve with pan juice.

COLORFUL STUFFED GREEN PEPPERS

Stuffed peppers is a dish which exists in different names and forms around the world. Most people have their favorite stuffed green pepper recipe passed down from their relatives. Green peppers are one of the most hated vegetables among children. Stuffing them with meat is one way clever mothers get their kids to eat peppers, and apparently it works.

½ pound each ground turkey and beef	1 package onion soup mix
	1 large can diced tomatoes
3 large green bell pepper	2 tablespoons Worcestershire sauce
1 teaspoon dried basil	¼ teaspoon salt
½ cup diced onions	1 can black beans drain, rinsed
2 teaspoons minced garlic	½ cup shredded cheese

Halve peppers lengthwise; remove stem ends, seeds and membranes. Immerse peppers into boiling water for 3 minutes. Sprinkle insides with dash of salt and invert on paper towels to drain. In large skillet cook meats, onion and garlic until meat is brown. Drain off fat. Stir in pepper, salt, Worcestershire sauce. Bring to boil. Reduce heat, simmer for 15-18 minutes. Fill peppers with meat mixture. Carefully place in 13x9 inch sprayed baking dish along with any remaining meat mixture. Bake in 375° oven about 15 minutes. Sprinkle tops with cheese; let peppers stand 2 minutes before serving.

COOKHOUSE ROAST BEEF

Roast beef is a cut of beef, which is roasted in an oven. It's often served in sandwiches and sometimes is used to make hash. In England, Canada, Ireland, and Australia roast beef is one of the meats traditionally served at Sunday Dinner and traditionally served "rare" or "pink" meaning that the centre of the joint is warmed, but not cooked so that it retains the red color of raw beef.

2 tablespoons butter	1 16-ounce bag frozen green beans
1 tablespoon olive oil	1 teaspoon garlic salt
1 large onion cut into wedges	3 cups boiling water
3 pounds boneless beef rump roast	2 envelopes onion soup mix
3 carrots cut into chunks	1 tablespoon cornstarch
3 potatoes cubed	1 teaspoon cold water
2 bay leaves	

Heat butter and oil in skillet. Add onion and beef. Brown beef roast on all sides. Transfer beef and onion to slow cooker. Arrange carrots, potatoes, green beans and bay leaves around beef; sprinkle with garlic salt. Combine soup mix with boiling water, stir until smooth.; pour soup mixture over beef and vegetables in slow cooker. Cover and cook on high until meat is very tender, about 3 ½ hours. In saucepan, combine cornstarch and cold water, stir to form paste. Remove 2 cups of hot liquid from slow cooker and place in saucepan, bring to a boil, stir until gravy is thickened. Slice beef and serve with gravy and vegetables.

CORNED BEEF

Corned beef IS Saint Patrick's Day for many Irish Americans and non Irish; a traditional meal of corned beef and cabbage. Corned beef is usually purchased precooked in delicatessens. The sandwich most made is the traditional corned beef on rye: a very thick sandwich with thinly sliced corned beef, rye bread with caraway seeds and mustard or horseradish. Also popular is the Reuben sandwich, consisting of corned beef, Swiss cheese, sauerkraut, and Thousand Island or Russian dressing on rye bread and grilled.

3 carrots cut into chunks	½ teaspoon black pepper
1 cup chopped celery	4 pounds corned beef
1 teaspoon salt	Water
2 bay leaves	1 onion cut in wedges
1 medium onion peeled and studded	½ head cabbage cut in wedges
with 4 whole cloves	4 potatoes peeled and chunked

Place carrots, celery in slow cooker; set corned beef on top of vegetables. Add salt, bay leaves, onion studded with cloves and pepper; add enough water to cover corned beef totally. Cover with lid and cook on low 8-10 hours or on high for 5-6 hours. Remove corned beef from cooker, remove and discard onion, cloves, carrots, celery and bay leaves. Place onion wedges, cabbage and potatoes; return corned beef in slow cooker. Cover with lid and cook for 2 hours on high. Remove corned beef, cool and slice on diagonal in thin slices. Serve with vegetables.

CORNED BEEF HASH

Hash is a mixture of beef; often leftovers of corned beef or roast beef, with onions, potatoes and spices mashed together and cooked, Corned beef hash is usually a breakfast food with eggs, biscuits and fried potatoes, hashbrowns or home fries. My dad and my husband could live off this dish, my challenge was finding the perfect combination that satisfied these tough critics.

3 pounds potatoes peeled, cooked,	¼ cup milk
diced	2 tablespoons flour
1 pound corned beef chopped	2 teaspoons dried parsley
2 diced onions	3 tablespoons canola oil

In large skillet, heat oil over moderate heat. Stir together potatoes, beef, onion, milk, flour and parsley, add to skillet. With spatula, pack mixture down firmly to make solid cake in skillet. Continue cooking hash, shaking skillet occasionally to prevent it from sticking, until underside is crusty and well browned: about 10 minutes. Cut into wedges and serve.

COTTAGE PIE—AMERICAN STYLE SHEPHERDS PIE

Cottage pie, also known as shepherd's pie, refers to an English meat pie with a crust made from mashed potato and beef. The term cottage pie is known to have been in use in 1791, when potatoes were introduced as an edible crop affordable for the poor, a similar dish is called cowboy pie.

1 ½ pounds ground beef	1 teaspoon Worcestershire sauce
1 onion chopped	½ teaspoon salt
1 stalk celery chopped	½ teaspoon black pepper
1 16-ounce bag frozen mixed	3 large russet potatoes
vegetables	2 tablespoons sour cream
1 stick butter	⅓ cup milk
¾ cup beef broth	

Peel and cube potatoes, boil in salted water until tender; drain and discard. Melt 4 tablespoons of butter in large skillet. Sauté onions until tender over medium heat, about 10 minutes, add beef and sauté until no longer pink. Add salt, pepper, Worcestershire sauce and beef broth. Cook uncovered over low heat for 20 minutes. Add vegetables and cool another 10 minutes. Mash potatoes in bowl with remainder of sour cream, butter and milk. Place beef mixture in baking dish and top with mashed potatoes. Cook in 400° oven until bubbling and brown, about 30 minutes.

COUNTRY FRIED STEAK

Ask the question "What is the difference between "country fried" and "chicken fried" steak—you will get a different answer from every person who dares answer. After traveling, asking and comparing—the biggest difference seems to be country fried is served with brown and/ or onion gravy instead of milk gravy. So that's how I have always served them.

2 pounds beef cubed steaks	2 eggs
¾ cup flour	½ cup canola oil
½ teaspoon salt	2 cups dry breadcrumbs
1 teaspoon onion powder	2 cups beef broth
½ teaspoon garlic powder	1 cup onions sliced
½ teaspoon black pepper	

Mix flour with salt, onion powder, garlic powder and pepper. Beat eggs. Heat oil in heavy skillet over medium high heat. Reserve 3 tablespoons of seasoned flour; set aside. Dredge steaks in remaining flour; dip in egg and into breadcrumbs; add to hot oil. Sear steaks well, turning to brown both sides. Reduce heat to medium, cover skillet and cook for 15 to 20 minutes, turning occasionally, until steaks are cooked through and tender; steak should be well done, but not dry. Remove steaks from pan and drain on paper towels; keep warm. Place onions in skillet and cook until tender but not brown. Remove from skillet on plate. Pour off all but 3 tablespoons of fat in skillet. Whisk reserved seasoned flour into 1 cup of beef broth. Pour broth mixture into skillet and fat. Stir well with wooden spoon and scrape bottom of pan to loosen browned bits. Stir in remainder of broth. Cook, stirring constantly until thick and bubbly. Then cook 2-3 minutes longer. Gravy: In medium saucepan, melt butter or margarine over medium heat. Add onions and mushrooms; cook and stir until tender. Add beef broth; simmer for 5 minutes, stirring occasionally. Combine water and cornstarch in a small cup; stir into broth. Cook and stir for 1 minute, or until thickened.

COUNTRY SMOTHERED STEAK

This steak is similar to country and chicken fried steak, but is then simmered in gravy, which makes a tougher cut of meat even more succulent and tender.

3 pounds boneless beef round
   steaks
½ cup flour
2 tablespoons shortening
1 teaspoon salt
¼ teaspoon black pepper

2 teaspoons Worcestershire sauce
1 cup chopped celery
½ cup chopped onions
2 cups beef broth
½ cup ketchup
1 teaspoon ground cloves

Trim excess fat from round steak; cut into serving size pieces. Sprinkle flour evenly on both sides of steak pieces, pound with meat mallet to tenderize and flatten. Melt shortening in oven proof skillet; brown steaks on both sides. Whisk together in bowl, salt, pepper, Worcestershire sauce, celery, onions, broth, ketchup and cloves until smooth; pour over steaks. Cover and bake in 350° oven for 2 to 2-½ hours or until round steak is tender, adding more water if needed.

DAD'S MEAT AND POTATOES GOULASH

Goulash is a savory beef stew originating in Hungary, and usually made with cuts of shank, shoulder or shin. While sometimes thickened with flour. My dad's German background kept this dish very simple, meat thickened with cooking potatoes.

1 pound ground beef
1 cup diced onions
4 cups peeled and cubed russet
   potatoes
1 cup diced celery

1 tablespoon minced garlic
½ teaspoon black pepper
1 teaspoon salt
Water

Cook ground beef until no longer pink in large skillet. Drain fat off beef; add onions, potatoes, celery, garlic, pepper and salt. Cover with water; bring to boil, occasionally stirring; boil for 5 minutes. Reduce heat and simmer until water has evaporated and cooked some of potatoes into a sauce.

FLANK STEAK

The first time I had this meat, I was in nursing school and it was a cheap meat to serve a crowd. This meant it required being oven cooked slow and long to be tender. I loved it smothered in its own gravy. Now it's been upgraded and although still a tough part of the cow, slicing on a 45° angle and some prep work makes it a wonderful fancier meat for company and able to be grilled.

Marinade:

1 ½ tablespoons mustard

3 ½ tablespoons red wine vinegar

½ teaspoon dried oregano

Salt and black pepper

¼ cup olive oil

1 ½ pounds beef flank steaks

1 tablespoon canola oil

1 tablespoon butter

1 teaspoon salt

½ teaspoon black pepper

1 tablespoon dried minced onion

1 cup beef broth

1 cup red wine

Whisk together in large bowl, mustard, vinegar, oregano, salt and pepper. Slowly drizzle in olive oil, whisking constantly until thickened; add flank steak to the marinade and turn it to coat well. cover and marinate in refrigerator for about 8 hours, turning the steak once or twice. Remove from the marinade, discard and pat meat dry. Sprinkle the steak on both sides with salt and pepper. Heat the oil and butter in a large oven-proof sauté pan over high heat. Once butters foam subsides, add steak and let it develop a rich brown crust on first side, 3-5 minutes. Turn it over and brown 2 minutes on second side. Mix together onion, beef broth and wine; pour over steak in pan. Put pan and steak in oven and cook in 350° oven for about 1 hour. Check doneness and add on time if needed. Let meat rest, loosely covered with foil, 5 minutes before slicing. To slice, hold the knife at an angle and cut very thin slices against the grain. Drizzle any accumulated juices over meat before serving.

GRILLED STEAK MARINADE

The verb: 'to marinate' something; the noun: 'a marinade'. Marinating, is the process of soaking foods in a seasoned, often acidic, liquid before cooking: the technique of adding flavor by immersion in liquid. The liquid in question, the 'marinade' can be acidic with ingredients such as vinegar, lemon juice, or wine, or savory with soy sauce, brine or other prepared sauces. Along with these liquids, a marinade often contains oils, herbs, and spices to further flavor the food items. It is commonly used to flavor foods and to tenderize tougher cuts of meat or harder vegetables such as beetroot and eggplant. The process may last seconds or days. Different marinades are used in different cuisines.

1 large can beer   1 ½ teaspoons black pepper
1 finely chopped onion   1 tablespoon minced garlic
2 tablespoons olive oil

Mix all ingredients in plastic zip loc bag. Add steaks and refrigerate for up to 6 hours, turning bag occasionally. Discard marinate and grill steaks.

HOME SWEET POT ROAST

Pot roast is a braised beef dish made by browning a roast-sized piece of tough beef to induce a reaction, then slow-cooking in an acidulated liquid in a covered dish. Boneless chuck roast and 7-bone pot roast are recommended because they are inexpensive, yet become tender after braising. As with all braises, the slow cooking tenderizes the tough meat, while the liquid exchanges its flavor with that of the beef. The result of a good pot roast should be tender, succulent meat and a rich liquid that lends itself to gravy. Pot roast is often served with carrots and/or potatoes simmered in the cooking liquid. Sauerbraten is a famous German variety of pot roast

4 pounds beef chuck pot roast	3 cups beef broth
¼ cup flour	6 peeled and quartered yams
½ teaspoon salt	1 peeled and cut in chunks rutabaga
½ teaspoon onion powder	2 peeled and cut in chunks turnips
Dash dried thyme	1 yellow onion cut in chunks
Dash garlic powder	½ cup beef broth or red wine
⅛ teaspoon black pepper	3 tablespoons flour mixed with
1 tablespoon olive oil	4 tablespoon cold water

In food storage bag, toss roast with flour, salt, onion powder, thyme, and garlic powder. Heat oil in Dutch oven or large saucepan; add roast and brown on all sides. Add beef broth and bring to simmer. Reduce heat to low, cover and simmer for 2 ½ hours. Add red wine or beef broth and vegetables. Cover and simmer for 45 minutes longer, or until vegetables are tender. Strain juices into saucepan and bring to boil; reduce heat to simmer. Simmer for 5 minutes. Combine flour water and whisk to make smooth mixture. Stir into simmering broth, a little at a time, until thickened as desired. Arrange sliced pot roast and vegetables on platter. Drizzle gravy over sliced beef or serve gravy on the side.

LIVER AND ONIONS

This is one of those meals I will only cook because my husband loves it. There are two kinds of people, those who absolutely it and those who can't stand it. It takes a little prep work, but is the best when you take the time to do it. Don't overcook, turn liver as little as possible and don't skip soaking in milk.

2 pounds sliced beef liver	2 cups flour
2 cups milk	½ teaspoon salt
¼ cup butter divided	½ teaspoon black pepper
2 large sweet onions sliced	

Gently rinse liver slices under cold water. Place them in medium bowl, pour milk to cover. Let stand for at least 1 hour and up to 2 hours. Melt 2 tablespoons of butter in large skillet over medium heat. Separate onion slices and sauté them in butter until soft. Remove onions and melt remaining butter in skillet. Season flour with salt and pepper; place in shallow dish. Drain milk from liver and coat each slice of liver with flour mixture. Turn heat in skillet to medium high and place the liver slices in the pan. Cook until nice and reduce heat to medium. Cook to taste.

OLD FASHION BEEF STEW

This is such an old recipe, simple to fix and smells wonderful. The two prerequisites for a dish to be considered beef stew is that it have beef as it's main component, and that it is cooked over a direct flame in a pot with a liquid base, Stewing meat has been a method of cooking that is older than almost any other. From the moment man made his first fire, almost immediately thereafter he began slow cooking meat over a low flame for long periods of time.

2 pounds beef chuck roast 1-inch pieces	3 cups peeled and cubed potatoes
2 tablespoons flour	2 cups peeled and chopped carrots
2 tablespoons butter	1 cup diced celery
3 tablespoons canola oil	1 cup chopped onions
1 cup vegetable juice	1 cup frozen green beans
3 cups water	1 cup frozen whole kernel corn
3 teaspoons instant beef bouillon	1 teaspoon black pepper
1 teaspoon Worcestershire sauce	1 teaspoon garlic powder
	1 teaspoon onion powder

Brown beef in skillet in butter and oil; add water, vegetable juice, beef bouillon and Worcestershire saucer; add black pepper, garlic powder and onion powder. Bring to simmer; cover and cook about 2 hours. Add vegetables and simmer covered until vegetables are tender, about 30 minutes longer.

I have seen a really good beef stew, a slice of freshly baked bread, spread with warm honey butter make even those who hate snow, smile, forget the falling temperature and admire the accumulating inches outside the frosty window.

OLD FASHION SWISS STEAK

Cube steak is the usual meat used in producing Swiss steak by most home cooks. It's the connective fibers that make the meat tough that are physically broken by the butcher and the braising process further breaks down the connective tissue in the meat. Swiss steak should be tender enough to be eaten without a knife.

3 pounds boneless beef chuck steak	1 28-ounce can diced tomatoes
Salt and black pepper	Canola oil
1 cup flour	1 tablespoon flour
2 sliced onions	1 cup cold water

Trim fat from steak; cut into 6 pieces 1 ½-inch thick. Season meat with salt and pepper; place on well-floured cutting board. Sprinkle more flour over steaks and pound with meat hammer to tenderize. Continue to turn, flour, and pound until 1 cup of flour is used. Heat oil in heavy skillet; brown onion in hot oil, remove; brown steaks on both sides. Place onion on top of steak, add tomatoes; cover and bake in 350° oven. Cook until tender, about 1 ½ to 2 hours; remove steak and onions to hot serving platter. Serve with gravy made by thickening skillet juices with flour blended with cold water to form a smooth paste. Stir flour and water into juices and bring to boil, cook 2 minutes or until thickened to gravy consistency.

ONE POT ROAST SUPPER

These days if I can make a meal by creating less to clean up, the whole meal seems to taste better.

1 cup cider vinegar	1 9-ounce box frozen green beans
2 tablespoons Worcestershire sauce	1 10-ounce bag frozen green peas
3 pounds beef chuck pot roast	1 package onion soup mix
2 stalks celery sliced	1 tablespoon liquid smoke
3 carrots cut in strips	1 teaspoon garlic powder
2 potatoes cubed	1 can beer
2 onions coarsely chopped	½ cup beef broth

Mix together vinegar and Worcestershire sauce; marinate roast in mixture in refrigerator for 2-4 hours. Remove roast and discard marinade. Place vegetables in slow cooker. Place roast on top of vegetables. Sprinkle with dry soup mix. Combine liquid smoke, garlic powder, beer and broth; pour over roast. Cover and cook on low for 7-8 hours or until vegetables are tender.

PEPPER STEAK

Evidence for the dish's existence in the US dates from at least 1948. The dish originated from Fujian cuisine, the original dish meat was pork and the seasonings were relatively light compared to pepper steak. A similar dish is found in Japanese Chinese cuisine.

1 tablespoon butter	2 large green bell peppers sliced
2 tablespoons olive oil	½ pound sliced mushrooms
½ cup chopped onions	2 tablespoons cornstarch
3 cloves garlic halved	¼ cup cold water
½ teaspoon black pepper	2 tablespoons soy sauce
1 cup beef broth	
2 pounds beef round steaks thin slices	

In skillet, melt butter in oil; sauté onions over medium heat. Add garlic, black pepper and bell peppers. When garlic is roasted, use fork and mash into oil. Remove vegetables using slotted spoon when tender, but not soft. Turn heat to high, brown steak; add mushrooms. Remove steak and mushrooms to vegetable dish when tender. Mix cold water and cornstarch until dissolved. Add beef broth, cornstarch mix and soy sauce scraping pan while stirring and bringing to a boil. Boil 1 minute; reduce heat to very low and simmer for 5 minutes. Add vegetables and steak; heat through; serve over rice or noodles.

RECEPTION SWEDISH MEATBALLS

Swedish meatballs are traditionally served with gravy, boiled potatoes, lingonberry jam, and sometimes fresh pickled cucumber. In the US, there are a number of variations, based on the assimilation of Swedes in the Midwest.

1 pound ground beef	½ cup milk
½ pound ground pork	¼ cup canola oil
½ cup minced onions	¼ cup flour
¾ cup fine dry breadcrumbs	½ teaspoon salt
1 tablespoon minced parsley	½ teaspoon garlic powder
1 teaspoon salt	¼ teaspoon black pepper
¼ teaspoon black pepper	1 teaspoon paprika
½ teaspoon garlic powder	2 cups boiling water
1 tablespoon Worcestershire sauce	¾ cup sour cream
1 egg	

Combine beef, pork, onions, breadcrumbs, parsley, salt, pepper, garlic powder, Worcestershire sauce, egg and milk. Shape into balls size of walnuts. Heat oil in skillet and brown meatballs. Reserve dripping and place meatballs in slow cooker; cover. Cook on high 10-15 minutes. Stir flour, salt, garlic powder, pepper and paprika into hot drippings in skillet and scrape bottom of skillet. Stir in water and add sour cream. When mixed well, pour over meatballs in slow cooker. Cover with lid and reduce heat to low. Cook 4-5 hours. Serve over noodles.

ROYAL STEAK AND VEGETABLE

The first slow cooker was a large cast iron pot suspended over a fireplace. These worked for hundreds or even thousands of years, but women still had to stoke the fire beneath it and continuously stir the pot

1 ½ pounds lean London broil or beef round steaks cut in strips	1 14 ½-ounce can tomatoes
	1 4-ounce can sliced mushrooms drained
⅓ cup flour	
1 teaspoon salt	1 tablespoon molasses
½ teaspoon black pepper	3 tablespoons soy sauce
1 onion sliced	2 cups frozen green beans

Toss steak strips with flour, salt and pepper; place in slow cooker. Add onion, tomatoes, mushrooms, molasses, and soy sauce. Cover and cook for 8 to 10 hours on low. Add green beans 30 to 45 minutes before serving. Good served with rice.

SAUERBRATEN SLOW COOKED

Sauerbraten is one of the best known German dishes and several regions boast local versions including: Bavaria, Rhineland, Saarland, Silesia, and Swabia. Regional variations of sauerbraten differ in the ingredients of their marinade, gravy, and traditional accompaniments.

4 pounds beef rump roast	1 10-ounce can beef broth
1 teaspoon salt	⅔ cup brown sugar
1 teaspoon black pepper	⅓ cup cider vinegar
2 onions sliced	6 gingersnaps crumbled
6 stalks diced celery	

Sprinkle roast on all sides with pepper and salt. Place roast in slow cooker and add onion, celery, broth, brown sugar and vinegar. Cover and cook on high for 5-6 hours. Remove roast and keep warm. Skim fat from cooker juices and stir in gingersnaps. Stir until sauce thickens and bubbles. Slice meat and spoon sauce over slices.

SLOW COOKER MEATLOAF

Adding the potatoes, not only cooks them in a wonderful juice, but completes the meal without using added pans or dishes.

2 pounds ground beef	1 package onion soup mix
½ pound bulk ground sausage	½ teaspoon liquid smoke
2 eggs	½ teaspoon Worcestershire sauce
1 teaspoon garlic powder	1 teaspoon dry mustard
¾ cup crushed saltine crackers	½ cup ketchup
2 tablespoons diced green bell peppers	½ teaspoon ground nutmeg
	Green bell pepper rings
2 tablespoons finely chopped celery	4 potatoes cubed

Place potatoes on bottom of slow cooker. Combine meats, eggs, garlic powder, peppers, celery, dry soup mix, liquid smoke, Worcestershire sauce, mustard and all but 2 tablespoons of ketchup; shape into loaf. Combine remaining ketchup and nutmeg; spoon over meat loaf. Place green pepper rings on top; cover and cook on low 8-12 hours.

STANDING RIB ROAST

Standing Rib Roast, otherwise known as prime rib, is a classic, specially popular on Christmas night. Of course, prime rib is a favorite menu item in restaurants year round so any time you serve it to guests, they're getting a special treat.

5 pounds standing beef rib roast	½ teaspoon garlic powder
½ tablespoon salt	½ teaspoon onion powder
½ teaspoon black pepper	1 teaspoon Mrs. Dash seasoning

Let roast stand at room temperature for at least 1 hour. Mix together salt, pepper, garlic, onion and Mrs. Dash. Rub roast all over with seasoning mixture. Place roast on rack in pan with rib side down and fatty side up. Place roast in 375° oven. DO NOT remove roast until ready to serve. Roast in 375° oven for 1 hour. Turn off oven. Leave roast in oven but do not open door another 3 hours. About 30 minutes before serving, turn oven to 375° to reheat roast.

TEXAS STYLE BARBECUE BEEF BRISKET

Briskets are one of the toughest cuts of beef, however with the proper cooking method, spices and time, this inexpensive boneless section can become the most tender and flavorable meat to serve.

4-6 cups mesquite wood chips	2 tablespoons mild molasses
2 tablespoons butter	½ teaspoon dry mustard mixed with
1 tablespoon canola oil	1 teaspoon water
¼ cup minced onions	¼ cup cider vinegar
1 teaspoon minced garlic	3 pounds beef brisket

1 ½ teaspoons chili powder	**RUB:**
2 cups tomato juice	4 teaspoons chili powder
½ cup white vinegar	½ teaspoon cayenne pepper
1 ½ teaspoons salt	2 teaspoons salt
1 teaspoon minced Chipotle chili	1 ½ teaspoons black pepper

Cook onions and garlic in butter and oil; add chili powder, tomato juice, white vinegar, salt, chipotle chili, molasses and mustard water. Bring to boil; simmer over medium heat until thick. Stir in ¼ teaspoon black pepper and cider vinegar. Divided to use some sauce while cooking meat and cool rest to room temperature to serve with cooked meat. Mix chili powder, cayenne pepper, salt and rest of black pepper together; rub into brisket and let it stand at room temperature for 1 hour. Soak wood ships for 1 hour in enough water to cover. Drain chips and arrange in grill. Place meat on rack in sprayed roasting pan and place pan on grill. Cover and grill for 2-2 ½ hours. Every 30 minutes brush meat with sauce. Thinly slice across grain and serve with more sauce.

TRAVEL COLLAGE

My cookbook shelves are a Collage: a random hodgepodge of my travels. They're full of stories, advice, tidbits, directions, guidelines, instructions, opinions, suggestions, secrets, procedures, techniques, recommendations and warnings. A valuable collection that forms a record of my culinary efforts, mistakes, collaborations, extravagances and lessons.

This section of collected works is priceless and irreplaceable: from pages found in shreds with ink barely readable to pristine family heirlooms. These manuscripts were stuffed in attics, closets, basements, flea markets and garage sales; forgotten to all. Some books are collectables, others historical, many are regional, from the simple to complex, lots are out of print, loads are food specific, a few famous, several organizational and all unique—many my husband's lovingly found and gifted to me.

In all of them—there's not a single barbecue recipe that is the same. Every family has their favorite even if it's just off a store shelf. Some will start with a bottle of sauce and add their family favorite secret ingredients. Some swear by a rub rather than a sauce, others slow cook the meat for days, others slap sauce on something quickly grilled and call it barbecue, then there are those who precook and add sauce when they serve it. Don't even start discussing the hot spice level—spicy seasonings is different than hot spicy; sweet could mean tomato sweet or honey sweet—smoky? is it real hickory wood or flavoring?

A new restaurant opening in the Juneau Alaska area promised to be a real smokehouse BBQ place and everyone was excited and hungry for that slow cooked, sauce-slathered taste. Unfortunately the owner used shortcuts by getting his menu items prepackaged from the warehouse stores. The chicken and coleslaw were bland, the pork and baked beans too sweet and the beef—a weird spicy. It could've been a success by having one type of sauce or any homemade sauce at all. The business was stampeded when it first opened—but closed in a few short months.

BBQ—Whether we agree on the secret ingredients or not, you just need to find a specific taste you enjoy and proudly share it with your family, friends and guest. "Viva la Difference" or should I say, "Viva La Unique".

Don't Squirm With The Term

Every recipe has one thing in common: following the list of necessary ingredients and the instructions—brief, sometimes abbreviated, orders on how to put the ingredients together and emerge with a steamy pot of soup, a crusty loaf of bread, a chewy batch of cookies.

Most terms are self-explanatory. Many others are quite simple, some complex. The science of cooking has a jargon all its own and the following definitions should help you wade through almost any recipe.

♦ Al dente—An Italian expression applied to processed pasta cooked just until enough resistance is left in it to be felt "by a tooth"; also applied to vegetables that have been cooked crisp by steaming, boiling, or stir-frying
♦ Au gratin—Topped with crumbs and/or cheese and browned in an oven or under broiler.
♦ Au jus—Served in its own juice.

   ♦ Bake—To cook, either covered or uncovered, in an oven.
   ♦ Barbecue—A cooking method involving grilling food over a fire. Usually some sort of rub, marinade, or sauce is brushed on the item before or during cooking
   ♦ Baste—To keep foods moist during cooking by pouring a liquid over them: meat drippings, melted fat, or other liquid.
   ♦ Beat—To make a mixture creamy, smooth, or filled with air by whipping it in a brisk motion.
   ♦ Bisque—A thick cream soup.

♦ Blanch—To precook a food briefly in boiling liquid, usually to loosen the skin; for example, you can drop tomatoes in boiling liquid for less than a minute, and the skin comes off easily.
♦ Blend—To stir two or more ingredients together until they are smooth and uniform.
♦ Boil—To cook at temperature -212° at sea level. When boiling a liquid, you will see bubbles forming rapidly, rising continually and breaking when they reach the surface of the liquid. You can either boil liquid, or can boil some other food in a liquid.

- Braise—To first brown meat quickly in fat and then cook it in a covered pan on top of the stove or in the oven; liquid may or may not be added.
- Bread—To coat a raw food is first dipped in beaten egg or milk or other liquid and then coated with breadcrumbs.
- Broil—To cook food placed directly under the source of heat or directly over an open fire.
- Broth—Broth and stock are interchangeable terms and mean a flavorful liquid made by gently cooking meat, seafood, or vegetables, often with herbs, in liquid, usually water
- Caramelize—The flavor of many foods: vegetables, meats, and seafood, is often enhanced by a gentle browning that caramelizes natural sugars and other compounds and intensifies their flavor. Meats for stews are usually browned to caramelize juices that if not caramelized are much less flavorful. Chopped vegetables, especially aromatic ones such as carrots and onions, are often caramelized—sometimes with cubes of meat—in a small amount of fat before liquid is added to enhance the flavor of soups, stews, and sauces.
- Chill—To put food in the refrigerator until it is cold throughout.
- Chop—To cut food in pieces about the size of small peas.
- Coat—To cover the back of a spoon with a layer of a thickened sauce or stirred custard.
- Cool—To remove a food from the source of heat and let it stand at room temperature until it reaches room temperature; food should not be put in the refrigerator to bring the temperature down more quickly.
- Cream—To mix one or more foods together until they are creamy and soft.
- Crimp-To seal the edges, usually piecrust, by pinching at intervals with fingers or pressing them together with a fork.
- Crudités-An assortment of raw vegetables served as appetizers, usually with dips
- Cut in—To use two knives or a pastry blender to add shortening or cold butter by cutting it into tiny pieces during the blending process.
- Deglaze—To add liquid to a pan in which foods have been sautéed or roasted in order to dissolve the bits and juices stuck to the bottom of the pan. The purpose of deglazing is to make a quick sauce or gravy for a roast, steak, chop, or a piece of seafood fillet or steak

♦ Degrease-To remove fat from the surface of stews, soups or stock. The food can be cooled in the refrigerator so the fat hardens and can be removed easily.

♦ Dice—To cut food in small cubes all of the same size and shape.

♦ Dredge—To coat raw meat with a dry mixture, usually flour or cornmeal prior to frying.

♦ Dutch oven—A cast-iron pot used for the preparation of stews, braises, and pot—roasts

♦ Entrée—The main course.

♦ Fold in—To gently add a new ingredient to an already-beaten mixture. The new ingredient is dumped on top of the mixture; with a large spoon or spatula, the new ingredient is brought down through the middle of the mixture, and the mixture is scraped off the bottom of the bowl and brought to the top.

♦ Fricassee—To braise small, individual serving pieces of meat or poultry in a little broth, sauce, or water.

♦ Fry—To cook food in hot fat; no water is added, and no cover is used.

♦ To pan-fry—food is cooked in a small amount of fat (a few tablespoons to half an inch) in a frying pan.

♦ Deep-fry—food is cooked in a large kettle that contains enough hot fat to cover the food or allow it to float.

♦ Glaze—To cover a food with a mixture that hardens, adds flavor, and makes the food look glossy or shiny.

♦ Grate—To cut food into fine particles, usually with the use of a grater.

♦ Grill—To cook food on a rack directly under or over the source of heat.

♦ Julienne—To cut and slice vegetables, fruits, cheeses and meats into match shaped slivers.

♦ Knead—To make a dough or dough-like substance smooth and elastic by folding, stretching, and pressing it continuously until it reaches the desired texture. (When fondant for candies is kneaded, it gets satiny instead of elastic.)

♦ Marinate—To make foods more flavorful or tender by allowing them to stand in a liquid or rub for hours or overnight; the food is generally completely covered.

Most marinades are a mixture of cooking oil and vinegar or lemon juice with a variety of spices added for flavor.

♦ Mince—To chop food in very fine pieces.

- Mix—To stir ingredients until they are very well blended.
- Pan-broil—To cook food in a heavy pan on top of the stove; the pan is usually ungreased, and any grease from the food is poured off as it accumulates so the food won't start to fry.
- Parboil—To cook a food in boiling liquid only until it is partly cooked.
- Pare—To remove the outermost skin of fruit or vegetable.
- Phyllo dough—Pastry made with very thin sheets of flour-and-water dough layered with butter and / or crumbs; similar to strudel. Also called filo dough
- Poach—To simmer in a hot liquid slowly; poaching is a gentle process, food holds its shape.
- Pot-roast—To brown a large piece of meat in fat quickly, and then cook it in a covered pan in the oven or on top of the stove; liquid is usually added to make the roast more tender.
- Puree—To blend a cooked fruit or vegetable until it is smooth and uniform throughout.
- Reduce or Reduction—technique of cooking liquids down so that some of the water they contain evaporates. Reduction is used to concentrate the flavor of a broth or sauce and, at times, to help thicken the sauce by concentrating ingredients such as natural gelatin.
- Refresh—To run cold water over food that has been parboiled in order to stop the cooking.
- Roast—To make a food in the oven, uncovered, without added liquid.
- Sauté—To cook a food quickly in melted butter until tender.
- Scald—To heat liquid to just below the boiling point, tiny bubbles appear at the edges.
- Scallop—To cook a food in a sauce; many scalloped foods are cooked in a cheese or a cream sauce and topped with browned crumbs.
- Sear—To brown meat rapidly by using extremely high heat.
- Shred—To cut food in narrow, long, small pieces, usually with a grater.
- Simmer—To cook a food in hot liquid just below the boiling point (usually above 185° but below 210°; bubbles form slowly, but break before they reach the surface.

- Soft Peaks—To beat egg whites or cream until peaks hold their shape, but droop slightly.
- Steam—To cook a food on a rack or in a perforated pan, and placed in a covered container that has a small amount of boiling water in the bottom. In some cases, the food is cooked in a container that creates pressure (called a pressure cooker).
- Steep—To simmer a food in liquid just below the boiling point over an extended period of time so the flavor or other element is extracted into the water.

- Stew—To simmer slowly in a small amount of liquid, usually for several hours.
- Stiff peaks—To beat egg whites or cream until it is moist and glossy and the peaks stand up straight without drooping.
- Stir—To use a spoon to thoroughly combine two or more ingredients.

- Toss—To mix lightly and gently, usually with a slight lifting motion.
- Whip—To beat a food rapidly so you add air to it.
- Zest—The thin, brightly colored outer part of the rind of citrus fruits. The oils make it ideal for use as a flavoring. Remove the zest with a grater, citrus zester, or vegetable peeler. Be careful to remove only the colored layer, not the bitter white pith beneath it.

Use a dry measure for powders, such as sugar, salt, and baking powder. Spoon or scoop the powder lightly into the cup and level by running a knife or spatula across the top to level the surface and scrape any excess back into the jar or canister. Measure a "heaping" or "rounded" tablespoon, teaspoon, or cup. This is not precise, but is generally a moderately sized, round mound, or heap of the dry ingredient in addition to the spoon. Measure a "scant" cup or spoon by filling the measure not completely full, or by shaking or pouring a little bit out.

For Flour, sift first and spoon into dry measure gently, without pressing or packing it in. Then level with a knife. Measure brown sugar by packing it moderately firmly in dry measure. With grated cheese or chopped nuts, pack loosely into a dry measure until they are about even with the rim.